THE BOLSHEVIK REVOLUTION

1917-1923

A HISTORY OF SOVIET RUSSIA
by Edward Hallett Carr
in Norton Paperback Editions

The Bolshevik Revolution, 1917–1923 (I)

The Bolshevik Revolution, 1917–1923 (II)

The Bolshevik Revolution, 1917–1923 (III)

A HISTORY OF SOVIET RUSSIA

THE BOLSHEVIK REVOLUTION
1917-1923

BY

EDWARD HALLETT CARR

★

VOLUME ONE

W. W. NORTON & COMPANY
New York • London

Printed in the United States of America

First published as a Norton paperback 1985
by arrangement with The Macmillan Company, New York

W. W. Norton & Company, Inc., 500 Fifth Avenue,
New York, N.Y. 10110
W. W. Norton & Company Ltd., 37 Great Russell Street,
London WC1B 3NU

ISBN 0-393-30195-8

1 2 3 4 5 6 7 8 9 0

PREFACE

THE temerity of an attempt to write a history of Russia since the October revolution of 1917 will be obvious to everyone ; and those who condone the attempt at all will show some indulgence towards faults of execution. A history of Soviet Russia written by an Englishman who has neither a Marxist nor a Russian background may seem a particularly hazardous enterprise. But the width and obviousness of the gap to be bridged has its compensations. Books written in Great Britain or the United States about western or central Europe are often marred by the unconscious assumption that the policies and institutions of, say, France or Italy or Germany can be understood in the light of British or American analogies. No sensible person will be tempted to measure the Russia of Lenin, Trotsky and Stalin by any yardstick borrowed from the Britain of MacDonald, Baldwin and Churchill or the America of Wilson, Hoover and Franklin Roosevelt. The historian of Soviet Russia will at every stage of his work be more than ordinarily conscious of the exacting character of the dual task imposed on every serious historian : to combine an imaginative understanding of the outlook and purpose of his dramatis personae with an overriding appreciation of the universal significance of the action.

My ambition has been to write the history not of the events of the revolution (these have already been chronicled by many hands), but of the political, social and economic order which emerged from it. Having this purpose in mind, I imagined a long introductory chapter in which I should have analysed the structure of Soviet society as it was established before Lenin's final withdrawal from the scene in the spring of 1923—a moment which approximately coincided with the foundation of the Union of Soviet Socialist Republics. But this framework proved on examination almost ludicrously inadequate to the magnitude of Lenin's achievement and of its influence on the future. The chapter was quickly replanned as a volume, and grew in process of writing into a major work under the title *The Bolshevik Revolution, 1917–1923*, to be completed in three volumes, of which the first contains Parts I to III. The second volume containing Part IV (" The Economic Order ") and the third volume containing Part V (" Soviet Russia and the World ") are far advanced and should be ready for publication next year. The second instalment of the whole project will be entitled *The Struggle for Power, 1923–1928*.

The Bolshevik Revolution, 1917–1923, though it will be complete in itself, none the less retains something of its character as the introductory stage of a larger enterprise. It purports to contain not an exhaustive record of the events of the period to which it relates, but an analysis of those events which moulded the main lines of further development. For example, the reader will find no consecutive narrative of the civil war, though I have had many occasions to discuss its course and consequences, especially in Part III of the present volume, and shall have many more in Part V. On the other hand, I have not hesitated to devote my opening chapters to events and controversies before 1917 which, even if their immediate consequences appear small, played a vital part in the later history of the revolution. John Reed's *Ten Days that Shook the World* (1919) and M. Philips Price's *My Reminiscences of the Russian Revolution* (1921) provide vivid pictures of the revolution itself ; and those in search of a comprehensive narrative in English of the period of the civil war will find it in W. H. Chamberlin's two-volume *History of the Russian Revolution, 1917–1921* (1935).

The writing of contemporary history has its pitfalls. But I have never been convinced that they are greater than those confronting the historian of the remoter past, when time has reduced the evidence to manageable proportions by a process of selection and attrition which in no way guarantees the survival of the fittest. It is commonly believed that the historian of Soviet Russia faces exceptional difficulties arising from the paucity, or unreliable character, of his sources. Whatever justification may exist for this belief in the period after 1928, it has no foundation in the period now in question, the materials for which are abundant and are on the whole marked by an unusual frankness both in the statement of facts and in the expression of opinions. Since the Soviet authorities at present pursue the mistaken policy of giving no encouragement to non-communist students of their history and institutions to visit the USSR and to work in its libraries, I have been obliged to draw mainly on the libraries of other countries. Among these the most richly endowed in this field are the libraries of the United States : I am therefore deeply indebted to the Institute for Advanced Study at Princeton, to Columbia University and to Stanford University for making it possible for me to visit the United States in 1948 and to travel widely in the country. The libraries of Columbia, Harvard and Stanford Universities, as well as New York Public Library and the Library of Congress, are all rich in Soviet material ; I am grateful to the librarians and staffs of all these institutions for their ready assistance and advice in the search for material.

The main part of my work has, however, been done in England ; and, while much has still to be achieved before adequate facilities for Soviet studies are developed in our major universities, I have been fortunate in the generous help of friends, the diversity of whose opinions has often contributed to the clarification of my own. Mr. Isaac Deutscher has read the whole of my MS., and given me the benefit of his mature knowledge and advice on innumerable points of fact and interpretation ; Mr. A. Rothstein, lecturer in the School of Slavonic and East European Studies, University of London, read several chapters and made valuable comments and criticisms ; Dr. R. Schlesinger, of the Department for the Study of the Social and Economic Institutions

of the USSR, University of Glasgow, performed the same service for
the chapter and note on the Bolshevik doctrine of self-determination,
and Mr. Rachmilevich for the first two chapters on early party history ;
Mrs. Jane Degras read the whole volume in proof and suggested many
corrections both of substance and of form ; Dr. Ilya Neustadt, formerly
assistant in the library of the London School of Economics, and now
lecturer in the University College, Leicester, was an invaluable guide
to the extensive resources of the library and a resourceful helper on
points of research ; and Mr. J. C. W. Horne, of the British Museum,
Dr. L. Loewenson, librarian of the School of Slavonic Studies, and the
library staff of the Royal Institute of International Affairs, have also
given me courteous and unfailing help in my unending quest for books.
I am conscious of having incurred to all these a debt which I cannot
adequately acknowledge in this Preface. It is perhaps less necessary
than usual on this occasion to add the customary *caveat* that none of
those who have helped or advised me is responsible either for my
mistakes or for my opinions : not one of them is likely to find himself
in agreement with everything I have written. My gratefulness to them
is none the less sincere and profound. I should also like to take this
opportunity to thank my publishers for having made it possible for
me to embark on this long-term undertaking.

Some technical details remain to be noted. Two constant bugbears
of writers on Russian subjects are the calendar and the system of transliteration. Events occurring in Russia before October 25/November 7,
1917, are here dated according to the Julian calendar at that time
current ; events occurring outside Russia are dated according to the
western calendar. Wherever confusion seemed possible, I have made
it clear which calendar I was using. Events occurring in Russia between
October 25/November 7, 1917, and February 1/14, 1918 (when Russia
adopted the western calendar) are dated in both styles. Events occurring after February 1/14, 1918, are dated according to the western
calendar. No system of transliteration is ever satisfactory except to the
philologist who has invented it ; the system which I have followed
approximates to that of the Library of Congress, shorn of a few of its
refinements. In proper names I have sometimes sacrificed system to
desire to avoid the outlandish. Thus I have written Herzen (not
Gertsen), Axelrod (not Aksel'rod), Zinoviev (not Zinov'ev), and
Orjonikidze (not Ordzhonikidze). Sometimes consistency has been
sacrificed to familiarity, as in Djugashvili (not Jugashvili or Dzhugash-
vili) and Jordania (not Zhordania) ; and Dzerzhinsky has been preferred
to Dzierzynski, the Polish form which he himself doubtless used when
he wrote in Latin script. On such points I have probably failed even
to be consistently inconsistent, but need plead for the indulgence only
of those who have not wrestled with these particular difficulties.

A bibliography of the main sources used for *The Bolshevik Revolution,
1917–1923*, will appear in the third volume. In the meanwhile it is
hoped that sufficient guidance will be found in the footnotes. No
single complete edition exists of the works of Marx and Engels in the

languages in which they were written. Of the projected *Historisch-Kritische Gesamtausgabe* under the auspices of the Marx-Engels-Lenin Institute only seven volumes of Part I (Early Writings) and four volumes of Part III (Marx-Engels correspondence) have been published: these I have used where applicable. Elsewhere I have used the virtually complete Russian translation of the works also published by the Marx-Engels-Lenin Institute. Of Lenin's works I have used the second edition (of which the third was a reprint), in preference to the still incomplete fourth edition, which omits nearly all the full and informative notes. Of Stalin's works, the first twelve volumes (out of sixteen projected) were available when the present volume went to press. The collected edition of Trotsky's works in course of publication in Moscow between 1925 and 1927 was not completed, but I have used this edition for writings included in it. Speeches of Lenin and Stalin at party or Soviet congresses, etc., have as a rule been quoted from the collected works and not from the official records of the congresses, etc., which are less accessible to the ordinary student : the transcriptions, where I have checked them, have proved reliable. Other speakers have been quoted from the official records. Owing to the incompleteness (and sometimes the illegibility) of files of Soviet newspapers in this country, I have occasionally been obliged to quote them from secondary sources without verification. Except for the collected works of Marx and Engels, Lenin, Trotsky and Stalin, I have given the publication date of sources cited. The place of publication has been noted only where uncertainty was likely to arise ; works in English are assumed to have been published in London unless otherwise noted, or unless the nature of the work (e.g. the official *Foreign Relations of the United States*) made such indication superfluous. The habit of using abbreviations of Soviet institutions (e.g. VTsIK, Comintern) was too convenient to be discarded. But I have always given the institution its full title on its first mention, and have appended a list of abbreviations at the end of the volume.

A full index will appear with the bibliography at the end of the third volume.

E. H. CARR

April 20, 1950

CONTENTS

PART I

THE MAN AND THE INSTRUMENT

PART II

THE CONSTITUTIONAL STRUCTURE

PART III

DISPERSAL AND REUNION

ix

PART I

THE MAN AND THE INSTRUMENT

CHAPTER I

THE FOUNDATIONS OF BOLSHEVISM

WHAT afterwards became the " Russian Communist Party (Bolsheviks) ", and, later still, the " All-Union Communist Party (Bolsheviks) ", traced back its origin to a tiny congress of nine men who, meeting at Minsk in March 1898, founded a " Russian [1] Social-Democratic Workers' Party ". The nine delegates represented local organizations at Petersburg, Moscow, Kiev and Ekaterinoslav, and the Jewish General Workers' Union in Russia and Poland, commonly called the " Bund ". The congress lasted three days — March 1–3, 1898. It appointed a central committee and decided to issue a party organ. But before anything else could be done, the police arrested all the principal participants, so that virtually nothing remained of this initial effort save a common name shared by a number of local committees and organizations which had no central rallying point and no other connexions with one another. None of the nine delegates at Minsk played any leading rôle in the subsequent history of the party. A " manifesto of the Russian Social-Democratic Workers' Party " issued after the dispersal of the congress was the work of Peter Struve, a Marxist intellectual. This remained its most substantial legacy to posterity.

The manifesto, after referring to the " life-giving hurricane of the 1848 revolution ", which had blown over Europe fifty years before, noted that the Russian working class was " entirely deprived of what its foreign comrades freely and peacefully enjoy — a share in the administration of the state, freedom of the spoken and written word, freedom of organization and assembly ". These were necessary instruments in the struggle " for its final liberation, against private property, for socialism ". In the west the bourgeoisie had won these freedoms. In Russia conditions were different :

[1] Not *Russkaya*, but *Rossiiskaya* to denote not ethnic Russia, but the whole territory of the Russian Empire.

3

The farther east one goes in Europe, the weaker, meaner and more cowardly in the political sense becomes the bourgeoisie, and the greater the cultural and political tasks which fall to the lot of the proletariat. On its strong shoulders the Russian working class must and will carry the work of conquering political liberty. This is an essential step, but only the first step, to the realization of the great historic mission of the proletariat, to the foundation of a social order in which there will be no place for the exploitation of man by man.[1]

The document thus unequivocally accepted the two stages of revolution, the bourgeois-democratic and the proletarian-socialist revolution, laid down in the *Communist Manifesto* just fifty years earlier. Its great merit was that it pointed for the first time to the fundamental dilemma of the Russian revolution — the incapacity of the Russian bourgeoisie to make its own revolution and the consequent extension of the rôle of the Russian proletariat to leadership in the bourgeois-democratic revolution. The main criticism afterwards made of it was that it failed to mention the dictatorship of the proletariat or to indicate the means by which the proletariat could be enabled to carry out its mission. The manifesto remained an academic exercise rather than a programme of action.

The congress at Minsk was the first concerted attempt to create a Russian Marxist party on Russian soil. For the past thirty years the leading Russian revolutionaries had been the *narodniks* — a composite name for a succession of revolutionary groups believing in the theory of peasant revolution and in the practice of terrorism against members of the autocracy. At the end of the 1870s a young revolutionary named Plekhanov broke with the *narodniks* on the issue of individual terrorism, which he rejected as futile, fled abroad, became a convert to Marxism, and in 1883 founded in Switzerland a Russian Marxist group under the name " The Liberation of Labour ". For the next fifteen years Plekhanov and his associates, of whom Axelrod and Vera Zasulich were the most active, waged unceasing literary war against the *narodniks*, applying to Russia the Marxist thesis that the revolution could come about only through the development of capitalism and as the achievement of the industrial proletariat. The rapid expansion of industry and factory life in Russia during

[1] *VKP(B) v Rezolyutsiyakh* (1941), i, 3-5.

these years and the beginning of industrial strikes added substance to a programme which might at the outset have seemed
unrealistic.   In the 1890s embryonic Marxist groups made their
appearance in Russia itself, and the year 1895 saw the foundation
in Petersburg of a League of Struggle for the Liberation of the
Working Class.   Among the members of this league was a young
and enthusiastic disciple of Plekhanov, Vladimir Ilich Ulyanov.

Vladimir Ulyanov had been born in 1870 in Simbirsk (which
many years later, was renamed Ulyanovsk), the son of a minor
official.   The younger generation of the family was early imbued
with the revolutionary tradition.   When Vladimir was seventeen,
his elder brother, Alexander, was executed for complicity in a plot
to assassinate Alexander III.   Vladimir Ulyanov studied at the
university of Kazan where he was converted to Marxism and
eventually expelled for revolutionary activities.   In the early
1890s he came to Petersburg to practise law and to complete his
Marxist education.   His earliest writings were a continuation of
Plekhanov's polemics against the *narodniks*, and in the winter
of 1894–1895 he was expounding Plekhanov's new work *On the
Question of the Development of the Monist View of History* [1] to an
admiring circle of young Marxists.

In the summer of 1895 young Ulyanov visited the master
himself in Switzerland, and, back in Petersburg, joined the League
of Struggle for the Liberation of the Working Class.   But the
league was not interested only in theory.   Ulyanov, like its other
members, engaged in the distribution of revolutionary pamphlets
to factory workers; and this led at the end of 1895 to his arrest,
his imprisonment for some months and his eventual exile to
Siberia, though owing to the laxity of police regulations the
sentence did not interrupt his literary activities.   During his exile
in Siberia his mind was turning over plans of party organization
which centred round the creation of a party newspaper to be
published abroad and smuggled into Russia.   He discussed these
plans with Nadezhda Krupskaya, who joined him in Siberia and
became his wife, with another social-democrat, Krzhizhanovsky,
who shared his place of exile, and with two others, Potresov and

---

[1] The ponderous title was chosen to avert suspicion from the contents,
the work being legally published in Russia with the sanction of the censorship.
The English translation (1947) bears the more informative title *In Defence of
Materialism*.   The author disguised himself under the pen-name of Beltov.

Martov, who were elsewhere in Siberia.[1] On their release from Siberia early in 1900, Ulyanov, Potresov and Martov, having collected much needed funds, went on to Geneva to seek Plekhanov's collaboration. Agreement was soon reached. A popular weekly named *Iskra* (" The Spark ") and a solid theoretical journal named *Zarya* (" The Dawn ") were to be published under the editorship of a board of six — Plekhanov, Axelrod and Zasulich, representing the " Liberation of Labour " group, together with Ulyanov, Potresov and Martov.

The first number of *Iskra* came from the press in Stuttgart[2] on December 1, 1900, the first issue of *Zarya* on April 1, 1901. Plekhanov's prestige and authority as the doyen of Russian Marxists made him, in his own eyes and in those of others, the presiding genius of the enterprise. The three members of the " Liberation of Labour " group were the only prospective collaborators mentioned by name in the preliminary announcement of *Iskra*, which was apparently based on a draft made by Ulyanov in Russia,[3] and the same three names — Plekhanov, Axelrod and Zasulich — also appeared alone on the title page of *Zarya*. The three junior editors were still quite unknown and had their spurs to win. Ulyanov, the most prolific writer among them, had published his earliest works under the pen-names " Ilin " and " Tulin " : since leaving Russia he had concealed his identity under the pseudonyms " Petrov " and " Frei ". An article appearing in *Zarya* in December 1901 was the first occasion for the use of a new signature, " Lenin ". The occasion was of symbolical importance. It was about this time that Lenin first began to emerge head and shoulders above his fellow-editors by his energy and by the clarity of his ideas. He alone knew exactly what he wanted : to establish an accepted body of revolutionary doctrine and an organized revolutionary party. The first of these aims required, in addition to filling the columns of *Iskra*, the promulgation of a party programme ; the second, the summoning of a party congress to take up the work begun and abandoned

[1] N. K. Krupskaya, *Memories of Lenin* [i] (Engl. transl. 1930), p. 39.
[2] Subsequent issues were printed in Munich down to December 1903, when publication was transferred to Geneva.
[3] Lenin, *Sochineniya*, iv, 37-41 ; *VKP(B) v Rezolyutsiyakh* (1941), i, 7-10. Martov confirms the existence of the original draft (Lenin, *Sochineniya*, iv, 554): there is no evidence to prove how much of it survived in the finished version.

in 1898. *Iskra* was designed to give, in the words of the preliminary announcement of its birth, " a definite physiognomy
and organization " to the scattered Russian social-democratic
movement :

> Before uniting, and in order to unite, we must first decisively
> and definitely draw a line of separation. Otherwise our union
> would be merely a fiction covering up the present confusion
> and preventing its radical removal. It will therefore be under-
> stood that we do not intend to make our organ a mere collection
> of variegated opinions. We shall on the contrary conduct it in
> the spirit of a strictly defined policy.[1]

By the middle of 1902 *Iskra* was able to lay before its readers a
draft party programme which represented a careful blend of the
views of the milder and more cautious Plekhanov and those of
the bolder and more uncompromising Lenin. About the same
time Lenin published his first major original work on revolutionary
doctrine and revolutionary organization, *What is to be Done?*
Early in 1903 preparations were far enough advanced to summon
a party congress to meet in Brussels in July of that year.

" Bolshevism as a stream of political thought and as a political
party ", Lenin was to write nearly twenty years later, " has existed
since 1903." [2] Its character was determined by the controversies
of the period in which it was conceived and brought to birth —
controversies in which Lenin's clear-headed genius, confident
persistence and polemical temperament gave him the outstanding
rôle. Before the congress met three ideological battles had been
fought and won. As against the *narodniks*, the Russian Social-
Democratic Workers' Party regarded the proletariat and not the
peasant as the driving force of the coming revolution ; as against
the " legal Marxists ", it preached revolutionary and socialist
action ; as against the so-called " Economists ", it put forward
in the name of the proletariat political as well as economic demands.
    The campaign against the *narodniks* was the main achievement
of Plekhanov. The first Russian revolutionaries of the 1860s,
building on the intellectual foundations laid by the pioneers of

---

[1] *VKP(B) v Rezolyutsiyakh* (1941), i, 9 ; Lenin, *Sochineniya*, iv, 39-40.
[2] *Ibid.* xxv, 174.

the 1840s, were materialists in the sense of the eighteenth-century Enlightenment and radicals in the tradition of the French revolution ; they lacked contact both with the Russian peasant and with the still numerically insignificant Russian factory worker. The Russian revolutionaries of the 1870s discovered the Russian peasant and found in him the prospective protagonist of the Russian revolution, which thus acquired for the first time a social as well as an intellectual content. Some of them were followers of Bakunin and turned towards anarchism and terrorism. Others were influenced by Marx (whose works began to penetrate Russia in the 1870s), but interpreted his teaching in a peculiarly Russian way, arguing that Russia, being a predominantly peasant country, would avoid the western stage of bourgeois capitalism and that the specifically Russian peasant commune would provide a direct transition from the feudalism of the past to the communism of the future. The distinction between the revolutionary radicals of the 1860s and the *narodniks* of the 1870s had some analogy with the famous argument in other fields of Russian thought between westerners and Slavophils. The westerners held that it was the destiny of Russia, as a backward country, to learn from the west and to advance through the same phases and by the same processes which had already marked the progress of the west. The Slavophils believed that Russia, backward no doubt but full of youthful vigour and in this respect superior to the already decaying west, had a peculiar destiny of her own to accomplish which would enable her to rise above the characteristic evils of western civilization.

Lenin's early writings against the *narodniks* did little more than drive home the arguments of Plekhanov. In the very first of them he proclaimed with youthful emphasis his own revolutionary faith in the proletariat :

It is on the industrial working class that the social-democrats centre their attention and their activity. When the advanced members of that class have assimilated the ideas of scientific socialism and the idea of the rôle of the Russian worker in history, when their ideas are widespread and the workers have created stable organizations that will transform the disconnected economic war of today into a conscious class-struggle — then will the Russian *worker*, rising at the head of all democratic elements, overthrow absolutism and lead the RUSSIAN PRO-

LETARIAT (by the side of the proletariat of ALL COUNTRIES) along the straight way of open political struggle towards a *Victorious Communist Revolution*.[1]

In the last decade of the nineteenth century Witte and foreign capitalists were busy intensifying the development of Russian industry and of the Russian proletariat and thus creating the conditions which would prove Plekhanov and Lenin right. The star of the industrial worker was rising, the star of the peasant waning, in the revolutionary firmament. It was not till 1905 that the problem of fitting the peasant into the revolutionary scheme again became a burning party issue.

The " legal Marxists " were a small group of intellectuals who, in the middle 1890s, began to expound Marxist doctrines in books and articles cast in such a form as to pass the Russian censorship. The rapid spread of Marxism among Russian intellectuals at this time was due to the expansion of Russian industry and to the absence of any bourgeois tradition or bourgeois political philosophy which could play in Russia the rôle of western liberalism. Marx had praised the growth of capitalism in feudal conditions as a progressive force. Marxism was acceptable to the nascent Russian middle class as an ideological reinforcement in the struggle against feudalism and autocracy, just as Marxism was later to have its appeal to the rising capitalist class in " backward " Asiatic countries as an ally in the struggle against foreign imperialism. But, in accepting Marxism, the Russian middle-class intellectual emptied it of any immediate revolutionary content, so that the authorities, who still feared the *narodniks* as the main revolutionary party, were not unwilling to tolerate these sworn enemies of the *narodniks* whose own programme seemed to carry no imminent threat. The outstanding figure among the " legal Marxists " was Peter Struve, the author of the manifesto of the Minsk congress. His *Critical Notes on the Question of the Economic Development of Russia*, published in 1894, were the original platform of the group, ending with the famous injunction to socialists not to concern themselves with unrealistic projects of " heaven-storming ", but to " learn in the school of capitalism ".[2]   Other

[1] Lenin, *Sochineniya*, i, 194.

[2] Struve occupied for some time an equivocal position, and was a contributor to the first numbers of *Iskra* ; after 1902 he severed all connexion with the party, and in later years became a bitter enemy of the revolution.

" legal Marxists " were Bulgakov and Berdyaev, subsequent con-
verts to Orthodox Christianity, and Tugan-Baranovsky, author of
a standard work on Russian factories. Diametrically opposed to
the *narodniks*, they accepted without qualification the Marxist
view of the development of bourgeois capitalism as a necessary
first stage in the eventual achievement of socialism ; and they
believed that in this respect Russia must learn from the west
and tread the western path. So far Lenin was in full agreement
with them. But their insistence on the necessity of the bourgeois
capitalist stage soon led them to regard this as an end in itself
and to substitute reform for revolution as the process through
which socialism would eventually be achieved, thus anticipating
the views of Bernstein and the German " revisionists " of Marxism. As Lenin summed up the matter long after, " they were
bourgeois democrats for whom the breach with *narodnism* meant a
transition from petty-bourgeois (or peasant) socialism not to proletarian socialism, as in our case, but to bourgeois liberalism ".[1]
    More substantial was the controversy with the so-called
" Economists " — a group of Russian social-democrats who exercised a powerful influence on the whole movement about the turn
of the century. The distinctive tenet of the " Economists " was
the sharp separation of economics from politics ; the former were
the affair of the workers, the latter of the intellectual leaders of
the party. According to this thesis the workers were interested
not in political, but only in economic, ends ; the class struggle
for them reduced itself to a form of trade unionism — a struggle
of men against masters for better conditions of work and social
improvements within the framework of the existing order.
Politics were the concern of the intellectuals ; but, since the only
conceivable political programme in contemporary Russia was a
programme of bourgeois reform, the party intellectuals were in
fact limited to the same ends as the bourgeois liberals and became
indistinguishable from them. In the words of the so-called *credo*
which came to be accepted as the manifesto of the group :

> Discussions about an independent workers' political party
> are nothing more than the product of a transfer of foreign tasks
> and foreign achievements to our soil. . . . A whole set of
> historical conditions prevents us from being western Marxists

[1] Lenin, *Sochineniya*, xii, 57.

and demands from us a different Marxism which is appropriate
and necessary in Russian conditions. The lack in every Russian
citizen of political feeling and sense evidently cannot be redeemed by discussions about politics or by appeals to a non-
existent force. This political sense can be gained only by
training, i.e. by participation in that life (however un-Marxist
it may be) which Russian reality offers. . . . For the Russian
Marxist there is only one way out : to support the economic
struggle of the proletariat and to participate in liberal opposition
activity.[1]

These heresies were denounced in the summer of 1899 by Lenin
and a group of his fellow-exiles in Siberia, who described them in a
counter-manifesto as a regression from the party manifesto of the
previous year, where " the work of conquering political liberty "
had been squarely placed on " the strong shoulders " of the
Russian worker.[2] In the following year Plekhanov produced a
vade-mecum of documents introduced by a preface of his own
which was designed to serve as the final exposure of " Economism " ; [3] and Martov, who had a talent for political satire, wrote
a Hymn of the Latest Russian Socialism :

> Flatter us not with your politics, ye demagogues of the
> toiling masses, prate not to us of your communisms ; we believe
> in the might of — caisses d'assistance.[4]

The controversy was carried on into the Iskra period, occupying
many columns of the new journal : and Lenin's What is to be
Done ?, after an initial sally against the " legal Marxists ", proceeded to a mass assault on " Economism " in all its ramifications :

> The idea of the social-democrat must be not a trade union
> secretary, but a tribune of the people. . . . A trade union policy of
> the working class is simply a bourgeois policy for the working class.[5]

Political as well as economic agitation was needed to arouse the
class-consciousness of the masses. Indeed the two could not be

---

[1] Ibid. ii, 479-480. According to the author of the document, Kuskova,
it was not intended for publication, nor was the title credo given to it by
her (ibid. ii, 638-639). The publicity it received was due to the fact that
Lenin and his companions in Siberia took it as the text for their attack on
" Economism ".
[2] Ibid. ii, 483-486.
[3] G. V. Plekhanov, Sochineniya, xii, 3-42.
[4] Quoted in E. Yaroslavsky, Istoriya VKP(B), i (1926), 252.
[5] Lenin, Sochineniya, iv, 423-426.

separated, since every class struggle was essentially political. Unlike the " legal Marxists ", who were in essence a bourgeois group advocating bourgeois policies through a Marxist idiom, the " Economists " had a policy of economic agitation and social reform for the workers and were to that extent a genuine workers' party. But they reached the same practical conclusion as the legal Marxists that it was necessary to postpone to an indefinite future the revolutionary socialist struggle of the proletariat and to concentrate meanwhile on a reformist democratic programme in alliance with the bourgeoisie. Lenin did not fail in later years to point out that they had in this respect anticipated the fundamental tenet of Menshevism.[1]

The underlying issue at stake in the controversy with the legal Marxists and the Economists was one which continued to dog the whole history of the Russian revolution. The tidy scheme of the *Communist Manifesto* provided for revolution by successive stages. First, the bourgeois revolution would overthrow the remains of the feudal order and of political absolutism, and establish bourgeois democracy and bourgeois capitalism, with its attendant phenomenon, an industrial proletariat ; then the proletariat, organizing itself under the conditions provided by bourgeois democracy, would proceed to the final revolution to overthrow bourgeois capitalism and establish socialism. On the other hand, Marx himself had seemed to have some doubts about the application of this scheme, which was the product of a brilliant generalization from English and French history, to the Germany of the 1840s, still awaiting her bourgeois revolution but already possessing a nascent industry and rapidly growing proletariat. In 1844 Marx had questioned the possibility of keeping the coming German revolution within the limits of a bourgeois revolution " which leaves the pillars of the house standing ", and declared that Germany could be emancipated only through the revolutionary proletariat.[2] In the *Communist Manifesto* itself he predicted that, owing to the " advanced con-

[1] Lenin, *Sochineniya*, xii, 69.

[2] This was the gist of the famous concluding passage of the essay *On the Critique of Hegel's Theory of Law*, ending with the prediction that " the signal for Germany's resurrection from the dead will be given by the crow of the Gallic cock " (*Karl Marx-Friedrich Engels: Historisch-Kritische Gesamtausgabe*, 1er Teil, i, i, 617-620).

ditions " and " developed proletariat " of contemporary Germany, the German bourgeois revolution would be " the immediate prelude to a proletarian revolution ". And after the fiasco of 1848 had revealed the helplessness of the German bourgeoisie, Marx drew the link between bourgeois and proletarian revolutions in Germany closer still. In his address to the Communist League in March 1850, he argued that the failure of 1848 had imposed a dual task on the German workers : first, to support the bourgeoisie in its democratic struggle against feudalism and to give to that struggle the acutest possible form ; and, secondly, to maintain an independent party ready to take up the socialist struggle against bourgeois capitalism as soon as the bourgeois-democratic revolution was completed. Moreover, while the two tasks were theoretically separate, the interest of the workers was to make the process continuous :

> While the democratic petty bourgeoisie wants to end the revolution as rapidly as possible . . . our interests and our task consist in making the revolution permanent until all the more or less possessing classes are removed from authority, until the proletariat wins state power, until the union of proletarians not only in one country, but in all the leading countries of the world, is sufficiently developed to put an end to competition between the proletarians of these countries, and until at the very least the chief productive forces are concentrated in the hands of the proletarians.

And Marx ended a long appeal with the phrase : " Their fighting slogan must be ' permanent revolution ' ".[1]

Russian Marxists in the 1890s thus had two courses open to them. Everyone agreed that Russia had not yet reached her bourgeois revolution ; and it could therefore be argued, as the legal Marxists and Economists argued, that at this stage the proletariat could, so far as the socialist revolution was concerned, only play a waiting game, and in the meanwhile act as a subsidiary ally of the bourgeoisie in its programme for the overthrow of feudalism and autocracy. The alternative was to apply to Russia

---

[1] Marx i Engels, *Sochineniya*, vii, 483, 489. The origin of this famous phrase is uncertain ; Marx used it for the first time in an article of 1844, in which he observed that Napoleon had " substituted permanent war for permanent revolution " (*Karl Marx-Friedrich Engels: Historisch-Kritische Gesamtausgabe*, 1ᵉʳ Teil, iii, 299) ; in 1850 he ascribed to Blanqui " a declaration of permanent revolution (Marx i Engels, *Sochineniya*, viii, 81).

some such scheme as Marx had propounded for Germany; and
Lenin seems to have been the first, in an article called *Tasks of
Russian Social-Democrats*, written in Siberia in 1898, to make
the application.   Here Lenin argued that the task of Russian
social-democracy was to lead the class struggle of the proletariat
" in both its manifestations " — in the democratic struggle against
absolutism, in which the proletariat would have an ally in the
bourgeoisie, and in the socialist struggle against capitalism, in
which the proletariat would fight alone.   While " all social-democrats recognize that the political revolution in Russia must precede
the socialist revolution ", it is none the less true that the democratic
task is " indissolubly linked with the socialist task ", so that " all
socialists in Russia must become *social-democrats* . . . and all true
and consistent *democrats* in Russia must become *social-democrats* ".[1]   Lenin preserved a complete theoretical separation
between the two revolutions.   Mindful of the absence in Russia
of the relatively advanced industrial development of Germany in
1848, he refrained from following Marx in his prediction of an
" immediate " succession of bourgeois and proletarian revolutions ; he preferred to say nothing at all about the interval between
them.   But the " indissoluble link " between the two tasks of
Russian social-democracy brought him near to Marx's conception
for Germany of a continuous process of revolution.   Lenin's
article was enthusiastically received by the " Liberation of Labour "
group in Geneva, and published there with a preface by Axelrod
praising it as a " direct commentary " on the party manifesto.[2]

Acceptance of the dual task of the proletariat, democratic and

---

[1] Lenin, *Sochineniya*, ii, 171-178.   The thesis of the " indissoluble link "
had a respectable ancestry in Russian thought.   Herzen, who, though rightly
accounted the progenitor of the *narodniks*, shows occasional traces of Marx's
influence, wrote in 1868 : " A republic which did not lead to socialism would
seem to us absurd, a transition taking itself for an end ; socialism which tried
to dispense with political liberty, with equality of rights, would quickly de-
generate into authoritarian communism " (*Polnoe Sobranie Sochinenii i Pisem*,
ed. M. K. Lemke, xx (1923), 132 : an obvious error in punctuation has been
corrected).   From a different angle, a Minister of the Interior under Alexander
III, D. Tolstoy, said in the 1880s : " Any attempt to introduce into Russia
western European parliamentary forms of government is doomed to failure.
If the Tsarist regime . . . is overthrown, its place will be taken by communism, the pure undisguised communism of Mr. Karl Marx who recently
died in London and whose theories I have studied with attention and interest "
(Bernhard von Bülow, *Denkwürdigkeiten* (1931), iv, 573).

[2] The preface is reprinted in Lenin, *Sochineniya*, ii, 603-605.

socialist, had its implications in terms of party organization. One of the issues in the controversy with the Economists was the so-called question of " spontaneity " [1] in the workers' movement. The *Communist Manifesto*, in attacking the utopian socialists, had opposed " the gradual, spontaneous class organization of the proletariat " to " an organization of society specially contrived by these inventors ". On the other hand, emphasis on " gradual " and " spontaneous " development might be pushed to a point where it amounted to a denial of the need for political action. " Spontaneity " thus became a catchword of the Economists, who held that the development of economic action among the masses (trade unionism, strikes, etc.) would make them " spontaneously " ripe for revolution. Orthodox social-democrats, as represented by Plekhanov and the " Liberation of Labour " group as well as by Lenin, argued not only that the workers should be encouraged to put forward political as well as economic demands, but that they should be imbued with a conscious revolutionary purpose and conduct a consciously planned revolutionary campaign. " Consciousness " was adopted as the opposing catchword to " spontaneity ".[2] According to Lenin, the weakness of the Russian workers' movement at the end of the century was that the " spontaneous " element had outstripped " consciousness ". Russia's rapid industrial development had provoked a wave of strikes against intolerable conditions in the factory. But the protest of the workers was not guided by any revolutionary consciousness or revolutionary theory.

The theoretical discussion on " spontaneity " and " consciousness " masked the vital practical issue of the nature and function of a revolutionary party which ultimately rent the Russian Social-Democratic Workers' Party in twain. What was one day to become Bolshevik doctrine developed gradually, and provoked no serious clashes of opinion within the party before the fateful congress of 1903. It was not moulded exclusively by Lenin. Plekhanov still enjoyed a unique authority as the theorist of the

---

[1] The Russian words *stikhiinyi* and *stikhiinost'* are conventionally but inadequately translated by " spontaneous " and " spontaneity ". They also convey the idea of untutored inspiration, of something innate and elemental.

[2] The controversy is also reflected in an early article of 1901 by Stalin, who wrote that " social-democracy took in hand this unconscious, spontaneous, unorganized movement " of the workers (*Sochineniya*, i, 14).

party, which Lenin was slow to contest. But from the foundation of *Iskra* onwards Lenin became more and more the pace-maker of advanced ideas within the party ; and it is in his writings that the evolution of party doctrine can be most clearly traced. The view consistently propounded in *Iskra* of the character of the party rested on two propositions to which Lenin returned over and over again. The first was that " without revolutionary theory there can be no revolutionary movement ".[1] The second was that " social-democratic consciousness " or " class political consciousness " was not a " spontaneous " growth, and could come to the worker only " from without ".[2] Both these propositions defined the relation of the party to the proletariat as a whole and had corollaries whose far-reaching implications were not immediately apparent.

The first proposition, which insisted on the supreme importance of theory, called for a party created by intellectuals and, at any rate at the outset, composed mainly of them. This, in Lenin's view, was an historically attested necessity :

> The history of all countries bears witness that by its own resources alone the working class is in a position to generate only a trade-union consciousness, i.e. a conviction of the necessity of coming together in unions, of carrying on a struggle with the masters, of securing from the government the promulgation of this or that law indispensable for the workers and so forth. The teaching of socialism has grown out of philosophical, historical and economic theories worked out by educated representatives of the possessing classes, of the intelligentsia. The founders of contemporary socialism, Marx and Engels, belonged themselves by their social origin to the bourgeois intelligentsia. Similarly in Russia the theoretical teaching of social-democracy has arisen altogether independently of the spontaneous growth of the workers' movement, has arisen as the natural and inevitable result of the development of thought among the revolutionary-socialist intelligentsia.[3]

[1] Lenin, *Sochineniya*, ii, 184, iv, 380.
[2] *Ibid.* iv, 384, 422.
[3] *Ibid.* iv, 384-385. Lenin's emphasis seems here to have led him into a phrase (" altogether independently ") which is doubtfully Marxist ; elsewhere he laid stress on the necessary social roots of every political doctrine. The same charge might be brought against a well-known passage in one of Marx's own early writings in which he spoke of the proletariat as " the material weapon of philosophy " for making the revolution (*Karl Marx-Friedrich Engels: Historisch-Kritische Gesamtausgabe*, 1er Teil, i, i, 619-620).

He invoked the authority of the " profoundly just and weighty words " of Kautsky, still the revered theoretical leader of German social-democracy:

> The contemporary socialist movement can come into being only on the basis of a profound scientific knowledge. . . . The bearer of this science is not the proletariat, but the *bourgeois intelligentsia*; contemporary socialism was born in the heads of individual members of this class.[1]

It is difficult to dissociate this attitude from a faint aroma of condescension, which was characteristic of Plekhanov and not at this time wholly absent from the writings of Lenin. The manifesto announcing the foundation of *Iskra*, in pursuing the campaign against the Economists, expressed contempt for " purely workers' literature ";[2] and looking back much later on this period, Lenin noted that, in Russia as elsewhere, the growth of a mass workers' movement had been a signal for the appearance of " opportunist " deviations in the Marxist camp.[3] Lenin and his early associates were intellectuals of the purest water; and their writings attained a high standard of learning and acumen. Zinoviev described the few workers in the early party organizations as " isolated phenomena ".[4] The 1905 revolution for the first time brought into the ranks of the party a significant number of workers.

The second proposition, which envisaged the party as a revolutionary élite imposing a revolutionary consciousness " from without " on the mass of the workers, drew a sharp distinction between the proletariat and the party. The class was an economic

---

[1] Lenin, *Sochineniya*, iv, 390-391.

[2] *VKP(B) v Rezolyutsiyakh* (1941), i, 10.

[3] Lenin, *Sochineniya*, xvii, 344. Marx had noted that " the workers, when they . . . give up work and become professional *littérateurs*, always make ' theoretical ' trouble " (Marx i Engels, *Sochineniya*, xxvi, 484-485). R. Michels, discussing the question on the basis of German and Italian experience, concludes that " whenever the marshal's baton has rested in the worker's horny hand, the army of workers has had a leadership less sure and less satisfactory for its purposes than when the leadership has been in the hands of men from other classes of society ", and adds explicitly: " Ultimately it is not so much the revisionist intellectuals as the leaders of the trade union movement, that is to say, proletarians by origin, who have been behind the reformist tendency in German social democracy " (*Zur Soziologie des Parteiwesens* (2nd ed. 1925), pp. 391, 408).

[4] G. Zinoviev, *Geschichte der Kommunistischen Partei Russlands* (1923), p. 85.

unit, the party a political or ideological unit ; [1] and it was in the nature of things that the party could be only a part of the class [2] — its vanguard and the champion of its interests.   It was Plekhanov who in the columns of *Iskra* coined the term " hegemony " to express the relation of the party to the proletariat.   He protested against the " confusion of the concept ' class ' with the concept ' party ' ", and added that " the whole working class is one thing, and quite another thing is the social-democratic party which represents only the leading and at the beginning numerically small detachment of the working class ".[3]   No serious Marxist ever believed that a small *élite* of revolutionaries could by itself make a revolution ; that would have been to fall into the heresy of " Blanquism ".[4]   No one insisted more powerfully than Lenin himself that without the masses no serious political action was possible.   But the party was never conceived by Lenin as a mass organization.   Much of its strength was due to the fact that it was more concerned to exclude than to include : quality rather than quantity was its aim.   The function of the party was to lead the workers.   " The spontaneous struggle of the proletariat will not become a genuine ' class struggle ' until this struggle is led by a strong organization of revolutionaries." [5]   The doctrine of spontaneity, which denied this rôle of leadership, was nicknamed " tail-endism " because it condemned the party to lag at the tail of the workers' movement.

The doctrine of the party as a repository of revolutionary

---

[1] As Lagardelle, the French socialist, put it, the class is held together by a *lien de nécessité*, the party by a *lien de volonté* (H. Lagardelle, *Le Socialisme Ouvrier* (1911), pp. 166-167).

[2] This was even declared to be the derivation of the word : " The word ' party ' comes from the Latin *pars* or part : and we Marxists say today that the party is part of a definite class " (G. Zinoviev, *Geschichte der Kommunistischen Partei Russlands* (1923), p. 10).

[3] G. V. Plekhanov, *Sochineniya*, xii, 80-81.

[4] " Blanquism " in nineteenth-century revolutionary parlance meant addiction to the isolated revolutionary conspiracy or *putsch* and neglect of methodical organization.   " A military conspiracy is Blanquism ", wrote Lenin in 1917, " *if* it is not organized by the party of a definite class, *if* its organizers have not taken into account the political factor in general and the international factors in particular " — and *if* the objective conditions are not propitious (Lenin, *Sochineniya*, xxi, 347).   A briefer, though perhaps less reliable, definition is suggested by Lenin's *obiter dictum* in 1917 : " We are not Blanquists : we are not in favour of seizure of power by a minority " (*ibid.* xx, 96).

[5] *Ibid.* iv, 465.

theory and revolutionary consciousness, leading and guiding a spontaneous workers' movement, was hammered out by Lenin and his colleagues in *Iskra* against a background of current controversy. It had, however, good Marxist warrant. Some such doctrine had inspired the first Communist League of the 1840s, a body whose membership never exceeded a few hundreds, and left its mark in at least one passage of the *Communist Manifesto* :

> The Communists are, practically, the most progressive and resolute section of the working class of all countries . . . ; they have, theoretically, the advantage over the great mass of the proletariat of understanding the line of advance, conditions, and general results of the proletarian movement.

Another passage of the *Communist Manifesto*, on the other hand, described the proletarian movement as " the independent self-conscious movement of the immense majority " ; and in later years, influenced partly by the failures of 1848 and partly by their English surroundings, Marx and Engels came to believe in a period of indoctrination of the masses as the necessary prelude of a proletarian revolution. The only organization sponsored by Marx and Engels after their arrival in England, the International Workingmen's Association (the so-called " First International "), was a mass association, not a revolutionary party, and was as remote as could well be imagined from the Communist League of their youth.

Such difference as there was between the Marx of the Communist League and the Marx of the First International was the effect not of an evolution of doctrine, but of a change of *milieu* from the Prussian police state of the 1840s to the bourgeois democracy of mid-Victorian England. It was thus logical that Lenin should in this respect have been a disciple of the earlier rather than of the later Marx. Lenin was from the outset a practical Russian revolutionary, whose revolutionary theory was framed in the light of Russian needs and Russian potentialities. The project of making the intelligentsia the spearhead of a proletarian revolution was even more apposite to Russian than to German conditions, not only because the weak and backward Russian proletariat stood even more than its German, and *a fortiori* than its western European, counterpart in need of such leadership, but because the Russian intelligentsia did not, like its western counterpart, possess social roots in the commercial bourgeoisie and was not therefore committed to any deep-seated bourgeois allegiance. The economically rootless Russian intelligentsia had already shown how its capacity for abstract revolutionary thinking could be harnessed to the political reality of social revolution. The " going to the people " movement of the 1870s, being exclusively directed to the most backward section of the population, the peasantry, was a fiasco. But it had its place in history as a first quixotic and desperate attempt to bridge the gulf between the masses and the revolutionary intelligentsia; and this could now be repeated with the proletarian masses. It was, however, when Lenin reached the details of party organization that Russian conditions most clearly influenced his thought. The nature of the Russian state precluded the formation of any kind of socialist, or even democratic, party on a western model and drove every democratic or socialist movement into secret and conspiratorial channels. Isolated revolutionary groups of workers and students formed by well-meaning amateurs fell easy victims to the Tsarist police. Such exploits were like " a campaign waged by gangs of peasants armed with clubs against a modern army ".[1]

> Against small groups of socialists seeking shelter up and down the broad Russian underworld [wrote Lenin at this time] stands the gigantic machine of the powerful contemporary state straining all its forces to crush socialism and democracy. We are convinced that we shall in the end break this police state. . . . But in order to carry on a systematic struggle against the government we must bring our revolutionary organization to the highest point of perfection.[2]

The making of revolution in Russia was a task for professional revolutionaries; and it was no accident that military metaphors so frequently appeared in discussions not only by Lenin, but by Plekhanov and other *Iskra* writers, of party organization.

The theme of party organization was finally developed by Lenin in the summer of 1902 in the pamphlet *What is to be Done?*, which drew the conclusions from the campaign against the Economists. In his treatment of this concrete topic Lenin ran further ahead of his *Iskra* colleagues than on any previous occasion. He compared the position of the Economists to that of the re-

---

[1] Lenin, *Sochineniya*, iv, 439.   [2] *Leninskii Sbornik*, iii (1925), 26.

visionists in Germany, of the " possibilists " in France and of
the Fabians in England ; it was the symptom of a profound
division in the social-democratic movement between a democratic
party of social reformers and a socialist party of true revolutionaries.[1] The one party conceived itself as an " organization of
workers ", the other as an " organization of revolutionaries ".
The difference was fundamental :

An organization of workers must be, first of all, occupational ;
secondly, it must be as broad as possible ; thirdly, it must be
as little secret as possible. . . . Conversely, an organization of
revolutionaries must contain primarily and chiefly people whose
occupation is revolutionary activity. . . . This organization
must necessarily be not very broad, and as secret as possible.[2]

Lenin faced the charge that such an organization was in contradiction with " the democratic principle ". The charge could
come only from foreign quarters ignorant of Russian realities.
The democratic principle as commonly interpreted required " full
publicity " and " election to all posts ". Neither of these requirements could be fulfilled by a revolutionary party working within
" the framework of our autocracy ". Lenin concluded :

The one serious organizational principle for workers in our
movement must be strictest secrecy, strictest choice of members,
training of professional revolutionaries. Once these qualities
are present something more than democracy is guaranteed :
complete comradely confidence among revolutionaries. . . . It
would be a great mistake to think that the impossibility of a
really " democratic " control makes the members of a revolutionary organization irresponsible. . . . They feel their *responsibility* very keenly, knowing by experience that in order to
rid itself of an unworthy member an organization of genuine
revolutionaries recoils from nothing.[3]

This principle was to be applied equally at all levels :

We must break completely with the tradition of a purely
workers' or trade union type of social-democratic organization
down to factory groups *inclusive*. The factory group or factory
committee . . . must consist of a very small number of
revolutionaries, receiving *direct from the* [*central*] *committee*
orders and powers to conduct the whole social-democratic party
work in the factory. All members of the factory committee

[1] Lenin, *Sochineniya*, iv, 366-367.   [2] *Ibid.* iv, 447.
[3] *Ibid.* iv, 466-469.

must regard themselves as agents of the [central] committee, bound to submit to all its directions, bound to observe all " laws and customs " of this " army in the field " into which they have entered and which they cannot leave without permission of the commander.[1]

Thus the whole emphasis came to rest on the need for a small, closely knit party under a strong central leadership to act in the name of the proletariat as the spearhead of revolution. The methods of the revolutionary struggle varied and must be determined empirically from time to time. What remained fixed and consistent was the central plan built up on a sound basis of theory, and executed, with the support of the masses, by a highly organized, disciplined and centrally directed party of professional revolutionaries.

Lenin, now in his early thirties, had reached the summit of his powers. The three years following his release from Siberia were years of feverish and incessant intellectual activity. These were the years in which the foundations of Bolshevism " as a stream of political thought and as a political party " were laid. The instrument carried the stamp of the man: it reflected its creator's simplicity, his unbending strength and, above all, his singleness of purpose. A well-known passage in Krupskaya's memoirs bears witness to that masterful concentration on a single end which was the hall-mark of Lenin's character. As a schoolboy he liked skating, but found that it tired him, so that he wanted to sleep afterwards. " This hindered my studies. So I gave up skating." After his return from Siberia he ceased to play chess because " chess gets hold of you too much, and hinders work ". At one time he had been fascinated by the study of Latin, but " it began to hinder other work, so I gave it up ".[2] After the revolution he told Gorky :

I can't listen to music too often. It affects your nerves, makes you want to say stupid, nice things and stroke the heads of people who could create such beauty while living in this vile hell. And now you mustn't stroke anyone's head — you might get your hand bitten off.[3]

[1] Lenin, *Sochineniya*, v, 185-186.
[2] Krupskaya, *Memories of Lenin* [i] (Engl. transl. 1930), p. 35.
[3] M. Gorky, *Days with Lenin* (Engl. transl. n.d.[? 1932]), p. 52.

If Lenin could lead and dominate men, it was because he himself throughout his life was led and dominated to an exceptional extent by a single thought and a single aim. This overwhelming sense of service to an idea accounted for the simplicity and modesty of demeanour which all remarked in him. He set an example of austerity and impersonality which long remained a standard of conduct for the party. No doubt Stalin was correct in noting this trait as " one of the strongest sides of Lenin as the new leader of the new masses ".[1] But there was no element of calculation in Lenin about an attitude which was deeply rooted in his character.

This whole-hearted simplicity and directness left their mark on Lenin's thinking. His immense learning, his analytical skill, his outstanding intellectual power in the marshalling of fact and argument were displayed without much concern for the subtler alternations of light and shade ; everything was clear-cut, brilliant, decisive. As Bukharin said in the last year of Lenin's life :

> Lenin is a strategist of genius. He knows that it is necessary to strike the principal enemy and not eclectically weave shade upon shade.[2]

In controversy he was apt to resort to a one-sided emphasis which he justified by the need to counteract similar one-sidedness in his adversary :

> The Economists bent the stick one way [he said at the second party congress, defending *What is to be Done?*]. In order to straighten the stick it was necessary to bend it the other way ; and this is what I did.[3]

Yet his ideas could be utopian to the point of naïvety, as in his reflexions on the disappearance of the state or on the replacement of bureaucracy by the personal service of citizens. The combination of a fundamental simplicity of thought and character with fanaticism in opinion and ruthlessness in action is strongly reminiscent of Robespierre. Lenin's self-assurance in the infallibility of his creed was rendered all the more formidable by his

---

[1] Stalin, *Sochineniya*, vi, 55.
[2] *Dvenadtsatyi S"ezd Rossiiskoi Kommunisticheskoi Partii (Bol'shevikov)* (1933), p. 563.
[3] Lenin, *Sochineniya*, vi, 23. *State and Revolution*, written fifteen years later, reveals the same technique (see p. 240 below).

lack of personal pretensions.   The denunciation of opponents,
and the attribution of their intellectual myopia to moral obliquity,
had been fixed in the Russian tradition since Belinsky and in the
revolutionary tradition since Marx, if not earlier.   But the fanaticism was none the less real because it was traditional ; and even
fellow-revolutionaries were shocked by the ruthlessness with
which Lenin excommunicated dissidents.   " A sectarian with a
serious Marxist training, a Marxist sectarian ", was the final
verdict of the bitterly hostile Potresov who regarded Lenin as
" constitutionally incapable of digesting opinions different from
his own ".[1]   But Lenin was no mere theorist of revolution.
Opinion was never divorced from action.   He was a practising
revolutionary ;   and, whatever might be said of doctrine, the
practice of revolution allowed of no mercy and no exceptions.

It was this union of theory and practice which made Lenin a
complex figure and accounted for his unique greatness.   Trotsky
in a well-known passage contrasted Marx, the man of theory, with
Lenin, the man of action :

> The whole of Marx appears in the *Communist Manifesto*,
> in the preface to the *Critique* [*of Political Economy*], in *Capital*.
> Even if he had never been destined to become the founder of
> the First International, he would still remain for all times the
> figure which we know today.   The whole of Lenin on the other
> hand appears in revolutionary action.   His scientific works are
> only a preparation for activity.   Even if he had never published
> a single book he would live on in history in the shape in which
> he has entered it : as the leader of the proletarian revolution,
> as the creator of the Third International.[2]

This estimate may require some corrective, especially for the
early period.   But it was Lenin himself who quoted in April
1917 : " Theory, my friend, is grey, but green is the everlasting
tree of life " ;[3] and it was Lenin who in November 1917 observed
with a sigh of relief that it is " more agreeable and useful to go
through the ' experiment of revolution ' than to write about it ".[4]
In the succeeding months he was constantly at odds with the
doctrinaires in his party.

[1] A. N. Potresov, *Posmertnyi Sbornik Proizvedenii* (Paris, 1937), pp. 294, 299.
[2] L. Trotsky, *O Lenine* (n.d. [1924]), p. 148.
[3] Lenin, *Sochineniya*, xx, 102.   [4] *Ibid.* xxi, 455.

It is not enough [he wrote at this time] to be a revolutionary and an advocate of socialism in general. It is necessary to know at every moment how to find the particular link in the chain which must be grasped with all one's strength in order to keep the whole chain in place and prepare to move on resolutely to the next link.[1]

After three years of revolutionary experience he could exclaim — it was no doubt an *obiter dictum* uttered in the heat of controversy — that " practice is a hundred times more important than any theory ".[2]   In the roll of Lenin's genius one of the largest entries would have to be devoted to his greatness as a political strategist and as a political tactician.   His far-sightedness in building up impregnable positions in advance was matched by an uncanny instinct which told him where and when and how to strike or to hold back.

If, however, Lenin was a great revolutionary — perhaps the greatest of all time — his genius was far more constructive than destructive.   The contribution of Lenin and the Bolsheviks to the overthrow of Tsarism was negligible.   It is only in an external sense that they can be held responsible for the overthrow of the Provisional Government.   From July 1917 its downfall had become inevitable; it was waiting only for its successor to appear. Bolshevism succeeded to a vacant throne.   The crucial moments of the interval between the February and October revolutions were Lenin's announcement at the first All-Russian Congress of Soviets in June that the Bolsheviks were willing to take power and Lenin's decision in September that the time was ripe to take it.   Lenin's major achievement came after the bloodless victory of the revolution in October 1917 and was that of a great constructive statesman.   But what he built, with all its merits and all its defects, was raised on foundations laid long before, and cannot be fully understood without some knowledge of those foundations.   The first of them were laid during the so-called " *Iskra* period " before Lenin's followers received their distinctive name at the second party congress.

---

[1] *Ibid.* xxii, 466.   [2] *Ibid.* xxvi, 71.

BOLSHEVIKS AND MENSHEVIKS

MAINLY as the result of the preparatory work done by the *Iskra* group, the second congress of the Russian Social-Democratic Workers' Party met in July and August 1903 under the chairmanship of Plekhanov, first in Brussels (whence it fled for fear of police persecution) and then in London. It was the real foundation congress of the party : but it also saw the famous split between Bolsheviks and Mensheviks which widened and deepened until it led to complete formal separation after 1912. The congress was attended by representatives of 25 recognized social-democratic organizations, each having 2 votes except the Jewish workers' organization, the Bund, which had 3 in virtue of the special status as an autonomous section of the party accorded to it by the first congress. As some organizations sent only one delegate the congress was actually composed of 43 voting delegates disposing in all of 51 votes. In addition there were 14 delegates from various organizations with consultative, but without voting, rights. Of the full delegates more than 30 were professed adherents of *Iskra*, and the congress was completely dominated by the *Iskra* group. So long as the *Iskra*-ites remained united, the only concerted opposition came from the delegates of the Bund, who were interested almost exclusively in the rights of national minorities and in upholding their own autonomous status in the party, and from two delegates with " Economist " leanings, Akimov and Martynov, who represented the Union of Russian Social-Democrats Abroad. The resolution to recognize *Iskra* as the central organ of the party was passed at an early stage of the congress with only two dissenting votes.[1]

The most important pieces of business before the congress were the adoption of a party programme and of a party statute.

[1] *Vtoroi S"ezd RSDRP* (1932), p. 155.

Plekhanov in the 1880s, and Lenin in the 1890s, had already made experiments in drafting a programme; and, when the *Iskra* group began to consolidate itself, the demand for a party programme was raised simultaneously with the demand for a fresh party congress. The discussions which went on through the early part of 1902 ranged Lenin, who stood for youth and no concessions to expediency, against Plekhanov, who preached tradition and caution even in the pursuit of revolution. A first draft by Plekhanov was severely criticized by Lenin, who described it as " not a programme for a party engaged in a practical struggle, but a declaration of principles — rather a programme for students ",[1] and produced a counter-draft of his own. A commission composed of other members of the *Iskra* group was entrusted with the task of conflation and rather surprisingly succeeded. Plekhanov's authority was still immense, and Lenin, still in the early thirties, was prepared — almost for the last time in his life — to compromise on a theoretical issue. Lenin accepted a less incisive formulation than his own of the advance of capitalism in Russia towards the inevitable climax of social revolution. But he secured the insertion of a cautious programme of agrarian reform, which had been altogether absent from Plekhanov's draft. Of the draft programme printed in *Iskra* on June 1, 1902, and submitted to the party congress in the following year, the first or theoretical part was, broadly speaking, Plekhanov's work stiffened here and there by Lenin, the second or practical part Lenin's, attenuated here and there by Plekhanov.[2]

The theoretical part of the programme began with the orthodox Marxist argument that the relations of production have now evolved to a point where bourgeois capitalism has become incompatible with further progress. As its contradictions multiply, " the number and solidarity of the proletarians [3] increase and

---

[1] Lenin, *Sochineniya*, v, 18.

[2] Lenin's own contributions are reprinted in Lenin, *Sochineniya*, v, 1-51, and a useful brief summary of the whole controversy will be found *ibid.* v, 398-399, note 1.

[3] Martynov proposed at the congress to amend this clause to read, " the number, solidarity and consciousness of the proletarians " (*Vtoroi S"ezd RSDRP* (1932), p. 116). This was an echo of the controversy about spontaneity and consciousness, and was accompanied by a vigorous attack on Lenin's *What is to be Done?* on the ground that it denied any spontaneously socialist impulse in the proletariat; Lenin was defended by Plekhanov, Martov and Trotsky, and the amendment was rejected.

their struggle with their exploiters becomes more acute ". Technical development thus " more and more rapidly creates the material possibility of a replacement of capitalist by socialist relations of production ", i.e. of a social revolution which would " abolish the division of society into classes " and " put an end to all forms of exploitation of one class of society by another ". The dictatorship of the proletariat, defined as " the conquest of political power by the proletariat ", was " the indispensable condition of this social revolution ". It was the first time that the dictatorship of the proletariat had been formally inscribed in any party programme. The practical and specifically Russian part of the programme related to immediate aims ; these, as the *Communist Manifesto* had said, would naturally vary from country to country. These aims fell into three groups — political demands (including equal and universal suffrage, freedom of conscience, speech, press, assembly and association, election of judges, separation of church and state, and free and universal education), economic demands of the workers (including the eight-hour day, prohibition of employment of children, limitations on work for women, state insurance for old age and incapacity, and prohibition of fines and payment in kind), and economic demands of the peasants (notably the return to them of the strips of land unjustly taken away from them at the time of the emancipation). These were evidently regarded by the framers of the programme as the most extreme demands compatible with obtaining the support of the radical bourgeoisie in the first stage of the revolution. The relation between these immediate aims and the ultimate goal of the classless society was not touched on. The programme ended by offering the support of the party to " any opposition or revolutionary movement directed against the existing social and political order in Russia " and demanding as a first step towards the realization of its aims " *the overthrow of the autocracy* and the calling of a *constituent assembly* freely elected by the whole people ". The programme was debated in detail by the congress and minor amendments made. But in the end only Akimov opposed its formal adoption.[1] It remained unaltered till 1919.

---

[1] *Vtoroi S"ezd RSDRP* (1932), pp. 258-259. The text of the programme as adopted will be found *ibid.* pp. 417-423, *VKP(B) v Rezolyutsiyakh* (1941), i, 19-23, and elsewhere.

The debate on the party statute ran at once into deep water on the first clause of the statute which defined the qualifications of membership. The commission which prepared the draft had split on a question of principle and offered two alternative texts, one put forward by Lenin, the other by Martov. Lenin had defined the qualifications of party membership in the following terms :

A member of the party is one who accepts its programme, and supports it both materially and by personal participation in one of its organizations.

Martov proposed the following alternative :

A member of the Russian Social Democratic Workers' Party is one who accepts its programme and supports it both materially and by regular cooperation under the leadership of one of its organizations.

The margin between the two drafts was narrow in form ; but the more precise formula on which Lenin insisted was a deliberate and challenging expression — and was known by all to be such — of his conception, already elaborated in *What is to be Done?*, of a small party of organized and disciplined professional revolutionaries. Feeling ran high ; and the distinction which emerged from this debate between " hard " and " soft " *Iskra*-ites [1] was the original form of the Bolshevik-Menshevik feud. Martov and Axelrod distinguished between " organization " and " party ". While the need for a conspiratorial organization was admitted, this could have a meaning only if it were the nucleus of a broad party of sympathizers. Lenin retorted that it was essential to draw a line between " chatterboxes " and " workers " : Martov's draft opened the door equally to both. Plekhanov came down rather nonchalantly on the side of Lenin. The other members of the *Iskra* board, Potresov and Zasulich, did not speak, but shared the views of Axelrod and Martov. Trotsky unexpectedly came out in favour of Martov.[2] At the end of a long and stubborn

[1] Lenin afterwards also classified them as " consistent " and " inconsistent " *Iskra*-ites (Lenin, *Sochineniya*, vi, 269).

[2] Trotsky came to Lenin in London in October 1902 and quickly attracted attention by his literary talent. Twice in the spring of 1903 Lenin proposed that he should be coopted on to the board of *Iskra*, but met a firm veto by Plekhanov (Krupskaya, *Memories of Lenin* [i] (Engl. transl. 1930), pp. 85-86, 92). According to Krupskaya, Lenin at the congress " least of all thought that Trotsky would waver " (*ibid.* p. 99).

debate Lenin's draft was rejected in a full vote of the congress by 28 votes to 23, and Martov's alternative carried by 28 votes to 22.[1] The remainder of the statute was accepted without much difficulty. The rather clumsy central organization of the party consisted of the board of the central organ (*Iskra*) as the custodian of party doctrine, a central committee to direct party work through the local organizations, and a party council of five composed of two nominees of each of these bodies and a president nominated by the party congress; the council was the supreme controlling organ responsible only to the biennial congress.[2]

The sequel of the crucial vote on the first clause of the statute was paradoxical. The majority had been made up of " soft " *Iskra*-ites and the delegates of the Bund and other extraneous organizations which had never been associated with *Iskra*. Within the *Iskra* group itself Lenin still commanded a majority. The debate on the party statute involved a decision on the relations of the Bund to the party. The rejection by an overwhelming majority of the claim of the Bund to " remain the sole representative of the Jewish proletariat " caused its delegates to withdraw in dudgeon after the twenty-seventh sitting of the congress (there were thirty-seven in all).[3] At the following sitting a decision to recognize in the statute only one " foreign " organization of the party, the League of Revolutionary Social-Democracy which was closely associated with *Iskra* (Lenin was its delegate at the congress), thus disfranchising the Union of Russian Social-Democrats Abroad, led to the withdrawal of Martynov and Akimov.[4] In taking these decisions all the *Iskra*-ites still stood together. But the withdrawal of seven delegates who had voted with the " softs " on the qualifications of party membership had the result of shifting the balance of votes in favour of the " hards ". It became apparent that Lenin would command a majority in the congress on the one important outstanding item of the agenda — the elections to the party organs — and that he would use this power to further the victory of his opinions. This discovery, rather than any overt incident, caused a sudden change in the climate of the congress. From the thirtieth sitting onwards

[1] *Vtoroi S"ezd RSDRP* (1932), pp. 263-285.
[2] The text of the statute will be found *ibid*. pp. 423-425, and *VKP(B) v (Rezolyutsiyakh* 1941), i, 24-25.
[3] *Vtoroi S"ezd RSDRP* (1932), pp. 324-325.   [4] *Ibid*. p. 334.

the proceedings were conducted in an atmosphere of intense bitterness.

Evidently an issue of substance was at stake. Yet it must be added that clauses of the party statute, drafted and put through the congress by the *Iskra* group as a whole, provided for an almost unlimited control by the central authority over local party organs, and that subsequent indignation at Lenin's conception of a centralized and disciplined party was the sequel, rather than the origin, of the feud. It transpired from the mutual recriminations between Lenin and Martov at the congress that Lenin's project to reduce the number of the *Iskra* board under the new dispensation from six to three, and to limit the membership of the party central committee to three, had been discussed in the board before the congress without encountering any objection of principle. It was only when this project emerged in the congress in the concrete form of a proposal to appoint Plekhanov, Lenin and Martov (two " hards " and one " soft ") to the *Iskra* board, and to elect secondary figures to the central committee, so that the control of the party by the board should be unchallenged, that opposition became implacable ; and it was at the congress that Martov first made the charge of " martial law within the party " with " exceptional laws against individual groups " which played so conspicuous a rôle in subsequent controversy.[1] The rest of the proceedings took the form of a series of votes and protests. The decision to elect three members of the *Iskra* board was taken by a majority of 25 votes to 2 with 17 abstaining. The majority then proceeded to elect Plekhanov, Martov and Lenin ; Martov rejected the proffered seat on the board ; and the minority refused to take any further part in the elections.[2] The central committee was composed exclusively of " hards " ; and Plekhanov was appointed president of the party council. On the strength of these results the victors were dubbed " Bolsheviks " or majority men, the dissentients " Mensheviks " or minority men. These names were destined to pass into history.

This was not, however, the end of the story. Plekhanov had stood firmly with Lenin through the turmoil of the congress.

[1] *Ibid.* p. 373.
[2] *Ibid.* p. 376. From this point onwards the two factions into which the congress had split began to hold separate meetings (Lenin, *Sochineniya*, vi, 56).

When a delegate tried to draw a distinction between Lenin's views and his own, he had replied a little pompously that, whereas Napoleon had made his marshals divorce their wives, nobody would succeed in divorcing him from Lenin.[1] But the earlier argument about the programme had already shown how easily the mildness of the older man might clash with the ruthlessness of the younger. Plekhanov was quickly shocked by the uncompromising consistency with which Lenin proposed to exploit the victory. The Mensheviks whom Lenin wished to excommunicate included most of Plekhanov's old friends and associates. Lenin's stringent party discipline had been approved by Plekhanov in principle, but, when it came to enforcement, proved alien to the less rigid notions of political organization which he had unconsciously imbibed during his long sojourn in the west. Unthinkably for Lenin, Plekhanov began to advocate reconciliation with the dissidents. Before the end of 1903 Lenin had resigned from the editorial board of *Iskra*;[2] Plekhanov had coopted on to it the former members rejected by the congress, Mensheviks all; *Iskra* had become a Menshevik organ; and Lenin, evicted from the party machine which the congress had placed within his grasp, was left to organize his Bolsheviks as an independent faction.

The next twelve months saw a series of scathing articles against Lenin from the pen of Plekhanov, as well as of his other former colleagues on *Iskra*. Plekhanov quickly overcame any embarrassment caused by his record of support for Lenin up to the end of the second congress, offering the lame excuse that he had disagreed with some passages in *What is to be Done?* when he first read it, but had the impression that Lenin had modified his views.[3] Lenin was now declared guilty of fostering " a sectarian spirit of exclusiveness ".[4] In an article entitled *Centralism or Bonapartism?* he was accused of " confusing the dictatorship of the proletariat with the dictatorship over the proletariat ", and of practising " Bonapartism, if not absolute monarchy in the old

---

[1] *Vtoroi S"ezd RSDRP* (1932), p. 138.
[2] According to Plekhanov Lenin sought a precedent in contemporary English politics : " Chamberlain left the ministry in order to strengthen his position ; I am doing the same " (G. V. Plekhanov, *Sochineniya*, xiii, 44).
[3] *Ibid.* xiii, 135-138.   [4] *Ibid.* xiii, 7.

pre-revolutionary style ".[1]   His view of the relation of the professional revolutionary to the masses was that not of Marx, but
of Bakunin.[2]   Martov, reverting to the idea which he had propounded at the congress, wrote a pamphlet on *The Struggle against
Martial Law in the Russian Social-Democratic Workers' Party.*
Vera Zasulich wrote that Louis XIV's idea of the state was
Lenin's idea of the party.[3]   The party printing-press, now under
Menshevik auspices, published a brilliantly vituperative pamphlet
by Trotsky entitled *Our Political Tasks* ; [4]   the present Menshevik
affiliations of the author were proclaimed by the dedication " To
my dear teacher Pavl Borisovich Axelrod ".   Lenin's methods
were attacked as " a dull caricature of the tragic intransigence of
Jacobinism " and a situation predicted in which " the party is
replaced by the organization of the party, the organization by the
central committee, and finally the central committee by the
dictator ".   The final chapter bore the title " The Dictatorship
over the Proletariat ".[5]   It was some time afterwards that Plekhanov in the *Journal of a Social Democrat* wrote that, if the
Bolshevik conception prevailed " everything will in the last resort
revolve round one man who *ex providentia* will unite all the powers
in himself ".[6]

Echoes of the split were soon heard in the German Social-
Democratic Party which had had its own troubles over the schism
of the " revisionists ".   The apparent unanimity of almost all the
prominent members of the Russian party — for Lenin's followers
were rank-and-filers with scarcely a known name among them —
won almost universal support for the Mensheviks.   Kautsky not
only refused to publish in the German social-democratic journal

---

[1] *Ibid.* xiii, 90-91.

[2] *Ibid.* xiii, 185.   [3] *Iskra*, No. 70, July 25, 1904.

[4] N. Trotsky, *Nashi Politicheskie Zadachi* (Geneva, 1904).   Trotsky at first
used the initial N. with his pseudonym, later reverting to his own initial L. ;
Lenin also sometimes used the fictitious initial N.

[5] It is fair to recall Trotsky's final verdict on this controversy nearly thirty
years later : " It was not for nothing that the words ' irreconcilable ' and
' unsparing ' occurred so frequently in Lenin's vocabulary.   Only the highest
concentration on the goal of revolution, free from everything pettily personal,
can justify this kind of personal ruthlessness. . . . His behaviour seemed to
me inadmissible, terrible, shocking.   Yet at the same time it was politically
correct and therefore indispensable from the point of view of organization "
(L. Trotsky, *Moya Zhizn* (Berlin, 1930), i, 187-188).

[6] G. V. Plekhanov, *Sochineniya*, xiii, 317.

Neue Zeit an article from Lenin defending the Bolshevik stand-point, but sent to the Menshevik *Iskra* for publication a copy of a letter roundly condemning Lenin's attitude.[1]   The most substantial attack on Lenin was an article in *Neue Zeit* in July 1904 by Rosa Luxemburg, who denounced his policy of " ultra-centralism " as bureaucratic and not democratic.   Diagnosing a specifically Russian character in Lenin's project, she spoke bitterly of " the ' ego ' crushed and pulverized by Russian absolutism " reappearing in the form of " the ' ego ' of the Russian revolu-tionary " which " stands on its head and proclaims itself anew the mighty consummator of history " ; and she offered a new argu-ment when she attacked the absolute powers of Lenin's party leadership as likely to " intensify most dangerously the con-servatism which naturally belongs to every such body ".[2]   Finally, Bebel, the veteran German party leader, made an offer of arbitra-tion, which was hastily accepted by the Mensheviks and no less summarily rejected by Lenin.[3]

Lenin remained apparently unmoved by all these attacks.[4] He had behind him the example and authority of Marx who, when criticized for his attacks on other German revolutionaries, had replied in his journal :

> Our task consists in unsparing criticism directed even more against our so-called " friends " than against open enemies; and in so acting we gladly renounce a cheap democratic popularity.[5]

In his reply to Martov at the congress itself Lenin had made a spirited defence of his uncompromising position :

> I am not in the least frightened by big words about " martial law " and " exceptional laws against particular persons and groups ", etc.   In dealing with unstable and warring elements we not only can, but are bound to, set up " martial law ", and our whole party statute, the whole policy of " central-ism " just approved by the congress, is nothing else than

[1] *Iskra*, No. 66, May 15, 1904.

[2] *Neue Zeit*, xxii (Vienna, 1903–1904), ii, 484-492, 529-535.

[3] Particulars of this episode will be found in Lenin, *Sochineniya*, vii, 450-452, note 44 ; *Leninskii Sbornik*, v (1926), 169-176, 182-183.

[4] Krupskaya in her memoirs (*Memories of Lenin* [i] (Engl. transl. 1930), p. 108) speaks of the personal pain caused to him by the break with Martov ; but this implies no shadow of political doubt.

[5] Marx i Engels, *Sochineniya*, viii, 445.

" martial law " to deal with such numerous sources of political
indiscipline.   Against political indiscipline special, even exceptional, laws are required ; and the step taken by the congress has set the right political course by creating a solid basis
for *such* laws and *such* measures.[1]

In a lengthy pamphlet, *One Step Forward, Two Steps Back*, pub-
lished at Geneva in the following year with the sub-title " On the
Crisis in our Party ", he refused to be intimidated by charges of
Jacobinism :

> A Jacobin, indissolubly united with the *organization* of a pro-
> letariat *conscious* of its class interests — that is a *revolutionary
> social-democrat*.[2]

In a searching analysis of the congress proceedings he showed
that the " soft " *Iskra*-ites had constantly found themselves in
embarrassing alliance with delegates, such as those of the Bund,
who were enemies both of *Iskra* and of any strong centralized
party organization ; and Lenin traced back their spiritual pedigree
to the " gentlemen-anarchists " who were the ancestors of *narodnism* in all its forms, including nihilism :

> This aristocratic anarchism has always been particularly
> congenial to the Russian nihilist.   Party organization seems to
> him some monstrous " factory ".   Subordination of the part
> to the whole and of a minority to the majority strikes him as
> " enslavement ". . . . The division of labour under the leader-
> ship of a central authority provokes him to tragi-comic outcries
> against people being turned into " cogs and screws ".[3]

He was not alarmed when the Mensheviks accused him of supporting the bureaucratic principle against the democratic principle.
If bureaucracy meant centralism and democracy " autonomism ",
then revolutionary social-democracy stood for the first against
the second.[4]   If there was any principle behind the views of the
Mensheviks it was " the principle of anarchism ".[5]

The notion of a centralized and disciplined party as the instrument of revolution was cardinal to Lenin's thought.   It had
inspired the foundation of *Iskra* as the focus for such a party ;
it had inspired *What is to be Done?* in which the doctrine of party
leadership of the masses was first expounded.   Lenin later called

[1] Lenin, *Sochineniya*, vi, 36.   [2] *Ibid.* vi, 303.   [3] *Ibid.* vi, 310.
        [4] *Ibid.* vi, 313.   [5] *Ibid.* vi, 321.

the system of party discipline which he advocated " democratic
centralism "; and the quip was easy that it was more remarkable
for " centralism " in the form of control by the leaders than for
" democracy " in the sense of control by the rank and file. But
there is some danger in regarding these centralizing tendencies
as peculiar to the Russian party or, within that party, peculiar to
Lenin. It was everywhere a period of the rapid extension of
large-scale organization; everywhere the interests of efficiency
and power appeared more and more to demand a concentration
of authority. In no great country were political parties immune
from these tendencies. Proletarian parties were particularly
subject to them : it was here that the argument was most often
heard that party members owed obedience to their own chosen
leaders and that indulgence in criticism was incompatible with
party loyalty.[1] Plekhanov, now Lenin's bitter enemy, had in his
day argued in the same strain :

> When we are told that social-democracy ought to guarantee
> full freedom of opinion to its members, it is forgotten that a
> political party is not an academy of science. . . . Freedom of
> opinion in the party can and should be limited precisely because
> a party is a freely constituted union of men of like mind. Once
> identity of opinion vanishes, dissolution becomes inevitable.[2]

It was not the proletariat but the bourgeoisie, Lenin argued,
which shrank from this necessary and salutary restraint. The
Mensheviks represented " bourgeois-intellectual individualism ",
the Bolsheviks " proletarian organization and discipline ".[3]

Nor was Lenin's answer to Menshevik criticism confined to
words. Undaunted by the isolation in which he had been left by
the breach with *Iskra*, unmoved by opposition or by defections,
he summoned a meeting of twenty-two Bolshevik stalwarts at
Geneva in August 1904, and created a " bureau of committees of
the majority " to serve as a new Bolshevik central organization.
At the end of the year he founded a new journal, *Vpered* (" For-

---

[1] R. Michels, *Zur Soziologie des Parteiwesens* (2nd ed. 1925), pp. 278-280,
quotes striking instances of these sentiments from German, French and Belgian
sources. He also uses the term " democratic centralism " (*ibid.* p. 227) in a
way which suggests that it was in current use in the early 1900s in the German
Social-Democratic Party.

[2] G. V. Plekhanov, *Sochineniya*, xii, 455.

[3] Lenin, *Sochineniya*, vi, 213.

ward "), to take the place of the renegade *Iskra*. His main anxiety was to forestall any hasty movement for reunion which might compromise the purity and independence of Bolshevik doctrine and taint it with the heresies of Menshevism. In party correspondence of the period he demanded " everywhere and most decisively schism, schism, schism ".[1] To split the party and to expel dissenters from the ranks rather than jeopardize unity even in minor particulars was the principle which Lenin applied and bequeathed to his successors. It was the result of profound intellectual conviction, and accorded perfectly with his masterful and self-confident personality. He returned to it again and again even when he had seemed momentarily to abandon it in the interests of conciliation. It was not for nothing that the tactics employed against the Mensheviks after 1903 became a model for the party to follow in times of internal crisis, or that the word " Menshevism " was afterwards adopted, by a more and more elastic extension of usage, to brand any kind of dissent within the party ranks. In April 1905, in defiance of the old central organs of the party, now exclusively Menshevik, a fresh party congress assembled in London. It was composed exclusively of Bolsheviks and was boycotted by the Mensheviks, who held a parallel conference of their own at Geneva. The rift had been pushed to its conclusion.

The occasion of the original split at the second congress left behind it a widespread impression that, since both wings of the party had together voted the party programme and had parted only on the statute, the dispute turned only on the issue of organization and not on the issue of party doctrine. If this was true at the outset, the split quickly widened and deepened. The teaching of Marx, from the *Communist Manifesto* onwards, contained both evolutionary or scientific or objective elements and revolutionary or propagandist or subjective elements. Marxism was at one and the same time a statement of the laws of social and economic development and an exhortation to resort both to non-violent and to violent action in order to further the fulfilment

---

[1] *Leninskii Sbornik*, v (1926), 149. " Schism " seems the only appropriate translation of the Russian word *raskol*, which is primarily used of religious dissent.

of those laws. The two aspects of Marxism could be reconciled on the view that human affairs are subject to a process of continuous evolution which, none the less, does not dispense with occasional discontinuous acts of revolution forming an essential part of the process. Nevertheless, the apparent discrepancy led to shifts of emphasis between two opposite views of historical development; such shifts occurred, indeed, in the writings of Marx himself. In the controversy which split the Russian disciples of Marx, Mensheviks accused Bolsheviks of overstepping the Marxist evolutionary scheme by attempting through conspiratorial means to organize a proletarian revolution for which, at the present bourgeois stage of Russian development, the objective conditions were lacking; Bolsheviks accused Mensheviks of regarding revolution as " a process of historical development " instead of as something to be consciously organized according to a deliberate plan.[1] The Mensheviks, analysing the course of the revolution and believing that this course could not be altered or expedited by conscious action, were primarily men of theory; in Bolshevik terminology they were *raisonneurs*, " dry-as-dust archivists ", the " party intelligentsia ".[2] The Bolsheviks were the men of action, engaged in the organization of revolution by legal or illegal means; Lenin, the spokesman and creator of Bolshevism, was from the first, in contrast to the Mensheviks, less interested in evolutionary theory than in revolutionary practice. It was not for nothing that Lenin always insisted that Marx must be interpreted dialectically and not dogmatically. If theory and practice were one, theory had meaning only in so far as it found expression in the practice of a particular time and place. Lenin, quoting Marx's famous *Theses on Feuerbach*, compared the Mensheviks with those philosophers who merely " interpreted the world differently ". The Bolsheviks, like good Marxists, sought to change it.[3]

The dispute between Bolsheviks and Mensheviks, though it appeared to turn on esoteric points of Marxist doctrine, raised

---

[1] Lenin's article of February 1905, *Should We Organize Revolution?* (*Sochineniya*, vii, 122-129), deals with this controversy.

[2] The last term actually occurs in a resolution of the fifth party conference of December 1908 (*VKP(B) v Rezolyutsiyakh* (1941), i, 125); for the rest, see Lenin, *Sochineniya*, viii, 49-50.

[3] *Ibid.* viii, 52.

issues fundamental to the history of the Russian revolution. The Mensheviks, clinging to the original Marxist sequence of bourgeois-democratic and proletarian-socialist revolutions, never really accepted Lenin's hypothesis, thrown out as early as 1898, of an indissoluble link between them. The bourgeois revolution had to come first; for it was only through the bourgeois revolution that capitalism could receive its full development in Russia, and, until that development occurred, the Russian proletariat could not become strong enough to initiate and carry out the socialist revolution. This formal separation between the two revolutions, however satisfying to the theorist, had consequences which would have proved embarrassing to more practical revolutionaries than the Mensheviks. Narrowing their horizon to the bourgeois revolution, the Mensheviks found difficulties in imparting to their political programme any socialist or proletarian appeal. The bourgeois revolution was the necessary and predestined precursor of the proletarian revolution, and was therefore, at long range, a vital interest of the proletariat. But the immediate effect would be to put in power those who were the oppressors of the proletariat and, once more at long range, its most formidable enemies. From this dilemma the Mensheviks could escape only by concentrating on a short-term policy of· support for the bourgeoisie in destroying the autocracy and completing the bourgeois revolution, and of pressure on the eventual bourgeois revolutionary government to accord to the proletariat such material alleviations of their lot as formed the staple of social policy in advanced capitalist countries (recognition of trade unions, the eight-hour day, social insurance and so forth).

In essence, therefore, as Lenin frequently pointed out, the Bolshevik argument against the Mensheviks repeated the controversies with the legal Marxists and the Economists against whom the whole party had formerly stood united; and it echoed the controversy with the " revisionists " in the German Social-Democratic Party. Wedded to the cut-and-dried thesis that Russia was on the eve of a bourgeois, but not of a socialist, revolution, the Mensheviks followed the legal Marxists in their emphasis on revolutionary theory and in their postponement of revolutionary action to some still remote future; they followed the Economists in preferring the economic concept of class to the political concept of party [1] and believing that the only concrete aim that could be offered to the workers at the present stage was the improvement of their economic lot ; they followed the German revisionists in advocating parliamentary pressure on a bourgeois government to secure reforms favourable to the workers rather than revolutionary action to overthrow it. Menshevism was not an isolated or accidental phenomenon. The Mensheviks came to stand for a series of ideas familiar in the practice of western European socialism — a legal opposition, progress through reform rather than revolution, compromise and cooperation with other parliamentary parties, economic agitation through trade unions. Menshevism was firmly rooted in western thought and western tradition (and, after all, Marx was a westerner). The Russian *narodniks*, like the Slavophils, had asserted the uniqueness of Russia's development ; unlike the west, Russia was destined to avoid the capitalist stage. Plekhanov, refuting the *narodniks*, based his whole teaching on the axiom that Russia must follow precisely the same development as the west. In this sense, he too was a whole-hearted westerner ; and the Mensheviks were Plekhanov's disciples. They always found it easier than the Bolsheviks to win sympathy and understanding among the social-democratic leaders of the west. It was a quip of Radek many years later that " western Europe begins with the Mensheviks ".[2]

It was symptomatic of this contrast that, when the Bolshevik and Menshevik wings of the party came to be clearly differentiated in Russia itself (which happened later and much less sharply than among the *émigrés*), the Mensheviks found their adherents among the most highly skilled and organized workers, the printers, the railwaymen and the steel-workers in the modern industrial centres of the south, whereas the Bolsheviks drew their main support

---

[1] This is the basis for the assertion of the former Menshevik leader Dan, that the Bolsheviks represented " the general-democratic and political tendencies of the movement ", the Mensheviks " its class and socialist tendencies " (F. Dan, *Proiskhozhdenie Bol'shevizma* (N.Y., 1946), p. 291).

[2] In the words of the current official history, the Mensheviks " wanted in Russia a party similar, let us say, to the German or French social-democratic party " and " fought the Bolsheviks just because they sensed something new in them, something unusual and different from the social-democrats of the west " (*History of the Communist Party of the Soviet Union* (Engl. transl. 1939), pp. 139-140). It should be remembered that in 1903 there were no political parties in the western sense in Russia : such parties existed only after 1905.

from the relatively unskilled labour of the mass industries — the old-fashioned heavy industry of the Petersburg region and the textile factories of Petersburg and Moscow. Most of the trade unions were predominantly Menshevik. The Economists had argued that, while the instructed workers of the west were capable of political indoctrination, only economic agitation could appeal to the mass of the Russian " factory proletariat " ; [1] and Lenin himself appeared to accept the view that the appeal of the Economists was to the " lowest and least developed strata of the proletariat ".[2] This diagnosis was, however, contradicted both by the experience of the west (where, from the days of the First International onwards, it was the most advanced section of the workers, the English trade unionists, who exalted the economic at the expense of the political struggle) and by contemporary Russian realities. The most highly skilled, educated, organized and privileged Russian workers, who approximated most nearly to the organized workers of the west, were least susceptible to revolutionary appeals and most easily induced to believe in the possibility of improving their economic lot within a bourgeois political framework. The unskilled mass of Russian factory workers who, standing in all respects at a lower level than the lowest grades of western industrial labour, had " nothing to lose but their chains ", were most readily accessible to the Bolshevik plea for political revolution as the sole avenue to economic improvement.

The failure of Menshevism, a failure marked both by tragedy and by futility, was a result of its alienation from Russian conditions. The Russian social and political order provided none of the soil in which a bourgeois-democratic régime could flourish. History rarely repeats itself ; and an interpretation of Marxism which supposed that the successive stages of revolution elsewhere in the world would precisely conform to a pattern established in western Europe was deterministic and therefore false. In Germany it proved impossible throughout the latter half of the nineteenth century to complete the bourgeois-democratic revolution in its classical form ; German social and political development was twisted and stultified by the abortion of 1848. In Russia, if

---

[1] This argument was used in Kuskova's *credo* (see p. 10 above).
[2] Lenin, *Sochineniya*, ii, 552.

the Mensheviks could have had their way, the bankruptcy of the German revolution in 1848 would have been matched by the bankruptcy of 1905. Nor was this merely because the German bourgeoisie of 1848 and the Russian bourgeoisie of 1905 were too weak and undeveloped to achieve their own revolutionary ambitions. That they were weak was undeniable. But a more significant cause of their hesitancy was that they were already conscious of the growing menace to themselves of an eventual proletarian revolution.[1] One reason why history so rarely repeats itself is that the dramatis personae at the second performance have prior knowledge of the *dénouement*. The Marxist scheme of revolution required the bourgeoisie to overthrow the feudal order as a prelude to its own overthrow by the proletariat. The weakness of the scheme was that, once it had penetrated the bourgeois consciousness, it could no longer be carried out.[2] Once bourgeois democracy was recognized as a stepping-stone to socialism, it could be brought into being only by those who believed also in socialism. This was the profound truth which Lenin expressed when he argued that only the proletariat could take the lead in carrying out the bourgeois revolution. The trouble was not that conditions in Russia were not yet ripe for the western revolutionary drama; it was that that drama had been played out in the west, and could no longer be re-acted elsewhere. The Mensheviks, who waited for conditions in Russia to ripen, were doomed to sterility and frustration.

The Bolshevik standpoint, though it took far more account of specifically Russian conditions and was thus spared the humiliation of failure, was also not free from inner contradictions. According to this standpoint the bourgeois-democratic revolution,

[1] Trotsky in a striking phrase describes the German bourgeoisie of 1848 as " shabbily wise with the experience of the French bourgeoisie " (*Perspektivi Russkoi Revolyutsii* (Berlin, n.d. [1917], p. 27).

[2] Lenin wrote bitterly at this time : " The European bourgeois began by fighting on the barricades for the republic ; then lived in exile, and afterwards became traitors to freedom, betrayed the revolution and entered the service of the constitutional monarchs. The Russian bourgeois want to ' learn from history ' and ' abridge the stages of development ' ; they want to betray the revolution at once, to become at once traitors to freedom. In intimate conversations they repeat to one another the words of Christ to Judas : ' What thou doest, do quickly ' " (*Sochineniya*, vii, 359). But why should the bourgeois fight on the barricades once he knows that the sequel to his victory is his own overthrow by the proletariat ?

though carried out by the proletariat with the support of the peasantry, was none the less essentially bourgeois in character : it was a stage which could not be skipped, and must not be confused with the subsequent proletarian-socialist revolution. That a revolution carried out in these conditions could and should adopt many measures which were in fact not socialist and were perfectly compatible with bourgeois capitalism — such as the distribution of land to the peasants, the eight-hour day or the separation of church and state — was, of course, undeniable : these measures and many like them were inscribed in the minimum programme of the party. But that such a revolution, boycotted or actively opposed by the bourgeoisie, could achieve that " bourgeois freedom and bourgeois progress " which Lenin himself had described as the only " path to real freedom for the proletariat and the peasantry ",[1] was a conception whose difficulties Lenin never appears seriously to have faced. In later speeches and writings he frequently denounced " bourgeois freedom " as a hollow sham. This involved him in no inconsistency, since he was speaking of two different epochs. So long as the bourgeoisie was a revolutionary force taking the offensive against the remnants of mediaevalism and feudalism, bourgeois freedom was real and progressive ; so soon as the bourgeoisie, having consolidated its power, was on the defensive against the rising forces of socialism and the proletariat, " bourgeois freedom " became reactionary and false. But the verbal contradiction helped to unmask the real problem. The Bolshevik argument required the establishment in Russia of a bourgeois freedom and bourgeois democracy which had and could have no social roots in Russia (since it would have to be established without the support of the bourgeoisie), and declared that failing this there could be no path to the higher freedom of socialism. The Menshevik scheme which waited for the Russian bourgeoisie to establish bourgeois freedom was scarcely more unreal than the Bolshevik scheme which required it to be established by a revolutionary dictatorship of the proletariat and the peasantry.

The tragic dilemma of the Russian revolution, which neither Mensheviks nor Bolsheviks could wholly solve, rested on an error of prognostication in the original Marxist scheme. Marx believed

[1] *Ibid.* viii, 34.

that bourgeois capitalism, once established, would everywhere run its full course, and that, when it began to decay through its own inherent contradictions, then and only then would it be overthrown by a socialist revolution. What in fact happened was that capitalism, in the countries where it was most fully and powerfully developed, built around itself a vast network of vested interests embracing a large sector of the industrial working class, so that, even after the process of decay had manifestly set in, it continued for a long period to resist without much difficulty the forces of revolution, whereas it was a nascent and immature capitalism which succumbed easily to the first revolutionary onslaught. The economic consequences of this departure from the preconceived plan were apparent : the young revolutionary government, instead of being able to take over the efficient industrial organization and trained man-power of a fully developed capitalism, was compelled to rely, for the building of the socialist order, on the inadequate resources of a backward country, so that the new socialism had to bear the handicap and the reproach of being a régime of scarcity and not, as Marxists had always expected, a régime of abundance. The political consequences were not less embarrassing : the new repositories of political power were a proletariat innocent of the political training and experience which are acquired under a bourgeois constitution from the exercise of universal suffrage and from association in trade unions and workers' organizations, and a peasantry mainly illiterate and almost wholly devoid of political consciousness. The difficulties of this situation, and the disappointments resulting from it, were attributed by the Mensheviks to the wilful abandonment by the Bolsheviks of the Marxist scheme of revolution. But that scheme was bound to break down when the proletarian revolution occurred in the most backward of capitalist countries. These embarrassments still lay in the future. But they were inherent in the fundamental issue between Bolsheviks and Mensheviks which the outbreak of the first Russian revolution of 1905 laid bare.

CHAPTER 3

1905 AND AFTER

THE split between Bolsheviks and Mensheviks meant that the Russian Social-Democratic Workers' Party confronted the first Russian revolution of 1905 in an enfeebled and discouraged mood. Neither faction could congratulate itself on the victory in this internecine strife.

> When the breach became a fact [wrote Lenin early in 1905], it was clear that we were *materially the weaker several times over.* . . . The Mensheviks have more money, more literature, more transport, more agents, more " names ", more collaborators. It would be unforgivable childishness not to see this.[1]

Yet a few months later a Menshevik agent in a confidential letter was speaking in still more contemptuous terms of the complete ineffectiveness of Menshevik literature and organization in Petersburg.[2] As the revolution was gathering momentum throughout Russia in the summer of 1905, the Bolsheviks held in London the exclusively Bolshevik congress, which they described, and which became known in history, as the third party congress. Lenin's principal lieutenants at the congress, Bogdanov and Lunacharsky, were to break with him three years later. Lunacharsky returned to the party in 1917; and the third congress brought on to the scene for the first time three other delegates who were to play a conspicuous rôle after the October revolution — Kamenev (one of five delegates from the Caucasus), Litvinov and Krasin. But the fact that every outstanding leader in the original party except Lenin had gone over — whether whole-heartedly, like Axelrod, Martov and Potresov, or half-heartedly, like Plekhanov and Trotsky — to the Menshevik camp placed Lenin in a position of unique authority. The only figure at the third congress capable of taking a stand independent of Lenin was Krasin, at this time the

---

[1] Lenin, *Sochineniya*, vii, 101.   [2] *Ibid.* viii, 500, note 120.

chief Bolshevik organizer in Russia itself; and Lunacharsky
regarded the principal achievement of the congress as " a complete fusion of the Bolsheviks of the Leninist Left wing with the
Bolshevik Right wing under Krasin ".[1] But the purely subaltern
rôle assigned to Lenin's adjutants is described in Lunacharsky's
own recollections of the report on armed insurrection which he
was called on to make to the congress :

> Vladimir Ilich gave me all the fundamental theses of the
> report. Not satisfied with that, he insisted that I should write
> my whole speech and give it to him to read in advance. The
> night before the sitting at which my report was to be given,
> Vladimir Ilich attentively read through my manuscript and
> returned it with two or three insignificant corrections — which
> was not surprising considering that, so far as I remember, I
> took the most precise and detailed indications of Vladimir Ilich
> as my starting point.[2]

The difference between Bolshevik and Menshevik attitudes to the
nascent revolution was marked in the respective resolutions of
the London congress and the Geneva conference. The congress
recognized the urgent need " to organize the proletariat for an
immediate struggle with the autocracy by means of armed insurrection ", and held that eventual participation in a provisional
revolutionary government might be permissible " for the purposes
of a ruthless struggle against all counter-revolutionary attempts
and of the defence of the independent interests of the working
class " — a decision destined to give trouble twelve years later.[3]
The Menshevik conference, on the other hand, considered that
the party " must not set itself the aim of seizing power or sharing
power in a provisional government, but must remain the party
of extreme revolutionary opposition ".[4]

This party strife played no part in events in Russia. The
revolution set in motion by the massacre before the Winter Palace
on January 9, 1905, slowly gathered momentum through the
spreading disorders of spring and summer till it reached its climax
in October with a wave of strikes, the promise by the Tsar of a
liberal constitution, and the formation of the first Soviets of
Workers' Deputies. The earliest of these new-fangled institutions

---

[1] *Proletarskaya Revolyutsiya*, No. 11 (46), 1925, p. 53.   [2] *Ibid.* p. 54.
[3] *VKP(B) v Rezolyutsiyakh* (1941), i, 45; see p. 72 below.
[4] *Iskra*, No. 100, May 15, 1905 (*Prilozhenie*).

seem to have been the result of spontaneous action by groups of workers on strike. Priority in time was claimed by the factory town of Ivanovo-Voznesensk ; [1] and during the next few weeks more or less organized Soviets sprang up in nearly all the main industrial centres. The Petersburg Soviet, which was one of the earliest, was also incomparably the most important. The history of the institution begins with its Petersburg prototype.

The Petersburg Soviet of Workers' Deputies was constituted on October 14, 1905, and had a career of fifty days. Its first president was Khrustalev-Nosar, a radical lawyer, who joined the Menshevik wing of the Social-Democratic Party during the period of the Soviet.[2] The Soviet quickly acquired an organization, issued a weekly newspaper (the *Izvestiya Soveta Rabochikh Deputatov*, ancestor of the more famous daily *Izvestiya* of 1917), and at its height numbered some 550 delegates, representing 250,000 workers. The most prominent social-democrat in its ranks was Trotsky, who quickly emerged as an energetic and resourceful leader and, when Khrustalev-Nosar was arrested at the end of November 1905,[3] became its president for the last few days of its existence. The weakness of the Soviet was, as Trotsky afterwards said, " the weakness of a purely urban revolution ". By the beginning of December the government felt strong enough to take action against it. Trotsky and the other leaders were arrested, and Trotsky's brilliant and defiant conduct of the defence before the court which tried them helped to build up the prestige of the Soviet as well as his own. The Petersburg Soviet had been composed mainly, though by no means exclusively, of social-democrats ; in so far as it took account of the feud within the party, it was either neutral or Menshevik. Everywhere in Russia the rôle of the Bolsheviks in the Soviets of 1905 was slight and undistinguished. Lenin himself had spoken of them guardedly as " not a workers' parliament and not an organ of proletarian self-government ", but " a fighting organization for the attainment of definite ends ".[4] As such they could be no more than

---

[1] *Proletarskaya Revolyutsiya*, No. 4 (39), 1925, pp. 125-137.
[2] L. Trotsky, *1905* (2nd ed. 1922), p. 198.
[3] Trotsky, *Sochineniya*, ii, i, 303.
[4] Lenin, *Sochineniya*, viii, 409. Trotsky himself said of the first meeting of the Petersburg Soviet that it " was more like a council of war than a parliament " (*1905* (2nd ed. 1922), p. 106).

a non-party auxiliary of the party in its struggle to achieve revolutionary ends, and might even be regarded with a slight tinge of jealousy as a rival organization.[1]   Lenin reached Petersburg early in November 1905.   But it is not certain that he ever appeared at the Petersburg Soviet; in any case he took no leading part in its work.[2]

The practical activity and heroism of the revolutionaries and the tragedy of their failure threw a grim light on the disunity in the party which aspired to lead the revolution.   The split in both London and Geneva had not yet gone deep among the rank and file of the party in Russia itself.[3]   In the Russia of 1905 social-democrats everywhere sank their differences and worked together without taking account of the differences which divided the party leaders.   During the summer, moves for reunion were made from both sides; as the movement grew with the relatively free conditions promised by the October constitution of 1905, Lenin became impressed by the increasing impatience of the rank and file of the party at the deadlock.[4]   " The former disputes of the pre-revolutionary period ", he wrote shortly afterwards, " were replaced by solidarity in practical questions." [5]   Just before the downfall of the Petersburg Soviet, Bolsheviks and Mensheviks so far buried the hatchet as to issue three numbers of a joint

[1] According to a party historian, " certain Bolsheviks, particularly in Petersburg . . . were inclined to look on them [i.e. the Soviets] as competitors of the party " (N. Popov, *Outline History of the Communist Party of the Soviet Union* (Engl. transl. n.d.), i, 163).

[2] On the strength of a book of reminiscences by an obscure author published in 1922, the second edition of Lenin's works credits Lenin with the authorship of a resolution on the lock-out adopted by the executive committee on November 14, 1905 (*Sochineniya*, viii, 391-392). The inclusion of the resolution in Trotsky's works (*Sochineniya*, ii, i, 298-299) is tantamount to a claim of authorship by Trotsky, which is intrinsically more probable.   An article by Lenin which appeared in *Novaya Zhizn'* on the subject on the following day, and was welcomed by Trotsky in *Nachalo* (Trotsky, *Sochineniya*, ii, i, 313), may have caused the confusion. The further statement in the second edition of Lenin's works (*Sochineniya*, viii, 513, note 175), based on some unpublished reminiscences, that Lenin spoke at the executive committee on the resolution, is still more improbable.   Krupskaya does not " remember Vladimir Ilich speaking in the Soviet of Workers' Deputies " (*Memories of Lenin* [i] (Engl. transl. 1930), p. 154) ; and he was certainly not a member of the executive committee.

[3] Krasin makes it clear that the Petersburg Bolsheviks were still working in harmony with the Mensheviks down to February 1905 (*Proletarskaya Revolyutsiya*, No. 1 (36), 1925, pp. 83-84).

[4] Lenin, *Sochineniya*, viii, 379.   [5] *Ibid.* ix, 123.

newspaper in its support, the *Severnyi Golos*.   In December 1905
a conference of Bolsheviks at Tammerfors in Finland — it was
the occasion of Stalin's first appearance at an all-Russian party
conference or congress and of his first meeting with Lenin —
approved a fusion between the central committees of the two
wings with a view to organizing a joint party congress.[1]   In
January and February 1906 the new joint committee was able
to announce active preparations for the congress, which met at
Stockholm in April.[2]   Officially described as the " unity " congress, it bore at the time no regular number in the party series
(since the Mensheviks contested the validity of the third all-
Bolshevik congress of 1905), though it was known in later literature as the fourth ; and a further joint congress (afterwards known
as the fifth) was held in London in April–May 1907.   The
Stockholm " unity " congress of April 1906 met at the climax of
the mood of optimism engendered by the October constitution
and the convocation of the first Duma, and yielded a Menshevik
majority.   At the London congress Bolsheviks outnumbered Mensheviks, though the balance was held by smaller groups, while
Trotsky, appearing at a congress for the first time since 1903,
claimed to stand " outside the fractions ".

Even before the London congress of 1907 recriminations
had broken out again between Bolsheviks and Mensheviks.   Lenin
accused Dan and other Menshevik leaders of a bargain with the
Kadets over the Duma elections, which he branded as " selling
workers' votes ", and was summoned to defend himself before a
party court against a charge of slandering party colleagues.[3]   A
fortnight after the London congress dispersed, the dissolution of
the second Duma in Petersburg ended the pretence of constitutional government and ushered in the Stolypin period of reaction

[1] *VKP(B) v Rezolyutsiyakh* (1941), i, 57-58.   No records of the conference
survived, but reminiscences of it are collected in *Trudy Pervoi Vsesoyuznoi
Konferentsii Istorikov-Marksistov* (1930), i, 210-247.   A delegate describes
Lenin's attitude to fusion as follows : " It seemed that the revolution was
wiping out the dividing line between the fractions, and many believed this.
But Lenin did not believe it.   If he accepted union as completely inevitable in
view of the voice of the masses and the formal necessity for it, he none the less
agreed to union with a heavy heart and did not take it seriously " (*ibid.* i,
234-235).   But this reads like an *ex post facto* judgment.

[2] The two announcements of the committee are in *Chetvertyi (Ob"edinitel'nyi)
S"ezd RSDRP* (1934), pp. 572-576.

[3] Lenin, *Sochineniya*, xi, 216-228.

and the strong hand. Formal unity was preserved at a party conference held in Paris at the end of December 1908; [1] and during the following year several numbers appeared of a new party journal, *Sotsial-Demokrat*, on the editorial board of which Martov sat side by side with Lenin, Kamenev and Zinoviev. Lenin's willingness at this time to temporize with the Mensheviks was probably not unconnected with trouble within the Bolshevik wing of the party. Bogdanov and Lunacharsky were the leading spirits in an " idealist " deviation which sought to reconcile socialism with religion and was fiercely demolished by Lenin in his one large philosophical work, *Materialism and Empirio-Criticism*. This deviation also had a political bias, being associated with a demand for a boycott by the social-democrats of the third Duma — the first instance in party history of that afterwards familiar phenomenon, a " Left opposition ".[2] Lenin doggedly fought down all his opponents; and if the Bolsheviks succeeded during these years in maintaining their existence as a coherent and organized group, their survival was due entirely to the single-minded and persistent self-confidence of one man. Meanwhile a meeting of the party central committee in Paris in January 1910 once more reaffirmed party unity on a basis of compromise between Bolsheviks and Mensheviks, this time against Lenin's vote.[3]

Beneath the outward forms of party unity, maintained with increasing difficulty from 1906 to 1911, lay differences which grew more, not less, profound with the lapse of time and the frustrating consciousness of defeat. The collapse of the glorious hopes of 1905 had been a heavy blow to the party. But sober analysis of what had happened in that year only served to show how irreconcilable the standpoints of the factions had become. Even the factions themselves began to disintegrate, so that it was no longer possible to speak of two sharply defined and opposite camps; and it was perhaps this general confusion rather than any underlying unity of opinion which prevented an open breach.

[1] *VKP(B) v Rezolyutsiyakh* (1941), i, 125-132.

[2] Lenin in 1920 set the episode of 1908 side by side with the dispute over Brest-Litovsk ten years later as the two major instances of " Left " deviations in the party (*Sochineniya*, xxv, 182).

[3] *VKP(B) v Rezolyutsiyakh* (1941), i, 154-160. What most angered Lenin was that the compromise involved the closing down of the separate Bolshevik " centre " and of the journal *Proletarii* which it had been issuing by way of corrective to the *Sotsial-Demokrat*.

The Mensheviks remained a large but loosely knit group, held together by a common philosophy rather than by a common programme of action. The Bolsheviks had more cohesion and a more clearly defined policy, but owed these advantages exclusively to the masterful determination of their leader. Among those who belonged to neither of the two main factions, the dominant figure was Trotsky, whose intellectual acumen gave him a position in the field of theory independent both of Bolsheviks and Mensheviks, though he lacked the support of any regular following. The controversies in the Russian Social-Democratic Workers' Party during these years on the lessons of 1905 and the future destinies of the Russian revolution turned on three different interpretations or applications of Marxist doctrine propounded respectively by the Mensheviks, by the Bolsheviks and by Trotsky.

The experience of 1905, while leaving untouched the fundamental problem of the application of the Marxist analysis to the Russian revolution, raised new issues and presented old issues in a new light. Kautsky described it as " a bourgeois revolution in an epoch when bourgeois ideals have come to complete bankruptcy, when bourgeois democracy has lost all faith in itself, when it is only on the soil of socialism that ideals can flourish and energy and enthusiasm develop ".[1] The driving force of the revolution came from the workers and, intermittently, from the peasants. Its tentative achievements — the granting of a constitution, the Duma, the formation of political parties — had been bourgeois. It had proved abortive — and by 1908 hardly anything remained of it — because the bourgeoisie had been incapable not merely of making a revolution, but of garnering the fruits of a revolution made for them by others. Recognition of the incapacity of the Russian bourgeoisie was common ground for all groups. But on the conclusions to be drawn from this recognition opinions were utterly divided. Did it call for a revaluation of the theoretical relation of the socialist to the bourgeois revolution, and therefore, in political terms, of the relation of the proletariat and of its party to the bourgeoisie? Would the Marxist scheme be strictly followed in the development of the Russian revolution, or might it undergo

[1] *Chetvertyi (Ob"edinitel'nyi) S"ezd RSDRP* (1934), p. 594.

some modification either owing to the preponderance of the peasantry in the Russian economy and the peculiar features of the agrarian problem, or owing to the ripening of the socialist revolution in more advanced European countries? Finally, the old question of the nature, functions and organization of the party continually recurred and lost none of its acuteness in the new setting.

Of the three groups, the Mensheviks had been the least affected by the experience of 1905. Nothing that happened in Russia in that year could alter their fidelity to what seemed to them the fundamental tenet of Marxism. The socialist revolution could be the work only of a strong proletariat; the Russian proletariat could become strong only through the development of Russian capitalism; Russian capitalism could be developed only through the victory of the bourgeois revolution. This syllogism implied not only the theoretical separateness of the two revolutions (which all groups were ready to concede), but an interval of time between them. It ruled out any policy of immediate preparation for a socialist revolution, and condemned the proletariat at the present stage to the rôle of a subsidiary ally of the bourgeoisie. The Mensheviks did not believe that the Russian proletariat could anticipate Marxist destiny by enlisting the alliance of the peasant masses. The peasantry remained for the Mensheviks an essentially anti-revolutionary force; any revolutionary policy which counted on its support was a reversion to the *narodnik* heresy of a peasant revolution. This argument could be reinforced by the experience of 1848, by numerous passages from Marx and Engels, and by the experience of 1905 when, as Trotsky himself said, the proletarian revolution was broken " on the bayonets of the peasant army ".[1] As regards the prospects of European revolution the Mensheviks had committed themselves at their conference of May 1905 :

> Only in one event would social-democracy on its own initiative direct its exertions towards acquiring power and holding it for as long as possible — namely in the event of revolution spreading to the advanced countries of western Europe, where conditions for the realization of socialism have already reached a certain ripeness. In this event the restricted

[1] L. Trotsky, *1905* (2nd ed. 1922), p. 267.

historical limits of the Russian revolution can be considerably widened, and the possibility will occur of advancing on the path of socialist transformations.[1]

But the phrase " a certain ripeness ", which Lenin criticized as unwarrantably pessimistic,[2] was typical of Menshevik caution. This resolution, adopted at a moment when the prospects of 1905 were still untarnished, remained the sole Menshevik pronouncement on the subject; and European revolution never occupied a conspicuous place in Menshevik thought — if only because the Mensheviks never regarded it as imminent.

It followed that a strain of pessimistic resignation was inherent in the Menshevism of this period. As Axelrod put it at the Stockholm congress :

> Social relations in Russia are as yet ripe only for a bourgeois revolution ; and the impulse of history drives the workers and revolutionaries themselves with much greater force towards bourgeois revolutionism, which turns both the one and the other into involuntary servants of the bourgeoisie, than towards a revolutionism which is in principle socialist and tactically and organizationally prepares the proletariat for political supremacy.[3]

And Martynov at the same congress defined the function of the party in the current period as being " to stir bourgeois democracy to political life, to push it forward and to radicalize bourgeois society ".[4] In terms of party organization, this meant continued opposition to conspiratorial action or to preparations for armed insurrection and, consequently, to Lenin's whole conception of a party of professional revolutionaries. Lenin contemptuously described the Mensheviks as men who " take a pace backwards or mark time on the same spot . . . not knowing how to define the conditions of a decisive victory ".[5]

The Bolshevik diagnosis of 1905 and of the lessons to be drawn from it was radically different. The massacre of January 9, 1905, had brought on the scene a " third force " in Russian politics which was one day destined to eclipse both the autocracy and the bourgeoisie, the proletariat :

---

[1] *Iskra*, No. 100, May 15, 1905 (*Prilozhenie*).
[2] Lenin, *Sochineniya*, viii, 83.
[3] *Chetvertyi (Ob"edinitel'nyi) S"ezd RSDRP* (1934), p. 260.
[4] *Ibid.* p. 204.   [5] Lenin, *Sochineniya*, viii, 99.

The proletariat has shown that it is . . . a force not only interested in the smashing of the autocracy, but *ready to proceed to a genuine smashing* of the autocracy. Since January 9/22, our workers' movement is *growing up* before our eyes into a national movement.[1]

Lenin accepted as unequivocally as the Mensheviks the bourgeois character of the incipient revolution and the necessity to pass through the stage of bourgeois democracy on the way to socialism :

He who seeks to advance towards socialism by any other road, by-passing political democracy, inevitably arrives at conclusions both economically and politically inept and reactionary. . . . We Marxists should know that there is not, and cannot be, any other path to real freedom for the proletariat and the peasantry than the road of bourgeois freedom and bourgeois progress.[2]

But he argued that the Russian bourgeoisie was neither able nor willing by itself to complete the bourgeois-democratic revolution, not only because it was weak, but because its support of revolution was " inconsistent, selfish and cowardly " ; owing to its fear of the proletariat, it was already half-way to becoming counter-revolutionary. The Menshevik policy of delay, far from improving the prospects of revolution, would make bourgeois resistance all the more stubborn. Henceforth the proletariat was the one consistently revolutionary class : " it alone is capable of going on reliably to the end, because it is prepared to go much further than the democratic revolution ". It must therefore take on itself, first of all, the task of completing the bourgeois revolution.[3]

The task imposed on the proletariat of completing the bourgeois-democratic revolution as a prelude to the consummation of its own socialist revolution could be fulfilled on two conditions ; and the elaboration of these was the main theme of Lenin's major work of the summer of 1905, *Two Tactics of Social-Democracy in the Democratic Revolution*. The first was an alliance between the proletariat and the peasantry. The peasantry, though not revolutionary in the sense assumed by the *narodniks* of being hostile to capitalism as such, was " at the present moment less interested in the unconditional defence of private property than

---

[1] Lenin, *Sochineniya*, vii, 109-110.   [2] *Ibid.* viii, 41, 104.
[3] *Ibid.* viii, 94.

in taking away the land-owners' land, which is one of the chief
forms of that property ".[1] Hence the peasantry could be harnessed
by the proletariat as its ally at the present stage : and this would
enable the proletariat to overthrow the autocracy and to complete
the bourgeois-democratic revolution in defiance of bourgeois luke-
warmness or bourgeois opposition. The result of this victory
would be not a socialist dictatorship of the proletariat, but a
" revolutionary-democratic dictatorship of the proletariat and the
peasantry ".[2] Lenin was, however, prepared to look even further
ahead than this. Once the bourgeois revolution was achieved by
this combination, the peasantry as a whole would no longer be
revolutionary and would not support the proletariat in its advance
towards the socialist revolution. At that stage it would be necessary for the proletariat, once more taking the lead, to split the
peasantry against itself and to enlist the support of the semi-
proletarian elements, i.e. the poor and landless peasants, against
the rich peasants who would have profited most by the division of
the landowners' estates. The whole programme was summarized
in an italicized passage of *Two Tactics of Social-Democracy* :

> The proletariat must carry through to completion the demo-
> cratic revolution by uniting to itself the mass of the peasantry, in
> order to crush by force the opposition of the autocracy and to
> paralyse the instability of the bourgeoisie. The proletariat must
> complete the socialist revolution by uniting to itself the mass of
> semi-proletarian elements in the population, in order to break by
> force the opposition of the bourgeoisie and to paralyse the instability
> of the peasantry and of the petty bourgeoisie.[3]

The second condition was not discussed at anything like the same
length, probably because Lenin was as usual expounding his
doctrine in the form of a polemic, and the second condition, unlike
the first, was not contested by his Menshevik adversaries. But it
had already been tentatively stated in an article of April 1905
and was repeated clearly enough in two passages of *Two Tactics
of Social-Democracy*. One result of the democratic revolution
would be to " carry the revolutionary conflagration into Europe " ;
and nothing would " so powerfully shorten the route to complete

---

[1] *Ibid.* viii, 94.
[2] This phrase was coined by Lenin in an article of April 1905 (*ibid.* vii, 196-
203) and repeated several times in *Two Tactics of Social-Democracy.*
[3] *Ibid.* viii, 96.

victory " in Russia. The establishment of the " revolutionary-democratic dictatorship of the proletariat and peasantry " would " give us the possibility to raise Europe, and the European socialist proletariat, throwing off the yoke of the bourgeoisie, will in its turn help us to complete the socialist revolution ".[1]

Lenin was careful throughout *Two Tactics of Social-Democracy* to uphold the distinction, practical as well as theoretical, between the two stages of the revolution. He even wrote that " this democratic revolution will not weaken, but will strengthen, the domination of the bourgeoisie "[2] — a prediction which seemed to commit him to the Menshevik belief in an extended interval between the two stages for the further development of capitalism. Nevertheless he specifically pointed to two elements of the transition from the democratic to the socialist stage — the support of the semi-proletarian section of the peasantry and the support of a socialist revolution in Europe ; and he showed how these two elements might be expected to grow out of the revolutionary-democratic dictatorship which would crown the first stage. He did therefore treat the two stages as in some sort a continuous process. Three months later, in September 1905, in a short article on *The Relation of Social-Democracy to the Peasant Movement*, he borrowed Marx's famous phrase of 1850 :

> From the democratic revolution we shall begin immediately and within the measure of our strength — the strength of the conscious and organized proletariat — to make the transition to the socialist revolution. We stand for uninterrupted revolution. We shall not stop half way.[3]

He never seems to have used the phrase again. But the idea remained. At the end of 1905, in some notes which were first published twenty years later, he sketched out once more the stages of the revolution in their logical sequence. The proletariat in alliance with the peasantry would complete the bourgeois revolution. This achievement would lead to a new stage in

[1] Lenin, *Sochineniya*, vii, 191, viii, 62, 83.
[2] *Ibid.* viii, 37.
[3] *Ibid.* viii, 186. Marx wrote " permanente Revolution " ; Russian writers sometimes used " permanentnaya " and sometimes the ordinary Russian word for " uninterrupted ", i.e. " nepreryvnaya ". In later controversy an attempt was made to distinguish between Trotsky's advocacy of " permanent " revolution and Lenin's acceptance of " uninterrupted " revolution. But there is no significance in the variation of terminology.

which the rich peasants and " a substantial part of the middle peasantry " would go over to the bourgeoisie, and the proletariat, with the sympathy of the poor peasantry, would struggle " for the preservation of its democratic victory in the interests of a socialist revolution ". This struggle would be hopeless " *unless the European socialist proletariat* came to the help of the Russian proletariat ". This was the key to the final victory. " The European workers will show us ' how it is done ', and then we together with them will make the socialist revolution." [1]

Of all the leading Russian social-democrats, Trotsky was the only one to play a conspicuous part in the events of the 1905 revolution. It was therefore natural that he should be strongly influenced by its lessons ; in this respect he stood at the opposite extreme to the Mensheviks. His collaboration with the Mensheviks after the split with Lenin in 1903 on the question of organization was brief. He had no natural sympathy with the passive strain in Menshevik doctrine.

> *Our struggle for the revolution* [he wrote immediately after January 9, 1905], *our preparation for the revolution, will be at the same time an unsparing struggle with liberalism for influence over the masses, for the leading rôle of the proletariat in the revolution.* In this struggle we shall have on our side a great force : the logic of the revolution itself.[2]

In February 1905 Trotsky returned to Russia as an active revolutionary. It was in the autumn of that year, at the height of his work in the Petersburg Soviet, that he outlined his theory in terms which added precision to Lenin's September formula of " uninterrupted revolution " :

> The vanguard position of the working class in the revolution, the direct connexion between it and the revolutionary countryside, the spell by which it conquers the army — all this pushes it inevitably to power. The complete victory of the

---

[1] *Ibid.* viii, 424-427. This conception of the interaction of east and west in bringing about the socialist revolution also had a recognizable Russian ancestry. Herzen wrote to Proudhon in 1855 : " Russia, less haughty than Savoy, will not *fard da se*, she needs the solidarity of the peoples of Europe, their help ; but, on the other hand, I am convinced that liberty will not come in the west so long as Russia remains enrolled as a soldier in the pay of the emperor of Petersburg " (*Polnoe Sobranie Sochinenii i Pisem*, ed. M. K. Lemke, viii (1919), 196).

[2] Trotsky, *Sochineniya*, ii, i, 57.

revolution means the victory of the proletariat. This in turn means the further uninterrupted advance of the revolution. The proletariat realizes the fundamental tasks of democracy, and the logic of its immediate struggle to safeguard its political supremacy causes purely socialist problems to arise at a given moment. Between the minimum and maximum programmes of social-democracy a revolutionary continuity is established. This is not a single stroke, it is not one day or one month, it is a whole historical epoch.[1]

And early in 1906, after his arrest, Trotsky wrote in prison a searching analysis under the title *Results and Prospects*, which he afterwards cited as " the only work in which I more or less systematically expounded my views of the development of the revolution ".[2]

In Trotsky's view the peculiarity of the Russian social structure was that capitalist industry had developed there as the result of foreign pressure and under the patronage of the state : hence a proletariat had been created without an independent bourgeois class of entrepreneurs. For this reason " in an economically backward country the proletariat may find itself in power earlier than in a leading capitalist country ", and " in Russia the ' worker ' may find himself in power earlier than his ' master ' ".[3] Nor did Trotsky merely regard this as theoretically possible. The experience of 1905 convinced him that this must in fact happen. He had seen the Russian factory owners reply to the demand for an eight-hour day by declaring a lock-out. The workers could

---

[1] Quoted from an article in *Nachalo* (October 1905) by L. Trotsky, *Permanentnaya Revolyutsiya* (Berlin, 1930), pp. 58, 90-91.

[2] L. Trotsky, *Permanentnaya Revolyutsiya* (Berlin, 1930), p. 39. *Results and Prospects* (*Itogi i Perspektivi*, a title borrowed from Parvus's article referred to on p. 61 below) was first published in Petersburg in 1906 in a volume of essays by Trotsky under the title *Nasha Revolyutsiya* ; neither the original nor a reprint published after the October revolution has been available. At the end of 1917 this essay was republished by itself in Russian in Berlin under the title *Perspektivi Russkoi Revolyutsii* : the last chapter and the last two sentences of the penultimate chapter predicting a European socialist revolution as a result of the war, and declaring this to be essential to the victory of the Russian revolution, were omitted out of respect for the German censorship. References in footnotes below are to this edition. In 1918 an abridged English translation of Trotsky's 1906 volume was published under the title *Our Revolution* (N.Y., 1918), including the greater part of this essay (pp. 73-144) ; the sentences from the penultimate chapter and the greater part of the last chapter omitted from the Berlin edition appear in this version.

[3] L. Trotsky, *Perspektivi Russkoi Revolyutsii* (Berlin, n.d. [1917]), pp. 36, 40.

enforce their demand, which was a legitimate and necessary demand of the bourgeois revolution, only by taking over the factories. " Once in power the proletariat inevitably by the whole logic of its position will be pushed into administering the economy as a state concern." [1] To suppose that social-democrats would take the lead in carrying through the bourgeois revolution and then retire, " giving place to bourgeois parties ", was " utopianism of the worst kind, a sort of revolutionary-philistine utopianism "; the proletariat, having taken power, would " fight for this power to the end ".[2] The completion of the bourgeois revolution would automatically involve a transition to the socialist revolution.

In a later article written in 1909 Trotsky defined the point at which Mensheviks and Bolsheviks respectively departed from his analysis :

> If the Mensheviks, starting from the abstraction, " our revolution is bourgeois ", arrive at the idea of adapting the whole tactics of the proletariat to the behaviour of the liberal bourgeoisie before its conquest of state power, the Bolsheviks, proceeding from an equally barren abstraction, " a democratic, not a socialist, dictatorship ", arrive at the idea of a bourgeois-democratic self-limitation of the proletariat in whose hands state power rests. It is true, there is a very significant difference between them in this respect : while the anti-revolutionary sides of Menshevism are already displayed in full force now, the anti-revolutionary traits of Bolshevism threaten enormous danger only in the event of a revolutionary victory.[3]

That Trotsky by a stroke of uncanny insight accurately predicted in this passage the attitude adopted by most of the Bolshevik leaders in Petrograd before Lenin's return in April 1917 is undeniable ; that Lenin himself continued up to the February revolution to adhere to the same doctrine of " self-limitation " cannot be so easily sustained. Lenin did not, it is true, take so clear and decisive a stand on this question as Trotsky ; his failure to do so was mainly responsible for the confusion in the Bolshevik ranks after February 1917. After 1906 Lenin engaged in polemics

[1] *Ibid.* p. 41.
[2] *Ibid.* pp. 51, 55.
[3] L. Trotsky, *1905* (2nd ed. 1922), p. 285. Trotsky, in the second edition, added to the last phrase a footnote to the effect that this did not happen because " Bolshevism under the leadership of Lenin undertook its ideological re-equipment (not without an internal struggle) in the spring of 1917 ".

on two or three occasions against Trotsky's theory of " permanent revolution ".   But Trotsky was probably right in holding that Lenin had never read *Results and Prospects*, which he quoted at second hand from an article by Martov ; [1] and these utterances did little to clarify Lenin's own position.   Lenin did not, any more than Trotsky, reject the prospect of a direct transition from the bourgeois to the socialist revolution.   But, whereas Trotsky believed that this transition would set in automatically and inevitably through the " logic " of the revolution itself, Lenin clung more firmly to the *terra firma* of the bourgeois revolution, and held that the transition to socialism would depend on the realization of the two extraneous conditions which he had laid down in 1905 : the support of the peasantry and the support of a European socialist revolution.   The main difference of doctrine between Lenin and Trotsky at this time was that Lenin made the beginning of the transition to socialism dependent on conditions which Trotsky regarded as necessary only for its final victory.

As regards the peasantry, the Marxist view of the incapacity of the peasantry to constitute a revolutionary party had been the starting-point of Plekhanov's polemic against the *narodniks*, and was firmly rooted in party doctrine.   Trotsky on the eve of 1905 had called the peasantry " a vast reservoir of potential revolutionary energy " [2] — which was as far as any social-democrat was likely to go at that time.   The experience of 1905, which inspired Trotsky's brilliant analysis of the rôle of the proletariat in the revolution, had given him a jaundiced view of the rôle of the peasantry.   Peasant risings had accompanied and supported the early stages of the revolutionary movement.   But at the critical moment it was the peasant in uniform who, remaining loyal to the Tsar and to his officers, had crushed the revolution of the urban proletariat.   Trotsky drew his conclusions from this diagnosis.   He accepted the indispensable importance of a peasant rising as an auxiliary to the main task of the proletariat.   But this did not imply that the peasantry was an independent political force in equal alliance with the proletariat : the correct formula was

[1] Lenin, *Sochineniya*, xiv, 44-47 ; L. Trotsky, *Permanentnaya Revolyutsiya* (Berlin, 1930), pp. 39-40.
[2] Trotsky, *Sochineniya*, ii, i, 20.   In the collected edition published in 1926 the phrase is printed in italics, which do not appear in the original version (N. Trotsky, *Do Devyatogo Yanvarya* (Geneva, 1905), p. 18).

that the proletariat would make the bourgeois revolution " supported by the peasant element and leading it "[1] — a formula which Lenin afterwards accepted as identical in substance with his own.[2] Nor did Trotsky agree with Lenin's formula for the government resulting from this revolution — a " revolutionary-democratic dictatorship of the proletariat and the peasantry " : this he dismissed in *Results and Prospects* as " unrealizable ".[3] The revolution led by the proletariat could result only in a " workers' government " in the sense of a government in which workers' representatives held the " dominant and leading position ".[4] Still less was it possible to contemplate a proletarian-peasant alliance as the instrument for carrying out the socialist revolution. A fundamental conflict of interest would destroy the partnership on the very threshold of common action ; for the revolutionary government in its agricultural policy would be driven to " the organization of cooperative production under communal control or directly for state account ",[5] and would have to impose these socialist measures on the peasantry. Trotsky thus demurred — though the difference between them was later much exaggerated — to both parts of Lenin's dual formula of an alliance with the peasantry as a whole for the achievement of the bourgeois revolution and of an alliance with the " semi-proletarian " elements of the peasantry for the achievement of the socialist revolution. The

---

[1] Trotsky, *Sochineniya*, ii, i, 448.

[2] Lenin, *Sochineniya*, xiv, 42.

[3] L. Trotsky, *Perspektivi Russkoi Revolyutsii* (Berlin, n.d. [1917]), p. 48.

[4] *Ibid.* p. 43. Parvus, a German social-democrat of Russian origin, in his preface to Trotsky's earlier pamphlet *Do Devyatogo Yanvarya*, had written in January 1905 : " If social-democracy places itself at the head of the revolutionary movement of the Russian proletariat, then this government [i.e. the " revolutionary provisional government "] will be social-democratic ". He added : " The social-democratic provisional government cannot complete the socialist revolution in Russia, but the very process of the liquidation of the autocracy and the establishment of the democratic republic will give it a favourable ground for political work ". This passage contained the nucleus of Trotsky's theory of " permanent revolution ". In the same preface Parvus wrote of the peasants : " They are only in a position to increase political anarchy in the country and thus to weaken the government, they cannot form a coherent revolutionary army ". An article by Parvus on similar lines, entitled *Itogi i Perspektivi*, appeared in *Iskra*, No. 85, January 27, 1905. Trotsky long afterwards stated that his views in 1905 " bordered closely on those of Parvus without, however, being identical with them " (*Permanentnaya Revolyutsiya* (Berlin, 1930), pp. 64-65).

[5] L. Trotsky, *Perspektivi Russkoi Revolyutsii* (Berlin, n.d. [1917]), p. 54.

major responsibility would rest at both stages on the proletariat.

On the necessity of a socialist revolution in Europe as the second condition of the consummation of the socialist revolution in Russia Mensheviks, Bolsheviks and Trotsky were in full agreement. Trotsky enunciated this condition unequivocally towards the end of *Results and Prospects* :

> Without the direct state support of the European proletariat the working class of Russia will not be able to maintain itself in power and convert its temporary supremacy into a lasting socialist dictatorship. We cannot doubt this for a moment. On the other hand there is no doubt that a socialist revolution in the west would allow us to turn the temporary supremacy of the working class directly into a socialist dictatorship.[1]

Lenin at this time went even further. He did not believe that the Russian proletariat could even begin — let alone, maintain — a socialist revolution in Russia without the support of the European proletariat. But both Lenin and Trotsky accepted without qualification the necessity of the European revolution for the final victory of socialism in Russia ; neither would have had any truck at this time with the conception of a victorious socialist revolution in Russia without a socialist revolution in Europe.

While, however, on issues of doctrine, Trotsky occupied positions only faintly distinguishable from those of Lenin, on the issue of organization he had remained faithful, ever since the split of 1903, to the Menshevik view. Not sharing Lenin's conception of a small, highly organized and highly disciplined party, he continued to regard the split as unjustified and to work for a restoration of party unity, choosing for himself the rôle of a conciliator "outside the fractions". This attitude constantly allied Trotsky, in spite of all doctrinal divergences, with the Mensheviks, whose conception of a mass party was not intolerant of differing shades of opinion within it, and as constantly embroiled him with Lenin, whose views of party unity had not wavered since 1903. Throughout the period from 1909 to 1914, Trotsky's efforts to bring the fractions back within the same fold were repeatedly countered by Lenin in the name of doctrinal purity and efficiency of organiza-

---

[1] L. Trotsky, *Perspektivi Russkoi Revolyutsii* (Berlin, n.d. [1917]), ends with the first sentence of this passage (see p. 58, note 2, above) : the two remaining sentences are quoted from L. Trotsky, *Our Revolution* (N.Y., 1918). p. 137.

tion; and the persistence of this strife produced a mutual exacerbation and a rich vocabulary of mutual vituperation. In 1903–1904 Trotsky had been the aggressor in the war of words.[1] Now, in the bitter controversies of 1911–1914, it was Lenin's turn to speak of Trotsky's " resounding but hollow phrases ",[2] and of his " incredible bombast ".[3] Refusal to bow to party discipline led to instability of opinion. " It is impossible to argue with Trotsky on any point of substance since he has no opinions "; he is always " creeping through the crack of this or that controversy and running from one side to the other ".[4] Trotsky was at this time less virulent than Lenin in public debate, but made up for this in a private letter of 1913 to the Georgian Menshevik Chkheidze, in which he wrote that " the whole foundation of Leninism at the present time is built on lying and falsification and carries within itself the poisoned element of its own disintegration ".[5] The reconciliation of 1917 never effaced these acrimonious exchanges from the memory of Trotsky's adversaries in the party.

Party divisions were thus acute and party fortunes at a low ebb when Lenin, in January 1912, assembled a small conference of his followers and sympathizers from Russia and from western Europe in Prague. Though it was attended by only fourteen voting delegates, all but two of them Bolsheviks, it proclaimed itself a " general party conference " and " the supreme organ of the party ". It noted the melancholy fact of the " disintegration and collapse of the majority of party organizations " under the stress of counter-revolutionary repression, intensified by the prolonged absence of " a working party centre "; it condemned as " liquidators " those who did not accept the Bolshevik policies

---

[1] See p. 33 above.

[2] Lenin, *Sochineniya*, xv, 11. The same phrase recurs later *ibid.* xviii, 381.

[3] *Ibid.* xv, 546. The Russian word *khlestakovshchina* is a strong one, being derived from Gogol's Khlestakov, the bombastic impostor in *Revizor*; in a letter to Gorky of this period Lenin calls Trotsky a " *poseur* " (*ibid.* xxviii, 523).

[4] *Ibid.* xv, 304, xvii, 469.

[5] *Lenin o Trotskom i o Trotskizme*, ed. M. Olminsky (2nd ed. 1925), pp. 217–219. This letter, intercepted by the censorship, was discovered in the archives after the revolution, and its publication was one of the sensations of the campaign against Trotsky after Lenin's death.

of action and organization; and it insisted on " the necessity of intensified work to build up again the illegal organization of the Russian Social-Democratic Workers' Party ". Nor did it neglect the possibilities of legal activity, offering three party slogans — all well within the limits of the bourgeois revolution — for the forthcoming elections to the fourth Duma : " a democratic republic, an eight-hour working day and the confiscation of all landowners' land ". But the most significant step taken by the Prague conference related to party organization. The central committee of the party appointed by the London congress in 1907, and representative of the different groups at that congress, had not met for two years and was virtually defunct. The conference, arrogating to itself the functions of a party congress, appointed a new central committee of six members, including Lenin, Zinoviev and Orjonikidze, and five substitutes or " candidates ", including Bubnov and Kalinin. It was an unconstitutional step. But it clearly marked the claim of the Bolsheviks to form by themselves, and to the exclusion of all " liquidators ", Menshevik and other, the Russian Social-Democratic Workers' Party. What had been attempted at the third congress in 1905 was done again. And this time there was no going back. Henceforth the Bolsheviks were no longer a faction within the party, but the party itself.[1]

One change made by the conference in the party statute allowed the central committee to coopt additional members. Under this regulation Stalin was coopted shortly after the conference,[2] and also became a member of a newly appointed " Russian bureau " to take charge of work in Russia itself. The

[1] The resolutions of the conference were issued as a pamphlet (*Vserossiiskaya Konferentsiya Ros. Sots.-Dem. Rab. Partii 1912 goda* (Paris, 1912)) and reprinted in *VKP(B) v Rezolyutsiyakh* (1941), i, 177-191. For reasons of secrecy they did not contain the list of members and candidates elected to the central committee. But these appear with slight variations between the two categories in all party histories down to the early 1930s (e.g. N. Popov, *Outline History of the Communist Party of the Soviet Union* (Engl. transl. n.d.), i, 274) and in Lenin, *Sochineniya*, xv, 651-654, note 167.

[2] The sources referred to at the end of the preceding note, as well as Krupskaya, *Memories of Lenin*, ii (Engl. transl. 1932), 79, record Stalin's cooption " soon after the conference ". The official history of 1938 (*History of the Communist Party of the Soviet Union (Bolsheviks)* (Engl. transl. 1939), p. 141), in defiance of all previous records, includes Stalin and Sverdlov among those elected to the central committee by the conference, and is followed in subsequent official accounts.

moment was crucial. On April 4, 1912, troops fired on striking workers of the Lena goldfields and there were more than 500 casualties. It was the worst massacre of the kind since January 9, 1905, and opened a new era of industrial unrest and agitation. One of the symptoms of renewed party activity was the foundation in Petersburg of a new Bolshevik newspaper, *Pravda*, the first number of which appeared on April 22, 1912. Another was Lenin's personal decision to change his place of residence from Paris to Cracow, in Austrian Poland, in order to be nearer the scene of action. The mounting tension in Russia during the next two years not only increased the possibilities and the prospects of revolutionary activity in Russia itself, but deepened the rift between Bolsheviks and Mensheviks. Lenin's high-handed action at Prague aroused indignation among other party groups. But nothing shook his determination to pursue an independent course. In August 1912 Trotsky summoned a gathering of Russian social-democrats of all shades of opinion at Vienna in the hope of once more paving the way for reunion. But the meeting was denounced and derided by the Bolsheviks with the result that the " August bloc " became a temporary coalition of Mensheviks, Trotskyites and minor groups against the Bolsheviks. It had no sequel except still further to exacerbate relations between Lenin and Trotsky. At no time did they write of each other in more bitter and venomous language than in the eighteen months which followed the August conference.

The war of 1914 was destined to serve as the forcing-house for the seeds of revolution. The immediate effect of its outbreak was to complicate immensely the task of the revolutionaries and to break up such rudimentary organization as they possessed. In Petersburg the Bolshevik and Menshevik deputies in the Duma momentarily united in a common declaration on behalf of the whole Russian Social-Democratic Workers' Party, refusing to vote for war credits ; on the government side the first act was the suppression of the anti-government press, including the Bolshevik *Pravda*. Even in western Europe freedom of propaganda was restricted to a handful of small neutral countries. Lenin, arrested and threatened with internment in Austria, took refuge in Switzerland and, being joined by Zinoviev, established at Berne what was quickly recognized as the authoritative centre of Bolshevism.

Lenin had no doubt about the party attitude to the war. Since the Stuttgart congress of 1907 the Second International, at Lenin's instigation, had been committed to an injunction to social-democrats, in the event of war, to " utilize the economic and political crisis caused by the war in order to . . . hasten the destruction of the class domination of the capitalist class ".[1] The defection of the socialists and social-democrats of western Europe who, almost to a man, supported their respective national governments in August 1914 was the blackest treason. It in no way shook Lenin's convictions. He reached Berne on September 5, 1914; and on the following day he assembled the small group of available Bolsheviks and read them a set of theses on the war, in which he explicitly declared that " from the point of view of the working class and of the toiling masses of all the peoples of Russia the defeat of the Tsarist monarchy and its armies would be the least evil ", and set forth the slogans which social-democrats must proclaim :

> Universal propaganda, extending to the army and to the theatre of military operations, for the socialist revolution and for the necessity of turning one's weapons not against one's brothers, the hired slaves of other countries, but against the reactionary and bourgeois governments of all countries. Unconditional necessity to organize illegal cells and groups in the armies of all nations for such propaganda in all languages. Ruthless struggle against the chauvinism and patriotism of the bourgeoisie of all countries without exception.[2]

In February 1915 a larger conference of Bolsheviks at Berne, attended by Bukharin, Krylenko and Pyatakov as well as by Lenin and Zinoviev, accepted and published a series of resolutions on similar lines.[3] But they remained an isolated group. Plekhanov preached national defence as a necessary prelude to reform, thus taking a stand indistinguishable from that of the social-democratic or labour parties of the Second International who had been branded by Lenin as " social-chauvinists "; and Menshevik opinion ranged all the way from this " Right " position of

[1] The party attitude towards war will be discussed in Part V.
[2] Lenin, *Sochineniya*, xviii, 44-46. The theses appeared in an amended and expanded form as an article in the party journal *Sotsial-Demokrat* for November 1, 1914 (*ibid.* xviii, 61-66).
[3] Lenin, *Sochineniya*, xviii, 124-128 ; Krupskaya, *Memories of Lenin*, ii (Engl. transl. 1932), 156-157.

Plekhanov to the " Left " position of Martov who declared himself
an internationalist and joined Lenin in denouncing the " imperialist war ". But between Bolshevism and this Menshevism of
the Left there was still an essential difference. Lenin wished to
end the war by a socialist revolution throughout Europe which
would enable Russia to pass on direct from the bourgeois revolution to the socialist revolution. Martov wished to end the war by
a bourgeois-democratic peace on the basis of national self-determination and without annexations and indemnities; and no
Menshevik, accepting the unqualified dogma of the bourgeois
character of the coming revolution in Russia, could go further
than this. Both Martov and Lenin attended the famous Zimmerwald conference of international socialists opposed to the war in
September 1915. The difference between them was the difference
between the " Zimmerwald majority " and the " Zimmerwald
Left ".

In Russia, after the initial measure of cooperation between
Bolsheviks and Mensheviks, the pressure of events and of opinion
gradually drove the two groups apart ; and the superior underground organization of the Bolsheviks, which, though severely
restricted by police persecution, never quite ceased to function,
told in their favour. At the end of September 1914, five
Bolshevik deputies of the Duma and other Bolshevik delegates
from various parts of Russia held a secret conference in Finland.
Inspired by Lenin's theses of August 24/September 6, 1914, they
adopted a resolution condemning — in somewhat general terms,
it is true — the government and the war. A month later the
Bolshevik deputies together with other prominent Bolsheviks,
including Kamenev, who had assembled for another conference,
were arrested and, early in 1915, exiled to Siberia.[1] Under
examination at the trial, both Kamenev and two of the deputies
claimed that they did not agree with Lenin's theses in so far as
these enjoined the party to work for a national defeat in the war.[2]
But where the Bolsheviks wavered, the Mensheviks in Russia
almost entirely disintegrated and became indistinguishable from
other " progressives ", combining a patriotic attitude towards the
war with a demand for " democratic " reforms.

[1] E. Yaroslavsky, *Istoriya VKP(B)*, iii (1929), 220-223.
[2] For Lenin's condemnation of this action see *Sochineniya*, xviii, 129.

The deportation of all the prominent Bolsheviks from Petrograd to Siberia, where Sverdlov, Stalin and Orjonikidze were already serving sentences of exile before the outbreak of war, virtually broke up the central Bolshevik organization in Russia. For eighteen months the so-called " Russian bureau " of the central committee ceased to exist. In the spring or summer of 1916 it was reconstituted by a party worker named Shlyapnikov who, living at the beginning of the war in Paris, had attended the Berne conference in 1915 and had later been sent by Lenin to Scandinavia to arrange for the smuggling of party literature into Russia. Shlyapnikov now returned to Petrograd and, coopting two young party members hitherto inconspicuous enough to have avoided molestation, Zalutsky and Molotov (a young intellectual from Kazan, whose real name was Skryabin and who had made his party début in the office of *Pravda* in 1912), formed a new " Russian bureau ".[1] There was, however, little to be done. Local committees in a few large centres still carried on surreptitious propaganda. But communications with the central committee in Switzerland were intermittent and precarious, though issues of the party journal *Sotsial-Demokrat*, published by Lenin at irregular intervals throughout the war, sometimes got through. In Russia, the party had no publication since the suppression of *Pravda* on the outbreak of war.

Lenin sat meanwhile in Switzerland writing and watching and waiting. Early in 1916 he moved from Berne to Zürich where he found more readily available material for *Imperialism as the Highest Stage of Capitalism*, his major work during the war. He also wrote much on the attitude of socialists to the war and on the question of national self-determination, which had been brought into prominence by allied propaganda, and on which party opinion was keenly divided. In April 1916 he attended a second conference of the Zimmerwald group at Kienthal. The proceedings seemed to show a slight move towards the Left among socialists opposed to the war, but no real unity of opinion or purpose. Lenin's confidence in the rightness of his creed never flagged. But the cramped monotony of existence and the inability to act sapped something of his optimism. In the autumn of 1911, at what seemed the darkest moment of reaction, he had

[1] E. Yaroslavsky, *Istoriya VKP(B)*, iii (1929), 234-235.

seen increasing signs that " the epoch of the rule of so-called peaceful bourgeois parliamentarianism is nearing its end to give place to the epoch of the revolutionary struggles of a proletariat organized and trained in the spirit of the Marxist idea, which will overthrow the rule of the bourgeoisie and establish the communist order ".[1] In January 1917, addressing a Swiss audience, he was doubtful whether " we, the old " (Lenin was forty-six) would " live to see the decisive battles of the coming revolution ".[2] Some six weeks later revolution broke out in Russia ; and, after more than a month of anxious waiting and troublesome negotiation, Lenin with a party of some twenty Bolsheviks, including Zinoviev, Radek, Sokolnikov and Safarov, travelled through Germany to Sweden by agreement with the German authorities in a railway coach sealed from communication with the outside world.[3] The party reached Petrograd on April 3, 1917.

[1] Lenin, *Sochineniya*, xv, 265.   [2] *Ibid.* xix, 357.
[3] A full account of the negotiations and of the journey is in Fritz Platten, *Die Reise Lenins durch Deutschland* (n.d. [? 1925]). The occasion was less dramatic and less sinister than it was afterwards made to appear. Shortly afterwards a much larger party of Russian *émigrés*, including a Menshevik group headed by Martov, made the same journey in the same conditions.

CHAPTER 4

FROM FEBRUARY TO OCTOBER [1]

THE February revolution of 1917 which overthrew the Romanov dynasty was the spontaneous outbreak of a multitude exasperated by the privations of the war and by manifest inequality in the distribution of burdens. It was welcomed and utilized by a broad stratum of the bourgeoisie and of the official class, which had lost confidence in the autocratic system of government and especially in the persons of the Tsar and of his advisers; it was from this section of the population that the first Provisional Government was drawn. The revolutionary parties played no direct part in the making of the revolution. They did not expect it, and were at first somewhat nonplussed by it. The creation at the moment of the revolution of a Petrograd Soviet of Workers' Deputies was a spontaneous act of groups of workers without central direction. It was a revival of the Petersburg Soviet which had played a brief but glorious rôle in the revolution of 1905, and was, like its predecessor, a non-party organization elected by factory workers, Social-Revolutionaries, Mensheviks and Bolsheviks being all represented in it. It did not at first aspire to governmental power, partly because its leaders took the hitherto accepted view that Russia was ripe only for a bourgeois, and not yet for a socialist, revolution, and partly because it had no sense of its own competence or preparedness to govern. The attitude of the Soviet was afterwards described by Lenin as a " *voluntary* surrender of state power to the bourgeoisie

---

[1] A history of this vital period is badly needed. In addition to official documents *Revolyutsiya 1917 goda: Khronika Sobytii* (6 vols. by various editors, 1923–1930) is an invaluable source-book; and there is a vast array of other first-hand material, including, from their own point of view, Milyukov's brilliant sketch in *Istoriya Vtoroi Russkoi Revolyutsii* (Sofia, 1921) and Trotsky's *History of the Russian Revolution.*

and *its* Provisional Government ".[1] The fact, however, that the
writ of the Soviet was recognized by an ever-increasing number
of workers and soldiers gave it, in spite of itself, a position of
authority which could not be ignored ; and this was the practical
and almost accidental basis of the so-called " dual power " set
up by the February revolution, when public authority was in
some sort exercised by two bodies whose attitude to each other
swung uneasily between rivalry and cooperation : the Provisional
Government, which was the legal successor of the Tsarist government and recognized as such by the outside world, and the self-
constituted and therefore revolutionary Soviets of Workers'
Deputies. The example of Petrograd was followed by the setting
up of Soviets in Moscow and other large cities and, somewhat
later, in country districts ; and this, in turn, led to the summoning
of a first " all-Russian conference " of Soviets at the end of
March 1917.

Of the two factions of the Russian Social-Democratic Workers'
Party it was the Mensheviks who at first profited most by the
February revolution. As in 1905, the promise of constitutional
government seemed to justify their programme and gave them
the advantage over the Bolsheviks. A bourgeois revolutionary
régime, enjoying the critical support of good Marxists until such
time as bourgeois capitalism had exhausted its potentialities and
the way was open for the socialist revolution — this was precisely
the Menshevik picture of the first stage in the revolutionary
process. Indeed the " dual power ", considered as a constitutional partnership between bourgeois government and proletarian
" legal opposition ", was essentially Menshevik in conception.
The main point of embarrassment for the Mensheviks was their
attitude to the war, on which they were not agreed among themselves. But a policy of pressing the bourgeois government to end
the war on a democratic programme without entering into precise
details of the ways and means of ending it seemed for the moment
to meet all requirements. The Mensheviks quickly emerged into
a predominant position in the Petrograd Soviet : its first president
was the Georgian Menshevik Chkheidze. The principal rivals of
the Mensheviks were the Social-Revolutionaries. It was not long

---

[1] Lenin, *Sochineniya*, xx, 114. V. Chernov, *The Great Russian Revolution*
(Engl. transl. N.Y., 1936), pp. 99-109, gives a similar analysis.

before the Soviets of Workers' Deputies became Soviets of Workers' and Soldiers' Deputies ; and, as the armies dissolved into struggling masses of peasants crying out for peace and land and counting on the Social-Revolutionaries, the traditional party of the peasant revolution, to fulfil their ambitions, the star of the Social-Revolutionaries (or SRs, as they were commonly called) continued to ascend.

The Bolsheviks seemed to have gained least.   The suddenness of the revolution had left the determination of Bolshevik policy in the hands of three men (two of them young and without experience) cut off not only from the party centre in Switzerland, but from the other experienced party leaders marooned in Siberia. The position was embarrassing.   On the one hand, they were committed by Lenin's theses of 1914 and by everything he had since written to the sensational policy, known to be distasteful even to many Bolsheviks, of advocating civil war and national defeatism.   On the other hand, the party resolution of 1905 had contemplated the establishment of a provisional revolutionary government as the result of a democratic revolution and had admitted that Bolshevik cooperation in such a government might be desirable " for the purposes of a ruthless struggle against all counter-revolutionary attempts and of the defence of the independent interests of the working class ".[1]   With so much guidance and no more, Shlyapnikov, Zalutsky and Molotov, constituting the Russian bureau of the central committee, drafted a party manifesto which was issued as a broadsheet on February 26, 1917, and appeared two days later as a supplement to the first issue of the *Izvestiya* of the Petrograd Soviet.[2]

All things considered, it was a creditable effort.   Since no provisional government had yet been proclaimed, the question of defining relations to it did not arise.   The manifesto called on the working class and the revolutionary army to create a " provisional revolutionary government ", which would establish a republic, introduce democratic reforms such as the eight-hour day, the confiscation of estates and the creation of a constituent assembly on a basis of universal suffrage and secret ballot, confiscate and distribute stocks of food, and " enter into negotiations with the

---

[1] See p. 46 above.
[2] The text is in Lenin, *Sochineniya*, xx, 600-601 : see also *ibid*. xx, 634.

proletariat of the belligerent countries for a revolutionary struggle of the peoples of all countries against their oppressors and enslavers . . . and for the termination of the bloody human slaughter which has been imposed on the enslaved peoples ". Factory workers and insurgent armies were urged to elect their representatives to this provisional revolutionary government. The appeal ended with salutes to " the red banner of revolution ", " the democratic republic ", " the revolutionary working class " and " the revolutionary people and insurgent army ". Lenin, who read extracts from this manifesto in the German press while he was still in Switzerland struggling to arrange for his journey to Russia, noted as " especially important and especially topical " the " perfectly correct idea of our central committee that the indispensable thing for peace is relations with the proletarians of all the belligerent countries ". [1]

The February revolution had removed all obstacles other than the shortage of man-power to a revival of the party journal. The publication of *Pravda* was resumed on March 5, 1917, under an editorial board consisting of Molotov, who as member of the bureau of the central committee bore the chief responsibility, Kalinin, valued perhaps, then as later, less for his intellectual qualities than for his prestige as a usable party member of peasant origin, and Eremeev, of whom little is known except that he had been a contributor to the *Pravda* of 1912.[2] The first issue was distributed free, the second sold 100,000 copies.[3] The views expressed in the first seven numbers of the new *Pravda* were broadly those of the party manifesto. It denounced the existing Provisional Government as " a government of capitalists and landowners ", and thought that the Soviet should convene a constituent assembly to establish a " democratic republic ". On the issue of the war, it published on March 10, 1917, a resolution of the bureau advocating a transformation of the imperialist war into a civil war for the liberation of the peoples from the yoke of the ruling classes, though it still refrained from the explicit advocacy of national defeatism. But it was not immune from backslidings. The same issue which printed this resolution printed an article by Olminsky which concluded :

[1] *Ibid.* xx, 31.
[2] A. Shlyapnikov, *Semnadtsatyi God*, ii (1924), 178.   [3] *Ibid.* ii, 114.

The [bourgeois] revolution is not yet completed. We live under the slogan of " striking together ". In party affairs, each party for itself; but all as one man for the common cause.

The position was complicated by the revival of the local Petrograd party committee, which, having for the first time acquired legal status, had attracted a large number of new recruits and exhibited a disconcerting variety of opinions. In general, the Petrograd committee stood further to the Right than the bureau. When on March 5, 1917, young Molotov appeared at one of its sessions as delegate of the bureau and proposed a resolution attacking the Provisional Government as counter-revolutionary and demanding its replacement by a government capable of carrying out a pro-gramme of democratic revolution, he failed to convince the majority of the committee, which adopted a text promising not to oppose the Provisional Government so long as " its actions corre-spond to the interests of the proletariat and of the broad democratic masses of the people ".[1]

This confused situation was worse confounded by the arrival in Petrograd from Siberia on March 13, 1917 — the day on which the seventh issue of *Pravda* appeared — of Kamenev, Stalin and Muranov. Kamenev was an experienced writer and had been appointed editor of the central party organ — at that time the *Rabochaya Gazeta* — by the Prague conference of 1912; Stalin, having been a member of the central committee of the party since 1912, replaced Shlyapnikov as senior party organizer in Petro-grad; Muranov was one of the Bolshevik deputies of the fourth Duma. All three had formerly worked on the old *Pravda*.[2] They at once took over the reins of authority from Shlyapnikov and his young colleagues; and *Pravda* of March 15, 1917, carried an announcement that Muranov had assumed the direction of the journal and that Stalin and Kamenev had joined the editorial

[1] *Pervyi Legal'nyi PK Bol'shevikov* (1927), pp. 18-19. The party com-mittee retained the name " Petersburg " in its title, refusing to recognize the change of name made in 1914 " for chauvinistic purposes " by the Tsarist govern-ment (*ibid.* p. 5).

[2] According to N. Popov, *Outline History of the Communist Party of the Soviet Union* (Engl. transl. n.d.), i, 277, all three were members of the editorial board of 1912. Stalin took part in bringing out the first issue (Stalin, *Sochineniya*, v, 130) and was arrested on the day it appeared, April 22, 1912. Kamenev was sent to Petersburg at the beginning of 1914 to take charge of *Pravda* (Krupskaya, *Memories of Lenin*, ii (Engl. transl. 1932), 126).

board. The former members of the board presumably remained, though with diminished influence and prerogatives.

These proceedings, however distasteful to the stop-gap leaders who had acquitted themselves well in a difficult situation,[1] were natural enough, and would have excited little interest but for the fact that the newcomers carried out a contentious change of policy. A brief article by Stalin in *Pravda* of March 14, 1917, was less remarkable for what was said than for what was omitted. It urged workers, peasants and soldiers to rally to the Soviets " as organs of the union and the power of the revolutionary forces of Russia ". But it did not mention either the Provisional Government or the war; and the cautious appeal to " maintain the rights that have been won in order finally to beat down the old powers and to move the Russian revolution forward " approached more nearly to the Menshevik formula of pressing the bourgeoisie forward from behind than to the Bolshevik formula of taking the lead.[2] The issue of the following day, which contained the announcement of the changes in the editorial board, carried on its front page a proclamation issued by the Petrograd Soviet " To the Peoples of the Whole World ", announcing that " we shall stoutly defend our own liberty " and that " the Russian revolution will not flinch before the bayonets of the aggressors ".[3] This was followed by a signed article from Kamenev :

> When army faces army, it would be the most inane policy to suggest to one of these armies to lay down its arms and go home. This would not be a policy of peace but a policy of slavery, which would be rejected with disgust by a free people.

A free people could only " answer bullet with bullet, shell with shell ". This whole-hearted endorsement of national defence signally confirmed Kamenev's statement in court over two years earlier that he did not share Lenin's position.[4]

According to Shlyapnikov, who at this point becomes our sole authority, *Pravda*'s change of front excited dismay among the Bolshevik factory workers, and a meeting was held at which

---

[1] Shlyapnikov betrayed his sense of grievance in his otherwise valuable memoirs ; Molotov kept silent — a habit which stood him in good stead throughout his career.

[2] Stalin, *Sochineniya*, iii, 1-3.

[3] Reprinted in A. Shlyapnikov, *Semnadtsatyi God*, ii (1924), 291.

[4] See p. 67 above ; the article is in Lenin, *Sochineniya*, xx, 601-602.

the bureau, the Petrograd committee and the exiles from Siberia were all represented.   In the course of the discussion, Stalin and Muranov disowned the views of Kamenev, who " submitted to the general decision and took up in the organization a ' moderate position ' ".[1] What resulted from the discussion seems to have been less a compromise than a deadlock ; for while *Pravda* published no more articles so outspokenly in favour of national defence as that of Kamenev, it equally refrained from any fundamental attack on the Provisional Government or on its war policy.[2] An older and more cautious editorial board had repressed the rash ardour displayed in the earlier issues and retired to a more comfortable position on the fence.   When a party conference was held to decide the line to be taken at the first all-Russian conference of Soviets at the end of March 1917, the proposal put forward by Stalin to " support the Provisional Government in its activity only in so far as it moves along the path of satisfying the working class and the revolutionary peasantry " scarcely differed in substance from the formula approved by the Menshevik majority at the conference of Soviets ; and most Bolsheviks shared the view expressed by Stalin that unification was possible " on a Zimmerwald-Kienthal line " with those Mensheviks who were against national " defencism ".[3]

More than seven years later, at the height of his controversy with Trotsky, Stalin confessed his error at this time.   After arguing that the party could neither seek the overthrow of the Provisional Government, since it was bound up with the Soviets, nor support it, since it was an imperialist government, Stalin continued :

> The party — its majority — . . . adopted a policy of pressure by the Soviets on the Provisional Government in the

[1] A. Shlyapnikov, *Semnadtsatyi God*, ii (1924), 185.

[2] The difference between the other editors and Kamenev was that they took up a neutral position, neither supporting nor opposing the Provisional Government, while Kamenev regarded this position as " impossible " and wished for open support (see his speech in *Pervyi Legal'nyi PK Bol'shevikov* (1927), p. 50).

[3] The proceedings of the all-Russian conference of Soviets are described in A. Shlyapnikov, *Semnadtsatyi God*, iii (1927), 211-249, and its resolutions are reprinted *ibid.* iii, 360-374.   The proceedings of the party conference have never been officially published.   But there is no reason to doubt the authenticity of the incomplete records published by Trotsky, *Stalinskaya Shkola Falsifikatsii* (Berlin, 1932), pp. 225-290, who obtained them from Zinoviev and Kamenev in 1925 ; for the quotations from the remarks of Stalin, who made the principal report at the conference, see *ibid.* pp. 235, 265-266.

question of peace, and did not decide at once to take the step forward from the old slogan of the dictatorship of the proletariat and peasantry to the new slogan of power for the Soviets. This half-and-half policy was intended to give the Soviets a chance to detect in the concrete questions of peace the imperialist nature of the Provisional Government and so to detach them from it. But it was a profoundly mistaken position since it bred pacifist illusions, added fuel to the flame of defencism and hindered the revolutionary uprising of the masses. This mistaken position I shared with other party comrades, and renounced it completely only in the middle of April when I adhered to Lenin's theses.[1]

The argument is not particularly convincing and attributes to subtlety of intention what was due to mere confusion. But sympathy may be felt with those who sought to hammer out a consistent Bolshevik policy in Petrograd in the March days of 1917. Nobody had yet contested the view that the Russian revolution was not, and could not be, other than a bourgeois revolution. This was the solid and accepted framework of doctrine into which policy had to fit. Yet it was difficult to discover within this framework any cogent reason to reject out of hand the Provisional Government, which was indubitably bourgeois, or to demand a transfer of power to the Soviets, which were essentially proletarian, or — least of all — to denounce the quest for a " democratic " peace and preach civil war and national defeat. The circle could not be squared. It was left to Lenin, before the eyes of his astonished followers, to smash the framework.

The scene of Lenin's arrival at the Finland station in Petrograd on the evening of April 3, 1917, has been recorded by at least four eye-witnesses.[2] He had been met at Beloostrov, the last

---

[1] Stalin, *Sochineniya*, vi, 333-334.

[2] *Izvestiya*, April 5, 1917 ; A. Shlyapnikov, *Semnadtsatyi God*, iii (1927), 257-259 : Raskolnikov in *Proletarskaya Revolyutsiya*, No. 13, 1923, pp. 220-226 ; N. Sukhanov, *Zapiski o Revolyutsii* (Berlin, 1922), iii, 14-15. Shlyapnikov's account shows anxiety to emphasize his own rôle as master of ceremonies and to score off Kamenev ; Raskolnikov was a matter-of-fact rank-and-file Bolshevik ; Sukhanov was a brilliant, though garrulous, writer of Menshevik affinities, who has left the most vivid and detailed extant account of the externals of the revolution. Krupskaya, *Memories of Lenin*, ii (Engl. transl. 1932), 211, records the meeting at Beloostrov. Both Raskolnikov and Zalezhsky (in *Proletarskaya Revolyutsiya*, No. 13, 1923, p. 155) notice the presence of Kollontai. None of the early accounts names any leading Bolshevik other than Shlyapnikov, Kamenev and Kollontai as present to receive the travellers.

station outside Petrograd, by a group representing the Russian
bureau of the central committee and headed by Shlyapnikov. In
the train Lenin plied Shlyapnikov with questions " about the
position of things in the party . . . about the causes of the turn-
over in *Pravda* towards ' defencism ', about the position of individual colleagues ". On arrival in Petrograd he was greeted by
members of the central committee and the Petrograd committee
of the party and of the staff of *Pravda*. Among them was
Kamenev, whom he at once began good-humouredly to chide :
" What is this you are writing in *Pravda*? We saw some of your
articles and roundly abused you." Alexandra Kollontai produced
a bouquet which Lenin carried awkwardly ; and the party proceeded to the former imperial waiting-room. Here Lenin was
officially welcomed by Chkheidze, the president of the Petrograd
Soviet, who, in a few carefully chosen words, expressed his hopes
for " a closing of the ranks of democracy " in defence of " our
revolution ". Lenin, turning vaguely away from the official party
towards the assembled crowds outside, addressed them as " dear
comrades, soldiers, sailors and workers ", greeted in their persons
" the victorious Russian revolution ", declared that the " robber
imperialist war " was the beginning of civil war all over Europe,
and concluded :

> Any day, if not today or tomorrow, the crash of the whole
> of European imperialism may come. The Russian revolution,
> made by you, has begun it and opened a new epoch. Hail the
> world-wide socialist revolution.[1]

As Sukhanov notes, it was not a reply to Chkheidze. It did not
even fit " the ' context ' of the Russian revolution as understood
by all without exception who had witnessed it or taken part in it ".
Lenin had spoken ; and his first words had been not of the
bourgeois, but of the socialist, revolution.

On the square outside the station there was a mass demonstration of Bolsheviks headed by an armoured car carrying the banner
of the party. Lenin, standing on the armoured car, addressed
the cheering crowds in similar terms and, later on the same evening, spoke for two hours to a party audience at party headquarters.

---

[1] Chkheidze's address was published in *Izvestiya*, April 5, 1917. Lenin's
address to the crowd was not reported, and this account suggests that it was
delivered before, not after, Chkheidze's speech.

The slowly mounting astonishment with which his words were
received by the other party leaders was described by an eye-
witness ten years later :

> It had been expected that Vladimir Ilich would arrive and
> call to order the Russian bureau of the central committee and
> especially comrade Molotov, who occupied a particularly irre-
> concilable position in regard to the Provisional Government.
> It turned out, however, that it was Molotov who was nearest
> of all to Ilich.[1]

On the following day there were more discussions at his sister's
flat and at the editorial offices of *Pravda* ; [2] and in the afternoon
he spoke before a gathering of social-democrats — Bolshevik,
Menshevik and independent — at the Tauride palace, where the
Soviet held its sessions. It was on this last occasion that Lenin
for the first time read the famous " April theses " which summarized his views; that Bogdanov interrupted with cries of " Delirium, the delirium of a madman "; that Goldenberg, another
former Bolshevik, declared that " Lenin had proposed himself as
candidate for a European throne vacant for 30 years, the throne
of Bakunin "; and that Steklov, the editor of *Izvestiya* and soon
to join the Bolsheviks, added that Lenin's speech consisted of
" abstract constructions " which he would soon abandon when he
had acquainted himself with the Russian situation. Lenin's speech
was attacked from all sides, only Kollontai speaking in support
of it ; and he left the hall without exercising his right of reply.[3]
On the same evening he re-read the theses to a gathering of
Bolshevik leaders, and once more found himself completely isolated.[4] The theses *On the Tasks of the Proletariat in the Present
Revolution* were published in *Pravda* of April 7, 1917.[5]

The key to Lenin's position was in the second of his theses :

> The peculiarity of the current moment in Russia consists
> in the *transition* from the first stage of the revolution, which
> gave power to the bourgeoisie as a result of the insufficient

[1] *Proletarskaya Revolyutsiya*, No. 4 (63), (1927), p. 157.
[2] A. Shlyapnikov, *Semnadtsatyi God*, iii (1927), 264.
[3] N. Sukhanov, *Zapiski o Revolyutsii* (Berlin, 1922), iii, 28-42 ; see also
Lenin, *Sochineniya*, xx, 99.
[4] N. Sukhanov, *Zapiski o Revolyutsii* (Berlin, 1922), iii, pp. 49-51 ; notes of
Lenin's remarks on this occasion were preserved and are in *Sochineniya*, xx, 76-83.
[5] *Ibid.* xx, 87-90.

consciousness and organization of the proletariat, *to its second stage*, which should give the power into the hands of the proletariat and poorest strata of the peasantry.

The negative conclusion of this was to reject the Provisional Government and its support of the war, and to abandon the folly of demanding that " this government, a government of capitalists, should *cease* to be imperialist ". The positive conclusion was to explain to the masses that " the Soviet of Workers' Deputies is the *one possible* form of revolutionary government ". So long as the Soviet was " subject to the influence of the bourgeoisie ", that is to say, so long as it contained a non-Bolshevik majority, this work of education was the main task of the party. But the goal was clear :

> Not a parliamentary republic — a return to that from the Soviet of Workers' Deputies would be a step backwards — but a republic of Soviets of Workers', Poor Peasants' and Peasants' Deputies throughout the country, growing from below upwards.

Lenin thus implied that the moment when the Bolsheviks, by means of mass education, secured a majority in the Soviet would be the moment of the passing of the revolution into its second, or socialist, phase. This implication was carried into the economic theses, which proposed the nationalization of all land and the transformation of large estates into model farms under the control of the Soviet, the fusion of existing banks into a national bank (a milder periphrasis for the nationalization of banks), and added as the third point :

> Not the " introduction " of socialism as our *immediate* task, but immediate transition merely to *control* by the Soviet of Workers' Deputies over the social production and distribution of products.

The theses ended with a proposal to revise the party programme and to change the name of the party from " social-democratic " to " communist ", and with a demand for the creation of a revolutionary International.

Lenin's cautious phraseology left room for a certain practical vagueness about the precise moment of the transition to socialism, but none for doubt about this transition as the main goal ; and it was on this point that the battle was at once joined. On the day after the publication of the theses, *Pravda* carried what appeared to be an editorial note signed by Kamenev emphasizing that they represented only Lenin's " *personal* opinion " and concluding :

> In so far as concerns Lenin's general scheme it appears to us unacceptable, since it starts from the assumption that the bourgeois revolution is *finished* and counts on the immediate transformation of this revolution into a socialist revolution.[1]

On the same day the Petrograd committee of the party discussed Lenin's theses and rejected them by 13 votes to 2, with 1 abstention.[2] The challenge had still to be taken up at the Petrograd " all-city " party conference on April 14, 1917, and at the all-Russian conference which was to follow ten days later. Meanwhile Lenin developed his views in a further article in *Pravda* and in two pamphlets, though the second of these was not published till some months later.

In Lenin's analysis the " dual power " consisted of two distinct governments. The Provisional Government was the government of the *bourgeoisie* ; the Soviets were a dictatorship formed by " the proletariat and the peasantry (dressed in soldiers' uniforms) ".[3] Since the transfer of power to this dual authority had taken place, it was " to this extent " true that " the bourgeois or bourgeois-democratic revolution is *finished* ", even though all the necessary bourgeois-democratic reforms had not yet been carried out ; " the revolutionary-democratic dictatorship of the proletariat and the peasantry has been realised " (" in a certain form and to a certain degree ", added Lenin cautiously in a footnote).[4] The peculiarity of the situation was the " interweaving " (Lenin used this word several times) of the bourgeois power of the Provisional Government and the (potential, if not actual) revolutionary dictatorship of the Soviets. The future turned on the struggle between the bourgeoisie and the proletariat for the peasant masses.[5] For the

[1] Reprinted in Lenin, *Sochineniya*, xx, 607-608.
[2] *Pervyi Legal'nyi PK Bol'shevikov* (1927), pp. 83-88.
[3] Lenin, *Sochineniya*, xx, 94.
[4] *Ibid.* xx, 100-101.
[5] For the past twenty years, wrote Lenin a few months later, " there has run through the whole political history of Russia like a red thread the question whether the working class is to lead the peasants forward to socialism or whether the liberal bourgeoisie is to drag them back into a compromise with capitalism " (*ibid.* xxi, 109-110).

moment " the fact of *class* cooperation between the bourgeoisie
and the peasantry " was decisive; the Soviets were still, in
accordance with the Menshevik view, " an annex of the bourgeois
government ". But if and when the peasantry seized the land for
itself (meaning, in class terms, that the peasantry would split away
from the bourgeoisie and ally itself with the révolutionary proletariat, and, in political terms, that the Bolsheviks would win a
majority in the Soviets), " then this will be a new stage of the
bourgeois-democratic revolution ".[1] Lenin's powerful argument
once more implied the transition to socialism, though it stopped
short of explicitly proclaiming it. He still regarded it as premature
to demand the overthrow of the Provisional Government. But
he emphasized that the " dual power " could be no more than a
transitional phase of struggl which must end in a victory for one
side or the other. " *There cannot be* two powers in the state." [2]
The Menshevik conception of partnership would not work.
Sooner or later the Soviets must overthrow the Provisional
Government or themselves be destroyed.

The Petrograd party conference proved to be a sort of rehearsal
for the all-Russian party conference, so that the issues were
debated twice over by the same protagonists and with the same
results in the smaller and in the larger assembly. The proceedings again demonstrated Lenin's immense power over the party,
a power resting not on rhetoric, but on clear-headed and incisive
argument conveying an irresistible impression of a unique mastery
of the situation. " Before Lenin arrived ", said a delegate at the
Petrograd conference, " all the comrades were wandering in the
dark." [3] Now only Kamenev presented a coherent defence of
the policies accepted by all the leading Bolsheviks in Petrograd
before the presentation of the April theses. The main issue was
narrowed down to the question whether, as Lenin proposed, the
party should work for the transfer of power to the Soviets, or
whether, as Kamenev desired, it should be content with " the
most watchful control " over the Provisional Government by the
Soviets, Kamenev being particularly severe on anything that
could be construed as incitement to overthrow the govern-

[1] Lenin, *Sochineniya*, xx, 102-103.   [2] *Ibid.* xx, 114.
[3] *Sed'maya* (" *Aprel'skaya* ") *Vserossiiskaya i Petrogradskaya Obshchegorod-
skaya Konferentsii RSDRP(B)* (1934), p. 11.

ment. In the decisive vote Kamenev's amendment was defeated by 20 votes to 6, with 9 abstentions.[1]

The all-Russian party conference (known in party history as the " April conference ") met ten days later under the shadow of a ministerial crisis. Milyukov's note of April 18, 1917, promising fidelity to the undertakings given to the allies by the Tsarist government, had raised a storm of protest which led to his enforced resignation. At the conference the tide flowed still more strongly in Lenin's favour. Stalin briefly, and Zinoviev at greater length, supported him against Kamenev.[2] Lenin at one moment held out an olive branch to Kamenev by saying that, though the Provisional Government must be overthrown, it could not be overthrown " at once or in the ordinary way ".[3] The main resolutions were passed by overwhelming majorities of the 150 delegates. With only seven abstentions, the conference declared that the advent of the Provisional Government " did not change and could not change " the imperialist character of Russia's participation in the war, and undertook to assist " the transfer of all state power in all belligerent countries into the hands of the revolutionary proletariat ". This was followed by a resolution, carried with only three dissentients and eight abstentions, condemning the Provisional Government for its " open collaboration " with the " bourgeois and land-owners' counter-revolution ", and demanding active preparations among the " proletarians of town and country " to bring about " the rapid transfer of all state power into the hands of the Soviets of workers' and soldiers' deputies or of other organs directly expressing the will of the majority of the people (organs of local self-government, constituent assembly, etc.)"[4] The most substantial opposition was manifested to the resolution containing an analysis of the " current situation "; for, even after it had accepted Lenin's policy, the party, long attuned to the conception of a bourgeois revolution as the proximate goal, still had its hesitations about proclaiming the transition to the socialist stage of the revolution. This resolution declared that " the objective conditions of the socialist revolution, which

[1] *Ibid.* p. 29.
[2] *Ibid.* pp. 87, 89-91 ; Stalin, *Sochineniya*, iii, 48-49.
[3] *Sed'maya* (" *Aprel'skaya* ") *Vserossiiskaya i Petrogradskaya Obshchegorodskaya Konferentsii RSDRP(B)* (1934), pp. 97-98 ; Lenin, *Sochineniya*, xx, 253.
[4] *VKP(B) v Rezolyutsiyakh* (1941), i, 226-229.

were undoubtedly present before the war in the most advanced countries, have ripened further and continue to ripen in consequence of the war with extreme rapidity "; that " the Russian revolution is only the first stage in the first of the proletarian revolutions inevitably resulting from the war " ; and that common action by the workers of different countries was the only way to guarantee " the most regular development and surest success of the world socialist revolution ". It then reverted to the old argument that, while the immediate realization of " the socialist transformation " was not possible in Russia, the proletariat should none the less refuse to support the bourgeoisie and should itself take the lead in carrying out the practical reforms requisite to complete the bourgeois revolution. This resolution was carried only by a majority of 71 to 39, with 8 abstentions.[1] Nor did anyone answer the question which only Rykov seems to have raised :

Whence will arise the sun of the socialist revolution? I think that with all existing conditions, with our standard of living, the initiation of the socialist revolution does not belong to us. We have not the strength, nor the objective conditions, for it.[2]

The adoption at the April conference of the slogan " all power to the Soviets ", though it did not betoken immediate revolutionary action, for the first time gave concrete shape and a constitutional mould to the Bolshevik scheme of revolution. Lenin's somewhat lukewarm attitude towards the Soviets in 1905 had been modified by their vigour and success in mobilizing popular support, and by the prestige which attached to them even after their downfall. In the spring of 1906 he referred to them as " new organs of *revolutionary power* " :

These organs were founded exclusively by the *revolutionary* strata of the population, they were founded outside all laws and regulations in an entirely revolutionary way as a product of primitive popular creativeness, as an exhibition of the independent action of the people.[3]

---

[1] *VKP(B) v Rezolyutsiyakh* (1941), i, 236-237.

[2] *Sed'maya* (" *Aprel'skaya* ") *Vserossiiskaya i Petrogradskaya Obshchegorodskaya Konferentsii RSDRP(B)* (1934), p. 93. The conference also elected a new central committee of nine — Lenin (104 votes), Zinoviev (101), Stalin (97), Kamenev (95), Milyutin, Nogin, Sverdlov, Smilga, Federov (*ibid.* p. 190).

[3] Lenin, *Sochineniya*, ix, 116.

They could thus be regarded as an approximation to Lenin's conception of a revolutionary-democratic dictatorship of the proletariat and the peasantry, and as the " *de facto* beginnings of a provisional government ".[1] But in the ensuing period of reaction and discouragement the memory of the Soviets faded and little was heard of them in party discussions. When Lenin delivered a long lecture on the 1905 revolution to a Swiss audience in January 1917, the Soviets were dismissed in three or four sentences, though it was still claimed for them that in some places they had " really functioned in the capacity of a new state power ".[2]

It was therefore understandable that the revival of the Petrograd Soviet in February 1917 should not at first, in view of Menshevik predominance in its ranks, have greatly excited the Bolshevik group in the capital : it was not mentioned in the first Bolshevik proclamation of February 26. But here a curious parallel occurs between Marx and Lenin. Marx's " dictatorship of the proletariat " remained, for twenty years after he first enunciated it, an abstract and disembodied conception, till Marx eventually discovered its embodiment in an institution created by men who were for the most part not his disciples, and regarded at the outset by Marx himself with thinly veiled suspicion : the Paris commune. Lenin had evolved all the essentials of his theory of revolution before Soviets had been heard of ; and his attitude to the first Petersburg Soviet — a non-party or, worse still, a Menshevik affair — was as hesitant as that of Marx to the commune. Yet the Soviets, raised to a pinnacle by their challenge to autocracy in 1905, became in the spring of 1917 the predestined repositories of the revolutionary power of which Lenin dreamed. The first of his *Letters from Afar* written from Switzerland in March 1917, and the only one of them to be published before his arrival in Petrograd, hailed the Petrograd Soviet as a " new, unofficial, undeveloped, still comparatively weak *workers' government* expressing the interests of the proletariat and of all the poorest part of the town and country population " ; and this view implied, as Lenin saw, that the situation was already " in transition from the first to the second stage of the revolution ".[3] The way was thus prepared for the April theses, in which recognition of this

[1] *Ibid.* x, 18.   [2] *Ibid.* xix, 353.   [3] *Ibid.* xx, 18.

transition was clearly connected with the new slogan " all power to the Soviets ". It was at this time that Lenin proclaimed the Soviets to be " a power *of the same type* as the Paris commune of 1871 " — a power whose source was " not a law previously discussed and passed by a parliament, but a direct initiative of the popular masses from below and on the spot, a direct ' usurpation ', to employ the current expression ".[1] Lenin thus triumphantly linked himself with Marx and the Soviets with the commune. The Soviets were not only a realization of the " revolutionary-democratic dictatorship "; they were, like the commune, a foretaste of the Marxist dictatorship of the proletariat.[2]

But the party line remained fluid on one point. The concluding words of the party programme adopted in 1903 and still unaltered in 1917 demanded " a constituent assembly elected by the whole people "; and the third all-Bolshevik party congress of 1905 had once more called for " the convening by way of revolution of a constituent assembly on the basis of universal equal and direct suffrage and with secrecy of the ballot ".[3] It is true that Lenin at the same time poked fun at those who believed in the " immediate birth " of a constituent assembly, and declared that " without armed insurrection a constituent assembly is a phantom, a phrase, a lie, a Frankfort talking-shop ".[4] But this essentially bourgeois-democratic institution continued none the less to occupy a cardinal place in Lenin's scheme of revolution. In April 1917 it would have been possible to argue that this plank in the party

---

[1] Lenin, *Sochineniya*, xx, 94. The same parallel was repeated at greater length *ibid*. xx, 107. It had already been drawn in an article of unknown authorship published in *Proletarii* in July 1905, with a postscript by Lenin (*ibid*. viii, 467-470). Lunacharsky long afterwards remembered " how excitedly and with what enthusiasm " Lenin, in the last days of 1905, had discovered in the Petrograd Soviet " a revival of the best tradition of the Paris commune ", and had declared that " to cover all Russia in fact with Soviets of workers ', and then of workers' and peasants ', deputies was to realize the best part of the political plans of the commune which had won the approval of Marx " (*Proletarskaya Revolyutsiya*, No. 11 (46), 1925, pp. 56-57) ; but this passage, written after Lenin's death, is hardly borne out by contemporary evidence.

[2] It is amusing to record that Lenin had once written somewhat patronizingly of the Paris commune as a body which " could not distinguish the elements of a democratic and a socialist revolution " and " confused the tasks of the struggle for a republic with the tasks of the struggle for socialism " (*Sochineniya*, viii, 81).

[3] *VKP(B) v Rezolyutsiyakh* (1941), i, 45.

[4] Lenin, *Sochineniya*, viii, 195, 242.

platform belonged to a period when the bourgeois revolution lay in the future and had been rendered obsolete by the advent of the February revolution. But this argument was never used, no doubt because neither Lenin himself nor — still less — his followers were prepared to commit themselves to the view that the bourgeois revolution had been completed. The resolution of the April conference had named both the Soviets and the constituent assembly as potential recipients of power, without apparently choosing between them ; and throughout the period from February to October 1917 the Bolsheviks, in common with all other Left groups, continued to voice the demand for the constituent assembly and to censure the Provisional Government for dilatoriness in convening it, unconscious of any inconsistency between this demand and the concurrent slogan " all power to the Soviets ". If this inconsistency — or this inability to choose — had been probed to the source, it might have thrown light on the initial dissensions in the party over the April theses. But for the present it reflected, not a division of opinion, but an uncertainty and lack of definition in the mind of the party leaders, including Lenin, on the character of the current revolutionary process. Events were left to prepare the eventual clarification.

From the moment of the April conference every move on the political chessboard seemed to play into the hands of the Bolsheviks and to justify Lenin's boldest calculations. Milyukov's note of April 18 had been a slap in the face not so much for the Bolsheviks as for those moderate elements in the Soviet which, while rejecting the Bolshevik policy of peace through civil war and national defeat, were none the less insistent on a renunciation of " imperialist " designs and on immediate efforts to secure a " democratic " peace. Milyukov's resignation brought about the downfall of the government. In the first Provisional Government Kerensky had been the only socialist minister ; and his equivocal position had been marked by his frequent attempts to disown responsibility for acts of other ministers. Early in May a new government was formed in which, though Lvov remained premier, six socialist ministers were included as representatives of the Soviet : two portfolios were held by SRs, two by Mensheviks and two by independent socialists.

This rearrangement was designed ostensibly to increase the

power and prestige of the Soviet by strengthening its control of the government. The results were quite different. The new government, still the prisoner of an administrative machine run by the bourgeoisie and by the old official class, hard pressed by the allies and faced by the quite insoluble problem of a democratic peace, could do little to satisfy the soldiers and workers who more and more clamoured for some token that an end to the war was at hand. The Soviet had hitherto been a coalition of socialist parties for the defence of the interests of the workers against the bourgeoisie. Now it could no longer win credit in their eyes by harassing a bourgeois government in which it was strongly represented.[1] Splits developed in the SR and Menshevik parties between those who supported and those who attacked the socialist ministers. Most important of all, the Bolsheviks were now the only party uncompromised by participation in a feeble bourgeois-socialist coalition and offering a clear-cut policy of peace at any price. The process by which they eventually won the confidence of the vast majority of soldiers and workers, and became the dominant power in the Soviets, had begun.

Early in May another significant event had occurred. Among the exiles now flocking back in large numbers, Trotsky reached Petrograd from the United States, having been delayed for five weeks by the British authorities. On the day after his arrival he spoke in the Petrograd Soviet; and his prestige as the outstanding figure of the original Soviet of 1905 at once made him a potential leader.[2] He joined a small social-democratic group called the "united social-democrats" (more commonly known as the *Mezhraiontsy*), which had existed in Petrograd since 1913 and claimed independence both of Bolsheviks and of Mensheviks. In the past his restless intellect and temperament had led him to quarrel with every party leadership. But now he thirsted for action, and saw in Lenin the only man of action on the scene, despising alike the SRs, the Mensheviks and those weak-kneed Bolsheviks who had hesitated to answer Lenin's call. Almost from the moment of his arrival it was clear that an alliance would

[1] Milyukov, smarting over his own expulsion from the government, bitingly remarks that "the moderate socialists took under their protection the principle of bourgeois democracy which the bourgeoisie had let fall from its hands" (P. N. Milyukov, *Istoriya Vtoroi Russkoi Revolyutsii* (Sofia, 1921), i, 57).

[2] *Revolyutsiya 1917 goda*, ii (ed. N. Avdeev, 1923), 108, 111-112.

be struck. The April conference itself had recognized the importance of " rapprochement and union with groups and movements
which really stand on the ground of internationalism ".[1]   On
May 10, 1917, Lenin in person attended a meeting of the
Mezhraiontsy and offered them a seat on the editorial board of
Pravda and on the organizing committee of the forthcoming party
congress, proposing also to extend the offer to Martov's group of
" internationalist " Mensheviks. According to notes taken by
Lenin at the time, Trotsky replied that he was in agreement " in
so far as Bolshevism internationalizes itself ", but added proudly :
" The Bolsheviks have de-bolshevized themselves, and I cannot
call myself a Bolshevik. It is impossible to demand of us a
recognition of Bolshevism." [2] The meeting led to no result. In
effect, Trotsky, faithful to his old policy of reconciliation all round,
wanted an amalgamation of the groups on equal terms and under
a new name. Lenin had no intention of weakening or diluting
the instrument which he had created ; the party must remain
supreme and intact. He could afford to wait.

The summer of 1917 in Petrograd was a period of incessant
conferences.   An all-Russian peasant congress in May was
dominated by the SRs and voted firmly for support of the Provisional Government. On the other hand, a conference of Petrograd factory workers at the end of the same month was the first
representative body to yield a Bolshevik majority — a foretaste
of what was to come. The beginning of June brought the first
All-Russian Congress of Soviets. Of its 822 delegates with voting
rights, the SRs accounted for 285, the Mensheviks for 248 and
the Bolsheviks for 105. Nearly 150 delegates belonged to various
minor groups, and 45 declared no party allegiance — an indication
that the political affiliations of many outlying Soviets were still
fluid. The Bolshevik leaders attended in full force ; Trotsky and
Lunacharsky were among the 10 delegates of the " united social-
democrats ", who solidly supported the Bolsheviks throughout
the three weeks of the congress.

The most dramatic moment of the congress occurred on its

---

[1] *VKP(B) v Rezolyutsiyakh* (1941), i, 234.
[2] *Leninskii Sbornik*, iv (1925), 301-303.

second day during the speech of the Menshevik Minister of Posts and Telegraphs, Tsereteli, and was thus reported in the official records :

> At the present moment there is no political party which would say : " Give the power into our hands, go away, we will take your place ". There is no such party in Russia. (Lenin from his seat : " There is.") [1]

The claim, or the threat, was not taken very seriously. The Bolsheviks were in a small minority at the congress, and Lenin's principal speech was frequently interrupted. The congress passed a vote of confidence in the Provisional Government, rejecting a Bolshevik resolution which demanded " the transfer of all state power into the hands of the All-Russian Soviet of Workers', Soldiers' and Peasants' Deputies ".[2] Not the least important decision of the congress was to give itself a regular constitution. The congress itself was to meet every three months, and created for current action a " central organ " in the form of an " All-Russian Central Executive Committee " (Vserossiiskii Tsentral'nyi Ispolnitel'nyi Komitet or, from its initials, VTsIK) [3] whose decisions would be binding on all Soviets in the intervals between congresses. VTsIK was elected forthwith on a proportional basis : of its 250 members 35 were Bolsheviks.[4]

Lenin's assertion of the Bolshevik willingness to take power was a declaration of war on the Provisional Government and was intended as such. The authority of the coalition was wilting : it was the period of what Trotsky called " the dual powerlessness ".[5] The next step was to test the state of mind of workers and soldiers in Petrograd. The Bolsheviks summoned their supporters to a street demonstration on June 9, 1917, but called it off in face of opposition in the congress. The congress itself then arranged a monster street demonstration in support of the Soviets on June 18, 1917. But not more than a handful of the banners carried expressed confidence in the Provisional Government, and it was said that the slogans inscribed on 90 per cent of them were Bolshevik.[6] A more serious popular rising began on July 3, 1917, at the moment when the government, hard pressed by the allies,

---

[1] *Pervyi Vserossiiskii S"ezd Sovetov* (1930), i, 65.
[2] *Ibid.* i, 285-289.   [3] *Ibid.* ii, 62, 70.
[4] A full list of members will be found *ibid.* ii, 423-426.
[5] Trotsky, *Sochineniya*, iii, i, 61.
[6] Krupskaya, *Memories of Lenin*, ii (Engl. transl. 1932), 225.

had ordered a large-scale military offensive in Galicia. The demonstrations lasted for four days and became seriously menacing. It was freely believed that this was the beginning of a serious Bolshevik attempt to seize power, though the party leaders insisted that it was a spontaneous demonstration which they themselves struggled to keep within bounds ; and Lenin himself argued that it was impossible to act so long as a majority still believed in " the petty bourgeois capitalist-controlled policy of the Mensheviks and SRs ".[1] This time, however, the government took up the challenge. Loyal troops were drafted into the capital ; *Pravda* was suppressed ; and orders were issued for the arrest of the three chief Bolshevik leaders. Kamenev was taken ; Lenin and Zinoviev went into hiding, and escaped to Finland.

Within the next few days the Galician offensive failed, with heavy losses ; another ministerial crisis led to the resignation of Lvov and the appointment of Kerensky as premier ; Trotsky and the *Mezhraiontsy*, some 4000 strong, at length joined the Bolsheviks ;[2] and there was a flood of further arrests, including Trotsky, Lunacharsky and Kollontai. At the end of July, 1917, with Lenin and other leaders still in hiding or in prison, the sixth party congress — the first since the London congress of 1907 — was held in Petrograd. Sverdlov presided ; and it fell to Stalin and Bukharin to make the main political reports.[3] Lenin had furnished guidance in a small pamphlet written since his retirement into hiding *On the Slogans*,[4] in which he argued for the withdrawal of the slogan " all power to the Soviets ". This had been devised in the days when a peaceful transfer to Soviets representing the proletariat and the peasantry still seemed possible. Since the July troubles it was clear that the bourgeoisie had declared for counter-revolution, and that it would fight : the existing

---

[1] Lenin, *Sochineniya*, xx, 551.
[2] The special character of this accession was subsequently recognized by a regulation that *Mezhraiontsy* should be allowed to count their period of membership of the organization as equivalent to party membership for the purpose of appointments for which a certain length of membership was required (see e.g. *Izvestiya Tsentral'nogo Komiteta Rossiiskoi Kommunisticheskoi Partii (Bol'shevikov)* No. 33, October 1921, p. 41).
[3] Trotsky had been designated before his arrest to make the report on the political situation eventually made by Bukharin, *Protokoly S"ezdov i Konferentsii VKP(B) : Shestoi S"ezd* (1927), p. 9.
[4] Lenin, *Sochineniya*, xxi, 33-38.

Soviets were tools of the bourgeoisie.   The congress, skilfully led
by Stalin in face of some opposition on this point, declared that
" all power to the Soviets " was " the slogan of the peaceful
development of the revolution, of the painless transfer of power
from the bourgeoisie to the workers and peasants ", and that
nothing would now avail short of the complete liquidation of the
counter-revolutionary bourgeoisie.   When Nogin, echoing the
doubt expressed by Rykov at the April conference, asked whether
the country had " really made such a leap in two months that
it is already prepared for socialism ", Stalin boldly replied that
" it would be unworthy pedantry to ask that Russia should ' wait '
with her socialist transformation till Europe ' begins ' ", and that
" the possibility is not excluded that Russia may be the country
which points the way to socialism " — an acceptance of Trotsky's
thesis of 1906.   At the same time there was a warning against
being provoked into " premature fighting ".[1]   With the leaders
dispersed, and the party itself threatened at any moment with
official persecution, the congress could do little but mark time.

The principal event of August 1917 was an all-party " state
conference " convened in Moscow by Kerensky to advise on the
state of the nation.   Composed of more than 2000 delegates drawn
from a variety of public bodies and organizations, it proved a
wordy fiasco.   It was followed at the end of August by the one
attempt of this period at a military *coup* from the Right — the
Kornilov insurrection.   Though the plot miscarried ignominiously
without a blow being struck, it caused a flurry of alarm in all the
Left parties and groups.   Even Lenin offered a compromise to
the Mensheviks and SRs : the Bolsheviks would resume their
support of the Soviets if they in their turn would finally break
with the bourgeois parties.   But this led to nothing.[2]   The Mensheviks and SRs convened a " democratic conference " to match
the " state conference " in Moscow ; and this created a " council

[1] *VKP(B) v Rezolyutsiyakh* (1941), i, 255-256; Stalin, *Sochineniya*, iii, 174, 186.
Stalin afterwards cited this occasion as one on which the party was right against
Lenin, who too hastily depreciated the value of the Soviets (*ibid.* vi, 340-341).

[2] Lenin's tentative proposal took the form of an article written in Finland
on September 1, 1917.   When it appeared in the party journal *Rabochii Put'*
on September 6, 1917, it carried a postscript containing the following passage :
" Perhaps the offer of a compromise is already too late.   Perhaps the few days in
which a peaceful development was *still* possible are *also* over.   Yes, it is evident
by all the signs that they are already past " (Lenin, *Sochineniya*, xxi, 132-136).

of the republic " (the so-called " pre-parliament ") designed to
fill the gap until the constituent assembly should meet. By this
time the Bolshevik star was rising rapidly. After the Kornilov
affair the Bolsheviks secured majorities in the Petrograd and
Moscow Soviets, though the SRs and Mensheviks still dominated
VTsIK. In the country, as the self-demobilized soldiers returned
to their homes, land-hunger grew more acute and peasant disorders
and the ransacking of estates more frequent ; and with this went a
discrediting of the SRs, who had done nothing, and a shift of
sympathy towards the Bolsheviks, who promised everything. The
conditions which Lenin had foreseen in his April theses as justify-
ing the transition to the second stage of the revolution were
maturing fast.

Lenin's first reaction was to revive the slogan " all power to
the Soviets ". This was done in an article written in the first
part of September and published on September 14, 1917, in
Rabochii Put'.[1] Then on September 12, 13 and 14, growing more
and more impatient in his enforced retreat, Lenin wrote two secret
letters in succession to the party central committee declaring the
time ripe for the Bolsheviks to seize power by armed force.[2]
Trotsky, released from prison in the middle of September, was
elected president of the Petrograd Soviet, which became the
principal focus of Bolshevik militancy. Throughout the next
month the battle over the April theses was repeated in a new
context. The first clash in the central committee occurred over
participation in the " democratic conference ", Kamenev and
Rykov supporting it and Trotsky and Stalin demanding a boycott.
The decision went in favour of participation and was severely
blamed by Lenin who applauded Trotsky's stand.[3] Towards the

---

[1] *Ibid.* xxi, 142-148.

[2] These letters were first published in 1921 under the title *The Bolsheviks
Must Take Power* and *Marxism and Insurrection*, and appear in the collected
edition of Lenin's works, *Sochineniya*, xxi, 193-199. The proceedings of the
central committee which received the letters on September 15, 1917, are briefly
recorded in *Protokoly Tsentral'nogo Komiteta RSDRP* (1929), pp. 64-65.
Kamenev moved to reject Lenin's proposals ; the committee was manifestly
embarrassed and, while rejecting Kamenev's motion, adjourned the question
of substance.

[3] *Protokoly Tsentral'nogo Komiteta RSDRP* (1929), pp. 70-71 ; Lenin,
Sochineniya, xxi, 219. The Bolsheviks afterwards withdrew from the " pre-
parliament " at its first meeting, Trotsky making a declaration of defiance
(Trotsky, *Sochineniya*, iii, i, 321-323).

end of September, 1917, Lenin, more and more excited and determined, moved up from Helsingfors to Viborg to be nearer the scene of action. A short article in *Rabochii Put'* entitled *The Crisis is Ripe* repeated previous arguments and added a new one : growing disorders in the belligerent countries and the beginning of mutinies in the German army and fleet made it clear that " we stand on the threshold of a world-wide proletarian revolution ".[1] But the most significant part of the article was a postscript not for publication, but for communication to members of the central committee. He accused them of ignoring his previous communications and offered his resignation from the central committee in order to regain his freedom to agitate among the rank and file of the party ; " for it is my profound conviction that if we ' wait ' for the congress of Soviets and let slip the present moment, we shall ruin the revolution ".[2]

Lenin's threat seems to have once more reduced the central committee to an embarrassed silence : there is no record of any answer. The personal touch was required to shake the prevailing inertia or scepticism. On October 9, 1917, Lenin came in disguise to Petrograd, and on the following day appeared at a meeting of the committee which was destined to become historic. His presence and reproaches of " indifference to the question of insurrection " sufficed to turn the scale. By a majority of 10 votes (Lenin, Trotsky, Stalin, Sverdlov, Uritsky, Dzerzhinsky, Kollantai, Bubnov, Sokolnikov, Lomov) to 2 (Kamenev and Zinoviev, now for the first time united in an inglorious partnership) the committee decided to prepare for armed insurrection and to appoint a " political bureau " to carry out the decision. This " politburo " (the first germ of what later became a permanent institution) consisted of seven persons : Lenin, Zinoviev, Kamenev, Trotsky, Stalin, Sokolnikov and Bubnov.[3] It is significant of the sense of solidarity among the party leaders at this time and of the requirements of party discipline that the two who had voted against the decision were none the less included as a matter of course in the executive organ. Six days later the Petrograd Soviet created a " military-revolutionary committee " under the presidency of Trotsky as president of the Soviet, with Podvoisky as

[1] Lenin, *Sochineniya*, xxi, 235-236.   [2] *Ibid.* xxi, 241.
[3] *Protokoly Tsentral'nogo Komiteta RSDRP* (1929), pp. 99-101.

his effective deputy; and it was this body rather than the party " politburo " which made the military preparations for the revolution.[1]

The battle was, however, still not finally won. On October 11, 1917, Kamenev and Zinoviev circulated a letter to all the principal Bolshevik organizations protesting against the decision for " armed insurrection ".[2] On October 16, Lenin once more stated the case for the immediate seizure of power to an enlarged meeting of the central committee attended by Bolsheviks from the Petrograd party committee, from the military organization of the Petrograd Soviet and from the trade unions and factory committees. Since the Kornilov affair, he argued, the masses had been behind the party. But the question was not one of a formal majority:

> The position is clear. Either a Kornilov dictatorship or a dictatorship of the proletariat and the poorest strata of the peasantry. We cannot be guided by the mood of the masses : that is changeable and unaccountable. We must be guided by an objective analysis and estimate of the revolution. The masses have given their confidence to the Bolsheviks and ask from them not words, but deeds.

Lenin reverted to the international, especially the German, situation which justified the conclusion that " if we come out now, we shall have on our side all proletarian Europe ". The discussion showed that, though the central committee might have been haltingly won over by Lenin's magnetism, the doubts of Kamenev and Zinoviev were still shared in wider party circles. Zinoviev and Kamenev repeated their objections. Stalin and other members of the central committee supported Lenin.

[1] The decision of the Petrograd Soviet to create a " military-revolutionary committee " preceded the decision of the central committee of October 10 ; far from being concerned with the preparation of armed insurrection, it actually originated from the Mensheviks. After October 10 the Bolsheviks took it up and converted it to their purposes. This committee was formally appointed on October 16, 1917, and began work four days later : by this time it was exclusively Bolshevik except for a single Left SR (Trotsky, *Sochineniya*, iii, ii, 91-92 ; *Istoriya Russkoi Revolyutsii*, ii (Berlin, 1933), ii, 121-122 ; according to the latter work (ii, ii, 171), the " politburo " appointed by the central committee never met).

[2] *Protokoly Tsentral'nogo Komiteta RSDRP* (1929), pp. 102-108 ; Lenin, *Sochineniya*, xxi, 494-498.

Here are two lines [said Stalin] : one is headed for the
victory of the revolution and leans on Europe : the other does
not believe in the revolution and counts only on being an
opposition. The Petrograd Soviet has already taken its stand
on the road to insurrection by refusing to sanction the removal
of the armies.[1]

The debate was somewhat unreal. Active preparations were being
pressed forward by the Petrograd Soviet and its military-revolutionary committee. But military preparations could not be discussed at such a gathering ; and neither Trotsky nor Podvoisky
spoke, if indeed they were present. The meeting reaffirmed by
19 votes to 2 the decision to proceed with the preparations for an
immediate insurrection, though a proposal of Zinoviev to await the
meeting of the second All-Russian Congress of Soviets, convened
for October 20 (but afterwards postponed to October 25), obtained
6 votes against 15.[2] At the conclusion of the meeting the central
committee met alone, and appointed a " military-revolutionary
centre " consisting of Sverdlov, Stalin, Bubnov, Uritsky and
Dzerzhinsky which was to form part of the military-revolutionary
committee of the Petrograd Soviet.[3] This was a curious early
instance of the fusion of party and Soviet institutions. Contemporary records make no further mention of the centre : it was
evidently intended as a contact group rather than as a separate
organ, and, like the " politburo " appointed a week earlier, never
seems to have come into existence.

At the end of the meeting of October 16, 1917, Kamenev resigned his membership of the central committee.[4] Two days later
he published in *Novaya Zhizn'*, a non-party journal of the Left,
a letter once more protesting, in his own name and that of Zinoviev, against the decision. The letter was not only a breach of
party discipline (since Kamenev was still a member of the party),
but a betrayal to the world of the party decision — though in the
state of disorganization and impotence into which the Provisional

---

[1] The reference is to an attempt by the Provisional Government to send
certain regiments of the Petrograd garrison to the front : the Petrograd garrison
early in the revolution declared its allegiance to the Petrograd Soviet and refused
to take orders not countersigned by it.

[2] *Protokoly Tsentral'nogo Komiteta RSDRP* (1929), pp. 111-125. The
record of this meeting is fuller than usual, but consists, like the others, of
secretary's notes and does not claim completeness or textual accuracy.

[3] *Ibid.* p. 124.   [4] *Ibid.* p. 125.

Government had now fallen the disclosure of preparations for an insurrection against it was perhaps as likely to intensify panic as to provoke effective counter-measures. The party, on the eve of the decisive action which was to put its fortunes to the supreme test, was threatened with a grave domestic crisis. Lenin, after the meeting of October 16, had retired once more into hiding. But on October 18 — the day of the publication in *Novaya Zhizn'* — he wrote a letter to members of the party describing the act of Kamenev and Zinoviev as " strike-breaking " and " a crime ", and declaring that he no longer regarded them as comrades and would demand their exclusion from the party. This was followed on the next day by a more detailed letter in the same sense to the central committee.[1] Trotsky, in an attempt to cover up Kamenev's indiscretion, publicly denied in the Petrograd Soviet that any decision had been taken for armed insurrection.[2] Kamenev, believing or pretending to believe that Trotsky had been converted to his view, declared that he agreed with every word Trotsky had said; and Zinoviev wrote in the same sense to the party journal *Rabochii Put'*. His letter was published on the morning of October 20, 1917, in the same issue which carried the last instalment of an article by Lenin vigorously attacking the views of Kamenev and Zinoviev, though without naming them.[3] Stalin tried to pour oil on the waters by appending an editorial note in the following terms :

> We in our turn express the hope that the declaration of comrade Zinoviev (as well as the declaration of comrade Kamenev in the Soviet) may be considered to close the question. The sharp tone of comrade Lenin's article does not alter the fact that in fundamentals we remain of one mind.[4]

Feelings therefore ran high when, in the absence of Lenin, the central committee met on October 20, 1917. Sverdlov read

[1] Lenin, *Sochineniya*, xxi, 350-356. These letters were published for the first time in 1927.

[2] Trotsky, *Sochineniya*, iii, ii, 31-33. Trotsky explained to the central committee the motive for his declaration (*Protokoly Tsentral'nogo Komiteta RSDRP* (1929), p. 123) ; Lenin afterwards endorsed his action (*Sochineniya*, xxi, 353).

[3] Zinoviev's letter is in *Protokoly Tsentral'nogo Komiteta RSDRP* (1929), p. 137 ; Lenin's article in *Sochineniya*, xxi, 334-349.

[4] *Protokoly Tsentral'nogo Komiteta RSDRP* (1929), p. 137. The note does not appear in Stalin's collected works, but its authorship is not disputed.

Lenin's letter to the committee. After a debate Kamenev's resignation was accepted by a majority of five to three; and a specific injunction was issued to Kamenev and Zinoviev to make no further public pronouncements against decisions of the central committee or of the party. Lenin's demand for their expulsion from the party was not taken up. Meanwhile Trotsky protested not only against the declarations of Kamenev and Zinoviev, but against the editorial note in *Rabochii Put'* which appeared to exculpate them. Sokolnikov declared that, though a member of the editorial board, he had no responsibility for the note and did not approve of it; and Stalin offered his resignation from the board. The committee prudently decided not to discuss the matter or accept the resignation, and passed to other business.[1] It was the first open clash between the future rivals.[2]

The critical moment was now at hand, being fixed by the decision to strike the blow before the second All-Russian Congress of Soviets met on the evening of October 25. On the eve of the appointed day the central committee met to put the final touch to some practical arrangements; and Kamenev — the decision of four days earlier having been reversed or forgotten — resumed his seat. Trotsky asked that members of the committee should be attached to the military-revolutionary committee of the Petrograd Soviet to look after postal and telegraphic and railway communications and to keep watch on the Provisional Government. Dzerzhinsky was detailed for railways, Bubnov for posts and telegraphs, Sverdlov for the Provisional Government; and Milyutin was put in charge of food supplies. An embryonic administration was taking shape within the party committee. In the early morning of October 25, 1917, the Bolshevik forces went into action. The key-points in the city were occupied; the members of the Provisional Government were prisoners or fugitives; in the afternoon Lenin announced to a meeting of the

---

[1] *Protokoly Tsentral'nogo Komiteta RSDRP* (1929), pp. 127-129.

[2] Stalin had thrown himself *con amore* into the bitter controversy between Lenin and Trotsky in the autumn of 1912, calling Trotsky in the columns of *Pravda* a " champion with false muscles " and a " comedian " (Stalin, *Sochineniya*, ii, 260 ; the former phrase is repeated a few weeks later, *ibid.* ii, 279). The first personal encounter between them (though they both were at the party congress in London in 1907) apparently occurred in Vienna early in 1913, when Trotsky long afterwards remembered a " glint of animosity " in Stalin's " yellow eyes " (L. Trotsky, *Stalin* (N.Y., 1946), p. 244).

Petrograd Soviet the triumph of " the workers' and peasants' revolution " ; [1] and in the evening the second All-Russian Congress of Soviets, proclaimed the transfer of all power throughout Russia to Soviets of Workers', Soldiers' and Peasants' Deputies. [2] On the evening of October 26, 1917, the second and last meeting of the congress adopted the decrees on peace and on the land, and approved the composition of the Council of People's Commissars, popularly known as Sovnarkom — the first Workers' and Peasants' Government.

For the organization of the almost bloodless victory of October 25/November 7, 1917, the Petrograd Soviet and its military-revolutionary committee were responsible. It was the military-revolutionary committee which took the power as it fell from the nerveless hands of the Provisional Government, and proclaimed to the world the achievement of the revolution.[3] As Stalin afterwards said, the congress of Soviets " only *received* the power from the hands of the Petrograd Soviet ".[4] All contemporary witnesses pay tribute to the energy and ability displayed by Trotsky at this time and to his services to the revolutionary cause. But the higher strategy of the revolution had been directed by Lenin through his chosen instrument, the Bolshevik wing of the Russian Social-Democratic Workers' Party. The victory, though won under the slogan " all power to the Soviets ", was a victory not only for the Soviets, but for Lenin and the Bolsheviks. Lenin and the party, the man and the instrument, were now indissolubly one. The triumph of the party seemed almost exclusively due to Lenin's consistent success in stamping his personal will upon it and in leading his often reluctant colleagues in his train. The prestige of Lenin's name had been firmly established ; the foundations had been laid of the ascendancy in the party of the single leader.

The relation of Lenin's policy to the wider issues raised by the Russian revolution opens an endless debate. The decision foreshadowed in Lenin's April theses and carried out at his instigation six months later to seize power on a socialist programme and on the foundations of an unfinished bourgeois revolution has been the subject of volumes of commentary and controversy. It has been treated as a prolongation of the Marxist line consistently

[1] Lenin, *Sochineniya*, xxii, 4-5.   [2] *Ibid.* xxii, 11-12.
[3] *Ibid.* xxii, 3.   [4] Stalin, *Sochineniya*, vi, 347.

pursued by the party since 1903, though the Bolsheviks in Petrograd in the confusion of the February revolution and in the absence of their leader had momentarily deviated from the line : this remains the official view.   It has been treated as a final abandonment by Lenin and the Bolsheviks of the Marxist line and a plunge, in defiance of Marx's teaching, into the adventure of a socialist revolution not resting on the foundations of a preceding bourgeois revolution : this was the Menshevik view.   It has been treated as a last-minute correction by Lenin, based on true Marxist principles, of a long-standing party deviation due to excessive devotion to the formal aspects of Marx's scheme of revolution : this was Trotsky's view.   Since these divergent views rested on different texts of Marx, on different interpretations of what Marx meant and on different estimates of what was required to apply Marx's meaning to Russian conditions, the argument proved inexhaustible and inconclusive.   The question hotly debated in later years between Bolsheviks and Mensheviks whether the course adopted by Lenin could and did lead to the socialist goal also turned on a point of interpretation : what was meant by socialism.

But behind these arguments conducted in conventional Marxist terminology lay the real problem which the makers of the October revolution had to face.   It may well have been true, as the rapid disintegration of the February revolution seemed to show, that bourgeois democracy and bourgeois capitalism on the western model, which was what the Mensheviks wanted and expected, could not be rooted in Russian soil, so that Lenin's policy was the only conceivable one in the empirical terms of current Russian politics.   To reject it as premature was to repeat, as Lenin once said, " the argument of the serf-owners about the unpreparedness of the peasants for freedom ".[1]   But what this policy committed its sponsors to was nothing less than to make a direct transition from the most backward to the most advanced forms of political and economic organization.   Politically, the programme involved an attempt to bridge the gap between autocracy and socialist democracy without the long experience and training in citizenship which bourgeois democracy, with all its faults, had afforded in the west.   Economically, it meant the creation of a socialist

[1] Lenin, *Sochineniya*, xx, 120.

economy in a country which had never possessed the resources in capital equipment and trained workers proper to a developed capitalist order. These grave handicaps the victorious October revolution had still to overcome. Its history is the record of its successes and failures in this enterprise.

PART II

THE CONSTITUTIONAL STRUCTURE

CHAPTER 5

THE TWO REVOLUTIONS

THE October revolution had triumphed with the Bolsheviks still divided on the scope of the revolution, and uncertain whether to regard it as bourgeois-democratic or as proletarian-socialist. The revolution, by overthrowing the Provisional Government, had consecrated the Soviets as the supreme repositories of revolutionary power. But this did not imply rejection of the ultimate authority of a constituent assembly, which was the characteristic organ of bourgeois democracy, and to whose early convocation the Bolsheviks, equally with the Provisional Government, were committed. The decree of October 26/November 8, 1917, which established the Council of People's Commissars, described it as a " provisional workers' and peasants' government " exercising authority " until the convocation of the Constituent Assembly "; and the decree on land opened with the statement that " the land question in all its magnitude can be settled only by the nation-wide Constituent Assembly ".[1] It is true that a laconic decree of the same date proclaiming that " all power belongs to the Soviets " added no such reservations; [2] and the Declaration of Rights of the Peoples of Russia promulgated a few days later announced the principles of a future " voluntary and honourable union of the peoples ", and promised the prompt elaboration of " concrete decrees " to give effect to them, without referring at all to the powers of the Constituent Assembly.[3] But in the heat of revolution such formal inconsistencies were not likely to be noticed. The Provisional Government, far more pedantic than its successor about constitutional proprieties, had itself flagrantly forestalled the functions of the constituent assembly by its decree of September 1, 1917, proclaiming Russia a republic.

[1] *Sobranie Uzakonenii, 1917-1918*, No. 1 (2nd ed.), arts. 1, 3.
[2] *Ibid.* No. 1 (2nd ed.), art. 5.　　　[3] *Ibid.* No. 2, art. 18.

The student of the documentary records of the October revolution will at once be struck by the infrequent and inconspicuous appearance of the words " socialism " and " socialist " in its earliest pronouncements. To defend " the revolution " or " the revolution of the workers and peasants " is a sufficient definition of purpose ; " revolutionary " is by itself an adjective of commendation (" revolutionary order ", " revolutionary justice "), " counter-revolutionary " the quintessence of evil.[1] Derivatives of the neutral word " democracy ", equally acceptable to supporters of the bourgeois and of the socialist revolution, appear four times in the initial proclamation of the second All-Russian Congress of Soviets of October 25/November 7, 1917 (" a democratic peace ", " democratization of the army "), and over and over again in the peace decree of the following day. " As a democratic government ", said Lenin in introducing the land decree to the same session of the congress, " we cannot evade the decision of the popular masses, even if we were not in agreement with it." [2] The vital first steps of the régime were thus taken under the banner not of socialism, but of democracy. A little later the epithet " democratic " was used to commend the system of election to the Soviets and to the Constituent Assembly and especially the " right of recall ",[3] as well as the principle of the election of judges.[4]

This emphasis on democracy was accompanied by a proclamation of socialism as the ultimate goal. The most revealing evidence of Lenin's attitude at the moment of the revolution is his speech at the Petrograd Soviet on the afternoon of October 25/November 7, 1917, announcing the triumph of the " workers' and peasants' revolution ". Having declared that " this third Russian revolution must lead in its final result to the victory of socialism ", he reverted in his concluding words to the two conditions which he had laid down long ago for the transition to socialism — the support of the peasants and the support of world revolution :

> We shall win the confidence of the peasants by a single decree abolishing the property of the landowners. The peasants

[1] The same quasi-religious fervour was attached to the words " revolution " and " revolutionary " at the time of the French revolution.

[2] Lenin, *Sochineniya*, xxii, 23.

[3] *Sobranie Uzakonenii, 1917–1918*, No. 3, art. 49.

[4] *Ibid.* No. 4, art. 50.

will understand that the salvation of the peasantry lies only in union with the workers. . . . We have the mass strength of organization which will conquer all and lead the proletariat to world revolution.

In Russia we must at once occupy ourselves with the building of the proletarian socialist state.

Hail the world-wide socialist revolution.[1]

The international aspect of the revolution was present to Lenin's mind with peculiar vividness at the moment of its victory in Russia. Ten days later he declared in his capacity as president of Sovnarkom:

We shall march firmly and unswervingly to the victory of socialism which will be sealed by the leading workers of the most civilized countries and give to the peoples solid peace and deliverance from all oppression and all exploitation.[2]

And the Declaration of Rights of the Toiling and Exploited People drafted by Lenin at the beginning of January 1918 proclaimed " the socialist organization of society and the victory of socialism in all countries " as part of the " fundamental task " of the Soviet order.[3] The achievement of socialism was still thought of by Lenin at this time primarily in terms of world revolution.

These hesitations about the scope and character of the October revolution are reflected in early constitutional terminology. The word " Russia " having been abandoned, there were difficulties in finding an appropriate name for the new authority. It called itself the " Provisional Workers' and Peasants' Government " or simply the " revolutionary government ", resting on " Soviet power " and on the triumph of the slogan " all power to the Soviets ". Only once in a particular context did it refer to itself as the " socialist government of Russia ".[4] The first fundamental

[1] Lenin, *Sochineniya*, xxii, 4-5. The only record of this speech is unfortunately a brief newspaper report.

[2] *Istoriya Sovetskoi Konstitutsii v Dekretakh* (1936), p. 34.

[3] *Sobranie Uzakonenii, 1917-1918*, No. 15, art. 215.

[4] The occasion was the ultimatum of December 4/17, 1917, to the Ukrainian Rada (see p. 295 below) ; the purpose was to distinguish itself clearly from the bourgeois government of the Ukraine. Stalin in his speech at the congress of the Finnish Social-Democratic Party on November 14/27, 1917, had referred to " the new socialist government " (Stalin, *Sochineniya*, iv, 2). Lenin in his *Theses on the Constituent Assembly* noted the strife between the Soviet Government and " the bourgeois nationalism of the Ukrainian Rada, the Finnish Seim, etc." as one of the factors hastening " the new grouping of class forces " and the consequent transition from bourgeois to socialist revolution (Lenin, *Sochineniya*, xxii, 132-133).

constitutional declaration in Soviet history is contained in the Declaration of Rights of the Toiling and Exploited People, which opens with the words :

> Russia is declared a republic of Soviets of workers', soldiers' and peasants' deputies. All power in the centre and locally belongs to these Soviets.

And the following clause for the first time names the country the " Soviet Russian republic ". It might be dangerous to draw conclusions from a terminology so fluctuating and uncertain. But whatever Lenin himself may have thought, the word " socialist " was still a bugbear to many of his supporters and allies.[1]   A substantial minority, if not a majority, of the party at this time seems clearly to have clung to the view, fervently held by Mensheviks and SRs alike, that the revolution had not yet fully completed its bourgeois stage and was consequently still unripe for its transition to socialism. On this view the October revolution was merely a continuation and deepening of the February revolution, and did not differ from it in principle or purpose. On this view it was legitimate to look forward to the Constituent Assembly as the crowning achievement of the democratic revolution.

Waverings within the party had not been ended by the victory of the revolution. At the moment of victory an all-Bolshevik government had been proclaimed. But in the first few days its authority was not established far outside Petrograd ; and under pressure from the executive committee of the railwaymen's union (Vikzhel for short), which controlled communications and aspired for some weeks to act as an independent power dictating terms to the government, the central committee of the party agreed to open negotiations with the SRs and Mensheviks for a coalition government of all parties represented in the Soviets. For Lenin this was merely a tactical manœuvre ;[2] for Kamenev and Zinoviev it was an admission of the correctness of the view taken by them

[1] Steinberg, then Left Social-Revolutionary People's Commissar for Justice, states in his sketchy and none too reliable *Souvenirs d'un Commissaire du Peuple, 1917–18* (Paris, 1930), pp. 65-66, that Lenin's original draft of the opening sentence of the Declaration of the Toiling and Exploited People inserted the word " socialist " before " republic ", and that it was struck out at the instance of the Left SRs, who thought that so solemn a document ought not to " contain any exaggeration ".

[2] Lenin called it " a diplomatic move to distract attention from operations of war " (*Protokoly Tsentral'nogo Komiteta RSDRP* (1929), p. 152).

on the eve of October 25 that the time was not yet ripe for a
specifically proletarian revolution. When, therefore, on November 1/14, 1917, Lenin proposed to abandon the negotiations as
futile, he encountered strong opposition from Kamenev, Zinoviev
and Rykov. In the debate in the party central committee he
received unequivocal support only from Trotsky ; but the majority
voted solidly for a resolution laying down conditions which
would of necessity lead to a breakdown of negotiations.[1] Kamenev
and Rykov, in their capacity as Bolshevik delegates to VTsIK,
failed to act on the decision. In a declaration of November 3/16,
1917, Lenin carried the issue on to the plane of party discipline ;
and three days later a formal ultimatum was delivered by the
central committee to its recalcitrant members. Five members of
the committee, Kamenev, Zinoviev, Rykov, Milyutin and Nogin,
at once resigned. The last three resigned their positions as People's
Commissars, and several lesser members of the government also
resigned. Of the recalcitrants only Zinoviev recanted forthwith
and was reinstated in the central committee.[2] A considerable
split among the party leaders had once more occurred at a critical
moment on an issue of tactics which was also an issue of doctrine.

Having surmounted this crisis and gradually extended its
authority over the northern and central provinces of European
Russia, the régime had now to face the elections to the Constituent
Assembly, fixed by the Provisional Government before its downfall for November 12/25, 1917. What Lenin thought about them
at this time is not certainly known.[3] But the party was deeply

[1] *Ibid.* (1929), pp. 148-156 ; Lenin, *Sochineniya*, xxii, pp. 36-37. It was on
the same day, according to Trotsky, that Lenin, speaking at a meeting of the
Petrograd Soviet of the impossibility of a coalition, said : " Trotsky understood
this, and from that time there has been no better Bolshevik ". What purports
to be a stenographic record of the meeting containing these words was published
in L. Trotsky, *Stalinskaya Shkola Fasifikatsii* (Berlin, 1932), pp. 116-124 :
according to Trotsky (*ibid.* pp. 112-116), it was actually printed for inclusion
in the volume *Pervyi Legal'nyi PK Bol'shevikov* (1927), but omitted at the last
moment on orders from the central committee ; he reproduces in facsimile part
of the printed proof with marginal annotations.

[2] Lenin. *Sochineniya*, xxii, 38-39, 57, 551-552 ; *Protokoly Tsentral'nogo
Komiteta RSDRP* (1929), pp. 170-177.

[3] According to Trotsky, *O Lenine* (n.d. [1924]), pp. 91-92, Lenin wished to
postpone them, but was overruled by Sverdlov and others ; Lenin himself,
writing in 1920, defended Bolshevik participation in the elections on the ground
that it had helped to " *prove* to the backward masses why such parliaments
deserve to be broken up " (*Sochineniya*, xxv, 202).

committed to them by its repeated utterances between the February and October revolutions; the official machine was in motion and would have proved difficult to reverse at the last moment. One of the first acts of Sovnarkom had been to confirm the date set by the Provisional Government.[1] Uritsky, one of the leading Bolsheviks, was appointed as commissar to supervise the work of the electoral commission appointed by the Provisional Government. The commission in its turn refused to cooperate with Uritsky and complained of having been placed under duress.[2] But the elections went forward and seem to have been conducted without interference from any side, though in some outlying districts they were not held at all.

The results justified any apprehensions that may already have been felt in the Bolshevik ranks. Of the 707 elected members of the assembly (out of a total of 808 originally provided for) the SRs could claim a comfortable majority — 410 in all. The Bolsheviks secured just under a quarter of the seats, i.e. 175. Most of the 86 members of the " national groups ", of which the Ukrainians formed the largest, were strongly anti-Bolshevik. The Kadets, the only surviving bourgeois party, had 17 seats, the Mensheviks 16.[3] If this could be read as a verdict on the government set up by the October revolution, it was a crushing vote of non-confidence.

The first effect of the defeat was to convince Lenin of the necessity of a compromise on the issue of a coalition. At the moment of the elections an All-Russian Congress of Peasants' Deputies was in session in Petrograd. At the first All-Russian Congress of Soviets in June 1917 a group of Left SRs had already rebelled against the party leadership and supported the Bolshevik minority, though this had had little effect on the party as a whole. Now at the All-Russian Congress of Peasants' Deputies Lenin and the other Bolshevik delegates were successful in bringing about a split in the ranks of the SRs. Agreement for a coalition

[1] *Sobranie Uzakonenii, 1917-1918*, No. 1 (2nd ed.), art. 8.
[2] *Vserossiiskoe Uchreditel'noe Sobranie*, ed. I. S. Malchevsky (1930), pp. 150-151.
[3] The figures are taken from *Vserossiiskoe Uchreditel'noe Sobranie*, ed. I. S. Malchevsky (1930), p. 115. The records were never completed and other figures are cited elsewhere, e.g. in M. V. Vishnyak, *Vserossiiskoe Uchreditel'noe Sobranie* (Paris, 1932); but the variations are unimportant.

was reached between the Bolsheviks and the Left wing, which secured a majority in the congress and whose most noteworthy figure was Spiridonova. It was an agreement, as Lenin emphatically remarked, " possible only on a socialist platform ".[1] On November 15/28, 1917, a joint meeting of VTsIK, of the Petrograd Soviet and of the executive committee of the peasants' congress was held to celebrate the act of union.[2] VTsIK already consisted of 108 members elected by the second All-Russian Congress of Soviets of Workers' and Soldiers' Deputies. Its membership was now doubled by the addition of an equal number of delegates elected by the peasants' congress; and 100 delegates of the army and the fleet as well as 50 from the trade unions were added to its ranks, raising the numbers to something over 350. It now became " the All-Russian Central Executive Committee of the Soviets of Workers', Soldiers' and Peasants' Deputies ". In order to complete the coalition, Left SRs were appointed to three People's Commissiariats — Agriculture, Justice, and Posts and Telegraphs — carrying membership of Sovnarkom, as well as to several minor government posts. About the same time the commissariats were transferred from party headquarters at Smolny to the premises of the old ministries; Bolshevik rule was rapidly fitting itself into the traditional framework of state power.

The agreement with the Left SRs not only reinforced the position of the Bolsheviks, but also provided them with their strongest argument to explain away the results of the elections to the Constituent Assembly — the potentially deceptive character of the SR vote. The SRs had gone to the polls as a single party presenting one list of candidates. Its election manifesto had been full of lofty principles and aims but, though published on the day after the October revolution, had been drafted before that event and failed to define the party attitude towards it.[3] Now three days after the election the larger section of the party had made a coalition with the Bolsheviks, and formally split away from the other section which maintained its bitter feud against the Bolsheviks. The proportion between Right and Left SRs in the

[1] Lenin, *Sochineniya*, xxii, 88.
[2] *Protokoly Zasedanii VTsIK 2 Sozyva* (1918), p. 64.
[3] The text, reprinted from the party newspaper *Delo Naroda*, of October 26/November 8, 1917, is in *Vserossiiskoe Uchreditel'noe Sobranie*, ed. I. S. Malchevsky (1930), pp. 165-168.

Constituent Assembly — 370 to 40 — was fortuitous. It was entirely different from the corresponding proportion in the membership of the peasants' congress, and did not necessarily represent the views of the electors on a vital point which had not been before them. " The people ", said Lenin, " voted for a party which no longer existed." [1] Reviewing the whole issue two years later Lenin found another argument which was more cogent than it appeared at first sight. He noted that in the large industrial cities the Bolsheviks had almost everywhere been ahead of the other parties. They secured an absolute majority in the two capitals taken together, the Kadets here being second and the SRs a poor third. But in matters of revolution the well-known principle applied : " the town inevitably leads the country after it ; the country inevitably follows the town ".[2] The elections to the Constituent Assembly, if they did not register the victory of the Bolsheviks, had clearly pointed the way to it for those who had eyes to see.

The results of the elections made it certain that the Constituent Assembly would serve as a rallying-point for opposition to the Soviet régime from both wings — from the surviving bourgeois supporters of the Provisional Government and from the dissident socialists. The Bolsheviks, well versed in revolutionary history, were alive to the precedent of the French Constituent Assembly of May 1848 whose function, three months after the February revolution, had been, in a well-known phrase from Marx's *Eighteenth Brumaire*, " to cut down the results of the revolution to a bourgeois standard " [3] and to prepare the way for the massacre of the workers by Cavaignac. An attempt was made in the name of former ministers of the Provisional Government, and in defiance of the Soviet Government, to convene the assembly on November 28/December 11, 1917. This was resisted by force.

[1] Lenin, *Sochineniya*, xxii, 97. The argument was developed at greater length in Lenin's speech at the congress of railwaymen in January 1918 immediately after the dissolution of the assembly (*ibid.* xxii, 226-231) : here Lenin somewhat tendentiously attributed the result " first and foremost " to the fact that the elections took place " on lists drawn up before the October revolution ".

[2] *Ibid.* xxiv, 634.

[3] Marx i Engels, *Sochineniya*, viii, 329.

Anti-Soviet forces under former Tsarist generals were beginning to mass in south Russia; and Sovnarkom, now thoroughly alarmed, issued a decree which accused the Kadets of providing " a ' legal ' cover for the Kadet-Kaledin counter-revolutionary insurrection ", declared the Kadet party " a party of enemies of the people ", and announced that " the political leaders of the counter-revolutionary civil war " would be arrested.[1] Though the Right SRs and many of the Mensheviks sided with the Kadets, the Bolsheviks did not as yet venture to apply measures of repression to other socialist parties.

From this time onwards the fate of the Constituent Assembly was the subject of constant preoccupation in party circles.[2] What appears to have been the first warning of Bolshevik intentions was given by Lenin in a speech to VTsIK on December 1/14, 1917 :

> We are asked to call the Constituent Assembly as originally conceived. No, thank you ! It was conceived against the people and we carried out the rising to make certain that it will not be used against the people. . . . When a revolutionary class is struggling against the propertied classes which offer resistance, that resistance has to be suppressed, and we shall suppress it by the same methods by which the propertied classes suppressed the proletariat. New methods have not been invented yet.[3]

And he followed up this declaration with a set of *Theses on the Constituent Assembly*, which appeared anonymously in *Pravda* of December 13/26, 1917, and constituted the most important brief analysis from his pen of the character of the October revolution.

The *Theses on the Constituent Assembly* brought uncompromisingly into the open what had been implicit in everything

---

[1] *Sobranie Uzakonenii, 1917-1918*, No. 4, art. 64.

[2] An inconclusive discussion took place in the central committee on November 29/December 12, 1917. At this time it was thought likely that the Constituent Assembly might split into two groups, one recognizing the Soviet Government, the other hostile to it. Bukharin raised the question whether the assembly should be convened at all. He answered it in the affirmative, since " constitutional illusions are still alive in the broad masses ". He then wished to expel the Kadets (the Right SRs were not mentioned) and to turn the Left rump into a " revolutionary convention ", in other words, to effect the transition from bourgeois to socialist revolution through the agency of the Constituent Assembly. Lenin appears to have taken no part in this discussion (*Protokoly Tsentral'nogo Komiteta RSDRP* (1929), pp. 180-184).

[3] Lenin, *Sochineniya*, xxii, 109-110.

Lenin had written since the famous April theses eight months earlier — the conviction that the bourgeois revolution in Russia was a spent force and that the right course was to turn one's back resolutely on it and pursue the road to socialism. He began by admitting that " in a bourgeois republic the constituent assembly is the highest form of the democratic principle ", so that its appearance in past party programmes, drawn up before the achievement of the bourgeois revolution, was " fully legitimate ". Ever since the February revolution of 1917, however, " revolutionary social-democracy " had been insisting that " a republic of Soviets is a higher form of the democratic principle than the customary bourgeois republic with its constituent assembly "; it was indeed " the only form capable of assuring the least painful transition to socialism ". This process of transition had been assisted, first, by the re-grouping of " class forces " due to the permeation of the army and peasantry with revolutionary ideas, secondly, by the struggle between the Soviet power and the bourgeois régime in the Ukraine (and in part, also, in Finland, White Russia and the Caucasus), and thirdly, by the counter-revolutionary rising of Kaledin and the Kadets which had " taken away all possibility of resolving the most acute questions in a formally democratic way ". These developments had created an inevitable clash between the Constituent Assembly and " the will and interest of the toiling and exploited classes who began on October 25 the socialist revolution against the bourgeoisie ". Thus " any attempt, direct or indirect, to look at the question of the Constituent Assembly from the formal, juridical standpoint, within the framework of bourgeois democracy " was treason to the proletariat, an error into which " a few of the Bolshevik leaders fall through failure to appraise the October rising and the tasks of the dictatorship of the proletariat ". All that was left for the Constituent Assembly was " an unconditional declaration of acceptance of the Soviet power, of the Soviet revolution ". Otherwise " a crisis in connexion with the Constituent Assembly can be solved only by revolutionary means ".[1]

There is no record of the discussion of Lenin's theses in the central committee of the party; but, whether or not formal discussion took place, they thenceforth became accepted party

[1] Lenin, *Sochineniya*, xxii, 131-134.

doctrine. For the Bolsheviks Lenin's *Theses on the Constituent Assembly* were a final tearing asunder of the veil of bourgeois constitutionalism. For the other socialist parties painful events were required to bring home to them what the proletarian revolution meant. The acceptance of the theses had two practical results. In the first place it made irrevocable the breach between the Bolsheviks and the socialist parties, which (except for the Left SRs) adhered to the view that the revolution was still in its democratic stage ; once the proletarian character of the revolution was accepted, those who maintained the democratic view logically and inevitably became counter-revolutionaries, in intention if not in action. Secondly, it sealed the fate of the Constituent Assembly, the crown of the democratic revolution, but an anachronism once that stage had been superseded by the proletarian socialist revolution. The burning issue of the " dual power ", the clash between the Soviets and the representative organs of bourgeois democracy which had raged since the February revolution, was resolved at last. The Constituent Assembly had now only to surrender or be wiped out. Any suggestion that the action taken against the assembly was the result of a sudden or unpremeditated decision prompted by anything that happened after the assembly met must be dismissed as erroneous. The action of the Bolsheviks was the outcome of a considered policy and of a clear-cut view of the progressive development of the revolution from its bourgeois-democratic to its proletarian-socialist phase.

The publication of Lenin's *Theses on the Constituent Assembly* was in the nature of a declaration of war on the assembly and on the political parties which were likely to control it. The actions of the next three weeks were so many tactical steps in a campaign whose main strategy had been decided. On December 17/30, 1917, came the arrest of the Right SR leader, Avxentiev, together with some of his followers, not, as a leading article in *Izvestiya* explained, " in his quality as a member of the Constituent Assembly ", but " for the organization of a counter-revolutionary conspiracy." [1] It was the first occasion on which such measures had been applied to representatives of a socialist party. On December 20, 1917/January 2, 1918, a decree of Sovnarkom convened the Constituent Assembly for January 5/18, 1918,

[1] *Izvestiya*, December 22, 1917/January 4, 1918.

subject to the attainment of a quorum of 400 members;[1] and two days later it was decided by a resolution of VTsIK to summon the third All-Russian Congress of Soviets for January 8/21, 1918, and an All-Russian Congress of Peasants' Deputies a few days later. Zinoviev, now once more Lenin's obedient henchman, pointed the decision by a clear enunciation of Leninist doctrine:

> We see in the rivalry of the Constituent Assembly and the Soviets the historical dispute between two revolutions, the bourgeois revolution and the socialist revolution. The elections to the Constituent Assembly are an echo of the first bourgeois revolution in February, but certainly not of the people's, the socialist, revolution.

The terms of the resolution were an avowed challenge. It denounced the slogan " all power to the Constituent Assembly " as the rallying-point of " elements all without exception counter-revolutionary " and as a screen for the watchword " down with the Soviets "; the purpose of the resolution was " to support with all the organized force of the Soviets the Left half of the Constituent Assembly against the Right, bourgeois and compromisers', half ".[2] The Menshevik Sukhanov dryly put the logical dilemma. If current events were part of the bourgeois revolution, then the Constituent Assembly should be fully supported; if they were in fact the socialist revolution, then it should not be summoned at all.[3] But the chosen tactics, though possibly the result of a compromise in the counsels of the party, were more dramatic. They were correctly diagnosed in a protest issued by the non-Bolshevik survivors of the first VTsIK appointed by the first All-Russian Congress of Soviets, which maintained a shadowy existence and still more shadowy claim to legitimacy: the third All-Russian Congress of Soviets was being summoned " in order to torpedo the Constituent Assembly ".[4]

---

[1] *Vserossiiskoe Uchreditel'noe Sobranie*, ed. I. S. Malchevsky (1930), pp. 144-145.

[2] *Protokoly Zasedanii VTsIK 2 Sozyva* (1918), pp. 176-177.

[3] *Ibid.* p. 179.

[4] The existence of the first VTsIK had been officially terminated by a resolution of the second VTsIK at its first meeting on October 27/November 9, 1917 (*Protokoly Zasedanii VTsIK 2 Sozyva* (1918), p. 4). It none the less continued to meet, and the records of its meetings from November 6/19, 1917, to January 11/24, 1918, were published in *Krasnyi Arkhiv*, No. 3 (10), 1925, pp. 99-113: most of its members were Mensheviks and Right SRs.

The preparations for the campaign were completed at a meeting of VTsIK on January 3/16, 1918,[1] when the Declaration of Rights of the Toiling and Exploited People was drafted for adoption by the Constituent Assembly. The declaration opened with the constitutional announcement already quoted :

1. Russia is declared a republic of Soviets of workers', soldiers' and peasants' deputies. All power in the centre and locally belongs to these Soviets.
2. The Russian Soviet Republic is established on the basis of a free union of free nations, as a federation of national Soviet republics.

Then, in a long enunciation of principles which was an endorsement, put into the mouth of the Constituent Assembly, of Soviet policy and legislation, it introduced two paragraphs which constituted an act of abdication on the part of the assembly :

Being elected on the basis of party lists compiled before the October revolution, when the people could not yet rise in its masses against the exploiters and, not having yet experienced the full force of the resistance of the exploiters in defence of their class privileges, had not yet undertaken in practical form the building of a socialist society, the Constituent Assembly would think it fundamentally incorrect, even from the formal standpoint, to set itself up against the Soviet power. . . .

Supporting the Soviet power and the decrees of the Council of People's Commissars, the Constituent Assembly recognises that its tasks are confined to the general working out of the fundamental principles of the socialist reconstruction of society.[2]

And lest the moral of this should be overlooked, *Izvestiya* of January 4/17, 1918, the day before the assembly met, carried the text of a resolution also emanating from VTsIK and couched in curt and unmistakable terms :

On the basis of all the achievements of the October revolution and in accordance with the Declaration of Rights of the Toiling and Exploited People adopted at the session of the Central Executive Committee on January 3, 1918, all power in the Russian republic belongs to the Soviets and Soviet institutions. Therefore any attempt on the part of any person or

---

[1] The record of this meeting is missing from the protocols of the second VTsIK.

[2] *Vserossiiskoe Uchreditel'noe Sobranie*, ed. I. S. Malchevsky (1930), pp. 4-6.

institution whatever to usurp this or that function of state power will be regarded as a counter-revolutionary act. Any such attempt will be crushed by all means at the disposal of the Soviet power, including the use of armed force.[1]

The outlawing of the Kadets and the arrest of several leading Right SRs had blunted the main potential offensive power of the Constituent Assembly. But a certain note of caution in the procedure adopted was due to the apprehension felt by some Bolsheviks, though not justified by the events, of the supposed prestige of the Constituent Assembly among the masses. When the assembly met on January 5/18, 1918, Sverdlov ousted from the tribune the oldest member of the assembly, who in accordance with tradition was about to open the proceedings, and in the name of VTsIK declared the assembly open. The French revolution, he said, had issued its Declaration of the Rights of Man and of the Citizen which was " a declaration of rights to the free exploitation of those not possessing the tools and means of production " ; the Russian revolution must issue its own declaration of rights. He then read the draft prepared two days earlier by VTsIK and briefly requested the assembly to adopt it.

The remainder of the proceedings served mainly to illustrate the unreality of the assembly and the fundamental differences of doctrine between those who composed it. Chernov, the Right SR leader, was elected president by a substantial majority over Spiridonova, the Left SR, who had Bolshevik support. Bukharin, for the Bolsheviks, spoke eloquently of the immediate issues of the socialist revolution :

> The watershed which at this moment divides this assembly into . . . two irreconcilable camps, camps of principle — this watershed runs along the line : for socialism or against socialism.

Chernov, in his speech from the chair, had proclaimed the " will to socialism " :

> But of what socialism was citizen Chernov speaking? Of the socialism which will come in 200 years, which will be made by our grandchildren? Was he speaking of that socialism? We speak of a living, active, creative socialism, about which we do not only want to speak, but which we want to realize. And that, comrades, is what is called being an active socialist.

[1] *Sobranie Uzakonenii, 1917–1918*, No. 14, art. 202.

Steinberg, the spokesman of the Left SRs, who was People's Commissar for Justice in Sovnarkom, evaded the issue of principle, but argued that the time had passed for a discussion of policy (which was what the Right SRs proposed) and that the only function of the assembly, as the " child of the people ", was to " submit to the will of the toiling people set forth in the programme of the Soviet of Workers' and Soldiers' Deputies ". The speech of Tsereteli for the Mensheviks was on a high plane of theoretical cogency and consistency. He argued, at enormous length, as the Mensheviks had argued for fourteen years, against " anarchic attempts to introduce a socialist economy in a backward country ", and protested that " the class struggle of the workers for their final liberation " could only be conducted under conditions of " popular sovereignty based on universal and equal suffrage ".[1] Speech-making went on unabated for nearly twelve hours. But little that was said had any relation to the world outside. The harsh challenge implicit in the Soviet declaration was ignored ; so was the concentration of effective power in the hands of the proletariat and of the Soviet Government. No alternative government capable of wielding power was suggested or could have been suggested. In these circumstances the debate could have no issue.

At midnight the Bolshevik declaration was rejected by a majority of 237 to 138 in favour of a motion of the Right SRs to discuss current questions of policy. The debate continued. Then, in the early hours of the morning, a Bolshevik, Raskolnikov, announced that in view of " the counter-revolutionary majority " in the assembly the Bolsheviks would leave it. An hour later the Left SRs also withdrew. Then the central committee of the Bolshevik party, which had remained in session elsewhere in the building, decided to act. The sailor in command of the military guard, Zheleznyakov by name, announced to the president of the assembly that he had received instructions to close the meeting " because the guard is tired ".[2] In the ensuing confusion a resolution on the agrarian question and an appeal to the allied Powers for peace were read to the assembly and declared carried. It was characteristic of the bankruptcy of the assembly that it

[1] *Vserossiiskoe Uchreditel'noe Sobranie*, ed. I. S. Malchevsky (1930), pp. 29-30, 34-35, 50-51.
[2] *Ibid.* p. 110. Apparently the instruction was received directly from Lenin (*ibid.* p. 217).

could do nothing more than repeat in substance what the second All-Russian Congress of Soviets had done on the morrow of the revolution ten weeks earlier. Then shortly before 5 A.M. it adjourned for twelve hours. It never met again. Later in the same day VTsIK, having listened to a two-hour speech from Lenin,[1] decreed its formal dissolution. Its reassembly was prevented by the simple method of placing a guard on the door of the Tauride palace.

Marx, in discussing Louis Bonaparte's *coup d'état* of December 2, 1851, commented in a famous passage on the procedure of his predecessors :

> Cromwell, when he dissolved the Long Parliament, walked alone into its midst, pulled out his watch in order that the body should not continue to exist one minute beyond the term fixed for it by him, and drove out each individual member with gay and humorous invectives. Napoleon, smaller than his proto-type, at least went into the legislative body on the 18th Brumaire and, though in a tremulous voice, read to it its sentence of death.[2]

Every period of history has its own dramatic symbols. The dismissal of the All-Russian Constituent Assembly by an armed sailor " because the guard is tired " was one of these. The contemptuous gesture masked a certain nervousness in Bolshevik circles as to the possible consequences of their high-handed action. A demonstration in favour of the Constituent Assembly at the moment of its meeting had been dispersed by troops, and several persons variously described as " peaceful demonstrators " and " armed conspirators " were killed.[3] But the act of dissolution passed almost without protest ; and the verdict of a Right member of the Soviet, equally unsympathetic to the SRs and to the Bolsheviks, seems to reflect accurately the prevailing mood :

> The impression of the " injustice " committed by the Bolsheviks against the Constituent Assembly was attenuated to a considerable extent by dissatisfaction with the Constituent Assembly itself, by its (as was said) " undignified behaviour ",

---

[1] Lenin, *Sochineniya*, xxii, 184-187.   [2] Marx i Engels, *Sochineniya*, viii, 398.
[3] *Pravda*, January 6/19, 1918. According to Sokolov, a SR member of the Constituent Assembly, the demonstration was organized by the SRs and the demonstrators were unarmed ; he adds that the people of Petrograd remained passive : " we could not drive them against the Bolshevik movement " (*Arkhiv Russkoi Revolyutsii* (Berlin), xiii (1924), 65-66).

and by the timidity and feebleness of its president Chernov. The Constituent Assembly was blamed more than the Bolsheviks who dispersed it.[1]

It was one more demonstration of the lack of any solid basis, or any broad popular support, in Russia for the institutions and principles of bourgeois democracy.

When, therefore, the third All-Russian Congress of Soviets opened at the Tauride palace on January 10/23, 1918, it found itself the natural, though self-constituted, heir to the Constituent Assembly, whose formal dissolution it at once confirmed. After the singing of the " Internationale ", the " Marseillaise " was also played " as a historical recollection of the path traversed ". The symbolism is explained by the enthusiastic compiler of the official records of the congress: " The Internationale has conquered the Marseillaise as the proletarian revolution leaves behind it the bourgeois revolution ".[2] The business of the congress, as Sverdlov, its president, informed it in his opening speech, was " to build the new life of the future and to create an all-Russian power "; it had to " decide whether this power is to have any link with the bourgeois order or whether the dictatorship of workers and peasants will be finally and irrevocably constituted ".[3] Lenin was, as usual, cautious in diagnosis, but firm in conclusion :

> He who has understood the meaning of the class struggle, the significance of the sabotage organized by the officials, knows that we cannot all at once make the leap to socialism. . . . I have no illusions about the fact that we have only begun the transitional period to socialism, that we have not yet arrived at socialism. But you will act correctly if you say that our state is a socialist republic of Soviets.[4]

Martov repeated once again the Menshevik argument :

> The full socialist transformation is possible only after prolonged work caused by the necessity to re-create a whole political organization of society, to strengthen the economic position of the country, and only after that to proceed to the realization of the slogans of socialism.[5]

[1] V. B. Stankevich, *Vospominaniya, 1914-1919* (Berlin, 1920), p. 302 ; the diagnosis of Sokolov in the account quoted in the preceding note is strikingly similar.

[2] *Tretii Vserossiiskii S"ezd Sovetov* (1918), p. 3.   [3] *Ibid.* p. 5.

[4] Lenin, *Sochineniya*, xxii, 209, 212.

[5] *Tretii Vserossiiskii S"ezd Sovetov* (1918), p. 35.

And Lenin in reply traced the course traversed in the past twelve years :

> The Bolsheviks talked of the bourgeois-democratic revolution in 1905. But now when the Soviets are in power, when the workers, soldiers and peasants . . . have said, " We will take the whole power and will ourselves undertake the building of a new life ", at such a time there can be no question of a bourgeois-democratic revolution. And this was already said by the Bolsheviks in congresses and meetings and conferences, in resolutions and decisions, in April last year.[1]

Politically, Lenin's argument could hardly be refuted. The October revolution had settled the question for good or ill. Whether the bourgeois revolution had been completed or not, whether the time was or was not ripe for the proletarian revolution — and whatever the ultimate consequences if these questions had to be answered in the negative sense — the proletarian revolution had in fact occurred. After October 1917 nobody could undo what had been done or force the revolution back into a bourgeois-democratic mould. Political development seemed to have outrun economic development. This was indeed the assumption which Lenin made on the eve of October :

> Owing to the revolution Russia in a few months has caught up the advanced countries in her *political* organization. But this is not enough. War is inexorable and puts the question with unsparing sharpness : either perish, or catch up and overtake the advanced countries *economically* as well.[2]

But the hypothesis of a suddenly acquired political maturity did some violence to the facts as well as to Marxist doctrine. Lenin himself was not unconscious of the embarrassment ; for, in his retrospect on the situation in the autumn of 1918, he offered a substantially different analysis from that given at the third All-Russian Congress of Soviets in January of the same year :

> Yes, our revolution is a bourgeois revolution *so long as* we march *with* the peasantry *as a whole*. . . . *At first* with " all " the peasantry against the monarchy, against the landowners, against mediaevalism (and, so far, the revolution remains bourgeois, bourgeois-democratic). *Then*, with the poorest peasantry, with the semi-proletariat, with all the exploited

---

[1] Lenin, *Sochineniya*, xxii, 221.   [2] *Ibid.* xxi, 191.

against capitalism, meaning also against the rich peasants, the *kulaks* and the speculators ; and, so far, the revolution becomes *socialist*.[1]

And Lenin continued, reviving after a long interval Marx's idea (though not the phrase itself) of " permanent " or " uninterrupted " revolution :

> To attempt to put up an artificial Chinese wall between one and the other, to separate one from the other by any other element *except* the degree of preparedness of the proletariat and the degree of its unity with the poor of the countryside, is the greatest perversion of Marxism, its vulgarization, its replacement by liberalism.[2]

Nor were these difficulties of analysis purely scholastic. They reflected the persistent dilemma of a socialist revolution struggling retrospectively to fill the empty place of bourgeois democracy and bourgeois capitalism in the Marxist scheme.

When the debate in the third All-Russian Congress of Soviets was over, the congress adopted the Declaration of Rights of the Toiling and Exploited People shorn of its last two paragraphs, which had become superfluous ; and, on the motion of the People's Commissar for Nationalities, Stalin, it passed, with only 24 dissentients and 3 abstentions in a congress of some 900 delegates, a resolution " On the Federal Institutions of the Russian Republic ", the first paragraph of which added a fresh foundation-stone for the Soviet order :

> The Russian Socialist Soviet Republic is created on the basis of a voluntary union of the peoples of Russia in the form of a federation of the Soviet republics of these peoples.[3]

The word " provisional ", hitherto officially attached to the title of the Workers' and Peasants' Government, disappeared. The congress instructed VTsIK to prepare for submission to the next congress a draft of " the fundamental principles of the constitution of the Russian Federal Republic ".

---

[1] *Ibid.* xxiii, 390-391. In March 1919 Lenin dated the transition more precisely : " Our revolution up to the formation of the committees of the poor, that is, up to the summer or even the autumn of 1918, was in large measure a bourgeois revolution " (*ibid.* xxiv, 125).

[2] *Ibid.* xxiii, 391.

[3] *Tretii Vserossiiskii S"ezd Sovetov* (1918), p. 82.

CHAPTER 6

THE CONSTITUTION OF THE RSFSR

THE decision of the hitherto anonymous " Workers' and Peasants' Government " to abandon its provisional status, to give itself both a geographical and an ideological designation, and to draw up for itself a formal constitution, marked a symbolical turning-point in its history. The new constitution did not so much create new forms of government as register and regularize those which were in course of being established by uncoordinated initiative in the aftermath of the revolutionary upheaval. The debates in the drafting commission reflected the frictions of a natural process of growth ; and the same flexibility enabled it to survive through a series of adjustments and transformations for eighteen revolutionary years   It would, however, be easy to exaggerate its importance in the eyes of its authors. The enthusiasm of the first months of the revolution had no great respect for constitutional forms. The period of the drafting of the constitution was one of grave and continuous crises both in economic and in external policy, which threatened the existence of the régime and left little leisure for smaller preoccupations. Finally, the republic for which the constitution was being drafted was still regarded by its rulers as a brief transitional stage on the way to a world-wide socialist republic or federation of republics. The constitution was scarcely expected to last as a working instrument. Its character and purpose are perhaps best described in a phrase applied by a modern historian to the Jacobin constitution of 1793 — a " political prospectus ".[1]

In these circumstances it is not surprising that the principal leaders themselves took no personal part in the work. The revision of the party programme, much discussed at this time though not in fact undertaken till a year later, occupied far more attention

---

[1] R. R. Palmer, *Twelve who Ruled* (Princeton, 1941), p. 42.

in party circles. Lenin's copious speeches and writings of these months will be searched in vain for any reference to constitution-making. It was the period of the Brest-Litovsk crisis and of the hurried transfer of the capital from Petrograd to Moscow. For more than two months, apart from several draft constitutions prepared in the commissariats of Internal Affairs and of Justice and elsewhere,[1] no progress was made; and nothing was ready for the fourth All-Russian Congress of Soviets when it met in March. Then on April 1, 1918, VTsIK decided after a short debate to create a commission to draft a constitution. Its president was Sverdlov, the party factotum and president of VTsIK; and its other members were Stalin, the party expert on the national question and the only representative of Sovnarkom on the commission; Bukharin and Pokrovsky, both party intellectuals; Steklov, a former waverer between Bolsheviks and Mensheviks, who had been secretary of the executive committee of the Petrograd Soviet after the February revolution and was now editor of *Izvestiya*; and representatives of the commissariats of Internal Affairs, Justice, Nationalities, War and National Economy.[2] The commission worked for three months and produced an agreed text. The result of its labours was published on July 3, 1918, the same day on which it was submitted for approval to the central committee of the party as a preliminary to its presentation to the fifth All-Russian Congress of Soviets.

The constitution began with general principles. The first four chapters recited textually the Declaration of Rights of the Toiling and Exploited People adopted by the third All-Russian Congress of Soviets. Chapter 5 enunciated a series of " general propositions ", including the federal character of the republic; the separation of church from state and school from church; freedom of speech, opinion and assembly for the workers, assured by placing at their disposal the technical means of producing papers, pamphlets and books as well as premises for meetings; the obligation for all citizens to work on the principle " he that does not

---

[1] Several of these drafts are preserved in appendices to G. S. Gurvich, *Istoriya Sovetskoi Konstitutsii* (1923); Gurvich was a member of the drafting commission, and his book is the main source for the drafting of the constitution.

[2] *Protokoly Zasedanii VTsIK 4ᵒᵒ Sozyva* (1920), pp. 4, 72-73. There was, properly speaking, no commissariat of National Economy: Bukharin represented the Supreme Council of National Economy.

work, neither shall he eat "; the obligation for all workers of military service in defence of the republic; the right of citizenship for all workers living on Russian territory and of asylum for foreigners persecuted on the ground of political or religious offences; and the abolition of all discrimination on grounds of race or nationality. The constitution then turned to practical arrangements. Chapters 6 to 8 dealt with organization at the centre. The supreme power was the All-Russian Congress of Soviets, composed of representatives of city Soviets on the basis of one deputy to every 25,000 voters and of provincial Soviets on the basis of one deputy to every 125,000 inhabitants. The All-Russian Congress elected the All-Russian Central Executive Committee (VTsIK) of not more than 200 members which exercised all powers of the congress when the congress was not in session. VTsIK appointed the Council of Peoples' Commissars (Sovnarkom), whose function was the "general administration of the affairs of the RSFSR", but also extended to the issuing of "decrees, orders and instructions". The ninth chapter defined the functions of the All-Russian Congress and of VTsIK, while chapters 10 to 12 related to the organization of regional, provincial, county and district congresses of Soviets and to the formation of city and village Soviets.[1] Chapter 13 confined the franchise to those who "earn their living by production or socially useful labour", soldiers and disabled persons, specifically excluding persons who employ hired labour, *rentiers*, private traders, monks and priests, and officials and agents of the former police. The remaining articles were concerned with routine matters of detail.

The making of constitutions is normally a battlefield of contending purposes, and the finished product bears on its face more or less obvious scars of the conflict. The controversy which lay behind the making of the first constitution of the RSFSR took three forms which were often barely distinguishable. It was a conflict between those who sought a weakening and those who sought a strengthening of state power; between those who desired a dispersal of power and initiative through local author-

[1] The translation "village Soviets" is consecrated by usage but may be seriously misleading, as is shown by the provision for "villages" of anything from 300 to "over 10,000" inhabitants. A *selo* is an inhabited rural locality of undefined area and population.

ities and those who desired a concentration of authority and discipline at the centre; and between those who sought to make federalism effective and those who, under whatever guise, sought to establish the "one and indivisible" republic. The former group was composed in part of Left SRs, who traditionally represented these trends, but not exclusively of them; its most effective spokesman in the drafting commission was Reisner, the representative of the People's Commissariat of Justice. Its views were, however, tinged with an unpractical utopianism, so that the sterner realists would probably have emerged victorious even if they had not found an incontrovertible argument in the emergencies of a struggling and gravely menaced revolutionary régime. But the pattern of much subsequent Soviet political controversy was set in the debates of the commission on the drafting of the constitution.

The Bolshevik doctrine of the state was entangled in a contradiction already inherent in Marxist teaching. Marx and Engels accepted to the full the traditional socialist hostility to the oppressive state, culminating in the belief that the state would die away altogether in conditions of socialism; at the same time they recognized the need to establish a powerful state machine to consummate and establish the victory of the revolution through the dictatorship of the proletariat. Lenin, who on the eve of the revolution devoted one of his ablest writings, under the title *State and Revolution*, to an analysis of the Marxist doctrine of the state, met the dilemma by regarding the dictatorship of the proletariat as a temporary expedient, necessary so long as the remnants of bourgeois power had not yet been eradicated, but destined, like any other form of state, to die away when the final goal of communism is achieved.[1] The Bolshevik leaders were thus able, while maintaining the deeply rooted socialist tradition of hostility to the state, to defend as a transitional measure that strengthening of state power, the paramount necessity of which became increasingly obvious in the dark winter of 1917–1918, and the still darker summer of 1918.

The distrust of the state and the opposition to bourgeois parliamentarianism which lay at the root of Marxist theory drove

[1] See Note A: "Lenin's Theory of the State", pp. 233-249 below.

many even of the Bolsheviks in the direction of syndicalism ; and the Left SRs had marked syndicalist leanings. So long as bourgeois democracy was a living tradition, Bolsheviks and syndicalists could find a certain amount of common ground in denouncing it. Both regarded the " citizen " of bourgeois democracy as an atomized abstraction, and treated man as essentially a member of a class of producers. It was not therefore surprising that the strongest assaults on the conception of a powerful Soviet state should have had a syndicalist complexion. Indeed the Soviets themselves, being in origin professional rather than territorial organizations, lent themselves easily to this tendency.[1] A draft constitution emanating in January 1918 from the Commissariat of Justice was a pure example of syndicalism. It proposed a republic whose constituent members would be five federations of workers — " land workers, industrial workers, employees of trading institutions, employees of the state, and employees of private persons ".[2] That this was no mere freak was shown by the speech of the spokesman of the Left SRs, Trutovsky, at the meeting of VTsIK which appointed the drafting commission. Trutovsky explicitly argued that a constitution was a bourgeois conception, that the socialist state could only be a " centre which regulates productive and economic relations ", and that the business of the commission was to work out " not properly speaking a constitution, but the mutual relations which must exist between different organs of power in so far as we can speak of power over persons ".[3] No vote on the question of principle was taken in VTsIK ; and Reisner continued throughout April 1918 to uphold these ideas in the drafting commission :

It is indispensable to keep in mind that territorial organization and territorial federalism cannot serve as a basis for the solution of state questions in a socialist republic. Our federation is not an alliance of territorial governments or states, but a federation of social-economic organizations. It is founded not

---

[1] Lenin once described " the theory that representation should be by industries " as " the germ of the Soviet system " (A. Ransome, *Six Weeks in Russia in 1919* (1919), pp. 80-81). The principle of " workers' control " in industry promulgated in the first months of the régime also had potential syndicalist implications.

[2] G. S. Gurvich, *Istoriya Sovetskoi Konstitutsii* (1923), pp. 102-107.

[3] *Protokoly Zasedanii VTsIK 4ᵉᵒ Sozyva* (1920), pp. 70-72.

on the territorial fetiches of state power, but on the real interests of the toiling classes of the Russian republic.[1]

In the final debate on the constitution in the fifth All-Russian Congress of Soviets one speaker wished to discard the terms " federation " and " republic " as smacking of the old discarded conception of the state and to call the new entity the " All-Russian Workers' Commune." [2]

These syndicalist aberrations led to the intervention of Stalin, who presented a set of theses to the drafting commission and secured their adoption by a majority vote as the basis of its work. They contained a reminder that " the plan of the constitution now being worked out by the commission must be temporary, being designed for the period of transition from the bourgeois to the socialist order ", and that it must therefore take account of " questions of the dictatorship of the proletariat and the poor peasantry, of the organization of power as an expression of this dictatorship, etc. — questions which have no relation to an established socialist order where there will be no classes or apparatus of power ".[3] The dying away of the state remained as an ultimate ideal. But in the intervening period the state form of the Socialist Soviet Republic was to conform to a pattern of territorial sovereignty familiar in the capitalist world. Article 9 of the finished constitution skilfully combined a recognition of the transitional character of Soviet state power with a reminder that, while it lasted, it must be strong :

> The principal aim of the constitution of the RSFSR, which is designed for the present transition period, consists in the establishment of the dictatorship of the urban and rural proletariat and the poorest peasantry in the form of a strong all-Russian Soviet power for the purpose of the complete crushing of the bourgeoisie, the abolition of the exploitation of man by man and the establishment of socialism, under which there will be neither division into classes nor state power.

Since, however, " the establishment of socialism " could be conceived only as an international event, the Russian federation was

[1] G. S. Gurvich, *Istoriya Sovetskoi Konstitutsii* (1923), p. 142.
[2] *Pyatyi Vserossiiskii S"ezd Sovetov* (1918), p. 193.
[3] G. S. Gurvich, *Istoriya Sovetskoi Konstitutsii* (1923), pp. 33, 146-147 ; these theses are not included in Stalin's collected works.

merely the first unit of an eventual world federation of socialist republics.[1] In this sense, too, it marked a " transition period ".

The underlying clash between the conception of a state in transition towards its own eventual dying away and a dictatorship of the proletariat powerful enough to crush bourgeois opposition was also reflected in the struggle between local self-government and centralization. The peculiarity of the Soviet structure lay in the fact that it was built up round Soviets which had already taken shape and acquired some degree of organization before they became constitutional organs of state power. It was emphasized again and again that the constitution merely registered forms spontaneously evolved by the masses themselves. In the words of the *rapporteur* to the fifth All-Russian Congress of Soviets, it " was realized in practice long before it was written down on paper ".[2] The Soviets were initially, and in part always remained, loose and informal assemblies without clearly defined functions. Village Soviets, created under no fixed or uniform rules,[3] combined to form rural district (*volost*) congresses of Soviets, and these again to form county (*uezd*) congresses of Soviets;[4] county congresses combined with city Soviets, created on a different and mainly professional basis, to form provincial congresses of Soviets ; and these in turn combined to form regional (*oblast'*) congresses.[5]

---

[1] It was thus logical that the constitution should extend rights of citizenship " to foreigners working within the territory of the RSFSR provided they belong to the working class or to the peasantry working without hired labour " (art. 20). This provision originated in a decree of VTsIK designed primarily for the benefit of German and Austro-Hungarian prisoners of war (*Protokoly Zasedanii VTsIK 4ᵍᵒ Sozyva* (1920), pp. 62-66).

[2] *Pyatyi Vserossiiskii S"ezd Sovetov* (1918), p. 190.

[3] The smallest Soviets were examples of " direct democracy ", i.e. bodies composed of all citizens (or, in the case of factory Soviets, of all workers in the factory) ; the larger Soviets consisted of delegates elected by the citizens or workers to represent them and in early days were sometimes distinguished from Soviets pure and simple by the use of the term " Sovdepi " (Soviets of deputies). Among " white " Russians " Sovdepia " was the current nickname of the territory of the Soviet republic.

[4] An amendment passed by the seventh All-Russian Congress of Soviets in December 1919, laid it down that the county congresses of Soviets should be composed of delegates of the city, as well as of the rural Soviets of the county (*S"ezdy Sovetov RSFSR v Postanovleniyakh* (1939), p. 149).

[5] The *oblast'* was an optional and not universal stage in the organization (*Sobranie Uzakonenii, 1917-1918*, No. 99, art. 1019).

The All-Russian Congress of Soviets was composed of delegates from either provincial or regional congresses and from the largest city Soviets which were outside the lower stages of the congress system. The local Soviet, urban or rural, was the supposed source of power, the congresses of Soviets at different levels and the All-Russian Congress of Soviets at the summit being emanations from it. The very informality of the system was regarded by Lenin as its main recommendation :

> All bureaucratic formalities and limitations disappear from the elections, and the masses themselves determine the ordering and timing of the elections with free right of recall of those elected.[1]

The Soviets constituted, like the Paris commune, a " new kind of state ", free from the obnoxious characteristics of the old bureaucratic state and designed to replace it. " All power on the spot ", ran the proclamation of the second All-Russian Congress of Soviets at the moment of the revolution, " passes to the Soviets of Workers', Soldiers' and Peasants' Deputies, who must ensure true revolutionary order." [2]

This idealized conception of authority did not survive the test of experience. The very spontaneity of the movement which had created Soviets in factory and village up and down the country meant that their independent acts were irregular, uncoordinated and disruptive of orderly administration. After the October revolution an attempt was made in a decree of the People's Commissariat of Internal Affairs to define the place of the local Soviets in the new order :

> Locally the Soviets are the organs of administration, the organs of local power : they must bring under their control all institutions of an administrative, economic, financial and cultural-educational character. . . .
> Each of these organizations, down to the smallest, is fully autonomous in questions of a local character, but conforms its activity to the general decrees and resolutions of the central power and to the resolutions of the larger Soviet organizations into the composition of which it enters. Thus is created a coherent organism of the republic of Soviets, uniform in all its parts.[3]

[1] Lenin, *Sochineniya*, xxii, 645.   [2] *Ibid.* xxii, p. 11.
[3] *Sobranie Uzakonenii*, *1917–1918*, No. 12, art. 79.

But it was easier in the first weeks of the revolution to issue such decrees than to secure their observance. In the first half of 1918, when the constitution of the RSFSR was in the making, signs of a general breakdown and dispersal of authority were manifest all over Russia. Lenin himself might pretend to make light of what happened when " some local Soviet sets up an independent republic " and call this " a disease of growth " and a " quite natural phenomenon of the transition from Tsarist Russia to the Russia of united Soviet organizations ".[1] But it was not seriously possible to ignore the necessity of restoring some kind of effective central authority if the country was to survive the difficulties crowding in on it from all sides.

The conditions of the moment therefore favoured those who in the drafting commission pleaded the cause of centralization. The initial debate turned on the question whether to begin by defining the powers of the local Soviets or those of the central organs. Stalin is said to have turned the discussion — it is not quite clear how — by invoking the federal principle.[2] A significant verbal antithesis between article 10 and article 12 of the finished constitution may reflect the keenness of the debate. According to the one, " all authority within the territory of the RSFSR is vested in the entire working population organized in urban and rural Soviets "; according to the other, " supreme authority in the RSFSR is vested in the All-Russian Congress of Soviets and, in the interval between congresses, in VTsIK ". But the same formal antithesis between the derivation of authority from below and the exercise of authority from above is implicit in any constitution claiming to rest on a basis of popular sovereignty; and the text of the constitution left no room for doubt. According to the instruction of the third All-Russian Congress of Soviets, " local matters " were to be " decided exclusively by the local Soviets ", and the central authorities were to be left to control the execution of " the fundamental principles of the federation " as well as of " measures of national importance ". The way in which this instruction was carried out in the final text was decisive. A long and comprehensive enumeration of seventeen " questions of national importance " falling within the competence

[1] Lenin, *Sochineniya*, xxiii, 19.
[2] G. S. Gurvich, *Istoriya Sovetskoi Konstitutsii* (1923), pp. 22-25.

of the All-Russian Congress of Soviets and of VTsIK was framed in such a way as to be illustrative rather than exhaustive, and followed by the precautionary rider that " in addition to the above-mentioned questions the All-Russian Congress of Soviets and VTsIK may decide on any other matter which they deem within their jurisdiction ".[1] This rider was the nearest thing in the constitution to an allocation of residuary powers.

A later chapter of the constitution defined in general terms the tasks of the local Soviets and the regional, provincial, county and district congresses of Soviets with their executive committees. These were :

(a) the carrying into effect of all resolutions of the corresponding higher organs of Soviet power ;

(b) the taking of all measures to improve the territory in question culturally and economically ;

(c) the settlement of all questions having a purely local significance ;

(d) the unification of all Soviet activity within the territory in question.

The effect of the last provision was to encourage the Soviets to absorb pre-revolutionary organs of local government and to transform themselves into local government organs of the normal pattern. The budgetary chapter of the constitution, which was a subject of controversy between the People's Commissariats of Internal Affairs and of Finance, contributed to the same result. A

---

[1] According to G. S. Gurvich, *Istoriya Sovetskoi Konstitutsii* (1923), p. 76 : " the illustrative and secondary character of the enumeration was fully recognized by its authors ". The enumeration was couched in terms which did not aspire to precise legal significance : it rested with the central authorities to establish the " general principles " of agrarian policy and of education, the " foundations " of the judicial system and the " fundamental laws " of labour and citizenship. The difficulty for western commentators arises from an attempt to fit these provisions into a framework of ideas totally foreign to them. The point has been well made in an English study of local government in Moscow : " The general principle which applies to all governing authorities in the Soviet Union is that no specific limitation is placed on their powers. There is nothing corresponding to the English doctrine of *ultra vires*, nor is an express authorization by some legal enactment or sovereign body necessary to permit action being taken. On the other hand, every Soviet or other organ is subject to the overriding control of higher authorities, there being no absolute autonomy in any sphere whatever. . . . The city Soviet has far more extensive powers than any English municipality, but at the same time it is not in possession of an absolute autonomy or an untrammelled discretion in regard to any of them " (E. D. Simon, etc., *Moscow in the Making* (1937), p. 36).

decree passed while the drafting commission was at work prohibited local Soviets from levying taxation on local organs of the central commissariats serving general state needs.[1] The constitution recognized the right of local Soviets to raise " taxes and levies exclusively for the needs of the local economy ". But all local revenue and expenditure were brought under direct or indirect central control, the budgets of the minor Soviets being reviewed by the provincial or regional Soviets or their executive committees, the budgets of the city, provincial and regional Soviets by the All-Russian Congress of Soviets or by VTsIK. What was in effect a monopoly of finance was enjoyed by the central government; and the granting of credits and subsidies was a powerful means of bringing local Soviets under the supervising authority of the People's Commissariat of Internal Affairs.[2]

The Soviets were thus firmly fitted into their place in the constitutional structure. On the one hand, they were the formal source of authority and the electoral colleges by which, through several intermediate stages, the delegates to the supreme All-Russian Congress of Soviets were chosen. On the other hand, they were organs of local government enjoying a large measure of local initiative, but subject in all their functions to ultimate control, through the same intermediate levels of authority, by the organs of the central government. It was this second and novel aspect of their position which at first gave some trouble. In June 1918 the interpretation of the slogan " all power to the Soviets " as meaning " all power to the local Soviets " was pronounced by an authoritative commentator to be " harmful " and

---

[1] *Sobranie Uzakonenii, 1917-1918*, No. 31, art. 408.

[2] This is explicitly stated by an official writer in *Pyat' Let Vlasti Sovetov* (1922), p. 262. Information on the actual working of the local Soviets and congresses of Soviets is scarce for the first years of the revolution. The best source is M. Vladimirsky, *Sovety, Ispolkomy i S"ezdy Sovetov* (i, 1920, ii, 1921), based on the material of the People's Commissariat of Internal Affairs. This shows that the provincial and county congresses of Soviets, together with their executive committees, met regularly and functioned in the manner provided for in the constitution, though with some irregularities of composition and procedure, but that regional and district congresses of Soviets (the highest and lowest grade respectively) were already falling into desuetude. In other words, practical experience quickly lightened the cumbrous constitutional structure by shedding the redundant props. Little is known of the working of the local " village " Soviets. Further information is said to be found in a later work, *Sovety v Epokhu Voennogo Kommunizma*, ed. V. P. Antonov-Saratovsky (1928), which has not been available.

" a thing of the past ".[1]   But the indiscipline of the local Soviets died hard.   Six months later it was still necessary to exhort them to " execute without demur and with strict accuracy all decisions and orders of the central authorities ".[2]

The third issue — between the federal and the unitary state — was not explicitly raised in the debates on the constitution, but was implicit in discussions of the interpretation to be given to the term " federal " in the title of the RSFSR.   The words " federal " and " federation ", while having a precise meaning in constitutional law, are politically neutral in colour.   In the American revolution the federalists were those who stood for union and a strong central authority ; in the French revolution they were Girondins who stood for a dispersal of authority and resisted Jacobin policies of centralization.[3]   It was the tradition of the French revolution which influenced nineteenth-century socialist views of " federation ".   In his address of 1850 to the Communist League Marx had written that, while German bourgeois democrats supported federation and sought to weaken the central power by strengthening the independence of the regions, " the workers must use their influence not only for the one and indivisible German republic, but for a decisive centralization of force within it in the hands of the state power ".[4]   Engels at the very end of his life, attacking the system of " petty states " under the federal constitutions of Germany and Switzerland, held that " the proletariat can make use only of the form of the one and indivisible republic ".[5]   On the other hand, Proudhon and the anarchists, invoking the other aspect of the French revolutionary tradition, freely used the words " federal " and " federation " without constitutional precision, but with a strong flavour of

---

[1] *Sovetskoe Pravo*, No. 3 (9), 1924, p. 29.
[2] Resolution of the Council of Workers' and Peasants' Defence quoted in R. Labry, *Une Législation Communiste* (1920), p. 22.
[3] H. Hintze, *Staatseinheit und Föderalismus im alten Frankreich und in der Revolution* (1928), is a learned presentation of the running conflict between " federalism " and the conception of " the nation, one and indivisible " at successive stages of the French revolution ; the victory of centralization was due, not to ideological preferences, but to military and economic pressures.   Interesting parallels to the Russian revolution suggest themselves.
[4] Marx i Engels, *Sochineniya*, viii, 487.   [5] *Ibid.* xvi, ii, 109-110.

emotional approval, to indicate a loose voluntary association of local units — the antithesis of the strong and centralized state. The position was complicated by the fact that the Communards of 1871, who, being for the most part Proudhonists rather than Marxists, had treated " federation " as the ultimate form of union between free communes and had been popularly known as " les fédérés ", also received the blessing of Marx :

> The commune was to be the political form of the smallest village. . . . The rural communes of every district were to administer their common affairs by an assembly of delegates in the central town, and these district assemblies were to send deputies to the " national delegation " in Paris. . . . The few but important functions which would remain to the central government . . . were to be handed over to communal, i.e. strictly responsible, officials.

This project, which served as a prototype for the Russian Soviets, fitted in well enough with the conception of local self-government and direct democracy as an antidote to a bureaucratic and tyrannical executive. But the context made it clear that Marx was thinking here in terms of the dying away of the state. There was no question of breaking up a great nation into " a federation of small states such as was dreamt of by Montesquieu and the Girondins " ; on the contrary, the unity of the nation was to " become a reality by the destruction of state power ".[1]

Marxist objections to federalism were inherited by Lenin and the Bolsheviks, and were reinforced by the long struggle with the Jewish Bund, which, following the precedent of Austrian social-democracy, wished to introduce the federal principle into the organization of the party. Even later, when prejudices against a federal constitution for the state had been overcome, Bolshevism never wavered in its insistence on a unitary, centralized Russian communist party. But at the outset objections to federalism were as rigidly maintained in state as in party organization. In 1903 Armenian social-democrats were rebuked by Lenin for advocating a federal Russian republic.[2] In 1913 Lenin noted that " Marxists are, of course, hostile to federation and decentralization " (he evidently drew no clear distinction between them) on the ground that " capitalism for its development demands as large

[1] Marx i Engels, *Sochineniya*, xiii, ii, 314.   [2] Lenin, *Sochineniya*, v, 242-243.

and as highly centralized states as possible ";[1] and in a letter of the same year he declared himself " against federation in principle ", adding that it " weakens the economic link and is an unsuitable form for a single state ".[2] The argument was not constitutional but practical. Federation meant decentralization ; the unitary state was praised as the instrument of centralization.

Like other political principles, opposition to federation was for Lenin never an absolute rule. It had, for instance, to be weighed against the principle of national self-determination.

> We are unconditionally, *other conditions being equal*, in favour of centralization and against the bourgeois ideal of federal relations [wrote Lenin in December 1914]. Nevertheless even in this case . . . it is not our business, not the business of democrats (to say nothing of socialists), to help Romanov-Bobrinsky-Purishkevich to strangle the Ukraine, etc.[3]

The party tradition continued, however, to be strongly weighted against federation. Stalin in an article of March 1917 *Against Federalism* declared that the trend was everywhere towards centralization.

> Is it not clear [he concluded] that federalism in Russia does not and cannot solve the national question, that it merely confuses and complicates it with quixotic ambitions to turn back the wheel of history ?[4]

Party orthodoxy was modified only by the victory of the revolution. In the first place, the Soviet system, purporting to follow the precedent of the Paris commune and professedly based on the voluntary organization of local organs to form a central authority, was the very essence of what nineteenth-century socialist writers had meant by federalism. Secondly, federation was the one political concept which could be invoked to satisfy the aspirations of the former dependent nations of the Tsarist empire and at the same time retain them within a Soviet framework ; once the right of national self-determination had been proclaimed, federalism became an indispensable corollary — or antidote. The turning-point coincided with Lenin's *State and Revolution*, written on the eve of the October revolution. Engels

---

[1] *Ibid.* xvii, 154.   [2] *Ibid.* xvii, 90.   [3] *Ibid.* xviii, 82.
[4] Stalin, *Sochineniya*, iii, 27 ; Stalin later recanted this view (*ibid.* iii, 28-31).

in the criticism of the Erfurt programme, in which he had declared so bluntly for the " one and indivisible republic ", had none the less admitted that " in England, where four nations live on two islands ", federation would be " a step forward ". Lenin, quoting this passage, described federation as " an exception and a hindrance to development " which may yet be " a ' step forward ' in certain special conditions ". And " among these special conditions the national question appears prominently ".[1] But the discussion that followed made it clear that the issue of federal or unitary state was still for Lenin a question not of constitutional form, but of the decentralization or centralization of power; and it was significant that this qualified conversion to federation occurred in a work in which he was largely concerned with the dying away of the state.

Such was the background of the federal aspects of Soviet constitution-making. The Declaration of Rights of the Toiling and Exploited People, drafted by VTsIK and presented by way of ultimatum to the Constituent Assembly, proclaimed the Russian Soviet republic as " a federation of national Soviet republics "; and, after the dissolution of the Constituent Assembly, the third All-Russian Congress of Soviets instructed VTsIK to draft " the fundamental principles of the constitution of the Russian Federal Republic ". The use of the term was doubtless due in part to its popular appeal. It even gave encouragement to syndicalist visions of a " federation of social-economic organizations ".[2] But the position was made clear in a statement by Stalin which was published in *Pravda* on April 3 and 4, 1918, while the drafting commission was at work. The Soviet federation did not represent, like the Swiss or American federations, a union of territories divided only by geographical environment or by historical accident; it was " a union of historically distinct territories differentiated by a special way of life, as well as by their national composition ". Whereas, moreover, bourgeois federation was " a transitional stage from independence to imperialist unification ", Soviet federation represented a transition, to be achieved " with the lapse of time ", from " forced unification " under the Tsars to " the voluntary and fraternal union of the working masses of all nations and peoples of Russia ". The ultimate goal was " the

[1] Lenin, *Sochineniya*, xxi, 419.   [2] See p. 128 above.

future *socialist* unitarism ".[1]   On Stalin's motion a resolution in similar terms was adopted by the drafting commission as the basis of its work.[2]   What clearly emerged was the view of federation not as a good in itself (that would have been too much at variance with established party doctrine), but as a convenient transitional stage, necessitated by the particular conditions of the national question in Russia, to something better.   This view was confirmed by the party programme, adopted a year later, which described " a federal union of states organized on the Soviet model " as " one of the transitional forms to complete unity ".[3]

These uncertainties were reflected in the curious fact that, while the RSFSR was freely referred to as a federation, and while the word " federal " appeared in its title and in the initial chapters of the constitution devoted to general principles, the word nowhere recurred in the body of the constitution.   The extent and composition of the federation, as well as much of its constitutional machinery, were undefined.   This was easily explicable by the precarious conditions in which the constitution was drafted.   In the spring and early summer of 1918 German armies were in occupation of the former Baltic provinces, of most of White Russia and of the whole Ukraine, and had penetrated even into the northern Caucasus and into Transcaucasia, where Baku stood out as a solitary islet of Bolshevik power.   A Bolshevik Turkestan was isolated from all communication with Europe.   Siberia, where Bolshevik authority seemed at one moment to be slowly consolidating itself, was completely cut off after May 1918 by the revolt of the Czech legions, which also led to the establishment of an anti-Bolshevik government on the Volga.   In these circumstances nearly everything in the constitution necessarily remained provisional.   The Declaration of Rights of the Toiling and Exploited People had left

to the workers and peasants of each nationality the right to make an independent decision, at their own plenipotentiary congress of Soviets, whether they desire, and, if so, on what basis, to participate in the federal government and in other Soviet institutions.

[1] Stalin, *Sochineniya*, iv, 66-73.
[2] *Ibid.* iv, 79-80 ; Stalin's original draft is preserved in G. S. Gurvich, *Istoriya Sovetskoi Konstitutsii* (1923), pp. 147-148.
[3] *VKP(B) v Rezolyutsiyakh* (1941), i, 287.

The resolution of the third All-Russian Congress of Soviets on the drafting of the constitution provided that " the order of participation of individual republics and separate regions in the federal government " should be determined when the republics and regions were eventually constituted. But this had not yet occurred; and a constitution could not well be made for a federation of indeterminate or non-existent units. What was in fact created in 1918 was a Russian republic of undefined territorial extent. Room was made in the general provisions of the constitution for the incorporation in it of " autonomous regions "; and it was laid down in article 11 of the constitution that the highest organs of an autonomous region, its congress of Soviets and executive committee, would have the same rank and status as the regional congress of Soviets and executive committee of any other region, Russian or non-Russian, of the RSFSR. In other words, federation was treated in the constitution, as in the earlier writings of Lenin and Stalin, as equivalent to decentralization. It was a matter of administrative organization rather than of the essential character of the constitution. The party resolution of 1913 on the national question had failed to distinguish between " broad regional autonomy " and " democratic local self-government "; [1] their identity was still assumed in Bolshevik thought. Of specifically federal machinery, as distinct from the division of powers between central and local organs of government, the constitution of 1918 contained no trace whatever. These arrangements may have been well enough designed to secure a reasonable degree of local self-government for national groups without endangering the essential unity of the RSFSR. But they were not federal in a constitutional sense.

The issue of the federal character of the constitution of the RSFSR illustrated the nature of the gulf between the theories that lay behind it and those inspiring the constitutions of bourgeois states or federations. The very notion of a constitutional act implied in western thought a law to which the state itself was subject; this conception was incompatible with a doctrine which regarded law as a creation of the state. Most constitutions of the

[1] *VKP(B) v Rezolyut:yakh* (1941), i, 211.

western world had been based on the assumption that the power
of the state was something which required to be limited and cir-
cumscribed by legal enactment in order to prevent abuse.
Constitutions were wrung from reluctant monarchs ; federations
were formed by units determined to allow the smallest possible
encroachments on their authority by the federal government. In
bourgeois constitutions such limitations might admittedly have
some value as affording the workers a certain protection against
the bourgeois state. But no such compromises had any place in
the Soviet constitution. In Stalin's words, " it came into being
not as a result of a deal with the bourgeoisie, but as a result of a
victorious revolution ".[1] It was the expression not of any balance
or bargain between conflicting forces, but of the dictatorship of
the proletariat. The absolute character of Bolshevik theory was
represented in the phrase " the autocracy of the people " — a sort
of parody on the title of the Tsar as " autocrat " (*samoderzhavets*)
— which figured prominently in the party programme of 1903
and was long current in party circles. Every state and every
government was an instrument of the supremacy of a ruling class.
The dictatorship of the proletariat, like every other form of state,
was in Lenin's phrase " a special kind of cudgel, nothing else " ;
its purpose was to beat down and crush the exploiting classes. It
followed that the powers conferred on this state by the constitution
were in their essence unlimited, undivided and absolute.

It was a deduction from this view that the Soviet constitution
involved no recognition of " constitutional safeguards " or of
rights of individual citizens against the state. The Declaration
of Rights of the Toiling and Exploited People was not a declaration of rights in the conventional sense ; it was the announcement
of a social and economic policy. This was perfectly logical.
Marxism rejected the bourgeois view that the freedom of the
individual could be guaranteed by the non-intervention of the
state in his activities ; such freedom in conditions of class rule
remained formal and ineffective. To bring true freedom to the
workers positive action was required. Thus under the constitution
of the RSFSR freedom of conscience was secured to the workers
by the separation of church from state, and of school from church ;
freedom of opinion by assuring to the workers " all technical and

[1] Stalin, *Sochineniya*, vii, 70.

material means for the publication of newspapers, pamphlets, books and all other printed works ", and for their distribution throughout the country ; freedom of assembly by putting at the disposal of the workers " all premises suitable for holding popular meetings with equipment, lighting and heating "; access to knowledge by " full, universal and free education ". The freedom of the worker was to be asserted, not against the state, but through the action of the state. What the constitution provided was the promise and guarantee of this action. The notion of an antithesis between individual and state was the natural assumption of a class society. The interest of the individual worker was the interest of the working class as a whole ; it would have been illogical and incongruous to set him in opposition to the workers' state.

It followed also that the constitution did not recognize any formal equality of rights. No such tradition existed in Russian constitutional practice. The subjects of the Tsars had been divided into five legally established " estates ", each enjoying a different legal status.[1]   A decree of November 10/23, 1917, abolished these distinctions and created a single legal category of citizens.[2]   But so long as economic classes existed in fact, equality between individual members of unequal classes, such as was recognized in bourgeois-democratic constitutions, remained, according to Bolshevik doctrine, essentially unreal. Equality between individuals could become real only in the classless society. The purpose of the dictatorship of the proletariat was not to establish formal equality between individual members of the bourgeoisie and of the working classes but to destroy the bourgeoisie as a class. The Soviets, which were the embodiment of that dictatorship, were class organs of the workers and peasants. Only workers and peasants were recruited into the Red Army. The rights accorded by the constitution were thus logically accorded to " the toilers " or " the working class and the poor peasantry " — and to them alone. The statement of " general principles " specifically justified discrimination :

[1] These " estates " (the Russian word *soslovie* is not adequately translated by " caste ", " class " or " guild ", partaking of the character of all three) were (1) " nobility " or " gentry ", (2) clergy, (3) merchants, (4) petty bourgeoisie (shopkeepers, clerks, artisans), (5) peasantry, including those who worked as unskilled labourers in towns and factories. The urban proletariat as such had no legal existence.   [2] *Sobranie Uzakonenii, 1917-1918*, No. 3, art. 31.

In the general interest of the working class the RSFSR deprives individuals or separate groups of any privileges which may be used by them to the detriment of the socialist revolution.

Hence no validity was conceded to such principles of bourgeois democracy as " one man, one vote " ; and the franchise " ceases to be a right and is transformed into a social function of the electors ".[1]   The constitution of the RSFSR excluded from the franchise " those who employ others for the sake of profit ", " those who live on income not arising from their own labour ", " private business men " and " monks and priests ", as well as criminals and imbeciles.   The decision not to exclude professional men and intellectuals from the franchise was much contested, and was inspired, as a commentator remarks, " not by considerations of so-called social justice, and still less by sentimental motives ", but by considerations of practical utility.[2]   The discriminatory franchise remained in force until 1936.

A more complicated example of discrimination was the difference between the voting rules in town and country for the All-Russian Congress of Soviets.   In the cities the number of delegates to the congress was fixed at one for every 25,000 *electors*, in the country at one for every 125,000 *inhabitants*.   The difference had its historical origin.   The All-Russian Congress of Soviets of Workers', Soldiers' and Peasants' Deputies, which was the sovereign organ of the RSFSR, resulted from the amalgamation of the All-Russian Congress of Soviets of Peasants' Deputies with the All-Russian Congress of Soviets of Workers' and Soldiers' Deputies which took place when agreement was reached between the Bolsheviks and the Left SRs in November 1917.   It was natural that both city and rural Soviets should retain the method of reckoning which suited their conditions and to which they were accustomed — the former by number of workers belonging to the Soviet, the latter by number of inhabitants of the area covered. The only difficulty was to fix the ratio between them.   What was in fact done was to retain the figure of one delegate for 25,000

[1] G. S. Gurvich, *Istoriya Sovetskoi Konstitutsii* (1923), p. 46.
[2] *Ibid.* p. 47.   One of the earlier drafts provided for a system of voting by *curiae*, under which the votes of workers and peasants would have been weighted as against those of craftsmen, government employees, scientists, artists and specialists ;   but this refinement was abandoned in the final version (*ibid.* pp. 161-162).

electors adopted by the organizers of the first All-Russian Congress of Soviets of Workers' and Soldiers' Deputies in June 1917,[1] and to raise the figure of one delegate to 150,000 inhabitants used by the All-Russian Congress of Soviets of Peasants' Deputies to a figure of one to 125,000. The ratio of one to five thus established was defended by Steklov at the session of VTsIK which approved the constitution as giving no precedence to the towns and making their representation barely equal to that of the countryside.[2] This argument was untenable ;[3] nor was it sustained by other Soviet spokesmen. Lenin spoke of " the inequality of workers and peasants " under the constitution, and justified it by its origin in the history of the Soviets.[4] The party programme adopted in 1919 specifically noted that " our Soviet constitution " reflected the leading rôle of the urban worker in the revolution " by retaining a certain preference for the industrial proletariat in comparison with the more dispersed petty-bourgeois masses in the country ".[5] Such issues were always to be considered from the empirical standpoint, not from that of formal or abstract equality. The more highly developed class-consciousness of the urban workers and, consequently, their greater effectiveness in the struggle against the bourgeoisie entitled them to a privileged franchise in the revolutionary state.

The absolute character of state power meant that this power was not only unlimited but indivisible. Marx, in an early work, described the familiar constitutional doctrine of the " separation of powers " as the product of an age in which " the royal power, the aristocracy and bourgeoisie are struggling for supremacy ",

---

[1] *Pervyi Vserossiiskii S"ezd Sovetov* (1930), i, xxiii-xxiv.

[2] *Pyatyi Vserossiiskii S"ezd Sovetov* (1918), p. 193.

[3] Since 51 per cent of the population were adults over twenty, the correct ratio of " electors " to " inhabitants " should *prima facie* have been approximately one to two : this was the ratio adopted for the elections to the Constituent Assembly in assigning seats to civilian constituencies on the basis of population and to army and fleet constituencies on the basis of the number of electors (*Proekt Polozheniya o Vyborakh v Uchreditel'noe Sobranie* (1917), ii, 33-36). Even allowing for the point made by Steklov that the percentage of adults was higher in the towns than in the country, the arithmetically correct ratio could not have been lower than two to five : the British Labour Delegation of 1920 was told that it was one to three (*British Labour Delegation to Russia, 1920 : Report* (1920), p. 128).

[4] Lenin, *Sochineniya*, xxiv, 146.

[5] *VKP(B) v Rezolyutsiyakh* (1941), i, 286.

elevated into an " eternal law ".[1] He later described Louis Bonaparte's *coup d'état* of December 2, 1851, as " a victory of the executive over the legislative power " in the sense that it was the victory of a ruling clique over the representative organ of the bourgeoisie as a whole.[2] But such distinctions would be swept away in a socialist revolution. Marx praised the Paris commune for having been " not a parliamentary but a working corporation which at one and the same time legislated and executed the laws ".[3] Lenin regarded the separation of executive from legislative as a specific characteristic of parliamentarianism, their fusion as a specific merit of the Soviet system.[4] Under the dictatorship of the proletariat the organs of state power were merely different instruments wielded by or on behalf of the workers for the achievement of the same purpose. The issue was stated at the time of the drafting of the constitution by Reisner, the spokesman of the People's Commissariat of Justice :

> The separation of powers into legislative, executive and judicial . . . corresponds to the structure of the bourgeois state where the principal task is the balancing of the main political forces, i.e. the possessing classes on the one hand and the toiling masses on the other. Being inevitably by its nature a compromise between exploiters and exploited, the bourgeois state has to balance and divide power. . . .
> The Russian socialist republic has no interest in any division or balancing of political forces for the simple reason that it bases itself on the domination of one all-embracing political force, i.e. the Russian proletariat and the peasant masses. This political force is engaged in the realization of a single end, the establishment of a socialist order, and this heroic struggle requires unity and concentration of power rather than division.[5]

It was therefore logical that the constitution of the RSFSR should recognize no separation of legislative and executive functions.

---

[1] *Karl Marx-Friedrich Engels: Historisch-Kritische Gesamtausgabe*, 1er Teil, v, 36.

[2] Marx i Engels, *Sochineniya*, viii, 403.

[3] *Ibid.* xiii, ii, 314.

[4] Lenin, *Sochineniya*, xxi, 258 ; xxii, 371. The same idea appears in the party programme of 1919, which describes the division between legislative and executive power as one of the " negative sides of parliamentarianism " (*VKP(B) v Rezolyutsiyakh* (1941), i, 285).

[5] Quoted in Bunyan and Fisher, *The Bolshevik Revolution, 1917-1918* (Stanford, 1934), p. 578.

The favourite comparison of VTsIK with Parliament and of Sovnarkom with the Cabinet ignores the absence of any distinction, either in the terms or in the working of the constitution, between the function of the two bodies, which were equally legislative and executive : indeed, there was logic in a proposal made during the discussions on the constitution for the fusion of the two bodies.[1] Equally little justification could be found in constitutional theory for a separate and independent judiciary as for a separate and independent executive. The constitution of the RSFSR made no specific provision at all for the exercise of the judicial function ; and the direct organization and control of the judiciary by the People's Commissariat of Justice clearly marked its subordination to the executive.[2] Every function of government was one; it should be exercised for a single purpose by a single undivided authority.

The definitions which appeared in the constitution of the competence of the All-Russian Congress of Soviets, VTsIK and Sovnarkom respectively, thus represented, in the main, differences not of function, but of rank in the hierarchy. The functions of the All-Russian Congress and of VTsIK were defined jointly in Article 49 of the constitution without any general attempt to distinguish between them. Two functions only—" the establishing, supplementing and modifying of the fundamental elements of the Soviet constitution " and " the ratification of peace treaties " — were reserved by Article 51 for the All-Russian Congress to the exclusion of VTsIK. Since, however, Article 49 had already conferred on VTsIK power to deal with " the confirmation, modification and supplementing of the constitution ", the first of these exceptions would seem to have turned on the delicate question which parts of the " fundamental law " of the RSFSR were " fundamental elements " and which were not. The exception made for the ratification of treaties probably followed the precedent of March 1918, when an extraordinary All-Russian

---

[1] It was originally made by Latsis in April 1918 (G. S. Gurvich, *Istoriya Sovetskoi Konstitutsii* (1923), p. 73) and repeated by Osinsky at the eighth party congress in 1919 (*Vos'moi S"ezd RKP(B)* (1933), p. 197).

[2] Reisner in the report already quoted observed that the independence of judges in bourgeois states merely made them " narrower and more intolerant defenders of the dominant class " (Bunyan and Fisher, *The Bolshevik Revolution, 1917–1918* (Stanford, 1934), p. 578).

Congress of Soviets was summoned to ratify the treaty of Brest-Litovsk. But, broadly speaking, the result of the constitution was to confer on VTsIK the exercise of all powers except when the large and unwieldy sovereign congress was actually in session.[1]

The minor frictions between the All-Russian Congress and VTsIK reflected in these constitutional niceties were of little moment compared with the major jealousies between VTsIK and Sovnarkom. According to a contemporary commentator, the first half of 1918 was " a time of very noticeable friction between the central institutions of the state, and especially between VTsIK and Sovnarkom ", and "the mutual relation of these two supreme institutions was moving, not without some internal struggle, towards the *de facto* predominance of Sovnarkom in domestic and foreign policy ".[2] When Sovnarkom first conferred legislative powers on itself by decree of October 30/November 12, 1917, it admitted two qualifications. The powers were valid only " from now on until the convocation of the Constituent Assembly "; and VTsIK had the right to " defer, modify or annul " any enactment of Sovnarkom.[3] Within a week of the passing of this decree the SRs were protesting in VTsIK against the issue of decrees by Sovnarkom without previous submission to VTsIK. After a debate in which both Lenin and Trotsky took part, a resolution recognizing the right of Sovnarkom to issue urgent decrees " without previous discussion by VTsIK " was carried by a narrow majority of 29 to 23.[4] But the same complaint was repeated at almost every meeting of VTsIK in November and December 1917. Thereafter the practice gradually acquired the force of habit ; and the gathering crisis and the resulting drive for centralized authority, which multiplied the number of enactments and intensified the need for prompt decision and action, worked powerfully on the side of the smaller organ. But the usurpation of authority by Sovnarkom was a major grievance of

[1] Sverdlov at the fifth All-Russian Congress of Soviets, referring to the abolition of the death penalty by decree of the second All-Russian Congress, went so far as to argue that VTsIK, being " the supreme organ or supreme power between congresses ", could not only repeal but override decrees of the congress (*Pyatyi Vserossiiskii S"ezd Sovetov* (1918), p. 49).

[2] G. S. Gurvich, *Istoriya Sovetskoi Konstitutsii* (1923), p. 67.

[3] *Sobranie Uzakonenii, 1917-1918*, No. 1 (2nd ed.), art. 12.

[4] *Protokoly Zasedanii VTsIK 2 Sozyva* (1918), pp. 28-32 ; Lenin, *Sochineniya*, xxii, 45-46 ; Trotsky, *Sochineniya*, iii, ii, 106-108.

the Left SRs, and even of some Bolsheviks, when the constitution was being drafted.

The text of the constitution, while it reflected this dispute, did little or nothing to settle it. By article 31, momentarily ignoring the All-Russian Congress, it made VTsIK " the supreme legislative, administrative and controlling organ of the RSFSR ", and by article 32 gave it " general direction of the Workers' and Peasants' Government and of all government organs throughout the country ". Under articles 37 and 38 Sovnarkom " has general direction of the affairs of the RSFSR " and " issues decrees, orders and instructions and takes all general measures necessary to secure prompt and orderly administration ". Under articles 40 and 41 all decisions " of general political significance " were to be submitted to VTsIK " for examination and ratification ", and VTsIK retained the right to " annul or suspend " any order of Sovnarkom. But these formal stipulations were mitigated by a " note " which allowed " measures of extreme urgency " to be " put into force on the sole authority of Sovnarkom ". The constitution, in effect, changed nothing, and left relations between the three main organs of central power to be hammered out in the light of experience. The danger of a deadlock, which the terms of the constitution itself seemed to invite, was removed by the single authority behind the constitution : the authority of the ruling party.

So acute an observer of political realities as Lenin could not fail to see in the concentration of power at the centre a threat to the principle of authority emanating " from below " and an encouragement to the endemic evil of bureaucracy. An attempt was made in the constitution to conjure this evil by attaching to each of the People's Commissars a " collegium " of five persons, apparently in the capacity of lay assessors, who had a right of appeal to Sovnarkom or to VTsIK against his decisions. But, though this arrangement escaped the universal discredit which rapidly overtook the same system as applied to industrial management, it proved of little practical significance. Lenin did not really put his faith in such safeguards. What he believed was that the centralization of authority carried with it its own antidote. The effect of the fusion of legislative and executive functions would mean the disappearance of the professional administrator as differentiated and divorced from the elected legislator. The advantage of the fusion would be " to unite in the persons of the elected representatives of the people both legislative and executive functions " — a combination which was the essence of " direct democracy ".[1] The revised party programme of 1919 included among " the negative sides of parliamentarianism " not only " the separation of the legislative and executive powers ", but " the divorce of representative institutions from the masses ". The Soviets seemed to Lenin to embody the notion of the masses of workers and peasants legislating for themselves, carrying out their own decisions, and administering their own affairs ; and this highly idealized picture of " direct democracy " helped to mask the increasingly stubborn reality of an immense accretion of bureaucratic power at the centre. But here, too, the ultimate sanction rested with the party, whose authority could always be invoked to remedy constitutional shortcomings.

The practical working of a constitution commonly depends not only on the principles inspiring its framers or on the rules laid down by them, but even more on the political conditions in which it is brought into operation. The changes which occurred in Soviet Russia during the preparation of the constitution were the continuation of a process which had been at work since the inception of the régime. But they were significant and decisive. When the main principles of the future constitution were enunciated by the third All-Russian Congress of Soviets after the dispersal of the Constituent Assembly in January 1918, the government was a coalition of Bolsheviks and Left SRs. When the drafting commission met in April, the Left SRs, though they had left the government, remained in the Soviets and were represented in the commission. When the fifth All-Russian Congress of Soviets finally approved the constitution in July 1918, the Left SRs had just been expelled and outlawed and the civil war had begun. The growth of the one-party state and the impact of the civil war, which for the next two years put the survival of the republic in almost daily jeopardy, destroyed the optimistic foundations on which the constitution had been built, and threw into the shade most of the controversies which had occupied the drafting commission. The needs of the army in the field and of security at

[1] Lenin, *Sochineniya*, xxi, 258.

home created an atmosphere inimical to constitutional niceties. The experience of much early Soviet legislation revealed a broad gulf between idealistic principles and the stern realities of practice. If this was also true of the constitution of the RSFSR, the circumstances of its birth went far to explain the rift.

The draft constitution was examined on July 3, 1918, by the central committee of the party, which made a few minor amendments. On Lenin's proposal the Declaration of Rights of the Toiling and Exploited People was incorporated in the constitution as a preamble.[1] This done, the draft was presented to the fifth All-Russian Congress of Soviets. The congress was interrupted for three days by the serious crisis arising from the murder of the German ambassador, Mirbach. Then, on July 10, 1918, it listened to an exposition of the new constitution by Steklov and endorsed it unanimously.[2] It came into force on its official publication in *Izvestiya* of July 19, 1918, as the " Constitution (Fundamental Law) of the Russian Socialist Federal Soviet Republic ".

[1] G. S. Gurvich, *Istoriya Sovetskoi Konstitutsii* (1923), pp. 90-91 ; Trotsky, *O Lenine* (n.d. [1924]), pp. 113-114, also records this intervention.
[2] *Pyatyi Vserossiiskii S"ezd Sovetov* (1918), pp. 183-195.

CHAPTER 7

CONSOLIDATING THE DICTATORSHIP

THE term "dictatorship of the proletariat "[1] applied by the Bolsheviks to the régime established by them in Russia after the October revolution, carried no specific constitutional implications. It defined the ruling class, but was neutral about the form of government through which that class exercised power. There was no opposition in this sense between dictatorship and representative government : the " dictatorship of the bourgeoisie ", which was the antithesis of the dictatorship of the proletariat, was generally exercised through the medium of representative government. The emotional overtones of the word " dictatorship " as associated with the rule of the few or of one man were absent from the minds of Marxists who used the phrase. On the contrary, the dictatorship of the proletariat would be the first régime in history in which power would be exercised by the class constituting a majority of the population — a condition to be satisfied in Russia by drawing the mass of the peasantry into alliance with the industrial proletariat. Moreover, since the dictatorship of the proletariat was the rule of the vast majority, it would require, once the bourgeoisie was struck down, less compulsion to maintain it than any previous order of society. Far from being a rule of violence, it would pave the way for the disappearance of the use of violence as a social sanction, i.e. for the dying away of the state.

Nothing in the first days of the revolution shattered this idealistic and optimistic mood. The almost effortless success of the Petrograd coup of October 25, 1917, seemed to show that it

---

[1] Its origin is uncertain. In 1849 Marx described Blanqui's " revolutionary socialism " as " a class dictatorship of the proletariat " (Marx i Engels, *Sochineniya*, viii, 81) ; in 1852 he adopted the term himself (see p. 235 below).

indeed had behind it the vast majority of the population.[1] The boast of the Bolsheviks that the revolution itself cost remarkably few lives, and that most of these were lost in attempts by their opponents to wrest the victory from them when it had already been won, was justified. By one of those acts of generosity which often attend the first hours of a revolution, the young officer cadets captured at the Winter Palace were allowed to go free on promising not to " take up arms against the people any more ".[2] Krasnov, the " white " general who helped Kerensky to organize his futile counter-offensive from Gatchina and was captured there, was released on parole — which he broke a few weeks later to participate in the civil war in the south; and that this clemency was no accidental freak is shown by a statement of Lenin ten days after the Bolshevik victory :

> We are reproached with using terror. But such terror as was used by the French revolutionaries who guillotined un-armed people we do not use and, I hope, shall not use. . . . When we have made arrests we have said : " We will let you go if you will sign a paper promising not to commit acts of sabotage ". And such signatures are given.[3]

The members of the Provisional Government who had been arrested and lodged in Peter-and-Paul fortress on the day of the revolution were quickly released and subjected only to a nominal form of supervision, which did not prevent them from conspiring actively against the new régime. Capital levies or forced loans extracted more or less at haphazard from the bourgeoisie, or such incidents as that of the threat to send fifteen wealthy Kharkov capitalists down the Donetz mines if they did not provide a million rubles to pay the Kharkov workers,[4] were evidence not so much of calculated ferocity as of the dilemma of inexperienced and determined men trying to create a workable administrative machine out of non-existent or recalcitrant material. In the desperate chaos of the first weeks of the revolution the new rulers

---

[1] In Moscow fairly serious resistance, mainly from the young officers' training corps, continued for a week ; almost everywhere else the transfer of power to the Bolsheviks, though delayed in the remoter centres for some weeks, took place peacefully.

[2] John Reed, *Ten Days that Shook the World* (N.Y., 1919), p. 101.

[3] Lenin, *Sochineniya*, xxii, 50.

[4] Antonov-Ovseenko, *Vospominaniya Grazhdanskoi Voiny* (1924), i, 178-179.

had little time for concerted action or even for consistent thinking and planning; almost every step taken by them was either a reaction to some pressing emergency or a reprisal for some action or threatened action against them.[1] In seeking to ride the storm they were themselves driven before it. Many cases of mob violence occurred in the cities and throughout the country. Many brutalities and atrocities were committed by revolutionaries[2] as well as by their adversaries. But no regular executions either by summary judgment or by normal judicial process appear to have taken place in the first three months of the régime. The first legislative act of the second All-Russian Congress of Soviets on the day after the revolution had been to abolish the death penalty at the front, where it had been restored by Kerensky in September 1917 under military pressure after its total abolition at the time of the February revolution.[3] The revolutionary tradition of opposition to the death sentence weakened and collapsed only after the outbreak of the civil war and open insurrection against the Soviet régime.[4]

[1] This was particularly true of the establishment of economic controls, which will be discussed in Part IV. In another sphere, even so obvious a measure as the separation of church from state was not announced till after Archbishop Tikhon had launched an anathema against the régime (*Sobranie Uzakonenii, 1917-1918*, No. 18, art. 263; A. I. Vvedensky, *Tserkov' i Gosudarstvo* (1923), pp. 114-116); even then, according to J. Sadoul, *Notes sur la Révolution Bolchevique* (1919), p. 222, it was opposed by many commissars for fear that " a religious war might be added to foreign war and civil war ".

[2] The most notorious of these, the murder of two former Kadet ministers while lying in hospital on January 7/20, 1918, was strongly condemned in the official press (Bunyan and Fisher, *The Bolshevik Revolution, 1917-1918* (Stanford, 1934), pp. 386-387). The sailors had an unenviable notoriety for the perpetration of atrocities in the revolution : it was the sailors of the Black Sea fleet who, having seized Sevastopol in February 1918, carried out a three-day massacre of its bourgeois population. But there are also plenty of records of military units getting out of hand. The reputation of the various " white " forces stood no higher : the Cossacks, including many of the Cossack leaders, were particularly feared for their cruelty.

[3] *Sobranie Uzakonenii, 1917-1918*, No. 1 (2nd ed.), art. 4.

[4] A curious essay might be written on the attitude of the Russian revolution to capital punishment. Russian prejudice against the infliction of the death sentence by judicial process was deep-rooted ; it had a religious origin and was reinforced by the teachings of western eighteenth-century writers, who, through Catherine II and her successors, left their mark on Russian political thought, though rarely on Russian political institutions. Down to the middle of the nineteenth century the prejudice was commonly circumvented by sentences to the knout or, in the case of mutinous soldiers, to running the gauntlet, which were in effect, but not in form, death sentences. When the jury system was

It would, however, be an error of a different order to suggest that the measures of repression eventually applied for the defence of the victorious revolution were forced on reluctant Bolshevik leaders in defiance of their cherished convictions. The principle of terror was embedded in the revolutionary tradition. Robespierre had dismissed, in words which Lenin would have echoed, the ordinary processes of law as insufficient to defend a revolution :

> Is it with the criminal code in one's hand that one must judge the salutary precautions demanded by the public safety in times of crisis brought about by the very impotence of the laws ?

And again :

> If the attribute of popular government in peace is virtue, the attribute of popular government in revolution is at one and the same time *virtue and terror*, virtue without which terror is fatal, terror without which virtue is impotent. The terror is nothing but justice, prompt, severe, inflexible ; it is thus an emanation of virtue.[1]

established in Russia in the 1860s, juries were notoriously reluctant to bring in verdicts which would entail the death sentence. Russian terrorist groups, down to and including the SRs, found no inconsistency in advocating assassination as a political weapon and, at the same time, denouncing capital punishment as a judicial institution. The Bolsheviks at first stoutly rejected this tradition. They were opposed to political assassination ; but at the second congress of the Russian Social-Democratic Party in 1903 a proposal to include the abolition of the death penalty in the party programme was rejected by a large majority amid cries of " And for Nicholas II ? " (*Vtoroi S"ezd RSDRP* (1932), pp. 193-194). Nevertheless as time went on many Russian social-democrats came to be affected by the same western nineteenth-century liberal humanitarianism which influenced the social-democratic and labour parties of western Europe : the Second International at its congress at Copenhagen in 1910 had unanimously condemned capital punishment. The February revolution in Russia was permeated with western liberal and social-democratic ideas ; and opposition to capital punishment became a leading plank in its programme. The restoration of the death penalty at the front in September 1917 was the occasion of Kerensky's famous retort to critics at the " democratic conference " that it would be time to condemn him when a death sentence was actually carried out. The Soviet criminal code of 1922 prescribed the death penalty for counter-revolutionary offences without naming it : it was referred to simply as " the highest measure of punishment ".

[1] *Discours et Rapports de Robespierre*, ed. C. Vellay (1908), pp. 197, 332. Lenin said in 1920 to the French communist Frossard : " A Frenchman has nothing to renounce in the Russian revolution, which in its methods and in its procedure recommences the French revolution " (*Humanité*, September 10, 1920). Compare Jefferson's defence of the terror : " In the struggle which was necessary

In the autumn of 1848 Marx declared that, after " the canni-
balism of the counter-revolution ", there was " only one means
to *curtail*, simplify and localize the bloody agony of the old society
and the bloody birth-pangs of the new, only one means — the
revolutionary terror ; " [1] and later he paid tribute to Hungary as
the first nation since 1793 which dared " to meet the cowardly
rage of the counter-revolution with revolutionary passion, the
terreur blanche with the *terreur rouge* ".[2] Bourgeois society, " however little heroic it may now appear ", had in its day " needed
heroism, self-sacrifice, terror, civil war and bloody battle-fields
to bring it into the world ".[3] In the second half of the nineteenth
century the growth of liberal humanitarian sentiment spread to
large sectors of the working class, particularly in England and
Germany ; traces of it can be found in the later writings of
Engels.[4] The programme of the German Communist Party
drafted by Rosa Luxemburg in December 1918 specifically
rejected terror :

> In bourgeois revolutions the shedding of blood, terror and
> political murder were the indispensable weapon of the rising
> classes. The proletarian revolution needs for its purposes no
> terror, it hates and abominates murder.[5]

But in Russia, at any rate, the doctrine of revolutionary terror
was never denied by any revolutionary party. The controversy

many guilty persons fell without the forms of trial, and, with them, some innocent.
These I deplore as much as anybody and shall deplore some of them to the day
of my death. But I deplore them as I should have done had they fallen in
battle. It was necessary to use the arm of the people, a machine not quite so
blind as balls and bombs, but blind to a certain degree " (*The Writings of
Thomas Jefferson*, ed. P. L. Ford (N.Y.), vi (1895), 153-154).

[1] *Karl Marx-Friedrich Engels : Historisch-Kritische Gesamtausgabe*, 1ᵉʳ Teil,
vii, 423.

[2] Marx i Engels, *Sochineniya*, vii, 271.   [3] *Ibid.* viii, 324.

[4] The best example of this trend of thought in the second generation of
German social-democracy was Kautsky, whose *Terrorismus und Kommunismus :
ein Beitrag zur Naturgeschichte der Revolution* (1919) was a diatribe against
the Bolshevik terror. Kautsky quoted passages from the later Engels, but
omitted the earlier passage in which Engels recorded with satisfaction that
" during the short period of the French revolution in which the proletariat was
at the helm of the state under the rule of the Mountain, it carried out its policy
by all means at its disposal, including grapeshot and the guillotine " (*Karl Marx-
Friedrich Engels : Historisch-Kritische Gesamtausgabe*, 1ᵉʳ Teil, vi, 348).

[5] *Bericht über den Gründungsparteitag der Kommunistischen Partei Deutsch-
lands (Spartakusbund)* (n.d. [1919]), p. 52.

which raged between Russian social-democrats and Russian social-revolutionaries on the subject turned not on the principle of terror but on the expediency of the assassination of individuals as a political weapon. The Mensheviks, owing in part to their disbelief in the immediate practicability of a proletarian revolution and in part to their closer affiliations with western social-democrats, were perhaps less predisposed than the Bolsheviks to the use of terror. After 1918, when the Bolsheviks began for the first time to use this weapon against other socialist parties, the Mensheviks, in common with the social-democratic parties of western Europe, were among its most vigorous and unsparing critics.

Reared in the Jacobin and Marxist schools of revolution, Lenin accepted the terror in principle, though in common with all Marxists he condemned as futile isolated terrorist acts :

> In principle [he wrote in 1901] we have never renounced terror and cannot renounce it. This is one of those military actions which may be completely advantageous and even essential at a certain moment of the battle in a certain situation of the army and in certain conditions. But the gist of the matter is that terror at the present time is applied not as one of the operations of an army in the field, closely connected and co-ordinated with the whole plan of the struggle, but as an independent method of individual attack divorced from any army.[1]

Two months before the October revolution he warned his followers that " any kind of revolutionary government could scarcely dispense with the death penalty as applied to *exploiters* (i.e. land-owners and capitalists) ", and reminded them that " the great bourgeois revolutionaries of France 125 years ago made their revolution great by means of the *terror* ".[2] In conformity with this view Lenin is said to have expressed consternation when the second All-Russian Congress of Soviets, on the motion of Kamenev, hastily abolished the death penalty at the front.[3] Lenin had his utopian moments. But he had a more realistic appreciation than Kamenev of what revolution meant, though some half-jesting remarks on the subject attributed to him scarcely carry the weight that has been placed on them.[4]

[1] Lenin, *Sochineniya*, iv, 108.   [2] *Ibid.* xxi, 173, 186.
[3] L. Trotsky, *O Lenine* (n.d. [1924]), p. 101.
[4] The following *boutade* is said to date from 1918 : " We'll ask the man Where do you stand on the question of the revolution? Are you for it or

The most militant pronouncements of the first weeks of the revolution came from Trotsky, whose role in the military-revolutionary committee and in the military organization of the October coup gave him a special title to speak. It was Trotsky who, after the suppression of the revolt of military cadets on the morrow of the revolution, issued a fierce public warning :

> We hold the cadets as prisoners and hostages. If our men fall into the hands of the enemy, let him know that for every worker and for every soldier we shall demand five cadets. . . . They thought that we should be passive, but we showed them that we could be merciless when it is a question of defending the conquests of the revolution.[1]

" We shall not enter into the kingdom of socialism in white gloves on a polished floor ", he told the All-Russian Congress of Peasants' Deputies ; [2] and on the occasion of the outlawry of the Kadet party he issued another warning :

> At the time of the French revolution more honest men than the Kadets were guillotined by the Jacobins for opposing the people. We have not executed anyone and do not intend to, but there are moments when the fury of the people is hard to control.[3]

It was Trotsky who, challenged in VTsIK on arrests and searches carried out by the new régime, retorted that " demands to forego all repressions at a time of civil war are demands to abandon the civil war ".[4] After the suppression of the Kadet party he added still more ominously :

> You protest against the mild terror which we are directing against our class enemies. But you should know that not later

against it ? ' If he is against it, we'll stand him up against the wall. If he is for it, we'll welcome him in our midst to work with us " (V. Adoratsky, *Vospominaniya o Lenine* (1939), pp. 66-67). After the revolution he asked in the manner of Henry II : " Is it impossible to find among us a Fouquier-Tinville to tame our wild counter-revolutionaries ? " (V. Bonch-Bruevich, *Na Boevykh Postakh Fevral'skoi i Oktyabr'skoi Revolyutsii* (1930), p. 195).

[1] *Izvestiya*, October 30/November 12, 1917, quoted in Bunyan and Fisher, *The Bolshevik Revolution, 1917-1918* (Stanford, 1934), p. 153.

[2] Trotsky, *Sochineniya*, iii, ii, 202.

[3] *Izvestiya*, December 6/19, 1917.

[4] *Protokoly Zasedanii VTsIK 2 Sozyva* (1918), p. 24. Trotsky developed this argument later in his polemic against Kautsky (*Terrorizm i Kommunizm* (1920), pp. 60-61).

than a month from now the terror will assume very violent forms after the example of the great French revolutionaries. The guillotine will be ready for our enemies and not merely the jail.[1]

Within a week of this speech, the All-Russian Cheka came into being. It was the offspring of the military-revolutionary committee of the Petrograd Soviet which had organized the October revolution. After victory had been won, the committee was transformed into a committee of VTsIK and remained in charge of various operations designed to consolidate the victory and to combat counter-revolution, including such abuses as "sabotage, concealment of supplies, deliberate holding up of cargoes, etc.".[2] Among its duties was the examination of suspects arrested on charges of counter-revolutionary activities ; and to deal with this it set up a special section under Dzerzhinsky, who, being military commandant of Smolny, was concerned with questions of security.[3] When the military-revolutionary committee was finally dissolved this section remained, and, by a decree of Sovnarkom of December 7/20, 1917, was reorganized as "the All-Russian Extraordinary Commission" (Cheka for short) for the purpose of "combating counter-revolution and sabotage".[4] The commission was composed of eight members under the presidency of Dzerzhinsky.[5] One of its first acts was to issue a circular to local Soviets, apprising them of its establishment, asking them to "send to it all information about organizations and persons whose activity is directed against the revolution and popular authority ",

---

[1] Quoted in Bunyan and Fisher, *The Bolshevik Revolution, 1917–1918* (Stanford, 1934), p. 362, from a SR newspaper: the speech does not appear in the records of VTsIK, where it is stated to have been delivered.

[2] These last attributes were added by an order of Sovnarkom of November 12/25, 1917 (Lenin, *Sochineniya*, xxii, 78).

[3] These activities are described by Joffe in an article in *Kommunisticheskii Internatsional*, No. 6, October 1919, cols. 777-782 : he and Uritsky were delegates on the committee from the central committee of the party. The account in *The History of the Civil War in the USSR*, ii (Engl. transl. 1947), 599-601, is based on unpublished official sources.

[4] The decree seems to have been kept secret and was published for the first time in *Pravda*, December 18, 1927, quoted in Bunyan and Fisher, *The Bolshevik Revolution, 1917–1918* (Stanford, 1934), pp. 297-298.

[5] M. Latsis, *Chrezvychainye Komissii po Bor'be s Kontrrevolyutsiei* (1921), p. 8.

and suggesting that they should create similar local commissions.[1]
A few days later a further decree created a revolutionary tribunal
to try those " who organize uprisings against the authority of the
Workers' and Peasants' Government, who actively oppose it or
do not obey it, or who call on others to oppose or disobey it ", as
well as civil servants guilty of sabotage or destruction or concealment of public property : the tribunal was to fix penalties in
accordance with " the circumstances of the case and the dictates
of the revolutionary conscience ".[2]

At the critical moment of a hard-fought struggle the establishment of these organs can hardly be regarded as unusual.
Within six weeks of the revolution Cossack armies and other
" white " forces were already mustering in south-eastern Russia ;
the Ukraine, egged on by French and British promises, was in a
state of all but open hostilities against the Soviet power ; the
Germans, in spite of the armistice, were a standing threat in the
west. The military danger made it essential to bring order out
of chaos at home. The first application of forced labour was to
bourgeois men and women sent to dig trenches for the defence
of the capital against the Germans. The three abuses against
which the Cheka turned its first energies were, according to one
of its members, the sabotage of administration by the bourgeoisie,
destruction and rioting by drunken mobs (the so-called " drunken
pogroms "), and banditry " under the flag of anarchism ".[3] Lenin
at this time reserved his fiercest anathemas for speculators and
wreckers on the economic front. He did not, it is true, publish
an article, written in January 1918 and afterwards found among
his papers, in which he advocated among other measures " putting
in prison ten rich men, a dozen swindlers and half-a-dozen workers
who keep out of the way of work ", and " shooting on the spot one
out of every ten found guilty of idling ".[4] But shortly afterwards,
in the struggle against hoarding of food, he declared that " until
we apply the terror — shooting on the spot — to speculators, we

[1] *Izvestiya*, No. 252 of December 15/28, 1917, quoted in *Revolutsiya 1917
goda*, vi (ed. I. N. Lyubimov, 1930), 350. Strictly speaking, the local commission was the Che-ka, the central body the Ve-Che-Ka (All-Russian Extraordinary Commission) ; but the abbreviation Cheka was commonly applied to
central or local organs indifferently.
[2] *Sobranie Uzakonenii, 1917–1918*, No. 12, art. 170.
[3] *Proletarskaya Revolyutsiya*, No. 10 (33), 1924, pp. 7-8.
[4] Lenin, *Sochineniya*, xxii, 166-167.

shall achieve nothing ";[1] and three months later he was still demanding " the arrest and *shooting* of takers of bribes, swindlers, etc." and arguing that there will be no famine in Russia if stocks are controlled and " any breach of the rules laid down is followed by the harshest punishment ".[2]

The development of the Cheka was a gradual and largely unpremeditated process. It grew out of a series of emergencies. When the Germans at Brest-Litovsk denounced the armistice and resumed their advance, the famous proclamation of February 22, 1918, declaring " the socialist fatherland in danger " was followed by an order from the Cheka to all local Soviets to " seek out, arrest and shoot immediately " all enemy agents, counter-revolutionary agitators and speculators.[3] At this time the total headquarters staff of the Cheka did not exceed 120 ;[4] and the degree of organization of the local commissions was, like everything else in these early days, largely a matter of chance. It was the transfer of the seat of government from Petrograd to Moscow which first conferred on the Cheka the attributes of a large and independent department of state. Dzerzhinsky, who, as chief security officer, was in charge of the move, set up his own headquarters in Moscow, not in the Kremlin, but in the premises of a large insurance company on Lubyanka Square, and established within it an " inner prison " for suspects. Thus equipped the Cheka quickly found work. Hitherto the régime had been saved by a confusion and lack of cohesion which afflicted its opponents even more than itself : counter-revolutionary organization did not yet exist. But the picture was soon to change. The Left SRs had voted in the fourth All-Russian Congress of Soviets against the ratification of the Brest-Litovsk treaty, and, when it was carried against them, withdrew their members from Sovnarkom.[5] One-party government was thus restored ; and though the Left SRs remained in

[1] Lenin, *Sochineniya*, xxii, 243.   [2] *Ibid.* xxii, 449, 493.

[3] *Pravda*, February 23, 1918, quoted in Bunyan and Fisher, *The Bolshevik Revolution, 1917–1918* (Stanford, 1934), p. 576.

[4] *Proletarskaya Revolyutsiya*, No. 10 (33), 1924, p. 11. In 1920 the vice-president of the Cheka told the British Labour delegation that at that time it had " throughout the country a staff of 4500 workers assisted by every member of the party who considers it a duty to inform the commission of any acts inimical to the government " (*British Labour Delegation to Russia, 1920: Report* (1920), p. 55).

[5] *Chetvertyi Chrezvychainyi Vserossiiskii S"ezd Sovetov* (1920), pp. 56-57.

the Soviets and in VTsIK, their loyalty was henceforth in doubt. In April 1918 foreign intervention began with the Japanese landing at Vladivostok, and provided a hope and rallying-point for all elements in Russia itself which were opposed to the régime. In the spring and summer of 1918 Moscow became a focus round which allied and German agents, fragmentary groups of the Right and Centre, and the surviving parties of the Left all wove their several, or sometimes joint, plots and intrigues against the Soviet Government.[1]

The first concerted action of the Cheka was taken against the anarchists — a name which covered sincere idealists whose philosophy found no outlet in action, as well as organized gangs whose political creed was little more than a cover for hooliganism. On the night of April 11-12, 1918, known anarchist centres in Moscow were surrounded by Cheka agents and Soviet troops, and called on to surrender arms in their possession; resistance occurred in a few places and was crushed with force. Some 600 persons were arrested, of whom one-quarter were immediately released. The offenders were branded not as anarchists but as " criminal elements ".[2] Emboldened by the prospect of allied intervention, the Right SRs at their party conference in Moscow in May 1918 openly advocated a policy designed " to overthrow the Bolshevik dictatorship and to establish a government based on universal suffrage and willing to accept allied assistance in the war against

[1] A sidelight on less topical preoccupations of the Cheka in the summer of 1918 is thrown by the Ukrainian anarchist Makhno, himself formerly a political prisoner : " The Cheka investigating commission of former political inmates of the Moscow prison applied to all former inmates of the prison with a request for any information about tyrannical supervisors. These were then arrested by the order of the Cheka and were at that moment under examination " (N. Makhno, *Pod Udarami Kontrrevolyutsii* (Paris, 1936), pp. 113-115).

[2] Reports of the action against the anarchists are collected in Bunyan and Fisher, *The Bolshevik Revolution, 1917-1918* (Stanford, 1934), pp. 582-586 ; see also R. H. Bruce Lockhart, *Memoirs of a British Agent* (1932), pp. 258-259, where the coup is described as a " first step towards the establishment of discipline " ; and J. Sadoul, *Notes sur la Révolution Bolchevique* (1919), pp. 275-276, where the "anarchist masses " are said to have been " recruited from the dregs of the population " and encouraged by the " reactionaries ". According to a statement by Dzerzhinsky in *Izvestiya*, April 16, 1918, not more than one per cent of those arrested were " ideological anarchists ". The official case was stated in VTsIK by a spokesman of the Cheka, who was himself not a Bolshevik but a Left SR, in reply to an interpellation (*Protokoly Zasedanii VTsIK 4ro Sozyva* (1920), pp. 153-156).

Germany " [1]   The Mensheviks, who lacked the SR tradition of conspiracy and violent action, temporized. Since December 1917 the party had been torn by internal dissensions. The old " defencists " led by Potresov had seceded, leaving two groups of " internationalists " headed respectively by Martov and Dan to reach an uneasy compromise. Their proceedings reflected the embarrassments of attempting at one and the same time to condemn the so-called " German orientation " of the Bolsheviks (the legacy of Menshevik opposition to Brest-Litovsk) and to reject the " Anglo-French orientation " which was the sole effective basis of an anti-Bolshevik policy; and their resolution was uncompromising only on one point — their hostility to the régime.[2] Their inconsistencies did not save them. By a decree of June 14, 1918, VTsIK excluded both Right SRs and Mensheviks from its ranks on the ground of their association with " notorious counter-revolutionaries " seeking to " organize armed attacks against the workers and peasants ", and recommended all Soviets to exclude them, thereby virtually eliminating them from participation in the governmental machine.[3]

This step left only two major parties in effective existence : the Bolsheviks themselves and the Left SRs, formerly, though since Brest-Litovsk no longer, members of the government coalition. In June 1918, however, relations between these two parties were also near to breaking-point. In the first place, the Bolsheviks, hard pressed to extract adequate supplies of grain from the country, had embarked on the policy of organizing committees of poor peasants against their richer fellows, among whom the SRs found their most solid supporters;[4] secondly, a new issue had flared up between them on the application of the death penalty. Since February, when the " socialist fatherland " had been proclaimed in danger, executions had been carried out by

[1] S. A. Piontkovsky, *Grazhdanskaya Voina v Rossii, 1918-1921* (1925), pp. 154-156.

[2] The resolution is in *Novaya Zhizn'*, June 10, 1918, pp. 79-81 ; I. Maisky, who was expelled from the Menshevik central committee for joining the so-called " Samara government ", makes a searching criticism of Menshevik hesitations at this time (*Demokraticheskaya Kontrrevolyutsiya* (1923), pp. 8-11).

[3] *Sobranie Uzakonenii, 1917-1918*, No. 44, art. 536. The issue of the decree was preceded by a long debate in VTsIK (*Protokoly Zasedanii VTsIK 4ᵉᵒ Sozyva* (1920), pp. 419-439).

[4] This question will be discussed in Part IV.

the Cheka — in what numbers cannot be determined [1] — without any regular or public judicial process. Both Right SRs and Mensheviks had from time to time protested against these proceedings. The Left SRs, retaining their membership of VTsIK and of the Soviets though not of Sovnarkom, were still represented in the Cheka and bore their share of responsibility for its actions. But when the revolutionary tribunal for the first time pronounced a death sentence — on a counter-revolutionary admiral named Shchastny [2] — the Left SRs sought to have the sentence quashed by VTsIK, and, when they failed, withdrew their representatives from the tribunal. It is, however, important to recognize the grounds on which the objection was taken. It was not founded on humanitarian considerations. The charge of being " Tolstoyans " was indignantly denied; for not only had the Left SRs participated in the work of the Cheka, but they had in the past been the prime instigators of assassination as a political weapon. Their case rested in part on the formal argument, which the Bolsheviks rejected as irrelevant, that the death sentence had been abolished by decree of the second All-Russian Congress of Soviets, [3] but mainly on opposition to the imposition of a death sentence by judicial process. The Left SRs admitted that it was sometimes legitimate and necessary to kill opponents, whether by assassination or by some special process such as that of the Cheka. But they were irrevocably opposed to the revival of " the old

[1] Sverdlov stated in July 1918 that " tens of death sentences have been carried out by us in all towns : in Petrograd, in Moscow and in the provinces " (*Pyatyi Vserossiiskii S"ezd Sovetov* (1918), p. 49). His argument against the Left SRs required him to stress the frequency of the occurrence : the usual motives for understatement were absent. The figure of twenty-two for the first six months given by M. Latsis, *Chrezvychainye Komissii po Bor'be s Kontr-revolyutsiei* (1921), p. 9, may conceivably be for the central Cheka in Moscow only : otherwise it is certainly too low.

[2] A review of the Shchastny affair is in D. F. White, *The Growth of the Red Army* (Princeton 1944), pp. 71-72 ; whether Shchastny tried merely to " save " the Baltic fleet from the Bolsheviks or to betray it to the Germans is a not very material point. The account of the charges against him in E. Sisson, *One Hundred Red Days* (Yale, 1931), p. 437, is of doubtful authenticity.

[3] Sverdlov refuted the formal argument on two grounds : that VTsIK in virtue of its full powers could reverse any resolution of the congress, and that the congress had abolished the death penalty at the front, but not elsewhere (*Pyatyi Vserossiiskii S"ezd Sovetov* (1918), p. 49). The second point was equivocal : the second All-Russian Congress of Soviets undoubtedly believed itself to be abolishing the only form of death penalty still in force.

accursed bourgeois state principle " implied in a regular process
of condemnation and execution by a court.[1] The argument
seemed fine-drawn ; and Krylenko neatly replied that the admiral
had not been " condemned to death " but only ordered to be
shot.[2] But it was a logical and consistent expression of the
anarchist background of social-revolutionary thought, which
accepted terrorism, but rejected the state.[3]

The situation was therefore exceedingly tense when the fifth
All-Russian Congress of Soviets met in Moscow at a critical
moment in history on July 4, 1918. Of the 1132 delegates with
voting powers, the Bolsheviks accounted for 745, the Left SRs
for 352, the remainder representing various small fractions.[4] The
proceedings at once developed into a duel between the two major
parties. The peasant issue was raised, but was less in evidence
than indignation at the suppression of rival parties and at the use
of the death penalty. The sharpest protests of all were heard
against the Brest-Litovsk treaty and the subservience of the
Soviet Government to Germany ; and the most animated clashes
of the congress occurred over Trotsky's insistence that it would
be madness to tolerate any attack on the German forces in the
Ukraine. On July 6, 1918, apparently in the hope of forcing a
breach, two Left SRs assassinated the German ambassador,
Mirbach. The murder was planned by SR members of the Cheka,
and the assassins gained admittance to the ambassador by producing papers purporting to have been signed by Dzerzhinsky.[5]

[1] The case was argued at length by Spiridonova at the fifth All-Russian
Congress of Soviets (*Pyatyi Vserossiiskii S''ezd Sovetov* (1918), pp. 59-61).

[2] *Izvestiya*, June 23, 1918.

[3] The Mensheviks, though not compromised by support of individual
terrorism, were also stung to deeper indignation at a single death sentence
pronounced by a legally constituted tribunal than at the dozens of executions
privately carried out by Cheka. It was the sentence on Shchastny which provoked a virulent pamphlet from Martov entitled *Doloi Smertnuyu Kazn'*
(" Down with the Death Penalty ") : " The beast has licked hot human blood.
The man-killing machine is brought into motion. . . . Plague-infected out-
casts . . . cannibal executioners." When the Menshevik authorities in Tiflis
fired on a workers' gathering, Lenin angrily retorted : " When we use shootings
they turn Tolstoyans and shed crocodile tears over our harshness. They have
forgotten how they helped Kerensky to drive the workers to the slaughter, keeping
the secret treaties hidden in their pockets " (Lenin, *Sochineniya*, xxii, 426).

[4] *Pyatyi Vserossiiskii S''ezd Sovetov* (1918), p. 163.

[5] *Proletarskaya Revolyutsiya*, No. 10 (33), 1924, p. 16. The protocols
of the central committee of the Left SRs of June 24, 1918, when the

This coup was followed by an attempt to seize power in Moscow and by insurrections in various provincial centres, of which that at Yaroslav was the most serious. Savinkov, the well-known SR terrorist, afterwards claimed to have been the organizer of these revolts, and to have been financed by funds supplied through the French military attaché in Moscow.[1]

Faced with treason on this large scale at a moment when allied forces were landing in Murmansk and Vladivostok, when the Czech legions had begun open hostilities against the Bolsheviks, and when the threat of war was looming on all sides, the Soviet Government was under no temptation to resort to half measures. The rising in Moscow was quickly put down. Most of the Left SR delegates to the fifth All-Russian Congress of Soviets were arrested, including Spiridonova, who admitted that Mirbach's assassins had acted on her instructions; thirteen of them who had been members of the Cheka were shot.[2] Several newspapers were suppressed. After three days of confusion the congress resumed its sittings and, having expressed approval of the actions of the government, passed a cautiously worded resolution to the effect that " in so far as certain sections of the Left SR party associate themselves with the attempt to involve Russia in war through the murder of Mirbach and the rising against the Soviet power, these organizations can have no place in the Soviets of Workers' and Peasants' Deputies ".[3] The concluding act of the congress on July 10, 1918, was to approve the constitution of the RSFSR, which thus came into force at the darkest and most dangerous moment in the history of the republic, when the open revolt of the last considerable independent party had driven the régime a long step further on the road to the one-party state.

Accounts of punitive measures taken by the Cheka are nearly

decision was taken to " organize a series of terrorist attacks on the leading representatives of German imperialism " were published in *Krasnaya Kniga Ve-che-ka* (1920), i, 129.

[1] *Boris Savinkov pered Voennoi Kollegiei Verkhovnogo Suda SSSR* (1924), pp. 55-59. On the other hand, Savinkov denied prior knowledge of the murder of Mirbach, which was the work of the Left SRs.

[2] *Krasnaya Kniga Ve-che-ka* (1920), i, 200-201 ; I. Steinberg, *Spiridonova: Revolutionary Terrorist* (1935), p. 216. Spiridonova herself was released a few months later, once more engaged in propaganda against the régime (*Pravda*, December 19, 1918), and was eventually banished to Tashkent.

[3] *Pyatyi Vserossiiskii S"ezd Sovetov* (1918), p. 209.

always fragmentary and unreliable. But some authentic information exists of the reprisals which followed the suppression of the
widespread provincial revolts of the summer of 1918. The
insurgents in Yaroslav held out for a fortnight, and 350 were shot
when the city was finally taken.[1] In the neighbouring town of
Murom, where the revolt collapsed at once, 10 leaders were shot
and a levy of a million rubles imposed on the bourgeoisie.[2] In
Nizhny-Novgorod, 700 " officers and gendarmes " were arrested,
and the local Cheka " broke up the white-guard organization . . .
by arresting almost its entire membership and shooting part of
it ".[3] On the night of July 16-17, 1918, the former Tsar and his
family were shot in Ekaterinburg by order of the Ural regional
Soviet. When the Czechs captured the town ten days later, the
Ural regional Cheka moved to Vyatka, where it arrested more than
400 persons and shot 35 who were " involved in counter-revolutionary plots ".[4] When a " *kulak* rising " occurred in August 1918
in Penza, Lenin himself telegraphed instructions " to put into
effect an unsparing mass terror against *kulaks*, priests, and white
guards, and to confine suspects in a camp outside the city ", and
recommended the taking of hostages who would " answer with
their life " for prompt and accurate deliveries of grain.[5] These
bald records undoubtedly conceal horrors and brutalities committed both in the heat of battle and in cold blood and common
to all parties, though specific accounts of them rarely carry conviction. Such occurrences, as well as the multiplication, exaggeration and sheer invention of them by opponents, are the invariable
concomitants of war and revolution waged with the fanatical
desperation which marked the struggle unleashed in Russia by
the events of October 1917.

The sanctions thus applied were frankly described by their
authors as " terror " and justified as measures of war. " The
Soviet power must guarantee its rear ", ran a resolution adopted
by VTsIK on July 29, 1918, after speeches by Lenin and Trotsky,

[1] *Pravda*, July 23, July 26, 1918, quoted in J. Bunyan, *Intervention, Civil
War, and Communism in Russia* (Baltimore, 1936), pp. 194, 228.
[2] *Ezhenedel'nik Chrezvychainykh Komissii*, No. 2, 1918, p. 30. Only six
numbers of this unique periodical appeared.
[3] *Ibid.* No. 1, 1918, pp. 21-22.
[4] *Ibid.* No. 1, 1918, pp. 18-19.
[5] Lenin, *Sochineniya*, xxix, 489.

" by putting the bourgeoisie under supervision and carrying out mass terror against it." [1] And Dzerzhinsky said in a press interview at this time :

> The Cheka is not a court. The Cheka is *the defence of the revolution* as the Red Army is ; as in the civil war the Red Army cannot stop to ask whether it may harm particular individuals, but must take into account only one thing, the victory of the revolution over the bourgeoisie, so the Cheka must defend the revolution and conquer the enemy even if its sword falls occasionally on the heads of the innocent.[2]

But the culmination of the terror was provoked by a further recourse of the SRs to the method of political assassination — this time against the Bolsheviks. Volodarsky, a Bolshevik leader famous in his day as a mob orator, had been killed in Petrograd in June 1918. On August 30, 1918, Uritsky was also assassinated in Petrograd, and Lenin seriously wounded in Moscow. All these assaults could be traced to SRs of one faction or the other. The indignation and the fear caused by them put fresh weapons into the hands of the Cheka.[3] Next day the British representative in Moscow was arrested on a charge of British complicity in counter-revolutionary plots,[4] and the British naval attaché was killed in an attack on the British Embassy in Petrograd. On September 2, 1918, VTsIK adopted a resolution on the murder of Uritsky and the assault on Lenin which concluded :

> All counter-revolutionaries and all who inspired them will be held responsible for every attempt on workers of the Soviet Government and upholders of the ideals of the socialist revolution. To the white terror of the enemies of the Workers' and

---

[1] *Protokoly Zasedanii VTsIK 4ᵒᵒ Sozyva* (1920), p. 83.

[2] Quoted in K. Radek, *Portrety i Pamflety* (1933), i, 50.

[3] Among the telegrams of protest addressed to VTsIK was one from the Tsaritsyn front signed by Stalin and Voroshilov : " The military council of the north Caucasian war sector, having learned of the criminal attempt by hirelings of the bourgeoisie on the life of the greatest revolutionary in the world, the tried leader and teacher of the proletariat, comrade Lenin, replies to this vile underhand attempt by the organization of open, mass, systematic terror against the bourgeoisie and its agents " (Stalin, *Sochineniya*, iv, 128).

[4] R. H. Bruce Lockhart, *Memoirs of a British Agent* (1932), pp. 314-316, contains what is virtually an admission of complicity ; if *Britain's Master Spy: Sidney Reilly's Narrative written by Himself* (1933) is authentic, the complicity went very far.

Peasants' Government the workers and peasants will reply by a mass red terror against the bourgeoisie and its agents.[1]

More than a coincidence of date recalls the Paris terror of September 2, 1793, when, following on the Duke of Brunswick's proclamation threatening foreign intervention and ruthless repression of the revolution, mass reprisals started in Paris in which 3000 aristocrats are said to have perished.   In both revolutions this date marked the turning-point after which the terror, hitherto sporadic and unorganized, became a deliberate instrument of policy.

No reliable estimate can be formed of the total of those who suffered in the " red terror " of the autumn of 1918.   The largest number of executions recorded at any one time and place were the 512 " counter-revolutionaries and white guards " (otherwise described as " hostages ") shot in Petrograd immediately on the announcement of the terror.[2]   Those shot in Moscow included " many Tsarist ministers and a whole list of high personages ".[3] Of numerous reports from the provinces perhaps the most revealing came from Kazan.   After stating that " punitive expeditions have been sent into every county ", it continued :

In Kazan proper only seven or eight people have been shot by the tribunal.   This is explained by the fact that the entire bourgeoisie, including the petty bourgeoisie, the priests and the monks, fled from the city.   Half of the city houses are deserted. The property of the fugitives is being confiscated for the benefit of the city poor.[4]

The essence of the terror was its class character.   It selected its victims on the ground, not of specific offences, but of their membership of the possessing classes.

The English bourgeois [exclaimed Lenin in his letter to the American workers] have forgotten their 1649, the French their 1793.   The terror was just and legitimate when it was applied by the bourgeoisie for its own advantage against the feudal lords.

[1] *Pyatyi Sozyv VTsIK* (1919), p. 11.
[2] *Izvestiya*, September 3, September 7, 1918.   *Ezhenedel'nik Chrezvychainykh Komissii*, No. 6, 1918, p. 19, gives 800 as the total number executed in Petrograd during the terror.
[3] *Proletarskaya Revolyutsiya*, No. 10 (33), 1924, p. 32.
[4] *Ezhenedel'nik Chrezvychainykh Komissii*, No. 4, 1918, p. 25.

The terror became monstrous and criminal when the workers and poor peasants dared to apply it against the bourgeoisie.[1] The Cheka, as one of its members explained, " does not judge, it strikes ". Those who compared the Cheka with the Tsarist Okhrana " have slept through the February and October revolutions, and expect others to do all the dirty work necessary for the construction of the new communist order, so that they can step in with unstained hands and clean, starched collars ". Moreover, since " the counter-revolutionaries are active in all spheres of life, . . . there is no sphere in which the Cheka does not operate ".[2]

The events of the summer of 1918 left the Bolsheviks without rivals or partners the ruling party in the state ; and they possessed in the Cheka an organ of absolute power. Yet a strong reluctance remained to use that power without restraint. The moment for the final extinction of the excluded parties had not yet arrived. The terror at this time was a capricious instrument ; and it is common to find parties against which the fiercest anathemas had been pronounced and most drastic measures taken continuing to survive and to enjoy a measure of tolerance. One of the first decrees of the new régime had authorized Sovnarkom to close down all newspapers preaching " open resistance or disobedience to the Workers' and Peasants' Government " ; [3] and in principle the bourgeois press ceased to exist. Yet in spite of this decree, and of the outlawing of the Kadet party at the end of 1917, the Kadet newspaper *Svoboda Rossii* was still being published in Moscow in the summer of 1918.[4] The Menshevik newspaper in Petrograd, *Novyi Luch*, was suppressed in February 1918 for its campaign of opposition to the Brest-Litovsk treaty. But, borrowing a technique used in the past by the Bolshevik press, it reappeared in April in Moscow under the new name of *Vpered*,

---

[1] Lenin, *Sochineniya*, xxiii, 185.

[2] M. Latsis, *Chrezvychainye Komissii po Bor'be s Kontrrevolyutsiei* (1921), pp. 8-23.

[3] *Sobranie Uzakonenii, 1917-1918*, No. 1 (2nd ed.), art. 17.

[4] It was this paper which gave currency to a supposed decree of an " anarchist club " at Saratov declaring all women " state property " (quoted in J. Bunyan, *Intervention, Civil War, and Communism in Russia* (Baltimore, 1936), p. 556) ; this report in various more or less garbled forms made the rounds of the foreign press.

and for some time continued its career without interference. Anarchist journals were published in Moscow long after the Cheka action against the anarchists in April 1918. Makhno, the Ukrainian anarchist, came to Moscow in the summer of 1918, had interviews with Lenin and Sverdlov, and freely visited the Moscow anarchists, among whom he found an atmosphere of " paper revolution ".[1] Practice was everywhere less consistent than theory. Before the end of 1918 other factors were leading to some mitigation of the excesses of the terror. The thirst for revenge had been slaked; fears of the counter-revolution at home were less acute; the German collapse had, momentarily at any rate, relieved external pressures. On the other hand, the encroachment of the Cheka on almost all branches of the administration excited the jealous resentment of local Soviets and of some central departments, notably the Commissariats of Justice and Internal Affairs;[2] and those responsible for economic policy, who were finding non-Bolshevik technicians more and more indispensable as " specialists ", could have little sympathy for a policy of indiscriminate terror against political opponents.

This was the mood when the sixth All-Russian Congress of Soviets, the first almost exclusively Bolshevik congress, met on the eve of the first anniversary of the revolution. It at once approved what was described as an " amnesty ", ordering the release of all those " detained by the organs for combating counter-revolution " unless a definite charge of counter-revolutionary activities were preferred against them within two weeks of their arrest, and of all hostages except those held by the central Cheka as a specific guarantee for " comrades in enemy hands ". The same resolution settled a disputed question of competence by giving the right of supervising its execution to VTsIK and to

[1] N. Makhno, *Pod Udarami Kontrrevolyutsii* (Paris, 1936), pp. 92-107, 119, 135; for Makhno see pp. 302-303 below. From the time of *State and Revolution* onwards Lenin always showed a certain tenderness for anarchists; in August 1919 he wrote that " very many anarchist workers are now becoming the most sincere supporters of the Soviet power " and attributed their former hostility to the betrayal of Marxist principles by the Second International (*Sochineniya*, xxiv, 437-438).

[2] Evidence of this bureaucratic feud is quoted in Bunyan and Fisher, *The Bolshevik Revolution, 1917–1918* (Stanford, 1934), pp. 580-581, and Bunyan, *Intervention, Civil War, and Communism in Russia* (Baltimore, 1936), pp. 259-260; constitutionally the Cheka was responsible only to Sovnarkom and to VTsIK.

local executive committees.[1] Having thus — on paper, at any rate — clipped the wings of the Cheka, the congress passed a further resolution " On Revolutionary Legality ", enjoining on " all citizens of the republic, and all organs and officials of the Soviet power " a strict observance of the laws, and giving citizens a right of appeal against any neglect or violation of their rights by officials. The injunction on officials and public institutions to observe the laws was, it is true, qualified by a carefully guarded exception in favour of measures required by " the special conditions of civil war and the struggle against counter-revolution ".[2] But the resolutions of the sixth All-Russian Congress of Soviets represent the first of a series of sincere, though ultimately unavailing, attempts to check the exercise of arbitrary power by the security organs of the republic and to confine them within the limits of legality.

The congress was followed by a further notable step on the path of conciliation. It was decided to hold out an olive branch to the excluded socialist parties — or to accept it when proffered by them. The exclusion of the Mensheviks from VTsIK and from the Soviets had not prevented the central committee of the party from holding a five-day conference in Moscow at the end of October 1918. The outbreak of the civil war and the open threat to the régime placed them in an embarrassing position, since, for all their hostility to the Bolsheviks, they had still less to hope from a restoration. They chose once more the path of compromise. The conference adopted a series of " theses and resolutions " recognizing the October revolution as " historically necessary " and as " a gigantic ferment setting the whole world in motion ", and renouncing " all political cooperation with classes hostile to democracy " ; at the same time, while promising " direct support of the military actions of the Soviet Government against foreign intervention ", the resolution demanded " the abrogation of the extraordinary organs of police repression and the extraordinary tribunals " and " the cessation of the political and economic terror ".[3] A public proclamation by the Mensheviks

---

[1] S"ezdy Sovetov RSFSR v Postanovleniyakh (1939), pp. 116-117.
[2] Ibid. p. 119. For greater solemnity this resolution appeared as a decree in Sobranie Uzakonenii, 1917-1918, No. 90, art. 908.
[3] The resolutions, which appeared in the press, are summarized in Lenin, Sochineniya, xxiii, 571-572. The protest against the terror was answered by

denouncing counter-revolution and foreign intervention [1] was
followed by an unusually conciliatory speech from Lenin, who
declared that no more was asked of the Mensheviks and SRs than
" neutrality and good-neighbour relations " and that it was important " to make use of those hesitating elements which the
bestialities of imperialism are driving towards us ".[2] On November 30, 1918, VTsIK passed a resolution annulling the exclusion
pronounced against the Mensheviks in the previous June, while
excepting from this act of grace " those groups of Mensheviks
who continue to be allied with the Russian and foreign bourgeoisie
against the Soviet power ".[3] The SRs made haste to follow the
Menshevik example. As an avowedly revolutionary and terrorist
party, they had even less than the Mensheviks to expect from
former Tsarist generals and their foreign backers : Kolchak had
just given short shrift to the SRs whom he had caught in western
Siberia. In February 1919 a conference of SRs at Petrograd
" decisively rejected any attempt to overthrow the Soviet power
by way of armed struggle " and denounced the Russian bourgeois
parties and " the imperialist countries of the Entente " ; and about
the same time the group of former SR members of the Constituent
Assembly who in 1918 had formed the so-called Samara government surrendered and were accorded an amnesty.[4] These
demonstrations of good-will evoked a resolution of VTsIK of
February 25, 1919, reinstating the SRs with the same reservation
against " all groups which directly or indirectly support external
and internal counter-revolution ".[5]

This uneasy compromise, based on the principle of toleration
for " loyal " Mensheviks and SRs, lasted after a fashion for two
years — so long as the prolongation of the civil war provided a
motive for restraint. But the proviso that it did not apply to those

---

Stalin in a long article in *Pravda* (Stalin, *Sochineniya*, iv, 134-145 : " How is it
possible to recognize the ' historical necessity ' of the October revolution and yet
fail to recognize the inevitable results and consequences which flow from it? ").

[1] Lenin, *Sochineniya*, xxiii, 571. The date of the proclamation there given
as September 26, 1918, should be November 14, 1918, as is correctly stated
ibid. xxiv, 760 ; it was published in *Pravda*, No. 251, of November 19, 1918 (not,
as wrongly stated *ibid.* xxiii, 571, November 26, which was the date of Lenin's
speech).

[2] *Ibid.* xxiii, 318-319, 323.   [3] *Ibid.* xxiv, 760.   [4] *Ibid.* xxiv, 760.

[5] *Ibid.* xxiv, 760-761. The meeting of VTsIK which took this decision is
described in A. Ransome, *Six Weeks in Russia in 1919* (1919), pp. 108-112.

" directly or indirectly " supporting counter-revolution gave it a fluidity of which the authorities freely availed themselves. When the eighth party congress met in March 1919 the atmosphere was already less friendly to the minority parties. One delegate openly protested against the " legalization " of Mensheviks and SRs; [1] and Lenin himself spoke in language quite different from that which he had used in the previous November :

> Very frequent changes are required of us in our line of conduct, which for the superficial observer may seem strange and incomprehensible. " What's this? " he will say. " Yesterday you were making promises to the petty bourgeoisie, and today Dzerzhinsky declares that Left SRs and Mensheviks will be put against the wall. What a contradiction ! " Yes, a contradiction. But there is also a contradiction in the behaviour of this same petty bourgeois democracy which does not know where to sit down, tries to sit between two stools, jumps from one to the other and falls over, now to the right, now to the left. . . . We say to it : " You are not a serious enemy. Our enemy is the bourgeoisie. But if you march with it, then we shall have to apply to you too the measures of the proletarian dictatorship." [2]

Immediately afterwards the SRs added fuel to the flames by once more splitting into several factions, one pledged to cooperation with the Bolsheviks, one hostile to them, while a third group under the old SR leader Chernov sought to establish " a third force equally removed from Bolshevism and restoration ".[3] From this time the Cheka played a cat-and-mouse game with the opposition parties, harrying and patronizing them by turn, alternately arresting and releasing their leaders and making their organized existence almost, but never quite, impossible. Dan, one of the Menshevik leaders, has left a detailed record of his adventures in the period 1919 to 1921, during which he was alternately arrested and released, was expelled from the capital under the guise of more or less mythical professional appointments in the provinces (he was a physician), returned to Moscow illicitly for political meetings, and on one occasion was recalled there officially to

---

[1] *Vos'moi S"ezd RKP(B)* (1933), pp. 33-34.

[2] Lenin, *Sochineniya*, xxiv, 120.

[3] The manifesto of the pro-Bolshevik group appeared in *Izvestiya*, May 3, 1919 (extracts in Lenin, *Sochineniya*, xxiv, 780) ; this group seceded from the party when the party council in June 1919 reverted to a policy of opposition to the régime (*ibid.* xxiv, 788-789).

attend the All-Russian Congress of Soviets.[1]   These harrying
tactics were not without effect.   So far as concerned the rank-and-
file Mensheviks, Stalin probably did not much exaggerate when
he described them at this time as " crossing over little by little
into the camp of the Soviet republic ".[2]

It was in these conditions that the Menshevik leaders were
present, by invitation though not as elected delegates, at the
seventh All-Russian Congress of Soviets in December 1919.
Dan made a brief ceremonial speech in which he spoke with sympathy of Soviet victories in the civil war and the repulse of
Yudenich before Petrograd and greeted " the single revolutionary
front . . . in all that concerns the defence of the revolution ".[3]
The more controversial utterance was reserved for Martov who
attacked violations of the Soviet constitution; diagnosed " an
apathy of the masses nourished and strengthened by centuries of
slavery under Tsars and serf-owners, a paralysis of civic consciousness, a readiness to throw all responsibility for one's fate on the
shoulders of the government " ; and read a declaration demanding
" a restoration of the working of the constitution . . . freedom of
the press, of association and of assembly . . . inviolability of the
person . . . abolition of executions without trial, of administrative arrests and cf official terror ".[4]   Lenin, in an effective debating
speech, replied that Martov's declaration meant " back to bourgeois
democracy and nothing else ", and that " when we hear such
declarations from people who announce their sympathy with us,
we say to ourselves : ' No, both terror and the Cheka are absolutely
indispensable ' ".[5]

Throughout 1920 the Mensheviks had party offices and a
club in Moscow (though " the Cheka occasionally raided the
premises, sealed them up, confiscated papers and arrested those
assembled "), and issued news-sheets and proclamations through
friendly printing establishments over the signature of the central
committee of the party.   In the local Soviet elections of that year
they secured 46 seats in the Moscow Soviet, 250 in Kharkov,
120 in Yaroslav, 78 in Kremenchug and smaller numbers in most

---

[1] F. Dan, *Dva Goda Skitanii* (Berlin, 1922).
[2] Stalin, *Sochineniya*, iv, 243-244.
[3] *7ⁱ Vserossiiskii S"ezd Sovetov* (1920), p. 20.
[4] *Ibid.* pp. 60-63.   [5] Lenin, *Sochineniya*, xxiv, 612-613.

of the other large towns.[1]   In May 1920 members of the British
Labour delegation visiting Moscow " were allowed complete
freedom to see politicians of opposition parties ",[2] and even
attended a session of the Menshevik central committee.   Some of
them were afterwards present at a meeting of 3000 workers
organized by the predominantly Menshevik printers' trade union
and addressed both by Menshevik and by Bolshevik orators.   In
the course of the meeting, Chernov, the SR leader, already wanted
by the Cheka, appeared in disguise on the platform and delivered
a harangue in which he compared socialism with primitive Christianity and the degeneracy of the Bolsheviks with that of the
mediaeval church.   According to Dan it was " the last such
meeting in Bolshevik Moscow ".[3]   In August 1920 a Menshevik
party conference was held openly in Moscow and even reported
in the Soviet press.[4]   Later still the Mensheviks continued to
control important trade unions and to act as an organized group
at congresses of the central council of trade unions.   The eighth
All-Russian Congress of Soviets in December 1920 was, however, the last to admit, without voting rights, delegates of the
Mensheviks and SRs as well as of a few minor groups.[5]   The
tone of the opposition speakers was more irreconcilable, and their
reception by the overwhelming Bolshevik majority at the congress more sharply hostile, than in the previous year.   Martov
had already left Russia, and had delivered in the autumn of 1920

---

[1] Y. Martov, *Geschichte der Russischen Sozial-Demokratie* (1926), p. 318.
A declaration of the Menshevik group in the Moscow Soviet on March 6, 1920,
attacking, among other things, the fairness of the elections, is published in
G. K. Gins, *Sibir', Soyuzniki i Kolchak* (Peking, 1921), ii, 564-565.

[2] B. Russell, *The Practice and Theory of Bolshevism* (1920), p. 26.

[3] F. Dan, *Dva Goda Skitanii* (Berlin, 1922), pp. 11-13.   Chernov gives the
text of his speech in *Mes tribulations en Russie* (Paris, 1921), pp. 55-60 ; Dan
describes it as " not very successful " and " excessively literary and abstract ".
A brief account of the meeting, together with the text of a speech by Kefali, a
member of the Menshevik central committee, is in *British Labour Delegation to
Russia, 1920: Report* (1920), pp. 63-65 : according to information subsequently
given to the delegation, the members of the council of the printers' union were
arrested in the following month (*ibid.* p. 71).

[4] F. Dan, *Dva Goda Skitanii* (Berlin, 1922), pp. 57-59.

[5] One delegate described himself as speaking for the " communist dissenters " (*Vos'moi Vserossiiskii S"ezd Sovetov* (1921), pp. 226-228) — a curious
product of the political confusion of the first years of the revolution and of the
encouragement given for a short time to religious dissenters as a weapon against
the Orthodox Church.

an effective fighting speech against Zinoviev and the Bolsheviks at the Halle congress of the German independent socialists.[1] The policy of qualified toleration of dissident parties in the Soviets was obviously wearing thin. The first months of 1921 brought the most serious internal crisis in Soviet history since the summer of 1918. The end of the civil war revealed the full extent of the losses and destruction which it had entailed and removed the restraints of loyalty which war commonly imposes; discontent with the régime became, for the first time outside political circles, widespread and vocal, extending both to peasants and to factory workers; the Kronstadt mutiny of the beginning of March 1921, was its expression and its symbol. At the tenth party congress in the same month, which approved the New Economic Policy (NEP), party discipline was tightened up to meet the emergency. The toleration of dissentient minorities outside the party became all the more anomalous. No formal decree similar to that of June 1918 was issued. But Lenin himself seems to have given the signal. In a pamphlet in defence of NEP published in May 1921 he wrote:

> As for non-party people who are nothing else but Mensheviks and SRs dressed up in modern, Kronstadt, non-party attire, we shall either keep them safely in prison or send them to Martov in Berlin for the free enjoyment of all the amenities of free democracy and for the free exchange of ideas with Chernov, Milyukov and the Georgian Mensheviks.[2]

According to a Menshevik source, the result of this hint was immediate:

> Repressions against social democrats began all over Russia. The only way to avoid persecution was to write a statement to the Bolshevik newspaper renouncing any connexion with the Social-Democratic Party. Many complied; but many also were banished to Solovki, to Suzdal, Siberia, Turkestan and so forth.[3]

Martyrs seem to have been few. No obstacles were placed in the way of the departure of the Menshevik leaders for Berlin, where

---

[1] This episode will be discussed in Part V.
[2] Lenin, *Sochineniya*, xxvi, 352.
[3] Y. Martov, *Geschichte der Russischen Sozial-Demokratie* (1926), p. 319. The writer (F. Dan in this section of the book) quotes Lenin's words in a slightly inaccurate form, and wrongly assigns them to Lenin's speech at the party congress.

in the spring of 1921 an important Menshevik centre was established with a Menshevik weekly journal, *Sotsialisticheskii Vestnik*.
The rank and file for the most part made their submission or
abandoned political activity. There is, however, a certain irony
in the fact that the extinction of organized political opposition to
Bolshevism from without coincided with the development of the
most important organized opposition within the party since the
days of Brest-Litovsk. Sharp differences of opinion continued to
exist. But they were now concentrated within the party. The
party had drawn into itself the whole political life of the country.
Its internal affairs were henceforth the political history of the
nation.

It is, however, once more significant of the flexibility of
Soviet policy, and of its empiricism in the choice of means, that
this same spring and summer of 1921, which saw the virtual
extinction of all independent parties in Soviet Russia, should have
witnessed the two most serious attempts made to bring about an
understanding between the Soviet power and the survivors of the
bourgeois intelligentsia remaining on Soviet soil. On the Soviet
side, NEP was the symptom of a willingness to compromise which
might be supposed to have its political counterpart ; on the other
side, many of those Russians hitherto hostile to the Soviet power,
whether in Russia or already in emigration, saw in NEP a surrender
of the hitherto uncompromising principles of Bolshevism which
might pave the way for a partial reconciliation. In April 1921 a
proposal was put forward for a joint public meeting to be followed
by a banquet between representatives of the Soviet Government
and of the bourgeois intelligentsia, at which the official spokesmen
were to explain the significance of NEP and the spokesmen of the
intelligentsia to welcome the change in policy. The plan broke
down owing to the intransigence of the representatives of the
intelligentsia who were unwilling to commit themselves to any
public blessing of Soviet action.[1] At the end of June 1921 news
of the catastrophic famine threatening the eastern provinces of
European Russia began to reach Moscow ; and a group of public
men and intellectuals approached the Soviet authorities with pro-

---

[1] The main source for this little documented episode is an article by E.
Kuskova, one of the representatives of the intelligentsia concerned in the
negotiations (*Volya Rossii* (Prague), No. 3, 1928, p. 56).

posals for an appeal to foreign countries for help. The magnitude of the impending disaster and the belief that a conciliatory gesture would favourably impress foreign opinion made the Soviet Government amenable to the project. A decree of July 21, 1921, set up an All-Russian Committee for Aid to the Hungry consisting of some sixty persons. These included Kamenev, the president of the committee, Rykov, Lunacharsky, Krasin, Maxim Gorky and a few other Bolsheviks, two former ministers of the Provisional Government, Kishkin and Prokopovich, some prominent Kadets and a large number of non-party intellectuals. It was to draw funds both from voluntary contributions and from a state subsidy, to collect supplies both in Russia and abroad, and to see to their distribution.[1]

Such a committee was unique in the history of the Soviet régime, and the difficulties inherent in it were quickly revealed. The *émigré* Russian press hailed the step as proof that the Soviet régime was in desperate straits and no longer able to maintain itself without bourgeois support; the British representative, newly arrived in Moscow, entered into relations with the committee over the head of the Soviet Government; and foreign governments showed an obvious inclination to treat it as an alternative government which might succeed to power once the Soviet régime was overthrown. The committee in fact did little but collect information and make publicity at home and abroad. On August 20, 1921, the Soviet Government concluded an agreement with Hoover's American Relief Administration (ARA) for the organization of famine relief. This success made the continued existence of the committee, from the Soviet point of view, not only superfluous, but dangerous; for ARA clearly hoped to use the relief programme to weaken the position of the Soviet Government and would seek as far as possible to deal with the predominantly bourgeois committee rather than with the Bolshevik authorities. At an earlier stage plans had been made for delegates of the committee to proceed to London and other foreign countries to solicit aid. This was now out of the question. The Soviet Government informed the committee that its work in Moscow was complete, and that its members should take their place in the organization of relief in the stricken regions. When the

---

[1] *Izvestiya*, July 23, 1921.

majority of the committee refused to accept this decision and insisted on the plan of sending delegates abroad, it was formally dissolved by a decree of August 27, 1921, and its leading bourgeois members arrested.[1] Thus ended the first and last attempt at cooperation between the Soviet régime and the surviving elements of the old order. It illustrated both the intensity of the mutual animosity between them and the way in which any independent force in Soviet Russia became, or could be plausibly suspected of becoming, a focus of foreign intervention against the régime.[2]

Before returning to the development of the party in its relation to the state, two further episodes must be recorded as marking stages in the consolidation of the dictatorship. The first was the abolition and transformation of the Cheka, which occurred in the spring of 1922. The second was the public trial of the SR leaders three months later.

Hostility to the Cheka came from two sources, both well represented in the party : from idealists who disapproved of the terror and of extra-judicial proceedings as a regular instrument of government though they had accepted them as necessary in an emergency, and from the vested interests of other branches of the administration which objected to the encroachment of a privileged and irregular institution on their normal functions. At the centre, this last objection was voiced by the Commissariats of Internal Affairs and of Justice ; in the regions, the local commissions of Cheka raised in its most acute form the chronic constitutional problem of the responsibility of local organs to the local Soviets. More generally, the end of the civil war had been followed by a relaxation of tension, of which NEP was the symptom in the economic field. The demobilization of the army should, it was felt, be crowned by a demobilization of the organ which had conducted the campaign, now triumphantly completed,

---

[1] The announcement of its dissolution with a brief statement of reasons appeared in *Izvestiya*, August 30, 1921.

[2] The longest connected account of the episode is an article by E. Kuskova, one of the members of the committee, in *Volya Rossii* (Prague), Nos. 3, 4, 5, 1928 : the Bolshevik case against the committee was stated in *Izvestiya Tsentral'nogo Komiteta Rossiiskoi Kommunisticheskoi Partii (Bol'shevikov)*, No. 34, November 15, 1921, p. 2.

on the home front. At the ninth All-Russian Congress of Soviets, Smirnov, an old Bolshevik who had been associated with opposition movements in the party from the " Left communists " of 1918 [1] onwards, proposed in the briefest of speeches a motion which, if the records are complete, was adopted without debate. It ran as follows :

> The Congress of Soviets takes note of the heroic work performed by the organs of the Cheka at the most acute moments of the civil war and the immense services rendered by it to the task of strengthening and defending the conquests of the October revolution against attacks from within and without.
> The Congress considers that the present strengthening of Soviet power within and without makes it possible to narrow the extent of the activity of the Cheka and its organs, reserving for the judicial organs the struggle against violations of the laws of the Soviet republics.
> Therefore the Congress of Soviets charges the presidium of VTsIK to review at the earliest date the statute of the Cheka and its organs in the sense of reorganizing them, of restricting their competence and of strengthening the principles of revolutionary legality. [2]

Except in the initial heat and enthusiasm of a revolution, fundamental issues of the mechanics of power are rarely discussed in public by those who exercise it. The future of the Cheka was such an issue. How far the acceptance of Smirnov's resolution by the party leaders at the congress of December 1921 was a tactical manœuvre, how far views were subsequently modified by the desperate famine whose effects did not reach their peak before the early months of 1922, or what forces were responsible for the ultimate decision, cannot be determined. But it is difficult to believe that, at a time when the introduction of NEP, through its toleration of capitalist and petty bourgeois elements, had increased the need for vigilance, the party leaders could seriously have thought of dispensing with so powerful an instrument of security. On February 8, 1922, VTsIK issued a decree abolishing the Cheka and its local commissions, transferring its functions to the People's Commissariat of Internal Affairs, and creating at the commissariat a " state political administration " (Gosudarst-

[1] See pp. 188-189 below.
[2] *Sobranie Uzakonenii, 1922*, No. 4, art. 42 ; *Devyatyi Vserossiiskii S"ezd Sovetov* (1922), p. 254.

vennoe Politicheskoe Upravlenie or GPU) to exercise these functions, with corresponding " political sections " in the provinces and in the autonomous republics and regions of the RSFSR. The dual responsibility of these sections to the GPU in Moscow and to the Soviet executive committees on the spot was defined in the usual vague terms which left no serious doubt of their subordination to the central organ. " Special army detachments " were placed at the disposal of the GPU, and among their functions was mentioned the task of " combating crime in the army and on the railways ". Finally, it was laid down that any person arrested by the GPU must, after two months, either be released or handed over to the judicial authorities for trial, unless special permission for his continued detention were obtained from the presidium of VTsIK.[1] This last provision was the escape-clause which enabled the GPU, where necessary, to avoid the trammels of legal procedure. But even this formality does not appear to have been observed for long; and after the creation of the Union of Soviet Socialist Republics in the following year, the nominal attachment to the Commissariat of Internal Affairs also disappeared. The transformation of February 1922, while it purported to transfer the quasi-judicial functions of the Cheka to the courts, in fact removed political offences altogether out of the scope of judicial procedure, and left the GPU more arbitrary powers to deal with such offences than the defunct Cheka had ever claimed or exercised. The GPU was not two months old when Lenin, at the eleventh party congress, criticized it for intervening in an economic transaction which did not appear to be its concern.[2]

The second landmark of 1922 was the trial of the SR leaders. The measures of repression applied to the Mensheviks in the previous year had descended equally on the SRs. But the SRs were of a different breed, and not so easily snuffed out. They were a revolutionary party with a tradition of underground conspiracy; and when the policy of opposition was resumed, some at least of them reverted to this tradition. The newly created GPU soon took a hand. In February 1922 it was announced that forty-seven leading SRs had been arrested on charges of conspiring against the Soviet power and would be brought to trial. The

---

[1] *Sobranie Uzakonenii*, *1922*, No. 16, art. 160.
[2] Lenin, *Sochinemiya*, xxvii, 249.

announcement made some stir abroad, especially in socialist circles. In April 1922 the matter was raised at a meeting in Berlin between representatives of the three Internationals — the solitary attempt at compromise between these rival bodies.[1] Bukharin and Radek, who represented the Russian party in the Comintern delegation, undertook that the death penalty would not be demanded against the SRs, and were publicly reproved by Lenin for their acquiescence in this intrusion into Soviet domestic affairs, though he admitted that the agreement must be kept.[2]

Before the trial could begin, Lenin had been laid low by his first stroke. The trial opened on June 8, 1922, lasted for two months, and secured international publicity through the presence of Vandervelde, the Belgian socialist, as principal counsel for the accused. It was the first great political trial of the régime. The general case against the SRs was formidable. Through Kerensky they were saddled with responsibility for every act of the Provisional Government; they had played a leading part in more than one " white " government during the civil war; the assassins of Mirbach and the author of the attempt on Lenin's life had been SRs; and, where concrete acts could not be proved, there were plenty of pronouncements by leading SRs in favour of acts of terror against the Soviet power. Vandervelde and his foreign colleagues abandoned the defence after a few days " at the request of the accused ", and issued a statement denouncing the tribunal and the prosecution for violation of the Berlin agreement.[3] Of the thirty-four defendants, a few were acquitted, and many sentenced to different terms and degrees of imprisonment. Fourteen were sentenced to death. Two of these were reprieved by a decree of VTsIK, and the sentences on the remainder suspended. It is noteworthy that throughout the proceedings it was not alleged that the SR party was in itself an illegal institution : evidence was brought against the defendants of acts which under any system of government would have been criminal. The decree of VTsIK of August 8, 1922, confirming and suspending the sentences, continued to imply recognition of a legal party :

---

[1] An account of this meeting will be given in Part V.
[2] Lenin, *Sochineniya*, xxvii, 277-280.
[3] E. Vandervelde et A. Wauters, *Le Procès des Socialistes-Révolutionnaires à Moscou* (Brussels, 1922), pp. 133-134.

If the party of the SRs in deed and in practice discontinues its underground-conspiratorial terrorist and military espionage activity leading to insurrection against the power of the workers and peasants, it will by so doing release from paying the supreme penalty those of its leading members who in the past led this work and reserved at the trial itself their right to continue it.[1]

The fiction of a legal opposition was, however, long since dead. Its demise cannot fairly be laid at the door of one party. If it was true that the Bolshevik régime was not prepared after the first few months to tolerate an organized opposition, it was equally true that no opposition party was prepared to remain within legal limits. The premise of dictatorship was common to both sides of the argument.

[1] *Protsess P. SR: Rechi Gosudarstvennykh Obvinitelei* (1922), pp. 243-244.

CHAPTER 8

THE ASCENDANCY OF THE PARTY

THE evolution after October 1917 of the Bolshevik wing of the Russian Social-Democratic Workers' Party, soon to become the " Russian Communist Party (Bolsheviks) ", was a process both of continuity and of change. The party throughout its history continued to bear the stamp which Lenin had imprinted on it, and constantly returned to the traditions and controversies of its youth. The October revolution changed it in some obvious, and some more subtle, ways. But here again it is difficult to distinguish between changes inherent in its nature as a party, or in particular as a revolutionary party, and changes peculiar to it or to the situation in which it had to operate. The three main developments which marked the period between the October revolution and the death of Lenin were the increase of authority in the hands of a small central party leadership ; the transformation of the party from a revolutionary organization directed to the overthrow of existing institutions into the directing nucleus of a governmental and administrative machine ; and, finally, the creation for it of a monopoly position through the elimination of other parties.

The tendency to concentrate power at the centre of any large organization, and the necessity of concentration as a condition of efficient working, has been a commonplace of modern political parties.[1] Parties, like the anarchists, which resisted it condemned themselves to political sterility ; other parties were, on the whole, successful in proportion to their willingness to accept the discipline of a strong central authority and management. This fact has disturbing implications for parties purporting to be organized on democratic lines. All organized political parties — and particularly parties representing the masses, where the rank and file

---

[1] See p. 36 above.

is widely separated from the leaders by the intellectual and technical qualifications required for leadership — have tended, however
democratic the principles on which they rest, to develop in the
direction of a closed oligarchy of leaders. A sociologist whose
material was derived mainly from study of the German Social-
Democratic Party and the Italian Socialist Party before 1914 has
diagnosed the symptoms :

> In every social relation nature itself creates domination and
> dependence. Thus every party organization represents a power-
> ful oligarchy resting on democratic feet. Everywhere are
> electors and elected. But everywhere, too, is the power of the
> elected leadership over the electing masses. The oligarchic
> structure of the building conceals the democratic foundation.[1]

When the Bolsheviks became a mass party after 1917 this process
set in rapidly. It was no doubt accelerated by the traditions of
secrecy and discipline established in the party before 1917, by
the special position which it gradually achieved after 1917 as a
monopoly party in the state, and perhaps also by the political
backwardness and inexperience of the Russian workers in comparison with their western counterparts. But the perspective will
be seriously distorted if the process is regarded as peculiarly
Russian or peculiarly Bolshevik. It was common, in greater or less
degree, to all political parties of the first half of the twentieth century.

The evolution of a revolutionary party into a governmental
party has been a feature of all victorious revolutions, and produces
some consequences so familiar that they may be called stereotyped.
The party, turning from the task of destruction to that of administration, discovers the virtues of law and order and of submission
to the rightful authority of the revolutionary power ; and it is
attacked from the Left by those who wish to carry on the revolution
in the name of former revolutionary principles which the government of the revolution is now alleged to be betraying. This
pattern was followed in the history of the Russian revolution. But

---

[1] R. Michels, *Zur Soziologie des Parteiwesens* (2nd ed. 1925), p. 504. And
again : " The further the official apparatus extends, i.e. the more members an
organization gets and the more its coffers are filled and its press grows, the more
is democracy thrust aside in it and replaced by the omnipotence of committees "
(*ibid*. p. 98). The charge of " Byzantinism " — a favourite taunt of critics of
the Bolsheviks — was heard in the German Social-Democratic Party as early
as 1908 (*ibid*. p. 148).

another and more distinctive feature resulted from the new interaction of party and state. The association between party and state
directly involved the party in every national crisis, and transformed
every call for national unity and national leadership into a call for
party unity and loyalty to the party leader. To close the ranks was,
for the party as for the nation, the natural reaction to the national
danger. Nor was it possible to separate Lenin the party leader
from Lenin the leader of the nation. The ascendancy which he
exercised was one of moral authority rather than of external power.
But it helped to establish in the party, as well as in the state, a
tradition of personal leadership which it was difficult to shake off.

The third important change was the acquisition by the party
of what was in effect a political monopoly in Soviet territory. No
political theory denies to a political party the right to impose rigid
conditions, whether of conduct or of creed, on its members and
to exclude those who fail to comply. This right, however, had
hitherto presupposed that the individual had the option of changing
his party allegiance, and that some alternative party had a comparable opportunity of influencing public affairs. Before the
revolution dissenting Bolsheviks could, and did, become Mensheviks or join other parties or political groups. In the first
months after the revolution this fluidity of membership between
the surviving parties — Bolsheviks and Mensheviks, Left and
Right SRs — was still to some extent operative. The Bolsheviks
were the ruling party, but still one of several parties. But after the
summer of 1918 other political parties existed only on sufferance,
their status becoming more and more precarious; and from 1921
onwards they virtually disappeared. Resignation or expulsion
from the sole remaining party henceforth normally meant — to
say the least — exclusion from any legal form of political activity.
Thus disputes within the party were liable to grow increasingly
bitter both because there was no other channel through which
dissentient opinions could be expressed and because such opinions
could now plausibly be attributed to former Mensheviks or SRs
who had entered the party for insincere or interested motives.[1]

---

[1] The resolution of the tenth party congress attributed the growth of
fractionalism to " the entry into the ranks of the party of elements which have
not fully absorbed the communist point of view " (*VKP(B) v Rezolyutsiyakh*
(1941), i, 375). Lenin's original draft of this resolution specifically mentioned
" former Mensheviks " (*Sochineniya*, xxvi, 262).

It became easy and natural to treat dissent as disloyalty. In the one-party state conceptions of party unity and party discipline developed hitherto unsuspected implications.

These changes developed by stages. In spite of Lenin's long-standing insistence on conformity of doctrine and on party discipline to enforce it, the original party statute adopted by the second party congress of 1903 and confirmed in a slightly revised form by the third congress of 1905 left implicit the obligation on members to submit to party decisions. In the revised party statute adopted by the sixth congress in August 1917 this obligation was made for the first time explicit. What is perhaps surprising is that the victory of the revolution appeared at first to relax the bounds of party discipline and to lead to an outburst of unfettered dissension and controversy unprecedented in the annals of the Bolshevik party and perhaps rare in those of any other. These controversies within the party, acute as they were, proceeded under the recognized rule that party members retained their freedom of action until, though only until, the party decision had been taken. The offence for which Kamenev and Zinoviev had been threatened with expulsion on the eve of the revolution was not that they had expressed dissentient views in the debates of the central committee preceding the decision, but that they had publicly challenged that decision when, by the vote of a majority, it had gone against them.[1] No party, facing such defiance, could reasonably be denied the right to apply sanctions. A few days after the victory of the revolution Lenin faced a further revolt, once more led by Kamenev and Zinoviev, against the policy (which was shortly afterwards relaxed in favour of the Left SRs) of excluding other parties from the Soviet Government ; and this crisis only ended with an ultimatum and several resignations.[2]

---

[1] Similarly in the trade union controversy of 1920-1921 the fault of Trotsky lay in the fact not that he had put forward untenable proposals, but that, when these proposals were rejected by a majority of the central committee, he had refused to serve on the commission appointed to work out a solution (*ibid.* xxvi, 88).

[2] See p. 109 above. The ultimatum delivered by the central committee on November 6/19, 1917, to Kamenev, Zinoviev, Ryazanov and Larin, demanded that they should " either immediately and in writing undertake to submit to the decisions of the central committee and carry out its policy in all their public actions or to abstain from all party public activity and relinquish all responsible posts in the workers' movement until the next party congress " (*Protokoly*

A winter of free speech and hard hitting in the central committee of the party culminated in the famous debates in February and March 1918 on the Brest-Litovsk negotiations with Germany and the signature of the Brest-Litovsk treaty. In these debates the point was reached where Dzerzhinsky expressed regret that the party was not strong enough to risk the resignation of Lenin, and Lomov, prepared to face even this contingency, openly said that " we must take power without Vladimir Ilich ".[1]

While, however, the initial effect of the revolution had been to encourage a freedom and publicity of discussion rarely practised by any party on vital issues of public policy, other forces soon began to operate in the opposite sense. The uncritical enthusiasm bred by the triumph of the revolution evaporated ; in the spring of 1918 economic difficulties were already acute ; and opposition began to come from Left groups within the party which accused the party leadership of opportunist tendencies and of an abandonment of Bolshevik principles. Thus the controversies over Brest-Litovsk gave birth to a group of " Left communists " which for a fortnight published in Petrograd an opposition daily newspaper *Kommunist*, and drew Lenin's fire at the seventh party congress convened to ratify the Brest-Litovsk treaty in March 1918:

> The serious crisis through which our party is passing in connexion with the formation within it of a Left opposition is one of the biggest crises through which the Russian revolution has passed.[2]

Defeated over Brest-Litovsk, it turned its attention to the critical economic situation, attacking Lenin's policy on such matters as the employment of specialists, the formation of industrial trusts and one-man management in industry ; and it was not unnaturally, though perhaps unjustly, suspected of intriguing with the Left SRs who had left Sovnarkom on the Brest-Litovsk issue.[3]   The

---

Tsentral'nogo Komiteta RSDRP (1929), p. 170). Zinoviev replied with a letter of submission ; the other three remained obdurate and were excluded from the central committee (*ibid.* pp. 175-177). Rykov, Milyutin and Nogin also resigned from the central committee and from their posts in Sovnarkom.

[1] *Ibid.* pp. 249-250.
[2] Lenin, *Sochineniya*, xxii, 321.
[3] During the bitter party controversies of December 1923 Zinoviev alleged that the Left SRs had proposed at this time to arrest Lenin and other members of Sovnarkom, that the plan had been seriously considered by the Left commun-

group secured control of the party organization in Moscow, and in April 1918 published two numbers of a new journal under the title *Kommunist*, described as the " Organ of the Moscow Regional Bureau of the Russian Communist Party (Bolsheviks) ".   The editors were Bukharin, Obolensky, Radek and V. Smirnov.[1]   The first number printed a long manifesto on the economic situation which had been read at a meeting of the group with the party leaders, including Lenin, on April 4, 1918.[2]   In the following month, the group was subjected to one of Lenin's most formidable broadsides in an article, *On "Left" Infantilism and the Petty-Bourgeois Spirit*, and faded away in the summer of 1918 when the conspiracy of the SRs and the beginning of the civil war frightened the party into a re-establishment of unity and self-discipline under Lenin's leadership.[3]

The seventh party congress, which decided to ratify Brest-Litovsk, also gave effect to the proposal made by Lenin a year earlier in his April theses to change the name of the party from " social-democratic " to " communist ".   Marx and Engels had expressed their dislike of the old title when the German workers' party adopted it in 1875 : already at that time the word " democracy ", even qualified by the adjective " social ", was beginning

ists and that Pyatakov had been designated to succeed Lenin (*Pravda*, December 16, 1923).   Stalin also referred to the same allegation (*ibid.* December 15, 1923).   A group of former Left communists, including Pyatakov and Radek, replied with a statement that the story had no foundation other than some remarks made in jest (*ibid.* January 3, 1924).   In 1937 Bukharin was charged with having organized a major plot against Lenin on this occasion.

[1] Among other participants named on the title page were Bubnov, Kosior, Kuibyshev, Pokrovsky, Preobrazhensky, Pyatakov, Sapronov, Safarov, Uritsky, Unshlikht and Yaroslavsky.

[2] According to a statement in *Kommunist*, No. 1, April 20, 1918, p. 13, Lenin on this occasion read a set of counter-theses and promised to publish them, but failed to do so.   The manifesto of the group is reprinted in Lenin, *Sochineniya*, xxii, 561-571 : its content will be discussed in Part IV.

[3] It is a symptom of the spirit of this period that at the height of this apparently bitter controversy, Bukharin should have appeared as principal delegate of the central committee of the party at the first All-Russian Congress of Councils of National Economy, and that Radek should have made a report to it on " the economic consequences of the Brest-Litovsk treaty " (*Trudy i Vserossiiskogo S"ezda Sovetov Narodnogo Khozyaistva* (1918), pp. 7, 14-23). Such elasticity was due partly to the extreme shortage of qualified men in the party, but partly also to the strong tradition that, however party members might dispute among themselves, they spoke in non-party organizations with the voice of the party.   Ryazanov on this occasion taunted Radek with " arguing against himself " and " executing an *Eiertanz* " (*ibid.* p. 34).

to lose its revolutionary connotation. Since 1914 the social-democrats of Europe, except for an insignificant minority, had abandoned the cause of world-wide proletarian revolution, and become bourgeois " reformists " and " chauvinists ". In December 1914 Lenin had enquired whether it would not be better to abandon the " stained and degraded " name of " social-democrats " and return to the Marxist name of " communists ".[1] It was time to mark the gulf between them, and to claim the Marxist heritage for the revolutionaries by reverting to the old Marxist title " communist ". The change had a dual significance. Internally, the party finally turned its back on the bourgeois stage of the revolution and set its face resolutely towards the communist goal. Externally, the change marked the division in the European workers' movement between those who clung to bourgeois policies of reform and those who stood for revolution through the proletariat : the split which Lenin had brought about in the Russian party in 1903 was now repeated on an international scale. There had been some reluctance within the party to alter the traditional name : but in March 1918 Lenin's followers finally ceased to call themselves the " Russian Social-Democratic Workers' Party " — a disputed title long shared with the Mensheviks and now abandoned to them — and became the " Russian Communist Party (Bolsheviks) ".[2]

The time had also come to tighten up party organization. The system of organization had long been described in party circles as " democratic centralism ",[3] a term intended to denote that double process by which authority flowed upwards from

[1] Lenin, *Sochineniya*, xviii, 73.

[2] *VKP(B) v Rezolyutsiyakh* (1941), i, 279.

[3] The term (for which see p. 36 above) was embodied in the party statute by the fifth party congress of 1907 (*ibid*. i, 108); a precise definition was first included in the party statute of 1934 (*ibid*. ii, 591) in the following terms :

(a) The application of the elective principle to all leading organs of the party, from the highest to the lowest ;

(b) The periodic accountability of the party organs to their respective party organizations ;

(c) Strict party discipline and subordination of the minority to the majority ;

(d) The absolutely binding character of the decision of the higher organs upon the lower organs and upon all party members.

party cells in town or factory or village through intermediate local or regional committees till it reached its apex in the central committee which was the organ of the sovereign congress, and discipline flowed downwards through the same channels, every party organ being subordinated to the organ above it and ultimately to the central committee. With the triumph of the revolution, the transformation of the party into a legal organization, and its large increase in membership, this conception could at length be fully realized on lines bearing a close resemblance to the organization of the Soviets. The supreme organ, the party congress, met in principle — and, during the first few years after the revolution, in fact — annually. The central committee, which was the main executive organ, met, according to the statute of 1917, " not less than once in two months ". When the revolution enabled the party to spread its net all over Russia, a vast hierarchy of central and local organizations was called into being. Beneath the " all-Russian " congress and its central committee, each constituent republic or region (*oblast*) had its regional conference and regional committee ; beneath them were the provincial conferences and provincial committees ; then came the county (*uezd*) conferences and committees and the district (*volost*) conferences and committees ; and last of all came the party cells, each with its " bureau ", in factories, in village communities, in the Red Army, in Soviet institutions — everywhere, indeed, where two or three party members could gather together. Though standing lowest in the hierarchy, the cells were by no means the least important element in the party machine. It is even more difficult to obtain an authentic picture of these than of the local Soviets which formed the lowest grade in the Soviet system. But in many respects they inherited the hard tradition of the small underground groups through which the party had made its influence felt in Tsarist Russia ; and the whole structure depended, at any rate in the early stages of the revolution, on their loyalty and effectiveness.[1]

Given the composition of the party and the turbulent conditions into which it was plunged within a few months of its revolutionary triumph, its evolution was inevitable. In the struggle latent in the term " democratic centralism " — the

[1] An important resolution of the tenth congress enumerated the functions of the cells (*ibid.* i, 370-371).

struggle between the flow of authority from the periphery to the centre and the imposition of discipline by the centre on the periphery, between democracy and efficiency — the second was bound to emerge as the predominant factor. So long as Lenin firmly held the reins, the two forces could be reconciled and run in double harness; and he himself was always impatient of those who tried to draw a contrast between authority " from above " and " from below ".[1] But the increasing ascendancy of Lenin's outstanding and self-confident personality in the critical years through which the new régime had to pass justified the tradition of strong leadership and helped to establish the need for it. Other forces were also at work. The strongest of all was the oppressive weight of the whole tradition of Russian administration and of the Russian social structure. Beyond question Lenin desired in principle, and even strove in practice, to initiate the rank and file of the party, and subsequently of the proletariat, into active participation in the affairs of the party and of the nation; and when he spoke, as he did on many occasions in his later years, of the " backwardness " and " lack of culture " of the Russian people, he was thinking in part of his failure to realize this dream. It was likely to take more than one generation to make any serious impression on so deep-seated a tradition of administrative direction from above. Nor did the Russian Communist Party differ as much in this respect as is sometimes supposed from political parties in other countries where controversial issues are fought out, and the party line determined, by a narrow circle of leaders rather than by any effective consultation of the rank and file.

[1] In 1920, after describing the way in which the party worked through the Soviet apparatus, he continued : " Such is the general mechanism of proletarian state power seen ' from above ', from the standpoint of the practical realization of the dictatorship. The reader will, it may be hoped, understand why the Russian Bolshevik, who knows this mechanism and has observed how this mechanism has grown up over a period of 25 years out of small, illegal, underground groups, cannot help regarding all talk about ' from above ' or ' from below ', the dictatorship of the leaders or the dictatorship of the masses, as ridiculous childish nonsense, comparable to the argument whether a man's left leg or right arm is more useful to him " (*Sochineniya*, xxv, 193). A few months later the central committee issued a circular letter on the " burning question " of the " upper " and " lower " ranks in the party ; it attributed the acuteness of the question partly to the large recent influx of young and untried members, partly to the " incorrect and often quite intolerable methods of work adopted by some responsible party workers " (*Izvestiya Tsentral'nogo Komiteta Rossiiskoi Kommunisticheskoi Partii* (*Bol'shevikov*), No. 21, September 4, 1920, pp. 1-3).

It was thus not surprising that the same irresistible tendency towards the concentration of authority which affected the Soviet organs, equally — though somewhat later in time — attacked those of the party. The formally sovereign party congress, though it met annually from 1917 to 1924, became too cumbersome, and its meetings too rare for the exercise of effective power; and its decline followed, though at a certain interval, that of its state counterpart, the All-Russian Congress of Soviets. The seventh party congress of March 1918 which voted for the ratification of Brest-Litovsk was the last to decide a vital issue of policy by a majority vote. The next few congresses continued to debate crucial issues and witnessed on occasion sharp exchanges of opinion : this was particularly true of the twelfth congress of 1923 — the first since the October revolution at which Lenin was not present. But even when discussions took place on the floor of the congress, the real decisions were reached elsewhere. Already in October 1917 it was the central committee which had taken the vital decision to seize power; and it was the central committee which succeeded to the authority of the congress. But even the central committee — like VTsIK, its counterpart in the Soviet system — failed in turn to retain its power, which was soon to be sapped by smaller and more effective organs. When Zinoviev in 1923 enthusiastically declared that " the central committee of our party in virtue of tradition, in virtue of the history of its 25 years of existence, constitutes a group which sucks into itself all that is most authoritative from the party ", he was describing a situation which was about to pass into history.[1]

The issue of centralization within the party first came into the open at the eighth party congress which met in March 1919 at the height of the civil war. The process had by this time gone a long way. Osinsky complained at the congress that all party work was centred round the central committee, and that " even the central committee as a collegiate organ does not, properly speaking, exist ", since " comrades Lenin and Sverdlov decide current questions by way of conversation with each other or with individual comrades in charge of this or that branch of Soviet work ".[2]

[1] *Dvenadtsatyi S"ezd Rossiiskoi Kommunisticheskoi Partii (Bol'shevikov)* (1923), p. 207.
[2] *Vos'moi S"ezd RKP(B)* (1933), pp. 165-166.

None the less, the civil war placed the party, as a resolution of the congress admitted, " in a position where the strictest centralism and severest discipline are an absolute necessity " ; [1] and it was particularly unfortunate that Sverdlov, hitherto the competent manager of the party machine, had died on the eve of the congress. The congress, accepting the need to strengthen the central authority, endeavoured to equip the central committee for its task both by limiting its numbers to nineteen (with eight " candidates ") and by prescribing fortnightly meetings. But it took at the same time the fateful step of creating three new organs which, though nominally emanations from the central committee, were destined, within the next three or four years, to divide its functions between them and to usurp all but the outward trappings of authority.

The first of these bodies was a Politburo of five members, whose name and character recalled the political bureau previously created at a moment of crisis on the eve of the October revolution. Its function was to " take decisions on questions not permitting of delay " and to report to the fortnightly meeting of the central committee. But it need hardly be said that the formal restriction of its competence to urgent questions, like the similar restriction of the powers of Sovnarkom in the constitution of the RSFSR, proved quite unreal ; the Politburo quickly became the principal source of major decisions of policy, which were executed through the machinery of the state. The second new body was an " organizational bureau " (Orgburo), also of five members, which was to meet three times a week and " conduct the whole organizational work of the party ". The third organ was a " secretariat of the central committee ", consisting of a " responsible secretary " and five " technical " assistants, whose functions were not further defined.[2] The dangers of a clash between Politburo, Orgburo and secretariat were reduced by the expedient of an interlocking membership. Krestinsky, who became the first " responsible secretary ", also had a seat on the Orgburo. One member of the Politburo was also to be a member of the Orgburo ; Stalin was chosen for this dual rôle. At the next congress in 1920 a

[1] *VKP(B) v Rezolyutsiyakh* (1941), i, 305.
[2] *Ibid.* i, 304. Hitherto the secretariat had been a purely routine organ supervised by Sverdlov (Lenin, *Sochineniya*, xxiv, 127-128).

further fateful step was taken. It was decided to strengthen the secretariat by giving it a membership of three " permanent workers ", all members of the central committee, and by entrust- ing to it " the conduct of current questions of an organizational and executive character ", only " the general direction of the organizational work " being reserved for the Orgburo.[1] The reinforced secretariat was to be composed of Krestinsky, Preobra- zhensky and Serebryakov.

It had not been generally foreseen that the main questions confronting this untried secretariat would be issues of party discipline. The dying away of the Left communist movement in the summer of 1918 under the impact of civil war did not betoken the end of opposition within the party. The Russian revolution had reached the point, common in the experience of all revolutions, when the party which had made the revolution was faced with the task of consolidating its power and of strengthen- ing the state machine ; and at such a moment opposition from the Left in the name of old revolutionary principles was inevitable and persistent. At the eighth party congress of March 1919, with the civil war at its height, a " military opposition " unsuccess- fully challenged Trotsky's policy of building up a new national conscript army with professional officers partly drawn from the old Tsarist army. At the ninth congress of March 1920 a group using the party slogan of " democratic centralism " objected to the introduction of one-man management in industry and secured the support of the trade unions in the person of Tomsky ; and this proved to be the starting-point of a new opposition movement. Its growth during the summer of 1920 was traced in a report of the central committee to the party congress in the following spring. Sometimes it took the form of clashes within the same party organ, sometimes of defiance of a provincial committee by the county organizations, sometimes of dissatisfaction among " the workers' part of certain provincial committees ", sometimes of disputes between workers' and peasants' organizations. The trouble was put down to several causes — " the terrible exhaustion of the working masses " from war, civil war, economic disorganiza- tion, cold and hunger ; the admission to the party of " sincere, devoted, but politically untrained workers and peasants " ; and

[1] *VKP(B) v Rezolyutsiyakh* (1941), i, 344.

the admission to the party of former members of other parties.[1]
Towards the end of the summer a commission was appointed to
look into the matter, including two of those who had figured in the
opposition at the previous congress, Ignatov and Sapronov, and
a resolution drafted by this commission was approved by an all-
Russian party conference in September 1920. The resolution spoke
in general terms of the need to improve contact between the rank
and file and the central authority, and to impart fresh vigour and
vitality to party life. But its most concrete recommendation was
to establish a " control commission side by side with the central
committee "; the function of the commission was " to receive
and examine complaints of all kinds ", to discuss them, if necessary, jointly with the central committee and to reply to them.
Pending the next party congress, the main control commission
was to consist of Dzerzhinsky, Muranov, Preobrazhensky and
four members appointed by the largest local party organizations ;
thereafter it was laid down that " in general members of the
central committee should not be elected to membership of the
control commission ".[2] Similar commissions were also to be
attached to the provincial party committees. A special " Kremlin
control commission " was set up to investigate " Kremlin privileges ", which were giving rise to complaints within the party,
and " to bring them, in so far as it was impossible to eliminate
them altogether, within limits which would be understood by
every party comrade ".[3] The central control commission inaugurated its work with a circular to all party members inviting
them " to communicate to it all offences against the party by
its members, *without for a moment being embarrassed by the position
or function of the persons incriminated* ".[4]

These measures did nothing to allay the growing unrest. In
the autumn of 1920, when the civil war was virtually over, the
most formidable dissentient group organized within the party
since the revolution came into being under the name of the

[1] *Izvestiya Tsentral'nogo Komiteta Rossiiskoi Kommunisticheskoi Partii
(Bol'shevikov)*, No. 29, March 7, 1921, pp. 4-6, reprinted in *Rabochaya Oppozitsiya: Materialy i Dokumenty* (1926), pp. 21-22.
[2] *VKP(B) v Rezolyutsiyakh* (1941), i, 351-353.
[3] *Izvestiya Tsentral'nogo Komiteta Rossiiskoi Kommunisticheskoi Partii
(Bol'shevikov)*, No. 26, December 20, 1920, p. 2.
[4] *Ibid.* No. 25, November 11, 1920, p. 1.

" workers' opposition ".   It was stronger in numbers than in leadership or programme.   Its only well-known leaders were Shlyapnikov, who, formerly himself a metal-worker and People's Commissar for Labour in the first Soviet Government, constituted himself the champion of the " workers ", and Kollontai, whose prestige no longer stood so high as in the early days of the revolution.   Its programme was a hotch-potch of current discontents, directed in the main against the growing centralization of economic and political controls, against the growing efficiency and ruthlessness of the machine.   It proposed the transfer of the control of industry and production from the state to the trade unions, thus appealing to the vague demand for " workers' control " and to the syndicalist trend endemic in certain sections of the party; it protested against the predominance of intellectuals in the party and called for a drastic purge of non-workers; and it wanted open election to all party posts and free discussions within the party with facilities for the dissemination of dissentient views. These criticisms and proposals, having been widely ventilated in the press and elsewhere during the winter of 1920–1921, were embodied in a pamphlet *The Workers' Opposition* by Kollontai, which was distributed to members of the party at the time of the tenth party congress in March 1921.[1]

The views of the workers' opposition made it one of the main wings in the controversy on the rôle of the trade unions which agitated the party throughout the winter of 1920–1921.   While the " workers' opposition " stood for the independence of the trade unions and their supremacy in the economic system, Trotsky, publicly ranged against Lenin for the first time since Brest-Litovsk, desired their open subordination to the state. Throughout the month of January 1921 *Pravda* carried, day after

---

[1] This pamphlet is no longer easily obtainable, but is extensively quoted in *Rabochaya Oppozitsiya: Materialy i Dokumenty* (1926) and in *Platforma Shlyapnikova i Medvedeva* (1927); see also Lenin, *Sochineniya*, xxvi, 632-634; xxvii, 494-496.   There is an English translation, *The Workers' Opposition in Russia* (n.d.).   The generalization of R. Michels about party dissensions, originally written before 1910, applies accurately to the workers' opposition : " The slogan of the majority is ' centralization ', that of minorities ' autonomy ' "; in order to reach their goal minorities are driven to conduct a struggle which at times takes the form of a struggle for freedom and even uses the terminology of heroes of freedom taking the field against the tyranny of tyrants " (*Zur Soziologie des Parteiwesens* (2nd ed. 1925), p. 228).

day, polemical articles in which the principal party leaders aired
diametrically opposite opinions.   The party published two
numbers of a special *Discussion Sheet* in order to provide a forum
for a more detailed exchange of views.   Lenin took alarm.   In
a pamphlet called *The Party Crisis* he spoke of the " fever " which
was shaking the party and asked whether the party organism was
" capable of healing itself completely and making a repetition of
the disease impossible or whether the disease will become chronic
and dangerous ".   He accused Trotsky of " creating a fraction
on an erroneous platform "; and, turning to the " workers'
opposition ", he enunciated the hitherto accepted party rule with
a qualification which was afterwards used to annul it :

> To form ourselves into different groups (especially before a
> congress) is of course permissible (and so is to canvass for votes).
> But it must be done within the limits of communism (and not
> syndicalism) and in such a way as not to provoke laughter.

He ended with a familiar warning of the exploitation by external
enemies of internal party dissensions :

> The capitalists of the *Entente* will undoubtedly try to take
> advantage of the disease in our party to launch a fresh attack
> and the Social-Revolutionaries to organize conspiracies and
> risings.   We are not afraid, since we shall all unite as one man,
> not fearing to recognize the disease, but conscious that it
> demands from us more discipline, more restraint, more firmness
> at every post.[1]

Before the long-awaited party congress met on March 8, 1921,
the Kronstadt mutiny — the most serious internal threat to the
régime since the revolution — had justified Lenin's fears and
added point to every appeal to close the party ranks.

The tenth party congress of March 1921 was decisive in the
history of the party and of the republic.   It met at a moment
when the easy hopes borne of the triumphant conclusion of the
civil war had been dashed, when economic crisis had appeared in
the stark form of failing food supplies, and when political insurrection had raised its head for the first time since the summer of
1918.   A sense of the precariousness of the situation pervaded

[1] Lenin, *Sochineniya*, xxvi, 87-94.

the congress. The least of its achievements was the settlement of the vexed dispute about the trade unions ; the announcement of NEP came at a late stage of the proceedings and was not discussed in any far-reaching way ; the real leitmotif of the congress, harped on by Lenin in nearly all his numerous utterances, was the overriding need for unity in the party. He struck it dramatically in his brief opening speech :

> Comrades, we have lived through a remarkable year, we have allowed ourselves the luxury of discussions and disputes within our party. For a party which is surrounded by the strongest and most powerful enemies embracing the whole capitalist world, for a party which carries on its shoulders an unheard of burden, this luxury was truly astounding. I do not know how you will assess it now. Has this luxury in your view been fully consistent with our material and moral resources ?

And later he turned with unwonted passion on the opposition :

> All these reflexions about freedom of speech and freedom of criticism which . . . abound in all the speeches of the " workers' opposition " constitute nine-tenths of the sense of speeches which have no real sense — nothing but words of this character. Comrades, do not let us talk only about words, but about their content. You cannot fool us with words like " freedom of criticism ". When we said that the party shows symptoms of disease, we meant that this diagnosis deserves threefold attention ; undoubtedly the disease is there. Help us to heal this disease. Tell us how you can heal it. We have spent a great deal of time in discussion, and I must say that now it is a great deal better to " discuss with rifles " than with the theses of the opposition. We need no opposition, comrades, now is not the time ! Either on this side, or on that — with a rifle, not with the opposition.[1]

The terminology was vague. The context allowed it to be supposed that all that Lenin was demanding was the exclusion from the party of those who persisted in their opposition, and who might be logically expected to find themselves on the other side of the barricades. Yet he conveyed, and intended to convey, that within the party ranks freedom of criticism was a " luxury " which easily degenerated into a " disease ", and that beyond those

---

[1] *Ibid.* xxvi, 200, 227.

ranks the only effective instrument of settling differences was the rifle. These conclusions may well have been correct in the conditions of crisis and armed insurrection which overshadowed the tenth congress. They had their roots in party doctrine; and Lenin helped to rivet them in the party tradition.

Two resolutions bearing on the theme of party unity and discipline were adopted by the congress. One, bearing the title, " On the Syndicalist and Anarchist Deviation [1] in our Party ", pronounced the dissemination of the ideas of the " workers' opposition " to be " incompatible with membership of the Russian Communist Party ". The resolution added, a little inconsequently, that " place should be found in special publications, miscellanies, etc. for the most detailed exchange of opinions among members of the party on all the questions concerned "; [2] and the congress, in a short separate resolution, refused to accept the resignation of members of the " workers' opposition " who had been re-elected to the central committee, and summoned them to " submit to party discipline ".[3] The other major resolution " On the Unity of the Party " insisted that all disputed issues in the party should be submitted " not to discussion by groups formed on some platform or other, but to discussion by all members of the party ". The central committee was instructed to bring about " the complete abolition of all fractionalism " : [4]

> The congress prescribes the immediate dissolution of all groups without exception forming themselves on this or that platform, and instructs all organizations to insist strictly on the inadmissibility of any kind of fractional activities. Nonfulfilment of this decision of the congress must entail unconditional and immediate exclusion from the party.

[1] This was apparently the first appearance of this famous word in the party vocabulary. Lenin explained it at the congress as follows: " A deviation (*uklon*) is not a fully formed movement. A deviation is something that can be corrected. People have strayed a little from the path or are beginning to stray, but it is still possible to correct it. That in my view is expressed by the Russian word *uklon* " (Lenin, *Sochineniya*, xxvi, 267).

[2] *VKP(B) v Rezolyutsiyakh* (1941), i, 366-368.

[3] *Ibid.* i, 368.

[4] The word " fractionalism " became a popular one in party vocabulary during the next few years. It was defined in the resolution as " the appearance of groups with special platforms and with the ambition to form in some degree a unit and to establish their own group discipline ". Thus " groups " were not in themselves illegitimate : " fractions " were.

Finally, the congress added a secret rider, which became famous as " point 7 ", in the following terms :

> In order to realize strict discipline within the party and in all Soviet work and to attain the greatest possible unity through the removal of all fractionalism, the congress gives the central committee full powers in case(s) of any breach of discipline or revival or toleration of fractionalism to apply all measures of party sanctions, including expulsion from the party, or, as regards members of the central committee, transfer to the status of candidates, or even, as an extreme measure, exclusion from the party. The application to members and candidates of the central committee and to members of the control commission of so extreme a measure is conditional on the summoning of a plenum of the central committee to which all candidates of the central committee and members of the control commission shall be invited. If such a general meeting of the responsible leaders of the party recognizes by a two-thirds majority the necessity of transferring a member of the central committee to the status of candidate or excluding him from the party, such a measure should be carried out immediately.[1]

The periphrastic drafting, the precautions against hasty action, and the decision to keep secret this final paragraph of the resolution,[2] were evidence of the reluctance with which the congress adopted this minatory measure. The hesitation was justified. The resolution, though a logical outcome of the passing of effective power from congress to central committee, was capital for the future of the party.

The tenth party congress was a milestone in the development of the power of the party machine. The current doctrine of party discipline required the party member, and especially the member of the central committee, to comply loyally with decisions of the party once they had been taken, subject to the extreme penalty of exclusion from the party. Until the decision was taken, he remained perfectly free, in accordance with the statute

---

[1] *Ibid.* i, 364-366. The resolution in the form in which it was submitted to the congress by Lenin will be found in Lenin, *Sochineniya*, xxvi, 259-261. The congress made only minor drafting changes : " point 7 " remained in the form in which it was originally drafted, presumably by Lenin himself.

[2] The party conference of January 1924, a few days before Lenin's death, decided on the proposal of Stalin to invite the central committee to publish the secret paragraph (*VKP(B) v Rezolyutsiyakh* (1941), i, 545).

of 1919,[1] to disseminate his opinions. As late as January 1921 Lenin had recognized the right of the party members " within the limits of communism " to form groups and canvass for votes. Two months later the darkening clouds of political and economic crisis at the tenth congress caused the withdrawal of this recognition. Henceforth the criticism of individuals or even of groups would be tolerated within the party, but the opposition must not organize : that would be to commit the sin of " fractionalism ". Even the composition of the central committee was in the last resort removed from the exclusive competence of the sovereign congress, since two-thirds of its members were now in a position to expel recalcitrant colleagues. The sum of these measures, approved and sponsored by Lenin himself in the crisis atmosphere of the tenth party congress of March 1921, was enormously to increase the disciplinary power of the inner group of party leaders.

These measures born of the party emergency eclipsed a multitude of good intentions inspired by the ending of the civil war, and made the introductory paragraphs of a long resolution on party organization somewhat unreal. The resolution referred to the " militarization ", to the " extreme organizational centralism " and to the " system of fighting commands " which had of necessity dominated party affairs during the civil war, and admitted that a " highly centralized apparatus created on the basis of the very backward cultural level of the masses " had been one of the " contradictions of war communism ". The civil war being now over, the tenth congress felt no further need for these anomalies and passed a resolution in favour of " workers' democracy " within the party. Party workers were to take their turn at the bench or the plough ; the discussion of party questions,

---

[1] The relevant passage ran : " Decisions of party centres must be carried out promptly and exactly. At the same time discussion within the party of all controversial questions of party life is completely free until such time as a decision has been taken." The statute went on to enumerate in an ascending scale penalties for failure to comply with decisions of higher party organs — " party censure, public censure, temporary removal from responsible party or Soviet work, temporary removal from all party or Soviet work, expulsion from the party, and expulsion from the party together with communication of the offence to the administrative and judicial authorities ". There was no question at this time of calling on dissentients to renounce their opinions or to confess themselves in the wrong : all that was required was compliance in action.

both particular and general, by local party organizations was to
be encouraged; and everything was to be done to realize " a
constant control by the public opinion of the party over the
work of its leading organs and a constant interaction in practice
between the latter and the whole party in its entirety, together
with the furtherance of strict accountability of the appropriate
party committees not only to the higher, but also to the lower
organizations ".[1]

But such aspirations were feebly reflected in the changes made
in the organization and membership of the central party organs.
The congress confirmed the resolution of the September conference on the establishment of a system of control commissions,
and attempted to define their scope and functions,[2] though it
became clear that the multiplication of central party organs was
little to the taste of many of the rank and file of the party.[3] The
existing central organs underwent minor but significant changes.
The fortnightly meetings of the central committee prescribed
by the eighth congress in 1919 [4] had fallen into desuetude.
The tenth congress required it to meet only every two months.
This made it easier to increase the membership to twenty-five. The
number of " candidates " entitled to attend meetings of the committee, but not to vote, was not laid down; on this occasion fifteen
were elected.[5] These changes marked no fresh development;
they were steps in the gradual transformation of the central com-

---

[1] *VKP(B) v Rezolyutsiyakh* (1941), i, 357-358, 360-361.
[2] *Ibid.* i, 368-369. The offences against which the work of the control commissions were directed are defined in the resolution as " bureaucratism, career-
ism, abuse by party members of their party or Soviet status, violation of comradely relations within the party, dissemination of unfounded and unverified
rumours, insinuations or other reports reflecting on the party or individual
members of it and destructive of the unity and authority of the party ".
[3] This emerges from remarks of spokesmen of the party leadership at the
congress (*Desyatyi S"ezd Rossiiskoi Kommunisticheskoi Partii* (1921), pp. 27, 42).
[4] *VKP(B) v Rezolyutsiyakh* (1941), i, 304.
[5] *Ibid.* i, 363; *Desyatyi S"ezd Rossiiskoi Kommunisticheskoi Partii* (1921),
p. 330. The central committee elected by the sixth party congress in August
1917 consisted of 21 members and 8 candidates (of whom 12 — 11 members and
one candidate — were present at the famous meeting of October 10 which decided
on armed insurrection). The seventh congress in March 1918 reduced the
membership to 15 with 8 candidates. Thereafter the membership continually
increased, and was fixed by a resolution of the twelfth congress in 1923 at 40
members and 15-20 candidates (*VKP(B) v Rezolyutsiyakh* (1941), i, 501).
Later it rose higher still.

mittee from the main working organ of the party into a grand
council of party chiefs. It was perhaps more significant that the
tenth congress raised the membership both of the Politburo and
of the Orgburo to seven with four " candidates ". The constitution of the secretariat was untouched, but a clean sweep was made
of the three secretaries of the past twelve months, who had
failed to cope with the opposition and supported Trotsky in
the trade-union controversy. Krestinsky, Preobrazhensky and
Serebryakov not only disappeared from the secretariat, but were
not even re-elected to the central committee — a sure mark of
disgrace. The three new secretaries were Molotov, Yaroslavsky
and Mikhailov; and these were also elected for the first time as
members of the central committee with a high quota of votes —
well above such old party leaders as Zinoviev and Kamenev.[1]
What rivalries and what calculations may have lain behind these
appointments can only be guessed. It is perhaps worth noting
that the three dispossessed members of the secretariat were to
become Stalin's enemies and two out of the three new members
his staunchest supporters. For the first time Stalin's hand may
with some plausibility be discerned in crucial party appointments.
How little attention was, however, generally paid to such matters
in the party is shown by some curious remarks of Ryazanov at the
congress itself. Ryazanov complained that " our nice comrade
Bukharin ", who was a pure theorist, had been called on to make
the report on party organization, and deduced that " there are no
specialists in organization in the central committee and the place
left vacant by Sverdlov is still unfilled ".[2] Meanwhile the growing significance of the secretariat in the party machine was
reflected in its constantly increasing staff. It had entered on
its functions in May 1919 with 30 workers. At the time of the
ninth party congress in March 1920 it had 150 workers; a year
later on the eve of the tenth congress the number had risen to

[1] The list of those elected with the votes cast for each was: Lenin 479,
Radek 475, Tomsky 472, Kalinin 470, Rudzutak 467, Stalin 458, Rykov 458,
Komarov 457, Molotov 453, Trotsky 452, Mikhailov 449, Bukharin 447,
Yaroslavsky 444, Dzerzhinsky 438, Orjonikidze 438, Petrovsky 436, Rakovsky
430, Zinoviev 423, Frunze 407, Kamenev 406, Voroshilov 383, Kutuzov 380,
Shlyapnikov 354, Tuntal 351, Artem 283. The high place of Tomsky and
Rudzutak was explained by the prominence of the trade-union question at the
congress (*Desyatyi S"ezd Rossiiskoi Kommunisticheskoi Partii* (1921), p. 221).

[2] *Ibid.* p. 161.

602, besides a military detachment of 140 men to act as guards and messengers.[1]

Hardly less important than the reorganization and strengthening of the secretariat was the initiation by the tenth congress of the first systematic " purge "[2] in the party ranks. The idea was implicit in Lenin's conception of the party. " Better ", he had already said at the 1903 congress, " that ten workers should not call themselves members of the party . . . than that one chatterbox should have the right and possibility to be a member of the party ".[3] Quality came before quantity ; above all the party must be kept pure. Its growth was for a long time exceedingly slow. On the eve of the 1905 revolution the Bolshevik wing of the party claimed no more than 8400 members. On the eve of the February revolution of 1917 the number was 23,600. A year later, after two revolutions, it had risen to 115,000 ; thereafter it rose steadily to 313,000 at the beginning of 1919, with corresponding figures of 431,000 and 585,000 for January 1920 and January 1921.[4] But it accorded with the party tradition that enthusiasm at this access of strength should be tempered by recognition of its dangers.

It was at the eighth party congress of March 1919 that the note of alarm was first struck. Nogin, a member of the central committee, spoke of " horrifying facts about the drunkenness, debauchery, corruption, robbery and irresponsible behaviour of many party workers, so that one's hair simply stands on end " ;[5] and a resolution of the congress recorded its conclusion in emphatic, though less highly coloured, terms :

> Elements which are not sufficiently communist or even directly parasitic are flowing into the party in a broad stream. The Russian Communist Party is in power, and this inevitably

---

[1] *Izvestiya Tsentral'nogo Komiteta Rossiiskoi Kommunisticheskoi Partii (Bol'-shevikov)*, No. 29, March 7, 1921, p. 7 ; the distribution of the 602 members of staff is given *ibid.* No. 28, March 5, 1921, p. 23.

[2] The traditional translation is slightly stronger than the original Russian *chistka*, which means a cleansing or purification.

[3] Lenin, *Sochineniya*, vi, 32-33.

[4] These figures are quoted from the official statistics of the statistical section of the party central committee by A. S. Bubnov, *VKP(B)* (1931), p. 612. The figures announced at party congresses were nearly always substantially higher (for instance, a total of 730,000 was claimed at the tenth Congress in March 1921), but did not presumably withstand the scrutiny of the party statisticians. None of these early figures can have had much claim to precise accuracy.

[5] *Vos'moi S"ezd RKP(B)* (1933), p. 170.

attracts to it, together with the better elements, careerist elements as well. . . .

A serious *purge* is indispensable in Soviet and party organizations.[1]

Lenin returned to the theme at the party conference of December 1919. After greeting the new members, " those thousands and hundreds of thousands who joined us while Yudenich was within a few versts of Petrograd and Denikin north of Orel ", he went on :

> Now that we have carried out such an expansion of the party, we must close the gates, we must be particularly cautious. We must say : Now, when the party is winning, we do not need new members. We know perfectly well that in a dissolving capitalist society a mass of noxious elements will fasten itself on to the party.[2]

The resumption of civil war in 1920 once more postponed action, and it was the tenth party congress of March 1921 which finally sanctioned the purge. Even then the cautious phraseology of the resolution suggests the need to appease rank-and-file objectors :

> An extreme necessity exists to turn the lever of party policy decisively towards the recruitment of workers and towards purging the party of non-communist elements by way of an accurate examination of each individual member of the Russian Communist Party, both in the light of his discharge of the work assigned to him and also in his capacity as a member of the Russian Communist Party.[3]

It was to be a scrutiny both of conduct and of convictions : Lenin himself went out of his way to record the opinion that " of the Mensheviks who entered the party after the beginning of 1918 not more than about one per cent should be left in the party, and that every one who is left should be checked three or four times ".[4]

In October 1921 the central committee of the party announced the beginning of the scrutiny, which was to be conducted under the supervision of a " central verification committee " of five members, including Zalutsky as president and Shlyapnikov as representative of the opposition, and five " candidates ", including

---

[1] *VKP(B) v Rezolyutsiyakh* (1941), i, 307.
[2] Lenin, *Sochineniya*, xxiv, 572.
[3] *VKP(B) v Rezolyutsiyakh* (1941), i, 359.   [4] Lenin, *Sochineniya*, xxvii, 13.

Molotov and Preobrazhcnsky.[1] This committee may be presumed to have acted as a court of appeal from the local party organizations charged with the task of sifting and cross-examining their members on the spot, and to have supervised the political aspect of the purge. This aspect was, however, kept on this occasion in the background. The report on the purge made to the eleventh party congress in March 1922 dwelt on misconduct and neglect of party duties as the main offences which had merited expulsion. Lenin's anathema against the Mensheviks can hardly have been ignored; but the prominence of former Mensheviks in the party at a later date suggests that it cannot have been fully applied. Numerically the purge was severe. Of rather more than 650,000 members 24 per cent suffered expulsion, bringing the total membership just under 500,000.[2] That the purge fell slightly more severely on intellectuals than on workers and peasants is shown by the calculation that, as a consequence of it, the proportion of workers and peasants in the party rose in the industrial provinces from 47 to 53 per cent, and in the agricultural provinces from 31 to 48 per cent.[3]

The purge of 1921–1922 coincided with a fresh period of internal stress and dissension within the party, centring round the acute controversies provoked by the introduction of NEP. The stringent resolutions of the tenth congress of March 1921 on party discipline and the tightening up of the party organization crushed the " workers' opposition " as an open group. But its members had not been convinced, and unrest in the party had not been quelled. The first overt trouble appears to have started from a one-man revolt. A certain Myasnikov, by origin a worker from Perm, who had acquired a following in party circles both in Petrograd and in the Urals, began to agitate for " freedom of the press from monarchists to anarchists inclusive ". In May 1921

---

[1] *Odinnadtsatyi S"ezd RKP(B)* (1936), pp. 722-725 ; Lenin, *Sochineniya*, xxvii, 532.

[2] The report on the purge is in *Odinnadtsatyi S"ezd RKP(B)* (1936), pp. 725-730. The results from Turkestan and from two provinces of the RSFSR did not arrive in time for inclusion, and the figures given in the report are therefore lower than those in the current party statistics.

[3] A. S. Bubnov, *VKP(B)* (1931), p. 557.

he wrote a memorandum in support of his views to the central committee of the party and followed this up with a published article. He was sufficiently important to receive a personal letter from Lenin attempting to dissuade him from the error of his ways.[1] Myasnikov, however, continued to agitate, and, when called to order by the Orgburo, published in his native Perm his own letter and article, Lenin's reply, and his reply to Lenin, together with a protest from local party members against the censure of the Orgburo. This was clearly too much. The machine moved slowly. But on February 20, 1922, the Politburo expelled Myasnikov from the party, with the right to apply for readmission after a year. For the first time the penalty approved by the tenth congress for " fractional activities " had been cautiously applied.

This episode would have been insignificant if it had not been accompanied by an outburst of renewed discontent in the party, inspired by the application of NEP : the party leadership was abandoning communism, was making concessions to the peasantry at the expense of the proletariat, and was becoming itself counter-revolutionary and bourgeois. The proposed grant of concessions to foreign capitalists was the most popular target ; and Shlyapnikov, still a member of the central committee of the party, was once more the protagonist of the opposition. In August 1921 Lenin convened a joint meeting of the central committee and of the control commission, in accordance with " point 7 " of the March resolution, and proposed Shlyapnikov's expulsion from the party. He just failed, however, to secure the necessary two-thirds majority — once more a token of the extreme dislike of severe measures against prominent party members ; and Shlyapnikov escaped with an admonition.[2] This was followed by the foundation in Moscow of a party " discussion club ", which quickly became a focus of opposition to NEP. A party conference in December 1921 exhorted party workers to explain to party members " the significance and rôle of party solidarity and discipline ", and to " illustrate the necessity of discipline by the

[1] Lenin, *Sochineniya*, xxvi, 472-475 : the history of the *affaire* Myasnikov will be found *ibid.* xxvi, 683-684, note 211.

[2] *Ibid.* xxvii, 538 ; out of 27 present at the meeting of the central committee, 17 voted for expulsion — one short of the necessary two-thirds (*Odinnadtsatyi S"ezd RKP(B)* (1936), p. 182).

example of our victories and defeats throughout the period of the historical development of the party ".[1]   The Moscow discussion club was dissolved on the initiative of the central control commission of the party in January 1922.[2]

It seemed likely, therefore, that, although the workers' opposition of 1921 was dead and buried, the eleventh party congress which was to meet in March 1922 would have to face at least as strong criticism and at least as grave a threat to party unity and discipline as its predecessor.   On the eve of the congress the critics of the official policy began to organize, and, conscious of the weakness of their position, had the desperate idea of seeking to mobilize the support of foreign communists by an appeal to the executive committee of Comintern (IKKI).   The appeal, which came to be known as " the declaration of the 22 ", detailed at some length the grievances of the opposition in terms plainly recalling the former workers' opposition to which half the present signatories had belonged :

> At a time when the forces of the bourgeois element press on us from all sides, when they penetrate even within the party, the social composition of which (40% workers, 60% non-proletarians) favours this, our leading centres conduct an irreconcilable, disintegrating struggle against all those, especially those proletarians, who permit themselves to form their own opinion, and apply all kinds of repressive measures to the expression of such opinion in party circles.
> The attempt to draw the proletarian masses towards the state is called " anarcho-syndicalism ", and its advocates are subjected to persecutions and disgrace. . . . The united forces of the party and trade union bureaucracy, availing themselves of their position and of their power, ignore the decisions of our congresses about the carrying into effect of the principles of workers' democracy.

The declaration ended :

> The position in our party is so grievous that it impels us to turn to you for help and in this way to remove the threat of a split which hangs over our party.[3]

---

[1] *VKP(B) v Rezolyutsiyakh* (1941), i, 413.
[2] Lenin, *Sochineniya*, xxvii, 536-537.
[3] *Rabochaya Oppozitsiya: Materialy i Dokumenty* (1926), pp. 59-60.

It was not difficult to dispose of the matter in IKKI by a soothing resolution which declared that the leadership of the Russian party fully recognized these dangers, and mildly condemned the opposition for endangering party unity by " knocking at an open door ".[1] But the eleventh party congress took a more serious view.   A commission consisting of Dzerzhinsky, Zinoviev and Stalin found no difficulty in convicting the twenty-two of the offence of organizing a fraction, and recommended the expulsion from the party of the five ringleaders (besides Myasnikov, who had already suffered this penalty) : Kollontai, Shlyapnikov, Medvedev, Mitin and Kuznetsov.[2]   On this report the congress decided to expel the two last, who were relatively obscure, and reprieved the first three.   It is significant that at this time, in spite of the resolutions of the tenth congress, the highest party organ — the last party congress to be attended by Lenin — was still reluctant to apply the penalty of expulsion to known and tried party members.   Notwithstanding the conditions of crisis and the strong appeals of the leaders, the tradition of toleration within the party died hard.

In spite of this leniency towards errant individuals, the eleventh congress showed no hesitation in once more tightening up the machinery of centralized control within the party.   Solts, the spokesman of the central control commission, expounded the case for party discipline by a brutally frank analogy :

> We knew very well how to talk about the democratization of an army which we had to disperse.   But when we needed our own army, we implanted in it the discipline which is obligatory for any army.[3]

But it was Lenin who created the sensation of the congress by returning in much more specific terms to last year's theme of " discussion with rifles ".   In his principal report he described NEP as a retreat — a difficult military operation calling for the most rigid discipline :

> Then discipline must be more conscious and is a hundred times more necessary, because, when a whole army retreats, it is

---

[1] *Kommunisticheskii Internatsional v Dokumentakh* (1933), pp. 275-276.
[2] *Odinnadtsatyi S"ezd RKP(B)* (1936), pp. 693-700.
[3] *Ibid.* p. 177.

not clear to it, it does not see, where it will stop, it sees only retreat ; then sometimes a few panic voices are enough to start everyone running. Then the danger is immense. When such a retreat is being carried out with a real army, machine-guns are brought out and, when the orderly retreat becomes disorderly, the command is given : " Fire ". And quite right. . . . At such a moment it is indispensable to punish strictly, severely, unsparingly the slightest breach of discipline.

Having explained that this necessity applied " not only to some of our affairs within the party ", Lenin launched an attack on Mensheviks, SRs and their foreign sympathizers, and declared that " for the public exhibition of Menshevism our revolutionary courts must shoot ".[1] Once more the text was ambiguous. But the use of what appeared to be the same threats against unruly party members as against Mensheviks and SRs was new and startling. Shlyapnikov complained that Lenin had threatened the opposition with " machine-guns " ; [2] and Lenin in his concluding speech attenuated a painful impression by explaining that the machine-guns were intended for " those people whom we call Mensheviks and SRs ", and that, so far as the party was concerned, " it is a question of party measures of discipline " [3] — such as the penalty of expulsion approved by the previous congress.

The final conclusions from Lenin's speech were thus not drawn at the congress, and Lenin himself would perhaps have shrunk from them. Nevertheless, the atmosphere had changed — even from the congress of the previous year. A monster resolution " On the Strengthening and the New Tasks of the Party " denounced the " cliques and groupings which in places have reduced party work to complete paralysis ", and exhorted the central committee " in struggling against such phenomena not to flinch from expulsions from the party ".[4] The congress adopted a new statute for the party control commissions, and declared that " the work of the control commissions must continue the activity of the verification commissions ", the implication being that the purge of 1921–1922 was to be transformed from a single operation into a continuous process.[5] More striking was perhaps a development

[1] Lenin, *Sochineniya*, xxvii, 239–240.
[2] *Odinnadtsatyi S"ezd RKP(B)* (1936), p. 107.
[3] Lenin, *Sochineniya*, xxvii, 262.
[4] *VKP(B) v Rezolyutsiyakh* (1941), i, 434.   [5] *Ibid.* i, 441–442.

of the functions of the central control commission which was
announced at the following congress a year later :

> We have coordinated our work with organs which by the
> nature of their activity are in close contact with the control
> commission : these are the judicial organs and the organs of
> the GPU. . . . Members of the party from time to time are
> arraigned in the courts or fall into the hands of the GPU. For
> this purpose we have established contact with the supreme court.
> It informs us of any comrade who is charged in a court. . . .
> Similarly with the GPU. We have arranged matters so that
> we have our investigator in the GPU, and as soon as the case
> of a communist is brought in he conducts it as an investigator
> of the control commission.[1]

The convenience was mutual. The GPU secured direct party
support : the party control commission could invoke the assistance
of the GPU for the furtherance of its own task. It is not unfair
to say that the main ultimate difference between the Cheka and
the GPU was that, whereas the former directed its activities exclusively against enemies outside the party, the GPU acted im-
partially against all enemies of the régime, among whom dissident
party members were now commonly the most important. The
difference was due not to any change in the character of the institution, but to the change which came over the political scene when
the party acquired a political monopoly in the Soviet state. It was
becoming more and more difficult to distinguish between disloyalty to the party and treason against the state.

Another event occurred as soon as the eleventh congress ended.
The central committee undertook a further remodelling of the
secretariat. On April 4, 1922, two days after the congress closed,
Pravda carried two modest paragraphs on its front page in the
space usually reserved for routine party announcements :

> The central committee elected by the eleventh congress
> of the Russian Communist Party has confirmed the secretariat of
> the central committee as follows : comrade Stalin (general
> secretary), comrade Molotov, and comrade Kuibyshev.
> The secretariat has fixed the following times of reception
> at the central committee from 12 to 3 : Monday — Molotov and
> Kuibyshev ; Tuesday — Stalin and Molotov ; Wednesday —

[1] *Dvenadtsatyi S"ezd Rossiiskoi Kommunisticheskoi Partii (Bol'shevikov)*
(1923), pp. 221-222.

Kuibyshev and Molotov; Thursday — Kuibyshev; Friday —
Stalin and Molotov; Saturday — Stalin and Kuibyshev.

The only novelty here was that the central committee had a
secretary-general with two assistants instead of three co-equal
secretaries. Molotov had been a secretary, and a member of the
Politburo, for the past year. Kuibyshev was a new-comer; the
eleventh congress had just elected him a candidate member of
the Politburo. Stalin's appointment had not been publicly
discussed, though it had presumably been canvassed in party
circles. Nothing suggests that it had aroused any opposition,
except perhaps an ill-tempered remark at the congress by Preobrazhensky, who, mentioning Stalin by name, asked whether it
was " thinkable that one man should be able to answer for the
work of two commissariats as well as for work in the Politburo,
the Orgburo and a dozen party committees." [1]   The announcement in *Pravda* seems to have attracted no great attention.

Nearly two months after the appointment of the new secretary-
general, on May 26, 1922, Lenin had a stroke, resulting in a
permanent incapacity which prevented him from resuming work
except for a brief period, and with much diminished force, in the
ensuing autumn and winter. These two events marked an epoch
in the history of the party. For more than twelve months the
acrimonious disputes of the past two years were stayed or were
carried on only behind the scenes. The uncertainties for the
future caused by Lenin's illness, Stalin's strong and efficient hand
on the helm and the marked improvement in the economic situation after the harvest of 1922, may all have contributed to this
interval of comparative calm. When acute dissensions broke out
once more in the summer and autumn of 1923 they took the new
form of an undisguised struggle for power, whose prize was
supreme control not merely of the party but of the state. Lenin
himself had so combined the two functions that they were no
longer distinguishable. As the party, by destroying its rivals, had
seemed to absorb the state, so the state now absorbed the party
into itself.

[1] *Odinnadtsatyi S"ezd RKP(B)* (1936), p. 89.

CHAPTER 9

PARTY AND STATE

THE concentration of power within the party matched a similar process in the organs of state. The same men, sharing the same traditions and the same purpose, directed the affairs of party and of state; the same incessant crisis and the same uninterrupted pressure of events weighed equally between 1917 and 1921 on party and on Soviet institutions. The outstanding developments of these years in the machinery of state — the concentration of central authority in the hands of Sovnarkom at the expense of the All-Russian Congress of Soviets and of VTsIK, and the concentration of authority at the centre at the expense of the local Soviets and congresses of Soviets and their organs — had actually preceded the corresponding developments in the party organization. For some time the lines of development in party and state ran parallel. Then, by an inevitable process they began to converge and, finally, to coincide. This process had been virtually completed before Lenin's death.

The shift in the balance of power within the central Soviet machine between the different central organs was far advanced when the constitution of 1918 was drafted. As was then already apparent, the sovereign All-Russian Congress of Soviets — a mass meeting of upwards of 1000 delegates — might reign but could not govern. The original intention to summon it every three months was silently abandoned after 1918 in favour of annual meetings;[1] and a speaker at the fifth All-Russian Congress in July 1918 complained that neither the president of VTsIK nor the president of Sovnarkom had troubled to make a report to the congress on the activities of these organs since the previous

[1] Not till 1921 did the ninth All-Russian Congress of Soviets make annual meetings the formal rule both for the All-Russian Congress and for provincial, county and district congresses.

congress.[1] But since the constitution extended almost all the functions of the congress concurrently to VTsIK, the transfer of power to VTsIK took place, on the whole, painlessly and uneventfully. The same fate befell the provincial and county congresses of Soviets. In spite of a resolution of the eighth party congress in 1919, deploring the tendency to relegate important decisions from Soviets to executive committees,[2] the process continued unchecked, effective power passing from the congresses of Soviets to the executive committees elected by them.

The power thus handed down from the All-Russian Congress of Soviets to VTsIK did not, however, remain with that organ. The self-aggrandizement of Sovnarkom, which had begun in the first days of the régime, could no longer be checked; and VTsIK was destined to experience, rather earlier than the central committee of the party, the same process of numerical expansion and loss of real authority. The membership of VTsIK, fixed by the constitution of 1918 at " not more than 200 ", was increased once more to 300 by a decree of the eighth All-Russian Congress of Soviets in 1920.[3] Originally intended to remain in more or less permanent session, its meetings became progressively rarer and were limited after 1921 to three sessions a year.[4] An attempt was made by the seventh All-Russian Congress in December 1919 to restore the authority of VTsIK by conferring special powers on its presidium, hitherto an informal managing committee of its principal officers, including its president, whose prestige derived from the fact that he was required on rare ceremonial occasions to discharge the formal duties of head of the state — a post occupied by Sverdlov and, after his death in 1919, by Kalinin. Under a constitutional amendment adopted by the seventh congress the presidium of VTsIK acquired specific functions, including the right in the intervals between the sessions of VTsIK " to ratify the decisions of Sovnarkom as well as to suspend the execution of such decisions "; [5] and at the eighth All-Russian Congress the further right was conferred on the presidium to annul resolutions of Sovnarkom and to " issue through administrative channels necessary regulations in the name of VTsIK ".[6] But these innova-

[1] *Pyatyi Vserossiiskii S"ezd Sovetov* (1918), pp. 81-82.
[2] *VKP(B) v Rezolyutsiyakh* (1941), i, 306.
[3] *S"ezdy Sovetov RSFSR v Postanovleniyakh* (1939), p. 176.
[4] *Ibid.* p. 219.　　[5] *Ibid.* p. 148.　　[6] *Ibid.* p. 176.

tions, while they ultimately weakened VTsIK by giving its presidium almost unlimited powers to act on its behalf, did nothing to shake the now impregnable position of Sovnarkom, which was no more amenable to control by the presidium of VTsIK than by VTsIK itself.

The provision in the constitution of 1918 that " measures of extreme urgency may be put into force on the sole authority of Sovnarkom " proved, as it was no doubt intended to prove, the escape-clause through which Sovnarkom could elude the unwieldy control of VTsIK. In a period of civil war and national emergency, all major decisions, whether legislative or executive, were likely to be " measures of extreme urgency " ; and Lenin, as president of Sovnarkom and an active participator in its work, conferred his personal prestige on the institution. From the middle of 1918 to the early summer of 1922, when Lenin's illness removed him from the active direction of affairs, Sovnarkom, whatever party authority may have been exercised over it behind the scenes, was the government of the RSFSR. It enjoyed not only full executive authority but unlimited powers of legislation by decree,[1] and owed only formal account to VTsIK or to the nominally sovereign body — the All-Russian Congress of Soviets. In December 1920 the Council of Labour and Defence (STO), a body hitherto concerned with supplies to the army,[2] was transformed into a commission of Sovnarkom and became, under the direct control of Sovnarkom, a sort of economic general staff; it was under the authority of STO that the first state planning commission was soon to be established. During 1921 the pressure of work on Sovnarkom was so great that a " small " Sovnarkom was brought into being to sit concurrently with the major body and take routine matters off its hands.[3] Sovnarkom had become the power-house from which all the machinery of government was set and kept in motion.

---

[1] According to G. Vernadsky, *A History of Russia* (New and Revised Ed., N.Y., 1944), p. 319, 1615 decrees were issued between 1917 and 1921 by Sovnarkom and only 375 by VTsIK.

[2] It was created by decree of November 30, 1918, as the Council of Workers' and Peasants' Defence (*Sobranie Uzakonenii, 1917-1918*, No. 91-92, art. 924), and was renamed Council of Labour and Defence in April 1920 when it also became concerned with the mobilization of labour for civilian work (Lenin, *Sochineniya*, xxvi, 619-620, note 23).

[3] The first official recognition of this body apparently occurs in a decree of October 6, 1921 (*Sobranie Uzakonenii, 1921*, No. 68, art. 532).

The concentration of the central Soviet power was accompanied by a second process which also had its parallel in party affairs : a concentration of authority at the centre, at the expense of local organs. This development also had already gone far when the constitution of the RSFSR was drafted. Its further progress, however, involved an issue which had been ignored in that constitution. The constitution made it clear that congresses of Soviets and their executive committees were subject to the control of the corresponding institutions of a higher category — village Soviets to rural district congresses of Soviets, district congresses to county and provincial congresses, and so on. But nothing was said of the subordination of local Soviets or congresses of Soviets or their executive committees to other central organs. The issue appears first to have become acute in the economic field. Sapronov at the eighth party congress in May 1919 complained that the Supreme Council of National Economy (Vesenkha) was pursuing a policy of " creating local Sovnarkhozy and cutting them off from the provincial executive committees ", saying to the latter when they protested : " You don't understand the first thing about production ". And the same speaker accused the central organs of using the financial weapon to bring local Soviet organs to heel.[1] In the emergency of the civil war, " revolutionary committees " were set up by decree of Sovnarkom of October 24, 1919, in regions affected by the war, and all local Soviet organs instructed to obey them.[2] This measure was denounced as unconstitutional at the seventh All-Russian Congress of Soviets in December 1919. The complaint was overruled. But the number of decrees of the following year on the status and rights of local Soviets[3] shows the sensitiveness of local opinion to encroachments from the centre and the difficulty of reaching a workable arrangement; and at the ninth party congress in March 1920 Sapronov once more contrasted the current " vertical centralism " with the " democratic centralism " which was the supposed basis of party and Soviet organization.[4] In December 1920 the rights of provincial executive committees in this respect

[1] *Vos'moi S"ezd RKP(B)* (1933), 205, 313-315 ; cf. p. 134 above.
[2] *Sobranie Uzakonenii, 1919*, No. 53, art. 508.
[3] *Sobranie Uzakonenii, 1920*, No. 1-2, art. 5 ; No. 11, art. 68 ; No. 20, art. 108; No. 26, art. 131.
[4] *Devyatyi S"ezd RKP(B)* (1934), p. 56.

were at length formally defined by the eighth All-Russian Congress of Soviets. These committees (but not lower Soviet organs) might suspend the operation of regulations issued by individual People's Commissariats (but not by Sovnarkom as a whole) " in exceptional circumstances or when such regulation is in clear contravention of a decision of Sovnarkom or of VTsIK or in other cases by resolution of the provincial executive committee ". The committee could, however, be held collectively responsible for any such act of suspension.[1]

The solution of the dilemma was ultimately found in a so-called system of " dual subordination ", the local organs being perforce satisfied with a formal authority which was not normally exercised. But the issue continued to cause friction from time to time; and as late as 1922 Lenin himself had to intervene in a serious dispute on the subject of judicial organization. In May 1922 the People's Commissar for Justice, Krylenko, drafted a decree providing that procurators throughout the country should be appointed by the procurator-general and be responsible to him rather than to the executive committee of the areas in which they exercised their functions. This proposal was subjected to hostile criticism in VTsIK on May 13, 1922, the system of " dual subordination " both to the procurator-general and to local executive committee being asked for. Some of the Bolsheviks shared this view; and Lenin came to the support of Krylenko with a memorandum arguing that, since " legality must be one " throughout the RSFSR, the case for the appointment and control of legal officers by the central authority was irrefutable. Thus called to order, VTsIK on May 26, 1922, on the occasion of the adoption of the first criminal code of the RSFSR, accepted the proposal; and one more step towards the formal concentration of power had been taken.[2]

By this time, however, questions of competence arising between different Soviet organs had become to this extent unreal that the ultimate power of decision rested with neither of the disputants

---

[1] S"ezdy Sovetov RSFSR v Postanovleniyakh (1939), p. 177. During the following year several cases are said to have occurred of " impeachments before the Supreme Judicial Tribunal of local food departments, economic councils, departments of health, etc., for arbitrarily setting aside in one way or another the decisions of the central authority " (A. Rothstein, The Soviet Constitution (1923), pp. 86-87). This suggests that suspension was not encouraged.

[2] Lenin, Sochineniya, xxvii, 298-301, 544-545.

but with the appropriate party organ. The parallel lines of
development of party and state institutions had converged to the
point where clear distinctions could no longer be drawn. If the
system of " dual subordination " worked, it was because central
Soviet organs and local executive committees both ultimately
recognized an authority outside the Soviet system. Like everything else in the RSFSR, relations between the Communist Party
and the Soviet state and its institutions had not been charted in
advance of the revolution. They had to be worked out gradually
in the strain and stress of a period of acute crisis. They were
formulated for the first time in categorical terms by the eighth
party congress in March 1919 :

> The Communist Party is the organization which unites in its
> ranks only the vanguard of the proletariat and of the poorest
> peasantry — that part of these classes which consciously strives
> to realize in practice the communist programme.
>   The Communist Party makes it its task to win decisive
> influence and complete leadership in all organizations of the
> workers : in trade unions, cooperatives, village communes, etc.
> The Communist Party strives especially to establish its pro-
> gramme and its complete leadership in the contemporary state
> organizations, which are the Soviets.
>   . . . The Russian Communist Party must win for itself
> undivided political mastery in the Soviets and practical control
> over all their work.[1]

These aims were already in course of achievement when this
resolution was adopted. They were achieved through two
different and distinct procedures. At the highest level the central
committee of the party — soon to be supplanted by the Politburo
created by the eighth congress itself — was the final arbiter of
public policy and the ultimate court of appeal in the whole complex
structure of government. At lower levels the party sought to
penetrate and permeate every administrative institution, public or
semi-public.

---

[1] *VKP(B) v Rezolyutsiyakh* (1941), i, 306. Zinoviev put the position still
more bluntly in the discussion which preceded the adoption of the resolution :
" Fundamental questions of policy, international and domestic, must be decided
by the central committee of our party, i.e. the Communist Party, which thus
carries these decisions through the Soviet organs. It carries them, of course,
cleverly and tactfully, not in such a way as to tread on the toes of Sovnarkom and
other Soviet institutions " (*Vos'moi S"ezd VKP(B)* (1933), p. 250) ; Zinoviev
held no governmental post except that of president of the Petrograd Soviet.

It would be a mistake to regard the relegation of all major political decisions to party organs as the result of any predetermined design. In the first weeks of the revolution Lenin showed every intention of making Sovnarkom the principal instrument of government, and important decisions were in fact taken there. The Bolsheviks had been the first to raise the slogan " all power to the Soviets " and, when the victory was won, made the Soviets the repository of the sovereign power of the state. But the Soviets were not exclusively — or, at the outset, even in majority — Bolshevik ; for a time the presence of members of other parties even in Sovnarkom [1] divorced its debates from the inner counsels of the party. It thus became the essential function of the party, in the words of the 1919 resolution, to " win for itself undivided political mastery in the Soviets ". The great decision to unleash the forces of revolution in October 1917 had been taken in the central committee of the party. The next contested issue of comparable importance — the conclusion of peace at Brest-Litovsk — was fought out, almost as a matter of course, in the same central committee. Thus early in the history of the régime it came to be taken for granted that the function of taking political decisions resided in the party.

> Today [Trotsky told the second congress of Comintern in 1920] we have received from the Polish Government proposals for the conclusion of peace. Who decides this question? We have Sovnarkom, but it must be subject to a certain control. What control? The control of the working class as a formless chaotic mass? No. The central committee of the party has been called together to discuss the proposal and decide whether to answer it.[2]

When the evolution of party affairs gradually transferred this authority from the central committee of the party to its Politburo, the latter quickly established its ascendancy over Sovnarkom and other major organs of government.[3] Successive party congresses

---

[1] The original Sovnarkom was exclusively Bolshevik ; three Left SRs joined it in November 1917, but resigned after the acceptance of the Brest-Litovsk treaty by the fourth All-Russian Congress of Soviets in March 1918.

[2] *Der Zweite Kongress der Kommunist-Internationale* (Hamburg, 1921), p. 94.

[3] A specialist working for the Soviet Government at this time has left specific testimony to this effect : " The two highest organs of the government which I knew — the Council of People's Commissars and the Council of Labour

devoted more and more of their attention to issues of public policy, great and small. The major decision to launch NEP was first publicly announced by Lenin to the tenth party congress. Party congresses made explicit recommendations even on quite minor issues of organization,[1] and on occasion even passed formal resolutions approving the policy of the Soviet Government or specific decrees of Sovnarkom.[2]

Party control of governmental policy at the highest level was complemented and made effective by the organized introduction of party members at all levels into every branch of the administrative apparatus. Key positions in the administration were filled by party nominations.[3] Long after the Mensheviks and SRs had been eliminated from the central organs of power, a substantial proportion of the membership of local Soviets and, still more, of other lesser public institutions, remained non-party or non-Bolshevik. This made it all the more necessary that the Bolshevik minority in such institutions should be highly organized and disciplined. The resolution of the eighth party congress had established this principle :

> In all Soviet organizations it is essential to form party fractions strictly subject to party discipline. Into these fractions all members of the Russian Communist Party working in a given Soviet institution must enter.[4]

And another resolution of the same congress enjoined the party " to introduce thousands more of its best workers into the network

and Defence — discussed practical ways to effect measures already decided on by this inner sanctum of the party, the Politburo " (S. Liberman, *Building Lenin's Russia* (Chicago, 1945), p. 13).

[1] The following item from the resolutions of the eighth party congress may be quoted as a sample : " The functions of the presidium of VTsIK are not worked out in the Soviet constitution. At the next congress of Soviets it is indispensable, on the foundation of all practical experience, to formulate precisely the rights and obligations of the presidium of VTsIK and to distinguish its sphere of action from that of Sovnarkom " (*VKP(B) v Rezolyutsiyakh* (1941), i, 305-306). In theory such resolutions were instructions to the party fraction at the congress ; in practice they were mandatory to the congress itself.

[2] An example will be found in the resolutions of the tenth party congress of 1921 (*ibid.* i, 391).

[3] Zinoviev explained at the twelfth party congress of 1923 that the presidents of the executive committees of provincial Soviets (*gubispolkomi*) were appointed by the central committee of the party, and that, if this were altered, " from that moment everything would be upside down " (*Dvenadtsatyi S"ezd Rossiiskoi Kommunisticheskoi Partii (Bol'shevikov)* (1923), p. 207).

[4] *VKP(B) v Rezolyutsiyakh* (1941), i, 306.

of the state administration (railways, food supplies, control, army, law-courts, etc.) ". At the same time party members were instructed to become active members of their trade unions.[1] At the next party congress, held when the first stage of the civil war had been triumphantly passed, new spheres of activity were pre-scribed for party members — in factories and workshops, in transport, " in the establishment of various forms of labour discipline ", in fuel organizations and in such matters as public dining-rooms, house committees, public baths, schools and welfare institutions.[2] " We administer Russia," said Kamenev at this congress, " and it is only through communists that we can ad-minister it." [3] Meanwhile, the last section of the party statute adopted in 1919, " On Fractions in Non-party Institutions and Organizations," prescribed the duties and functions of party members participating in " congresses, conferences or elective organs (Soviet, trade union, cooperative and so forth) ". They were enjoined to constitute themselves into " organized fractions " and to " vote solidly together in the general meeting of the organization in question ". The claims of discipline were strongest of all when party members found themselves in contact with non-party members of official or semi-official organizations. The fractions were " completely subordinate to the corresponding party organizations " and conformed their action to party decisions and instructions.[4]

It was no part of the original intention of those who made these arrangements to obliterate the dividing line between party and state. The resolution of the eighth party congress which had first defined relations between them laid it down that confusion of their functions would lead to " disastrous results " : it was the duty of the party " to *lead* the activity of the Soviets, but not to

---

[1] *VKP(B) v Rezolyutsiyakh* (1941), i, 303-304.   [2] *Ibid.* i, 342.
[3] *Devyatyi S"ezd RKP(B)* (1934), p. 325.
[4] *VKP(B) v Rezolyutsiyakh* (1941), i, 322-323. Left-wing parties every-where have been particularly insistent on their delegates in representative assemblies voting in accordance not with private convictions, but with party decisions. In the Social-Democratic Party in the German Reichstag the *Fraktionszwang* was rigorously enforced. The famous vote of August 4, 1914, in support of war credits was unanimous, but was preceded by a discussion within the fraction in which 78 voted in favour of support and 14 against it : Haase, who read the party declaration in the Reichstag, was actually one of those who had voted against it in the fraction.

replace them ".[1] Yet the discharge of this duty inevitably tended
more and more to place the ultimate responsibility for decisions
on the organs of the party rather than on those of the state.
Lenin complained at the eleventh party congress of the habit of
constant appeals from Sovnarkom to the Politburo, and spoke of
the need " to enhance the authority of Sovnarkom ".[2] As late as
March 1922 the eleventh congress in its main resolution declared
it " possible and indispensable to unburden the party of a series
of questions of a purely Soviet character which it has taken on its
shoulders in the preceding period ", asked for " a far more precise
distinction between its current work and the work of the Soviet
organs, between its own apparatus and the apparatus of the
Soviets ", and wished to " raise and strengthen the activity of
Sovnarkom ".[3] But these pious wishes provided a handle for
those who — especially in the economic field — sought to detach
the administrative organs of the state from the control of the
party ; and the following congress found it necessary to give a
warning against so broad an interpretation of these texts as might
create dangers for the overriding authority of the party.[4]

The tide of party encroachment on Soviet functions was indeed
too powerful to be stemmed ; and Lenin, with his customary
realism, faced and accepted what could not be altered. " As the
governing party ", he had already written in 1921, " we could not
help fusing the Soviet ' authorities ' with the party ' authorities '
— with us they are fused and they will be." [5] In one of his last
articles in *Pravda*, early in 1923, he invoked the conduct of foreign
affairs as a successful example of unity between party and Soviet
institutions :

> Why indeed should the two not be united if this is what
> the interest of business demands? Has anyone ever failed to
> notice that, in a commissariat like Narkomindel, such a union
> produces enormous advantages and has been practised from
> the very start? Does not the Politburo discuss from the party
> point of view many questions, small and great, of the " moves "
> from our side in reply to " moves " of foreign Powers in order
> to counteract their — well, let us say, cleverness, not to use a

[1] *Ibid.* i, 306.
[2] Lenin, *Sochineniya*, xxvii, 257-258.
[3] *VKP(B) v Rezolyutsiyakh* (1941), i, 416.   [4] *Ibid.* i, 473.
[5] Lenin, *Sochineniya*, xxvi, 208.

less polite expression? Is not this flexible union of Soviet with party element a source of enormous strength in our policy? I think that something which has justified itself, established itself in our external policy, and become so much a habit that in this sphere it provokes no doubts at all, will be at least equally in place (I think, far more in place) if applied to our whole state apparatus.[1]

After Lenin's death the tradition of fusion had become so firmly established that important decisions came to be announced almost indifferently by party or by government, and decrees were sometimes issued jointly in the name of the party central committee and of VTsIK or Sovnarkom.

If Lenin was driven by practical necessities to recognize a constantly growing concentration of authority, there is no evidence that he wavered in his belief in the antidote of " direct democracy ". But he began to understand that progress would be slower than he had at first hoped and the bogey of bureaucracy more difficult to conjure. The Soviet system was praised now for its educational function :

> Only in the Soviets does the mass of the exploited begin really to learn, not from books, but from their own practical experience, the business of socialist construction, the creation of new social discipline, the free union of free workers.[2]

In April 1921 Sovnarkom issued a decree whose declared motive was " to maintain the link between Soviet institutions and the broad masses of the workers, to enliven the Soviet apparatus and gradually to liberate it from bureaucratic elements ". The decree sought, among other things, to bring working women and peasant women into the sections of the executive committees of the congresses of Soviets ; the women were to be employed in adminis-

---

[1] Lenin, *Sochineniya*, xxvii, 413. Three months later, in the debate on Georgia at the twelfth party congress, some significant remarks were made by Enukidze : " I am perfectly familiar with the mutual relations between central Soviet organs and the central party organ of the RSFSR, and I will say flatly that no Soviet institution on the territory of the RSFSR enjoys such freedom of action as the Georgian Sovnarkom or Georgian TsIK in Georgia. There a whole series of most important questions of significance to the republic goes through without the knowledge of the Georgian central [party] committee or the committee of the Transcaucasian region — a thing which does not happen with us and should not happen so long as the party directs all policy '"(*Dvenadtsatyi S"ezd Rossiiskoi Kommunisticheskoi Partii* (1923), pp. 538-539).

[2] Lenin, *Sochineniya*, xxv, 315.

trative work for two months, after which they would be returned
to their normal employment unless it was desired to retain them
permanently.   But the most interesting point about an unpractical
project was that the women were to be drafted " through the
women workers' sections of the Russian Communist Party ".[1]
The last public act of Lenin's career was a bold plan for merging
party and state functions in a manner designed to counteract the
evils of bureaucracy.   Under the Tsars, the office of state con-
troller, originally created to check financial irregularities, had
acquired a general supervision over the working of the administration.   A decree establishing a People's Commissariat of State
Control was issued a few weeks after the revolution, and further
powers were given to the institution by a decree of March 1918.[2]
But no People's Commissar was appointed, and the commissariat
does not appear to have existed except on paper.   Presently the
party took a hand in the question.   The resolution of the eighth
party congress of March 1919 which first attempted to define
relations between party and state contained a paragraph prescribing
that " control in the Soviet republic should be radically reorganized in order to create a genuine practical control of a socialist
character ", adding that the leading rôle in the exercise of this
control must fall to " party organizations and trade unions ".[3]
Zinoviev, who introduced the resolution, suggested that the new
organ should " push its feelers into all branches of Soviet construction, and have a special section concerned with the simplifica-
tion and perfection of our machine ".[4]   Another speaker described
the existing state control as " a pre-flood institution carrying on
with all its old officials, with all kinds of counter-revolutionary
elements, etc." [5]   The resolution resulted in a joint decree of
VTsIK and Sovnarkom of April 9, 1919, establishing a People's
Commissariat of State Control.[6]   This time the decision took
effect.   The commissar for the new department, as Zinoviev had
already announced at the congress,[7] was Stalin, who thus secured,

---

[1] *Sobranie Uzakonenii, 1921*, No. 35, art. 186.   This is perhaps the earliest
instance of the assignment of a function to the party in an official decree.
[2] *Sobranie Uzakonenii, 1917–1918*, No. 6, arts. 91-92 ; No. 30, art. 393.
[3] *VKP(B) v Rezolyutsiyakh* (1941), i, 306.
[4] *Vos'moi S"ezd RKP(B)* (1933), p. 251.   [5] *Ibid.* p. 210.
[6] *Sobranie Uzakonenii, 1919*, No. 12, art. 122.
[7] *Vos'moi S"ezd RKP(B)* (1933), p. 225.

simultaneously with his dual appointment to the newly created Politburo and Orgburo of the party,[1] his first commanding position in the machinery of the state.

The task of the new commissariat was, however, delicate and controversial; and it did not long survive in its existing form. By a decree of VTsIK of February 7, 1920, it was transformed into a People's Commissariat of Workers' and Peasants' Inspection (Rabkrin or RKI) and given an entirely novel character. While the People's Commissar remained unchanged, " the struggle with bureaucratism and corruption in Soviet institutions " was now to be carried on by workers and peasants elected by the same constituents who elected delegates to the Soviets. The elections were to be only for short periods " so that gradually all the workers, men and women, in a given enterprise and all peasants may be drawn into the tasks of the inspection ".[2] Such was Lenin's conception of the use of direct democracy as a safeguard against bureaucracy. A curious clause in the decree gave the trade unions the right to protest against any candidate elected to work in Rabkrin and to propose the substitution of some other person. In April 1920 the third All-Russian Congress of Trade Unions decided to participate actively in the work of Rabkrin.[3] It may be surmised that trade-union participation was a means of giving coherence to what might otherwise have been a nebulous and unpractical project.

The career of Rabkrin continued to be stormy. A first " all-Russian conference of responsible workers of Rabkrin " met in Moscow in October 1920 and was addressed by Stalin, who claimed that it had incurred " hatred from some hide-bound officials and even from some communists who had listened to the voice of these officials ".[4] One of the difficulties was the recruitment of suitable personnel for this late-comer among the commissariats. Even Lenin, who looked to Rabkrin as an important instrument in the struggle again bureaucracy, admitted that it

---

[1] See p. 194 above.
[2] *Sobranie Uzakonenii*, 1920, No. 16, art. 94. The decree was based on a proposal originally put forward by a Moscow delegate at the seventh All-Russian Congress of Soviets in December 1919 (7[i] *Vserossiiskii S"ezd Sovetov* (1920), p. 211).
[3] *Tretii Vserossiiskii S"ezd Professional'nykh Soyuzov* (1921), i, 118.
[4] Stalin, *Sochineniya*, iv, 368.

" exists rather as an aspiration ", since " the best workers have been taken for the front ".[1] In the autumn of 1921 a report of Rabkrin on the fuel shortage incurred Lenin's censure; and Stalin replied in the capacity of a departmental chief tactfully defending a subordinate.[2] Rabkrin was regarded with increasing suspicion in many party circles. Lenin had defended Stalin against Preobrazhensky's attack at the eleventh party congress in March 1922; [3] but when Lenin, a few weeks later, proposed to make Rabkrin the channel for a new system of checking the execution of decrees of Sovnarkom and of the Council of Labour and Defence, Trotsky launched a savage attack on it, observing that " those working in Rabkrin are chiefly workers who have come to grief in other fields " and complaining of " an extreme prevalence of intrigue in the organs of Rabkrin which has long become a by-word throughout the country ". Lenin calmly replied that what was required was to improve Rabkrin, not to abolish it.[4]

It would be hazardous to speculate whether the growing general discontent with Rabkrin or the strong personal mistrust of Stalin which Lenin developed was mainly responsible for what appears to have been a sudden change of Lenin's attitude during the last few months of his working life. His last two articles, written or dictated in the first weeks of 1923, were an undisguised attack on Rabkrin in its existing form, and a proposal to the forthcoming twelfth party congress to reform it by amalgamating it with the central control commission of the party. The second article, the last which Lenin wrote, was particularly severe :

> The People's Commissariat of Workers' and Peasants' Inspection does not at present enjoy a vestige of authority. Everyone knows that there are no worse equipped institutions than the institutions of our Rabkrin, and that in conditions as

[1] Lenin, *Sochineniya*, xxv, 495.

[2] *Ibid.* xxvii, 14-20, 501. Stalin's letter is not included in his own collected works, presumably because it was no longer seemly, twenty-five years later, to have differed from Lenin even on a routine matter.

[3] See p. 213 above ; Lenin, *Sochineniya*, xxvii, 263-264.

[4] Lenin's original proposal is in *Sochineniya*, xxvii, 287 ; Trotsky's letter *ibid.* xxvii, 542-543. Lenin's comment on Trotsky's criticism is one of the few documents in the collected works published — without explanation — in extract only and out of its chronological order (*ibid.* xxvii, 289). Lenin mentions the number of officials of Rabkrin at this time as 12,000.

they are nothing at all can be expected of this commissariat.
. . . Either it is not worth spending time on one of those
reorganizations, of which we have had so many, of so hopeless
a concern as Rabkrin, or we must really set ourselves the task
of creating by slow, difficult and unusual methods, and not
without repeated verification, something really exemplary,
something capable of inspiring anyone and everyone with
respect — and not only because ranks and titles call for it.[1]

Stalin skilfully turned the implied rebuke by warmly endorsing
Lenin's plan of reform. The twelfth congress, meeting in April
1923 after Lenin had been laid low by his second stroke, adopted
an interlocking arrangement which amounted to a complete fusion
of the state and party institutions. In the first place, the character
of the party control commission, hitherto restricted like the
Politburo and the Orgburo to seven members, was completely
changed by the enlargement of its membership to fifty, " mainly
workers and peasants ", and by the appointment of a presidium
of nine to direct it. Secondly, it was laid down that the Commissar for Workers' and Peasants' Inspection should be appointed
by the central committee of the party and drawn, if possible, from
the presidium of the control commission. Thirdly, members of
the control commission were to be appointed to the collegia of the
various People's Commissariats as well as to Rabkrin.[2] The
commissariat received extended powers when it was transformed
by a decree of November 12, 1923, into a commissariat of the
USSR.[3] But in substance its authority had been merged in that
of the central control commission of the party. The control commission, strengthened by its recent working arrangement with the
GPU,[4] was thus in a position to exercise through Rabkrin direct
constitutional supervision over every activity of the Soviet
administration.

Stalin's report on organization at the twelfth party congress
drew attention to the growing importance of another institution.
As Stalin naïvely but significantly observed, a " good political
line " was only half the battle : it was also necessary to recruit

[1] Lenin, *Sochineniya*, xxvii, 406-418.
[2] *VKP(B) v Rezolyutsiyakh* (1941), i, 502. These decisions are preceded by
a long resolution " On the Tasks of the RKI and Central Control Commission "
(*ibid.* i, 498-499).
[3] *Sobranie Uzakonenii, 1923*, No. 109-110, art. 1042.
[4] See p. 212 above.

the right workers to carry out the directives.[1] Since 1920 or e of
the three party secretaries had been in charge of what was called
the " account and distribution section " (Uchraspred) which kept
account of the party's man-power and supervised its distribution
— " mobilizations, transfers and appointments of members of
the party."[2]   With the end of the civil war and the process of
demobilization the scope of Uchraspred broadened; and its
report to the tenth party congress in March 1921 showed that in
rather less than 12 months it had been responsible for transfers
and appointments of 42,000 party members.[3]   At this time it
was concerned with " mass mobilizations " rather than individual
appointments, which were left to the regional and provincial
committees.   But as the administrative machine grew, and
management of the national economy became one of its major
functions, specialised appointments grew more important, and it
was indispensable, as Stalin observed, " to know every worker
inside out ".   For this purpose the central committee decided,
some time before the twelfth congress, to " broaden" the machinery
of Uchraspred " in order to give the party the possibility to equip
the directing organs of our principal enterprises with communists
and thus to make real the party leadership of the state machine ".
Uchraspred thus became an inconspicuous but powerful focus of
the control exercised by the party over the organs of state, political
and economic.   It also proved, under the management of the
general secretary, a serviceable instrument for building up Stalin's
personal authority in the state as well as in the party machine.
Stalin's remarks at the twelfth congress were one of the rare
glimpses accorded to the outside world of the levers by which
the machine was operated.

Before the end of Lenin's life, therefore, the authority of the
party over every aspect of policy and every branch of administration had been openly recognized and proclaimed.   At the highest
level the predominance of the party as the ultimate source of policy
was assured by the supremacy of the Politburo; in the working
of the administrative machine the commissariats were subject to

---

[1] Stalin, *Sochineniya*, v, 210-213.
[2] The first report of Uchraspred is in *Izvestiya Tsentral'nogo Komiteta Rossiiskoi Kommunisticheskoi Partii (Bol'shevikov)*, No. 22, Sept. 18, 1920, pp. 12-15, a brief account of its functions *ibid*. No. 23, September 23, 1920, p. 1.
[3] *Ibid*. No. 28, March 5, 1921, p. 13.

the control of the Commissariat of Workers' and Peasants' Inspection and, through it, of the central control commission of the party; at the lowest level, party " fractions ", subject to party instructions and discipline, participated actively in the work of every official or semi-official body of any importance. Moreover, the party exercised in such organizations as the trade unions and the cooperatives, and even in major industrial establishments, the same functions of leadership as it performed in relation to the state. Just as the autonomy of the constituent republics and territories of the RSFSR (and later of the Soviet Union) was qualified by the dependence of all on decisions of policy taken by the central authorities of the ubiquitous party, so the independence enjoyed by trade unions and cooperatives in relation to organs of the state was qualified by the same common subordination to the will of the party.

The formula in which this complicated nexus of institutions and functions was expressed varied from time to time. According to Lenin :

> The party, so to speak, embodies in itself the vanguard of the proletariat. This vanguard makes the dictatorship of the proletariat a reality ; and without having such a foundation as the trade unions who make the dictatorship real, it is impossible to give reality to governmental functions. Reality is given to them through a series of special institutions of a new type, namely through the apparatus of the Soviets.[1]

In 1919 he made a trenchant retort to those who assailed the " dictatorship of one party " :

> Yes, the dictatorship of one party ! We stand upon it and cannot depart from this ground, since this is the party which in the course of decades has won for itself the position of vanguard of the whole factory and industrial proletariat.[2]

He poked fun at those who treated " the dictatorship of one party " as a bugbear, and added that " the dictatorship of the working class is carried into effect by the party of the Bolsheviks which since 1905 or earlier has been united with the whole revolutionary proletariat ".[3]   Later he described the attempt to distinguish

---

[1] Lenin, *Sochineniya*, xxvi, 64. A confused situation is revealed by a clumsiness of style rare in Lenin's writings : the verb *osushchestvlyat'* (to make real) occurs four times in four lines.

[2] *Ibid.* xxiv, 423.   [3] *Ibid.* xxiv, 436.

between the dictatorship of the class and the dictatorship of the party as proof of " an unbelievable and inextricable confusion of thought ".[1] This formula continued to satisfy the party for some years. At the twelfth congress in 1923, with Lenin no longer present, Zinoviev made light of " comrades who think that the dictatorship of the party is a thing to be realized in practice but not spoken about ", and proceeded to develop the doctrine of the dictatorship of the party as a dictatorship of the central committee :

> We need a *single* strong, powerful central committee which is leader of everything. . . . The central committee is the central committee because it is the same central committee for the Soviets, and for the trade unions, and for the cooperatives, and for the provincial executive committees and for the whole working class. In this consists its rôle of leadership, in this is expressed the dictatorship of the party.[2]

And the congress resolution declared that " the dictatorship of the working class cannot be assured otherwise than in the form of dictatorship of its leading vanguard, i.e. the Communist Party ".[3]

This time, however, Zinoviev's heavy-handedness provoked its reaction. Stalin, for his part, was concerned to resist the encroachment, not of the party on the state (that was anyhow a lost cause), but of the central committee on the working organs of the party, including the secretariat ; and the dictatorship of the central committee was a doctrine little to his taste.[4] At the congress he cautiously described the view that " the party gives orders . . . and the army, i.e. the working class, executes those orders " as " radically false ", and developed at length the metaphor of seven " transmission belts " from the party to the working class : trade unions, cooperatives, leagues of youth, conferences of women delegates, schools, the press and the army.[5] A year

---

[1] *Ibid.* xxv, 188.

[2] *Dvenadtsatyi S"ezd Rossiiskoi Kommunisticheskoi Partii* (*Bol'shevikov*) (1923), pp. 41, 207.

[3] *VKP(B) v Rezolyutsiyakh* (1941), i, 473.

[4] According to L. Trotsky, *Stalin* (N.Y., 1946), p. 367, it was immediately after the twelfth congress that Zinoviev began to devise schemes to reduce the importance of the secretariat in the party machine.

[5] Stalin, *Sochineniya*, v, 198-205. Nearly three years later Stalin developed this idea in a slightly different form : there are now five " leads " or " levers " through which the dictatorship of the proletariat makes itself effective — trade unions, Soviets, cooperatives, the league of youth and the party (*ibid.* viii, 32-35).

later he boldly described the dictatorship of the party as " non-sense ", and attributed its appearance in the resolution of the twelfth congress to an " oversight ".[1]   But, whatever the formula of the moment, the essential fact was nowhere questioned.   It was the Russian Communist Party (Bolsheviks) which gave life and direction and motive power to every form of public activity in the USSR and whose decisions were binding on every organization of a public or semi-public character.   Every significant struggle for power henceforth took place within the bosom of the party.

[1] Stalin, *Sochineniya*, vi, 258.

NOTE A

LENIN'S THEORY OF THE STATE

THE conception of the state as a necessary evil springing from man's fallen nature was rooted in the Christian tradition. The Middle Ages recognized a balance between ecclesiastical and political power, each supreme in its sphere but the former enjoying pre-eminence. It was only when the Reformation subordinated church to state, and the modern state came into being, that the protest against the abuses of political power passed over to the secular arm. Thomas More in his *Utopia* traced the evils of government to the institution of private property and anticipated an analysis of the state which came to be widely accepted more than three centuries later :

> Therefore I must say that, as I hope for mercy, I can have no other notion of all the other governments that I see or know, than that they are a conspiracy of the rich, who on pretence of managing the public only pursue their private ends, and devise all the ways and arts they can find out ; first, that they may, without danger, preserve all that they have so ill acquired, and then that they may engage the poor to toil and labour for them at as low rates as possible, and oppress them as much as they please.

This remained, however, an isolated flash of intuition ; and it was not till the eighteenth century that the modern socialist view of the state began to take shape. According to the Christian tradition, the state was evil but necessary because man's nature was evil ; according to the rational faith in nature preached by the Enlightenment, the state was unnatural and therefore evil. Marked traces of this view are found, among others, in Morelly and Rousseau ; but it was William Godwin who, in his *Enquiry Concerning Political Justice*, produced what rightly ranks as the bible of anarchism. According to Godwin property, marriage and the state are all offences against nature and reason.

> Above all [he writes], we should not forget that government is an evil, an usurpation upon the private judgment and individual conscience of mankind ; and that, however we may be obliged to admit it as a necessary evil for the present, it behoves us, as the friends of reason and the human species, to admit as little of it as

233

possible, and carefully to observe whether, in consequence of the gradual illumination of the human mind, that little may not hereafter be diminished.[1]

And later in the same work he becomes bolder and roundly proposes " to annihilate the quackery of government ". From this time forward the leading radical and socialist writers — Saint-Simon, Robert Owen, Fourier, Leroux, Proudhon — are all preoccupied with the super-session of the state and its transformation into a society of producers and consumers. It was left to Moses Hess, an early radical associate of Marx, to translate these ideas into the Hegelian terminology which was common form among young German intellectuals of the 1840s. He believed that, so long as the state existed, whatever the form of government, there would always be rulers and serfs, and that this opposition would continue " until the state, which is the condition of polarity, abolishes itself dialectically and gives place to unified social life, which is the condition of community ".[2]

Marx quickly reached the conception of the state as the instrument through which the ruling class pursued and protected its interests. In one of his earliest writings against the estate owners of the Rhineland he described " the organs of the State ", in the hyperbolic style of his juvenile period, as " the ears, eyes, hands and legs by which the interest of the forest owner listens, watches, judges, defends, seizes, runs ".[3] The modern state " exists only for the sake of private property " ; it is " nothing more than the form of organization which the bourgeois necessarily adopt both for internal and external purposes for the mutual guarantee of their property and interests ".[4] But private property in its capitalist phase produces its own antithesis, the property-less proletariat which is destined to destroy it. As Hess had said, the state is the expression of this contradiction, of this conflict between classes. When this contradiction is resolved by the overthrow of private property and the victory of the proletariat (which will, through the consummation of its own victory, cease to be a proletariat), society will no longer be divided into classes, and the state will have no further *raison d'être*. The state is thus a " substitute " for collectivism.[5] The first concise statement of Marx's position occurred in *The Poverty of Philosophy*, published in 1847 :

> In place of the old bourgeois society the working class will set up, in the course of its development, the kind of association which

---

[1] Godwin, *Enquiry Concerning Political Justice* (1793), p. 380.
[2] *Einundzwanzig Bogen aus der Schweiz* (Zürich, 1843), p. 88.
[3] *Karl Marx-Friedrich Engels: Historisch-Kritische Gesamtausgabe*, 1er Teil, i, i, 287.
[4] *Ibid.* v, 52.   [5] *Ibid.* v, 64.

excludes classes and their mutual opposition ; there will no longer
be any political power properly so-called, since it is political power
which is the official expression of the opposition of classes within
bourgeois society.[1]

The first work of Marx's maturity, the *Communist Manifesto*, recorded
the same conclusions, looking forward to the day when, the difference
between classes having been wiped out, " social power will lose its
political character ". But it was more immediately concerned with the
next practical step, which was that the proletariat should " establish its
supremacy by overthrowing the bourgeoisie ", and the state become
identical with " the proletariat organized as the ruling class ". This
was the idea which Marx crystallized four years later in the famous
slogan of " the dictatorship of the proletariat ". But he added at the
same time that this dictatorship was " only a transition to the abolition
of all classes and to the classless society ".[2] Twenty years later, when
Marx, in the famous address on *The Civil War in France*, discovered in
the Paris commune an imperfect but recognizable prototype of the
dictatorship of the proletariat, he still wrote of the state as " a parasitic
growth " and of the " abolition of state power ", which " now becomes
superfluous " ;[3] and Engels added later the more specific comment :

> The victorious proletariat, like the commune, will be obliged
> immediately to lop off the worst sides of this evil, until a generation
> which has grown up in new free social conditions finds itself in a
> position to throw overboard all this clutter of statehood." [4]

Marx therefore never retracted, or could have retracted, the opinion
that state power is an expression of class antagonisms — an evil that
will disappear in the eventual classless society. He showed, however,
less personal interest in the description of this ultimate goal than in
the analysis of immediate measures necessary to establish the dictatorship of the proletariat ; and it was left to Engels to produce the most
finished exposition of the Marxist doctrine of the state :

> When there are no longer social classes which have to be kept
> in subjection, when there is no longer a rule of one class over another
> and a struggle for existence rooted in the present anarchy of pro-

---

[1] *Ibid.* vi, 227.

[2] Marx i Engels, *Sochineniya*, xxv, 146 : the passage occurs in a private
letter of March 5, 1852, to Weydemeyer. Marx did not use the phrase again until,
more than twenty years later, he wrote in the *Critique of the Gotha Programme*
of 1875 that during the period of transition from capitalism to communism the
state would be " nothing else but *the revolutionary dictatorship* of the proletariat "
(*ibid.* xv, 283). The *Critique* was known in party circles, but not published
during Marx's lifetime.

[3] Marx i Engels, *Sochineniya*, xiii, ii, 315-316.   [4] *Ibid.* xvi, ii, 94.

duction, when the clashes and violence resulting from it have been removed, then there will be nobody to crush and restrain, and then the necessity for state power, which at present performs this function, will vanish.   The first act in which the state will appear as the real representative of the whole society — the conversion of the means of production into social property — will be its last independent act in its capacity as a state.   Intervention of state power in social relations will become gradually superfluous and will end of itself. The administration of men will be replaced by the administration of things and by the management of the productive processes.   The state is not " abolished ", it *dies away*.[1]

It was Engels also who wrote a few years later :

> With the disappearance of classes the state will inevitably disappear.   Society, which will organize production anew on the basis of a free and equal association of producers, will send the whole state machine to the place where it will then belong : to the museum of antiquities, along with the spinning-wheel and the bronze axe.[2]

The doctrine of the state which emerged from the writings of Marx and Engels was thus twofold.   In the long run, the traditional socialist view of the state as an evil in itself, a product of contradiction and an instrument of oppression, which can have no place in the communist order of the future, was maintained in its entirety.   In the short run, it was argued that the proletariat, having destroyed the bourgeois state instrument by revolutionary means, would need to set up a temporary state instrument of their own — the dictatorship of the proletariat —

[1] Marx i Engels, *Sochineniya*, xiv, 284.   The distinction between the " government of man " and the " administration of things " had long been familiar in socialist thought.   It was popularized by Saint-Simon, who wrote that human society was " destined to pass from the governmental or military regime to the *administrative* or *industrial* regime after having made sufficient progress in the positive sciences and in industry " (*Œuvres de Saint-Simon et d'Enfantin*, xxxvii (1875), 87).   The phrase already had anarchist implications. Elsewhere Saint-Simon wrote : " No useful action is exercised by man other than the action of man on things.   The action of man on man is always in itself harmful to the species " (*ibid*. xx (1869), 192).

[2] Marx i Engels, *Sochineniya*, xvi, i, 149.   A modern writer compares the attitude of Marx with that of St. Augustine : " The state becomes the expression of an immoral principle, of egotistical class interest. . . . The state —this *civitas diaboli* — must therefore be overcome, must ' die away ', and give place to a condition of classless and stateless ' society ', a *civitas dei*.   Between the conception of Saint Augustine and that of Marxism there is really only the difference that the former cautiously removes his ideal into the other world, while the latter forces it into this world by a causal law of development " (H. Kelsen, *Sozialismus und Staat* (2nd ed. 1923), pp. 32-33).   The essence of Marxist philosophy, i.e. its causal derivation of utopia from reality, of the *sollen* from the *sein*, resides in this " difference ".

until such time as the last vestiges of bourgeois society had been eradicated and the classless socialist order firmly established.   A working distinction was thus drawn between the eventual communist society, when all inequalities between man and man would have disappeared and the state no longer exist, and what came to be variously known as " socialism " or " the first stage of communism ", when the last vestiges of the bourgeois order were not yet eradicated and the state took the form of a dictatorship of the proletariat.   This distinction was one day to assume a capital importance in party doctrine.

One further refinement of the Marxist doctrine of the state particularly influenced Lenin.   The essence of the state was the division of society into two conflicting classes — rulers and ruled.   Engels, in his denunciation of Bakunin's secret revolutionary " alliance ", reproached him with putting a gap between those who directed and those who were directed and restoring the " authoritarian state " ;[1] and in his *Origin of the Family, Private Property, and the State*, he described the state as a " force proceeding out of society, but placing itself above it and becoming more and more estranged from it ".[2]   This raised the familiar problem of bureaucracy.   In the opinion of Engels the Paris commune had found the answers to it :

> In the first place it appointed to all official posts in administration, in the judiciary, in public education, persons elected by universal suffrage, and also introduced the right to recall those elected at any time by a decision of the electors.   Secondly it paid to all officials from the highest to the lowest only the same wages paid to other workers.

These measures Engels described as " a blowing up of the old state power and its replacement by a new, truly democratic, power ".[3] Here was the origin of Lenin's favourite thesis of the need to replace bureaucracy, as the characteristic instrument of the state, by the self-administration of the workers.

In the thirty years after Marx's death the doctrine of the state became a touchstone which divided the European workers' movement into two radically conflicting groups — the anarchists and the state socialists.

The anarchists started from the traditional socialist rejection of the state.   They rejected it on precisely the same ground as Marx, namely, that it was an instrument in the hands of a ruling and oppressive class. They also looked to the same ultimate solution — the replacement of the state " by the organization of productive forces and economic

---

[1] Marx i Engels, *Sochineniya*, xiii, ii, 550-551.
[2] *Ibid.* xvi, i, 145.   [3] *Ibid.* xvi, ii, 93.

services ".[1] But they extended their rejection of the state to any provisional or temporary form of state. Lenin quoted a dictum of Engels on this point :

> The anti-authoritarians demand that the authoritarian political state should be destroyed on the spot, even before the destruction of the social relations which gave birth to it. They demand that the first act of the social revolution should be the destruction of authority. Have these people ever seen a revolution ? A revolution is beyond doubt the most authoritarian thing imaginable.[2]

Their consistent rejection of authority made the anarchists irreconcilable opponents of the " dictatorship of the proletariat " — an issue which expressed itself in the feud between Marx and Bakunin. The syndicalists, refining on the crude dogmatism of the anarchists, believed that the future organization of society would be based not on any system of territorial states but on a nexus of trade unions and associations of producers. The aim of syndicalism, as defined by its most distinguished philosopher, was " to wrest from the state and the commune, one by one, all their attributions in order to enrich the proletarian organizations in course of formation, particularly the syndicates ",[3] or, put more curtly, " to suppress the state ".[4] In the matter of immediate tactics, the syndicalist movement rejected all forms of political action. The state would collapse as the result of revolutionary economic action by the workers, taking the form of the general strike ; any constructive programme for the state contradicted the nature and principles of syndicalism. These tendencies predominated in France and the other Latin countries, where Marxism had never struck firm roots.

On the other hand, the German social-democrats moved no less decisively towards an interpretation of Marxism diametrically opposite to the views of the anarchists and syndicalists. Reared in a Prussian-Hegelian respect for the power of the state, and in a Marxist contempt for the disciples of Bakunin, they allowed themselves to be convinced by the astute policies of Bismarck and by the fiery eloquence of Lassalle that the state could be made to serve the interests of the workers. They soon began to diverge from the strict Marxist position in two significant respects. They relegated to the limbo of utopia the whole notion of the " dying away " of the state, thus abandoning the fundamental socialist tradition of the state ; and, instead of insisting, like Marx, that the proletariat must smash the bourgeois state machine by

[1] Bakunin, Œuvres, ii (1907), 39.
[2] Marx i Engels, Sochineniya, xv, 136-137 ; Lenin, Sochineniya, xxi, 412.
[3] G. Sorel, Matériaux d'une Théorie du Prolétariat (1919), p. 132.
[4] G. Sorel, Reflections on Violence (Engl. transl. 1916), p. 190.

revolutionary means and set up a state instrument — the dictatorship of the proletariat — of its own, they came to believe in the possibility of taking over the existing state machine and transforming and converting it to proletarian purposes. In the 1890s Eduard Bernstein became the leader of a revisionist group in the German Social-Democratic Party, standing openly for the attainment of socialism through a process of reform in cooperation with the bourgeois state. The inherent strength of this movement was shown by the fact that Kautsky and his followers, who originally fought it in the name of orthodox Marxism, ultimately went over to a position indistinguishable from it. Marx's rejection of the state was dismissed, in Lenin's words, " as a naïvety which had outlived its day ", just as the Christians, having attained the position of a state religion, " forgot about the naïveties of primitive Christianity with its democratic revolutionary spirit ".[1] The German social-democrats thus approached more nearly to the standpoint of the English radicals, trade unionists and Fabians, who had never been Marxists and never whole-heartedly adhered to the anti-state tradition of European socialism. The combined influence of the German and English groups in the Second International paved the way for that alliance between socialism and nationalism which rent the International asunder on the outbreak of war in 1914.

Lenin remained, at any rate up to the October revolution, a consistent Marxist in his attitude to the state, steering an even course between the Scylla of anarchism and the Charybdis of state worship. He explained his position with exemplary clarity in one of the *Letters From Afar* which he wrote from Switzerland in the interval between the February revolution and his return to Russia :

> We need revolutionary *power*, we need (for a certain period of transition) the *state*. Therein we differ from the anarchists. The difference between revolutionary Marxists and anarchists lies not only in the fact that the former stand for huge, centralised, communist production, while the latter are for decentralised, small-scale production. No, the difference as to government authority and the state consists in this, that we stand *for* the revolutionary utilisation of revolutionary forms of the state in our struggle for socialism, while the anarchists are *against* it.
>
> We need the state. But we need none of those types of state varying from a constitutional monarchy to the most democratic republic which the bourgeoisie has established anywhere. And herein lies the difference between us and the opportunists and Kautskians of the old, decaying socialist parties who have distorted

---

[1] Lenin, *Sochineniya*, xxi, 398-399. The Russian communists of a later date were not wholly immune from the temptation which had overtaken the Christians and the German social-democrats.

or forgotten the lessons of the Paris commune and the analysis of these lessons by Marx and Engels.[1]

At the moment of his return to Russia at the beginning of April 1917 he added still more emphatically :

> Marxism is distinguished from anarchism by its recognition of the indispensability of the state and of state power in the revolutionary period in general and in the era of the transition from capitalism to socialism in particular.
>
> Marxism is distinguished from the petty bourgeois opportunist " social-democracy " of Messrs. Plekhanov, Kautsky and Co. by its recognition of the indispensability in the said periods, not of a state such as an ordinary parliamentary republic, but of a state such as the Paris commune.[2]

When, however, in the late summer of 1917 Lenin, then in hiding in Finland, sat down to write his major work on the Marxist doctrine of the state, he was more preoccupied with the second than with the first of these heresies. Anarchist and syndicalist objections to political action or to an eventual dictatorship of the proletariat were not much in the picture ;[3] it was the loyalty of so-called social-democrats to the national state, their abandonment of the fundamental socialist tenet of hostility to the state, which had broken the international solidarity of the workers of Europe and driven them to engage in fratricidal strife at the behest of the ruling classes of their respective nations. Hence the emphasis in *State and Revolution*, written by Lenin in August-September 1917 but not published till the following year, was somewhat one-sided. The argument against the anarchists in defence of the dictatorship of the proletariat occupied only a few hurried paragraphs ; the bulk of the pamphlet was an assault on those pseudo-Marxists who refused to recognize, first, that the state is a product of class antagonisms and an instrument of class domination, doomed to disappear with the disappearance of classes themselves, and, secondly, that the immediate goal is not the taking over of the bourgeois state machine, but its destruction and replacement by a transitional dictatorship of the proletariat which will pave the way for the ultimate disappearance of classes and of the state. The dictatorship of the proletariat bridged the period from the revolutionary overthrow of the bourgeois state to the final establishment of the classless and stateless society, " from the state to the no-state ".[4] Nor was this any less true of democracy than of any

[1] Lenin, *Sochineniya*, xx, 34-35.   [2] *Ibid.* xx, 120.

[3] Lenin attributed the " insignificant influence " of anarchism in contemporary Russia, partly to the Bolshevik campaign against it, partly to the fact that anarchism in Russia had had ample opportunity in the 1870s to demonstrate its unreliability and futility (*ibid.* xxv, 180).

[4] *Ibid.* xxi, 408.

other form of state. On the contrary, " *every* state is *non-*free and *non-*popular ", and " the completer the democracy, the nearer is the moment when it becomes superfluous ".[1]

All this came straight from Marx and Engels ; and the most interesting passages in *State and Revolution* were those which threw some light on the way in which Lenin conceived the transition. He taunted the anarchists, in words borrowed from Engels, for supposing that the state can be abolished " overnight " ;[2] the transition would occupy " a whole historical period ".[3] Yet this period was thought of in finite terms ; in 1918 he put it at " ten years or perhaps more ", and in his speech on the Red Square on May 1, 1919, he predicted that " a majority of those present who have not passed the age of 30 or 35 will see the dawn of communism, from which we are still far ".[4] Later he wrote that " ten or twenty years sooner or later make no difference when measured by the scale of world history ".[5] But more important than any question of time was Lenin's emphatic assertion in *State and Revolution* that the " dying away " of the state will begin forthwith :

> According to Marx, what the proletariat needs is only a state in process of dying away, i.e. so constituted that it will at once begin to die away and cannot help dying away. . . . The proletarian state will begin to die away immediately after its victory, since in a society without class contradictions, the state is unnecessary and impossible.[6]

Whatever the duration of the process, Lenin at this time clearly expected it to be progressive and continuous.

These theoretical views influenced Lenin's attitude after the revolution towards the constitutional structure of the transitional dictatorship of the proletariat. The state structure set up by the victorious revolution had to satisfy divergent purposes which contained from the start the seeds of a mutual incompatibility. It had to be strong and ruthless in order to crush the last resistance of the bourgeoisie and complete the repression of the minority in the interests of the majority ; it had at the same time to prepare for its own dying away and even to begin that process at once :

> This period is inevitably a period of unprecedentedly bitter class struggle, of unprecedentedly acute forms of it ; consequently the state of this period must inevitably be democratic *in a new way* (for proletarians and the unpropertied in general) and dictatorial *in a new way* (against the bourgeoisie). . . . The dictatorship of one class is indispensable not only for every class society, not only for the *pro-letariat* when it has overthrown the bourgeoisie, but for the whole

[1] *Ibid.* xxi, 382, 557.   [2] *Ibid.* xxi. 410.   [3] *Ibid* xxi, 393.

[4] *Ibid.* xxii, 466, xxiv, 270.   [5] *Ibid.* xxv, 199.   [6] *Ibid.* xxi, 385, 388.

historical period which separates capitalism from the " classless society ", from communism.[1]

Lenin never recognized any difficulty of principle in reconciling the quasi-voluntary association of the workers implied in the dying away of the state with the concentration of power necessary for the exercise of a ruthless dictatorship over the bourgeoisie. Of the ruthlessness of the dictatorship he spoke in uncompromising terms. He recognized that one of the causes of the defeat of the commune was its failure to crush bourgeois resistance " decisively enough ".[2] The dictatorship of the proletariat, like any other state, would be an instrument not of freedom, but of repression — the repression not, as in other states, of the majority, but of an intransigent minority. A trenchant passage from Engels was twice quoted by Lenin in his essay :

> So long as the proletariat still *needs* the state, it needs it not in the interests of freedom, but in the interests of the repression of its opponents, and when it becomes possible to speak of freedom, the state as such ceases to exist.[3]

And Lenin himself epigrammatically added :

> So long as the state exists there is no freedom ; when freedom exists there will be no state.[4]

But repressive though the dictatorship of the proletariat was, it was unique in being a dictatorship exercised by a majority over a minority ; and this not only gave it its democratic character,[5] but enormously simplified its working :

> The repression of a minority of exploiters by a majority of former wage-slaves is so relatively simple, easy and natural that it will cost far less blood than the repression of risings of slaves, serfs and hired workers, and work out far cheaper for humanity. And it coincides with the extension of democracy to such an overwhelming majority of the population that the need for a *special machinery* of repression begins to vanish. The exploiters are naturally not in a position to crush the people without a most complicated machine to carry out the task. But the people can crush the exploiters with very simple

---

[1] Lenin, *Sochineniya*, xxi, 392-393. [2] *Ibid.* xxi, 398.

[3] *Ibid.* xxi, 414, 431.

[4] *Ibid.* xxi, 436. In a famous phrase used more than once by Lenin the state is " a machine or a cudgel ", " a special cudgel, nothing more ", which the ruling class uses to crush other classes (*ibid.* xxiv, 377, xxv, 5).

[5] The dictatorship of the proletariat was thus distinguished from all forms of dictatorship resting on the conception of a superior and privileged *élite* ; even " the dictatorship of the party ", though the phrase was at one time used by Lenin, was later condemned as heterodox (see pp. 231-232 above).

" machinery ", almost without " machinery ", without a special apparatus, through the *simple* organization of the armed masses (like the Soviets of Workers' and Soldiers' Deputies).[1]

From this angle Lenin approached the old problem of bureaucracy. The evil of the state as something, in the words of Engels, " proceeding out of society but standing above it "[2] was epitomized for Lenin in " the privileged position of officials as the organs of state power ".[3] He appears to have thought of bureaucracy as specifically bourgeois. " From absolutist half-Asiatic Russia down to cultured, free, civilized England," he wrote in an early work, " everywhere we see this institution constituting the indispensable organ of bourgeois society."[4] Bureaucracy and the standing army were described in *State and Revolution* as " the two most characteristic institutions " of the bourgeois period of " centralized state power "; [5] in capitalist conditions even party and trade union officials " show a tendency to be perverted into bureaucrats, i.e. privileged persons divorced from the masses and standing *above* the masses ".[6] In the April theses, issued immediately on his return to Petrograd, Lenin demanded " abolition of the police, the army, the bureaucracy ".[7] In *State and Revolution* he invoked the example of ancient democracy, where the citizens themselves were administrators.

Under socialism, much of " primitive " democracy will inevitably revive, since for the first time in the history of civilized societies the *mass* of the population will be raised to *independent* participation not only in voting and elections, *but in day to day administration*. Under socialism *all* will administer in turn and will quickly become accustomed to nobody administering.[8]

It was in this spirit that Lenin praised the Soviets in September 1917 as the embodiment of a new state form in which a " direct democracy " of the workers could be realized :

[1] *Ibid.* xxi, 432. Lenin might perhaps have remembered Rousseau's aphorism in the *Contrat Social*: " Il est contre l'ordre naturel que le grand nombre gouverne and que le petit soit gouverné ".

[2] Marx i Engels, *Sochineniya*, xvi, i, 145.

[3] Lenin, *Sochineniya*, xxi, 378.   [4] *Ibid.* ii, 179.

[5] *Ibid.* xxi, 388.   [6] *Ibid.* xxi, 451.   [7] *Ibid.* xx, 88.

[8] *Ibid.* xxi, 452. It is hardly necessary to recall that Rousseau in the *Contrat Social* regarded direct democracy as the only true democracy ("A l'instant qu'un peuple se donne des représentants, il n'est plus libre "). This idea was familiar to many nineteenth-century socialists, e.g. V. Considérant : " Si le peuple délègue sa souveraineté, il l'abdique. Le peuple ne se gouverne plus lui-même, on le gouverne " (*La Solution, ou le Gouvernement Direct du Peuple*, p. 13). The principle of the revocability of deputies at any moment by their electors, as a mitigation of the evil of representative government, goes back at least as far as Babeuf, and found its place in article 78 of the constitution of the RSFSR.

" Power to the Soviets " — this means a radical re-fashioning of the whole old state apparatus, of that apparatus of officialdom which puts the brake on everything democratic, the destruction of that apparatus and its replacement by the new, popular, i.e. truly democratic apparatus of the Soviets, i.e. of the organized and armed majority of the people, of workers, soldiers and peasants, the reserving to the majority of the people of initiative and independence not only in the election of deputies, but in the administration of the state, in the realization of reforms and transformations.[1]

It was in this spirit that he drafted his appeal " To the Population " a few days after the October revolution :

Comrade Workers! Remember that *you yourselves* now administer the state. Nobody will help you if you yourselves do not unite and take *all the affairs* of the state into *your own* hands. *Your* Soviets are henceforth the organs of state power, organs with full powers, organs of decision.[2]

If bureaucracy was a specific product of bourgeois society, then there was nothing extravagant in the supposition that it would disappear when that society was overthrown.

The same principles applied to the management of economic affairs, of production and distribution. Lenin first expounded his views on this point in the pamphlet *Will the Bolsheviks Retain State Power?* written in September 1917. Apart from the repressive apparatus of the state " there was also in the modern state an apparatus closely bound up with the banks and syndicates, an apparatus which performs a mass of accounting and registration ". This belonged to the category of the " administration of things ", and could and must not be destroyed ; for this was a large part of the vital apparatus of the socialist order. " *Without the big banks socialism would be unrealisable.*" No difficulty need arise either in taking over the employees now engaged in this work or in recruiting the far larger numbers which would be necessary under the proletarian state, " since capitalism has simplified the functions of accounting and control, reduced them to comparatively straightforward entries comprehensible to every literate person ".[3] In *State and Revolution* he emphatically repeated this belief, and linked it with an eloquent vision of the process by which the state apparatus might be expected to die away :

Thus, when *all* learn to administer and in fact independently administer socialized production, and independently carry out the checking and control of the boneheads, lordlings, sharpers and such like " defenders of the capitalist tradition ", then evasion of this

[1] Lenin, *Sochineniya*, xxi, 143-144.   [2] *Ibid.* xxii, 55.
[3] *Ibid.* xxi, 260-261.

checking and control by the whole people will inevitably become so immeasurably difficult, so rare an exception, and will in all probability be visited by such swift and condign punishment (since the armed workers are practical people and not sentimental intellectuals, and will not allow themselves to be trifled with), that the *necessity* of observing the uncomplicated fundamental rules of every human society will soon become a *habit*.[1]

How far were Lenin's views expressed on the eve of the revolution modified by the experience of the revolution itself? Its immediate effect was to quicken the belief in the possibility of an immediate transition to socialism. Looking back from the vantage point of 1921, Lenin confessed that in the winter of 1917–1918 the Bolshevik leaders were, without exception, swayed by " presuppositions, not always perhaps openly expressed, but always silently taken for granted, about an immediate transition to the building of socialism ".[2] But before long the picture radically changed. During the winter the administrative and economic machine was running down at an alarming rate. The danger to the revolution came not from organized resistance, but from a breakdown of all authority. The appeal in *State and Revolution* to " smash the bourgeois state machine " now seemed singularly out of date ; that part of the revolutionary programme had succeeded beyond all expectation. The question was what to put in the place of the machine that had been destroyed. " The need to destroy the old state ", Lenin told Bukharin in April 1918, was " a matter of yesterday " : what was now required was " to create the state of the commune ".[3] Lenin had long ago laid down two conditions for the transition to socialism — the support of the peasantry and the support of a European revolution. The hope of realizing these conditions had been the ground of his optimism. The hope had not been fulfilled. At home, the peasantry had supported the revolution as the power which had given them the land. But, once this was achieved, and now that the main demand of the revolutionary régime on the peasant was for the delivery of food to the towns with no visible prospect of an adequate return, the peasantry relapsed into sullen obstruction and even carried a part of the urban workers with them into an attitude

---

[1] Lenin, *Sochineniya*, xxi, 441. The notion of the simplicity of economic administration has a long ancestry, going back to the nature school of the eighteenth century ; Morelly, *Le Code de la Nature* (ed. É. Dolléans, 1910), p. 39, refers to it as " une simple opération de calcul et de combinaison et, par conséquent, susceptible d'un très-bel ordre " ; Buonarotti, *Conspiration pour l'Égalité, dite de Babeuf* (1828), i, 214, as " une affaire de calcul, susceptible de l'ordre le plus exact et de la marche la plus regulière ". The importance of the rôle of the banks was a favourite idea of Saint-Simon ; its influence on the economic policy of the Soviet régime will be discussed in Part IV.

[2] Lenin, *Sochineniya*, xxvii, 60.   [3] *Ibid.* xxii, 488.

of passive opposition. Abroad, the European proletariat still allowed itself to be led by its imperialist governments to internecine slaughter, and the first faint symptoms of revolution failed altogether to mature. The new régime thus found itself isolated at home amid a predominantly indifferent and sometimes unfriendly rural population — the dictatorship not of the " vast majority ", but of a determined minority — and surrounded by a capitalist world united in its hostility to Bolshevism, though temporarily divided against itself. Lenin never openly admitted these disappointments, or perhaps even admitted them to himself. But they were responsible for the apparent contradictions between the theory of *State and Revolution* and the practice of the first year of the régime. Lenin was faced with a situation in which the old state machine had been destroyed and the conditions for the building of the socialist order had failed to mature.

It was in these circumstances that Lenin sounded a first note of warning at the seventh party congress in March 1918. He resisted as premature Bukharin'a proposal that the revised party programme should contain some description of " the developed socialist order in which there is no state " :

> For the present we stand unconditionally for the state ; and as for giving a description of socialism in its developed form, where there will be no state — nothing can be imagined about it except that then will be realized the principle " from each according to his capacities, to each according to his needs ". But we are a long way from that. . . . We shall come to it in the end if we come to socialism.

And again :

> When will the state begin to die away? We shall have time to hold more than two congresses before we can say, See how our state is dying away. Till then it is too soon. To proclaim in advance the dying away of the state will be a violation of historical perspective.[1]

A little later Lenin emphasized once more that " between capitalism and communism lies a certain period of transition ", that " it is impossible to destroy classes all at once ", and that " classes remain and will remain throughout the epoch of the dictatorship of the proletariat ".[2] The Lenin of *State and Revolution* had thrown into relief the prospective dying away of the state ; and in January 1919 he believed that " even now " the organization of Soviet power " clearly shows the transition towards the complete abolition of all power, of any state ".[3] But the Lenin of the years from 1918 to 1922 was more

---

[1] Lenin, *Sochineniya*, xxii, 364-365.   [2] *Ibid.* xxiv, 507, 513.
[3] *Ibid.* xxii, 215.

concerned to dwell on the need to strengthen the state in the transitional period of the dictatorship of the proletariat.

The most striking illustration of the change of emphasis was found in the evolution of his attitude towards bureaucracy. In one passage of *State and Revolution* he had already shown himself conscious of the charge to which his sanguine expectations might expose him :

> To abolish bureaucracy at once, everywhere and finally cannot be thought of. That is utopian. But to *destroy* at once the old bureaucratic machine and to begin immediately to build up a new machine which will permit of the gradual extinction of every kind of bureaucracy, that is *not* utopian, that is the experience of the commune, that is the direct matter-of-fact task of the revolutionary proletariat.[1]

Even before the October revolution he had written that it would be necessary to take the " capitalists " and " *compel them to work in* the new framework of state organization . . . to put them to the new state service ".[2] During the next three years — the period of the civil war — the struggle for efficiency in administration, the fiasco of workers' control in industry and the discovery that in every field, from war to economic organization, the technical skills of the bourgeois specialist were indispensable to the working of the administrative machine caused him to beat a retreat from the conception of the management of public affairs by workers in their spare time. At the beginning of 1921, on the eve of the introduction of NEP, Lenin expressed himself in terms which read like an explicit repudiation of his own earlier position :

> Can every worker know how to administer the state? Practical people know that this is a fairy tale. . . . The trade unions are a school of communism and administration. When they [i.e. the workers] have spent these years at school, they will learn, but it progresses slowly. . . . How many workers have been engaged in administration? A few thousands all over Russia, and no more.[3]

It was this dilemma which, as Lenin confessed, had compelled the Bolsheviks, instead of destroying the old state machine root and branch, to take over " hundreds of thousands of old officials, inherited from the Tsar and from bourgeois society, who work in part consciously, in part unconsciously, against us ".[4]

Faced with these difficulties Lenin returned the more persistently to his original antidote — the active participation of the rank and file in administration as the sole way of realizing democracy and countering bureaucracy. The process would be slower than he had hoped, but was all the more necessary :

[1] *Ibid.* xxi, 402.   [2] *Ibid.* xxi, 263.   [3] *Ibid.* xxvi, 103.   [4] *Ibid.* xxvii, 353.

The further development of the Soviet state organization [he wrote in April 1918] must consist in every member of the Soviet being obliged to undertake constant work in the administration of the state in addition to his participation in the meetings of the Soviet, and, consequently, in drawing the whole population individually and gradually both towards participation in the Soviet organization . . . and towards taking a share in the service of state administration.[1]

In the last two or three years of Lenin's life the campaign against bureaucracy assumed immense importance, not only for Lenin the administrator, but for Lenin the political thinker. It was the practical expression of the campaign against state power of which *State and Revolution* had been the theoretical exposition. It provided the practical answer to the question how the state could in fact die away. This could happen only when every citizen was willing and able to shoulder his own share of the work of administration, simplified as that work would be when the " government of men " had been transformed into an " administration of things ". In the words of the party programme of 1919:

> Conducting the most resolute struggle against bureaucratism, the Russian Communist Party advocates for the complete overcoming of this evil the following measures:
>
> (1) an obligatory call on every member of the Soviet for the fulfilment of a definite task in the administration of the state;
> (2) a systematic variation in these tasks in order that they may gradually cover all branches of the administration;
> (3) a gradual drawing of the whole working population individually into work in the administration of the state.
>
> The full and universal application of all these measures, which represents a further step on the road trodden by the Paris commune, and the simplification of the functions of administration accompanied by a rise in the cultural level of the workers will lead to the abolition of state power.[2]

It would, therefore, be a fundamental error to suppose that the experience of power brought any radical change in Lenin's philosophy of the state. The dying away of the state was in Marxist doctrine dependent on the elimination of classes and the establishment of a socialist order of economic planning and economic abundance; and this in turn was dependent on the fulfilment of conditions which had to be empirically determined at any given moment and in any given place. Theory could in itself give no ground for certainty about the right course of action or the prospect for the immediate future. Lenin could perfectly well admit, without stultifying himself or discrediting

[1] Lenin, *Sochineniya*, xxii, 465.   [2] *VKP(B) v Rezolyutsiyakh* (1941), i, 286.

the theory, that he had miscalculated the rate of the process of transformation. Nevertheless, it was also true that Lenin's theory of the state reflected the dichotomy in Marxist thought, which combined a highly realist and relativist analysis of the historical process with an uncompromisingly absolute vision of the ultimate goal, and strove to bridge the gap between them by a chain of causal development. This transformation of reality into utopia, of the relative into the absolute, of incessant class conflict into the classless society, and of the ruthless use of state power into the stateless society, was the essence of what Marx and Lenin believed. In so far as this was inconsistent, the inconsistency was fundamental; and there is no point in convicting Lenin, as is often done, of inconsistency of detail in his attitude to the state.

Nor does the theory appear to involve belief, as is sometimes suggested, in a radical change in human nature. The liberal doctrine of the harmony of interests did not suggest the nature of men would change, but that their natural egoism would be found in suitable conditions to serve the interests of society. This is the political doctrine which has the closest analogies with the doctrine of the dying away of the state; and Adam Smith has not escaped in recent years the charge of utopianism commonly levelled at Marx and Engels and Lenin. Both doctrines assume that the state will be superfluous in so far as, given the appropriate economic organization of society, human beings will find it natural to work together with one another for the common good. It is the context in which human nature displays itself rather than human nature itself which will be changed. In this sense both doctrines are consistent with belief in an economic order determining a superstructure of political ideology and behaviour.

PART III

DISPERSAL AND REUNION

CHAPTER 10

POLICY, DOCTRINE, MACHINERY

(a) Outlines of Policy

THE great Russian Empire, when the Bolsheviks took possession of it, was in a process of rapid disintegration — the
result of internal turmoil and of defeat in war. The immediate effect of the revolution was to accelerate the process. For
several weeks the writ of Petrograd scarcely ran outside the great
cities of northern and central Russia. The first two months
brought the beginnings of an expansion of Soviet power southward
through the Ukraine and eastward into Siberia. But this incipient
recovery was quickly interrupted. The Brest-Litovsk treaty of
March 1918 lopped off not only those western appendages of the
former Tsarist realm whose independence the Soviet Government
had spontaneously recognized, but a large slice of predominantly
Russian territory. The summer of 1918 saw the beginning of civil
war and of British, French, Japanese and American intervention,
which long outlasted the German collapse, and for more than two
years forcibly divided the country between several conflicting
authorities. By the end of 1918 the Russian Socialist Federal
Soviet Republic was confined within approximately the same
boundaries as mediaeval Muscovy before the conquests of Ivan
the Terrible; and few people — few perhaps even of the Bolsheviks themselves — believed that the régime could survive. Yet
just four years later the diverse units of the former Tsarist empire
were with a few exceptions gathered once more into the fold of
the Union of Soviet Socialist Republics; and the cohesion of the
newly established unit was destined to prove at least as strong as
that of the defunct empire. This consummation, which could
have been foreseen by none in the dark days of 1918 or 1919,
was an outstanding tribute to Lenin's genius as a constructive
statesman.

The vast European and Asiatic land-mass which had constituted the Russian Empire and, with some minor curtailments, was to form the Soviet Union, was inhabited by a population of extraordinary linguistic and ethnic diversity. Within its confines geographers and philologists discovered nearly 200 more or less distinct peoples and languages.[1] At the census of 1897 the Great Russians formed only 43 per cent of the total population. After the revolution the severance of the non-Russian western provinces gave them a small majority in what remained : they provided about 75,000,000, or 52 per cent of a total population of about 140,000,000.[2] The next largest groups, the 30,000,000 Ukrainians (or Little Russians) and the 4,500,000 White Russians were closely allied to the Great Russians in race, speech and sentiment. These three Slav groups, possessing a large measure of underlying natural cohesion, accounted for 110,000,000 out of the 140,000,000 inhabitants of the whole territory. The 30,000,000 non-Slavs lacked any kind of cohesion, racial, linguistic or political, among themselves. The largest group, the Uzbeks, was only 5,000,000 strong ; and some 8,000,000 to 10,000,000 of the non-Slavs were still in the primitive tribal or nomadic stage.

This conglomeration of peoples was held together by a ruling military and bureaucratic caste centred round the " Tsar of all the Russias ". Into this caste certain non-Russian elements found ready admittance, notably the German landowners of Latvia and Estonia and the Polish landowners of Poland, Lithuania, White Russia and the Ukraine ; but the conditions of this admittance were the use of the Russian language and the assimilation of the Russian tradition and outlook. The lower ranks of the administration, swollen by the growth of the bureaucratic machine, were recruited from the petty bourgeoisie, Russian and — on the same conditions — non-Russian ; and at a different level, native khans, begs and mullahs were the agents of an indirect rule over the more primitive Muslim peoples of the Tsar's dominions. Thus the groups which might have furnished the leadership of national

[1] A full list, together with the numbers of each group as shown in the 1926 census, will be found in F. Lorimer, *The Population of the Soviet Union* (League of Nations, Geneva, 1946), Table 23, pp. 55-61.
[2] These estimates were cited by Stalin in 1921 (*Sochineniya*, v, 114) : they were broadly confirmed by the census figures of 1926, when the total population had risen to 147,000,000.

movements among the subject peoples tended to be absorbed into the administrative machine and to enjoy the more or less privileged status which this promotion carried with it. As the experience of 1905 showed, these groups were for the most part inhibited from an active nationalism by fear of the revolutionary violence of their own workers and peasants, against which Tsarist power was a sure protection ; and the Russian markets were the foundation of their economic prosperity. Thus the demands made before 1917 in the name of the subject peoples rarely went beyond a mild degree of autonomy. It was only when the revolution destroyed both the symbols of unity and the reality of a common interest that the whole edifice crumbled into ruin. What happened in 1917 was due not so much to a deliberate break-away of the periphery as to a disintegration of the centre, " not a falling away of the parts, but a collapse of the old Russia ".[1]

The task which confronted the Bolsheviks of reassembling the scattered fragments of the Tsarist empire might well have proved insuperable but for one propitious natural factor. The racial and linguistic diversity which favoured dispersal at the outset was compensated by the immense preponderance of the Great Russian element, which acted like a magnet on the whole mass. It was this circumstance which eventually made it possible to arrest and reverse the disintegration of the Romanov dominions after 1917, whereas the break-up of the Habsburg empire proved irreparable. The situation in Russia had in certain respects a closer resemblance to that of north Germany. On the Ukrainians and White Russians the Great Russians exercised the same compulsive centralizing influence as was exercised by Prussia in the

---

[1] V. Stankevich, *Sud'by Narodov Rossii* (Berlin, 1921), p. 16. The " anarchic " tendencies of the Slav peoples and the need for a strong power to impose statehood on them have been a favourite theme of Russian historians ; it recurs in a well-known passage of Gorky's reminiscences of Tolstoy : " What is called Tolstoy's ' anarchism ' essentially and fundamentally expressed our Slav anti-stateism, which again is really a national characteristic and desire, ingrained in our flesh from old times, to scatter nomadically. . . . We break away, always along the line of least resistance ; we see that this is pernicious, but still we crawl further and further away from one another — and these mournful cockroach journeyings are called ' the history of Russia ', of a state which has been established almost incidentally, mechanically, to the surprise of the majority of its honest-minded citizens by the forces of the Variags, Tatars, Baltic Germans and petty constables " (M. Gorky, *Reminiscences of Tolstoy, Chekhov and Andreev* (Engl. transl. 1934), p. 47).

German Confederation; some Ukrainians, like the Bavarians, may have resented the predominance of their more powerful and vigorous kinsmen, but were neither strong enough nor united enough in their separatism to assert themselves effectively for long. The first stage in the process of reassembly was therefore to weld together the three Slav peoples, forming nearly four-fifths of the whole. Once they were united, the force of attraction on the uncoordinated and far less highly developed agglomeration of non-Slav peoples was likely to prove irresistible. And these unifying influences were reinforced and given social and economic substance by the concentration of industrial and commercial power in Great Russian hands. The industrial centres which dominated the economic life of the whole country either lay within the Great Russian core or represented Great Russian outposts in " alien " territory.

Another factor soon entered into the picture. Growing recognition of the practical need for a reunion of the dispersed territories of the defunct empire coincided with a resurgence of Russian patriotism which came as a paradoxical and unexpected reinforcement of Bolshevik policy. The anarchy of the revolution had prompted the extreme demand for separation; and it soon became clear that that demand could be sustained only with the support of foreign arms and foreign money, so that those whose pride had revolted against dependence on Petrograd or Moscow found themselves the satellites and hirelings of Germany or of the allies or successively of both. That was the story in the Ukraine, in Transcaucasia and even on the shores of the Baltic. Since both Great Britain and Japan were suspected of wanting a weak Russia, the view that bourgeois nationalism was an instrument for the dismemberment of Russia at the behest, and in the interest, of foreign Powers became difficult to refute. Even the " white " generals who sought to reconstitute the unity of Russia fell under the same condemnation of playing a foreign game. In the bitterness of defeat they too turned against their foreign backers. The *locus classicus* on this point was the remark attributed to Kolchak on the eve of his downfall in a discussion on the national gold reserve held by him : " I would rather leave the gold to the Bolsheviks than hand it over to the allies ".[1] Especially

---

[1] G. K. Gins, *Sibir', Soyuzniki i Kolchak* (Peking, 1921), ii, 332.

after the Polish war of 1920 the Bolsheviks came to be widely accepted as defenders of the Russian heritage and architects of a reunited Russia.

These centralizing impulses would not, however, have availed by themselves to set in motion the process of reunion. The Slav, and especially the Great Russian, element provided the indispensable hard core round which the dispersed territories could once more coalesce. But the striking thing was that these impulses should have been felt to so large an extent at the periphery as well as at the centre. In 1918 the old loyalties had seemed extinct among the former subject peoples. The tide of nationalism was in full flood. But Lenin had long recognized the revolutionary factors in nationalism, and had foreseen that the only safe course would be to welcome and harness the torrent. The civil war brilliantly justified Lenin's thesis. Unqualified recognition of the right of secession not only enabled the Soviet régime — as nothing else could have done — to ride the torrent of a disruptive nationalism, but raised its prestige high above that of the " white " generals who, bred in the pan-Russian tradition of the Tsars, refused any concession to the subject nationalities ; in the borderlands where other than Russian, or other than Great Russian, elements predominated, and where the decisive campaigns of the civil war were fought, this factor told heavily in favour of the Soviet cause.

Do not forget [said Stalin with an unusual warmth of emotion] that, if in the rear of Kolchak, Denikin, Wrangel and Yudenich we had not had the so-called " aliens ", if we had not had the former oppressed peoples who undermined the rear of these generals by their silent sympathy with the Russian proletariat — and this, comrades, is a special factor in our growth, this silent sympathy ; nobody sees it or hears it, but it decides everything — if it had not been for this sympathy, we should not have beaten one of these generals. While we were marching against them, the collapse began in their rear. Why? Because these generals relied on the " colonizing " element among the Cossacks, they offered to the oppressed peoples a prospect of further oppression, and the oppressed peoples were obliged to come forward and embrace us, seeing that we unfurled the banner of the liberation of these oppressed peoples.[1]

[1] Stalin, *Sochineniya*, v, 246.

Moreover, the eventual identification of nationalism in the Bolshevik programme with social reform — meaning, over the great
part of the former Russian Empire, a redistribution of the land
— was an all-important asset. It persuaded peasants whose
nationalism had been mainly an expression of social and economic
grievances to align themselves under Bolshevik (even if this meant
Russian) leadership against counter-revolutionary attempts to
restore the previous social order. Whatever national or linguistic
diversities might separate them, the peasants everywhere were in
overwhelming majority opposed to a counter-revolution which
would have returned the land to its former owners ; and, so long
as fear of counter-revolution was not extinct, the community of
interest between the Russian workers and the peasant masses of
the subject peoples on which Bolshevik propaganda insisted had
a perfectly solid basis. The same forces were at work in the few
industrial centres where capitalist development had produced a
non-Russian proletariat — in Riga, in Reval, in Baku. The combination between the recognition of a formal right of national
self-determination and the recognition of a real need for unity in
pursuit of common social and economic ends, which was the
essence of the Bolshevik doctrine of nationalism, proved a vital
contribution to the Soviet victory in the civil war.

The twelfth party congress of 1923, reviewing the whole
process at the time of its completion, distinguished three successive
stages in Soviet nationalities policy. The first stage was the
breaking of " the chains of national oppression " by the October
revolution, which " won for the Russian proletariat the confidence
of its brothers of other nations, not only in Russia, but in Europe
and in Asia ". The second was the period of intervention and
civil war, when the peoples of Russia were united by the needs of
self-defence and " cooperation between them took the form of a
military alliance ". In the third and final stage, following the
victorious end of the civil war, cooperation " took on this time
the character of a military-economic and political union of the
peoples ".[1] These stages were logical rather than chronological.
Owing to local conditions and the vagaries of the civil war, the
second stage was far advanced among some of the western peoples
while the first stage had hardly begun in the east ; and the approach

[1] *VKP(B) v Rezolyutsiyakh* (1941), i, 492-493.

to the final stage, ordered and leisurely in some regions, was abrupt and violent in others. But the classification has the merit of throwing into relief both the regularity of the process and the confused and contradictory nature of the phenomena contributing to it. Later accounts tended to depict a continuous process of development in which the initial motions of secession and dispersal were a cunningly premeditated prelude to the final act of reunion. This was an error of diagnosis which exaggerated the foresight of the Bolshevik leaders, and concealed the dual character of the process. In part, no doubt, the policy followed was an expression of loyalty to the principle of national self-determination, enforced by Lenin's will, like so many other policies of this time, on his wavering followers. Lenin realized that it was necessary to accept and overtrump the bourgeois doctrine of self-determination by applying it without reserve to the nations of the Russian Empire, and that this bold plan provided the best and, indeed, the only chance of ultimately reconstituting the former unity, " not by force, but by voluntary agreement ".[1] But it is also necessary to remember that in the first three or four months after October 1917 the writ of the Soviet Government scarcely ran outside a few major centres, and that between the summer of 1918 and the beginning of 1920 it was continually fighting with its back to the wall. At a moment when the Russian Empire was in dissolution and no power could have held it together, wholesale recognition of claims to national independence provided an excellent way of making a virtue of a necessity. At a moment when the civil war was raging over those outlying sectors of Russian territory which were mainly occupied by the non-Russian peoples, it was a means of enlisting local populations as allies against those who sought to re-create the Russian Empire. Finally, when victory in the civil war was won and the time came to restore order out of chaos, Soviet nationalities policy was flexible enough to provide a basis on which Moscow could support its friends and allies among the non-Russian peoples and once more weave together the scattered territories in a framework of voluntary reunion. But to attribute the whole process to a cunning calculation by the leaders or to a deliberate manipulation of theory in the interests of policy is to misunderstand the nature of the underlying forces at work.

[1] Lenin, *Sochineniya*, xxi, 317.

(b) *Doctrine in Evolution*

The seizure of power presented the Bolsheviks with the task of reconciling the apparent contradiction between the disintegrating tendencies of national self-determination and the demand for closer integration implicit in international capitalism as well as in international socialism. Bourgeois statesmen who were wrestling with the same problem at the same time could explain only on grounds of practical convenience why some nations should be encouraged to exercise the right of self-determination and others should not. But this purely empirical criterion was not open to Marxists. What was done must be buttressed on a basis of theory; and this was found in an historical approach which recognized not only stages of development in time but the presence of different stages simultaneously in different countries, so that variations of policy might be justified and required at different periods or in different places at the same period. A consistent flexibility in Bolshevik practice could thus be opposed to the unexplained inconsistencies of the bourgeois attitude towards different claims to self-determination.

The Bolshevik doctrine of national self-determination, like other Bolshevik doctrines of political right, was conditional and dynamic. The precise content of the right of self-determination depended on the character of the society in which the right was claimed and exercised. In the nineteenth century it had been asserted by bourgeois democracy against the survivals of feudal autocracy. It was to this extent progressive, and bourgeoisie and workers shared a common interest in liberation from alien rule; and in Russia this struggle had not yet been completed in 1917. In the twentieth century the right of national self-determination, though essentially a bourgeois-democratic right, was also being asserted by colonial and semi-colonial peoples against the imperialism of the more advanced bourgeois-democratic Powers, so that a natural alliance existed between the Russian proletariat seeking, after the defection of the Russian bourgeoisie, to complete the Russian bourgeois revolution, and bourgeois elements and workers of the colonial countries seeking to create their own bourgeois revolution through the process of national liberation. But all this had to be read in the light of the transition initiated in Russia in October 1917 from the bourgeois to the socialist stage of the revolution. The workers' movement was essentially international; for the proletariat the achievement of nationhood, though a necessary and progressive step, was valid only as a component part of its international socialist programme. At the socialist stage of the revolution, while the bourgeoisie still appeared as the champions of absolute separation, the workers recognized the superior claims of the international solidarity of the proletarian revolution, and so organized the nation as to make it a contributory factor to the victory of international socialism. The right of national self-determination was still recognized. But whether the workers who now spoke for the nation would decide to exercise it, and with what reservations, depended on the view taken of the wider interests of the proletariat throughout the world. Such was the theory of national self-determination elaborated by Lenin and the Bolsheviks before the October revolution on the foundations laid by Marx.[1]

Its practical application was a gradual process. The party conference of April 1917, when the Bolshevik leaders had gathered in Petrograd after the February revolution, was noteworthy for Stalin's first appearance as *rapporteur* on the national question. The party as a whole had not yet had time to digest the refinements which Lenin had introduced since 1914 into party doctrine, and was still in the state of confusion created by the April theses of 1917 with their announcement of the move forward from the bourgeois to the socialist revolution. Stalin was still content in the main to treat national self-determination as a problem of the bourgeois revolution against feudalism, and national oppression as something which could be progressively removed even under bourgeois democracy.[2] Pyatakov, who had returned to Petrograd with Lenin and was familiar with recent controversies, condemned Stalin for taking into account only " national oppression of the old kind . . . national oppression of the old period ". But he also

---

[1] See Note B : " The Bolshevik Doctrine of Self-Determination " (pp. 410-428 below).

[2] Stalin, *Sochineniya*, iii, 49-55. In an article in *Pravda* on March 25, 1917, Stalin had explicitly identified national liberation with the bourgeois revolution : " To remove the feudal aristocracy from the political scene, to take away its power — this means to liquidate national oppression, to create the *actual* conditions necessary for national freedom " (*ibid.* iii, 17).

revived the "Polish heresy" by denying that national self-determination could have any place in a socialist programme; and he found so much support in the conference that the drafting commission, by seven votes to two, put forward a resolution which declared that the national question could only be solved by "the method of socialist revolution under the slogan 'away with frontiers'", rejected the solution of "splitting up great state formations into small national states", and branded the right of national self-determination as "simply a phrase without definite content ".[1] This revolt brought Lenin on the scene with a strong attack on Pyatakov.[2] He swayed the conference sufficiently to secure the rejection of the Pyatakov draft and the adoption by a substantial majority of a resolution on well-worn lines reasserting the right of "all nations forming part of Russia" to "free separation and the creation of an independent state ".[3] But the task of working out the implications of national self-determination under a socialist order still lay ahead. Nor was the party at this time called on to take any practical stand on national self-determination except to condemn the Provisional Government for its temporizing attitude towards the claims of Finland and the Ukraine.[4]

The seizure of power by the Bolsheviks did not at once take the national question out of its bourgeois setting. The first few weeks after the October revolution left little time, and provided no occasion, for a reconsideration of the Bolshevik doctrine of

[1] Sed'maya (" Aprel'skaya ") Vserossiiskaya i Petrogradskaya Obshchegorod-skaya Konferentsii RSDRP(B) (1934), pp. 194, 269-271 ; for the " Polish heresy " see pp. 422-423 below. Rosa Luxemburg stuck firmly to this view till the end of her life : Ukrainian nationalism was described by her in the autumn of 1918 as " the ridiculous farce of a few university professors and students " which " Lenin and Co. by their doctrinaire agitation for ' self-determination to the point of . . .', etc. have artificially inflated into a political factor " (Archiv für die Geschichte des Sozializmus und der Arbeiterbewegung (Leipzig), xiii (1928), 285-286).

[2] Lenin, Sochineniya, xx, 275-278.

[3] VKP(B) v Rezolyutsiyakh (1941), i, 233.

[4] The first All-Russian Congress of Soviets in June 1917, which had a SR majority, urged the Provisional Government to issue a declaration recognizing " the right of self-determination for all nations to the point of secession ", but added the qualification " to be reached by way of agreement in the all-national constituent assembly " (Pervyi Vserossiiskii S"ezd Sovetov (1931), ii, 168). It added a similar qualification to its resolution on the independence of Finland (ibid. ii, 184-185) ; Kollontai criticized both resolutions on behalf of the Bolsheviks.

self-determination, whether as applied to the rapidly dissolving framework of the Tsarist empire, or to the semi-colonial foreign countries in contact with the new Soviet Government. The nationalities policy, like most policies of the new régime, took at first the form of public pronouncements rather than of administrative action. The peace decree of the second All-Russian Congress of Soviets called for peace " without annexations ", and defined as annexation " any union of a small or weak nationality with a great or powerful state without the precisely, clearly and willingly expressed consent and desire of that nationality ", at whatever time or in whatever conditions such union might have taken place. The application of this doctrine to the subject peoples of the Tsarist empire was pointed by a reference in another passage to " the annexations of the Great Russians ".[1] The first specific pronouncement was the Declaration of Rights of the Peoples of Russia of November 2/15, 1917,[2] followed a few weeks later by a special appeal " To all Muslim Toilers of Russia and the East ".[3] These documents all proclaimed without reservation or qualification the right of self-determination for all peoples.

> They tell us [wrote Lenin at this time] that Russia will be partitioned, will fall apart into separate republics, but we have no reason to fear this. However many independent republics there may be, we shall not be afraid. What is important for us is not where the state frontier passes, but that the union of workers of all nations shall be preserved for the struggle with the bourgeoisie of whatever nation.[4]

On the other hand, the Declaration of Rights of the Toiling and Exploited People of January 1918, which was adopted by the third All-Russian Congress of Soviets and embodied in the constitution of the RSFSR, added that " all the nations of Russia " had " the right of unfettered decision whether and on what basis to participate in the federal government and in the other federal Soviet institutions "; [5] and this was amplified in the resolution of the same congress " On the Federal Institutions of the Russian Republic ".[6] Thus early was " federation " (the word being used

---

[1] *Sobranie Uzakonenii, 1917–1918*, No. 1 (2nd ed.), art. 2.
[2] *Ibid*. No. 2 (2nd ed.), art. 18.   [3] *Ibid*. No. 6, annex 2.
[4] Lenin, *Sochineniya*, xxii, 100.
[5] *Sobranie Uzakonenii*, No. 15, art. 215.
[6] *S"ezdy Sovetov RSFSR v Postanovleniyakh* (1939), pp. 44–45.

without regard for constitutional niceties) established as the appropriate form through which the self-determining peoples could once more be gathered of their own free will into a single fold. But all this remained within the orbit of the bourgeois revolution; it was sufficient — and cost nothing — to invoke bourgeois-democratic principles in order to discredit bourgeois-democratic practice.

The invocation of the principle of national self-determination in former territories of the Russian Empire was, however, soon to provoke embarrassing questions. Some of these had been foreseen — by Stalin among others. In April 1917, when he was emphasizing the validity of bourgeois claims to national self-determination, Stalin appeared clearly to recognize that no objection could be raised to the secession of Transcaucasia, even if this were to result in the establishment of a bourgeois régime there.

> I personally would be opposed to the secession of Transcaucasia, bearing in mind the general level of development in Transcaucasia and in Russia, the conditions of the struggle of the proletariat, and so forth. But if, nevertheless, the peoples of Transcaucasia were to demand secession, they would, of course, secede, and would not encounter opposition on our part.[1]

Yet already in 1913 he had raised the awkward question of the right or duty of the party to interfere in exactly this situation:

> The Transcaucasian Tatars as a nation may assemble, let us say, in their Diet and, succumbing to the influence of their beys and mullahs, decide to restore the old order of things and to secede from the state. According to the meaning of the clause on self-determination they are fully entitled to do so. But will this be in the interest of the toiling strata of the Tatar nation? Can social-democrats remain indifferent when the beys and mullahs take the lead of the masses in the solution of the national problem? Should not social-democrats interfere in the matter and influence the will of the nation in a definite way? Should they not come forward with a definite plan for the solution of the problem which would be most advantageous to the Tatar masses?[2]

---

[1] Stalin, *Sochineniya*, iii, 52-53.
[2] *Ibid.* ii, 312-313. The "Transcaucasian Tatars" are the Azerbaijani Turks: the Russian habit of calling them "Tatars" has no racial or historical justification.

It is true that Stalin in 1913 was thinking purely in terms of propaganda and the party line, whereas in 1917 he was already thinking in terms of action by the state ; it may be true that in 1913 he was thinking primarily as a member of a Transcaucasian nation and in 1917 already as a Great Russian. It is also true that he did not in 1913 frankly answer his own rhetorical questions in the affirmative, but hedged by adding that " all these are questions the solution of which will depend on the concrete historical conditions in which the given nation finds itself ". Nevertheless, it was clear that this was one of the points at which the edges of party doctrine were blurred and uncertain. It was also clear, from the way in which Stalin formulated the issue in 1913, that party pressure to " interfere " in doubtful cases might be severe.

The practical issue arose in December 1917, when a bourgeois Ukrainian government, whose claim to national self-determination the Soviet Government did not contest, adopted a hostile attitude towards Petrograd, conducted negotiations with a French military mission and lent support to Kaledin, the Cossack leader who had come out in open opposition to the Soviet power. Stalin at once drew what seemed the common-sense conclusion :

> To invoke the principle of self-determination in order to support the revolt of Kaledin and the policy of disarming revolutionary Soviet armies, as the general secretariat now does, is to make a mockery of self-determination and of the elementary principles of democracy.[1]

This rough-and-ready answer did not, however, dispose of doctrinal embarrassments. At the third All-Russian Congress of Soviets, Martov, the Menshevik leader, enquired why at the Brest-Litovsk negotiations national plebiscites were being demanded " in Poland, Courland, Lithuania, etc.", whereas it was argued that " in the Ukraine, Caucasus, Finland, etc." the right to vote should be given only to the workers (the constitution of the RSFSR, which contained a similar limitation, was not yet drafted). The reply returned by Preobrazhensky was that the first-named countries had not yet " thrown off the autocratic yoke " and " reached the democratic stage ", whereas " the Ukraine, the Caucasus, etc. have passed the stage of bourgeois

[1] *Revolyutsiya 1917 goda*, vi (ed. I. N. Lyubimov, 1930), 306.

parliamentarianism"; and, Stalin added, "it would be senseless to demand Soviet power in the western regions while Soviets do not yet exist there, while there is as yet no socialist revolution there ".[1] It was the only possible answer that tallied with party doctrine. But it involved the assumption that the revolution had now passed on from the bourgeois to the socialist stage. With the dissolution of the Constituent Assembly this assumption could — indeed, must — now be openly made. Bolshevik doctrine had to be readjusted to the transition; the mere assertion of a right of self-determination for all nations, irrespective of their class structure or stage of development, no longer sufficed.

Stalin's report to the congress on the national question was a first attempt at this crucial readjustment. He argued that the clashes between Sovnarkom and the borderlands "arose not around questions of national character but specifically around the question of power ".[2] Bourgeois governments were simply trying to "disguise in a national costume the struggle with the power of the working masses ". The conclusion was clear :

> All this points to the necessity of interpreting the principle of self-determination as a right not of the bourgeoisie, but of the working masses of the given nation. The principle of self-determination must be an instrument in the struggle for socialism and must be subordinated to the principles of socialism.[3]

This was the test. On the strength of this argument the proletariat of the Ukraine, of White Russia and of the Baltic countries could be assisted to exercise the right of national determination as against the competing claims of the local bourgeoisie. It was not surprising that Stalin should have rallied to a doctrine which enjoyed at this time wide popularity in party circles and was

[1] *Tretii Vserossiiskii S"ezd Sovetov* (1918), pp. 77, 80 ; Stalin, *Sochineniya*, iv, 36. Martov's point had already been made by Troyanovsky at the session of the Constituent Assembly (*Vserossiiskoe Uchreditel'noe Sobranie*, ed. I. S. Malchevsky (1930), p. 98).

[2] What exactly Stalin meant by this distinction is not clear : pursued to its logical conclusion, it would involve the Austrian thesis of a separation of national aspirations from political power. A few months later Stalin himself denounced "the thick-headedness of Austrian social-democrats like Bauer and Renner ", who "failed to understand the indissoluble bond between the national question and the question of power " (*Sochineniya*, iv, 165).

[3] *Ibid.* iv, 31-32. The records of this congress are incomplete and only a summary, not a full text, of the proceedings has been preserved.

especially associated with the name of Bukharin.[1] In December 1918 he repeated emphatically that " the slogan ' all power to the national bourgeoisie ' is being replaced by the slogan of proletarian socialism, ' all power to the working masses of the oppressed nationalities ' ".[2] This view rarely found expression in official documents, but an appeal to the Karelian people in 1920 spoke of " the self-determination of the toiling masses ".[3]

A first unpromising and abortive attempt was made in the spring of 1918 to apply the thesis of self-determination for the workers to the Tatars and Bashkirs.[4] After the German collapse of November 1918, the thesis was applied under Stalin's aegis in the Ukraine (for which it had originally been formulated), in White Russia (where it remained largely unreal) and in the Baltic states (where it was reversed just over a year later, under pressure of British naval power, in favour of recognition of bourgeois national governments). Throughout the non-Russian borderlands the issue of self-determination became inextricably intertwined with the issue of the civil war. If it was true that Bolshevik régimes could never have been established in the Ukraine or White Russia or the Baltic states without the direct intervention of Moscow, it was equally true that the bourgeois régimes in these countries, which were too often accepted without question in western Europe as qualified to speak for the inarticulate masses of their nations, could also never have maintained themselves without the backing of foreign governments interested in fostering centres of opposition to the Bolsheviks. What was depicted as a struggle between a national proletariat and peasantry and a national bourgeoisie was in fact a struggle between the Russian

[1] It appeared in two famous text-books of the period, N. Bukharin, *Programma Kommunistov* (1918), ch. xix, and Bukharin and Preobrazhensky, *Azbuka Kommunizma* (1919), ch. vii, § 59; the "dividing line between Bukharin's thesis of self-determination for the workers " and the Polish thesis of " no self-determination for nations " was tenuous, and tended to vanish.

[2] Stalin, *Sochineniya*, iv, 177.

[3] *Politika Sovetskoi Vlasti po Natsional'nomu Voprosu* (1920), p. 50, art. 72. The anarchists also stood for self-determination " not in the sense of ' self-determination of nations ', but in the sense of ' self-determination of the workers ' " (P. Arshinov, *Istoriya Makhnovskogo Dvizheniya* (Berlin, 1923), p. 204). Early writings of Lenin, e.g. *Sochineniya*, v, 243 (" we ourselves are concerned for our part with the self-determination not of peoples and nations, but of the *proletariat* in every nationality ", cf. *ibid.* v, 337), can be quoted to the same effect ; but he never seems to have returned to this formula after 1905.

[4] See p. 320 below.

Bolsheviks, on the one hand, and Russian and foreign anti-Bolsheviks, on the other, for the controlling influence over the territory concerned. The choice was not between dependence and independence, but between dependence on Moscow or dependence on the bourgeois governments of the capitalist world. The relative strength of the local forces on either side was never tested and could not be tested. Even for these local forces nationalism was also subordinate to the social issue which lay beneath it ; bourgeois and revolutionaries alike eagerly sought outside allies in the struggle to defend or overthrow the social order. Everywhere, and in whatever guise the battle was fought, the real issue was the life or death of the revolution. Lenin was no more prepared at this time than any other Bolshevik — or than any anti-Bolshevik — to treat national self-determination as a question of abstract principle or to take it out of the context of the civil war.

The 1918 slogan of " self-determination for the workers " was, however, not destined to be permanent. Whatever its utility in a few regions possessing an industrial working class of Bolshevik, or potentially Bolshevik, sympathies, whether Russian (as in the Ukraine) or indigenous (as in Latvia and Estonia), it could not be so conveniently applied to the large non-Russian populations of Eastern Europe and Asia among whom the appeal to national self-determination was also being heard. For himself, Lenin had never abandoned the more flexible line laid down in a party resolution as long ago as 1913 ; and it was to this that he returned when the next serious discussion of the national question took place at the eighth party congress in March 1919, which drafted and adopted a new party programme. Stalin, engrossed at this time in military affairs, did not speak on this or any other part of the programme. Bukharin, rather maliciously quoting the authority of Stalin's report at the third All-Russian Congress of Soviets, once more demanded " self-determination for the working classes of every nationality ". He admitted that he wanted a formula which would cover the claims of " Hottentots, Bushmen, negroes and Hindus ", but not those of the Polish bourgeoisie.[1] Pyatakov again denounced self-determination as a bourgeois slogan which " unites all counter-revolutionary forces ", and

[1] *Vos'moi S''ezd RKP(B)* (1933), p. 49.

thought that " once we unite economically and build one apparatus, one Supreme Council of National Economy, one railway
administration, one bank, etc., all this notorious self-determination
is not worth one rotten egg ".[1] Lenin almost single-handed defended the old party position. The slogan " self-determination
for the working masses " was false because it applied only where
a cleavage had already been established between proletariat and
bourgeoisie. The right of self-determination must be accorded to
nations in which the cleavage had not yet occurred — for example,
the Bashkirs and other backward peoples of the former Tsarist
empire — and would help to hasten it. It must be accorded to
countries like Poland where the communists did not yet form a
majority of the working class. Only thus could the Russian
proletariat escape the charge of " Great Russian chauvinism
masked under the name of communism ".[2]

Lenin had his way ; and the articles on the national question
in the party programme of 1919 constituted the most authoritative
brief exposition of party doctrine on the subject in its finished
form. The first two articles established for the first time the
identity of principle and policy as applied to the nationalities of
the former Russian Empire and to those oppressed by other
imperialist powers — the link between Soviet domestic and foreign
policy :

1. The cornerstone is the policy of drawing together the proletarians and semi-proletarians of the various nationalities
   for the purpose of waging a joint revolutionary struggle for
   the overthrow of the landlords and the bourgeoisie.

2. In order to overcome the distrust felt by the toiling masses
   of oppressed countries towards the proletariat of states
   which oppress these countries, it is necessary to abolish
   all privileges enjoyed by any national group whatsoever, to
   establish complete equality of rights for all nationalities, to
   recognize the right of colonies and non-sovereign nations
   to secession.[3]

[1] *Ibid.* pp. 80-81.   [2] Lenin, *Sochineniya*, xxiv, 135-139.
[3] As Stalin pointed out two years later, this resolution dropped the " absolutely vague slogan " of self-determination, and substituted the specific formula of " state secession " (Stalin, *Sochineniya*, v, 42-43). The term " self-
determination " continued none the less in official use ; it occurred, for example,
in the treaty between the RSFSR and Bokhara of March 4, 1921 (*Sobranie
Uzakonenii, 1921*, No. 73, art. 595), in the treaty of peace between the RSFSR,

Next, by a somewhat abrupt transition, came a clause tentatively offering a stepping-stone to ultimate unity :

> 3. With the same aim in view the party proposes, as one of the transitional forms to complete unity, a federal union of states organized on the Soviet model.

Finally, the vital distinction between the two historical epochs of bourgeois and socialist revolutions was introduced for the first time into a party resolution on the national question :

> 4. On the question who is to express the nation's will to secede, the Russian Communist Party adopts the class-historical viewpoint, taking into consideration the stage of historical development of the given nation : whether it is evolving from mediaevalism to bourgeois democracy or from bourgeois democracy to Soviet or proletarian democracy, etc.

The resolution concluded with an unnumbered paragraph combining the warning against an " imperialist " attitude on the part of the proletariat of " oppressing " nations with a further reminder of unity as the ultimate goal :

> In any case, the proletariat of the nations which have been oppressing nations must exercise special caution and pay special attention to the survivals of national sentiment among the toiling masses of oppressed or non-sovereign nations. Only by pursuing such a policy will it be possible to create conditions for really lasting, voluntary unity among nationally differentiated elements of the international proletariat, as has been shown by the experience of the union of a number of national Soviet republics around Soviet Russia.[1]

the Ukraine and Poland of March 18, 1921 (*RSFSR : Sbornik Deistvuyushchikh Dogovorov*, ii (1921), No. 51, p. 43), and in the treaty between the three Transcaucasian republics of March 12, 1922, forming the Transcaucasian federation (*Istoriya Sovetskoi Konstitutsii v Dekretakh* (1936), p. 208).

[1] *VKP(B) v Rezolyutsiyakh* (1941), i, 286-287. The concluding paragraph was an echo of the argument used by Marx fifty years earlier in urging on English workers the duty to support the liberation of Ireland. Lenin had used the same argument in 1918 in application to the Ukraine : " We are for the closest union of the workers of all countries against the capitalists — both ' their own ' and those of other countries. But precisely in order that this union may be voluntary, the Russian worker, who has not in any respect or at any time any confidence either in the Russian or in the Ukrainian bourgeoisie, stands for the right of self-determination of the Ukrainians, *not forcing* his friendship on them, but winning it by treating them as an equal, an ally and a brother in the struggle for socialism " (*Sochineniya*, xx, 535).

It was the all-important fourth paragraph which provided the formula for the transition from bourgeois to proletarian democracy. So long as the national bourgeoisie was struggling to emancipate itself from " mediaevalism ", it was the legitimate bearer of " the nation's will to secede " and had the support of the proletariat; and this might apply to support given by the proletariat to the bourgeoisie of other nations as well as of its own. But when the struggle against mediaevalism (i.e. the bourgeois revolution) was completed, and the stage was set for the transition " from bourgeois democracy to Soviet or proletarian democracy ", then the proletariat became the only legitimate bearer of " the nation's will to secede "; and this would obviously be exercised only with the most careful regard for the overriding principle of the international unity of the proletariat and of the breaking down of national barriers in the socialist order. The two potentially conflicting principles of nationalism and internationalism which had been enunciated in the *Communist Manifesto* were thus reconciled in the achievement of the first proletarian revolution. Applying this doctrine to the Russian revolution, there was nothing inconsistent in a policy which began, so long as the last strongholds of the feudal order had not yet been overthrown, by unqualified recognition of the rights of self-determination and secession, and then, when the civil war had been won and the building of the socialist order was taken in hand, passed over to the task of reassembling the scattered national units within the framework of the Soviet Union.[1]

In practice the application of this theoretical scheme was no doubt less simple. In theory the choice depended on the answer to the question whether in the given historical situation the decision on secession rested with the bourgeois nation or inde-

[1] What appears to be the same difference in attitude towards different national aspirations is expressed by a bourgeois writer : " Whereas in the east we may still appraise it [i.e. nationalism], morally and economically, as a positive and progressive force, in Europe it already belongs, morally and economically, to a past phase of development. Progress in Europe can come only from the supersession of political nationalism. Nationalism and state patriotism here have fulfilled their historical function and lost their ethical meaning " (Hans Kohn, *Nationalism and Imperialism in the Hither East* (Engl. transl. 1932), p. 51). The distinction here drawn between two continents in different stages of historical development is more pointedly expressed by the Bolsheviks as a distinction between two stages which normally follow each other in the same country.

pendently with the proletariat of the nation. In practice the two policies were pursued side by side. In Estonia, Latvia and Lithuania independent Soviet republics were recognized in 1918 and independent bourgeois republics in 1920. In Georgia a bourgeois republic was recognized in 1920 and a Soviet republic in 1921. In general, the initial recognition of the right of self-determination and secession was accorded after 1917 willingly, sincerely and, on the whole, unreservedly. But where the workers of a seceding unit were too few, too weak or too unreliable to set in motion the process of reunion and reassembly (or, to put it in other words, where there were no spontaneous signs of the beginning of the second period), and where military or economic necessities made it imperative to hasten this process, the temptation was clearly great for the party, in Stalin's words of 1913, " to come forward with a definite plan " to redress the situation in the ultimate interest of the workers. And the party could, after 1917, as it could not when Stalin wrote, carry any such plan into execution by invoking the power of the Soviet state. Intervention in the Baltic countries in the winter of 1918-1919 may have been due to an honest over-estimate of Bolshevik prospects in a region where the workers' movement had always been strong. Intervention in the Ukraine in 1919 and again in 1920 may have been a legitimate measure of self-defence against a government which had already invoked foreign intervention. Intervention in the backward regions of the lower Volga or of central Asia may have been inspired by the sheer necessity of establishing some sort of order. Intervention in Georgia in 1921 was a rounding off of the sovietization of Transcaucasia ; and, with the allies still holding Constantinople, fears of a resumption of allied intrusion in the Caucasus through a friendly and subservient Georgia were less chimerical than they afterwards came to appear. Nevertheless, whatever grounds may have existed to justify intervention in particular cases, the scale on which it occurred clearly put some strain on the party doctrine of national self-determination.

While, however, Bolshevik nationalities' policy was not free from those empirical impurities which normally distinguish the application of a theory from the theory itself, it was still possible to point to substantial advances on bourgeois practice, as well as on bourgeois theory. The recognition of the right of subject nationalities to political emancipation, which was the sole content of the bourgeois theory of national self-determination, had been coupled with a belief in *laissez-faire* capitalism, which implied the continuance of existing economic inequalities and of the exploitation, under whatever political form, of the subject by the ruling nationalities. Bourgeois capitalism was thus an insuperable barrier to the creation of those conditions in which alone the bourgeois doctrine of national self-determination could have any practical meaning. As the result of this contradiction, " bourgeois society ", in the words of the resolution of the tenth party congress of March 1921, " is completely bankrupt as regards a solution of the national question ".[1] The assumption underlying bourgeois theory and bourgeois practice had been that political emancipation was the path to economic welfare. This assumption had been proved false. Bolshevik theory and practice rested on the assumption that economic progress was the path to political emancipation, and that real (and not merely formal) equality for the former subject nationalities was the path of economic progress.[2]

In an article of May 1921, two months after the tenth party congress, Stalin reviewed the four distinguishing features of the communist attitude to the national question as it had been evolved since the October revolution. The first was the close association between the " national " and " colonial " questions, so that emancipation of the peoples of Europe was bound up with that of the African and Asiatic peoples; this was symptomatic of the growing importance of the Eastern peoples as the cardinal point of Soviet nationalities policy. The second was that the " vague " slogan of self-determination had been replaced by recognition of the right of nations to secede and to form independent states; this disposed of the sham Austrian solution of national cultural autonomy. The third was the association of national oppression

---

[1] *VKP(B) v Rezolyutsiyakh* (1941), i, 383.

[2] A British colonial administrator, apparently unacquainted with Bolshevik theory and practice, has some observations worth quoting in this context: " Liberals looked to freedom as a key to economic progress, and regarded economic progress as a *cause* of native welfare, leading *automatically* to political independence. Modern colonial theory regards economic progress as a *condition* of native welfare, and native welfare as a *condition* of political advancement, but recognizes the need for state intervention to further economic progress. Liberals thought to promote welfare through freedom; the modern tendency is to promote welfare even at the expense of freedom " (J. S. Furnivall, *Colonial Policy and Practice* (1948), p. 288).

with capitalism; emancipation from both would necessarily be simultaneous. (Stalin had travelled far in the four years since, in April 1917, he had associated national oppression primarily with feudalism.) The fourth was acceptance of the principle of " real, and not merely juridical, equalization of nations (helping and encouraging the backward nations to raise themselves to the cultural and economic level of the more advanced nations) "; and Stalin concluded the article by enunciating five elementary points required to make national equality effective :

1. The study of the economic conditions, social life and culture of the backward nations and peoples ;
2. The development of their culture ;
3. Their political education ;
4. Their gradual and painless incorporation into the higher forms of economic life ; and
5. The organization of economic cooperation between the toilers of the backward and the advanced nationalities.[1]

This emphasis on " real " (meaning, in particular, economic) equality between nations became henceforth the essence of the party doctrine of national self-determination under socialism. Lenin had established the rôle of national self-determination in the bourgeois order and in the period of transition from the bourgeois to the socialist order. But, beyond the hypothesis announced in the party programme of " voluntary unity between the nationally differentiated elements of the international proletariat ", little had been said about the place of nations under socialism. Yet, even if nations were eventually doomed to disappear with the dying away of the state, there would be a long intervening period during which nations would certainly retain their significance.[2] According to the argument now developed, the right of self-determination, which presented itself in the period of the bourgeois revolution as a demand for liberation, became in the socialist period a demand for the equality of all national groups within the socialist order. In the Bolshevik view, contemporary nationalism was in the main the product of the inequalities between nations resulting from imperialist oppression

[1] Stalin, *Sochineniya*, v, 52-59.
[2] " National and state differences between peoples and countries . . . will remain very, very long after the realization of the dictatorship of the proletariat on a world scale " (Lenin, *Sochineniya*, xxv, 227).

and exploitation; and in such conditions national self-determination could only take the form of a right of secession. Under socialism, when a real and not merely formal equality had been created between men, and therefore between nations, the right of secession, while not formally abrogated, would become meaningless and would not be exercised.

Under socialism, therefore, the content of the right of national self-determination partakes essentially of the nature of equality; and the evolution of the doctrine repeats the dilemma familiar to those who, since the French revolution, have sought to reconcile liberty and equality. The pursuit of liberty involves inequality, and liberty, once it ceases to be purely formal, is confined to those who benefit from the unequal division. The acceptance of a limitation of liberty is a condition of equality. The issue of freedom for nations returns to the unending debate about the nature of political freedom. Freedom can be no more unconditional for nations than for men: it depends on the free recognition and acceptance of the necessary demands of contemporary society.[1] The ultimate expression of the Bolshevik doctrine of national self-determination is a union of equal nations in a socialist federation.

(c) Machinery

The first act of the Bolshevik revolution in the national question was to appoint Josef Vissarionovich Djugashvili-Stalin (both names were still used) as People's Commissar for the Affairs of Nationalities. The appointment was without precedent, though the Provisional Government in its last pronouncement on the subject had foreshadowed the formation of " a council for national affairs with representation of all the nationalities of Russia for the purpose of preparing material on the national question for the

---

[1] The British authority, already quoted on p. 273 above, may be once more invoked on this point: " The environment has changed and not the people; they still, if left to themselves, would try to reproduce their old environment. But they have been brought into contact with the modern world and cannot get away from it. All the king's horses and all the king's men cannot set the clock back. They can get what they want only if they want what in the conditions of the modern world they *must* want. A fundamental problem of autonomy is to change the people so that they shall come to want, or at least voluntarily to accept, those conditions which the welfare of the modern world requires " (J. S. Furnivall, *Colonial Policy and Practice* (1948), p. 442).

Constituent Assembly ".[1] It was clearly meant to herald a new attitude. Two months earlier Lenin had described the " national and agrarian questions " as " the root questions for the petty bourgeois masses of the population of Russia at the present time ".[2] Stalin afterwards referred to " peace, the agrarian revolution, and freedom for the nationalities " as " the three principal factors which rallied the peasants of more than 20 nationalities of vast Russia round the red flag of the Russian proletariat ".[3] Nor was the importance of the national question exclusively domestic. Liberation and national self-determination for subject peoples also became a cardinal point in Soviet foreign policy.

The People's Commissariat of Nationalities (Narkomnats) was the instrument through which the new policy was applied. Its initial organization was simplicity itself. Whenever the affairs of any nation or nationality formerly belonging to the Russian Empire became in any way acute, the People's Commissariat set up a special department under the direction of a member of the nation in question to deal with them — a form of organization designed, no doubt somewhat naïvely, but sincerely enough, to foster the management of national affairs by the nation concerned. These special departments were at first described as " commissariats " and later as sections. But from the outset they formed part of Narkomnats and were subordinate to it. The first such department to be established was a Polish commissariat in November 1917. Its functions were described as " affairs of liquidation, army affairs, refugees, etc. "; and by a subsequent decree government institutions were instructed to issue no orders or decrees relating to Polish affairs without previous consultation with this commissariat.[4] Its immediate successor was a Lithuanian commissariat, whose creation was apparently prompted by the number of refugees evacuated from Lithuania in face of the German advance. One function of the commissariats seems to have been to watch and control the activities of existing national

---

[1] *Revolyutsiya i Natsional'nyi Vopros : Dokumenty i Materialy*, ed. S. M. Dimanshtein, iii (1930), 56.

[2] Lenin, *Sochineniya*, xxi, 254.   [3] Stalin, *Sochineniya*, v, 113.

[4] Both decrees are in *Politika Sovetskoi Vlasti po Natsional'nomu Voprosu* (1920), p. 86, arts. 114, 116, the second also in *Sobranie Uzakonenii, 1917–1918*, No. 4, art. 67.

institutions on Russian soil. Thus all Polish institutions were brought under the supervision of the Polish commissar; all Lettish " social, charitable, religious and similar institutions " in Moscow were required to register with the Lettish commissar; and the Armenian commissar was given jurisdiction over the Armenian Institute in Moscow.[1] In January 1918 a " temporary commissariat for Jewish national affairs " and a " commissariat for internal Muslim affairs "[2] were brought into being with Jewish and Muslim commissars respectively. These decrees suggested an inclination to experiment with a non-territorial and " cultural " approach to the national question. But such an approach would have been incompatible with fundamental Bolshevik doctrine; and thereafter commissariats and sections were organized exclusively on a territorial basis.[3]

The system received its full development in 1918. In March 1918 the establishment of White Russian and Lettish commissariats served to provide a focus for White Russians and Letts who had moved into Russia and to stimulate national resistance in territories still in German occupation. The same motives inspired the creation of Ukrainian and Estonian commissariats in May 1918. An official publication of Narkomnats records that its main activity in these early days was to maintain contact through underground channels with national movements in territories held by the Germans or by the counter-revolutionaries.[4] Next the system was applied to stimulate and canalize communist

[1] *Politika Sovetskoi Vlasti po Natsional'nomu Voprosu* (1920), p. 87, art. 118 (also in *Sobranie Uzakonenii, 1917-1918*, No. 19, art. 291); p. 52, art. 75; p. 16, art. 15 (also in *Sobranie Uzakonenii, 1919*, No. 10-11, art. 109).

[2] Literally " commissariat for the affairs of the Muslims of internal Russia " : desire to disclaim responsibility for the Muslim world in general is noteworthy. The two decrees are in *Sobranie Uzakonenii, 1917-1918*, No. 17, arts. 243, 252.

[3] The Muslim commissariat disappeared in 1920 after separate commissariats had been created for most of the Muslim nationalities. The Jewish commissariat, renamed the " Jewish section " in 1920, continued to exist and to issue pronouncements on Jewish affairs generally, sometimes in conjunction with the Jewish section of the Russian Communist Party : some of these are collected in *Politika Sovetskoi Vlasti po Natsional'nomu Voprosu* (1920), pp. 31-35.

[4] *Natsional'nyi Vopros v Sovetskoi Rossii* (1921), pp. 28-29. As late as the summer of 1920 Narkomnats was busy arranging for the publication of newspaper articles, leaflets and appeals in local languages against the Polish invaders, and explaining " why the white guards are bringing the chains of moral and material slavery first of all to the small nations " (*Politika Sovetskoi Vlasti po Natsional'nomu Voprosu* (1920), pp. 146-147, art. 180; p. 148, art. 184).

loyalties among peoples whose geographical situation and stage
of development fitted them for autonomy rather than independence. Narkomnats soon comprised commissariats or sections for
the Tatar-Bashkirs, the Kazakhs, the Chuvashes, the Mountaineers
of the Caucasus, the Muslims of Transcaucasia (the Azerbaijani),
the Mordovtsy, the Volga Germans and other still smaller national
units. Even Czechoslovak and Yugoslav commissariats were set
up to deal with the numerous Czechs, Slovaks and southern Slavs
in Soviet territory.[1]

The People's Commissariat for Affairs of Nationalities was
thus in outward form a galaxy of national commissariats or sections
each under its own national chief.[2] The appearances suggested
that these chiefs were regarded as ambassadors pleading their
respective national causes in Moscow; the word " petition " is
actually applied in a decree of VTsIK of 1919 to a request put
forward by the commissar for Kazakh affairs.[3] But appearances
were deceptive. These posts, which were extremely hard to fill,[4]
were apt to go to sturdy Bolsheviks whose party loyalties were
stronger than their national affiliations, and who, established at
headquarters in Moscow, were more interested in carrying out
the policy of the centre in the national regions than in pressing
awkward national desiderata at headquarters. Pestkovsky, the

---

[1] References to the decrees setting up other commissariats and divisions
will be found in the relevant sections of *Politika Sovetskoi Vlasti po Natsional'-
nomu Voprosu* (1920). A corresponding organization of " national sections "
was set up within the Russian Communist Party, each with its " central bureau "
attached to the secretariat: Czechoslovak, German, Yugoslav, Hungarian,
Polish, Lettish, Lithuanian, Estonian, Jewish and Mari sections, as well as a
section for the Turki-speaking peoples were in existence in 1920 (*Izvestiya
Tsentral'nogo Komiteta Rossiiskoi Kommunisticheskoi Partii* (*Bol'shevikov*), No.
28, March 5, 1921, pp. 17-23.

[2] Eighteen commissariats or sections are listed with the names of their
chiefs in *Zhizn' Natsional'nostei*, No. 1, November 9, 1918 ; a few of the smaller
commissariats or divisions representing the more backward nationalities appear
to have had Russian chiefs, presumably in default of any suitable national
candidate.

[3] *Politika Sovetskoi Vlasti po Natsional'nomu Voprosu* (1920), p. 42, art. 63.

[4] " I remember the organization of the Muslim commissariat ", wrote one
of the leading officials of Narkomnats two years later. " How difficult it was
to find suitable Bolsheviks to put at the head of it ! Only in connexion with the
Constituent Assembly, when Bolshevik delegates arrived for it, only thanks to
that, did we succeed in organizing a general commissariat for all Muslims. We
had the same difficulties with the organization of the White Russian commissariat, and of the Jewish, since the old socialist parties then existing were all
against us " (*Zhizn' Natsional'nostei*, No. 42 (50), November 2, 1919).

deputy People's Commissar under Stalin, has left explicit testimony on the prevalence in the hierarchy of Narkomnats of an " international " attitude to the national question :

> The collegium of the People's Commissariat of Nationalities consisted of these russified non-Russians who opposed their abstract internationalism to the real needs of development of the oppressed nationalities. Actually this policy supported the old tradition of russification and was a special danger in the conditions of the civil war.[1]

According to Pestkovsky, Stalin at this time was the one supporter of Lenin's policy in the collegium of Narkomnats and was frequently outvoted by his colleagues, who were " Leftists " and adherents of the " abstract internationalism " of the Polish heresy.[2] In the spring of 1918 Stalin, under the orders of the party central committee, had the task of imposing a Tatar-Bashkir republic on sceptical colleagues and recalcitrant Tatars and Bashkirs.[3] If Narkomnats seemed to some of the nationalities to be an inadequate champion of their rights and interests, it seemed to many old Bolsheviks to be engaged, under Lenin's inspiration and Stalin's direction, on a reactionary policy of creating nationalities and stimulating national feelings where none existed.

As the new régime consolidated itself, and as the national question took on a new urgency under the impact of the civil war, the functions and machinery of Narkomnats were further extended. In November 1918 it issued the first number of a weekly journal, *Zhizn' Natsional'nostei* (" Life of the Nationalities "), devoted to the policy of the commissariat.[4] A month later it initiated the system of attaching sections of its own to the administrative organs of the autonomous territories. These local sections had no constitutional status and were perhaps rather in the position

---

[1] Quoted in L. Trotsky, *Stalin* (N.Y., 1946), p. 257.

[2] *Ibid.* p. 257. It is noteworthy that as late as June 1919 the official journal of Narkomnats carried a leading article signed by Pestkovsky in which Rosa Luxemburg's views on the national question were warmly eulogized, without a hint that these views had been flayed by Lenin at frequent intervals for the past ten years (*Zhizn' Natsional'nostei*, No. 22 (30), June 15, 1919).

[3] See p. 320, note 4 below.

[4] *Zhizn' Natsional'nostei* continued to be issued by the commissariat with gradually decreasing regularity down to February 1922, when it changed its format and became an independent periodical : it continued intermittently till January 1924.

of the embassy of a dominant Power in a nominally sovereign, but *de facto* dependent, country. But the definition of their functions in the decree instituting them was the first attempt at a systematic outline of the scope of Narkomnats. The functions of these local sections were :

(a) The carrying into effect of the principles of Soviet power in the milieu of the respective nations and in their own language ;

(b) The carrying into effect of all decisions of the People's Commissariat of Nationalities ;

(c) The taking of all measures to raise the cultural level and class consciousness of the working masses of the nations inhabiting the given territory ;

(d) The struggle with counter-revolution in its national manifestations (struggle with " national "-bourgeois governments, etc.) [1]

Narkomnats, in the words of another of its early decrees, was to be " a centre of ideas for socialist work ".[2] But the radiation of ideas was mainly from the centre to the localities, not vice versa.

The defeat of Kolchak and Denikin, the recovery of lost territories and the establishment within the RSFSR of numerous autonomous republics and regions led in May 1920 to what was officially described as a " reorganization of the People's Commissariat of Nationalities ".[3] The effect of the reform was to give the nationalities, at any rate on paper, a larger measure of control over the central organ. Each nationality, through its national congress of Soviets, was henceforth to elect representatives to a Council of Nationalities ; and this body, presided over by the People's Commissar for Nationalities, was placed " at the head of " Narkomnats, becoming, in the words of the official journal of the commissariat, " a sort of parliament of nationalities ".[4] In addition to the national " sections " (no longer

---

[1] *Politika Sovetskoi Vlasti po Natsional'nomu Voprosu* (1920), p. 145, art. 175.

[2] *Ibid.* p. 82, art. 108.

[3] *Sobranie Uzakonenii, 1920*, No. 45, art. 202. The decree is also to be found, together with two " instructions " of Narkomnats for carrying it out, in *Politika Sovetskoi Vlasti po Natsional'nomu Voprosu* (1920), pp. 147-148, arts. 181-183.

[4] *Zhizn' Natsional'nostei*, No. 15 (72), May 23, 1920. The statute of Narkomnats drawn up in 1921 (*Konstitutsii i Konstitutsionnye Akty RSFSR, 1918-1937* (1940), pp. 106-108) described it with perhaps greater accuracy as " a consultative representative organ attached to Narkomnats ".

to be called " commissariats ") in Narkomnats there was to be a single " section of national minorities " to look after groups not numerous enough or compact enough to have territories of their own — Finns, Poles, Letts, Chinese, Koreans, etc. As in most constitutional arrangements of the period, the division of authority was vague and indeterminate. On the one hand, the nationalities might reasonably feel that they had secured a more direct channel of access to the centre; on the other hand, they now found their access limited to a single channel.[1] Finally, when, in the autumn of 1920, the policy was adopted of putting relations between the RSFSR and the outlying Soviet republics on a treaty basis, Narkomnats acquired the right to maintain its representatives " in friendly republics not entering into the composition of the federation on the basis of agreements made by VTsIK with these republics ".[2] This constitutional innovation gave Narkomnats a footing in what were theoretically foreign relations. But by this time the dividing line between the autonomous national republics within the RSFSR and the independent national republics linked in alliance with it was becoming blurred.

The first formal statute of Narkomnats, approved by VTsIK and Sovnarkom in May 1921,[3] defined its functions on well established lines :

(a) To guarantee the peaceful cohabitation and fraternal collaboration of all nationalities and tribes of the RSFSR and also of the friendly treaty Soviet republics ;

(b) To assist their material and spiritual development with regard to the peculiarities of their way of life, culture and economic condition ;

(c) To watch over the application in practice of the national policy of the Soviet power.

The political functions of Narkomnats — the fitting of the autonomous republics and regions into the structure of the RSFSR and the adaptation of the independent republics to that

[1] This was made explicit by a further decree of November 4, 1920, which also stipulated that " the personal composition of the representations is confirmed by VTsIK " (*Sobranie Uzakonenii*, *1920*, No. 87, art. 438). Down to this time some of the nationalities had had special representatives attached to VTsIK : these were now withdrawn or transferred to Narkomnats.

[2] *Ibid.* No. 99, art. 529.

[3] *Konstitutsii i Konstitutsionnye Akty RSFSR, 1918-1937* (1940), pp. 106-108.

structure — remained the most important and most exacting parts of its task. But the extent and variety of its work can be illustrated from its multifarious decrees and from the columns of its official journal. It concerned itself with such details as an instruction to district and village Soviets in the Chuvash region to organize meetings of the population in order to read out to them newspapers, leaflets and proclamations in Chuvash, and to institute " a bureau for the receipt of complaints in the Chuvash language ",[1] or the admission of Votyaks to a party school.[2] Education, propaganda and the encouragement of national literature were continually insisted on ; and in 1920 " the preparation of new cadres of Soviet workers of the national group in question " was added to the list of functions.[3] Finally, under the statute of May 1921, Narkomnats was placed in charge of the Society for the Study of the East, of the newly founded Communist University of Toilers of the East [4] and of the Petrograd Institute of Living Oriental Languages — a symptom of the importance which, since 1920, the eastern peoples had assumed in Soviet national policies.

It was not long before the emphasis shifted from political and cultural to economic reconstruction. As early as April 1920 a writer in the official journal of Narkomnats complained that " when the question is raised of the east, of the eastern republics or of the republics in general, it is looked at first of all through ' economic eyes '. Turkestan means cotton, lemons, etc. ; Kirgizia wool, cattle ; Bashkiria timber, hides, cattle." [5] In the following year the inception of NEP and the first discussions of regional planning made economic questions a major issue of all Soviet policy ; and the grave famine of the winter of 1921–1922 raged most severely in the territories of some of the eastern republics and regions of the RSFSR. When a revised statute for Narkomnats was issued in the summer of 1922,[6] a new clause had been added to the definition of its functions :

[1] *Politika Sovetskoi Vlasti po Natsional'nomu Voprosu* (1920), p. 130, arts. 162-163.
[2] *Ibid.* p. 26, art. 32.   [3] *Ibid.* p. 149, art. 186.
[4] After the abolition of Narkomnats this university was placed under the control of Comintern.
[5] *Zhizn' Natsional'nostei*, No. 11 (68), April 18, 1920.
[6] *Konstitutsii i Konstitutsionnye Akty RSFSR, 1918–1937* (1940), pp. 134-138.

The guaranteeing of conditions favourable to the development of the productive resources of the national-territorial units and the defence of their economic interests in the new economic structure.

In its last period Narkomnats was organized not only in national sections, but in functional departments of agriculture, labour, education, army, press, forestry, social security and so forth.[1] Nothing could be more misleading than to think of Soviet nationalities policy as operative mainly in the cultural sphere. Such national rights as were implicit in the Soviet conception of national autonomy applied both to political and to economic questions. If Narkomnats seemed at any given moment more concerned with one aspect of national autonomy than another this was simply because Soviet policy as a whole was at that moment directed particularly to that aspect.

On the other hand, as the Soviet administrative machine became better organized, a commissariat which had no direct administrative functions of its own but cut across those of most other commissariats was bound to prove an awkward anomaly. It had long had its critics. Six months after the decree of May 1920 creating the Council of Nationalities it was admitted that " owing to circumstances outside the control of Narkomnats " the Council had not yet " entered fully on its functions ".[2] In December 1920, at the first (and only) All-Russian Congress of Nationalities, the acting commissar, Kamensky, drew a gloomy picture of the understaffing of Narkomnats, of the constant absence of its chiefs, including Stalin, on special missions, and of the mobilization for war service of its local workers, and raised the question whether it should not be closed altogether.[3] It was always a moot point whether the nationalities would regard Narkomnats as their advocate and protector or merely as the instrument of a central power seeking to organize and limit their rights.

Moreover, as the emphasis of Soviet policy, reflected in the conduct of that policy by Narkomnats, shifted from the cultural to the political and from the political to the economic, the chances of friction between Narkomnats and other Soviet institutions were

---

[1] The list is taken from the authoritative text-book, *Sovetskoe Gosudarstvennoe Pravo*, ed. A. Vyshinsky (1938), p. 364.

[2] *Zhizn' Natsional'nostei*, No. 35 (92), November 7, 1920.

[3] *Ibid.* No. 42 (98), December 31, 1920, No. 1 (99), January 13, 1921.

inevitably multiplied. The number of early decrees and resolutions regulating relations between Narkomnats and the People's Commissariat of Education [1] suggests the difficulty of securing coordination and smooth working even in this limited sphere. Evidence is scanty for the later period ; but it can hardly have been less difficult to fit the claims of Narkomnats into those of major political and economic organs. Relations between the local organs of commissariats in the provinces and the local Soviets and their executive committees were a constant source of difficulty in the early years of the Soviet system ; and the local sections of Narkomnats are unlikely to have been an exception to this rule. Friction between the representatives of Narkomnats and of Narkomindel in the independent republics led to a decree of June 8, 1922, appointing the former " counsellors " on the diplomatic establishment.[2] Friction of another kind is suggested by an order of Sovnarkom to the Moscow housing authorities " to reserve for Narkomnats as a matter of great urgency accommodation for all its delegations." [3] The revised statute of 1922 gave Narkomnats the right " to establish federal committees for the affairs of particular People's Commissariats ", with the laudable purpose of " bringing the activity of the central people's commissariats into harmony with their work in the autonomous republics and regions " [4] — an interference which, however well justified from the standpoint of the nationalities, is unlikely to have been welcomed by the commissariats concerned. In particular, the cardinal importance now assigned to economic policy and the first developments of planning encouraged the view that authority could be more efficiently decentralized through a system of economic rather than of national regions. In general, the nationalities question seemed, with the stabilization of the political system, to have lost some of its initial acuteness and significance. The drawbacks of a special People's Commissariat of Nationalities began to outweigh the advantages. When the Soviet Union was formed in the first half of 1923, the Council of Nationalities was introduced

---

[1] *Politika Sovetskoi Vlasti po Natsional'nomu Voprosu* (1920), pp. 153-161, arts. 194-204.

[2] *Sobranie Uzakonenii, 1922*, No. 40, art. 474.

[3] *Politika Sovetskoi Vlasti po Natsional'nomu Voprosu* (1920), p. 150, art. 189.

[4] *Konstitutsii i Konstitutsionnye Akty RSFSR, 1918–1937* (1940), p. 136.

into the new constitution as the second chamber of VTsIK; and on the day after the new constitution came into force Narkomnats was abolished.[1]

Seen in retrospect Narkomnats was an instrument well designed to enlist the support of the non-Russian nationalities for policies of cooperation and eventually of reunion with Moscow, and to secure the execution of these policies in a way most likely to placate them, or not unnecessarily to offend them. In that sense it guaranteed respect for the rights of non-Russian groups remaining within the Soviet system; it encouraged their languages and cultures and the development of their educational systems; in economic matters it provided a channel for making their views known and could broadly be regarded as their protector. But as time went on, any tendency to seek the main function of the sections of Narkomnats in " the juridical defence of the legal rights of the nationalities represented by them " was expressly deprecated.[2] Whatever its original intention, the essential character of Narkomnats as an organ of the central government made it primarily an instrument of centralization; in this respect its development may not unfairly be associated, not only with the whole evolution of the Soviet constitutional structure, but also with the personality and opinions of its first and only commissar, who, however great his loyalty to Lenin's national policy, emerged as a strong centralizer. It was an instrument for maintaining a point of assembly during troubled times between the dispersed fragments of the former Russian Empire, and for bringing them nearly all back, when the troubles were past, into the fold of the Soviet Union. It had then, in the words of the decree abolishing it, " completed its fundamental mission of preparation for the work of forming the national republics and regions and uniting them into a union of republics "; and its existence was logically terminated.

---

[1] *Sobranie Uzakonenii, 1923*, No. 66, art. 639. The decree was issued by the central executive committee of the RSFSR, not by the new VTsIK of the USSR.

[2] *Politika Sovetskoi Vlasti po Natsional'nomu Voprosu* (1920), p. 148, art. 185.

SELF-DETERMINATION IN PRACTICE

(a) The Western Borderlands

THE only parts of the Tsarist empire where the demand for complete national independence followed immediately on the February revolution were Poland and Finland. Each of these countries possessed a well-developed and numerous native ruling class — in Poland, landowning and feudal, in Finland, commercial and bourgeois — which had led the national movement and was capable of managing the affairs of the nation. Before 1917 the demand in both countries had been for national autonomy rather than for national independence; and this limitation had been due partly to disbelief in the practicability of the more far-reaching alternative and partly, perhaps, to fear of the social revolution which complete independence might unleash. Lenin had diagnosed the second of these causes some years earlier:

> There are two nations in Russia which are most cultivated and, in virtue of a whole series of historical and social conditions, most differentiated, and which could most easily and " naturally " exercise their right to separation. The experience of the revolution of 1905 showed that even in these two nations the ruling classes, the landowners and the bourgeoisie, renounce the revolutionary struggle for freedom and seek a rapprochement with the ruling classes in Russia and with the Tsarist monarchy *out of fear* of the revolutionary proletariat of Finland and Poland.[1]

But, once revolution broke out in Russia itself, these inhibitions disappeared and the demand for national independence developed rapidly. The reaction of the Provisional Government was, how-

[1] Lenin, *Sochineniya*, xvi, 508. The Prague conference of 1912 had adopted a resolution of " complete solidarity with the fraternal Finnish Social-Democratic Party " in the common struggle for " the overthrow of Tsarism and the freedom of the Russian and the Finnish peoples ". The issue of self-determination or independence was not raised (*VKP(B) v Rezolyutsiyakh* (1941), i, 191).

ever, not uniform in the two cases. Poland was by this time wholly under German occupation, and the central Powers were already offering independence to a puppet Polish state. The Russian Provisional Government could hardly do less, and was in a position to promise without any immediate obligation to perform. It issued a proclamation committing itself to the recognition of an independent Poland, though the proclamation was, as the cautious Milyukov, then Russian Minister for Foreign Affairs, afterwards admitted, not couched in " precise juridical language " and reserved the right of a future Russian constituent assembly " to give its consent to the modification of Russian territory which will be indispensable for the formation of a free Poland ".[1] About Finland, which still lay outside the zone of military operations, the Provisional Government temporized, and was more than once reproached by the Bolsheviks for its grudging attitude.[2]

After the October revolution the Soviet Government unconditionally accepted the independence of Poland, and no formal steps were thought necessary to regularize it, though ten months later a decree cancelling a long list of past agreements with Germany and Austria-Hungary, including agreements on such matters as copyright, extradition, mutual recognition of consular certificates and sanitary inspection, also contained the following clause:

> All treaties and acts concluded by the government of the former Russian Empire with the government of the kingdom of Prussia or of the Austro-Hungarian Empire concerning Poland, in view of their incompatibility with the principle of the self-determination of nations and with the revolutionary sense of right of the Russian people, which recognizes the indefeasible right of the Polish people to independence and unity, are hereby irrevocably rescinded.[3]

Finland presented more serious embarrassments. While the Finnish bourgeois government seemed firmly in the saddle, the

---

[1] P. Milyukov, *Istoriya Vtoroi Russkoi Revolyutsii* (Sofia, 1921), i, 64. The proclamation is in *Revolyutsiya i Natsional'nyi Vopros: Dokumenty i Materialy*, ed. S. M. Dimanshtein, iii (1930), pp. 57-58; there are translations in S. Filasiewicz, *La Question Polonaise pendant la Guerre Mondiale* (1920), No. 75, and P. Roth, *Die Entstehung des polnischen Staates* (1926), pp. 127-128.

[2] Lenin, *Sochineniya*, xx, 323-325, 495.

[3] *Sobranie Uzakonenii, 1917-1918*, No. 64, art. 698. The date of the decree is August 29, 1918: it presumably arose out of the signature in Berlin on August 27, 1918, of three Soviet-German treaties supplementary to Brest-Litovsk.

Finnish social-democrats were a strong, organized party. There were Russian troops still in Finland who could have aided their Finnish comrades. The moment might well have seemed ripe for a proletarian revolution. This belief clearly inspired the appearance of Stalin at a congress of the Finnish Social-Democratic Party in Helsingfors on November 14/27, 1917, where he made his first public speech as People's Commissar for Nationalities.[1] None the less, the principle of national self-determination, including the right of secession, was clear and Bolshevik promises incontrovertible. When the Finnish Government pressed its claim, the Soviet Government had no option but to recognize the national independence of Finland. The resolution to that effect adopted by Sovnarkom on December 18/31, 1917, was confirmed by VTsIK four days later.[2] That the decision caused some misgivings is shown by Stalin's half-hearted defence of it during the discussion in VTsIK :

> In fact the Council of People's Commissars against its will gave freedom not to the people, but to the bourgeoisie, of Finland, which by a strange confluence of circumstances has received its independence from the hands of socialist Russia. The Finnish workers and social-democrats found themselves in the position of having to receive freedom not directly from the hands of socialists, but with the aid of the Finnish bourgeoisie.

Stalin described this as " the tragedy of the Finnish proletariat ", and attributed it to " the indecision and incomprehensible cowardice " of the Finnish social-democrats.[3]

Thus reproached and thus encouraged, the Finnish social-democrats attempted to seize power by a revolutionary coup in January 1918, and in the civil war which followed received aid from the Soviet forces still in Finland. The Soviet Government found itself in the anomalous situation of recognizing both the bourgeois government of a neighbouring country and an embryonic workers' government which was seeking to overthrow it. On March 1, 1918, a treaty was even concluded between the " Russian Federal Soviet Republic " and the " Finnish Socialist Workers' Republic."[4] It was not the only, or even the first, occasion of the

[1] Stalin, *Sochineniya*, iv, 1-5.
[2] *Sobranie Uzakonenii, 1917-1918*, No. 11, art. 163.
[3] Stalin, *Sochineniya*, iv, 22-24.
[4] Klyuchnikov i Sabanin, *Mezhdunarodnaya Politika*, ii (1926), 120-121.

kind; a similar situation had already arisen a few weeks earlier in the Ukraine. Nor had the convenient division of functions between the Soviet Government and Comintern yet been invented. But this dilemma had no bearing on the formal issue of Finnish independence, since it might equally well have arisen in a foreign country. The Finnish civil war was fought with great bitterness and did not end until the arrival of German troops called in by the Finnish bourgeois government to settle the issue. Thereafter the bourgeois régime in Finland was firmly established, and relations between Soviet Russia and Finland were those of separate and independent states.

Lenin in his utterances of 1917 frequently coupled the Ukraine with Poland and Finland as a nation whose claim to independence was unreservedly accepted by the Bolsheviks. In an article of June 1917, he denounced the Provisional Government for not carrying out its " elementary democratic duty " by declaring " for the autonomy and for the complete freedom of secession of the Ukraine ".[1] The parallel was, however, far from perfect. The peculiar national texture and history of the Ukrainian population — peasantry, proletariat and intelligentsia — created in the Ukrainian national movement ambiguities and cross-currents from which the Polish and Finnish movements were exempt.

The Ukrainian peasantry was not only the vast majority of the population, but the only section having a long tradition behind it. Its social and economic animosities — always the foundation of peasant nationalism — were directed against the landowners, predominantly Polish west of the Dnieper and elsewhere Russian, and against traders and usurers, almost exclusively Jewish. Its orthodox religion united it with the Russian Church, and made Polish Catholicism as well as Jewry alien to it. Ukrainian nationalism was therefore anti-Semitic and anti-Polish in complexion even more than anti-Russian. The seventeenth century Cossack leader, Bohdan Khmelnitsky, who was a popular national hero, though himself of Polish origin, had led the Ukrainian peasants against their Polish masters and had done homage to Moscow. The Ukrainian, or Little Russian, peasants were conscious of their

[1] Lenin, *Sochineniya*, xx, 539-541.

separateness from the Great Russians; but they recognized themselves as Russians in the wider sense, and spoke a recognizably cognate language. The political supremacy of Moscow or Petrograd might be resented. Kiev was a more ancient capital than either; but Kiev, too, was a Russian capital. A Ukrainian nationalism which relied first and foremost on a sentiment of hostility to Russia had no strong appeal to the peasantry.

At the next level the situation was complicated by the lack of an indigenous Ukrainian proletariat. The new industrial centres, which became increasingly important after the turn of the century, were populated in large part by immigrants from the north, both workers and management; Kharkov, the largest industrial city of the Ukraine, was also the most Great Russian. This element, combined with the official and professional class, gave a predominantly Great Russian background to the urban culture of the Ukraine. The effect on the situation in 1917 was characteristic. Throughout Russia the strength of the Bolsheviks lay among the urban population and the industrial workers. In the Ukraine these groups were not only weak in numbers — the elections to the Constituent Assembly in November 1917 gave the Bolsheviks only 750,000 votes in the Ukraine — but were predominantly Great Russian.[1] This gave Bolshevism in the Ukraine the double handicap of being an alien movement as well as a movement of townsmen. The coincidence of the national division with the cleavage between town and country proved equally embarrassing for the nationalists and for the Bolsheviks.

The Ukrainian national movement evoked at this stage no widespread response either from the peasant or from the industrial worker. It remained the creation of a small but devoted band of intellectuals drawn predominantly from the teaching and literary professions and from the priesthood, and ranging from university professors to village schoolmasters; and it received encouragement and support from the same classes of the Ukrainian population in east Galicia across the Austrian frontier. In this form Ukrainian nationalism was directed against the oppression, no longer of the Polish landowner or of the Jewish merchant, but of

---

[1] This condition persisted: as late as 1923 it was observed that " the composition of the party [in the Ukraine] is Russian-Jewish " (*Dvenadtsatyi S"ezd Rossiiskoi Kommunisticheskoi Partii (Bol'shevikov)* (1923), p. 562).

the Russian bureaucrat. But even here some qualification is required. The first champions of the movement were moved by hatred of the Tsars rather than of Great Russians as such : they were revolutionaries as much as nationalists, carrying, as a Russian governor-general said in the 1880s, the works of Shev-chenko, the Ukrainian national poet, in one pocket and the works of Karl Marx in the other,[1] though tradition and a peasant back-ground allied them with the *narodniks* or the anarchists rather than with the Marxists.   Increasing economic prosperity, as well as the force of foreign example, gradually detached the movement from the cause of social revolution. The first years of the twentieth century witnessed the growth, here as elsewhere in Russia, of an intelligentsia inspired by the ideals of liberal democracy, which combined readily enough with Ukrainian nationalism. But this group remained too small, too much isolated from the masses, and therefore politically too ineffective, to form the nucleus of a native ruling class.   Unable to make any social-revolutionary appeal to the masses, it was compelled to rely for its national appeal on a campaign against the political and cultural oppression of Moscow. This was real enough ; the ban on Ukrainian literature and the Ukrainian newspapers imposed in the 1870s was relaxed in 1905, only to be reimposed in full force in 1914. But such restrictions meant little to the peasant and less than nothing to the Great Russian industrial worker, so that the movement, lacking any solid support at home, was compelled to seek foreign patronage, turning successively to the Austrians,[2] to the French, to the Germans and, finally, to the Poles ; and these expedients ended by discrediting a movement whose protagonists so readily sold themselves to foreign Powers. And behind these domestic weaknesses and embarrass-ments of Ukrainian nationalism lay the bare fact of the economic dependence of the Ukraine on the Russian market and of the economic importance of the Ukraine to any Russian state. The Ukraine contained one-fifth of the population of Tsarist Russia ; its land was the most fertile in Russia, its industries among the most modern ; its industrial man-power, as well as its industrial management, was mainly Great Russian ; its coal and iron, so

---

[1] Quoted in W. Kolarcz, *Myths and Realities in Eastern Europe* (1946), p. 68.

[2] The first " union for the liberation of the Ukraine " was organized in Vienna after the outbreak of war in 1914.

long as the resources of the Urals were relatively undeveloped, were indispensable to Russian industry as a whole. Had the Ukrainian claim to secession been as clear-cut as that of Poland or of Finland, it would have been far more difficult to reconcile with economic realities. But it is fair to recognize that the claims themselves were not comparable. Trotsky afterwards taunted the Russian bourgeoisie under Kerensky with having been unwilling " to agree to the ' autonomy ' of the wheat of the Ukraine, the coal of the Don and the ore of Krivoi Rog ".[1] But the economic interdependence of industrial Russia and the Ukraine was a fact which transcended forms of social or political organization.

This rudimentary national movement received a strong impetus from the February revolution. It found three leaders : Hrushevsky, a learned professor whose *History of the Ukraine* provided a literary and historical basis for the movement; Vinnichenko, a revolutionary intellectual who had played some part in the events of 1905; and Petlyura, a self-made man who had tried many trades, journalism being the most recent. The first two were sincere nationalists, the third an energetic adventurer. In March 1917 a central Ukrainian Ràda (or Soviet) representing social-revolutionaries, social-democrats, social-federalists (a Ukrainian radical group) and national minorities constituted itself under the presidency of Hrushevsky. In April it secured the blessing of a national Ukrainian congress. It appears to have had no formally representative character; and at first, in conformity with the mainly social and cultural character of the movement, no political functions were claimed or exercised. But by slow steps the Rada emerged as an embryonic national assembly of some 600 members. On June 13, 1917, after vain attempts to negotiate with the Provisional Government in Petrograd, it issued a decree (the " first universal ") proclaiming an " autonomous Ukrainian republic ", though " without separating from Russia and without breaking away from the Russian state ", and established a " general secretariat " with Vinnichenko at its head, which soon assumed the form and functions of a national government. The Provisional Government in Petrograd, whose tactics throughout had been those of procrastination, partially and grudgingly conceded the claim to autonomy, always subject to the eventual verdict of the Constituent

[1] L. Trotsky, *Istoriya Russkoi Revolyutsii*, ii (Berlin, 1933), ii, 48.

Assembly. But this was a symptom rather of the weakness of the Provisional Government than of any great strength in the Rada and the general secretariat.[1]

After the October revolution in Petrograd the virtual breakdown of authority at the centre further stimulated the movement towards independence. On November 7/20, 1917, the Rada proclaimed a Ukrainian People's Republic, though the proclamation (the " third universal ") specifically repeated the intention " not to separate from the Russian republic and to maintain its unity " and to aid it to " become a federation of equal and free peoples ".[2] The general secretariat now became a regular government, with Vinnichenko as its prime minister and Petlyura as its secretary for military affairs. But given the declared policy of the Soviet Government, all this did not necessarily imply a breach between Kiev and Petrograd ; and correct relations were maintained for some time. Nor was the process of separation pressed very far in practice. As late as November 29/December 12, 1917, the Rada was demanding funds from the State Bank in Petrograd for the payment of its railway employees.[3] Failure to comply with this request compelled the Rada to issue its first currency notes in December 1917.[4]

Before the revolution was a month old, however, relations were already seriously strained. Soviets had made their appearance in various parts of the Ukraine during the summer of 1917, notably a Soviet of Workers' Deputies and a separate Soldiers' Soviet in Kiev.[5] After the October revolution these united, and the encouragement given to them by the Soviet Government in Petro-

---

[1] Documents of this period are translated in F. A. Golder, *Documents of Russian History* (1927), pp. 435-443 ; the fullest account of the Ukrainian parties is given by B. Krupnyckyj, *Geschichte der Ukraine* (Leipzig, 1939), pp. 283-284. The " first universal " is in *Revolyutsiya i Natsional'nyi Vopros : Dokumenty i Materialy*, ed. S. M. Dimanshtein, iii (1930), 161-164.

[2] Klyuchnikov i Sabanin, *Mezhdunarodnaya Politika*, ii (1926), 432-435 ; a proclamation on national defence is erroneously cited in *Revolyutsiya i Natsional'nyi Vopros : Dokumenty i Materialy*, ed. S. M. Dimanshtein, iii (1930), 196-197, as the " third universal ". According to a member of the Bund, it was the insistence of the Bundist and Menshevik members of the Rada which secured the inclusion in the proclamation of the proviso about maintaining the unity of Russia (M. G. Rafes, *Dva Goda Revolyutsii na Ukraine* (1920), p. 57).

[3] *Revolyutsiya 1917 goda*, ed. I. N. Lyubimov (1930), vi, 236-237.

[4] Vinnichenko, *Vidrodzheniya Natsii* (Vienna, 1920), ii, 230.

[5] E. Bosh, *God Bor'by* (1925), pp. 54-57.

grad [1] led to charges of deliberate attempts to undermine the Rada's authority. The breaking-point came with the organization of an anti-Bolshevik army on the Don by the "white" generals Kornilov and Kaledin, the latter being the ataman of the Don Cossacks.[2] The specific grievances of the Soviet Government against the Rada took a predominantly military form. The Rada was endeavouring to effect a separation of the armies by recalling all Ukrainian units to the Ukraine and thus helping further to disorganize existing fronts and confuse the procedure of demobilization; it was disarming Soviet and Red Guard units on Ukrainian soil; and it was refusing to allow Soviet forces to pass

----

[1] An article by Stalin in *Pravda* of November 24/December 7, 1917, contained an urgent appeal " to create a regional congress of workers', peasants' and soldiers' deputies in the Ukraine " : the article is not reprinted in Stalin's collected works.

[2] The Cossacks were descendants of frontier settlers who, at different times from the fifteenth to the eighteenth century, had acquired land by seizure or by grant of the Tsars in the exposed borderlands of the Muscovite empire, holding it in return for a perpetual obligation to perform military service. In the nineteenth century they had become a mainstay of the régime. They were organized in a dozen large military communities, known as *voiska* or hordes, extending from the Don through Central Asia to eastern Siberia. At the head of each community was an elected ataman who enjoyed quasi-dictatorial powers, though nominally responsible to an elected council. On the day after the October revolution, Kaledin, ataman of the Don Cossacks, proclaimed an independent Cossack government on the Don : similar steps were taken by the atamans of the Kuban and Terek Cossacks. Dutov, ataman of the Orenburg Cossacks, and Semenov, ataman of the Ussuri Cossacks, also organized anti-Bolshevik forces in the first winter of the revolution. The Cossacks of south Russia were the nucleus of what became under Kornilov, and later under Denikin, the " white " volunteer army.

Inequalities of land tenure had, however, created divisions of interest between well-to-do and poor Cossacks ; and disaffection, stimulated by war-weariness, began to appear among the rank-and-file Cossacks after the February revolution. M. Philips Price, *War and Revolution in Asiatic Russia* (1918), pp. 294-295, describes a revolt of the Cossacks of the north Caucasus against their leaders in March 1917. The Bolsheviks were able to exploit this discontent. The decree on land of October 26/November 8, 1917, exempted from expropriation " lands of Cossacks who are simple soldiers ". Shortly afterwards a delegation of Cossacks received encouragement from Lenin and Trotsky to divide up the lands of great Cossack landowners and form Cossack Soviets (John Reed, *Ten Days that Shook the World* (N.Y., 1919), p. 288). In November 1917 five Cossack representatives were brought into VTsIK, and the congress of Soviets from its third session onwards became the " All-Russian Congress of Soviets of Workers', Peasants', Cossacks' and Soldiers' Deputies " (*Tretii Vserossiiskii S"ezd Sovetov* (1918), p. 81). In December 1917 a decree addressed " To all Toiling Cossacks " abolished the obligation of military service and limitations on freedom of movement, offered uniform and equipment to those

through the Ukraine to form a front against the " whites ", while giving passage to Cossack formations on their way to join Kaledin on the Don.[1]   The conclusion of the armistice with the central Powers at Brest-Litovsk on December 2/15, 1917, relieved the strain on the slender military resources of the Soviet Government. On December 4/17, 1917, a long communication was despatched to the Ukrainian Rada and simultaneously made public.   It began by according recognition, in the name of the principle of self-determination, to the " People's Ukrainian Republic ", but went on to accuse the Rada of pursuing an " equivocal bourgeois policy which has long expressed itself in a refusal by the Rada to recognize the Soviets and Soviet power in the Ukraine ", and demanded the immediate abandonment of the three practices enumerated above.   It also included the positive demand that the Rada should " render assistance to the revolutionary armies in their struggle with the counter-revolutionary Kadet-Kaledin rising ".   If these questions were not satisfactorily answered within forty-eight hours the Rada would be considered to be " in a state of open war against the Soviet power in Russia and in the Ukraine ".[2]   And behind

prepared to serve voluntarily and promised a settlement of the land question (*Sobranie Uzakonenii, 1917–1918*, No. 8, art. 68).   In February 1918 the younger Don Cossacks had " responded to Bolshevik propaganda and risen against their fathers and the Kaledin government " (*Foreign Relations of the United States, 1918: Russia*, ii (1932), 621).   In September 1918 a Cossack section of VTsIK was created and issued a journal entitled *Klich Trudovykh Kazakov* : its report for the first year of its activities (*Kazachii Otdel : Kratkii Istoricheskii Ocherk i Otchet Kazach'ego Otdela VTsIK po Oktyabr' 1919 g.* (1919)) is a valuable source. During the civil war numerous appeals were made to the Cossacks to support the revolution, culminating in one from the seventh All-Russian Congress of Soviets in November 1919 (7ᵗ *Vserossiiskii S"ezd Sovetov* (1920), pp. 55–56).   It is difficult to judge of the effect of these efforts ; certainly the weight of the Cossack forces was on the side of the " whites ".   After the civil war the Cossack communities were gradually assimilated to the rest of the population.   But the Cossacks retained their title as one of the four constituent groups of the Soviet power till the foundation of the USSR, when the names of the separate groups dropped out of use.   The rôle of the Cossacks in the revolution would provide the subject for a useful monograph; further sources are quoted in Bunyan and Fisher, *The Bolshevik Revolution, 1917–1918* (Stanford, 1934), pp. 401–406, and there is an informative article in *Zhizn' Natsional'nostei*, No. 6 (63), February 15, 1920.

[1] In a subsequent report to VTsIK Stalin insisted that it was these three questions, and not the question of self-determination (on which " Sovnarkom goes further than the Rada, admitting even the right of separation "), that caused the breach (Stalin, *Sochineniya*, iv, 15–17).

[2] The text is printed in *Sobranie Uzakonenii, 1917–1918*, No. 6, art. 90, and in Lenin, *Sochineniya*, xxii, 121–123.   According to the notes in the latter the body of the declaration was drafted by Lenin, the concluding ultimatum by

these political recriminations loomed the growing threat of hunger in Petrograd and Moscow and the urgent need for Ukrainian grain. " If you want food," wrote Radek in *Pravda*, " cry ' Death to the Rada '." [1]

The threat from Petrograd produced its predestined reaction. The inherent tendency of the Ukrainian national movement, faced with superior Russian power, to place itself under foreign patronage was once more illustrated. A French military mission under General Tabouis had been for some time in Kiev. Exactly at what moment efforts began to induce the Rada " to reconstitute a force of resistance and remain faithful to the allies " is not known. But these efforts are referred to in what appears to be the first formal communication from General Tabouis to Vinnichenko, which is dated December 5/18, 1917 — the day after the ultimatum from Petrograd — and asks for particulars of the " financial and technical aid " which the Ukrainian Republic would desire to receive from France.[2] The fact of a Franco-Ukrainian agreement quickly became known in Petrograd, where Stalin published in *Pravda* on December 15/28, 1917, what purported to be an intercepted telegram from the French mission to the Rada.[3] In Kiev General Tabouis announced his appointment as commissioner of the French Republic to the government of the Ukrainian Republic, and on December 29, 1917/January 11, 1918, informed Vinnichenko that France would support the Ukrainian Republic with all its moral and material forces. A similar declaration was made about the same time by a British representative at Kiev.[4]

Trotsky (*ibid*. xxii, 591). The causes of the break are discussed by Stalin at greater length in an article in *Pravda* (Stalin, *Sochineniya*, iv, 6-14). According to M. Philips Price, *My Reminiscences of the Russian Revolution* (1921), pp. 198-199, Pyatakov, himself of Ukrainian birth, was the leading advocate of military action against the Rada : he was opposed to the principle of national self-determination (see pp. 262, 268-269 above).

[1] *Pravda*, Jan. 2/15, 1918.

[2] Vinnichenko, *Vidrodzheniya Natsii* (Vienna, 1920), ii, 232-233.

[3] Stalin, *Sochineniya*, iv, 19-21. The impressions current in Petrograd at the time are vividly recorded in M. Philips Price, *My Reminiscences of the Russian Revolution* (1921), pp. 194-195.

[4] This correspondence is printed by Vinnichenko, *Vidrodzheniya Natsii* (Vienna, 1920), ii, 235-243, who is careful to point out that it actually antedates the proclamation of Ukrainian independence in the " fourth universal " of January 9/22, 1918. On January 7, 1918, the French Government informed Washington that it had decided to recognize the Rada " as an independent government " (*Foreign Relations of the United States, 1918: Russia* ii (1932), 655).

On the Bolshevik side, the decision implicit in the ultimatum of December 4/17, 1917, to break with the Rada required the speedy building up of an alternative authority in the Ukraine. On the day preceding the ultimatum an All-Ukrainian Congress of Workers', Soldiers' and Peasants' Deputies opened in Kiev. In preparation for the congress, the local Bolshevik party had met and renamed itself the " Russian Social-Democratic Workers' Party (Bolsheviks) of the Social-Democracy of the Ukraine " — a hybrid title which rather clumsily aimed at reconciling party unity with a concession to Ukrainian national feeling; but this did not save the Bolsheviks at the congress from being shouted down by the supporters of the Rada.[1] An unsatisfactory reply from the Rada to the ultimatum [2] was not followed by an open break, partly because neither side really wanted war, partly because the Soviet Government had now found a better means of handling the situation. The Bolsheviks of the Ukraine retired from Kiev, where the power of the Rada was still beyond challenge, to Kharkov, where on December 11/24, 1917, they convened a new All-Ukrainian Congress of Soviets. Two days later a " central executive committee of the Ukraine " elected by the congress telegraphed to the government in Petrograd that it had " assumed full powers in the Ukraine ";[3] it was composed mainly of Bolsheviks with a sprinkling of Left SRs.[4]

From this point onward the Soviet Government frankly pursued a double policy. On the one hand, it greeted this new authority as " the genuine government of the People's Ukrainian Republic ", and undertook to afford it all possible support both " in the struggle for peace " and " in the transfer of all lands, factories, workshops and banks to the toiling people of the Ukraine ".[5] Yet this did not prevent a continuance of the negotiations through various intermediaries with the Rada,[6] or the reluctant recognition of the credentials of the Rada's delegation at the peace conference of Brest-Litovsk, which could not have

[1] *Revolyutsiya 1917 goda*, vi, ed. I. N. Lyubimov (1930), 269-271.
[2] The text of this reply and of the exchanges that followed it is given, *ibid.* pp. 289-292.
[3] *Protokoly Zasedanii VTsIK 2 Sozyva* (1918), pp. 158-159; E. Bosh, *God Bor'by* (1925), p. 81, where the telegram is correctly dated.
[4] For the list see *ibid.* p. 91.
[5] *Izvestiya*, December 17/30, 1917, quoted in Lenin, *Sochineniya*, xxii, 592
[6] *Revolyutsiya 1917 goda*, vi, ed. I. N. Lyubimov (1930), 375-376, 414.

been withheld without throwing doubt on the sincerity of Bolshevik protestations of devotion to the cause of national self-determination.[1] But by this time, as Vinnichenko frankly admitted, " the vast majority of the Ukrainian population was against us ".[2] The area of the Rada's authority rapidly contracted as more and more of its forces disbanded themselves or went over to the Bolsheviks. On January 9/22, 1918, it issued a " fourth universal " proclaiming at length the Ukrainian Republic as " an independent, free and sovereign state of the Ukrainian people ", and its independence was recognized by the German Government ten days later.[3] While, however, these formalities were being exchanged, Soviet armies were surrounding Kiev, which they entered on January 26/February 8, 1918. The Rada was overthrown ; and a few days later the new Ukrainian Soviet Government was installed there.[4]

This was not, however, the end of the story. The rule of the Ukrainian Soviet Government lasted for less than three weeks, during which it did little to propitiate the population or to remove the impression of an occupation by " an external foreign force ".[5] At the moment when the Rada was being dispossessed in Kiev,

[1] The anomaly of the situation is illustrated by the fact that, as late as December 28, 1917/January 10, 1918, many days after the recognition by Petrograd of the Soviet régime in the Ukraine, Trotsky declared at Brest-Litovsk in reply to Kühlmann that, having recognized the right of self-determination, the Russian delegation raised no objection to the participation of the Ukrainian delegation at the peace conference (*Mirnye Peregovory v Brest-Litovske*, i (1920), 52). At a later stage the Russian delegation attempted to introduce delegates of the Kharkov government to the conference, but this was resisted both by the Rada delegation and by the Germans.

[2] Vinnichenko, *Vidrodzheniya Natsii* (Vienna, 1920), ii, 216 ; Hrushevsky, *History of the Ukraine* (Engl. transl. Yale, 1941), pp. 534-535, writes of the effect of Bolshevik propaganda on the Ukrainian armed forces.

[3] Vinnichenko, *Vidrodzheniya Natsii* (Vienna, 1920), ii, 244-252.

[4] The main authority for these events is the contemporary press : some excerpts are collected in Lenin, *Sochineniya*, xxii, pp. 591-592. Interesting sidelights will be found in Vinnichenko, *op. cit.* ii, 252-256, and in M. Philips Price, *My Reminiscences of the Russian Revolution* (1921), pp. 198-203, 233-235. A report of the United States consul at Kiev on the Bolshevik capture of the city is published in *Foreign Relations of the United States, 1918 : Russia*, ii (1932), 675-676.

[5] M. G. Rafes, *Dva Goda Revolyutsii na Ukraine* (1920), p. 77 ; according to M. Philips Price, *My Reminiscences of the Russian Revolution* (1921), pp. 202-203, the few disciplined Soviet troops had been sent to the Don front, and the Soviet armies in the Ukraine were scratch levies of adventurers of all kinds who " without any interest or knowledge of the Ukraine . . . pretended to act as ' liberators of the Ukrainian people ' ".

its delegates were signing a treaty of peace with Germany at Brest-Litovsk. True to the tradition of seeking foreign protection against the power of Petrograd, the Rada on February 12, 1918, appealed for help to Germany.[1] The German armies quickly swept over the Ukraine; and on March 2, 1918, the Bolsheviks abandoned Kiev to the forces of the Rada under Petlyura. But neither the religious thanksgiving celebrated by Petlyura nor the eloquence of Hrushevsky, who returned to Kiev as president of the Rada, concealed the " bitter truth ", admitted by Vinnichenko, that the Rada owed its restoration to " German heavy guns ".[2] Nor did its complacency save it for long. At the end of April the Rada was contemptuously dismissed in favour of a more effective or more compliant German-sponsored Ukrainian government under the hetman Skoropadsky.

The new régime was a German military convenience. In so far as it had any significance in the interplay of domestic forces in the Ukraine it represented the interests of large landowners and well-to-do peasants, whose surplus production offered to the German occupying authorities the last hope of replenishing empty German granaries. It was a frankly reactionary régime which offered little to the Ukrainian nationalists and nothing to the advocates of social reform. This did not prevent the continuance of peace negotiations between it and the Soviet Government.[3] There was nothing to choose from the Soviet point of view between a German-sponsored Rada and a German-sponsored hetman ; and a Soviet delegation pursued inconclusive discussions at Kiev through the summer of 1918. The unwillingness of the Bolsheviks to resume the war against the Germans in the Ukraine was one of the grievances on which the Left SRs harped at the fifth All-Russian Congress of Soviets in Moscow. The assassination of Eichhorn, the German general in the Ukraine, was, like that of Mirbach, an unsuccessful attempt to disturb Soviet-German relations.

[1] Vinnichenko, *Vidrodzheniya Natsii* (Vienna, 1920), ii, 301 ; text in *Izvestiya*, February 19, 1918. According to M. G. Rafes, *Dva Goda Revolyutsii na Ukraine* (1920), p. 70, there had already been a strong party in the Rada at the time of the agreement with General Tabouis in December 1917 which believed that only German aid could keep the Bolsheviks out.

[2] Vinnichenko, *Vidrodzheniya Natsii* (Vienna, 1920), ii, 296, 299-302.

[3] Stalin, who was initially in charge of these negotiations, defended them in a statement to *Izvestiya* (*Sochineniya*, iv, 82-84).

The authority of Skoropadsky over the Ukraine endured till the German military collapse of November 1918. Thereafter the history of the previous winter repeated itself. Elements of the old Rada re-established themselves at Kiev as a " Ukrainian director- ate " with Vinnichenko as president and Petlyura, now emerging in the character of a would-be dictator, as commander-in-chief. French aid was once more invoked. But General d'Anselm com- manding the French forces at Odessa had little to offer but words ; and even these were less encouraging than the promises of General Tabouis a year earlier.[1] The only novel feature in the situation was the proclamation, now that the authority of the central Powers had collapsed, of the inclusion in the Ukrainian Republic of the so-called " western Ukraine ", the former Austrian province of east Galicia. A bone of contention was thus created between the Ukraine and Poland.

It was significant of the lack of organized support for the Bolsheviks in the Ukraine itself that, even in the chaos created by the downfall of the German power and the flight of Skoro- padsky, they were unable to effect a direct seizure of power. Nevertheless, Bolshevik tactics were bolder than before. Within a few days of the German collapse, a " provisional workers' and peasants' government of the Ukraine " under Pyatakov constituted itself at Kursk on the northern frontier. On November 29, 1918, it issued a manifesto announcing its assumption of power and the transfer of the land to the peasants and of the factories to the " Ukrainian toiling masses " ;[2] in Kharkov a Soviet seized power after a three-day general strike at the beginning of December ;[3] and presently Bolshevik armies began their southward advance. In reply to protests of the " directorate " Chicherin in a note of January 6, 1919, disclaimed responsibility for Pyatakov's government and its armies which were " completely independ-

---

[1] An extremely cautious statement by General d'Anselm promising French aid to all " well-disposed elements " for the restoration of Russia is quoted in Vinnichenko, *Vidrodzheniya Natsii* (Vienna, 1920), iii, 267-268. On the other hand, the Bolsheviks in a note to the Paris peace conference of February 1919 gave a circumstantial account of an alleged agreement between Petlyura and the French military command (*L'Ukraine Soviétiste* (Berlin, 1922), pp. 15-16).

[2] *Politika Sovetskoi Vlasti po Natsional'nomu Voprosu* (1920), pp. 109-111, art. 147 ; an article by Stalin of December 1, 1918, entitled *The Ukraine is being Liberated*, is in *Sochineniya*, iv, 174-176.

[3] Stalin, *Sochineniya*, iv, 180.

ent ".[1] Ten days later the " directorate " declared war on Moscow, apparently against the wishes of Vinnichenko,[2] who resigned shortly afterwards. But this did nothing to delay the Soviet armies, which established themselves in Kharkov and then, in February 1919, fought their way back into Kiev as they had done just a year before. They were greeted by the population with every show of enthusiasm.[3] The members of the expelled " directorate " transferred their main activities to the peace conference in Paris, where their pleas fell on the deaf ears of statesmen more interested in the cause of Poland or of " white " generals pledged to reconstitute the unity of the Russian Empire than in that of Ukrainian nationalism.

The capital of the Soviet Ukraine was now established at Kharkov, its most important industrial centre; and Pyatakov, who, though a native of the Ukraine, seems to have shown too little sympathy for the claims of Ukrainian independence,[4] was replaced as head of the Ukrainian Soviet Government by Rakovsky. On March 10, 1919, a constitution of the Ukrainian Socialist Soviet Republic was officially adopted by the third All-Ukrainian Congress of Soviets. It did not diverge in any important particular from its prototype, the constitution of the RSFSR.[5] The weakness of an independent Ukrainian SSR was revealed by the list of members of the presidium of the third All-Ukrainian Congress of Soviets who signed its constitution. Rakovsky, Pyatakov, Bubnov and Kviring were well-known Bolsheviks, but their credentials as spokesmen for a Ukrainian nation were not very substantial.[6] Meanwhile external conditions were in-

---

[1] Vinnichenko, *Vidrodzheniya Natsii* (Vienna, 1920), iii, 205-208; for Vinnichenko's reply of January 9, 1919, accusing the Moscow government of pursuing the old Tsarist policy of imperialism, see *ibid.* iii, 213-218.

[2] *Ibid.* iii, 230.   [3] *Ibid.* iii, 328.

[4] This is probably the meaning of the statement of a competent reporter that " the views of the Pyatakov government were further left than those of its supporters " (Arthur Ransome, *Six Weeks in Russia in 1919* (1919), p. 22).

[5] *Politika Sovetskoi Vlasti po Natsional'nomu Voprosu* (1920), pp. 113-116, art. 151; *Istoriya Sovetskoi Konstitutsii v Dekretakh* (1936), pp. 115-121.

[6] Among other well-known Bolsheviks included in Rakovsky's government were Artem, Voroshilov, Mezhlauk and Podvoisky (full list in *L'Ukraine Soviétiste* (Berlin, 1922), pp. 9-10). Some of these had, like Trotsky and Zinoviev, been born in the Ukraine, but hardly regarded themselves as Ukrainians. Rakovsky was of Rumanian origin, had been active in the Rumanian Social-Democratic Party during the war of 1914-1918, and appeared at the third All-Russian Congress of Soviets in January 1918 as the bearer of greetings from

auspicious in every respect. Fighting continued for some time in the west, where Petlyura's retreating forces distinguished themselves by ruthless massacres of the large Jewish population.[1] In the eastern Ukraine a peasant leader of outstanding abilities, the anarchist, Nestor Makhno, had organized a group of partisans in 1918 for guerilla warfare against Skoropadsky: this group now swelled into an organized movement with an army some thousands strong, controlling at different times wide stretches of country and fighting now on the side of the Bolsheviks and now against them.[2]

" the social-democracy of Rumania " (*Tretii Vserossiiskii S"ezd Sovetov* (1918), pp. 10-11). There was nothing exceptional about this ; party workers were freely transferred from one field to another at a time when reliable workers were few, and national distinctions seemed unimportant. At the first All-Russian Congress of Soviets in June 1917 Zinoviev had spoken on behalf of the Ukrainian section of the party.

[1] According to a Jewish writer, a member of the Rada called anti-Semitism at this time " our principal trump ", and said that " no Bolshevism can stand against our anti-Semitism " (M. G. Rafes, *Dva Goda Revolyutsii na Ukraine* (1920), p. 132).

[2] Nestor Makhno was one of the leaders of a group of " anarchist-communists " established in the Ukrainian village of Gulyai-Pole in the province of Ekaterinoslav in 1905. Two years later, following peasant disturbances provoked by the Stolypin reforms, Makhno was sent to Siberia. Returning in 1917 he reorganized the group on the lines of a peasant commune, and in the autumn of 1918 built up a partisan organization to resist the Skoropadsky régime and its German and Austrian backers. His force rapidly swelled in numbers, and from 1918 to 1921 fought successively, and sometimes simultaneously, against the Ukrainian directorate, Denikin, Wrangel and the Bolsheviks. His memoirs in Russian were subsequently published in Paris in three volumes (the last two of them posthumous) under separate titles : *Russkaya Revolyutsiya na Ukraine* (1929) ; *Pod Udarami Kontrrevolyutsii* (1936) ; *Ukrainskaya Revolyutsiya* (1937). The memoirs end at December 1918, and a promised fourth volume containing Makhno's notes and articles on the later period does not appear to have been published. The editor of the second and third volumes explains, in his preface to the second, that Makhno " had only an elementary education and no command of the literary language ", so that the memoirs probably present a somewhat too finished and coherent account of an enigmatic figure. He depicts himself as a convinced anarchist who rejected all state authority as oppressive and counter-revolutionary ; but this did not prevent him from exercising stern military discipline in his own movement. He idealized the peasant, but was non-political, being equally opposed to the landowners, to the Cossacks, to the bourgeoisie, to the Ukrainian nationalists (it is said that he did not himself speak Ukrainian) and to the Constituent Assembly, which he called " a card game of all the political parties " (*Russkaya Revolyutsiya na Ukraine* (1929), p. 18). He cooperated with the Bolsheviks for brief periods but resisted all attempts by them to establish their authority in the Ukraine. His activities were confined mainly to the Ukraine east of the Dnieper : Makhno, notwithstanding his anarchism, appears to have inherited something of the Cossack

Pockets of German troops still remained here and there on Ukrainian soil. French detachments had been landed on the Black Sea coast and in the Crimea. In July Denikin's " volunteer army " with allied backing began its northward advance. The Red Army retreated, and in September Kiev was again occupied by the forces, first of Petlyura, then of Denikin himself. Disorganization was now complete. Hunger, typhus and other diseases swept the Ukraine.[1] Several independent military leaders, of whom Makhno was merely the most formidable, ranged the countryside with bands varying in character from organized armies to predatory gangs. Among the peasants, discontent with Soviet rule was forgotten in hatred of the harsher oppression of Denikin's occupying forces.

The defeat of Denikin led in December 1919 to the recapture of Kiev by the Red Army. A " military-revolutionary committee " of five members, three of them Bolsheviks, was installed under a decree signed by Rakovsky as president of the Ukrainian Sovnarkom;[2] and for the third time the attempt was made to consolidate a Soviet régime in the Ukraine. By February 1920 Soviet authority had been re-established in the main centres. But even this was not the end of the period of troubles. In December 1919 the discomfited Petlyura, defeated by the Bolsheviks, ignored by the allies in Paris and spurned by Denikin, turned to the one conceivable alternative source of moral and material support — Poland. Poland, opposed to a reincorporation of the Ukraine in a united Russia whether under Soviet rule or under that of Denikin, found in Petlyura the sole remaining figurehead of Ukrainian separatism ; Petlyura cynically abandoned the Ukrainian claim to east Galicia in exchange for the ambition of ruling the Ukraine as a satellite unit in a Polish Empire. Petlyura's agreement with the Polish Government, which was

tradition of independent military communities which was particularly strong in this region. An informative account of the movement by one of his followers (P. Arshinov, *Istoriya Makhnovskogo Dvizheniya* (Berlin, 1923)) is marred by excessive hero-worship ; the antidote is provided by a Soviet publication, M. Kabanda, *Makhnovshchina* (n.d. [?1925]).

[1] References to the severity of the typhus epidemic in the winter of 1919-1920 occur in P. Arshinov, *Istoriya Makhnovskogo Dvizheniya* (Berlin, 1923), pp. 156, 158.

[2] *Zhizn' Natsional'nostei*, No. 48 (56), December 21, 1919 ; *Oktyabr'skaya Revolyutsiya: Pervoe Pyatiletie* (Kharkov, 1922), p. 117.

concluded in Warsaw on December 2, 1919,[1] marked the ultimate
bankruptcy of Ukrainian bourgeois nationalism, since the rudimentary national feelings of the Ukrainian peasantry had been
stimulated mainly by hostility to the Polish landowner. But it
opened the way for a fresh incursion into the Ukraine, this time
by Polish armies, which occupied Kiev for some six weeks in
May-June 1920. This time, however, the defeat and expulsion
of the invader brought the Ukraine immunity from foreign invasion for two decades. It took the best part of another year
to restore order throughout the Ukraine,[2] and sporadic fighting
with partisans did not end till Makhno crossed the frontier
into Rumania on August 28, 1921, with the last remnant of his
forces.[3] Then at last in undisputed possession of the country,
the Soviet régime appeared to offer to the Ukrainian population not only the blessings of peace, but a government more
tolerable than any which it had experienced in these turbulent
years.

Thus the Soviet Ukraine was brought to its difficult birth.
The right of national self-determination and secession had been
officially vindicated. But whereas in Finland the bourgeois ruling
class had been strong enough to win recognition as representing
the Finnish nation, in the Ukraine the revolution had been hurried
on a step further and the bourgeoisie ousted in favour of a
" dictatorship of the toiling and exploited masses of the proletariat and the poor peasants " (the term occurs in the first article
of the Ukrainian constitution), which thus became the repository
of Ukrainian national independence. The interest of Petrograd
in such a solution was obvious. Yet the evidence also supports the
conclusion that Ukrainian bourgeois nationalism had been weighed
and found wanting. It had no national workers' movement to
which it could appeal. It failed to win the peasants owing to its
failure to espouse the cause not merely of social revolution, but
of social reform on any significant scale — a failure frankly and
repeatedly admitted by Vinnichenko, the most honest of its

---

[1] Vinnichenko, *Vidrodzheniya Natsii* (Vienna, 1920), iii, 474-476.
[2] An ultimatum sent to Makhno in November 1920, after the collapse of
Wrangel, by the Soviet commander Frunze, demanding the incorporation of
Makhno's forces in the Red Army is in M. P. Frunze, *Sobranie Sochinenii*, i (1929),
176-180 ; the ultimatum was rejected.
[3] P. Arshinov, *Istoriya Makhnovskogo Dvizheniya* (Berlin, 1923), p. 200.

leaders.[1] Its weakness made it constantly amenable to foreign pressure and thus precluded any real freedom of action. Its final bankruptcy came in 1920 when its last active leader Petlyura made his pact with the Poles, the national enemies of the Ukrainian peasant.

The Ukrainian bourgeoisie had proved even less capable than the Great Russian bourgeoisie of bringing about a bourgeois revolution. Its failure left the succession open. Except for the Bolsheviks there were no serious candidates in the field; and the disintegration one after another of all the forces opposed to them showed that the Bolsheviks were at any rate accepted by the Ukrainian masses as the least of possible evils. This did not, however, make a solution easy. The only effective choice which confronted the Soviet Government at the beginning of 1918 and again at the beginning of 1919 was between direct incorporation of the Ukraine in the Russian Soviet unit and an attempt to satisfy Ukrainian national aspirations by creating a separate Ukrainian Soviet unit. The second alternative was dictated by the principles which they had publicly proclaimed before the revolution and by Lenin's firmly held belief that the largest measure of dispersal in the name of national self-determination was the surest road to an ultimate union of hearts. Of Lenin's personal struggle to impart reality to the policy of an independent Soviet Ukraine there is ample evidence. When Soviet authority was about to be established there for the third time after Denikin's defeat in December 1919, a resolution " on the Soviet power in the Ukraine " drafted by Lenin and approved by the central

[1] The following are typical quotations from Vinnichenko's *Vidrodzheniya Natsii* (Vienna, 1920): " So long as we fought the Russian Bolsheviks, the Muscovites, we were victorious everywhere, but so soon as we came into contact with our own Bolsheviks, we lost all our strength " (ii, 155); the Rada showed no inclination " to liberate the toiling masses from the social oppression which was inimical to the nation and to the toiling class " (ii, 158); the fault of the Rada was to " develop in the mind of the masses a conflict between the national and the social idea " (ii, 219). Vinnichenko admits " the extraordinarily acute antipathy of the popular masses to the central Rada " at the time of the expulsion of the Rada by the Bolsheviks in February 1918; and he adds the pathetic confession that " what was terrible and strange in all this was that they derided at the same time everything Ukrainian — Ukrainian language, music, schools, newspapers and books " (ii, 259-260). The failure to provide a social content for Ukrainian nationalism ended by discrediting its other aspirations. M. G. Rafes, *Dva Goda Revolyutsii na Ukraine* (1920), p. 78, also speaks of the hostility aroused by the Rada's policy of " Ukrainization ".

committee was submitted to a special party conference in Moscow. It was concerned primarily with the attitude of the Soviet administration to the Ukrainian national question and to the Ukrainian peasant. It denounced " artificial attempts to push back the Ukrainian language into a secondary place ", demanding that all officials should be able to speak Ukrainian; and it prescribed the distribution of former large estates to the peasants, the creation of Soviet farms " only in strictly necessary proportions," and the requisition of grain " only in strictly limited amounts ". But it encountered stiff opposition at the conference from the Bolshevik leaders in the Ukraine. Rakovsky argued that large-scale Soviet farms should be the foundation of the Soviet order; Bubnov, one of his colleagues in the Ukrainian Sovnarkom, regarded the demand that officials should speak Ukrainian as an exaggeration of the importance of Ukrainian nationalism; and Bubnov, Manuilsky and others protested against any compromise with the *Borot'bisti*, a Ukrainian peasant party of SR complexion which was seeking an alliance with the Bolsheviks.[1] Lenin's resolution was carried; and in March 1920 the *Borot'bisti* were admitted to the Communist Party.[2] But, where the opposition of the men on the spot was so keen and so far-reaching, the difficulties of applying the party line could not be easily overcome.

Nor would it be fair to attribute these difficulties to the blindness or obstinacy of a few individuals. Ukrainian national aspirations could not be satisfied within a bourgeois framework. But when the Bolsheviks, by setting up the Ukrainian SSR, announced the transition from the bourgeois to the proletarian revolution, the Ukrainian national problem presented itself in a new and almost equally intractable form. It was an essential of Bolshevik doctrine that the proletariat could alone lead the peasantry on the revolutionary path; and in the absence of a native Ukrainian proletariat, the national content of social revolution in the Ukraine remained artificial and in some degree

---

[1] The resolution is in *VKP(B) v Rezolyutsiyakh* (1941), i, 316-318, and Lenin, *Sochineniya*, xxiv, 552-554. The records of the conference were not published, and Lenin's main speech on the Ukrainian question is lost; his brief summing up is in *Sochineniya*, xxiv, 557-578. Other information about the proceedings from unpublished archives will be found, *ibid.* xxiv, 815-816, note 171, 818-819, note 178.

[2] Stalin, *Sochineniya*, iv, 304.

fictitious.   For the Ukrainian bourgeois intellectual, the blot on the new régime was that its leaders were still predominantly Great Russian, in spirit and in training, if not by birth.   This impression was not quickly removed.   The winning over of a few of the former Ukrainian nationalists, notably the veteran Hrushevsky, who returned to Kiev in 1923 to become president of the new Ukrainian Academy of Sciences, thinly veiled the Great Russian complexion of the administration of the Soviet Ukraine.   For the Ukrainian peasant, the handicap of the new régime was that it was a régime of townsmen.   This handicap was less keenly felt in the period of reconciliation with the peasantry which was symbolized by NEP.   Later, when proletarian pressure on the peasant was resumed, and the discontents of the Ukrainian peasant coincided with those of the Ukrainian intellectual, the truth was once more illustrated that the national problem became acute when it acquired a social and economic content.

The establishment of a White Russian SSR in February 1919, almost at the same moment as that of the Ukrainian SSR, represented a further application of the policy of dispersal in the name of national self-determination.   The problem was simpler than in the Ukraine, since there were no more than the beginnings of a White Russian bourgeois nationalist movement; but this very fact made the solution more artificial.   The Ukrainian pattern was closely followed.   As early as March 1917 a White Russian national congress had issued a declaration favouring a " federal republican democratic order " for Russia, and set up a White Russian national committee.[1]   In August 1917 a bourgeois White Russian Rada was established at Minsk;[2] and its delegates actually appeared early in January 1918 at the third All-Russian Congress of Soviets, only to find themselves denied a hearing and their mandates disallowed.[3]   In the last days of 1917 striking events had occurred in Minsk.   A Bolshevik military-revolutionary committee, which came into existence after the October revolution, had overthrown

[1] *Revolyutsiya i Natsional'nyi Vopros: Dokumenty i Materialy*, ed. S. M. Dimanshtein, iii (1930), 267, 271-272.
[2] *Ibid.* iii, 275-276.
[3] *Tretii Vserossiiskii S"ezd Sovetov* (1918), pp. 64, 87.

the Rada, established a " Council of People's Commissars of the western region and front " and proclaimed the right of " the toiling people of White Russia to national self-determination ".[1] For a few weeks a rudimentary Soviet government ruled in Minsk.[2] But in February 1918 the advancing German armies overthrew it, and, anxious in their turn to pay lip-service to the fashionable doctrine of national self-determination, installed a White Russian Rada of their own. Later in the year congresses of White Russian refugees were convened in Moscow and proclaimed their unalterable desire for union with the Russian Soviet Republic.[3]

No further practical issue arose until the German armies behind the frontier accepted at Brest-Litovsk began to disintegrate in November 1918. Provision had then to be made for the government of the liberated territory ; and, as in the Ukraine, the choice lay here between its incorporation in the Russian unit and the creation of a separate White Russian unit. The same considerations dictated the same decision. It was taken by the central committee of the party and the necessary instructions were conveyed by Stalin to the local communist leader, Myasnikov by name, on December 25, 1918.[4] On January 1, 1919, a " pro-

---

[1] *Revolyutsiya 1917 goda*, vi, ed. I. N. Lyubimov, 1930, 457-458. At Brest-Litovsk Hoffmann countered Trotsky's appeals to the principle of national self-determination by alleging that " on the night of December 30-31 the first White Russian congress at Minsk, which insisted on the right of White Russians to self-determination, was broken up by the Bolsheviks with bayonets and machine guns " (*Mirnye Peregovory v Brest-Litovske*, i (1920), 95).

[2] *Proletarskaya Revolyutsiya*, No. 3 (74), 1928, pp. 61-130.

[3] References to these congresses in the contemporary press are cited in *Voprosy Istorii* No. 1, 1947, p. 11.

[4] The most complete available account of the foundation of the White Russian SSR is contained in an article devoted to the celebration of Stalin's sixtieth birthday (*Istorik Marksist*, No. 1, 1940, pp. 63-78). The following is a brief summary of the main facts there stated :

On December 25, 1918, after the retreat of the German armies from White Russian territory, Stalin had a telephone conversation with Myasnikov, president of the regional committee of the Communist Party for the north-western region :

Comrade Stalin informed Myasnikov of the decision of the central committee of the Communist Party about the foundation of a White Russian Socialist Soviet Republic and summoned the president of the regional committee to Moscow. . . . He intimated that the provinces of Kovno and Vilna should go to the Lithuanian Soviet Government. Comrade Stalin also put forward the fundamental principles of the formation of the White Russian SSR and of the work of the Communist Party of White Russia.

The intimations of comrade Stalin were discussed at a party conference

visional government of the White Russian independent Soviet republic " proclaimed its authority in Minsk and declared the " venal bourgeois White Russian Rada " outside the law.[1] Exactly a month later the first White Russian Congress of Soviets of Workers', Soldiers' and Peasants' Deputies assembled at Minsk and on February 4, 1919, adopted a constitution of the White Russian SSR and set up a White Russian government.[2]   The

[of the north-western region] in which Myasnikov took part. They formed the basis of the construction of the White Russian SSR and Communist Party and guided the Bolsheviks of White Russia in their struggle against bourgeois White Russian nationalists.

The Government of the White Russian SSR was to consist of 15 persons (subsequently the membership of the government was increased to 17). Comrade Stalin also concerned himself with the personal recruitment of those concerned.

A central bureau of the Communist Party of the White Russian republic was formed. The president of the central bureau was also the president of the central committee of the party and of the Soviet Government. Comrade Stalin drafted the manifesto of the provisional Workers' and Peasants' Soviet Government of White Russia and made a number of important corrections in it.

When the members of the provisional White Russian Soviet Government left for Smolensk, comrade Stalin wrote to Myasnikov :—" To-day the White Russians leave for Smolensk. They are bringing with them a manifesto. You are requested by the central committee of the party and by Lenin to receive them as younger brothers, perhaps still inexperienced, but ready to give their life to party and Soviet work."

After these preparations, an extraordinary party conference of the north-western region met on December 31st, immediately declared itself to be the first congress of the Communist Party of White Russia, and decided to proclaim an independent socialist republic of White Russia. Some dissenting communists (" Zhilunovich and his group "), who apparently objected to this essay in national self-determination, resigned from the party.

The circumstances in which this account was published may have justified some exaggeration of Stalin's personal rôle, but there is no reason to doubt its substantial accuracy.

A. F. Myasnikov was a party worker who had no personal connexion with White Russia, being by birth an Armenian. Later he was president of the Sovnarkom of the Armenian SSR, and in that capacity read at the ninth All-Russian Congress of Soviets in December 1921 a declaration in the name of the three Transcaucasian republics (*Devyatyi Vserossiiskii S"ezd Sovetov* (1922), p. 186). He is not to be confused with G. I. Myasnikov who was expelled from the party for breaches of party discipline in February 1922 (see pp. 207-208 above).

[1] *Istoriya Sovetskoi Konstitutsii v Dekretakh* (1936), pp. 99-102. The Rada retired to Grodno where it continued for some time to enjoy the patronage of the Polish Government.

[2] The constitution will be found *ibid.* pp. 111-114 ; the list of the government in *Zhizn' Natsional'nostei*, No. 5 (13), February 16, 1919.

work was done in such haste that the constitution, framed on the same plan as that of the RSFSR, defined the functions of the Congress of Soviets and a central executive committee, but failed to include provisions either for local Soviets or for a Sovnarkom.

Like the Ukraine, White Russia had to pass through a further period of tribulation even after her establishment as a socialist Soviet republic. During the spring of 1919 plans were made for a federation between the equally young and almost equally feeble White Russian and Lithuanian republics.[1] But in April 1919 a Polish advance extinguished the Lithuanian SSR; and Polish armies occupied a part of the territory claimed by White Russia, taking Minsk itself in August 1919. In the Polish-Soviet war of 1920 the White Russian republic was liberated by the advance of Soviet troops into Poland and celebrated the victory on August 1, 1920, by a flamboyant proclamation.[2] The Polish-Soviet armistice of October 1920 (confirmed in this respect by the treaty of Riga of March 18, 1921) once more deprived White Russia of the western part of her territory. But this time the decision was final, and a period of peace set in. In December 1920 the second White Russian Congress of Soviets repaired the omissions in the constitution of February 1919 by adopting a series of "supplements".[3]

"To the White Russians", observes a recent historian, "nationhood came as an almost unsolicited gift of the Russian revolution."[4] A writer in the official journal of Narkomnats admitted that the White Russian workers and peasants "always considered themselves a part of the working people of Russia, and only an insignificant part of the petty bourgeois White Russian intelligentsia stood for the independence of White Russia".[5] But nationhood was, in Bolshevik theory, a normal and useful, if not indispensable, stage of historical development; and if a White Russian nation did not yet exist, analogy suggested that it was in an advanced state of gestation. This was the rather dubious argu-

[1] Stalin, *Sochineniya*, iv, pp. 228-229; *Zhizn' Natsional'nostei*, No. 6 (14), February 23, 1919.
[2] *Istoriya Sovetskoi Konstitutsii v Dekretakh* (1936), pp. 140-142.
[3] *Ibid.* pp. 155-160.
[4] D. S. Mirsky, *Russia: a Social History* (1932), p. 278.
[5] *Zhizn' Natsional'nostei*, No. 10 (67), April 6, 1920.

ment with which Stalin two years later at a party congress, defended himself against the charge of " artificially cultivating a White Russian nationality " :

> Some forty years ago Riga was a German town ; but since towns grow by drawing on the country, and the country is the preserver of nationality, Riga is now a purely Lettish town. Some fifty years ago all the towns of Hungary had a German character ; now they are Magyarised. The same will happen with White Russia, in the towns of which non-White Russians still predominate.[1]

This was perhaps the most extreme example, at any rate in Europe, of the invocation of the principle of national self-determination for the purpose of stimulating national consciousness rather than of satisfying it.

The case of Estonia and Latvia fell midway between Finland, on the one hand, and the Ukraine and White Russia on the other. Both countries were of Lilliputian dimensions, having populations of 1,250,000 and 1,750,000 respectively ; but their languages, different from each other and akin neither to Teuton nor to Slav, gave them a distinctive position. In both countries a small but authentic bourgeois nationalist movement had grown up in protest against the domination of German merchants, industrialists and landowners — far weaker and less firmly established than its counterpart in Finland, but stronger and more determined than in the Ukraine. In both countries Soviet régimes had been proclaimed at the moment of the October revolution, but had been quickly swept away by the advancing German armies. On the German collapse in November 1918 bourgeois national governments were installed in Riga and Tallinn. But their duration was brief. On November 29, 1918, came the proclamation of an Estonian Soviet Government at Narva, to be followed by the proclamation of a Lettish Soviet Government three weeks later. Soviet armies, native and Russian, began to move in from the

---

[1] Stalin, *Sochineniya*, v, 49. Stalin long afterwards reiterated that " elements of nations " already existed in the pre-capitalist period, though only as a " potential " (*ibid.* xi, 336). Lenin in 1913 argued, with specific reference to " Poland, Lithuania, the Ukraine, White Russia, etc.", that " to tear away towns for the ' national ' reason from the villages and districts which gravitate towards them would be silly and impossible " (*Sochineniya*, xvii, 158) ; but the only practical conclusion which he drew at that time was that " Marxists must not stand wholly and exclusively on the ground of the ' national-territorial ' principle ".

east. This was the period at which the slogan of " self-determination for the workers " was officially current ; and Stalin's announcement of policy was clear and unequivocal :

> Soviet Russia has never looked on the western regions as its
> own possessions. It has always considered that these regions
> constitute the inalienable possession of the working masses of
> the nationalities that inhabit them, that these masses have a full
> right of freely determining their political destiny. Of course
> this does not preclude — it presupposes — help of every kind
> from Soviet Russia to our Estonian comrades in their struggle
> for the liberation of workers' Estonia from the yoke of the
> bourgeoisie.[1]

The Estonian Soviet Republic was recognized by Petrograd on
December 8, 1918, the Latvian Soviet Republic on December 22,
1918.[2] Early in January 1919 Soviet power had been established
as far as Riga.

So far the Ukrainian precedent had been followed ; and as
Riga had a large native industrial proletariat, the foundations of
Soviet power seemed more solid on the shores of the Baltic than
in the Ukraine. But here the ubiquity of British naval power
was the decisive factor. With the termination of hostilities against
Germany British naval units appeared in the Baltic. The Estonian
Soviet Republic collapsed in January 1919. The Latvian Soviet
Republic held out in Riga for five months and then succumbed to
the threat of British naval guns. In both countries the bourgeois
governments, restored under British patronage, had time to consolidate their authority. Thereafter, the Yudenich adventure [3]
once liquidated, the Soviet Government reconsidered its attitude.
The two bourgeois governments had shown greater strength and
cohesion than had been expected ; and their hostility to Yudenich

---

[1] Stalin, *Sochineniya*, iv, 178. The article containing this declaration
ppeared both in *Pravda* and in *Zhizn' Natsional'nostei*.

[2] The proclamations are in *Politika Sovetskoi Vlasti po Natsional'nomu
Voprosu* (1920), pp. 52-54, art. 76 ; pp. 133-134, art. 168 ; the decrees of
recognition in Klyuchnikov i Sabanin, *Mezhdunarodnaya Politika*, ii (1926),
206-208. These were decrees of Sovnarkom : they were confirmed for greater
solemnity by a resolution of VTsIK (*ibid.* ii, 208-209).

[3] In October 1919 the " white " General Yudenich, with British support,
launched from bases in Estonia an offensive against Petrograd which narrowly
failed of its object. Since Yudenich's aims included the restoration of the
Russian Empire within its former boundaries, his campaign met with no
sympathy from the Estonian and Latvian Governments.

had shown that they were not altogether unfriendly to the Soviet Republic. Above all, now that foreign trade was beginning to come within the orbit of Soviet policy (the allied blockade was lifted in January 1920), there would be some advantage in treating the ports of Riga and Tallinn as a sort of no-man's-land between the capitalist and the Soviet worlds. It was decided to follow the Finnish rather than the Ukrainian precedent, to drop the project of Estonian and Latvian Soviet republics and to recognize the bourgeois governments as beneficiaries of the right of national self-determination. Peace treaties were concluded with Estonia on February 2, 1920,[1] and with Latvia on August 11, 1920.[2] The régime thus established lasted for just twenty years.

The third Baltic country, Lithuania, followed the destiny of Latvia and Estonia with a few variations. A bourgeois national council, the Taryba, was set up during the winter of 1917-1918. Like the White Russian Rada of February 1918, it was essentially a German creation, and, with the compliance of the German occupying authorities, proclaimed the independence of Lithuania on February 16, 1918.[3] After the German collapse a provisional workers' and peasants' government was proclaimed in Lithuania,[4] and — somewhat prematurely — recognized by Petrograd at the same time as its more fully developed Latvian counterpart, on December 22, 1918.[5] In the following month the bourgeois Taryba was actually evicted from Vilna, and Soviet power established there. In April 1919 the capture of Vilna by the Polish army put an end both to projects for a federation between Lithuanian and White Russian Soviet Republics, and to the existence of Soviet Lithuania. A year and three months later, when Soviet armies retook Vilna in the course of the Polish war, other counsels had come into fashion. On July 12, 1920, a

---

[1] *Sobranie Uzakonenii, 1920*, No. 7, art. 44. The first Soviet approach to the bourgeois Estonian Government had been made in September 1919, but rejected by the latter on the ground that it did not wish to act independently of its neighbours (Klyuchnikov i Sabanin, *Mezhdunarodnaya Politika*, ii (1926), 344-346, 387-388); similar overtures at the same time to Finland, Latvia, and Lithuania were apparently ignored (*ibid.* ii, 383-384).

[2] *Sobranie Uzakonenii, 1920*, No. 95, art. 514.

[3] The official Lithuanian documents for this period are collected in P. Klimas, *Le Développement de l'État Lithuanien* (Paris, 1919).

[4] *Istorik Marksist*, No. 2-3, 1935, pp. 50-52.

[5] *Sobranie Uzakonenii, 1917-1918*, No. 98, art. 1006.

treaty of peace, parallel with the Estonian and Latvian treaties of the same year, was signed with a bourgeois Lithuanian Government; [1] and, though this did not save Lithuania later in the same year from losing Vilna to the Polish freebooter Zeligowski, Soviet recognition was not withdrawn from the Lithuanian Government, which transferred its seat to Kovno.

Lithuania, though slightly larger and more populous than Latvia or Estonia, was an almost exclusively peasant country, without a proletariat and with only a small handful of intellectuals. Its claim to independence, whether under bourgeois or under Soviet auspices, rested on precarious foundations, drawing the major part of its support, moral and material, from a large Lithuanian population in the United States. The main interest of Lithuanian independence for Soviet Russia was negative. Were Lithuania not independent, it was likely to fall within the Polish orbit; on the other hand, an independent Lithuania could be a thorn in the side of Poland. Here, therefore, it was a Soviet interest to give the widest possible scope to the principle of national self-determination.

(b) The Eastern Borderlands

The western borderlands of the RSFSR were inhabited by peoples who, whether Slav or non-Slav, stood within the wide circle of European civilization, shared the Russian tradition and had attained standards of culture and material welfare not lower, and sometimes appreciably higher, than the Great Russians themselves. The question of their relation to a predominantly Great Russian central unit was analogous to that presented in western Europe, say, by the Czechs in the Habsburg empire before 1918 or by the Slovaks and Sudeten Germans in Czechoslovakia after 1918. The alternative solutions of secession, federation, autonomy or integral incorporation were all open, and arguments could be adduced for each. But, whatever the solution, the issues raised were of the same nature as those known to western Europe as " minorities " questions. The eastern borderlands, meaning the lands of the Volga basin and of the northern slopes of the Caucasus, and Central Asia east of the Caspian Sea, presented problems of a different order. The populations of these regions, by their

[1] *Sobranie Uzakonenii, 1920*, No. 96, art. 515.

origins, by their language and by the still remaining vestiges of a mediaeval Mongol civilization, belonged to Asia rather than to Europe. Some ten millions of them were still nomadic, and primitive tribal organization was not extinct. Standards of living and culture set them far beneath the Russians and the peoples of the western borderlands. Here the sparsely scattered Russian inhabitants played the part of settlers and colonizers. Engels had written in the 1850s of these regions :

> Russian rule for all its nastiness, all its Slav slovenliness, has a civilizing significance for the Black and Caspian seas, for Central Asia, for the Bashkirs and Tatars.[1]

The issues raised by their relation to the central unit, or by projects for their emancipation, were in western terms not " minorities " but " colonial " questions. In Soviet literature the " national " and " colonial " questions were commonly linked together.

In the western borderlands the application of the principle of self-determination had resulted before the end of 1920 in the recognition of independent non-Soviet republics in Poland, Finland, Estonia, Latvia and Lithuania, and in the establishment of independent Ukrainian and White Russian Soviet Republics in close but still undefined relations with the Russian Soviet Republic. In the east the solution was less clear cut, partly owing to the inherent complexities of the situation, partly owing to the varying incidence of the civil war. But the broad pattern remained everywhere the same. The first stage of the revolution had proclaimed the principle of national self-determination, taking the practical form of a demand for autonomy rather than for complete independence. The Bolsheviks, by asserting this principle more vigorously and more consistently than the Provisional Government, at first secured unqualified support from the national movements of the eastern peoples. But when these same Bolsheviks, after the October revolution, appeared in the form of a Russian government (however disguised in name) ruling from Petrograd, and when, by passing over to the second stage of the revolution, they explicitly or implicitly challenged the existing social order, the self-constituted national leaders transferred their

[1] *Karl Marx-Friedrich Engels: Historisch-Kritische Gesamtausgabe*, III^{er} Teil, i, 206.

allegiance to the forces of counter-revolution. This step had, however, the same sequel as in the Ukraine. None of the " white " generals who led the campaign against the Soviet Government had any sympathy for the national aspirations of the backward peoples of the former Russian Empire, which they were fighting to reconstitute, so that the national leaders of these peoples found themselves between the devil who promised them only a return to the Tsarist yoke and the deep sea of social revolution. Hence the civil war sealed the bankruptcy of what may be called by analogy the " bourgeois " national movements of the eastern peoples, and hastened the Soviet authorities on the path of transition from national to social revolution.

Broadly speaking, the civil war marked the dividing line between the two phases of Soviet policy in the eastern borderlands. Unrest among the Muslim peoples of the Tsarist empire had begun to make itself felt even before the February revolution.[1] Among the Tatars of the Volga, who alone possessed the rudiments of a commercial middle class, among their immediate neighbours, the Bashkirs, formerly nomadic, but now mainly settled in agriculture and forestry, and among the still predominantly nomadic Kazakhs (incorrectly known to nineteenth-century writers by the more familiar name of Kirgiz),[2] who occupied the vast steppes stretching eastward from Kazan far across Central Asia, incipient national movements, fostered by tiny groups of intellectuals, had existed since the revolution of 1905.

[1] S. M. Dimanshtein, an official of Narkomnats, has an account of the effects of the 1905 revolution among these peoples in *Revolyutsiya i Natsional'nosti*, Nos. 8 and 9, 1930, and No. 1, 1931. His statement that they called themselves Muslims because their tribal or national names " did not please Russian officialdom " (*ibid*. No. 1, 1931, p. 73) is, however, only partially correct : the consciousness of many of them was as much religious as national.

[2] " Kazakh " was the original name of the mainly nomadic Turki-speaking inhabitants of the vast and thinly populated Central Asian steppes stretching eastward and north-eastward from the Caspian Sea. In the eighteenth and nineteenth centuries, however, the name was popularly bestowed on the colonies of military settlers, mainly Russian, in the outlying or newly conquered regions of the empire (in western parlance " Cossacks ") ; and the original Kazakhs came to be called by Russian and western writers " Kirgiz ", the name of a much smaller settled, but also Turki-speaking, people in the mountain country on the borders of Sinkiang. The Soviet Government and Soviet writers restored their rightful name to the Kazakhs of Central Asia, and called their territory Kazakhstan, though the name Kirgiz was still officially applied to them until the later 1920s.

These movements were fanned by the colonizing policy of the Tsarist régime which, partly by settling the natives and partly by importing settlers from elsewhere, had sought to extend and improve the cultivation of the soil. The filching of their traditional grazing grounds from the Kazakhs for occupation by Russian settlers was a perennial source of embitterment, and, followed by attempts to mobilize the population for labour during the war, had led to a serious Kazakh rebellion in 1916. Further south, among the more settled population of Khiva, Bokhara and Turkestan — the relics of the mediaeval empire of Gengis Khan — the same ferment was at work. During the winter of 1916–1917 the semi-independent khan of Bokhara had been compelled to call in Russian armies to repress a rebellion of his subjects.

These symptoms were the precursors of the general movement of 1917. In May of that year a first all-Russian Muslim congress met in Petrograd to demand not national independence but national autonomy, the main controversy being between a majority which demanded " a democratic republic on national-territorial-federal principles " and a minority which would have been content with cultural autonomy within a unitary Russian state.[1] In the confusion then prevailing throughout Russia the different Muslim peoples set to work to realize their ambitions. A second all-Russian Muslim congress, meeting in Kazan in July 1917, was mainly controlled by the Tatars who, as the most advanced of the Muslim peoples, sought to dominate the Muslim national movement and even played with pan-Turanian aspirations. A Bashkir congress was held simultaneously at Orenburg to demand autonomy for the Bashkirs. About the same time a Kazakh congress assembled, also in Orenburg, and set up a national council under the traditional name of Alash-Orda (" the Horde of Alash ", the probably mythical ancestor of the Kazakhs) ; and a programme was issued declaring that " Russia should become a democratic federal republic " with Kazakhstan as an autonomous unit.[2] At various dates in the summer of 1917 the smaller Muslim nationalities of the Volga basin, the Mari, the

---

[1] *Revolyutsiya i Natsional'nyi Vopros : Dokumenty i Materialy* ed. S. M. Dimanshtein, iii (1930), 294-305.

[2] *Ibid.* iii, 315-317, 328, 363-365.

Votyaks and the Chuvashes, held congresses and put forward similar claims ;[1] and two congresses of the Muslim tribes of the northern Caucasus took place at Vladikavkaz in May and September.[2] None of these was revolutionary in the social sense, and nearly all of them (the Kazakh movement was perhaps an exception) had a more or less marked religious flavour. Of the Bashkir Congress it was recorded that it was composed of mullahs, elders and *kulaks*, a fee of 50 roubles a head being charged for admission ;[3] and the Muslims of the northern Caucasus elected a mullah named Gotsinsky as their leader with the title of Mufti.[4]

In these circumstances it was not surprising that the national question in the east should at first have presented itself to the Soviet leaders almost exclusively in its Muslim guise. The first act of the Soviet Government in this sphere was to follow up the general Declaration of Rights of the Peoples of Russia with a special appeal " To all Muslim Toilers of Russia and the East ". Having announced that the burning desire of the Russian people was " to obtain an honourable peace and to aid the oppressed peoples of the world in order to bring them independence ", it continued :

> Muslims of Russia, Tatars of the Volga and the Crimea, Kirgiz [i.e. Kazakhs] and Sarts of Siberia and Turkestan, Turks and Tatars of Transcaucasia, Chechens and Mountaineers of the Caucasus, and all you whose mosques and oratories have been destroyed, whose beliefs and customs have been trampled under foot by the Tsars and the oppressors of Russia. Your beliefs and usages, your national and cultural institutions are henceforth free and inviolable. Organize your national life in complete freedom. You have the right. Know that your rights, like those of all the peoples of Russia, are under the powerful safeguard of the revolution and of its organs, the Soviets of workers, soldiers and peasants. Lend your support to this revolution and to its government.

It then passed to the cause of the Muslims of the east beyond the old Russian border, who were abjured to overthrow their oppressors and also promised aid.[5] A decree of January 19, 1918,

---

[1] *Revolyutsiya i Natsional'nyi Vopros: Dokumenty i Materialy*, ed. S. M. Dimanshtein, iii (1930), 414-428.   [2] *Ibid.* iii, 372-377.
[3] S. Atnagulov, *Bashkiriya* (1925), p. 57.
[4] *Revolyutsiya i Natsional'nyi Vopros: Dokumenty i Materialy*, ed. S. M. Dimanshtein, iii (1930), 377.
[5] Klyuchnikov i Sabanin, *Mezhdunarodnaya Politika*, ii (1926), 94-96 ; French translation in *Revue du Monde Musulman*, li (1922), 7-9. The fact that

created the commissariat for internal Muslim affairs: the commissar was a Tatar, his chief assistants a Tatar and Bashkir respectively.[1] A significant gesture of this period was the handing over to " the regional congress of Muslims at Petrograd " of the so-called " sacred Koran of Osman " which had formerly been brought from Samarkand to the imperial library.[2]   Another was the issue by the commissariat of Muslim affairs, on the occasion of the rupture at Brest-Litovsk and the renewed German offensive, of an appeal " to the Muslim revolutionary people " to " hasten to the red banner of the Muslim socialist army ".[3]   A congress of Muslim communist organizations held in Moscow in November 1918 set up a " central bureau of Muslim communist organizations " which issued propaganda material in many languages, including a daily paper in Turkish, sent out agitators and organized local printing presses.[4]   A second congress in November 1919 was addressed by both Lenin and Stalin in person.[5]

The second stage of Soviet policy, which set in early in 1918, was marked, in the east as in the Ukraine, by active intervention against the " bourgeois " national governments which had sprung into life in the interval between the February and October revolution.   These governments, like the Ukrainian Rada, tended after October to turn against the Soviet Government in Petrograd, whether because it was thought to threaten the existing social order or because, being a Russian government, it was regarded as naturally inimical to the former subject peoples.   A Bashkir government under one Validov, which had proclaimed an autonomous Bashkir state after the October revolution, went over to the Orenburg Cossacks who were in open warfare against the

the wrongs of " Indians " and " Armenians " are mentioned in the last part of the declaration suggests that the term " Muslim " had become the symbol in Bolshevik eyes for all peoples of the east.

[1] *Sobranie Uzakonenii, 1917-1918*, No. 17, art. 243.

[2] *Ibid*. No. 6, art. 103.   The ultimate result of the gesture has been the disappearance of this famous Koran, the present whereabouts of which are unknown.

[3] *Politika Sovetskoi Vlasti po Natsional'nomu Voprosu* (1920), p. 80, art. 99.

[4] *Vos'moi S"ezd RKP(B)* (1933), pp. 433-434.   The name of the bureau was changed in March 1919 to " central bureau of communist organizations of peoples of the east " (*Zhizn' Natsional'nostei*, No. 8 (16), March 9, 1919): by this time it had been placed under the authority of Narkomnats.

[5] Lenin, *Sochineniya*, xxiv, 542-551 ; Stalin, *Sochineniya*, iv, 279-280.

Soviet Government; [1] and this was typical of the prevailing attitude of the " nationalists ". The split led the Soviet Government to seek support among the quasi-" proletarian " (the term being, strictly speaking, as inappropriate here as the term " bourgeois ") elements in the regions concerned and to foster their incipient discontent and aspirations — the eastern counterpart of the western policy of " self-determination for the workers ". This period, unlike its predecessor, was marked by vigorous attacks on the Muslim religion and its traditions and practices, partly, no doubt, on ideological grounds, but partly also to destroy the influence of the mullahs, who had often been the backbone of the " bourgeois " national movements. The autonomous governments of the Tatars and Bashkirs were supplanted by the proclamation in March 1918 of a joint " Tatar-Bashkir Soviet republic of the Russian Soviet Federation " [2] which would also have embraced the Chuvashes and the Maris; and this was followed by a decree of April 13, 1918, dissolving the former Tatar national council and by the arrest of Tatar leaders. [3] According to one account this policy was adopted by VTsIK and imposed by Stalin on Narkomnats in face of strong opposition from his colleagues there. [4] That it was designed to serve as a precedent was shown by an important declaration signed by Stalin as People's Commissar for Nationalities and addressed " To the Soviets of Kazan, Ufa, Orenburg and Ekaterinburg, to the Sovnarkom of Turkestan and others ". Observing that " the revolution begun at the centre has been spreading in the borderlands, especially in the eastern borderlands, with some delay ", the declaration notes that " special measures are necessary to draw the toiling and

[1] S. Atnagulov, *Bashkiriya* (1925), pp. 56–59. An article in *Voprosy Istorii*, No. 4, 1948, p. 26, gives the date of the agreement between Validov and Dutov, the ataman of the Orenburg Cossacks, as November 11/24, 1917.

[2] The proclamation took the form of a decree of Sovnarkom (*Sobranie Uzakonenii, 1917–1918*, No. 30, art. 394). The " commissariat for the affairs of the Muslims of internal Russia " was to appoint a commission to organize and convene " a constituent congress of Soviets " for the new republic. Strictly speaking, no " Russian Soviet Federation " was yet in existence; the constitution of the RSFSR was at this time still in process of drafting.

[3] *Revue du Monde Musulman*, li (1922), 131.

[4] Pestkovsky, quoted in L. Trotsky, *Stalin* (N.Y., 1946), pp. 262–263. This appears to be confirmed by an article in *Voprosy Istorii*, No. 4, 1948, p. 34, which speaks of " the opposition on the one hand of Bashkir bourgeois nationalists and on the other hand of Bukharinites who rejected national self-determination ".

exploited masses of these borderlands into the process of revolutionary development ".   Since " the bourgeois-national groups demand autonomy in order to convert it into a weapon for the oppression of their own masses ", salvation can be found only in " organizing local congresses of Soviets and proclaiming Soviet autonomy ".[1]

The policy of an enforced sovietization of the eastern borderlands, based on the hypothetical support of native revolutionary masses hostile both to bourgeois nationalism and to Islam, proved a fiasco. Though the influence of the mullahs and bourgeois intellectuals who headed the embryonic national movements can easily be exaggerated, especially among the nomadic peoples, there was even less understanding or sympathy for the purposes and methods of the Bolsheviks ; and plans hatched in Moscow by men familiar with western conditions had little appeal to communities engaged in primitive agriculture or to nomads whose problems were the insufficiency of their flocks and denial of access to grazing grounds.[2] It was impossible to obtain any serious Tatar or Bashkir backing for the proposed Tatar-Bashkir Soviet republic ; the Chuvashes, who, according to a local historian, wanted neither independence nor autonomy, protested against their inclusion in it ;[3] and, though preparatory work was being done in Moscow in May 1918,[4] the republic never in fact came into being.   The civil war descended on a scene of widespread anarchy and confused and conflicting aspirations ;   and in June the anti-Bolshevik Samara

[1] *Politika Sovetskoi Vlasti po Natsional'nomu Voprosu* (1920), pp. 8-9, art. 4.

[2] The situation at this period in Kazakhstan was described by a writer in the official journal of Narkomnats : " The principles of the second revolution were incomprehensible to the Kirgiz [i.e. the Kazakhs] because neither capitalism nor class differentiation existed among them ; even their idea of property was different ; for example, many ordinary objects of daily use were considered in Kirgizia [i.e. Kazakhstan] as common property ". At the same time the October revolution horrified the Kazakhs by its external manifestations. The forms which the Bolshevik movement took in central Russia were unknown to the Kazakhs, while in the borderlands " it was followed by violence, plundering and abuses, as well as by a quite peculiar form of dictatorship. Thus in reality the movement in the borderlands was often not a revolution, as is generally understood, but pure anarchy." The same writer adds in regard to Soviet organizations which had seized power in Semipalatinsk and other towns in Kazakhstan : " The members of these organizations were simply adventurers who took the name of Bolsheviks, and often behaved in a shocking manner ". (*Zhizn' Natsional'nostei*, No. 29 (37), August 3, 1919).

[3] D. P. Petrov, *Chuvashiya* (1926), p. 70.

[4] Stalin, *Sochineniya*, iv, 85-92.

government began to extend its authority over a large part of the middle and lower Volga. The only constructive achievement of the year 1918 in all this region related to a non-Muslim community on its western confines. In October 1918 the 400,000 Germans of the Volga were allowed to constitute themselves as an autonomous " workers' commune " with its own congress of Soviets and executive committee.[1]

In other Muslim communities a similar policy was pursued, with the same inconclusive results. In the Crimea a " directorate " set up by a Tatar national assembly, formed in the interval between the February and October revolutions, was overthrown by the Bolsheviks in January 1918, the taking of Sevastopol being long remembered for the atrocities which accompanied it; and a Tatar Soviet republic of the Crimea was proclaimed in its place. But this was short-lived. The Germans, advancing through the Ukraine, set up a puppet government in the Crimea under a Russian general named Sulkevich, whose rule, like that of Skoropadsky in the Ukraine, ended with the downfall of German power in November 1918. Thereupon a group of " white " refugees from Bolshevik rule, a majority of them Kadets, formed a government of the Crimea which was pan-Russian in composition and sentiment and had no pretension to represent the Crimean Tatars. This government, dividing its authority somewhat uneasily with Denikin's military administration, and enjoying some measure of recognition and support from the allies, maintained its position till after Denikin's defeat.[2] In the northern Caucasus and in Dagestan an intermittent struggle was waged throughout 1918 between Bolsheviks and local nationalists, the latter aided and abetted by the Turks, till Denikin's armies swept over the region in the spring and summer of 1919, outdoing all the hardships and horrors inflicted in the earlier stages of the struggle.[3]

[1] *Sobranie Uzakonenii, 1917–1918*, No. 79, art. 831. The commune was soon transformed into an autonomous region of the RSFSR, and later, at the end of 1923, into an autonomous SSR (*Sobranie Uzakonenii, 1924*, No. 7, art. 33).

[2] An account of this short-lived Crimean government was afterwards published by its foreign minister (M. Vinaver, *Nashe Pravitel'stvo*, Paris, 1928).

[3] The fullest source for the complicated history of Dagestan from 1917 to April 1920 is E. Samursky, *Dagestan* (1925), pp. 61–76; see also *Revue du Monde Musulman*, li (1922), 79–84; Stalin, *Sochineniya*, iv, 97–99, 106–114. A picturesque but confused account of events in the northern Caucasus was given by a delegate to the Baku congress of eastern peoples (*1⁵ᵗ S"ezd Narodov Vostoka* (1921), pp. 93–95).

The first Soviet moves after the landslide of 1918 were dictated by the exigencies of the civil war and by the opportunities which it offered. By March 1919 the centres of fighting had moved away from the Volga. The Bashkirs, exposed to the persecutions both of Kolchak and of Dutov, the ataman of the Orenburg Cossacks,[1] were ready to listen to overtures from Moscow; and an agreement was concluded between the RSFSR and the government of an " Autonomous Bashkir Soviet Republic " under the leadership of Validov, temporarily restored to high favour.[2] Further east similar influences were at work. The Kazakh Alash-Orda split into two, one section going over to the Bolsheviks. In June 1919 a decree was issued setting up a " revolutionary committee " for the administration of Kazakh territory, providing for separate jurisdiction over the Russian and Kazakh communities. The decree attempted for the first time to meet Kazakh agrarian grievances. While not evicting Russian settlers already in possession, it forbade any further settlement at the expense of the Kazakhs even on lands already allocated for settlement — a standstill in the arbitrary taking over of Kazakh land, though not a radical, still less a revolutionary, solution.[3] This measure was clearly designed to rally the support of wavering Kazakhs in the civil war. The Alash-Orda was declared dissolved.[4] A month later a pro-

[1] According to the notes to Stalin, *Marxism and the National and Colonial Question* (Engl. transl. 2nd ed. 1936), p. 297, " the great power of Kolchak, who, incidentally, issued a decree abolishing the autonomy of Bashkiria, compelled Validov's government in 1919 under the pressure of the masses to declare adherence to the Soviet Government "; this is confirmed in substance by V. Chernov, *Mes tribulations en Russie* (Paris, 1921), p. 10.

[2] *Sobranie Uzakonenii, 1919*, No. 46, art. 451. During the summer of 1919 Bashkiria was once more overrun by " Kolchak's bands ", and it was not till August 1919 that Soviet authority was finally established (*Politika Sovetskoi Vlasti po Natsional'nomu Voprosu* (1920), pp. 19-20, arts. 18-19). Validov appeared at the seventh All-Russian Congress of Soviets in Moscow in December 1919 as spokesman of " Bashkir proletariat and Bashkir and Kirgiz [i.e. Kazakh] poor peasants " and celebrated the exploits of the Red Bashkir army in defending " the proletarian capital, Petrograd " against Yudenich (7[i] *Vserossiiskii S"ezd Sovetov* (1920), p. 17). At this time he posed as a communist and was trying to form an independent Bashkir Communist Party (S. Atnagulov, *Bashkiriya* (1925), pp. 71-72). For Validov see further p. 326, note 3 below.

[3] *Sobranie Uzakonenii, 1919*, No. 36, art. 354.

[4] Castagné, a hostile witness, characteristically mentions the dissolution of Alash-Orda, but not the June decree; he adds that " the struggle which everywhere else in Russia was an affair of classes became among the Kazakhs a struggle of clans and tribes " (*Revue du Monde Musulman*, li (1922), 175-177).

clamation was issued to the Kalmyks, an isolated, mainly nomadic group some 200,000 strong, speaking a Mongol language and Buddhist in religion, living round the head of the Caspian Sea near Astrakhan : it announced the intention to convene a Kalmyk workers' congress, and appealed for enlistment in the Red Army to fight against Denikin.[1]   This was followed by a decree, almost identical in language with that issued a few days earlier to the Kazakhs, assuring to the " toiling Kalmyk people " the full enjoyment of their land and forbidding the allocation of any further Kalmyk land to Russian settlers.[2]   But these enactments of 1919, for the most part, served purposes of propaganda and exhortation rather than the establishment of working social and political institutions; and throughout the eastern borderlands little or nothing was created at this time that proved durable.

The opposition which the Bolsheviks continued to encounter almost everywhere in the eastern borderlands down to the end of 1919 was in large part the product of fluctuating military fortunes.   So long as the fate of the Soviet régime was in the balance, and so long as its hold on these regions remained intermittent and precarious, the local populations were unlikely to rally to it.   But the opposition was intensified by the intransigent attitude of Soviet emissaries towards the Muslim religion.   The Soviet leaders had had little knowledge of the eastern parts of the vast domain which they had so unexpectedly acquired.   They had in their minds a vague picture of oppressed peoples awaiting emancipation from superstitious mullahs as eagerly as from Tsarist administrators; and they were astonished to discover that, while the hold of Islam over the nomadic peoples and in parts of Central Asia was little more than nominal, it remained elsewhere a tenacious and vigorous institution which offered far fiercer resistance than the Orthodox Church to new beliefs and new practices.[3]   In regions where it was strong — notably in the

[1] *Politika Sovetskoi Vlasti po Natsional'nomu Voprosu* (1920), pp. 38-39, art. 56.

[2] *Sobranie Uzakonenii, 1919*, No. 37, art. 368. An account of the development of Soviet Kalmykia, perhaps too rosy in detail, but conveying a clear general picture, is in T. K. Borisov, *Kalmykiya* (1926).

[3] A well-known Muslim Bolshevik of this period states that a Muslim *mechet'*, or parish, averaged 700 to 1000 inhabitants and had a mullah and two assistants, whereas the Orthodox priest had on an average 10,000 to 12,000 parishioners (M. Sultan-Galiev, *Metody Antireligioznoi Propagandy Sredi Musul'man* (1922), p. 4).

northern Caucasus [1] — the Muslim religion was a social, legal and political as well as religious institution regulating the daily way of life of its members in almost every particular. The imams and mullahs were judges, law-givers, teachers and intellectuals, as well as political and sometimes military leaders. That this authority was usually wielded over a population enjoying low economic and cultural standards of life gave the Bolsheviks a case against them; but it made the problem all the harder to face. By the end of 1919 the Soviet authorities seem to have reached the conclusion that the only course was to divide the priesthood against itself by wooing the support of its younger members.[2] This involved a compromise with Islam; in other words, an abandonment of the stiff ideological attitude of the civil-war period and a return to the toleration of the first winter of the revolution.

The year 1920 marked a sharp change in relations between Moscow and the eastern borderlands. Hitherto Soviet policy had looked primarily to the west, which had been at first the source of hopes for world revolution and later the source of danger to the survival of the régime. But the main danger was now over, though it revived for a moment in the Polish invasion of May 1920. The defeat of Kolchak and Denikin made it possible for the first time to bring order to the eastern borderlands, and to embark on Lenin's project of drawing the revolutionary masses of the exploited nations of the east into an alliance with the revolutionary workers and peasants of Russia. The weight of Soviet policy shifted decisively from west to east. The congress of eastern peoples in Baku in September 1920 inaugurated the crusade of the eastern nations under Soviet leadership against the imperialism of the west.

The same moment brought a corresponding change of attitude among the eastern peoples themselves. In all these regions the ultimate effect of the civil war waged by the " whites " with foreign backing had been to consolidate the prestige and authority of the Russian Soviet Government. In Russian and non-Russian areas

---

[1] E. Samursky, *Dagestan* (1925), pp. 126-137, draws a vivid picture of Muslim power in Dagestan, where it successfully resisted effective Soviet penetration from 1917 to 1921.

[2] Examples of this policy are given *ibid.* pp. 133-136.

alike, the scarcely veiled ambition of the " white " generals to restore the old system of land tenure and industrial ownership won the hesitating sympathy of a majority of peasants and workers for the Soviet cause. In the non-Russian areas their determination to restore the unity of the Russian Empire with its tradition of the complete political and cultural subordination of non-Russian elements made a sombre contrast with Soviet promises of unfettered national self-determination, conditioned though these were by certain political and social presuppositions. In 1918 and 1919 the Muslim peoples had been generally recalcitrant to the Soviet power. Experience of the heavier hand of the " white " armies was one of the factors which from 1920 onwards made them more amenable to Soviet pressure and guidance.

In pursuance of this policy decrees were issued by VTsIK in the course of May 1920 creating Bashkir and Tatar Autonomous SSRs and a Chuvash Autonomous Region;[1] and these were followed later in the year by the creation of a Kazakh Autonomous SSR and a Kalmyk Autonomous Region.[2] This did not mean that difficulties were at an end. Organization was everywhere embryonic; and boundaries were often still in dispute. In some places opposition from " bourgeois nationalist " elements had still to be crushed by force. In Bashkiria the creation in May 1920 of the Bashkir Autonomous SSR, which involved the removal of the capable and troublesome Validov, was followed by serious trouble throughout the summer and autumn of 1920, including a movement for the restoration of the Validov government. Conditions of anarchy and civil war prevailed throughout the territory; according to one authority, " a general Bashkir rising was narrowly averted ".[3] In Kazakhstan the land question re-

---

[1] *Sobranie Uzakonenii, 1920*, No. 45, art. 203; No. 51, art. 222; No. 59, art. 267.

[2] *Politika Sovetskoi Vlasti po Natsional'nomu Voprosu* (1920), p. 44, art. 65; p. 41, art. 60.

[3] S. Atnagulov, *Bashkiriya* (1925), pp. 72-74; further details are added by the notes to Stalin, *Marxism and the National and Colonial Question* (Engl. transl. 2nd ed. 1936), pp. 297-298, and by Castagné in *Revue du Monde Musulman*, li (1922), 162-163. In the autumn of 1921 the central committee of the party had to deal with disputes between two groups of party workers in Bashkiria who " had taken on a national colour and engaged in fierce mutual strife ". Goloshchekin, a member of the central committee, was sent to Bashkiria, but " did not succeed in fully quelling these disputes " (*Izvestiya Tsentral'nogo Komiteta Rossiiskoi Kommunisticheskoi Partii (Bol'shevikov)*, No. 34, November

mained particularly acute, and since the Russian settlers and even the settled Kazakhs tended to support the régime set up on the initiative of Moscow, while the Kazakh nomads, in so far as they were at all politically conscious, regarded the Russian Bolshevik as the natural successor of the Russian Tsar, the obstacles to any far-reaching agrarian reform were serious. There were, moreover, solid reasons to resist the break up of cultivated holdings for the purpose of restoring land to Kazakh nomads, whether for grazing or for settlement; for such a step, however just and however politically expedient, could hardly result in anything but an immediate decline in production. Accurate information on the extent to which a redistribution of land taken from the Kazakhs actually took place is not obtainable. But it is certain that the famine of 1921 struck Kazakhstan, as well as the whole Volga region, with particular severity.[1]

In the northern Caucasus a general settlement was also reached before the end of 1920. Down to the autumn of that year the scene was still one of confusion. The mullah Gotsinsky still defied the Soviet power in Dagestan;[2] and further to the west the Cossacks of the Terek region rose in the rear of the Soviet forces facing Wrangel in the Don basin, and once more cut the vital communications between Moscow and Baku.[3] But by October 1920 an armistice was signed with Poland; the

---

1921, p. 5). Bashkiria became a sort of test case and controversy continued to rage round it, e.g. in *Proletarskaya Revolyutsiya*, Nos. 11 (58) and 12 (59), 1926; Nos. 3 (74) and 5 (76), 1928. The reminiscences of participants in the civil war are collected in *Grazhdanskaya Voina v Bashkirii* (Ufa, 1932). Further study of these sources might well throw fresh light on Soviet policy in the eastern borderlands at this period. Validov was a typical figure of the tiny bourgeois intelligentsia of these regions. A bourgeois nationalist opposed to social revolution of any far-reaching kind, he was driven over to the Bolsheviks during the civil war by the contempt of the " whites " for the claims of the small nationalities; when the civil war was over, he once more became anti-Bolshevik. He afterwards joined the Basmachi in Central Asia (see p. 332 below); became a well-known pan-Turanian propagandist and settled down at a German university; returned to Turkey and was condemned there in 1944 for treasonable pan-Turanian activities; and, finally, made his peace with the Turkish authorities, and published in Turkish in 1948 a strongly anti-Russian history of Turkestan under the title *Turkestan Tarihi*, of which an English translation is projected.

[1] Some rather disjointed notes by Castagné on events in Kazakhstan in 1920 and 1921 are in *Revue du Monde Musulman*, li (1922), 182-191: he was no longer in Central Asia at this time.

[2] Stalin, *Sochineniya*, iv, 397.   [3] *Ibid.* iv, 400.

armies of Wrangel were in full retreat towards the Crimea; and Stalin had defined in *Pravda* the new policy of " Soviet autonomy ".[1] In the same month Stalin set forth on an extended tour of the northern Caucasus. On November 13, 1920, he addressed a congress of the peoples of Dagestan at Temir-Khan-Shure, their temporary capital. The voice of authority was undisguised and unmistakable. Now that Wrangel had been defeated and peace concluded with Poland, " the Soviet Government is able to concern itself with the question of the autonomy of the Dagestan people ". It followed that Dagestan "should be governed according to its own peculiarities, its own way of life and customs ". Religious customs and practices would be undisturbed : " the Soviet Government considers the *shariat* as fully valid customary law ". On the other hand, " the autonomy of Dagestan does not mean and cannot mean its separation from Soviet Russia ".[2] Four days later a similar congress of the peoples of the Terek region, grouped together under the common name of " Mountaineers ", was held at Vladikavkaz. Here Stalin came " to declare the will of the Soviet Government in regard to the conditions of life of the peoples of the Terek and their relations with the Cossacks ". He had penalties as well as rewards to announce. Experience had shown that " the living together of the Mountaineers and the Cossacks within the limits of a single administrative unit led to endless disturbances ". The recent treachery of some of the Cossacks had compelled the Soviet authorities to expel the offending communities and to settle Mountaineers on their lands. It had now been decided to complete the process of separation between Cossacks and Mountaineers, making the river Terek the frontier-line between the Ukraine and a new autonomous Socialist Soviet Republic of the Mountaineers.[3] The sequel of the congresses at Temir-Khan-Shure and Vladikavkaz was the creation two months later by decree of VTsIK of two autonomous socialist Soviet republics — Dagestan, and the republic of the Mountaineers; the latter,

---

[1] See pp. 383-384 below.   [2] Stalin, *Sochineniya*, iv, 394-397.
[3] *Ibid.* iv, 399-403. This interesting instance of a transfer of populations appears to have been partly a reprisal and partly a precaution against future disturbances. There is no record to show on what scale transfers were actually carried out; nor is it clear whether Mountaineers were transferred from the north to the south bank of the Terek as well as Cossacks from south to north.

which had its capital at Vladikavkaz, was afterwards subdivided by the formation of several autonomous regions.[1]

The settlement reached throughout the eastern borderlands in the winter of 1920–1921 was the sequel of the crowning victory of Soviet arms in the civil war. The issue of power had been decided. Moscow was the ultimate source of authority and it was time to settle down under forms of government acceptable to Moscow and under rulers who, whether Russian or native, would work in harmony with Moscow. In all these territories autonomy was a reasonable solution of the administrative problem, since none of them could on any count be said to possess the elements of independence; and the degree of autonomy to be enjoyed in practice was limited not so much by the niggardliness of the sovereign power as by the limited capacity of the local authority. The constitutional form of the settlement was significant. No kind of agreement or stipulation was made for any of these territories between the central and the local power. Autonomy was granted in each case by a unilateral decision of the central authority. Thus the question of status was settled within the constitution of the RSFSR; the issue of the ultimate form of a wider union of socialist Soviet republics did not arise in the eastern European borderlands.

Of all the borderlands in this region, the Crimea was the last to be settled. Its history during the years of revolution had been particularly chequered. It was the last refuge of Wrangel, the last of the " white " generals; and after his final eviction at the end of 1920 the turbulent Tatar population continued for nearly a year to defy the Soviet administration. Finally, a decree of October 18, 1921, constituted a Crimean Autonomous SSR as a member of the RSFSR.[2]

(c) Central Asia

The region commonly known before 1914 as Russian Turkestan was a broad strip of territory running eastwards from the Caspian Sea along the northern frontiers of Persia, Afghanistan

---

[1] The acts of January 20, 1921, constituting the Dagestan Autonomous SSR and the Mountaineers' Autonomous SSR are in *Sobranie Uzakonenii, 1921*, No. 5, art. 39, and No. 6, art. 41 ; for eventual subdivisions see *Revue du Monde Musulman*, li (1922), 95-100.

[2] *Sobranie Uzakonenii, 1921*, No. 69, art. 556.

and India, and abutting on Sinkiang (the so-called " Chinese Turkestan ") in the east. It had formed part of the mediaeval empire of Gengis Khan; and its principal cities, Tashkent, Samarkand, Kokand, Bokhara, Khiva and Merv were full of the traditions and monuments of an ancient civilization. History, as well as a settled way of life, thus sharply distinguished the people of Turkestan from the nomad Kazakhs of the steppe country to the north, from whom they differed little in racial origin and speech. Except for the small Iranian group of Tajiks in the south-east, the population of Turkestan was uniformly of Turkish origin and spoke Turki dialects. The later division into Turkmen in the west, Uzbeks in the centre and Kirgiz in the east was partly a matter of administrative convenience; it was a product of local jealousies rather than of profound racial or linguistic or historical differences. Turkestan had been incorporated in the Tsarist empire only in the 1870s; the amir of Bokhara and the khan of Khiva had retained a nominal independence to the last. The remoteness of these provinces and their comparatively recent acquisition rendered Russian control here unusually weak. But Turkestan had become an important commercial centre, especially with the introduction of the cotton crop; and a total population of some 12,000,000 included 500,000 Russian immigrants.

Tashkent was the administrative centre of Turkestan and the home of the largest Russian colony; it was through Tashkent that the influence of Europe was chiefly radiated. The disturbing influences of the war of 1914 were intensified by the Kazakh rebellion of 1916 across the northern border, and by the presence in Turkestan of large masses of German and especially Austrian prisoners of war who even before the revolution were subjected to no very effective control. The February revolution was followed by the formation at Tashkent of a " Turkestan committee ", composed of officials and supporters of the Provisional Government, and of a Soviet of Workers' and Soldiers' Deputies of more radical complexion, whose president, Broido by name, though at this time still a Menshevik, was to play some part in Soviet eastern policy in the next few years.[1] Both these bodies were exclusively

[1] Broido was one of the five members of the collegium of Narkomnats, and afterward became director of the Communist University of Toilers of the East in Moscow.

or mainly Russian in composition. The only organized Muslim party in Turkestan, the Ulema, was composed of mullahs and landowners, and was even less disposed to the cause of social revolution than the Muslim movements of the Volga basin. As elsewhere in the Russian Empire the general breakdown of authority precipitated a demand for autonomy. Already in September 1917 a local coup by the central executive committee of the Tashkent Soviet overthrew the authorities of the Provisional Government. Tashkent thus became the seat of the first Soviet (though not yet Bolshevik) government to be established in the former dominions of the Tsars.[1] Within a few weeks of these events a rising of the Orenburg Cossacks under their ataman Dutov severed communications between Europe and Central Asia for the best part of two years. Throughout this time European Russia was deprived of the oil and cotton of Turkestan, and Turkestan was deprived of essential supplies of grain, so that famine occurred over large parts of Central Asia. In these difficult conditions the revolution in Turkestan was left to work itself out with little or no interference from the centre.[2]

The revolutionary movement at Tashkent was at the outset confined to the Russian colony. A resolution of the Tashkent congress of Soviets of November 19/December 2, 1917, expressly excluded Muslims from governmental posts ;[3] and one of the first acts of the new government was to suppress a revolt in the native quarters of the city. Meanwhile, however, a congress of

[1] *Proletarskaya Revolyutsiya*, No. 10 (33), 1924, pp. 138-161.

[2] The most satisfactory authority for the period is G. Safarov, *Kolonial'naya Revolyutsiya: Opyt' Türkestana* (1921) ; there is also a concise narrative by Castagné (who was himself in Turkestan until the summer of 1920) in *Revue du Monde Musulman*, l (1922), 28-73. What should be a valuable source 'or these events, *Pobeda Velikoi Oktyabr'skoi Sotsialisticheskoi Revolyutsii v Turkestane: Sbornik Dokumentov* (Tashkent, 1947), has not been available. A reviewer of this work in *Partiinaya Zhizn'*, No. 4, 1948, complains that it gives the impression " that the struggle of the toilers of Turkestan was cut off from the all-Russian revolutionary struggle, and that, in the first period of the existence of Soviet power, Turkestan, surrounded on all sides by enemies, was left to its fate " ; but he offers no serious evidence that this impression does not correspond to the facts. Safarov called Turkestan from 1917 to 1919 " the ideal ' closed commercial state ' of Johann Gottlieb Fichte " (*op. cit.* p. 75). Broido himself wrote in a contemporary journal : " For nearly two years Turkestan was left to itself. For nearly two years not only no Red Army help came from the centre in Moscow but there were practically no relations at all " (*Novyi Vostok*, ii (1922), 79).

[3] G. Safarov, *Kolonial'naya Revolyutsiya : Opyt' Turkestana* (1921), p. 70.

Muslims had met in Kokand, the chief town of the province of Fergana, and had proclaimed an autonomous Turkestan " in union with a federal democratic Russian republic ".[1]   The Tashkent government took the offensive and, after savage fighting, defeated its rival and captured Kokand.[2]   For the next five years Fergana was in a state of anarchy, being terrorized by the Basmachi — a generic regional name for bands of outlaws and adventurers who took to the mountains and lived mainly on banditry.[3]   On the other hand, a Soviet offensive against Bokhara which counted in vain on the aid of a " young Bokhara " party, a bourgeois nationalist group with pan-Turanian pretensions, failed; and on March 25, 1918, the Tashkent government concluded a treaty with the amir, recognizing him as an independent Power.[4]   Further west, the khan of Khiva was also left in temporary enjoyment of his independence:[5] and in the Turkmen territory east of the Caspian a short-lived anti-Bolshevik Russian government composed mainly of SRs established itself in June 1918 with the support of a small British force, which moved up through Persia and occupied Merv.[6]   Meanwhile the Tashkent government was completely surrounded by hostile or potentially hostile territory.   Another serious rebellion against it occurred in Tashkent in January 1919 and provoked fierce reprisals.   Its almost miraculous survival appears to have been the work of a few capable and ruthless men in a situation where no alternative power was readily available.

[1] G. Safarov, *Kolonial'naya Revolyutsiya: Opyt' Turkestana* (1921), p. 71.

[2] A full account of the Kokand government and its fate is given by P. Alexenkov in *Revolyutsiya v Srednei Azii: Sbornik* (Tashkent), i (1928), 21-40 ; ii (1929), 43-81, including the act of surrender which was signed on February 22, 1918. Among the items in the Kokand government's programme were the maintenance of private property, of the *shariat*, and of the seclusion of women. It received support from some bourgeois Russians hostile to the Bolsheviks. But in this struggle between revolutionary Russians and conservative Muslims national feeling seems in general to have counted most.

[3] For short first-hand accounts of the Basmachi see *Revue du Monde Musulman*, li (1922), 236-243 ; *Novyi Vostok*, ii (1922), 274-278.

[4] *Revue du Monde Musulman*, li (1922), 217-218.

[5] Events in Khiva from 1917–1920 are described in *Novyi Vostok*, iii (1923), 241-257.

[6] An account of this " government ", which lasted from August 1918 to March or April 1919, is given by Castagné in *Revue du Monde Musulman*, li (1922), 192-201 ; for the British share see *Journal of the Central Asian Society*, ix (1922), ii, 96-110.

The Communist Party in Turkestan was a young organization. Before the October revolution social-democrats were rare in Turkestan and no distinction was made between Bolsheviks and Mensheviks. Not till June 1918 did the Turkestan Bolsheviks hold their first modest congress of some forty delegates. Paucity of numbers was, moreover, the least of the weaknesses of the new party. Born after the victory of the revolution, it had not served its apprenticeship as a fighting organization. It was, so to speak, an " official " party from the first, and the quality of its membership suffered accordingly. The Russian colony in Turkestan fell into two main categories. The first consisted of officials, merchants and members of the intelligentsia ; the second of Russian workers, most of them railwaymen. Both these groups had their reasons for joining the party, which also included, according to one witness, such anomalous figures as " the communist priest, the Russian police-officer and the *kulak* from Semirechie who still employs dozens of hired labourers, has hundreds of heads of cattle and hunts down Kazakhs like wild beasts ".[1] The Turkestan Bolsheviks, fired by Russian example, quickly gained the ascendancy. But left to their own devices, and deprived of direct guidance from Moscow, they fell into two major heresies. In the first place, like the Mensheviks, they regarded the peasants as essentially counter-revolutionary and rejected the Leninist doctrine of an alliance between the proletariat and the poor peasantry to drive home the revolution against the landowners and the bourgeoisie. Secondly, they retained enough of the mentality of a ruling race to look down on the Muslim masses and to exclude them as far as possible from active participation in affairs of government,[2] with the natural result that the few Muslim members of the party became on their side strongly nationalist in sentiment. Thus the party exhibited samples both of a " Great Russian chauvinism " and of a Muslim

---

[1] *Desyatyi S"ezd Rossiiskoi Kommunisticheskoi Partii* (1921), p. 105. Semirechie was the north-eastern province of Kazakhstan : the *kulaks* were the Russian peasants settled on land taken from the Kazakhs.

[2] The fifth congress of Soviets in May 1918 had formally removed the ban on the admission of Muslims to governmental posts, but " only occasional representatives of Kirgiz and Uzbeks or, more often, Tatars attained positions of power " (G. Safarov, *Kolonial'naya Revolyutsiya: Opyt' Turkestana* (1921), p. 85); trade unions admitted only Russian workers (*ibid.* p. 115). The provision of the constitution of the RSFSR excluding employers of hired labour from the Soviet franchise was not applied in Turkestan.

nationalism which were equally anathema to sound party doctrine.

> Militant Great Russian chauvinism [wrote Broido in 1920] and the defensive nationalism of the enslaved colonial masses shot through with mistrust of the Russians — that is the fundamental and characteristic feature of Turkestan reality.[1]

Meanwhile the eighth congress of the parent party had met in Moscow in March 1919, and, in the course of adopting a new party programme, had had a long discussion on nationalities policy. Though Turkestan was not mentioned, a few delegates may have been aware of a discrepancy between proceedings at Tashkent and the principles enunciated at the congress; and it was at this time that Moscow first began to take cognizance of events in remote Central Asia. On June 1, 1919, an article in the official journal of Narkomnats drew attention to the importance of Turkestan as a starting-point for the liberation of the East; and a fortnight later a further article declared that " Turkestan, the outpost of communism in Asia, awaits help from the centre ".[2] On July 12, 1919, a telegram from the central committee of the party drew the attention of the Tashkent government to the necessity of " drawing the native Turkestan population into governmental work on a broad proportional basis " and of " stopping the requisitioning of Muslim property without the consent of regional Muslim organizations ".[3] According to a British officer stationed in Tashkent at the time, the first request was received with consternation; to fill 95 per cent of administrative posts with natives of Turkestan would have meant " an end of the Bolshevik government ".[4] Mutual understanding between Moscow and Tashkent was a slow growth. In October 1919, when after nearly two years' interval communications were once

---

[1] *Zhizn' Natsional'nostei*, No. 23 (80), July 18, 1920. An account of the growth of the party and of its first two congresses (June and December 1918) is given by P. Antropov in *Revolyutsiya v Srednei Azii : Sbornik* (Tashkent), i (1928), 7-20, ii (1929), 10-42. The best statement of its divisions and doctrinal weaknesses is contained in some notes by Frunze written during his stay in Turkestan (1919-1920) and published in his collected works (M. P. Frunze, *Sobranie Sochinenii*, i (1929), 119-121).

[2] *Zhizn' Natsional'nostei*, No. 20 (28), June 1, 1919; No. 22 (30), June 15, 1919.

[3] Lenin, *Sochineniya*, xxiv, 811.

[4] F. M. Bailey, *Mission to Tashkent* (1946), pp. 190-191.

more established,[1] VTsIK and Sovnarkom by a joint resolution appointed a commission to proceed to Turkestan in an endeavour to clear up the situation.[2] The resolution reminded it that :

> The self-determination of the peoples of Turkestan and the abolition of all national inequality and all privileges of one national group over another constitute the foundation of all the policy of the Soviet government of Russia and serve as a guiding principle in all the work of its organs. . . . It is only through such work that the mistrust of the native toiling masses of Turkestan for the workers and peasants of Russia, bred by many years' domination of Russian Tsarism, can be finally overcome.[3]

The mandate of the commission was reinforced by a letter from Lenin to " communist comrades in Turkestan " exhorting them to " establish comradely relations with the peoples of Turkestan " and to " eradicate all traces of Great Russian imperialism ".[4] At the end of January 1920 the first " Red train " left Moscow for Turkestan with a full complement of propagandists and literature in the local languages.[5]

The arrival of the commission, and no doubt the reinforcement to the prestige and power of the central government through the defeat of Kolchak and Denikin, led to a rapid improvement during 1920.   Units of the Red Army were now available for the first time to stiffen local levies ; and the hitherto independent principalities of Khiva and Bokhara could be brought into line.   The khan of Khiva was driven out, and April 1920 saw the birth of a Soviet, though not yet socialist, republic of Khorezm (a revival of the ancient name of Khiva).[6] About the same time the amir of Bokhara succumbed to the " young Bokhara " movement while

---

[1] The recapture of Ashkabad by the Bolsheviks in October 1919 opened the route across the Caspian ; the railway through Orenburg was not cleared till the following spring.

[2] The members of the commission included Eliava (a recent Georgian convert from Menshevism), Frunze (who was appointed commander-in-chief on the Turkestan front), Kuibyshev, Rudzutak, Boky and Goloshchekin (G. Safarov, *Kolonial'naya Revolyutsiya: Opyt' Turkestana* (1921), p. 105).

[3] Lenin, *Sochineniya*, xxiv, 810-811.

[4] *Ibid.* xxiv, 531.

[5] *Zhizn' Natsional'nostei*, No. 4 (61), February 1, 1920.

[6] Castagné (*Revue du Monde Musulman*, li (1922), 207) puts these events in the first half of 1919, but adds that they were immediately followed by negotiations for a treaty with Moscow (which was concluded in September 1920); he seems to have misdated them by a year.

Bolshevik forces under the command of Frunze were advancing on his capital:[1] and on October 5, 1920, the first " congress of Bokhara workers " met in the old palace of the amir in Bokhara.[2] It was at this point, according to one witness, that the influence of the " young Bokhara " movement, which consisted of " the younger generation of enlightened merchants who drew their inspiration from the young Turks and were dreaming of a national renaissance " began to yield to that of an embryonic Bokharan communist party whose leader was Faizulla Khozaev.[3] In December 1920 a Bokharan delegate appeared in Moscow to bring the greetings of " Soviet Bokhara " to the eighth All-Russian Congress of Soviets.[4] The establishment of Soviet régimes in Khorezm and in Bokhara was quickly followed by the conclusion of treaties with the RSFSR.[5]

The commission from Moscow — and particularly Frunze, its military member — had evidently played a large part in organizing these victories. It proved difficult, however, to impose more than an outward semblance of unity and orthodoxy on the local party, or to apply in Turkestan the " eastern " policy of wooing the alliance of the Muslim peoples which had been adopted in the other eastern borderlands from 1920 onwards. In the summer of that year a letter from the party central committee to party organizations in Turkestan declared that it was " first and foremost the duty of Russian communists to win the confidence of the toiling and oppressed peoples ".[6] Attempts were made to break down national discrimination.[7] But there were few trained communists in Turkestan ; and doctrines handed down from Moscow seemed inapplicable in a country where the principle of national equality and non-discrimination would subordinate a small and relatively progressive Russian minority to the backward peasant

[1] M. P. Frunze, *Sobranie Sochinenii*, i (1929), 142-143 ; *Revue du Monde Musulman*, li (1922), 219.

[2] *Novyi Vostok*, ii (1922), 272.

[3] A. Barmine, *One Who Survived* (1945), p. 103.

[4] *Vos'moi Vserossiiskii S"ezd Sovetov* (1921), pp. 225-226.

[5] See pp. 388-389 below.

[6] G. Safarov, *Kolonial'naya Revolyutsiya: Opyt' Turkestana* (1921), p. 133.

[7] Two examples of a more conciliatory national policy quoted by Castagné (*Revue du Monde Musulman*, l (1922), 68-69) illustrate the complications of life in Turkestan : in the winter of 1920–1921, Friday was substituted for Sunday as the weekly rest day, and the postal authorities for the first time accepted telegrams in local languages.

masses as represented by a handful of nationally minded Muslim intellectuals.   The situation invited abuses which could not be quickly eradicated.   Safarov, one of the few " old Bolsheviks " who had visited Turkestan, wrote in 1920 :

> From the first days of the revolution Soviet power established itself in Turkestan as the might of a thin layer of Russian railway workers.   Even now the impression is widespread that only the Russian can be the bearer of the proletarian dictatorship in Turkestan. . . . National inequality in Turkestan, inequality between Europeans and natives, is found at every step. . . . In Turkestan there have been some peculiar communists, and they have not yet all gone.[1]

A few weeks later a Muslim delegate from Turkestan made a frank speech on the same theme at the Baku congress of eastern peoples.   Complaining that Zinoviev, Radek and other revolutionary leaders had never been in Turkestan, and referring to the " inadequacies " of Soviet policy for the past three years, he demanded the removal of " your colonists now working under the guise of communism " (the report records applause and cries of " Bravo " at this point), and continued :

> There are among you, comrades, people who under the mask of communism ruin the whole Soviet power and spoil the whole Soviet policy in the east.[2]

The indictment was repeated at the tenth party congress of March 1921 in Moscow, when Safarov, as one of the delegates from Turkestan, criticized once more the composition of the local party and demanded a more active struggle both against Great Russian chauvinism and against Muslim nationalism.[3]   As late

---

[1] *Pravda*, June 20, 1920.   At the tenth party congress in Moscow in March 1921 Safarov related that in the previous summer he had seen the following notice in a small town of Turkestan : " Since divine service today is being performed by a communist priest, all members of the Communist Party are invited to the service " (*Desyatyi S"ezd Rossiiskoi Kommunisticheskoi Partii* (1921), p. 104).   Broido noted the existence of Muslim communists who " pray at the appointed hours " and of a Russian archimandrite who " presides over a county committee or edits a party and Soviet journal " (*Zhizn' Natsional'nostei*, No. 23 (80), July 18, 1920).

[2] *I*[vi] *S"ezd Narodov Vostoka* (1921), pp. 85-91.

[3] *Desyatyi S"ezd Rossiiskoi Kommunisticheskoi Partii* (1921), pp. 163-168. Stalin made no direct reply to Safarov at the congress while accepting most of his amendments to the resolution on the nationalities question ; on a previous

as January 1922 the party central committee was still publicly
exhorting the Turkestan communists to get rid of the " colonist
deviation ", and warning them that Turkestan could not be allowed
to become " a Russian Ulster — the colonists' *fronde* of a national
minority counting on support from the centre ".[1]

The national problem was still therefore unsettled when, on
April 11, 1921, a decree of VTsIK created a Turkestan Socialist
Soviet Republic as an autonomous unit of the RSFSR,[2] though
the hesitations which accompanied the decision were shown by
the despatch to Tashkent of " a temporary commission for the
affairs of Turkestan ", responsible to VTsIK and to Sovnarkom,
for " the practical carrying out of the policy of Soviet power in
the national question ".[3] The new republic embraced the part
of Central Asia from the Caspian Sea on the west to Sinkiang on
the east, from the frontiers of Persia and Afghanistan on the south
to the confines of Kazakhstan on the north. The supreme organ
of the republic was the " Congress of Soviets of Workers',
Dehkans', Peasants', Red Army and Cossacks' Deputies ", the
conspicuous inclusion of the " dehkans ", or Muslim peasants,
being manifestly intended to proclaim the new policy of national
equality. The new régime failed to bring immediate peace. In
the autumn of 1921 Enver Pasha suddenly appeared on the scene
to place himself at the head of a serious rebellion in eastern
Bokhara. Appealing to the pan-Turanian aspirations of the
" young Bokhara " movement and of many of the Muslim communities of Turkestan, he effected a junction with the Basmachi
and raised the eastern part of the country against Tashkent.[4]
The revolt was finally quelled after many months' fighting, in the

occasion Stalin had minimized the charge of " great Power chauvinism " and
spoken critically of " nationalistic survivals " among Turki-speaking communists
(*Sochineniya*, v, 1-3).

[1] *Zhizn' Natsional'nostei*, No. 3 (132), January 26, 1922.

[2] *Sobranie Uzakonenii, 1921*, No. 32, art. 172.

[3] *Ibid*. No. 32, art. 173. The members of the commission were Tomsky
and Rudzutak, recently protagonists in the trade-union controversy at the tenth
party congress in March 1921 ; A. Barmine, *One Who Survived* (1945), p. 99,
describes a visit to them in Tashkent.

[4] The fullest account of the Basmachi rebellion, with some picturesque
details about Enver's pan-Islamic pretensions, is in *Novyi Vostok*, ii (1922),
274-284. According to Castagné, *Revue du Monde Musulman*, li (1922), 228-229,
Enver was invited by the Bolsheviks to mediate with the rebels, but went over
to them instead ; but the writer was no longer in Central Asia at this time and
his sources are not always reliable.

course of which Enver himself was killed on August 4, 1922 — a trivial end to a melodramatic career. Thereafter the Soviet authority was gradually re-established. It was not till after the formation of the Soviet Union and the death of Lenin that it was decided to ease the problem of government in Turkestan and to grant a wider scope to national aspirations by breaking it up into four separate national republics. This occasion was also taken to carry out a promise made in 1920 to the newly formed Kazakh autonomous republic to transfer to it, " in accordance with a declaration of the will of the population ",[1] the Kazakh lands hitherto included in Turkestan.

(d) The Transcaucasian Republics

The situation in Transcaucasia was complicated by the dual character of the national problem. The region contained, like the western borderlands, advanced peoples whose claim to national independence could not be rejected out of hand, and, like the eastern borderlands, primitive peoples whose stage of development limited them to the most elementary form of local autonomy. Apart from a substantial immigrant population of Russians and Turks, Transcaucasia was the home of some eight indigenous national groups, of whom the three largest — the Georgians, the Armenians and the Azerbaijani — were each less than 2,000,000 strong ; and the intermingling of different peoples had been a common source of conflict. The economic and social structure was equally variegated. Peasant standards of life were low, even in comparison with European Russia ; they were lowest of all in Azerbaijan. Feudal systems of land tenure survived among the *beks* of Muslim Azerbaijan and the princes of Christian Georgia ; Armenia, and to a much smaller extent Georgia, possessed a commercial class and a radical intelligentsia, but virtually no proletariat apart from a handful of railway workers ; in Baku the oil industry had attracted a large Russian as well as a large Armenian colony and a proletariat which was partly indigenous, partly Russian.

The ethnic frontiers dividing the three main national groups were in many places ill-defined. Armenia suffered particularly

[1] *Politika Sovetskoi Vlasti po Natsional'nomu Voprosu* (1920), p. 44, art. 65.

in this respect owing to the frequent persecution and dispersal of Armenian populations by Turkey. There were more Armenians in Georgia and Azerbaijan than in the Armenian republic as ultimately constituted: Tiflis, the Georgian capital, had a larger Armenian population than any other city, and contained more Armenians than Georgians. In these circumstances national animosities were as often directed against rival national groups as against the comparatively inconspicuous Russian power:

> If . . . there is no serious *anti-Russian* nationalism in Georgia [wrote Stalin in 1912] it is primarily because there are no Russian landlords there or a Russian big bourgeoisie to supply the fuel for such nationalism among the masses. In Georgia there is an *anti-Armenian* nationalism; but this is because there is an Armenian big bourgeoisie there which, beating the small and still unconsolidated Georgian bourgeoisie, drives the latter to anti-Armenian nationalism.[1]

The February revolution, both by stimulating national movements and by paralysing Russian control, opened the door to a prolonged period of disturbance and chaos. Nowhere, however, in the former Tsarist empire did a solution on national lines appear at first sight less promising or less practicable. A regional congress of Caucasian Bolsheviks held at Tiflis in September 1917 came to the conclusion that, in view of the variety, small numbers and geographical intermingling of the nations of the Caucasus it could not " recommend either separation or the formation of federal states by the Caucasian nationalities ".[2]

The first result of the October revolution was the establishment at Tiflis on November 15/28, 1917, of a " Transcaucasian commissariat ", whose authority derived from a Transcaucasian assembly, composed by an ingenious arrangement of the representatives elected by the Transcaucasian provinces to the Constituent Assembly in Petrograd together with supplementary representatives chosen by the different parties in the same proportions. The commissariat embodied an uneasy coalition between the Azerbaijani chiefs and Georgian landowners, who hoped to substitute their authority for the defunct Russian power, and the

[1] Stalin, *Sochineniya*, ii, 307.
[2] *Revolyutsiya i Natsional'nyi Vopros: Dokumenty i Materialy*, ed. S. M. Dimanshtein, iii (1930), 411-412.

Georgian radical intelligentsia, which nourished national aspirations and also hoped to provide the ruling class of a future nation.[1] Its composition and driving force were predominantly Georgian. Its president was the Georgian radical politician Gegechkori ; and it functioned side by side with a " regional centre " of local Soviets of Workers', Peasants' and Soldiers' Deputies which was presided over by the Georgian Menshevik leader, Jordania.   The commissariat did not at first purport to constitute a government or claim independence for Transcaucasia.   Its first proclamation, issued on November 18/December 1, 1917, in the name of " Transcaucasian revolutionary democracy ", asserted " the full self-determination of nationalities proclaimed by the Russian revolution ", but only claimed to exercise authority pending the convocation of the Constituent Assembly in Petrograd.[2]   But its outlook was essentially anti-Bolshevik ; and its refusal, after the dissolution of the Constituent Assembly, to recognize the Russian Soviet Government gave it, whatever its professions, a *de facto* independent status.

Meanwhile an armistice with the Turks had been signed on December 5/18, 1917, and the last Russian armies on the Turkish front melted away.   The Brest-Litovsk treaty of March 3, 1918, in the negotiation of which Transcaucasia had had no part, contained a provision for the cession to Turkey of the Georgian provinces of Kars and Batum and the mainly Armenian district of Ardahan.   It was loudly denounced by leading Georgian spokesmen ;[3] and the Transcaucasian commissariat officially protested against the cession of Transcaucasian provinces by an act concluded without its knowledge or consent.[4]   Turkey hastened to take over her new gains, occupying Batum on April 15, 1918, and showed some ambition to extend them.   Faced by the necessity of countering the Turkish menace and without hope of Russian support, the Transcaucasian assembly on April 22 proclaimed an

---

[1] Stalin, *Sochineniya*, iv, 53.

[2] The most complete source for these events is the volume of *Dokumenty i Materialy po Istorii Zakavkaz'ya i Gruzii*, published by the Georgian Government in Tiflis in 1919 ; for the proclamation of November 18 December 1, 1917, see pp. 8-10.

[3] *Dokumenty i Materialy* (Tiflis, 1919), pp. 164, 168, 171.

[4] Z. Avalishvili, *The Independence of Georgia in International Politics* (n.d. [? 1940]), p. 27.   This is an English translation of a book by a Georgian bourgeois diplomat, published in Paris in Russian in 1924.

independent Transcaucasian Federal Republic.[1] Its writ purported to run throughout the Transcaucasian provinces of the
former Tsarist empire, except for the areas ceded to Turkey at
Brest-Litovsk and for the town of Baku. In Baku, thanks mainly
to the large colony of workers, Russian and other, in the oil
industry, the Bolsheviks obtained a firm footing in the first winter
of the revolution. A regular Soviet government, headed by
Shaumyan, an old Bolshevik and a friend of Lenin, was established in April 1918 and enjoyed the support of a large part of
the substantial Armenian community, which feared the Turkophil
Azerbaijani population of the hinterland. In these conditions it
survived for some four months. On the other hand, a statement
by Stalin in May 1918 that Baku, as " the citadel of Soviet power
in Transcaucasia ", had " grouped around itself the whole of
eastern Transcaucasia from Lenkoran and Kuba to Elizavetpol "[2]
seems to have been little more than wishful thinking.

The experiment in Transcaucasian unity was short-lived.
When a conference to conclude peace with Turkey met at Batum
in May 1918, the underlying animosities between the three
members of the Transcaucasian Republic quickly came to light.
The Georgians expected the unqualified support of their partners
in resisting the Turkish claim to Batum. But Armenia's grievances against Georgia were as keenly felt as her grievances against
the Turk, and the Azerbaijani preferred their Turkish kinsmen
and co-religionists to their Christian partners. Jealousy of
Georgia's dominant rôle in the republic was common to Armenia
and to Azerbaijan. In each of the three countries these national
frictions were fanned and exploited by the ruling party — the
Mensheviks in Georgia, the Dashnaks in Armenia and the Musa-
wat (" equality ") party in Azerbaijan. Cooperation soon broke
down. On May 26, 1918, the Transcaucasian assembly met to
dissolve the republic; and on the same day a Georgian national
assembly proclaimed an independent Georgian republic.[3] Inde-

[1] The proceedings of the assembly are in *Dokumenty i Materialy* (Tiflis,
1919), pp. 200-222. The president of the assembly was the well-known
Georgian Menshevik Chkheidze; the prime minister of the new government
another Georgian named Chkhenkeli.
[2] Stalin, *Sochineniya*, iv, 96.
[3] The speeches of the Georgian spokesman Tsereteli at the last session of
the Transcaucasian assembly are in *Dokumenty i Materialy* (Tiflis, 1919),
pp. 317-330, the declaration of Georgian independence *ibid.* pp. 336-338 : the

pendent Armenian and Azerbaijani republics were proclaimed two days later.

The independence of these new creations proved even less durable than that of the Transcaucasian Republic. Within the next few weeks Turkish forces overran the greater part of Armenia and Azerbaijan. Independent Armenia ceased to exist even in name ; and the government of Azerbaijan became a puppet of the Turkish military command. Georgia saved herself from the same fate by seeking the patronage and protection of Turkey's ally, Germany. On May 28, 1918, a German-Georgian treaty was signed under which Georgia accepted the Brest-Litovsk frontiers but secured a tacit German guarantee against further Turkish encroachments. Germany undertook to appoint diplomatic and consular officers in Georgia, though she refrained from formal recognition of Georgian independence, apparently out of respect for Russian susceptibilities.[1] Germany thus secured control of the important Transcaucasian railway which carried the oil of Baku to the Black Sea ; and Georgia agreed to place all her raw materials, manganese being by far the most important of them, at the disposal of Germany for the duration of the war. Strengthened by this alliance Georgia concluded a peace treaty with Turkey on June 4, 1918.[2] A German garrison was established in Tiflis ; and the Soviet-German treaty supplementary to Brest-Litovsk which was signed in Berlin on August 27, 1918, contained a clause by which the Soviet Government consented to German recognition of an independent Georgia.

latter is also in Klyuchnikov i Sabanin, *Mezhdunarodnaya Politika*, ii (1926), 435-436. The declaration reproaches the Russian Soviet Government with having opened " Georgia's frontiers to invasion by the enemy and ceded Georgian territory to him ", and cites the Soviet decree recognizing " the freedom of each people forming part of Russia to choose a suitable political régime, including entire separation from Russia ". The faintly apologetic tone of both documents betrays a strong vein of uncertainty about the ultimate prospects of independence.

[1] An incident in the brief career of the Transcaucasian Republic was an offer by the local German commander, General von Lossow, to mediate between it and the Russian Soviet Republic. This offer was accepted by Chicherin, *Dokumenty i Materialy* (Tiflis, 1919), pp. 302-303, but came to nothing, presumably owing to the dissolution of the Transcaucasian Republic.

[2] The German-Georgian treaties are printed *ibid.* pp. 339-342. The main Georgian-Turkish treaty is omitted, apparently through an oversight, since a break occurs in the text between pp. 352 and 353. There are odd discrepancies between the text and the table of contents at this point : the latter omits the German treaties altogether.

The reason which enabled Georgia to assert a nominal, and to some extent real, independence at a time when Armenia and Azerbaijan were virtually extinguished as independent entities was partly accidental. Germany was interested in Georgian manganese, and was also concerned to maintain her footing in the Caucasus to supervise her unreliable ally and to watch Russia; and for these reasons she was willing to cast the mantle of German power over the Georgian Republic. But Georgia also enjoyed certain inherent advantages over the other two Transcaucasian national groups. Georgia possessed the remnants of a native Georgian aristocracy and the elements of a native Georgian bourgeoisie and intelligentsia which gave it a certain national cohesion. In Georgia even the Social-Democratic Party was a vigorous native growth, and produced several notable figures besides Stalin himself, though, like most Russian social-democratic groups outside the great industrial areas, it was mainly Menshevik in composition and in leadership. The appointment of Jordania, the party leader and president of the Soviet, as head of the government in June 1918 ended the duality of government and Soviet, and confirmed the Mensheviks as the ruling power. The question whether Georgia, in the absence of external intervention from any quarter, could in these years have established an effective independence as a tiny bourgeois republic remains academic. But her claims were somewhat less unreal than those of the other two main Transcaucasian peoples.

The summer of 1918 had thus seen Transcaucasia partitioned between Germany and Turkey with Russia totally excluded, except for the precarious Soviet hold on the town of Baku. The collapse of the central Powers in the autumn of that year had the effect of substituting British for German and Turkish power. British forces under General Dunsterville had already advanced from Persia into Azerbaijan, and actually entered Baku at the end of August 1918, only to retire on September 15 before the advancing Turks.[1] When both German and Turkish resistance collapsed six weeks later, British forces advanced once more and occupied

---

[1] These operations are vividly described, with naïve but occasionally illuminating political comment, in L. C. Dunsterville, *The Adventures of Dunsterforce* (1920). A Russian translation under the title *Britanskii Imperializm v Baku i Persii, 1917–1918*, was published in Tiflis in 1920. The twenty-six Soviet commissars who had constituted the government of Baku

Baku and the principal towns of Transcaucasia in time to nip in the bud in December 1918 an incipient frontier war between Georgia and Armenia.[1]   On December 31, 1918, the British Government informed a Georgian delegation that they " view with sympathy the proclamation of the independence of the Georgian Republic and are ready to urge its recognition at the peace conference "; and national governments of Armenia and Azerbaijan, resuscitated by the downfall of Turkey, and enjoying a less conspicuous degree of British patronage, also sent delegations to the peace conference in Paris.   Here, however, the issue was complicated by the support given to Kolchak and Denikin who were unwilling to recognize Transcaucasian independence. It was only after the defeat of the principal " white " armies that the Supreme Council decided in January 1920, at the instance of Curzon, on the *de facto* recognition of Georgia, Azerbaijan and Armenia.   But fine words in Paris meant little in Transcaucasia. Before the end of 1919 British troops had been withdrawn from the whole area (except the port of Batum, where they stayed till July 1920).   In the absence of foreign support, and even of elementary agreement among themselves, the independent bourgeois Transcaucasian republics had no capacity for survival.

The significant feature of Transcaucasian politics since the October revolution had been the absence of Russian power.   The vacuum had been filled in form by independent local governments, in reality by the military power, first of Germany and Turkey, then of Great Britain.   When Britain finally withdrew, Russian power was ready to step into its place.   The three Transcaucasian republics had been boycotted by the Soviet Government as puppets of a foreign Power.   They now succumbed in the order of their weakness.   At the end of April 1920 the Azerbaijan Government left in power by the retiring British troops, the

from April to July 1918 fled before the arrival of the British forces in Baku. But in September they fell into the hands of the anti-Bolshevik authorities of Transcaspia and were murdered — with, it was alleged, the complicity or tacit approval of the local British military commander.   This act became a *cause célèbre*, and responsibility for it was still being discussed in correspondence between the British and Soviet Governments four years later (Cmd. 1846 (1923)).

[1] It is amusing to record that the Georgian Government, on the same day on which it sent a formal protest against the entry of British troops into Georgia (December 22, 1918), also appealed to the British military mission for assistance in preventing Armenian attacks on Georgian territory (*Dokumenty i Materialy* (Tiflis, 1919), pp. 425-426, 478-479).

recipient of allied recognition in January 1920, was overthrown without much difficulty by a communist rising in Baku. A " military-revolutionary committee ", acting in the name of the revolutionary proletariat of Baku and the toiling peasantry of Azerbaijan, denounced the defunct government as traitors and appealed to Moscow to conclude " a fraternal alliance for the common struggle against world imperialism ". Aid was quickly forthcoming. An Azerbaijani Socialist Soviet Republic was proclaimed; and Kirov, Orjonikidze and Mikoyan — a Russian, a Georgian and an Armenian — arrived to lay the foundation of Soviet power in Transcaucasia.[1] For the moment, however, with the Polish war just beginning, the Soviet authorities preferred caution and refrained from seeking further gains. On May 7, 1920, they rather unexpectedly signed a treaty with the bourgeois Georgian Government, which thus secured Soviet recognition at the price of itself recognizing the Soviet Republic of Azerbaijan.[2] From the Soviet standpoint it was not a new departure ; the same policy had been pursued in the agreements with the bourgeois governments of the Baltic states. But it was none the less difficult to believe that the Soviet power, having got its foothold across the Caucasus, could confine its scope to Azerbaijan, or that Georgia could remain indefinitely as an unallocated bone of contention between Soviet Russia and a revived Turkey.

The second stage came in Armenia. Owing to fear and hatred of the Turks the Armenians were traditionally Russophil, without regard to the régime of the moment ; alone of the Transcausian governments, the Dashnak government of Armenia had contrived to have amicable relations with Denikin. The re-establishment of Russian power in Soviet guise in Azerbaijan had a powerful effect in Armenia and provoked a combined peasant and Bolshevik

[1] The fullest account of this episode is in M. D. Bagirov, *Iz Istorii Bol'-shevistskoi Organizatsii v Baku i Azerbaidzhane* (1946), pp. 193-198 : the appeals of the Azerbaijani military-revolutionary committee and of the central committee of the Azerbaijani Communist Party are in Klyuchnikov i Sabanin, *Mezhdunarodnaya Politika*, iii (1928), i, 21-22.

[2] *Sobranie Uzakonenii, 1920*, No. 64, art. 282. On April 30, 1920, Jordania, speaking in the Georgian Constituent Assembly of the Azerbaijan coup, had observed that " if the people itself sympathizes with the invasion of its country by a foreign force, action against that force would be a violation on our part of the rights of the people concerned " (Z. Avalishvili, *The Independence of Georgia in International Politics* (n.d. [? 1940]), p. 260). This conciliatory utterance doubtless paved the way for the Soviet-Georgian agreement.

rising, which was easily suppressed.¹ Trouble, however, soon
came from Turkey. The moral support of the allies and the
long-drawn-out and finally unrealized hope of an American or
allied " mandate " over Armenia had been the principal assets
of the Armenian Government. In the summer of 1920, with the
withdrawal of the last allied forces from Transcaucasia, these
visions faded away. The belated signature of the Sèvres treaty
on August 10, 1920, gave Armenia formal recognition by the
puppet Turkish Government in Constantinople, but inflicted an
unforgettable insult on Kemal and the Turkish nationalists. In
October 1920 fighting broke out over a frontier dispute, and
Turkish troops seized Kars and Alexandropol. In Armenia it
was widely believed that there was collusion between the Turkish
nationalists and Soviet Russia to overthrow the Dashnak govern-
ment.² Had such collusion existed, more favourable results might
have been expected for Soviet Russia. As it was, the Turkish
advance continued. It was only late in November, when the
Turkish victory was all but complete and the Armenian Government in dissolution, that Soviet forces advanced from the
north-east, bringing with them a revolutionary committee which
proclaimed itself the government of a new Armenian Socialist
Republic with its capital at Erivan.³ The new government quickly

¹ An account of this episode is given by B. A. Bor'yan, *Armeniya, Mezhdunarodnaya Diplomatiya, i SSSR* (1929), ii, 88-114. The writer, an Armenian
Bolshevik, is verbose and more interested in theories than in facts, but uses
sources otherwise difficult of access, including Armenian documents, and is
not wholly uncritical. According to *Kommunisticheskii Internatsional*, No. 13,
September 1920, col. 2549, a Bolshevik " revolutionary committee " seized
power in Alexandropol on May 3, 1920, and a week later proclaimed a Soviet
Armenia, but failed to follow up its initial success. The same source (*ibid.* col.
2547) estimates the membership of the Armenian section of the Russian
Communist Party (there was no independent Armenian communist party) at
this time at 3000, most of them resident outside Armenia.
² B. A. Bor'yan, *Armeniya, Mezhdunarodnaya Diplomatiya, i SSSR* (1929),
twice records the prevalence of this belief (ii, 121, 136) which he attributes to
Dashnak propaganda : he himself rejects it. The anti-Bolshevik literature of
the period contains several circumstantial stories of a secret treaty between
Soviet Russia and Turkey for the elimination of the Transcaucasian republics ;
none of them rests on reliable evidence.
³ " The revolutionary committee of Armenia was formed on the frontier
of Azerbaijan and Armenia and had no real power : its only overt act was the
issue of the declaration proclaiming a socialist Soviet republic of Armenia "
(B. A. Bor'yan, *Armeniya, Mezhdunarodnaya Diplomatiya, i SSSR* (1929), ii,
122-123).

received recognition from Moscow and, thus strengthened, was able to conclude a treaty of peace with Turkey on December 2, 1920.[1] A truncated Armenia survived as an independent Soviet republic. The régime was, however, not established without further resistance. In the middle of February 1921 the population rose against its new rulers, seizing Erivan and the other principal towns. The revolutionary committee, in the words of the Armenian Bolshevik historian, " recognizing its own impotence, called Soviet Russia to its aid, and, saving itself by flight under cover of a small detachment, handed over to the Red Army the task of saving Armenia ". The rising is said to have been provoked by the severity of the grain requisitions ; and it was not till the beginning of April, after the promulgation of NEP, that order was fully restored.[2] The respective parts played by economic and by national discontents in this rebellion can only be guessed.

The Georgian Menshevik republic still remained, and in the last few months of its life made some unexpected and conspicuous excursions into the international arena. In September 1920 it received a delegation of some of the most distinguished social-democrat and labour leaders of western Europe, including Kautsky, Vandervelde and Ramsay MacDonald. It was a moment when communists throughout Europe, egged on by Comintern, were seeking to split socialist parties. Feeling ran high. The purpose of the Georgian trip was to collect material for anti-Bolshevik propaganda ; and the Georgians were assiduous suppliers.[3] Georgia, now well in the swim of international politics, made a strong, though unsuccessful, bid for admission to the League of Nations at its first assembly in December 1920, and secured *de jure* recognition from the Supreme Council of the allies in the following month. This eagerness to curry favour with the principal enemies of Soviet Russia was hardly prudent. At the Baku congress of eastern peoples in September 1920, held at the moment when Georgia was receiving the western social-democrats, one of the Bolshevik orators launched a vigorous

[1] Klyuchnikov i Sabanin, *Mezhdunarodnaya Politika*, iii (1928), i, 75.
[2] B. A. Bor'yan, *Armeniya, Mezhdunarodnaya Diplomatiya, i SSSR* (1929), ii, 133-140, 158-159.
[3] The visit of the delegation left an extensive anti-Bolshevik literature behind it, including books by Kautsky and Vandervelde.

attack on the attitude of the Menshevik republic towards its minorities and its neighbours. Charges were made of " destroying and exterminating " the Osetians, of " burning whole villages " in Abkhazia, and of putting forward chauvinistic claims to Azerbaijani and Armenian territory; and it was recalled how Georgia at the end of 1918 had " begun a war with Armenia which was only stopped by the intervention of England ".[1] Stalin, during his visit to the Caucasus in October 1920, remarked that, with the conclusion of peace between Soviet Russia and Poland, the Entente might be expected to transfer its military operations to the south, " in which case it is quite possible that Georgia, in accordance with her obligations as a kept mistress of the Entente, will not refuse to render service ".[2]   In November 1920 the official journal of Narkomnats complained that, though the Communist Party had been legalized in Georgia after the Soviet-Georgian treaty of May 1920, so many communists had been arrested that no one was left at party headquarters in Tiflis but a woman clerk.[3]

Ominous reproaches continued to appear throughout the winter in the Soviet press; and Soviet armies were massed in adjacent territories. A frontier dispute with Soviet Armenia caused a local outbreak of hostilities. On February 21, 1921, Soviet and Georgian Bolshevik forces crossed the frontier; two days later Turkey presented an ultimatum, demanding the cession of the two districts of Ardahan and Artvin, which was complied with; on February 25, 1921, Tiflis fell, and a Georgian Socialist Soviet Republic was proclaimed by the victors.[4]   Except for mopping up campaigns in the troubled regions of Turkestan, it was the last military operation of the Red Army in the territories which were soon to form the USSR; and it was the last instance of forced sovietization for nearly twenty years, when foreign war once again loomed threateningly on the horizon.   Lenin's unusual anxiety on this occasion was expressed in a letter to Orjonikidze of March 3, 1921, recommending not only " a policy of concessions in relation to the Georgian intelligentsia and small traders ", but

[1] *I*^{vi} *S"ezd Narodov Vostoka* (1921), p. 149.
[2] Stalin, *Sochineniya*, iv, 379-380.
[3] *Zhizn' Natsional'nostei*, No. 34 (91), November 3, 1920.
[4] Klyuchnikov i Sabanin, *Mezhdunarodnaya Politika*, iii (1928), i, 86-87, 91.

even " a coalition with Jordania or similar Georgian Mensheviks ".[1]
The coalition was not realized, though an amnesty was proclaimed
for the Mensheviks. By the middle of March resistance had ceased
throughout the country, and the Georgian bourgeois and Menshevik politicians fled to Paris, where the first and last minister
of the Georgian Menshevik republic had presented his credentials
on the day when Tiflis fell to the Bolsheviks. During the course
of 1921 the three minority districts of Ajaria (comprising the port
of Batum), Abkhazia and Yugo-Osetia were constituted as autonomous republics and an autonomous region respectively within
the Georgian SSR.

(e) Siberia

In the European, Central Asian and Transcaucasian regions
of the former Russian Empire where independent authorities were
established after 1917, national movements, however embryonic,
had existed, so that the process of dispersal, though set in motion
or furthered by conditions of civil war and foreign invasion, had
at any rate some ostensible national foundations. In Siberia,
where the inhabitants of the developed belt along the railway
were mainly Russian colonists, and primitive native tribes were
scattered over vast, thinly populated areas, no effective nationalist
or separatist movements arose. Buryat-Mongolia became an
autonomous region in 1922 and an autonomous republic in the
following year.[2] The vast territory of the Yakuts in north-eastern
Siberia was recognized as an autonomous republic in 1922, though
much of the country was in open rebellion till the end of 1923.[3]
But apart from these minor exceptions, the independent authorities

----

[1] Lenin, *Sochineniya*, xxvi, 187. It may be surmised that Lenin, on the eve
of the introduction of NEP and of the signature of the trade agreement with
Great Britain, was not thinking much about Georgia, and that this surprising
readiness to temporize with Mensheviks was due to a desire to reduce the danger
of international complications. Lenin continued down to the end of his life to
regard Georgia as a sore spot of Soviet policy.

[2] See p. 359, note 2 below.

[3] The account of this rebellion, which lasted from February 1921 to
November 1923, in *Proletarskaya Revolyutsiya*, No. 5 (76), 1928, pp. 66-102,
is more informative about incidents than 'about underlying causes. But the
statement that the rebellion was started by " white " officers is probably true ;
according to *Zhizn' Natsional'nostei*, No. 18 (116), September 16, 1921, it " had
a clearly marked nationalist character, though among the rebels were not only
Russian, but even a few Magyar officers ".

which made their appearance from time to time were either the products of temporary political expediency or professed aspirants to rule over a reconstituted Russian Empire.

The six months after the October revolution were marked by a kind of interregnum in Siberia. Soviet power asserted itself sporadically and spasmodically ; local Soviets, having more or less intermittent contact with Moscow and with other local authorities, civil or military, exercised an undefined control in most areas. This indeterminate situation was broken by foreign military action. On April 5, 1918, Japanese forces landed in Vladivostok, nominally to protect Japanese lives and property,[1] and subsequently advanced along the Trans-Siberian railway as far as Lake Baikal. In May 1918 the Czech legions, composed of former Czech prisoners of war, whose evacuation through Vladivostok had been negotiated with the Soviet Government, clashed with the Bolsheviks in western Siberia and took organized military action to safeguard their position. Not without allied encouragement they moved westward on to the Volga, thus sealing off the whole of Siberia from the Soviet power and temporarily annexing to Siberia certain regions of eastern European Russia. The Czechs occupied the key point of Samara on June 8, 1918.

In these conditions various anti-Bolshevik " governments " began to crystallize throughout eastern European and Asiatic Russia. A group of former members of the Constituent Assembly, all socialists, almost all Right SRs but including a few Mensheviks, set up a provisional government at Samara under the protection of the Czech legion. In Omsk a Siberian government of bourgeois complexion was established in July 1918, and for the next four months exercised a measure of authority over western Siberia.[2] Further east Semenov, the ataman of the Siberian Cossacks, collected an army in Harbin during the winter of 1917 and in March 1918 marched into Siberia. His initial move was apparently made with French support. But on the arrival of Japanese occupying forces in the summer of 1918 he quickly came to terms with them, and, with their connivance, established himself at Chita, whence he dominated a considerable part of Trans-Baikalia.

[1] *Foreign Relations of the United States, 1918: Russia,* ii (1932), 100.
[2] The fullest account of this government, written by one of its members, is in G. K. Gins, *Sibir', Soyuzniki i Kolchak* (Peking, 1921), i, 102-131.

The first attempt to consolidate these separate interventions by creating a single anti-Bolshevik authority was made at a conference at Ufa in September 1918. Semenov, no doubt at the instance of his Japanese patrons, boycotted the conference. But it was attended by representatives of the Siberian government at Omsk, of the Samara government, of so-called national Kazakh, Turco-Tatar and Bashkir governments, of several Cossack military governments and of other minor authorities of somewhat uncertain jurisdiction; and on September 23, 1918, it signed an act constituting a " provisional all-Russian government ". Pending the convocation of a constituent assembly, the government was to be in the hands of a directorate of five, with Avxentiev, the Right SR leader, as its president.[1] It fixed its seat at Omsk. The conference had not, however, passed without ominous portents. While it was sitting, Soviet armies recaptured Kazan and Simbirsk from the Czechs. Samara itself fell early in October.[2] The authority of the new " all-Russian " government was quickly confined within the bounds of western Siberia. Here it held sway for less than two months. On November 18, 1918, Admiral Kolchak, recently arrived from Vladivostok, overthrew it by force and, with British support, assumed the title of " supreme ruler ". As one result of this step, most of the surviving members of the Samara government made their peace with the Bolsheviks.

The Kolchak episode lasted from November 1918 till the first days of 1920. Semenov refused to submit to him as he had refused to submit to the Siberian government; and, when in December 1918 Kolchak issued an order to deprive Semenov of his command and enforce his compliance, the Japanese military authorities let it be known that they would tolerate no interference by Kolchak — whom they regarded as an English tool — east of Lake Baikal.[3]   Further west, Kolchak enjoyed varying success, but

[1] The fullest accounts of the Ufa conference are in G. K. Gins, *Sibir'*, *Soyuzniki i Kolchak* (Peking, 1921), i, 207-255, and V. G. Boldyrev, *Direktoriya*, *Kolchak, Interventy* (Novonikolaevsk, 1925), pp. 35-53 ; the text of the act is in Boldyrev, *op. cit.* pp. 493-497 (translation in *Foreign Relations of the United States, 1918: Russia*, ii (1932), 406-409).   Boldyrev was commander of the forces of the directorate.   After the Kolchak *coup*, he retired to Japan, and reappeared in Vladivostok in 1920 as a " white " Russian who was *persona grata* to the Japanese general staff ; in 1922 he surrendered to the Bolsheviks and was amnestied ; his memoirs, cited above, were published under Soviet editorship.

[2] *Foreign Relations of the United States, 1918: Russia*, ii (1932), 381, 409-410.

[3] G. K. Gins, *Sibir'*, *Soyuzniki i Kolchak* (Peking, 1921), ii, 38.

antagonized all Russian parties, other than those of the extreme
Right, by his ruthless treatment of political opponents and by
savage punitive expeditions adopted as a reprisal for recurrent
peasant disorders. The summit of his career was reached in the
summer of 1919 when he secured a qualified recognition from
the allies as *de facto* ruler of Russia, the other " white " generals,
including Semenov, formally accepting his supreme authority.
But in the autumn of 1919 the position behind the front became
critical : " peasant revolts spread all over Siberia like an unbroken
sea ".[1] In October Soviet troops assumed the offensive and the
motley Kolchak forces soon began to disintegrate. Omsk was
evacuated on November 10, 1919, and captured by the Bolsheviks
a few days later.[2] At this moment the Czech legions, in a note
to the allies, renounced all further responsibility for the maintenance of order along the railway and asked for immediate evacuation. The demand was justified by a frank denunciation of the
Kolchak régime :

> Under the protection of Czecho-Slovak bayonets local
> Russian military organs commit acts which horrify the whole
> civilized world. The burning of villages, the beating up of
> peaceful Russian citizens by whole military detachments,
> the shooting without trial of representatives of democracy
> on a simple suspicion of political unreliability, are a daily
> phenomenon.[3]

In Irkutsk, where Kolchak momentarily established himself, the
situation rapidly became desperate. On December 24, 1919, a
rising occurred which ended, on January 5, 1920, with the formal
disbandment of Kolchak's government and the assumption of
power by a local " political centre " of predominantly SR complexion.[4] Kolchak, who had fled to Verkhne-Udinsk, signed an
order handing over his supreme powers to Denikin, and military

---

[1] *Ibid.* ii, 397.

[2] *Ibid.* ii, 413 (where " October " is a misprint for " November ") ; *Foreign Relations of the United States, 1919: Russia* (1937), p. 225.

[3] The text of the note is in G. K. Gins, *Sibir', Soyuzniki i Kolchak* (Peking, 1921), ii, pp. 441-442. According to the same authority, the Czech delegate, when reproached by members of the Kolchak government with the fact that Czech troops had also participated in these excesses, replied : " That is true, and it is just because our army is being demoralized by contact with yours that we are trying to withdraw it quickly " (*ibid.* ii, 529).

[4] *Ibid.* ii, 501.

and civil authority over Siberia to his old enemy, Semenov.[1] The " political centre " was quickly found to lack serious backing ; and on January 22, 1920, an act was signed transferring power to a Bolshevik " military revolutionary committee ", which undertook to convene a Soviet of workers', soldiers' and peasants' deputies.[2] Kolchak himself was stopped by the Czechs in an attempt to escape eastwards, and surrendered to the " military-revolutionary committee ". He was tried and shot on February 7, 1920.[3]

The downfall of Kolchak, the completion of the evacuation of the Czech legion and the withdrawal of the British and French missions, left the Bolsheviks and the Japanese face to face as the only effective forces in Siberia. The sequel showed that this unexpected confrontation was equally unwelcome to both, and that both shrank from the direct clash threatened by it. On the Russian side, victory over Kolchak and Denikin had given fresh confidence and released large military forces. But in the first part of 1920, with increasingly serious dislocations of internal administrative and economic machinery, and with the growing menace of an attack from Poland, the Soviet Government had reason to shrink from the responsibility of taking over vast new territories in Siberia, apart from the certain hostility, and probable opposition, of Japan to such a course. On the other hand, the recognition of the autonomy or independence of outlying regions was now firmly rooted in Bolshevik doctrine and practice ; and an expedient framed on these lines was likely to have a ready appeal. On the Japanese side, isolated and conspicuous intervention in Siberia after the withdrawal of the other allies accorded ill with the cautious policy favoured at this period by the Japanese

[1] G. K. Gins, op. cit. ii, 565-566 ; the act making the transfer to Semenov is reproduced in facsimile in B. Borisov, Dal'nyi Vostok (Vienna, 1921), pp. 15-16. A small body of Kolchak troops under a General Kappel escaped from the debacle, and by a sensational march through Yakutia and across the ice-bound lake Baikal (afterwards referred to as the " ice campaign "), succeeded in joining Semenov (G. K. Gins, op. cit. ii, 550-554). The " Kappelevtsy " held together and remained a turbulent element in the politics of eastern Siberia for another two years, being distinguished for their particularly ruthless treatment of any Bolsheviks with whom they came in contact. According to one account (Revolyutsiya na Dal'nem Vostoke (1923), p. 100), they included many Tatars and Bashkirs originally recruited from Ufa.

[2] P. S. Parfenov, Bor'ba za Dal'nyi Vostok (1928), pp. 60-61.
[3] For the text of the sentence see ibid. pp. 64-65.

Government. The situation at the beginning of 1920 brought to a head a rift gradually opening in Japanese policy between a military group which sought to prolong indefinitely the occupation of Siberia and a civilian group, perhaps supported by naval influence, which wanted to see the end of an embarrassing commitment. The first group urged the desirability of keeping Russia divided and holding Bolshevism at arm's length; the second feared the permanent antagonism of Great Britain and the United States which continued occupation might entail. During the first half of 1920 the second of the groups gradually acquired the ascendancy.

This was the background which gave reality to the apparently far-fetched project of a " buffer state " for eastern Siberia. It originated during the brief reign of the " political centre " at Irkutsk, and was a characteristic attempt to create a half-way house between Bolshevism and the bourgeois world. The centre decided to send a delegation to make this proposal to the Soviet military command now advancing rapidly eastward; and it prudently invited the leader of the Irkutsk Bolsheviks, Krasnoshchekov, to accompany the delegation. Krasnoshchekov, who was of Russian Jewish birth, had spent many years in Chicago and returned to Siberia after the February revolution. The negotiations took place at Tomsk on January 19, 1920, and were brilliantly successful. The SR head of the Irkutsk delegation assured the Soviet delegates, on the basis of his talks with American representatives, that " America was ready to admit the existence of a buffer state with the inclusion in its organ of power of a representative of the communist forces ". Agreement was reached on the creation of the buffer state, which undertook to clear the railway of foreign military detachments " by way of diplomatic negotiations ", and to hand over Kolchak, his staff and the gold reserves to the " Soviet power ". This agreement was confirmed from Moscow over the signatures of Lenin and Trotsky on January 21, 1920. Krasnoshchekov was appointed plenipotentiary of the Soviet Government to the " political centre ".[1]

---

[1] The best account of this episode, including the document as published in the Irkutsk press, is *ibid.* pp. 55-57; see also G. K. Gins, *Sibir', Soyuzniki i Kolchak* (Peking, 1921), ii, 545-546. H. K. Norton, *The Far Eastern Republic of Siberia* (1923), adds details apparently derived from personal contacts with individuals concerned, but lacks political understanding; he constantly magnifies the rôle of Krasnoshchekov.

It was the success of the Bolshevik committee at Irkutsk, during Krasnoshchekov's absence, in overthrowing the " political centre " which wrecked this ingenious scheme. Within a few weeks the Red Army had reached Irkutsk and the authority of the Soviet Government was firmly established up to this point. But Krasnoshchekov, nothing daunted, moved on to Verkhne-Udinsk ; and there on April 6, 1920, a " constituent assembly " of representatives of " all the people of the trans-Baikal territory " proclaimed an independent democratic Far Eastern Republic.[1] Krasnoshchekov, laying down his diplomatic rôle, became prime minister and minister for foreign affairs in the Far Eastern Government. One of his associates was " Bill " Shatov, a well-known American revolutionary leader, also of Russian Jewish birth. The new republic was formally recognized by the Soviet Government on May 14, 1920.[2]

The Japanese reaction was more hesitant. The decision to evacuate Siberia apparently became known at the beginning of March 1920 ; [3] and the withdrawal from advanced positions began about that time. The situation was complicated at this point by the so-called " Nikolaevsk incident " of March 1920, when the port of Nikolaevsk at the mouth of the Amur opposite Sakhalin fell into the hands of a Bolshevik partisan leader, Tryapitsyn by name, with the annihilation or capture of the Japanese garrison.[4]

[1] An English version of the declaration is in *A Short Outline History of the Far Eastern Republic* (Washington, 1922), pp. 40-42. According to H. K. Norton (*The Far Eastern Republic of Siberia* (1923), p. 136), it was originally drafted in English by Krasnoshchekov, who was more at home in English than in his native tongue.

[2] Klyuchnikov i Sabanin, *Mezhdunarodnaya Politika*, iii (1928), i, 24.

[3] *Revolyutsiya na Dal'nem Vostoke* (1923), p. 102.

[4] Exactly what happened at Nikolaevsk in March 1920 is difficult to establish. Late in February 1920 Tryapitsyn's army occupied the town, and arrived at some *modus vivendi* with the Japanese garrison. According to most Soviet versions, the trouble in March began with a treacherous attack by the Japanese in violation of this agreement : Tryapitsyn then rounded up the garrison, killing some Japanese civilians in the process. The rest of the story is undisputed. Tryapitsyn remained in possession of Nikolaevsk till May, when the Japanese despatched an expedition by sea to dislodge him. Learning of the approach of superior forces, Tryapitsyn massacred the whole Japanese population, including his Japanese prisoners, looted the town and burned it to the ground before leaving. At the beginning of July he was caught by the Red Army and shot, with his principal assistants. The uncertainties of the record are due partly to confusion between the events of March and those of May, partly to the fact that Soviet apologists, in their anxiety to condemn the Japanese reprisals

Ostensibly as a reprisal for this episode, substantial Japanese forces were landed at Vladivostok on April 4-6, 1920, and occupied other centres in the maritime province, amid scenes of wanton violence and destruction; and on April 29 a humiliating agreement, providing for an extended Japanese occupation of the maritime province and a withdrawal of all Russian forces to a distance of thirty versts from the Japanese zone, was forced on the local " white " Russian government.[1]   These steps marked a partial victory for the Japanese military party and a determination, which was maintained for the next two years, to keep a firm hold on Vladivostok and the Pacific coast.   But they did not alter the general policy of withdrawal from more advanced positions. During the summer the Japanese forces gradually abandoned the whole of eastern Siberia beyond the maritime province.

This policy had as its natural corollary the acceptance of the " buffer state ".   In May 1920, about the same time as the Soviet Government's recognition of the Far Eastern Republic, the Japanese commander in Siberia issued a statement in which, after expressing a general desire to withdraw Japanese armies from " the Russian Far East ", he advocated the establishment in Trans-Baikalia, " between the Japanese armies and the Bolsheviks advancing in an easterly direction, of a neutral zone free from the

of April, are not agreed whether to justify Tryapitsyn's action in March on the ground of Japanese provocation or to denounce him as an " anarchist " and an " adventurer " for whose actions the Bolsheviks could not reasonably be held responsible.   Thus two contradictory versions by different hands are included (apparently by oversight, since there is no editorial comment) in *Revolyutsiya na Dal'nem Vostoke* (1923), pp. 26-62, 119.   The former version — which accepts Tryapitsyn as a Bolshevik leader, minimizes the killing of civilians in March and stresses Japanese provocation — is the more plausible and is in general corroborated by P. S. Parfenov (*Bor'ba za Dal'nyi Vostok* (1928), pp. 95-97, 164-167). It does not seem to have occurred to the Bolsheviks to disown Tryapitsyn till after the May atrocities.   Parfenov (*ibid.* pp. 197-200) prints the July judgment of a military court on Tryapitsyn and his assistants from the contemporary local press.   It transpires from this that his age was twenty-three and that his principal accomplice was a woman of twenty-one.   According to an article in *Proletarskaya Revolyutsiya*, No. 5 (28), 1924, Tryapitsyn established a regular " commune " during his tenure of power in Nikolaevsk.   Material relating to the Nikolaevsk affair is translated in E. Varneck and H. H. Fisher, *The Testimony of Kolchak and other Siberian Material* (Stanford, 1935), pp. 331-364.

[1] The text is in V. G. Boldyrev, *Direktoriya, Kolchak, Interventy* (Novonikolaevsk, 1925), pp. 498-500.   The agreement was signed by Boldyrev as the local Russian commander with the commander-in-chief of the Japanese forces.

interference of the armies on both sides ".[1]   This declaration led,
after some further delays, to the opening of direct negotiations
between the Japanese military command and a delegation of the
Far Eastern Republic.   On July 17, 1920, the " Gongotta agreement " (so called from the station on the trans-Siberian railway
40 versts west of Chita where the negotiations took place) was
finally concluded between them.   It accepted the view that the
" best means to the establishment of tranquillity and order is the
formation of a buffer state with a single government, without
interference by armed force in the affairs of this state on the part
of other states ".   On the other hand :

> This buffer state cannot in international and economic matters
> live in isolation from civilised and highly industrial states.
> Between the Russian territory of the Far East and Japan there
> exists the closest bond of interests, so that the buffer state cannot
> fail to have the intention of closest friendship and cooperation
> with Japan.

Further, the new republic would not be communist and would
have a " popular, broadly democratic character ".   The Russians
agreed not to admit Soviet Russian armies to its territory, and
Japan agreed to withdraw her troops from Trans-Baikalia.   Both
parties were to endeavour to prevent conflicts in the territory of
the Far East and " only in extreme cases " to resort to " decisive
measures ".[2]

The immediate effect of this agreement was to give the Far
Eastern Republic a free hand against Semenov, whose importance
for Japan had ended with the elimination of Kolchak and his
British backers.   In October 1920, after the Japanese withdrawal,
Semenov was routed and driven out of Chita, which now became
the centre of the republic.   Here a congress of Far Eastern delegates was hastily summoned, and early in November 1920 issued
what was in effect a recapitulation of the Verkhne-Udinsk
declaration of April 6 constituting former Russian territory east
of Lake Baikal as an independent Far Eastern Republic.[3]   In
December a formal agreement with the Soviet Government fixed

[1] P. S. Parfenov, Bor'ba za Dal'nyi Vostok (1928), p. 200.

[2] V. G. Boldyrev, Direktoriya, Kolchak, Interventy (Novonikolaevsk, 1925),
pp. 363-364.

[3] Ibid. pp. 379-381 : English version in A Short Outline History of the Far
Eastern Republic (Washington, 1922), pp. 45-46.

the frontiers between the republic and the RSFSR.[1] Elections
to a constituent assembly in January 1921 yielded 180 seats to a
" peasant majority party ", which formed a bloc with the communists, and 92 to the communists themselves, these two groups
receiving more than two-thirds of the total vote.   SRs and
Mensheviks each had less than a score of seats.   Thirteen seats
were won by Buryat-Mongols, who came out in the assembly with
a demand for " self-determination and complete autonomy ".[2]
The meetings of the assembly were stormy from the outset.   SRs
and Mensheviks accused the government, composed equally of
peasants and of communists, of instituting a reign of terror and
of being tools of the Far Eastern bureau of the Russian Communist
Party, and were accused in their turn of accepting Japanese
subsidies.   The constitution adopted on April 17, 1921,[3] preserved bourgeois-democratic forms.   A government was installed
consisting of majority peasants and communists, together with a
council of ministers responsible to it;[4] and the fiction of complete independence from Moscow was preserved.   But Blucher,
one of the leading Red Army generals against Kolchak, was first
commander-in-chief of the armed forces of the republic;[5] and
this post was later held by Uborevich,[6] subsequently a well-known
general of the Soviet Union.   Whatever may be true of the
political leaders and the civil administration, there is no reason to
doubt that the army was from the first directly controlled from
Moscow.

[1] *RSFSR: Sbornik Deistvuyushchikh Dogovorov*, ii (1921), 78 ; *A Short
Outline History of the Far Eastern Republic* (Washington, 1922), pp. 47-48.
[2] P. S. Parfenov, *Bor'ba za Dal'nyi Vostok* (1928), p. 289 ; H. K. Norton,
The Far Eastern Republic of Siberia (1923), p. 157. In January 1922 the Buryat-
Mongols on the territory of the RSFSR were constituted as an " autonomous
region " (*Sobranie Uzakonenii, 1922*, No. 6, art. 59) ; it is to be inferred that a
similar step was taken by the Far Eastern Republic, since, after the reincorporation of that republic in the RSFSR, the Buryat-Mongols of the autonomous
regions in both republics were united in the summer of 1923 to form a single
Buryat-Mongol Autonomous Socialist Soviet Republic (*Sobranie Uzakonenii,
1924*, No. 1, arts. 10-11).
[3] English translation in H. K. Norton, *The Far Eastern Republic of Siberia*
(1923), pp. 282-307.
[4] P. S. Parfenov, *Bor'ba za Dal'nyi Vostok* (1928), pp. 305-308.
[5] V. G. Boldyrev, *Direktoriya, Kolchak, Interventy* (Novonikolaevsk, 1925),
p. 446.
[6] M. Pavlovich, *RSFSR v Imperialisticheskom Okruzhenii: Yaponskii Imperializm na Dal'nem Vostoke* (1922), p. 107.

The Japanese Government had no cause to congratulate itself on these developments. It had been outmanœuvred by superior diplomacy, and the boasted " buffer state " against Moscow and against Bolshevism was no longer a buffer. Negotiations had long been in progress between Chita and Vladivostok for the effective incorporation of the maritime province in the new republic; and the maritime province had already participated in the elections to the Far Eastern Constituent Assembly. In April 1921 it transpired, apparently for the first time, that the frontier of the republic had been so drawn as to leave the peninsula of Kamchatka to the RSFSR. The purpose was to enable the RSFSR to negotiate a concession to exploit the mineral resources of Kamchatka with an American financier. In Japanese eyes it must have seemed not merely a confession of the unsubstantial nature of the buffer republic, but a direct threat to Japanese interests. The reply of the Japanese authorities was to strengthen the defences of the maritime province. The weak local government at Vladivostok, which was displaying so untimely an inclination to join the Far Eastern Republic, was overthrown in April 1921 in favour of a more amenable government of predominantly Right complexion under a nonentity named Merkulov. Both Semenov and the " Kappelevtsy " once more appeared conspicuously in Vladivostok, and the Far Eastern Republic was afterwards in possession of a document of uncertain authenticity purporting to be an agreement between the Japanese authorities and the white Russian military forces to open an offensive against the republic, not later than July 1, 1921.[1]

The threat was averted by the increasing pressure exercised on Japan from the English-speaking world. In the summer of 1921 it was announced that the Great Powers proposed to convene a conference on Pacific affairs in Washington in the coming autumn.[2] The Soviet Government had at first great difficulty in guessing whether this would turn out to be the act of friend or

[1] The document, dated June 9, 1921, was presented to the Washington conference by the delegates of the Far Eastern Republic and is printed in M. Pavlovich, *RSFSR v Imperialisticheskom Okruzhenii: Yaponskii Imperializm na Dal'nem Vostoke* (1922), pp. 67-69. The main argument against its authenticity is that it was never carried out.

[2] The original American proposal had been for a conference on the reduction of armaments ; the Pacific question was added as the result of a British proposal in July 1921.

foe. The first reactions of the Soviet press and of Comintern were wholly hostile.[1] An attempt was made to secure representation of Soviet interests in the guise of an official invitation to the Far Eastern Republic. The recall to Moscow at this time of Krasnoshchekov and Shatov, who played no further part in the affairs of the republic,[2] may have been due to tardy realization that a government which included former American revolutionary agitators was unlikely to enjoy much favour at Washington. But the attempt failed, and American hostility to any dealings with the RSFSR remained insuperable. On the other hand, the American Government was known to be putting pressure on the Japanese Government to terminate its occupation of Russian territory and the conference might be expected to accentuate this pressure.[3] It was the shadow of the impending conference which induced Japan to enter into negotiations of undefined scope with the Far Eastern Republic. These negotiations began in Dairen on August 26, 1921, and continued throughout the winter and throughout the duration of the Washington conference.

The Dairen conference was completely barren of result. The final Japanese demands were formulated in seventeen clauses with three additional secret clauses. The more important of these demands were that the Far Eastern Republic should undertake to maintain no armaments or fortifications of any kind, and no naval units anywhere on the Pacific, and that it should " engage to the Japanese Government for all time not to introduce a communist régime on its territory, and to preserve the principle of private property in relation not only to Japanese subjects, but to its own citizens ". In return for these undertakings the Japanese Government would do no more than promise to evacuate the maritime province " at the time which it would find necessary and convenient to itself "; the evacuation of northern Sakhalin would

---

[1] See articles in *Izvestiya*, August 2, 1921, and in *Ekonomicheskaya Zhizn'*, August 10, 1921 (summarized in L. Pasvolsky, *Russia in the Far East* (N.Y. 1922), pp. 124-127), and theses of IKKI published in *Pravda*, September 1, 1921 (summarized *ibid.* pp. 127-129).

[2] P. S. Parfenov, *Bor'ba za Dal'nyi Vostok* (1928), p. 327 : available evidence reveals no motive for this step.

[3] A memorandum from the State Department to the Japanese Embassy in Washington of May 31, 1921, and an evasive Japanese reply of July 8, 1921, are in *Foreign Relations of the United States, 1921*, ii (1936), 702-705, 707-710.

be dependent not only on a settlement of the Nikolaevsk affair but also on the granting of a lease of the island to Japan for a period of eighty years.[1] If Japan hoped that the Dairen conference would serve the purpose of removing this issue from the orbit of Washington, this hope was disappointed. The Far Eastern Government addressed to Washington, and to the world at large, a stream of protests which easily found receptive hearers; and an unofficial delegation of the republic appeared, with American encouragement, in the corridors of the conference. On the other hand, the Russian calculation that concessions at Dairen were no longer necessary proved correct. Private undertakings were extracted from the Japanese delegates at Washington by the American Government that the evacuation both of the maritime province and of the northern part of Sakhalin was contemplated in the near future.[2]

It was thus the pressure of the Washington conference, and not the feeble proceedings at Dairen, which decided the Japanese Government, in this as in other matters, to avoid further friction with the English-speaking Powers and to pursue a policy of appeasement. The Dairen negotiations were wound up without result in April 1922. But less than three months later the Japanese Government announced that its troops would be withdrawn from the Russian mainland by November 1, 1922, and indicated its willingness to negotiate not only with the Far Eastern Republic but with the RSFSR itself.[3] The Soviet Government marked the importance of the occasion by the appointment of Joffe, its most astute and experienced diplomat, as its plenipotentiary. Joffe displayed all his skill and stubbornness at the conference, which opened at Changchun in Manchuria on September 4, 1922. But Soviet hopes of extracting material concessions and diplomatic recognition were disappointed. Neither side budged; and the conference quickly broke down on the issues of

[1] The text of this document is in P. S. Parfenov, *Bor'ba za Dal'nyi Vostok* (1928), pp. 331-333.

[2] The public statements of both delegations in the official records (*Conference on the Limitation of Armaments* (Washington, 1922), pp. 853-859) were somewhat less explicit, no doubt for face-saving reasons.

[3] The note of the Japanese consul in Chita to Yanson, the Foreign Minister of the Far Eastern Republic, dated July 19, 1922, and the reply of July 23, 1922, signed jointly by Karakhan on behalf of the RSFSR and Yanson on behalf of the Far Eastern Republic, are published in *Novyi Vostok*, ii (1922), 40-41.

northern Sakhalin, of Japanese fishing rights in Russian waters and of the disposal of Japanese war stores in Vladivostok. Joffe's intransigence was partly dictated by the perfectly correct calculation that Japan could no longer go back on her pledge to the Washington Powers. The end of the conference was followed on September 14, 1922, by a deprecatory statement from the Japanese Ministry of Foreign Affairs :

> Notwithstanding the breakdown of the Changchun conference the Japanese armies in Vladivostok will be completely evacuated before the end of October in accordance with previous declarations of the Japanese Government. In view of the declarations of Joffe that Japan intends to annex Sakhalin, the Ministry of Foreign Affairs declares that, in accordance with the obligation assumed by Japan at the Washington conference, Japan does not intend to impugn the territorial rights of Russia, and occupies Sakhalin only as a guarantee for the settlement of the Nikolaevsk question. In view of this the Japanese Government would desire to warn the Powers participating in the Washington conference against an erroneous interpretation of the intentions of Japan.[1]

The evacuation of the maritime province took place at the end of October : the " white " government installed in May 1921 at once collapsed ; and the authority of the Far Eastern Republic was established throughout eastern Siberia from Baikal to the Pacific. The questions of northern Sakhalin and of the fishing rights remained to trouble Soviet-Japanese relations. But the withdrawal of Japan deprived the " buffer state " of any further meaning, even as a symbol ; and on November 10, 1922, the assembly voted it out of existence, and proclaimed its incorporation in the RSFSR.[2] This constituted a further step towards the reunion in a single whole of the dispersed elements of the former Russian Empire.

[1] P. S. Parfenov, *Bor'ba za Dal'nyi Vostok* (1928), pp. 350-351 ; Joffe's own story of the conference is in *Novyi Vostok*, iv (1923), 1-11 ; the account in A. J. Toynbee, *Survey of International Affairs, 1920-1923* (1925), pp. 442-444, adds some details from the contemporary press.

[2] The official declaration, dated November 14, 1922, was published in *Izvestiya*, November 21, 1922 : Lenin hailed it with satisfaction in his last public speech (*Sochineniya*, xxvii, 361). The decree of VTsIK accepting it is in Klyuchnikov i Sabanin, *Mezhdunarodnaya Politika*, iii (1928), i, 206.

CHAPTER 12

THE BALANCE-SHEET OF SELF-DETERMINATION

THE year 1920 was a turning-point in the history of Soviet nationalities policy. It marked the end of the civil war and the beginning of the period of consolidation and reconstruction; it marked also a decisive shift of emphasis from west to east. Both these changes helped the evolution in the conception of national rights which was implicit in the advance from the bourgeois to the proletarian revolution. " The right to separate ", in the phrase once used by Lenin, was being replaced by the " right to unite ". In principle, it was unthinkable that any socialist nation should wish to secede from the socialist community of nations; in practice, it was unthinkable by the end of 1920 that anyone not irrevocably hostile to the Soviet order should wish to break up such unity as had already been achieved. Unity was as necessary for full economic development as it had been for military security. The plain interest of the workers and the peasants was unity on the widest possible basis (with " workers of all countries, unite " as the ultimate goal). In order to make the workers and the peasants understand this interest, what was necessary was to eradicate all traces of that past inequality and discrimination between nations which had been, in the Bolshevik view, the fount and origin of nationalism, to ensure that nothing of it should reappear in the future. Thus, from the moment of the triumph of the revolution the essence of the Bolshevik doctrine of national self-determination passed over almost insensibly from the concept of liberty to the concept of equality, which alone seemed to offer a radical solution.

Bolshevism long remained faithful to the international outlook of the original socialist thinkers. Equality between nations was deeply rooted in the teaching and practice of the first Bolshevik

leaders, who would have been inexpressibly shocked at the idea
that any position of influence in the government or in the party was
more readily accessible to a Great Russian than, say, to a White
Russian, a Georgian or an Armenian.   Party doctrine and party
practice alike unsparingly condemned discrimination ; and most
of the party leaders were guilty not of insincerity but rather of a
breath-taking and uncritical optimism.   The mood of the early
months is not unfairly expressed in an article by a member of the
collegium of Narkomnats in the official journal of the commissariat :

> The danger of enforced russification has vanished.   No one
> is interested any longer in strengthening one nation at the
> expense of another. . . . No one thinks of attacking anyone or
> depriving him of his national rights.[1]

The absolute rejection of any discrimination between individuals
on ground of nation, race or colour remained a fixed and rigidly
asserted principle in Bolshevik policy and practice, and became
a powerful asset in all dealings with former subject peoples.   But
this was not by itself enough.   The positive aspect of the policy
of equality was the provision of aid to the more backward nations
to enable them to bridge the gap separating them from their more
advanced partners.   This comprised material aid, education in
all its forms, the loan of technical experts and advisers and the
training of members of the backward nation to serve as its future
experts.   Since the directors of the Soviet economy were, above
all, anxious to increase production throughout the Soviet lands,
this policy was likely to be limited only by the shortage of resources, though, where such vast divergences between levels of
civilization and culture existed, " the abolition of actual inequality
between nations " could, as the resolution of the tenth party
congress of 1921 said, only be " a prolonged process ".[2]

For the Marxist the fundamental element in bringing about
a real, as opposed to a formal, equality between all nations entering
into the Soviet state or group of states was the equal distribution
of productive processes over the whole territory.   Hitherto the
development of Russian industry had concentrated the more
advanced forms of production mainly in a few centres of European
Russia, treating the outlying borderlands as sources for the supply

---

[1] *Zhizn' Natsional'nostei*, No. 8, December 29, 1918.

[2] *VKP(B) v Rezolyutsiyakh* (1941), i, 386.

of food and raw material; and this had been the predominant pattern throughout the capitalist world, where inhibitions due to vested interests and fears of competition slowed up, or altogether prevented, the development of industrial production in colonial and semi-colonial countries. Capitalism had thus tended to stabilize inequalities between nations. No such inhibitions impeded the eagerness of the Soviet régime to develop the higher forms of industrial production throughout the territories under its control. Nor was the desire to expand industrial output the sole motive at work. The Soviet leaders retained throughout the earlier years a firm conviction that the industrial worker constituted the bulwark of Soviet power in the sense that he could be relied on to support it in face of the wavering loyalties and potentially counter-revolutionary inclinations of the peasant; and it therefore became a matter of high political expediency to plant industry in as many of the outlying territories as possible. If Turkestan cotton, instead of being spun exclusively in the mills of Petersburg and Moscow, now also fed textile factories in Turkestan, this innovation served from the Bolshevik standpoint several purposes. It increased the total production of textiles by opening up a new region of production; it offered Turkestan the prospect of escape from the " colonial " status of a supplier of natural products, the badge of inferiority, to the more highly developed and coveted status of an industrial producer; and it provided for the growth in Turkestan of an indigenous proletariat which would one day become a sure support of the Soviet régime and ideology. The promotion of economic equality between nations in the sense of an equal distribution between them of an expanded industrial production was thus deeply rooted in the Bolshevik outlook. And, in the conditions inherited by the Bolsheviks from the Tsarist order, this outlook had as its necessary corollary a policy of favouring the outlying and still mainly agricultural borderlands at the expense of the older industrial core by allocating to them a disproportionate share in new industrial development. It was this development which gave point to the Bolshevik claim that Soviet nationalities policy was different in kind from any pursued by capitalist countries, and that it alone aimed not merely at a formal recognition of equality, but at creating the economic environment which made equality possible

and real. To preach equality between nations was in itself a hollow
pretence unless the presuppositions of such equality were freely
accepted. Equality between nations meant breaking down the
line of demarcation between industrial and agricultural nations.

This was, however, a long-term policy, and the equalizing
process had many obstacles to encounter. Intentions were sincere, and achievements real; but progress could only be gradual.
Existing inequalities always have a natural tendency to perpetuate
themselves and to resist every effort to overcome them. There
was thus in this early period a constant process of contradiction
and struggle between the aims of policy and the machinery through
which that policy had to be carried out. The growing concentration of authority and administrative control at the centre had the
inevitable effect, however illogical this might appear, of subordinat-
ing the other nationalities to the Great Russian core round which
they were assembled. It was not enough that members of the
lesser nationalities should have as large a proportion as was due
to them, or sometimes perhaps a larger proportion, of posts of
influence and authority in the administrative machine. Many
non-Russian occupants of these posts assimilated themselves without effort and without deliberate intention to the outlook of the
numerically preponderant Great Russian group; those who resisted assimilation were less likely to make successful careers.
Moscow was the administrative capital — the centre where the
major decisions were taken. The bureaucratic mentality against
whose spread Lenin inveighed tended almost automatically to
become a Great Russian mentality.

> The fact is [remarked Rakovsky in 1923] that our central
> organs begin to look on the administration of the whole country
> from the point of view of office convenience. Of course, it is
> inconvenient to administer 20 republics, but if there were only
> one, if by pressing a single button one could administer the
> whole country, that would be convenient.[1]

Centralization meant standardization; and the standards adopted
were naturally Great Russian standards. Nor is it surprising that
the Ukraine should have been the spearhead of opposition to this
tendency. Not only was the Ukraine the only one of the republics

---

[1] *Dvenadtsatyi S"ezd Rossiiskoi Kommunisticheskoi Partii (Bol'shevikov)*
(1923), p. 532.

which, economically and culturally, could rival the status and attainments of the RSFSR; the Ukraine was also the one of the non-Great Russian regions which had least to gain from the policy of the industrial development of the borderlands, since her industrial development was already a matter of history. The Ukrainian nationalist might therefore feel that he had the worst of both worlds. The Ukraine hardly shared at all in the material benefits which Soviet nationalities policy was bringing to the " backward " regions; on the other hand, the " Great Russian chauvinism " of the bureaucratic machine in Moscow showed little willingness to recognize the Ukraine as an equal partner in the central direction of affairs.

Strong, and partly successful, efforts were made to counteract these tendencies in the administrative machine. In other institutions fewer precautions were taken to assuage national susceptibilities. The first of these institutions was the Red Army. It does not appear that any of the republics, once the Soviet form of government was established, aspired to maintain an independent army of its own.[1] From the first, detachments were recruited for the Red Army both from constituent republics of the RSFSR and from the independent republics allied to it; and natives of the Asiatic republics, who had been exempted from conscription under the Tsars, were mobilized with the rest.[2] It was this unified Red Army which, during the civil war, defended and liberated the territory of the independent republics, where the brunt of the fighting and the worst devastation occurred. Rakovsky himself at the ninth All-Russian Congress of Soviets in December 1921, speaking in the name of the White Russian, Azerbaijani, Georgian and Armenian republics, as well as of the Ukraine, had pointed the moral and called for a strengthening of the Red Army to prevent a repetition of the catastrophe.[3] The Red Army thus became an instrument not merely of unification, but of unification through a distinctively Great Russian symbol.

---

[1] The *Borot'bisti* (see p. 306) demanded a separate Ukrainian army (N. Popov, *Ocherk Istorii Kommunisticheskoi Partii (Bol'shevikov) Ukrainy* (5th ed. 1933), pp. 214-215).

[2] An article in *Zhizn' Natsional'nostei*, No. 32 (89), October 17, 1920, discusses difficulties of bringing Turkestan Muslims into the Red Army, but adds that " many tens of thousands " of them were then in training in a camp outside Tashkent.

[3] *Devyatyi Vserossiikii S"ezd Sovetov* (1922), pp. 208-209.

Skrypnik the Ukrainian complained at the twelfth party congress that the Red Army " is and remains an instrument for the russification of the Ukrainian population and of the whole non-Russian population " ; and the congress included in its resolution on the national question a clause recommending " practical measures for the organization of national military detachments, while observing all precautions necessary to guarantee the full capacity of the republics to defend themselves ".[1] But the final qualification was significant. There is no trace of any " measures " taken to carry out the recommendations ; the efficiency of national defence could always be invoked as an over-riding necessity.

The precedent of the army was reinforced by the trade unions. The predominance of the Great Russian element among the workers made the trade unions from the outset a powerful unifying factor on a Great Russian foundation. The case was stated by Ryazanov at the first All-Russian Congress of Trade Unions :

> He who would build socialism in Russia can build it only if, while allowing the possibility of the free, autonomous development of each of its parts, he at the same time strengthens the social-economic link which holds us all together, and without which the workers of Petrograd are torn asunder from those of Moscow, those of Petrograd and Moscow from the workers of the Don, the workers of the Don from those of Siberia.[2]

At the third congress, held in April 1920, Tomsky gave an account of the work of the trade unions in the recently liberated areas of the Ukraine, the Urals and Siberia :

> Our instructors followed the Red Army. The first to appear after the Red Army detachments in towns liberated from the " whites " were instructors of the central council of trade unions, instructors of the central committee of the textile workers, of the leather workers, of the metal workers, of the railway men.

Pressure had come from the Ukraine for a separate organization for the Ukrainian unions or a special status for them in the all-Russian organization. In spite of the " strong opposition of Right elements ", however, the central council had stood firm for " unity and centralism ".[3] Clearly, if " workers of the world,

---

[1] *Dvenadtsatyi S"ezd Rossiiskoi Kommunisticheskoi Partii (Bol'shevikov)* (1923), p. 523 ; *VKP(B) v Rezolyutsiyakh* (1941), i, 496.

[2] *Pervyi Vserossiiskii S"ezd Professional'nykh Soyuzov* (1918), p. 27.

[3] *Tretii Vserossiiskii S"ezd Professional'nykh Soyuzov* (1921), i, 29-30.

unite " meant anything, it ought at least to mean the unity of the
workers of the former Russian Empire. The case for trade union
unity was incontrovertible. But unity naturally meant an organization under predominantly Great Russian control.

Most important of all, the Russian Communist Party played
the same unifying rôle as the army and the trade unions. From
1903 onwards, when the demand of the Jewish Bund for an
autonomous status was rejected by the second party congress,
Lenin had insisted on unity of organization as a keystone of party
doctrine.[1] After the October revolution it was laid down by a
resolution of the eighth party congress in 1919 that the recognition of separate Ukrainian, Latvian, Lithuanian and White Russian
Soviet republics provided no ground for the organization of independent communist parties, even " on a basis of federation ",
and that " the central committees of the Ukrainian, Lettish and
Lithuanian communists enjoy the rights of regional committees
of the party and are wholly subordinated to the central committee of
the Russian Communist Party ".[2] Even the proposal made on the
formation of the USSR to change the name of the party to " All-
Union Communist Party (Bolsheviks) " encountered obstruction,
of which Skrypnik complained at the twelfth party congress in
1923.[3] It was eventually carried into effect by the fourteenth congress at the end of 1925. But the objections were natural enough.
The party as a whole was proud of its Russian name and tradition.

The centralizing influence of such institutions as the army,
the trade unions and the party was perhaps the most important
of the many factors, conscious and unconscious, that lay behind
the phenomenon of " Great Russian chauvinism ". " Scratch
many a communist and you will find a Great Russian chauvinist ",
Lenin had said in the debate on the party programme at the eighth
party congress in 1919 ;[4] and from this time onwards the cant
phrase was used to denote the attitude of those communists who,
unconsciously inheriting a pre-revolutionary Russian tradition or

[1] See p. 420 below.
[2] VKP(B) v Rezolyutsiyakh (1941), i, 304-305. When, on the other hand,
Latvia and Lithuania were recognized in 1920 as independent bourgeois
republics, the communist parties of these countries also became independent.
[3] Dvenadtsatyi S"ezd Rossiiskoi Kommunisticheskoi Partii (Bol'shevikov)
(1923), p. 524.
[4] Lenin, Sochineniya, xxiv, 155.

through a deliberate denial of the significance of nationality, be-littled the national claims of the Ukrainians, the White Russians and the non-Slav peoples of the former Tsarist empire. " Great Russian chauvinism " was once more condemned at the party congresses of 1921 and 1923. Yet Stalin himself at the latter congress described it as " the fundamental force which is putting the brake on the union of the republics ", and declared that it was " growing daily and hourly " and " seeking to sweep away everything non-Russian, to concentrate all the threads of the administration round the Russian element and to squeeze out the non-Russian ".[1] The rallying of patriotic Russian sentiment behind the Bolsheviks in the later stages of the civil war — the unspoken alliance between Russian nationalism and communist internationalism which made its first appearance in the Soviet-Polish war of 1920 — had prepared the way for a process which had its economic counterpart in NEP. The increasing influx into Soviet institutions, as " specialists " or civil servants, of members of the former privileged classes, had moved Lenin to a note of warning at the eleventh party congress in 1922. He compared the Bolsheviks to a conquering nation which had been overcome by the superior culture of the conquered. " Their culture is wretched, trivial, but still greater than ours." It was not the responsible communists who were " managing " the vast bureaucratic machine; they themselves, without knowing it, were being " managed ".[2] The absorption of bourgeois and even aristocratic elements into the bureaucracy had a two-way influence. It betokened not only the reconciliation of these " former people " with the Soviet régime, but also a less negative attitude on the part of the régime to traditions of the " Russian " past. Far from refuting the charges made by Rakovsky and Skrypnik at the twelfth party congress, Stalin himself spoke of the danger with emphatic frankness :

It is no accident, comrades, that the *smenovekhovtsy* [3] have acquired a mass of supporters among Soviet officials. It is no

---

[1] Stalin, *Sochineniya*, v, 244-245.   [2] Lenin, *Sochineniya*, xxvii, 244-245.

[3] *Smena Vekh* (" A Changing of Landmarks ") was the title of a collection of articles by Russian *émigrés* published in Prague in 1921, advocating a qualified reconciliation with the Soviet régime; a weekly journal of the same name started publication in Paris in the autumn of 1921, declaring itself " open to all representatives of the Russian intelligentsia who accept the October revolution, irrespective of the ideological grounds of their acceptance ". The

accident also that these gentlemen, the *smenovekhovtsy*, praise the communist-Bolsheviks, as if to say : Talk as much as you like of Bolshevism, prate as much as you like of your international tendencies, but we know that you will achjeve what Denikin did not succeed in achieving, that you Bolsheviks have restored the idea of great Russia, or at any rate will restore it. All this is no accident. It is no accident also that this idea has penetrated even some of our party institutions.[1]

The leitmotif of Russian unity which had first drawn these discordant elements together in the civil war continued to play a rôle in policy after its victorious conclusion.

Incongruously, too, " Great Russian chauvinism " derived indirect encouragement from Marxist doctrine — or from current distortions of it — in two different forms. The first was a revival of the old Polish heresy which rejected nationalism and national self-determination as incompatible with the class struggle and the world solidarity of the proletariat. Lenin again and again pointed out that this view consecrated the privileges of the dominant nation by ruling out any challenge to the *status quo* on the ground of the national aspirations of others. It was rejected by the April conference of the party in 1917 and by the eighth party congress in 1919. But no condemnation finally killed it. Its popularity among officials of Narkomnats has already been discussed.[2] As late as 1923 Rakovsky offered the twelfth party congress an imaginary diatribe by this type of communist :

We are a country which has already passed beyond nationality, we are a country . . . where material and economic culture is opposed to national culture. National culture is for

main impulse to this step had come from the patriotic feelings aroused by the Soviet-Polish war and from Lenin's announcement of NEP, which was thought to betoken an abandonment of dogmatic communism. Ustryalov, the most distinguished of the *smenovekhovtsy*, expressed the spirit of Great Russian chauvinism in its purest form : " Only a ' physically ' powerful state can possess a great culture. The natures of ' small powers ' have the possibility to be elegant, honourable, even ' heroic ', but they are organically incapable of being great. This requires a grand style, a grand sweep, a grand scale of thought and action — ' the brush of a Michelangelo '. A German, a Russian, an English ' messianism ' is possible. But, let us say, a Serb, Rumanian or Portuguese messianism grates on the ear like a false note " (*Smena Vekh* (Prague, 2nd ed. 1922), pp. 57-58).

[1] Stalin, *Sochineniya*, v, 244.   [2] See p. 279 above.

backward countries who are on the other side of the barricade, for capitalist countries; we are a communist country.[1]

The picture may be overdrawn, but is broadly convincing; and this attitude, while purporting to deny nationalism in the name of Marx, flowed easily into the channels of Great Russian chauvinism.

The second encouragement received from Marxist doctrine was due to the structure of population in the former Tsarist empire. Throughout what remained of the empire after the secession of Poland, Finland and the Baltic states — and notably in the Ukraine, the only heavy industrial region outside Muscovy — a majority of the industrial proletariat was Great Russian, whereas the other nationalities were predominantly or exclusively of peasant composition. Relations between the industrial proletariat and the peasantry were always, in one form or another, the most delicate issue in Soviet domestic policy; and, since Marxist doctrine recognized the revolutionary pre-eminence of the proletariat, and treated the peasant as a subsidiary and sometimes unreliable ally, the preference accorded by " Great Russian chauvinism " to the Great Russian accorded all too easily with the preference given in Marxist orthodoxy to the proletarian, and could all too easily disguise itself in Marxist trappings. It was in this sense that the resolution of the twelfth party congress declared that in some of the national republics " the partnership (*smychka*) between town and country, between the working class and the peasantry, meets its most serious obstacle in the survivals of Great Russian chauvinism both in party and in Soviet organs ".[2] Yet after all, as Stalin himself pointed out to the congress, " the political foundation of the dictatorship of the proletariat is constituted first and chiefly by the central regions which are industrial and not by the borderlands which represent peasant countries "; and though Stalin was arguing against those who, like Bukharin and Rakovsky, were seeking to " bend the stick in the direction of the peasant borderlands to the detriment of the proletarian regions ", the temptation to bend the stick in the opposite direction must have been at least equally strong.[3] To rate the claims of

---

[1] *Dvenadtsatyi S"ezd Rossiiskoi Kommunisticheskoi Partii (Bol'shevikov)* (1923), p. 530.

[2] *VKP(B) v Rezolyutsiyakh* (1941), i, 494.   [3] Stalin, *Sochineniya*, v, 265.

the peasant borderlands somewhat below those of the Great Russian industrial core could easily be represented not only as plain common sense, but as a reflexion of the Marxist doctrine of the pre-eminence of the proletariat and of Marx's and Engels' own attitude to the peasant nationalities of 1848.

Great Russian prejudices, whatever excuse could be made for them, were the main source of a tactless behaviour on the part of Soviet officials which was a subject of frequent complaint. In 1919 the official journal of Narkomnats recorded that " some comrades think the foundation of republics a mistake on our part ", and continued with outspoken frankness :

> Wrong results were often achieved thanks to the unskilful tactics of those who worked in the separated territories. The artificiality of the separation showed too clearly. Often a Great Russian spirit was crudely displayed. Through the thin layer of independence was visible the hegemony of Moscow.[1]

Other communists " thought that such national republics are created only for a very short period in order to work off in the quickest possible time the nationalist tendencies of the local population ".[2] In 1923 a resolution of the twelfth party congress noted that " a union of republics is regarded by a significant proportion of Soviet officials at the centre and in the localities not as a union of equal state units, but as a step towards the liquidation of those republics ".[3] But more serious, perhaps, were those gestures of bureaucratic or national superiority which no official disapproval ever entirely suppressed. Rakovsky, at the same congress, quoted the incident of a high Ukrainian official who, as he was leaving a congress at which he had voted for a resolution asserting the equal rights of the Ukrainian language, replied curtly to a question addressed to him in Ukrainian : " Speak to me in an intelligible language ".[4]

Such avoidable errors occupy a large space in the literature of these early years. But criticisms based on them generally ignore the magnitude of the equalizing process which the régime had

---

[1] *Zhizn' Natsional'nostei*, No. 33 (41), August 31, 1919.
[2] S. Atnagulov, *Bashkiriya* (1925), p. 71.
[3] *VKP(B) v Rezolyutsiyakh* (1941), i, 495.
[4] *Dvenadtsatyi S"ezd Rossiiskoi Kommunisticheskoi Partii (Bol'shevikov)* (1923), p. 526.

undertaken, and the real and unavoidable obstacles which had to be surmounted in the translation into practice of declared Bolshevik policy. What long remained the gravest difficulty in the way of political equality among the nations of the Soviet system was discussed in detail by Stalin at the moment when the end of the civil war was in sight and policy could be reframed on a more lasting basis.

One of the most serious obstacles [wrote Stalin in October 1920] to the realisation of Soviet autonomy is the acute shortage of intellectual forces of local origin in the border regions, the shortage of instructors in every branch of Soviet and party work without exception. This shortage cannot but hamper both educational and revolutionary constructive work in the border lands. But for this very reason it would be unwise and harmful to alienate the all too small groups of native intellectuals, who perhaps would like to serve the masses of the people but are unable to do so, perhaps because, not being communists, they believe themselves to be surrounded by an atmosphere of mistrust and are afraid of possible measures of repression. The policy of drawing such groups into Soviet work, the policy of recruiting them for economic, agrarian, food-administrative and similar posts, with the purpose of their gradual sovietisation, may be successfully applied. . . .
But the employment of national groups of intellectuals will still be far from sufficient to satisfy the demand for instructors. We must simultaneously develop in the border regions a wide network of lecture courses and schools in every branch of administration in order to create cadres of instructors from among local people. For it is clear that without such cadres the organization of native schools, courts, administration and other institutions in the native tongue will be rendered difficult in the extreme.[1]

These difficulties were an unescapable legacy of the past. Few members of any of the subject nations of the Tsarist empire now remaining within the Soviet orbit had participated in the work of government or possessed a significant intelligentsia or a potential ruling class. Many of these nations were primitive peoples, wholly without political experience. In such cases autonomy often proved unreal, and its first forms had to be imposed from without. But this was due to the weakness in resources and experience of the national group on which the

[1] Stalin, *Sochineniya*, iv, 360-361.

autonomy was conferred rather than to any desire of the central government to limit its scope and effectiveness. Such experiments could be justified, not by the extent of real autonomy immediately enjoyed, but by the opportunity which they afforded for the slow work of training " backward " peoples in the responsibilities of government. Such conditions explain familiar anomalies of which much has been made by critics of Soviet policy. It is indeed not certain that, when lists of members of " national " governments are produced showing a majority of Russian names, the bearers of those names were necessarily Russians ; Russian names, and names with Russian forms, were current among many of the non-Russian nationalities.[1] But there are authenticated cases such as the appointment of Dimanshtein, the Jewish member of the collegium of Narkomnats, as a member of the first Kazakh military-revolutionary committee,[2] and of Vainshtein, one of the leaders of the Jewish Bund, as first president of the TsIK of the Bashkir Autonomous SSR ; [3] and these were certainly not isolated instances in the earlier years, when frequent transfers of party workers from one field to another were common practice.[4] But such instances were proof of nothing more sinister than an acute shortage of competent workers in every branch of the administration.

Nor could much present help be found in Stalin's suggestion to utilize non-communist " native intellectuals ". In the few countries within the Soviet orbit where a national intelligentsia existed in sufficient numbers to provide administrators for an autonomous or independent national state — Georgia, Armenia and, more doubtfully, the Ukraine — it was at this time predominantly anti-Bolshevik, having formed the backbone of the bourgeois governments which the Bolsheviks had overthrown. In White Russia, as late as 1923, it was reported that " the teachers

---

[1] Thus Castagné purports to show from a list of names that of the thirteen members of the first Sovnarkom of the Mountaineers' Republic at least nine were Russians (*Revue du Monde Musulman*, li (1922), p. 93) ; W. R. Batsell, *Soviet Rule in Russia* (N.Y. 1929), p. 129, offers similar evidence for the Tatar Autonomous SSR.

[2] *Novyi Vostok*, v (1924), 225.

[3] F. Dan, *Dva Goda Skitanii* (Berlin, 1922), p. 69. Desire to remove from Moscow a leader of a former Menshevik organization, whose loyalty to Bolshevism was not beyond suspicion, may have played its part in this appointment.

[4] See p. 301, note 6 above.

are to a large extent infected with the *narodnik* deviation, and through lack of confidence in these teachers the whole school system is a failure ".[1] When the government was taken over by, or in the name of, the workers and peasants, a shortage of trained local leaders loyal to the new régime and capable of shouldering the burdens of administration was inevitable ; and the lacuna was filled by bringing in leaders from the RSFSR. But this was never regarded as anything but a temporary and forced expedient. If criticism is to be made of the policy of the Soviet Government on this point, it is perhaps that it went too far in encouraging the resuscitation of primitive or half-decayed languages and cultures as a basis for a national autonomy which was bound to prove largely fictitious, at any rate for some years to come, rather than that it failed to do the utmost which these conditions allowed to make equality real. In some autonomous republics and regions of the RSFSR the national group formed only a bare majority, or even a minority, of the population, and it was the Russian element which might reasonably have complained of its inferior status.

The obvious imperfections in the working of the system were thus due far more to the weakness in resources and experience of the national groups on which autonomy was conferred than to any desire of the central government to limit the scope of their opportunities. They were the price paid for the attempt to accomplish in a single generation a process of levelling up which might otherwise have been the work of centuries. Reproaches were constantly directed from the centre against the inefficiency of autonomous institutions in the national regions or republics. As late as June 1922 Stalin, in the name of the central committee of the party, accused the party organs in the Kazakh SSR of " passivity and a pessimistic frame of mind ", and Soviet organs in the same republic of " stagnation deepened by the presence of small and petty cliques ".[2] Such defects were endemic in the " backward " regions and republics. They were a legacy of the past, and cannot be fairly laid to the door of any preconceived policy. The Soviet system offered, at any rate in the early years, as large a measure of local autonomy as the nations concerned could make effective ;

[1] *Dvenadtsatyi S"ezd Rossiiskoi Kommunisticheskoi Partii (Bol'shevikov)* (1923), p. 565.
[2] *Zhizn' Natsional'nostei*, No. 12 (147), June 15, 1922. This communication is not included in Stalin's collected works.

and it stood as firmly as the enormous preponderance of the Great Russian element allowed for the principle of equality and non-discrimination between different nations. Meanwhile its economic policy was, through the more even spread of industrial development, building up the conditions of a more real equality for the future, though this was necessarily a long-term project whose concrete results were scarcely visible in this early period.

The Bolshevik policy of national self-determination had completed its evolution from the recognition of the right of secession in a bourgeois society to the recognition of equality between nations and the cessation of the exploitation of one nation by another in a socialist community of nations. The link between them was Lenin's postulate of the " voluntary union " through which this consummation would be reached, and which made union an expression and not a denial of the self-determining will of the nation. The postulate rested on Lenin's firm personal conviction that, under socialism, the element of coercion would disappear from government and be replaced by voluntary acceptance of administrative rules. Whatever the ultimate philosophical validity of this conception, it must be said that it was not realized in the period of history under consideration, during which the principles of coercion and voluntary acceptance continued to exist side by side — as at other periods, in varying proportions — in all processes of government. What could be said in favour of the Bolshevik nationalities policy was not that it could be carried into effect without the use of force : manifestly it could not, though it perhaps enabled order to be established in Russia with less application of direct force than would have been required on any other hypothesis, and to this extent implied a larger element of voluntary acceptance than any other policy could conceivably have done. What could be said in its favour was that the bourgeois theory of self-determination had by 1919 reached an impasse from which no escape was possible ; that the capitalist order, in the form which it had assumed of a division of labour between advanced or industrial nations and backward or colonial nations, had rendered real equality between nations unattainable ; and that the conception of reunion in a socialist order between really and not merely formally equal nations was a bold and imaginative attempt to break the deadlock. The importance of the policy lay in the steps taken to establish equality by obliterating the division between industrial and agricultural nations. It was, no doubt, all the easier to accept and enforce the principle of equality and non-discrimination on national grounds precisely because there were other grounds on which inequality was proclaimed and discrimination practised. Stalin himself had once spoken of ending divisions between nations in order to open the way to the division of classes.[1] National differences became less important in proportion as social differences within the nation were emphasized. But it would be difficult to exaggerate the significance of Soviet nationalties policy either in its historical setting or in its ultimate influence. It was at the outset the crucial factor in Lenin's astonishing achievement of the reassembly of nearly all the former dominions of the Tsars after the disintegration and dispersal of war, revolution and civil war; and it long remained an effective ingredient of Soviet foreign policy in many parts of the world.

[1] Stalin, *Sochineniya*, ii, 362.

CHAPTER 13

THROUGH ALLIANCE TO FEDERATION

WHEN the civil war was finally extinguished towards the end of 1920, the principle of independence or autonomy had been extended to the whole of the former Russian Empire, which now fell into three categories. Certain former Russian territories — Poland, Finland, the three Baltic states recognized as independent, Bessarabia seized by Rumania, and the strip of territory ceded to Turkey at Brest-Litovsk — had passed for the time being altogether out of the orbit of Moscow. Of the remainder, the Russian Socialist Federal Soviet Republic formed a single nucleus incorporating nearly twenty autonomous units inhabited by non-Russian, mainly Muslim, peoples; the RSFSR alone accounted for 92 per cent of the area, and 70 per cent of the population, eventually to be included in the USSR. The rest was divided into no less than eight separate states, whose nominal independence was effective in varying degrees. These were the Ukrainian and White Russian Socialist Soviet Republics; the Azerbaijani, Armenian and Georgian Socialist Soviet Republics;[1] the Far Eastern Republic, with its capital at Chita; and the two Central Asian Soviet Republics of Khorezm and Bokhara. These external trappings of dispersal served, however, to mask a movement towards reunion which was already far advanced. The end of the civil war marked the transition from the second of the three periods retrospectively recorded in the party resolution of 1923, " cooperation in the form of a military alliance ", to the third, the " military-economic and political union of the peoples ", which was ultimately to be completed in the form of the Union of Soviet Socialist Republics.

The second of these periods, representing the specifically

---

[1] The Armenian SSR dated from December 1920, the Georgian SSR from February 1921.

military phase of reunion, had arisen directly out of the civil war
and begun in the western borderlands, where the emergency was
most acute. In January 1919, even before Kiev had been won
back, the provisional Soviet Government of the Ukraine issued
a declaration of its " solidarity with the Soviet Russian Federal
Republic, the cradle of world revolution ", and forecast the unification of the Ukrainian Soviet Republic with Soviet Russia on
the principles of socialist federation; the first White Russian
Congress of Soviets in February 1919 expressed a similar aspiration; [1] and Stalin deduced from these symptoms the encouraging
conclusion that " through the independent Soviet republics the
peoples of Russia are coming to a new voluntary brotherly unity ".[2]
Military events first forced the issue in the Ukraine. On May 18,
1919, the central executive committee of the Soviet Ukraine issued,
" in conjunction with the Kiev Soviet of Workers' Deputies, the
Kiev County Congress of Peasants' Deputies, and representatives
of the Kiev trade unions and factory shop committees " (an
agglomeration of authority betokening a particularly significant
occasion), a decree enunciating two general principles :

(1) All armed struggle against the enemies of the Soviet
republics should be unified in all existing Soviet republics ;
(2) All material resources necessary for the conduct of this
struggle should be concentrated round a centre common
to all the republics.[3]

On June 1, 1919, a decree of VTsIK in Moscow, while " recognizing the independence, liberty and self-determination of the
toiling masses of the Ukraine, Latvia, Lithuania, White Russia
and Crimea ", cited the Ukrainian resolution of May 18 and
unspecified " proposals of the Soviet Governments of Latvia,
Lithuania and White Russia ", and, on the strength of these,
proclaimed the necessity of a " military union "[4] between the
socialist Soviet republics of these countries and the RSFSR.
The union was to involve a fusion of " military organizations and

---

[1] *Istoriya Sovetskoi Konstitutsii v Dekretakh* (1936), pp. 103-104, 109-110.
[2] Stalin, *Sochineniya*, iv, 229.
[3] *Istoriya Sovetskoi Konstitutsii v Dekretakh* (1936), p. 122.
[4] This is apparently the first use in this context of the word *soyuz* which
does duty in Russian for both " alliance " and " union ". The confusion of
terminology is significant of a lack of precision in Russian constitutional thought,
and helped in this case to bridge the transition from one status to another.

military command, of the councils of national economy, of railway administration and economic structure, of finances, and of people's commissariats of labour ". The decree concluded by appointing a commission to negotiate the carrying out of this project.[1]

Within a few weeks of the issue of this decree the tide of civil war had swept over most of the territories with which it purported to deal. Like so many enactments of the period, the decree of June 1, 1919, remained on paper : the commission which was to have worked out the terms of the proposed union is not known to have met. Nevertheless, the moral was not lost. The decree of June 1, 1919, though void of concrete result, was an unconscious, almost accidental, foreshadowing of the process through which the new entity of the USSR would one day be created. It contained the notion of a " union " or " alliance " between the component parts of the former Russian Empire ; it established the principle of a " close union " between certain vital people's commissariats ; and it presupposed the right of Moscow, armed with some kind of formal prior concurrence of the other units of the alliance, to take constitutional decisions binding on all.[2] Military necessity had put the issue in a form which suited and confirmed Bolshevik theory. National self-determination was conditional on the unity of the workers of all nations in the revolutionary struggle and therefore subordinate to it : if failure to establish unity between the workers of different nations and regions of the former Russian Empire enabled counter-revolution to triumph, that would mean the end of self-determination for all. The argument naturally begged the question what manner of national self-determination would be achieved through the victory of the revolution. But in terms of the immediate military emergency it was valid and irrefutable. Nor did its validity pass

---

[1] *Sobranie Uzakonenii, 1919*, No. 21, art. 264. In the enumeration of the territories to which this decree applied, the Crimea was mentioned in three passages and omitted in two, which may suggest that its inclusion was an after-thought. Its inclusion was anomalous, since it never, like the other countries named, enjoyed the status of an independent Soviet republic. It later became an autonomous republic of the RSFSR.

[2] A resolution drafted by Lenin and approved by the party conference of December 1919 boldly described the Ukrainian resolution of May 18 and the decree of VIsIK of June 1 of the same year as constituting a " federal link " between the RSFSR and the Ukraine (Lenin, *Sochineniya*, xxiv, 552 ; *VKP(B) v Rezolyutsiyakh* (1941), i, 316).

with the immediate emergency, since socialist nations lived in lasting peril of capitalist attack.[1] The need for unity was perennial, and found expression in the unity of the Red Army. Once that unity was accepted as an obvious military necessity, and once the prestige of that army had been established through its victory in the civil war, the battle for unity — and unity on a Russian base — was more than half won.

The way was thus cleared for the development of an *ad hoc* military alliance into a permanent " military-economic and political union of the peoples ". The third and final stage of the process began automatically and almost accidentally as territories were liberated from bourgeois governments or occupying armies and the need arose to put their relations with the RSFSR on a more permanent basis. A resolution of VTsIK, published on February 15, 1920, described " the establishment of normal relations between the RSFSR and the autonomous Soviet republics and, in general, the non-Russian nationalities " as being " one of the most important tasks of VTsIK ", and set up a commission " to work out questions of the federal structure of the RSFSR ".[2] The Bashkir, Tatar, Kazakh and Kalmyk autonomous republics dated from the summer of 1920. Progress, though delayed by the war with Poland and the campaign against Wrangel, was made from the centre outward. On September 30, 1920, a treaty of " military-economic alliance " together with five supplementary treaties were concluded between the RSFSR and the Azerbaijani SSR which had come into existence just six months before ; and ten days later Stalin, as People's Commissar for Affairs of Nationalities, made an important pronouncement of policy in the form of an article in *Pravda*.[3]

Stalin began with the argument of military necessity :

Three years of revolution and civil war in Russia have shown that without the mutual support of central Russia and her

---

[1] A resolution of the tenth party congress of 1921 deduced the case for unity from the danger of capitalist attack (*ibid.* i, 384).

[2] *Zhizn' Natsional'nostei*, No. 6 (61, *leg.* 63), February 15, 1920.

[3] Stalin, *Sochineniya*, iv, 351-363 : it also appeared in the current issue of *Zhizn' Natsional'nostei*. The importance of this article in the history of the formation of the USSR was marked by a lecture devoted to it on its twentieth anniversary, October 10, 1940, at the Institute of Law of the Soviet Academy of Sciences, and published in *Sovetskoe Gosudarstvo i Pravo*, No. 11, 1940, pp. 1-10.

borderlands the victory of the revolution is impossible, the liberation of Russia from the claws of imperialism is impossible.

Only two alternatives were open to the border countries : to line up with Russia or to line up with the Entente. The writer continued with a rather ponderous irony :

> The so-called independence of so-called independent Georgia, Armenia, Poland, Finland, etc., is only a deceptive appearance masking the complete dependence of these — pardon the word — states on this or that group of imperialists.

If a majority of any of these nations demanded secession, Russia, as in the case of Finland, would presumably acquiesce. But the question was no longer one of rights, which were indisputable, but of the interests of the masses of the people ; and " the interests of the masses of the people say that the demand for the separation of the borderlands at the present stage of the revolution is profoundly counter-revolutionary ".

Brushing aside the idea of mere " cultural-national autonomy ", Stalin then advocated the solution of " *regional* autonomy of the borderlands " — an autonomy which must be effective both in the cultural and in the economic sense. But the main point of interest at the moment was the relation of " Soviet autonomy " to the unfinished " administrative redistribution of Russia ". Stalin praised the elasticity of " Soviet autonomy " which extended " from a narrow administrative autonomy (Volga Germans, Chuvashes, Karelians) . . . to a broad political autonomy (Bashkirs, Volga Tatars, Kirgiz), from this broad political autonomy to its still wider form (Ukraine, Turkestan), and from the Ukrainian type of autonomy to the highest form of autonomy, to treaty relations (Azerbaijan) ". What was significant here was, first, that Stalin made no substantive distinction, but only one of degree, either between the autonomous regions and autonomous republics of the RSFSR, or between the autonomous republics of the RSFSR and formally independent republics like the Ukraine and Azerbaijan, and, secondly, that he singled out the recently concluded treaty of " military-economic alliance " with Azerbaijan as the " highest form of autonomy ". The line of policy which, over the next two years, was to lead to the creation of the USSR was plainly foreshadowed in this enumeration. More careful attention would be paid in the future to the constitutional difference, which was rigidly maintained, between autonomous units of the RSFSR and the treaty republics. But the main course had been clearly charted in Stalin's article of October 1920. In the first category the lesser peoples would continue to be organized as autonomous units of the RSFSR; Stalin, when he wrote the article, was about to undertake a journey whose principal purpose was the "administrative redistribution" of the multifarious peoples of the northern Caucasus.[1] In the second category, Azerbaijan and the other seven independent republics would be organized on the basis of treaty relations with the RSFSR, of which the Azerbaijani treaties of September 30, 1920, were the prototype.

The Azerbaijani model was clumsy but direct. The main treaty established the principle of a " close military and financial-economic union " (or " alliance ") between the two states, and bound them to carry out in the shortest time a unification (1) of military organization and military command, (2) of the organs controlling the national economy and foreign trade, (3) of the supply organs, (4) of rail and water transport and of the postal-telegraphic administration and (5) of finance. The military item was presumably dealt with in an unpublished convention. The other items were covered by five supplementary treaties signed simultaneously with the main treaty. In three of the supplementary treaties (finance, foreign trade and national economy) the competent organ of the RSFSR appointed its plenipotentiary to the Azerbaijani Sovnarkom (or, for national economy, Sovnarkhoz) " with the right of a deciding vote "; in the other two treaties unification was achieved by slightly differing provisions.[2] But the emphasis on unification of economic and financial policy was obvious throughout. This was an early model, and Azerbaijan was a weak and backward country. The six treaties, like their successors between the RSFSR and other independent Soviet republics, were concluded as treaties between sovereign states and signed by the respective commissars for foreign affairs in the forms recognized by international law. But the result of the union

---

[1] See p. 328 above.

[2] The six treaties are in *RSFSR : Sbornik Deistvuyushchikh Dogovorov*, i (1921), Nos. 1-6, pp. 1-12.

could hardly be other than the dependence of Azerbaijan on the RSFSR. No great care was thought necessary in the text to mask this reality.

The next treaty in the series was concluded three months later with the Ukrainian SSR, whose long ordeal of successive foreign occupations had ended with the defeat of the Polish invaders in July 1920. As Azerbaijan (except for the Russian and cosmopolitan city of Baku, which cared little for the national aspirations of the country) was perhaps the poorest and weakest of the eight republics, so the Ukraine was certainly the strongest and the most insistent in her claim to formal independence and equality. The Ukrainian treaty had a certain solemnity and significance in that it was signed in Moscow on December 28, 1920, during the eighth All-Russian Congress of Soviets, and received the formal ratification of the congress; it was the only one of these treaties to be signed by Lenin himself on behalf of the RSFSR. Rakovsky, at this time president of the Ukrainian Sovnarkom and principal Ukrainian delegate to the congress, stressed the transition from military to economic union :

> There is no doubt whatever that our future policy will go along the path of unification, and especially now, in the period of Soviet economic construction, this integration and unification are just as indispensable as earlier in the period of military defence, perhaps even more indispensable.[1]

The wording was more elaborate than that of the Azerbaijani treaty. The preamble paid homage to " the right of nations to self-determination proclaimed by the great proletarian revolution ", and recognized " the independence and sovereignty of each of the contracting parties " as well as " the necessity to unite their forces for purposes of defence and also in the interests of their economic construction ". The machinery set up by the treaty (everything being covered this time by a single instrument) carefully avoided any direct implication of dependence. Military and naval affairs, national economy, foreign trade, finance, labour, communications and posts and telegraphs were entrusted to " unified commissariats " of both republics. These unified commissariats " enter into the composition of the Sovnarkom of the RSFSR and are represented in the Sovnarkom of the Ukrainian

[1] *Vos'moi Vserossiiskii S"ezd Sovetov* (1921), p. 232.

SSR by plenipotentiaries who are confirmed and controlled by the Ukrainian central executive committee and congress of Soviets ". On the other hand, the Ukrainian SSR had its representatives in VTsIK and in the All-Russian Congress of Soviets, in which ultimate authority over the unified commissariats resided. By a refinement introduced during the discussion at the eighth All-Russian Congress of Soviets, the representatives of one party in the congress of Soviets of the other party were to have no voting rights when matters affecting non-unified commissariats were in question.[1]

The year 1921 saw three more republics brought within the same system — the White Russian, the Georgian and the Armenian SSR. The White Russian treaty signed on January 16, 1921, was identical in terms with the Ukrainian treaty.[2] But, in the matter of finance at least, the comparatively loose Ukrainian model seems to have proved insufficiently strict for the more backward White Russian republic, which can hardly have possessed many financial experts ; and six months later a treaty was concluded on the Azerbaijani model, under which a representative of the Russian Commissariat of Finance sat in the White Russian Sovnarkom with the right of a deciding vote, with the new and additional provision that the budgets of the unified commissariats should be submitted to the Narkomfin and Sovnarkom of the RSFSR for confirmation and for eventual inclusion in the budget of the RSFSR.[3] Meanwhile, the treaty of May 21, 1921, with the Georgian SSR followed the Ukrainian pattern with only a few variants.[4] The treaty with the Armenian SSR, signed on September 30, 1921, was confined exclusively to financial matters, and stood half-way between the shared control of the Ukrainian model and the subordinate status of Azerbaijan and White Russia.[5] These differences of form certainly implied differences of substance. But the variations probably occurred not so much in the

[1] *RSFSR : Sbornik Deistvuyushchikh Dogovorov*, i (1921), No. 8, pp. 15-16 ; *Vos'moi Vserossiiskii S"ezd Sovetov* (1921), p. 234.

[2] *RSFSR : Sbornik Deistvuyushchikh Dogovorov*, i (1921), No. 7, pp. 13-14 ; W. R. Batsell, *Soviet Rule in Russia* (N.Y. 1929), p. 204, misdates the treaty January 16, 1920, being misled by a misprint in the heading of the treaty in the *Sbornik*, though the date is correctly given there in the text.

[3] *RSFSR : Sbornik Deistvuyushchikh Dogovorov*, ii (1921), No. 41, pp. 7-8.

[4] Klyuchnikov i Sabanin, *Mezhdunarodnaya Politika*, iii (1928), i, 22-23.

[5] *RSFSR : Sbornik Deistvuyushchikh Dogovorov*, ii (1921), No. 40, pp. 5-6.

degree of unification achieved as in the extent to which the allied republics were able to contribute effectively to the working of the unified system.

The remaining three republics — the Khorezm, Bokharan and Far Eastern Republics — were in the anomalous position of not being " socialist Soviet republics "; the two first were people's Soviet republics, the third a democratic republic. Khorezm (the former Khiva) and Bokhara had never been formally incorporated in the Tsarist empire; and, partly perhaps because of the turbulent conditions still prevailing there, partly because of their backward social development, Moscow showed a strong inclination to respect their " foreign " status for the present. Treaties of alliance and economic agreements were concluded by the RSFSR with Khorezm on September 13, 1920,[1] and with Bokhara on March 4, 1921.[2] In the military sphere, provision was made for " military-political " conventions to establish " a common plan and common leadership and preparations which will guarantee the fulfilment of the tasks of defending the independence and freedom of both republics ".[3] So far the pattern was familiar, though it may be doubted whether these military clauses had much immediate application, since the Red Army was actively engaged in Bokhara against the Basmachi till the late summer of 1922.

The economic provisions, to which the major part of the treaties was devoted, were, on the other hand, quite different from those in the treaties with socialist republics. Here there could be no question of a unification of organs. All foreign trade was to be conducted, not by private persons, but by state institutions; and the republics were to give no industrial or commercial rights in their territories to any state except the RSFSR or another Soviet republic. For the rest, great emphasis was laid on the renunciation by the RSFSR of all property rights or concessions of the former Russian Empire in the territory of the two republics, including the land of the Russian colonists settled before the

---

[1] *RSFSR : Sbornik Deistvuyushchikh Dogovorov*, i (1921), Nos. 9-10, pp. 17-26.

[2] *Ibid.* ii (1921), Nos. 42-43, pp. 7-14.

[3] The phrase is quoted from the Khorezm treaty; the Bokharan treaty merely refers back to an unpublished military convention of November 1920. The proposed new conventions, if concluded, were not published.

revolution in Bokhara, who could, however, apparently retain their land by opting for Bokharan citizenship; and substantial lump-sum payments were promised by way of subsidy to both republics — 500,000,000 rubles to Khorezm, and a sum to be fixed by subsequent agreement to Bokhara. These treaties may in practice have represented as great a degree of dependence on the RSFSR for Khorezm and Bokhara as for the independent socialist Soviet republics or for the autonomous republics, or even perhaps greater. But the formal ties were of a different order, and belonged to the conception of " foreign relations " rather than of " federal union ". It was several years before the two republics were thought ripe for introduction into the unified system.

The constitutional outcome of all these arrangements cannot easily be defined : what resulted from the treaties with the Ukrainian and White Russian republics and the three Trans-caucasian republics had some features of an alliance, some of a federation and some of a unitary state.[1] But this vagueness was characteristic of all Soviet constitutional documents of the period. The provision in the Ukrainian and White Russian treaties to admit Ukrainian and White Russian representatives to the All-Russian Congress of Soviets and to VTsIK had no counterpart in the Asiatic treaties. None the less, delegates of Azerbaijan, Georgia and Armenia, as well as of the Ukraine and White Russia, were present, without any objection being taken, at the ninth All-Russian Congress of Soviets in December 1921 ;[2] and the congress decided that " in view of . . . the desire of independent Soviet republics to have their representatives in the supreme legislative organ of the republic ", the number of members of VTsIK should be increased accordingly.[3] This gave a formal basis for the issue by VTsIK of decrees which were treated, apparently without further formality, as binding throughout the territories of the allied republics.

The other significant innovation was the emphasis laid in all

---

[1] The curious may find in this uncertainty of status a case of history repeating itself. Generations of historians had debated the question whether the treaty of Pereyaslavl of 1654 constituted a personal union between Muscovy and the Ukraine or an incorporation of the Ukraine in the Muscovite empire.

[2] Rakovsky, on this occasion, made, in the name of all five republics, the declaration about the Red Army, quoted on p. 368 above.

[3] *S"ezdy Sovetov RSFSR v Postanovleniyakh* (1939), p. 219.

the treaties on economic unity. As Stalin put it, in his subsequent review of the process, it was " the meagreness of the economic resources remaining at the disposal of the republics " which compelled them " to combine these meagre resources so as to employ them more rationally and to develop the main branches of production ".[1] The economic aftermath of the civil war completed the process which the military exigencies of the war itself had begun. Already in March 1920 the slogan " everything for the front " had given way to the slogan " everything for the national economy ".[2] Even earlier, the seventh All-Russian Congress of Soviets had appointed an " administrative-territorial commission " to redraw local boundaries on lines more in harmony with economic groupings.[3] Thereafter this subject was constantly in view. A plan which emanated from the State Planning Commission for the division of European Russia into twelve economic regions and Asiatic Russia into nine, was cautiously blessed by the twelfth party congress in April 1923 as a " preliminary working hypothesis, needing to be supplemented, checked and elaborated on the basis of experience."[4] The creation of these regions, cutting across all political divisions, including those drawn on national lines, provided a fresh illustration of the contradiction between the long-term and short-term aims of Soviet nationalities policy. The demands of economic unity, which was an essential condition of economic progress for the " backward " nations, and therefore of real equality in the future, came into conflict with the disintegrating influences exercised by present national aspirations.

The diplomatic stage of unification lagged behind the military and economic stages; for here there had been no specific cause or impulse to unite. None of the treaties between the RSFSR and the other Soviet republics included foreign affairs in the list of unified commissariats; and, since the unified control of foreign affairs was a traditional hall-mark of federation, its omission here emphasized the character of the relation now established as

---

[1] Stalin, *Sochineniya*, v, 146. [2] *Ibid.* iv, 295.
[3] *S"ezdy Sovetov RSFSR v Postanovleniyakh* (1939), p. 152.
[4] *VKP(B) v Rezolyutsiyakh* (1941), i, 497; *Zhizn' Natsional'nostei*, No. 12 (147), June 15, 1922, had printed a protest from the president of the Chuvash regional executive committee, who observed that, " if the autonomous regions and republics are to enjoy only political rights, there is no point in calling them autonomous national regions and republics ".

an alliance rather than a federation. In practice, the Ukraine was the only republic to make any wide use of the licence to conduct its own foreign relations, concluding treaties with such other states as recognized it [1] and maintaining its own diplomatic representatives for a short period in Prague, Berlin and Warsaw.

Apart, however, from the practical obstacles to the organization of independent foreign offices and diplomatic services by backward and impecunious republics not recognized by any important foreign countries, the relation between these republics and the RSFSR would by itself have precluded any serious attempt to conduct a separate foreign policy. The treaties created a formal union so close that the common attitude to the outside world could, on any matter of importance, only be determined by a common authority and represented through a single channel. But nothing like uniformity of procedure had yet been established. The Soviet delegation which signed the treaty of peace with Poland at Riga on March 18, 1921, was a joint delegation of the RSFSR and the Ukrainian SSR, the Russian delegation also holding full powers from the White Russian SSR.[2] Two days earlier the RSFSR had signed at Moscow a treaty with Turkey determining the frontier between Turkey and the three Transcaucasian republics, and even effecting several territorial changes, without any formal participation of the republics either in the negotiation or in the conclusion of the treaty. The point had, however, not been overlooked. The last article but one of the treaty ran as follows :

> Russia engages herself to take in relation to the Transcaucasian republics the necessary steps to bring about the recognition by these republics, in treaties which will be concluded by them with Turkey, of the articles of the present treaty directly affecting them.[3]

Later in the year, when the republics of Armenia, Azerbaijan and Georgia redeemed this vicarious promise by concluding a treaty with Turkey at Kars, it was specifically noted in the preamble that they had carried on the negotiations " with the participation of the

[1] See, for instance, a treaty with Estonia of November 25, 1921, published in *League of Nations: Treaty Series*, xi (1922), No. 294. In the autumn of 1921 Frunze went on special mission as Ukrainian delegate to Angora to conclude a treaty with Turkey (M. P. Frunze, *Sobranie Sochinenii*, i (1929), 274).

[2] *Sbornik Deistvuyushchikh Dogovorov RSFSR*, ii (1921), No. 51, p. 53.

[3] *Ibid.* ii, No. 52, pp. 72-77.

RSFSR ",[1] whose delegate also signed the treaty.

This confusion of procedure could not, however, continue. Early in 1922 the issue was brought to a head by the invitation of the western allied Powers to the RSFSR to attend the forthcoming European conference at Genoa — an invitation which took no account of the constitutional status of other Soviet governments. On February 22, 1922, the eight republics entered into an agreement empowering the RSFSR to " represent and defend " their interests at the forthcoming international conference at Genoa, and to sign not only any agreement concluded there, but " all international agreements of any kind directly or indirectly connected with this conference with states represented at the said conference and with any other states, and to take all measures resulting therefrom ".[2] This wide authority amply filled the gap left by the omission of foreign affairs from the list of " unified commissariats ". If there was any resistance to this merging of diplomatic functions, it came from the Ukraine, the only republic strong enough to indulge in gestures of diplomatic independence; and a soothing statement from Yakovlev, acting Ukrainian Commissar for Foreign Affairs, in the summer of 1922 was palpably designed to assuage opposition :

> The foreign policy of the Ukraine has not and cannot have any interests other than those common with Russia, which is just such a proletarian state as the Ukraine. The heroic struggle of Russia, in complete alliance with the Ukraine, on all fronts against domestic and foreign imperialists, is now giving place to an equally united diplomatic front. The Ukraine is independent in her foreign policy where her own specific interests are concerned. But, in questions which are of common political and economic interest to all Soviet republics, the Russian as well as the Ukrainian Commissariats for Foreign Affairs act as the united federal power.[3]

---

[1] Klyuchnikov i Sabanin, *Mezhdunarodnaya Politika*, iii (1928), i, 139.

[2] *RSFSR: Sbornik Deistvuyushchikh Dogovorov*, iii (1921), No. 1, pp. 1-3. It is significant that the same forces of common regional economic interest operated even beyond the circle of Soviet republics; on March 29-30, 1922, delegates of the RSFSR, Poland, Estonia and Latvia met in Riga to " coordinate the action of their representatives " at the Genoa conference (*Conférence de Moscou sur la Limitation des Armaments* (Moscow, 1923), pp. 139-141).

[3] Quoted from *Izvestiya* of August 13, 1922, in A. L. P. Dennis, *Foreign Policies of Soviet Russia* (1924), p. 189.

The last occasion on which the formality of separate representation was observed was at Berlin in November 1922, when the Ukraine, White Russia, Georgia, Azerbaijan, Armenia and the Far Eastern Republic signed with Germany a treaty extending to them the provisions of the treaty of Rapallo.[1] In December 1922, when a conference of eastern European Powers for the reduction of armaments met in Moscow, Litvinov informed it that " since the armed forces of all the Soviet republics constitute a single whole, the Russian delegate has full powers to negotiate a reduction of them".[2]

Before the end of 1922, therefore, the process of reunion was virtually complete and was beginning to be taken for granted. It remained only to clothe it in the appropriate constitutional garb. The dividing line between the independent republics linked in treaty relations with the RSFSR and the autonomous republics within the RSFSR was not in practice very great. The logical course would no doubt have been to assimilate them to one another, either by making the treaty republics autonomous units of an enlarged RSFSR, or by removing the autonomous republics from the aegis of the RSFSR and making them units, side by side with the RSFSR and the treaty republics, of the larger union.[3] But the logical rarely coincides with the politically expedient. · The first solution would have been resented by the treaty republics, and especially by the Ukraine, as a derogation from their formally independent status and an act of submission to " Russia "; the second solution would have weakened the RSFSR as the essential linchpin of the whole structure and incurred the hostility of all the vested interests in its existing predominance. Hence a compromise had to be framed which diverged as little as possible from the *status quo*. The RSFSR remained as a "federation" embracing at this time eight autonomous republics and thirteen autonomous regions,[4] and entered as a unit, on formally equal terms with

---

[1] Klyuchnikov i Sabanin, *Mezhdunarodnaya Politika*, iii (1928), i, 206.

[2] *Conférence de Moscou pour la Limitation des Armaments* (Moscow, 1923), p. 64.

[3] The second proposal was actually made in the nationalities section of the twelfth party congress in April 1923, apparently as an adjunct to the proposal of the Georgian " deviators " that the republics of the Transcaucasian federation should enter the USSR as separate units (Stalin, *Sochineniya*, v, 269-270).

[4] The Bashkir, Tatar, Kazakh, Turkestan, Mountaineers', Dagestan, Crimean and Yakut autonomous republics; the Chuvash, Mari, Kalmyk, Votyak, Komi, Kabardino-Balkarsh, Buryat-Mongol, Karachaevo-Cherkessian, Oirak, Adygeisk, Chechensk, Karelian and Volga German autonomous regions

the independent socialist Soviet republics, into the wider federation.

In order to pave the way for this solution, the three small Transcaucasian republics were required to combine into a local federal unit; and this apparently trivial step became the occasion of serious friction between Armenia and Georgia, between rival groups of Georgian Bolsheviks, between rival groups within the central committee of the party itself and, finally, between Stalin and the now almost incapacitated Lenin. The controversy was in part a sequel of the events of February 1921, when Georgia was taken over by the Bolsheviks and Lenin had so surprisingly, and vainly, come out for a coalition with the Mensheviks.[1] But it also reflected the intensity of Georgian nationalism and recent Menshevik affiliations, which made Georgia, hardly less than the Ukraine, a kernel of separatist " national " resistance to the Soviet power. It was the difficulty, from the Soviet point of view, of solving the Georgian problem without the crude and undisguised application of force to politically conscious groups of Georgians loudly voicing the claims of national self-determination, which caused embarrassment and division in the party leadership.

From the moment when all three Transcaucasian republics had been brought within the Soviet fold, Armenia, conscious of her military and economic weakness and isolation, had pressed for some form of federation or union between them;[2] and Georgia, proud of an independent tradition, had objected to a move which would tend to level out economic conditions between herself and her poorer neighbours and to increase the influence of her own large and despised Armenian minority. The difference of view was reflected in the respective constitutions of the two republics; for, whereas the constitution of the Armenian SSR spoke of the strengthening of relations with its neighbours, the

(the last being still officially designated a " workers' commune "). The list is in *Pyat' Let Vlasti Sovetov* (1922), p. 227 (to which is added the Chechensk region formed in November 1922). The number of republics and regions increased considerably later. Two autonomous republics (Abkhazia and Ajaria) and one autonomous region (Yugo-Osetia), originally part of Georgia, were included in the Transcaucasian SFSR.

[1] See pp. 349-350 above.

[2] B. A. Bor'yan, *Armeniya, Mezhdunarodnaya Diplomatiya, i SSSR* (1929), ii, 319, quotes pronouncements in this sense from the protocols of the first and second Armenian congresses of Soviets held in 1921 and 1922 respectively.

constitution of the Georgian SSR merely declared its solidarity
with all existing Soviet republics and its readiness to enter into
" a single international socialist Soviet republic ".[1] Here as elsewhere, however, economic necessity worked strongly on the side
of unification. Within a few weeks of the taking over of Georgia in
February 1921 the Georgian railways, the vital link in Transcaucasian communications, were incorporated with those of the other
two republics in the Soviet system, apparently in the face of
protests from the Georgian Bolsheviks and with the introduction of large numbers of Russian railway workers.[2] As early as
April 1921 Lenin, faced with the danger of an economic collapse,
urgently recommended the creation of a " regional economic
organ for the whole of Transcaucasia ".[3] A few days later,
obviously preoccupied with the success of NEP, he published
in *Pravda Gruzii* an article in which he appeared to warn the
Transcaucasian and Caucasian peoples against the extremes of
war communism. It was not, he explained, necessary to copy
" our tactics " in detail, but rather to imitate the spirit and to
profit by the example of the years from 1917 to 1921. What was
required was " more flexibility, caution, conciliatoriness in regard
to the petty bourgeoisie, the intelligentsia and especially the
peasantry . . . a slower, more cautious, more systematic approach
to socialism ". The most urgent needs were to improve the
position of the peasant and to undertake works of electrification
and irrigation.[4] The mood of 1921 was set strongly towards NEP,
with its relaxation of centralized discipline and control. Not much
was done in Georgia for the rest of the year. Famine raged in
the Volga provinces of European Russia and was a warning against
any abrupt change in systems of cultivation. It was afterwards
complained that not even a beginning had been made in Georgia
with the work of agrarian reform.[5]

In December 1921, under the direct impetus of a visit from

---

[1] Quoted *ibid.* ii, 333.

[2] These particulars come from an *ex parte* statement at the twelfth party
congress, but were not seriously challenged (*Dvenadtsatyi S"ezd Rossiiskoi
Kommunisticheskoi Partii (Bol'shevikov)* (1923), pp. 535-536) ; according to
Enukidze (*ibid.* p. 540) the action was taken with the approval of the president
of the Georgian Bolshevik military-revolutionary committee.

[3] Lenin, *Sochineniya*, xxvi, 188.   [4] *Ibid.* xxvi, 191-192.

[5] *Dvenadtsatyi S"ezd Rossiiskoi Kommunisticheskoi Partii (Bol'shevikov)*
(1923), p. 162.

Orjonikidze as the Georgian specialist of the party, a new campaign was opened; and an eventful year began with the arrest of Mensheviks who had remained active in Georgia after the amnesty of March 1921.[1] On March 12, 1922, under continued pressure from the centre, the three republics concluded a treaty forming a Federation of Socialist Soviet Republics of Transcaucasia (FSSRZ) with a " plenipotentiary conference " as the supreme federal organ. " Direction of economic policy " was one of the functions placed by the treaty under federal control; and Lenin's plea of a year before for a " regional economic organ " was at length satisfied by the creation of a " supreme economic council ".[2] No sooner had this been achieved than orders came from party headquarters in Moscow that what was needed was not a federation of republics but a single federal republic. This threw the local communists, who had reluctantly accepted federation, into a state of confusion and revolt. In the summer of 1922 a special commission was sent down to Georgia by the central committee, composed of Dzerzhinsky, Mitskevich-Kaptsukas and Manuilsky (a Pole, a Lithuanian and a Ukrainian), to pass judgment and restore discipline. In the autumn the local communist leaders, Mdivani and Makharadze, were relieved of their posts and recalled to Moscow and a new Georgian party committee constituted. The obstacles having thus been removed, a first Transcaucasian Congress of Soviets met in Tiflis, and, on December 13, 1922, adopted the constitution of a Transcaucasian Socialist Federal Soviet Republic (ZSFSR), closely modelled on that of the RSFSR.[3] The national recalcitrance of the Georgians had been curbed, and a suitable unit created for the formation of the broader union.[4]

[1] It would be impossible on the basis of now accessible material to unravel in detail the tangled story of what happened in Georgia, and in the party about Georgia, during the twelve months from December 1921 to December 1922. But the broad outlines are clear from the prolonged debates of the twelfth party congress of April 1923, in which all sides spoke their minds with considerable frankness — the last occasion of so much plain speaking at a party congress.

[2] The treaty itself is in *Istoriya Sovetskoi Konstitutsii v Dekretakh* (1936), pp. 208-210; the statute of the " supreme economic council " is translated from another source in W. R. Batsell, *Soviet Rule in Russia* (N.Y. 1929), pp. 403-408, where, however, the " council " has become a " conference ".

[3] *Istoriya Sovetskoi Konstitutsii v Dekretakh* (1936), pp. 223-232.

[4] At the twelfth party congress of April 1923, these proceedings were attacked by Mdivani, Makharadze and Bukharin, and defended by Stalin,

Through these proceedings the eight independent units in the Soviet constellation were reduced to six. A further convenient reduction was effected by the reincorporation of the Far Eastern Republic in the RSFSR. Of the remaining five, the republics of Khorezm and Bokhara, not yet socialist, were not eligible for inclusion in the union, and retained their allied status. Of the three that were left, the Ukrainian SSR and the Transcaucasian SFSR simultaneously passed resolutions on December 13, 1922 (the very day of the formation of the Transcaucasian SFSR), in favour of creating a union of socialist Soviet republics; and the White Russian SSR followed three days later.[1] On December 26, 1922, the tenth All-Russian Congress of Soviets, on a motion by Stalin, passed a resolution in similar terms.[2] On December 30, 1922, the delegates of the RSFSR, of the Ukrainian and White Russian SSRs and of the Transcaucasian SFSR constituted themselves by anticipation the first congress of Soviets of the USSR. The occasion marked, as Stalin said in the main speech of the day, " the triumph of new Russia over old Russia, over Russia the gendarme of Europe, over Russia the butcher of Asia ";[3] and he proceeded to read a solemn declaration and a draft treaty " on the organization of a Union of Soviet Socialist Republics ".[4] The declaration enumerated the three motives for union — economic, military and ideological :

Orjonikidze and Enukidze. The delicate feature of the situation was that Lenin was believed, before succumbing to his second stroke, to have promised his support to Mdivani : a letter of his, criticizing the policy of Stalin and Dzerzhinsky, was circulated to members of the congress, though not published. Trotsky, who did not speak on the subject at the congress, afterwards claimed to have been in Lenin's confidence and to have shared his views. The episode will be further discussed in the second instalment of the present work : *The Struggle for Power, 1923–1928.*

[1] The documents are in *Istoriya Sovetskoi Konstitutsii v Dekretakh* (1936), pp. 233-240 : Stalin, in a statement to *Pravda* on November 18, 1922, declared that the initiative had come from the republics themselves three months earlier (Stalin, *Sochineniya*, v, 138).

[2] *Sobranie Uzakonenii, 1923*, No. 28, art. 325 ; *Istoriya Sovetskoi Konstitutsii v Dekretakh* (1936), pp. 241-242 ; Stalin, *Sochineniya*, v, 145-155. This resolution introduced for the first time the title " Union of Soviet Socialist Republics " ; the constituent republics of the union, as well as the autonomous republics, were " Socialist Soviet Republics ". No explanation of the inversion ever seems to have been given.

[3] Stalin, *Sochineniya*, v, 158.

[4] *Istoriya Sovetskoi Konstitutsii v Dekretakh* (1936), pp. 244-250 ; Stalin, *Sochineniya*, v, 393-401.

Devastated fields, factories at a stand-still, destroyed productive powers and exhausted economic resources, which
remain as the legacy of the war, render insufficient the separate
efforts of separate republics in economic reconstruction. The
restoration of the national economy has proved incompatible with
the separate existence of the republics.

On the other hand, the instability of the international
situation and the danger of new attacks make inevitable the
creation of a united front of Soviet republics in face of capitalist
encirclement.

Finally the very structure of Soviet power, which is international by its class nature, drives the working masses of the
Soviet republics along the path of union into a single socialist
family.

All these circumstances imperatively demand the unification
of the Soviet republics into a single union state capable of
guaranteeing external security, internal economic progress and
freedom of national development for the peoples.

The rest of the proceedings were brief and formal. Frunze,
speaking on behalf of the three allied republics, approved the
draft treaty, but called for " supplementary guarantees that the
act accepted by us really is an act establishing without any mistake new and firm mutual relations which will allow each state
entering into the union to display the maximum of energy and
independence in the interests of the common cause ".[1] Greetings
were brought to the congress by delegates of the Soviet republics
of Bokhara and Khorezm, who expressed the modest hope that
they might one day qualify, as socialist republics, for admission
to the union,[2] and by Kirov, introduced by the president as " a
Baku worker ", on behalf of the proletariat of the Transcaucasian
SFSR.[3] The congress then unanimously approved the treaty,
elected a central executive committee — the first VTsIK of the
USSR — and instructed it to draft a constitution for the union.
The treaty just approved had already laid down its main outlines.

[1] *1 S"ezd Sovetov Soyuza Sovetskikh Sotsialisticheskikh Respublik* (1923),
p. 11.
[2] *Ibid.* p. 13. The hope was realized by the creation of the Uzbek and
Turkmen SSRs in 1925
[3] *Ibid.* p. 15.

CHAPTER 14

THE CONSTITUTION OF THE USSR

ON January 10, 1923, the presidium of the new VTsIK elected by the first All-Union Congress of Soviets appointed a commission of 13 to draft the terms of the constitution. The commission was quickly enlarged to 25, the RSFSR providing 14 members, the Ukrainian SSR 5, and the Transcaucasian and White Russian SSR 3 each.[1] Since 5 of the 14 delegates of the RSFSR were drawn from the autonomous republics, this meant that only 9 members of the commission were Great Russians — a point with which Enukidze made play when he eventually presented its report to VTsIK. In fact, as the sequel showed, the crucial decisions on the constitution did not rest either with the commission or with any organ of state, but rather with the Politburo or with some informal group of leaders within the party.

A project which deposed the RSFSR from its unique position and subordinated it, side by side with its now equal partners, to the common central authority of the USSR, had a flattering appeal to those partners, and especially to the Ukrainian SSR, the most powerful and most sensitive of them. But Frunze had already voiced the apprehensions of the republics; and gradual recognition that the new USSR might prove to be little more than the old RSFSR writ large, and endowed with enhanced prestige and wider power, caused a sharp reaction. Counter-drafts submitted to the drafting commission of VTsIK by the Ukrainian and White Russian central executive committees, which were afterwards made public, were in effect a challenge to the whole principle of a centralized authority and could scarcely be reconciled with the principles of union accepted in the previous December.[2] The

---

[1] *Vtoraya Sessiya Tsentral'nogo Ispolnitel'nogo Komiteta Sovetskikh Sotsialisticheskikh Respublik* (1923), pp. 11-12.

[2] The rejected drafts are in V. I. Ignatiev, *Sovetskii Stroi* (1928), pp. 123-137.

Council of Nationalities attached to Narkomnats served as a quasi-representative body through which the views of the diverse nationalities of the RSFSR could find expression. In February 1923 the proposal was put forward in the drafting commission to convert this council into an organ of the USSR, making it, in accordance with the precedent of other federal constitutions, into a second chamber of VTsIK. This proposal was fiercely resisted by some of the Russian delegates ; [1] and a deadlock seemed likely to ensue in the commission.

As in most delicate situations, it was left for the party to take a hand; the twelfth party congress, held in April 1923 while the controversy was at its height, showed itself keenly sensitive to criticism from the republics. Stalin, who had recently been under fire from Lenin for displaying undue intransigence in his handling of the Georgian question, was particularly eager to efface any such impression and to go more than half-way to meet the claims of the nationalities. The congress came out strongly against potential manifestations of " Great-Power chauvinism ". Overlooking for a moment the paragraph in the party programme which commended " a federal union of states organized on the Soviet model " as " one of the transitional forms to complete unity ", the congress strongly condemned those who took this view of the USSR now in course of formation :

> The union of republics is regarded by a considerable number of Soviet officials, both central and local, not as a union of equal state units with a mandate to guarantee the free development of the national republics, but as a step towards the liquidation of the republics, as a beginning of the so-called " one and indivisible " republic.

Such behaviour was branded as " anti-proletarian and reactionary " and penalties threatened for its continuance.[2] The congress specifically commended the project for " a special organ of representation of the nationalities on the principle of equality ".[3] But this left open the question, Equality between whom? According to the official plan, the Council of Nationalities was to be composed

---

[1] Stalin afterwards recorded of this occasion that " speeches were delivered which did not tally with communism, speeches which had nothing to do with internationalism " (Stalin, *Sochineniya*, v, 244-245).

[2] *VKP(B) v Rezolyutsiyakh* (1941), i, 505-506.   [3] *Ibid.* i, 496.

of representatives of all republics, whether federated or autonomous, and of the autonomous regions. According to another plan, it was to be composed exclusively of representatives of the four federated republics.[1] Rakovsky, the Ukrainian delegate, complained that, under the official plan, the RSFSR had more than three times as many representatives as the other three federated republics taken together, and proposed a new refinement, borrowed from the Weimar constitution of the German Reich, under which no single " state unit " could have more than two-fifths of the total representation. Stalin rejected all these projects on the ground that the new organ was to be a council not of states but of nationalities.[2] Under the arrangements finally made, the All-Union Central Executive Committee (VTsIK) was divided into two chambers. One — the Council of the Union — consisted of 371 members elected by the All-Union Congress from representatives of the constituent republics in proportion to the population of each;[3] the other — the Council of Nationalities — was composed of 131 delegates, five from each union republic or autonomous republic and one from each autonomous region, elected by the executive committee of the republic or region. The Council of Nationalities thus embodied a formal recognition of the equality not of the states but of the nations constituting the union, irrespective of population. The two chambers shared on an equal footing the rights and functions of VTsIK, which did not substantially differ, either in theory or in practice, from those of its predecessor, the VTsIK of the RSFSR. Every act of VTsIK required the concurrence of both chambers, voting separately. Differences of opinion between them, if they could not be reconciled in a joint session,[4] had to be referred to an ordinary or extraordinary All-Union Congress of Soviets.

[1] *Dvenadtsatyi S"ezd Rossiiskoi Kommunisticheskoi Partii* (*Bol'shevikov*) (1923), p. 599.

[2] Stalin, *Sochineniya*, v, 277-278.

[3] The number was increased by the second All-Union Congress of Soviets to 414.

[4] Even in " joint " sessions the chambers of VTsIK voted separately and a majority was required in each for an agreed decision. Provision was also made for " plenary " sessions for the election of officers and for questions of procedure, where the chambers voted together and only a majority of the joint body was required : this, however, was cancelled by an amendment adopted at the second All-Union Congress of Soviets.

The resolution of the party congress was a directive to the drafting commission to proceed with its work on the lines laid down. Thus stimulated, the commission completed its task, submitting an agreed draft to VTsIK for approval at the beginning of July. Apart from the innovation of the Council of Nationalities as a second chamber, the " fundamental law (constitution) of the Union of Soviet Socialist Republics "[1] presented comparatively few original features. It was a straightforward attempt to apply to the enlarged area of the new union the well-tried principles of the constitution of the RSFSR. Sovereign authority was transferred to the new All-Union Congress of Soviets, the All-Russian Congress of Soviets remaining the supreme organ of the RSFSR in its now subordinate capacity as a member of the union ; the All-Union Central Executive Committee took over the functions and the familiar short name (VTsIK) of the All-Russian Central Executive Committee, the latter being relegated to the subordinate rôle ; and what had been the Sovnarkom of the RSFSR became the Sovnarkom of the USSR,[2] the RSFSR like the other constituent republics having a minor Sovnarkom of its own. The central institutions of the RSFSR were thus converted, with some new accretions of personnel but in substance unchanged, into central institutions of the USSR. The real continuity was between the RSFSR of the old dispensation and the USSR, not between the RSFSR of the old dispensation and the subordinate RSFSR of the new.

The period of four years since the drafting of the constitution of the RSFSR had brought important changes in the constitutional structure, notably the creation within the RSFSR of a number of autonomous republics and autonomous regions. When the constitution came into force in July 1918, civil war was about to sweep over most of those areas of predominantly non-Russian population where autonomous units of the federation might have come into

---

[1] The text, as finally adopted by VTsIK on July 6, 1923, is in *Istoriya Sovetskoi Konstitutsii v Dekretakh* (1936), pp. 244-250, 255-267 ; an English version appeared in *British and Foreign State Papers*, cxx (1924), 889-902.

[2] Various bodies, formerly attached to the Sovnarkom of the RSFSR, of which the Council of Labour and Defence and the State Planning Commission were the most important, were thus henceforth attached to the Sovnarkom of the USSR. They were not mentioned in the constitution, and no formal provision seems to have been made for their transfer, which was taken for granted. This was one of several formal anomalies of the transition.

being, and soon diverted all attention to the military struggle. But after eighteen months of fighting, the collapse of Denikin and Kolchak reopened the issue. As the result of the appointment by VTsIK, in February 1920, of a commission to " work out questions of the federal construction of the RSFSR ",[1] a standard form of constitution was devised and applied in the next two years, with local variations, to autonomous republics in the Volga region (the republics of the Bashkirs and Tatars), in the Caucasus (Dagestan and the republic of the Mountaineers, Abkhazia and Ajaria), in Central Asia (Kazakhstan and Turkestan) and in the Crimea. Each of the autonomous republics had not only its own congress of Soviets and its executive committee, but its own people's commissariats, forming a republican Sovnarkom ;[2] and it was in the division of powers between these commissariats and the central authorities that the chief constitutional interest of the experiment resided. In all cases a tripartite classification was established. Foreign affairs and foreign trade were exclusively reserved to the central authorities ; so also were military affairs and " the conduct of the struggle against counter-revolution " by the all-Russian Cheka (and later by the GPU), subject in some cases to consultation with the local authorities. Next came a category of functions in which the people's commissariats of the republics were directly responsible to the corresponding organs of the RSFSR ; these normally included the principal commissariats concerned in the economic life of the country. The remaining commissariats of the autonomous republics were independent, subject to the general supervising authority of VTsIK, which was sometimes reserved and sometimes left to be understood.

These constitutional arrangements within the RSFSR had already served as a model in formulating relations between the RSFSR and other socialist Soviet republics.[3] They now served as a basis for the structure of the USSR. Under the constitution of 1923 the people's commissariats of the USSR and of the republics were divided into the familiar three categories. The first category was formed by five all-union commissariats which

[1] See p. 383 above.
[2] The " autonomous regions " had no such organs and present no constitutional interest ; they had the same status and structure as any other " region " (oblast') under the constitution.
[3] See pp. 384-385 above.

had no counterpart in the republics, so that the subjects treated by them — foreign affairs, defence, foreign trade, communications and posts and telegraphs — fell within the exclusive competence of the USSR. Here the central authority had exclusive control both of the framing and of the execution of decisions. The second category of " unified commissariats " — the name only was new — included the Supreme Council of National Economy, and the Commissariats of Labour, Food, Finance and Workers' and Peasants' Inspection.[1] In these cases both the USSR and the republic had commissariats, the commissariat of the republic being the agent and local department of the corresponding commissariat of the USSR. Here the commissariat of the republic was responsible for the execution locally of decisions taken by the central authority.[2] Into the same category also fell the Unified State Political Administration (OGPU) created by a short special chapter of the constitution for the purpose of " uniting the revolutionary efforts of the union republics in the struggle with political and economic counter-revolution, espionage and banditism ". Replacing the GPU of the RSFSR, the OGPU was " attached to the Sovnarkom of the USSR " but worked through " representatives attached to the Sovnarkom of the union republics "; it thus had the form of a unified commissariat. Finally, the six commissariats of Internal Affairs, Justice, Education, Health, Social Welfare and Nationalities formed a third category. These were organs of the republics and had no union counterpart, though the constitution reserved for the union the establishment of " the bases of the courts of justice and legal procedure as well as of the civil and criminal legislation of the union ", of " the fundamental labour laws ", of " general principles in the domain of popular education ", and of " general measures for the protection of public

---

[1] The constitution of the USSR made the supreme organs of the union responsible for " the establishment of the foundations and the general plan of the whole national economy ". The growing concentration of economic policy was one of the main centralizing forces at work in the constitution of the USSR.

[2] That this division of powers aroused apprehension in the republics is suggested by a cautious passage in the resolution of the twelfth party congress of April 1923 : " The fusion of commissariats is a test for the Soviet machine of government ; if this experiment developed in practice a great-Power tendency, the party would be compelled to take the most decisive measures against such a perversion, and even to raise the question of reconsidering the fusion of certain commissariats " (*VKP(B) v Rezolyutsiyakh* (1941), i, 505).

health ". Each constituent republic had its own Sovnarkom consisting of the commissars of the non-union commissariats and of
the " unified " commissariats; and the all-union commissariats
had the right to appoint delegates to sit on the Sovnarkom of each
republic. The Sovnarkoms of the republics, in so far as they
functioned effectively as corporate entities, thus tended to become
the local executive organs of the central authority. The central
executive committees of the republics had equally little power
against the Sovnarkom of the USSR. Under the constitution they
were entitled to protest against its decrees and resolutions to
VTsIK but " without suspending their execution ".

Another innovation on the 1918 constitution of the RSFSR
was registered in the chapter on judicial organization. The 1923
constitution of the USSR provided for the establishment of a
Supreme Court " attached to the Central Executive Committee of
the USSR " for the purpose of " strengthening revolutionary
legality and coordinating the efforts of the union republics in the
struggle against counter-revolution ". But, though the judiciary
thus acquired a certain formal independence, its rôle as the servant
of the executive was safeguarded by the provision that the pro-
curator of the Supreme Court, a nominee of the presidium of
VTsIK, had the right of appeal to the presidium against decisions
of the court. The Marxist theory of law as an instrument of state
power was thus maintained intact. It was in accordance with the
same spirit that no provision had been made in the 1918 constitution of the RSFSR for any judicial interpretation of the constitution. The 1923 constitution of the USSR allowed the Supreme
Court " to give opinions at the demand of the TsIK of the USSR
on the legality of resolutions of union republics from the point
of view of the constitution ". But no such way was offered of
testing the legality of any act of the organs of the union; and the
relation between the union and its constituent members was indicated by the provision that " the USSR safeguards the rights of
the union republics ". Ultimate authority rested with the All-
Union Congress of Soviets, or, more specifically, with VTsIK.
It was not possible for any act of these bodies, any more than of
the British Parliament, to be *ultra vires*.

It was a corollary of these arrangements that the right of
amending the constitution was vested not in the constituent

republics, but absolutely in the central authority.[1] The only specific provision made by the constitution of 1923 for its own amendment related to a division of authority between the All-Union Congress of Soviets and VTsIK, the former having, under article 2, exclusive competence for " the confirmation and amendment of the fundamental principles " of the constitution. This vague definition of function implicitly admitted the competence of VTsIK or its presidium to amend the constitution in matters not involving " fundamental principles "; and as time went on, this competence was freely exercised. For example, the decree of May 9, 1924, abolishing the union and republic Commissariats of Food and establishing " unified " Commissariats of Internal Trade, was issued by the Presidium of VTsIK; the decree of November 18, 1925, fusing the Commissariats of Internal and Foreign Trade into a single Commissariat of Trade, involving some consequential constitutional amendments, was issued jointly by VTsIK and Sovnarkom. On the other hand, the fourth All-Union Congress of Soviets itself amended article 11 of the constitution, which prescribed annual meetings of the congress, by making them biennial. The general conclusion is that the process of amendments to the constitution was governed by the same considerations of convenience, and subject to the same uncertainties of competence, as the ordinary process of legislation. From the standpoint of constitutional law the discrepancy was covered by the obligation of VTsIK to submit all decrees, including constitutional amendments, to the ensuing congress of Soviets for ratification. But this obligation did not delay their entry into force, and remained in practice a formality.

To sum up the changes in the Soviet structure resulting from the 1923 constitution is a difficult task. The student is confronted at the outset by one curious paradox. The RSFSR had the word " federal " in its title and was constantly referred to as such; yet it was, in strict constitutional terms, a unitary state, incorporating a number of subordinate, though partially autonomous, units. In the constitution of the USSR, and in official documents relating to it, the words " federal " and " federation " were avoided. Yet

[1] The constitution admitted one exception to this general principle: the right of secession accorded to the constituent republics could not be repealed, nor could the boundaries of the republics be changed, without their consent (art. 6).

the USSR was, in essential points, a federation. It was created by agreement between formally equally sovereign states ; and the constitution formally recognized the continuing sovereignty of the units of the federation, which was " restricted only within limits laid down in the constitution ". The constitution provided on orthodox federal lines for a division of competence between the authorities of the USSR and those of the republics, and on certain matters for concurrent jurisdiction (the " unified commissariats "). It even recognized a right not normally accorded to the constituent units of a federation, the right of secession, and explicitly provided that this right could not be abridged without the consent of all the republics. The bicameral assembly was a familiar device in federations to safeguard the rights of member states. In all these respects a large measure of formal satisfaction was offered to the Soviet republics constituting the USSR.

It is none the less possible to hold that the dropping of the term " federal " from the title of the USSR was more significant than the adoption of these federal forms. In the documents of the period the USSR was described with the emphasis of frequent repetition as " a single union state ". The 1923 constitution of the USSR marked, in comparison with the 1918 constitution of the RSFSR, a step forward in the direction of centralization both in the increased number of questions placed within the competence of the central government and in the greater stringency of its overriding power ; it was a further step in the process of concentration which had been steadily at work since the early days of the regime. No constitutional safeguards of the rights of the republics were powerful enough to resist this tendency towards centralization. The degree of uniformity imposed in practice by the constitution can indeed easily be exaggerated. The units of the USSR, especially if the autonomous republics and regions are included in that category, revealed a far greater diversity of economic, political and cultural development than has been present in any other federation in the course of history ; and this fact alone makes the application of uniform standards of measurement difficult or irrelevant. The Council of Nationalities, tracing its descent from the body which had grown up under the auspices of Narkomnats, may have signally failed to satisfy the aspirations of Ukrainian nationalists, and yet have represented an immense advance to the awakening political consciousness of the Kazakhs of the steppe or of Mountaineers of the Caucasus. In constitutional terms the provision for a bicameral representative assembly proved to be little more than an attempt to transplant to the uncongenial soil of the USSR the constitutional usages and devices of the bourgeois world. No contentious debates on matters of substance took place in either chamber, and no difference of opinion between them was ever registered. Decrees continued to be adopted by VTsIK and issued in its name; but neither the two chambers of VTsIK nor its joint presidium took major decisions or wielded constitutional power more effective than that of a drafting committee. In short, the constitution of 1923 shared what must necessarily seem the unreality of all constitutional forms under the Soviet system of government, once the system is criticized in terms of western constitutional law. These forms played their part in the conduct of the administration, central and local, and in the formation and presentation of opinion. But the major decisions of policy, and the debates which preceded such decisions, lay outside the constitutional framework.

The increasing concentration of power in the successive constitutions of the RSFSR and USSR, the tendency for federal forms to be eclipsed by the reality of a unitary state, and the ineffectiveness of constitutional checks were in one sense a concession to the prolonged national emergency. A struggle for existence whose outcome is constantly in doubt never creates an atmosphere favourable to a decentralization of authority or to a mitigation of its rigours. Moreover, at this period the notion of state power as a temporary instrument, ruthlessly wielded so long as the struggle went on, but destined to die away once the battle for the socialist order was won, was still vividly present to the mind of many Bolsheviks and excused ·any measures which seemed to need extenuation. Nor were strong centralizing tendencies confined to the Soviet Union. Indeed, Soviet experience confirms the conclusion of a recent general treatise on federal government:

> War and economic crisis, if they recur frequently, will almost certainly turn federal governments into unitary governments. . . . The growth of social services may, but need not, tend towards the same end.[1]

[1] K. C. Wheare, *Federal Government* (1946), p. 255.

The concentration of power at the centre was characteristic of the period rather than of the institutions of any one country. In the Soviet Union its roots were predominantly economic. A significant paragraph in article 1 of the constitution made the supreme organs of the union responsible for " the establishment of the foundations of the general plan of the whole national economy "; and four out of the five " unified " commissariats dealt with economic matters.

The constitution of the USSR as framed by the drafting commission on the directives of the twelfth party congress was adopted by VTsIK at its meeting on July 6, 1923, and came immediately into force. It still required formal confirmation by the second All-Union Congress of Soviets, and this was given on January 31, 1924, ten days after Lenin's death.[1]

[1] *Vtoroi S"ezd Sovetov Soyuza Sovetskikh Sotsialisticheskikh Respublik* (1924), pp. 129-136. This was the occasion of the two minor amendments mentioned on p. 401, notes 3 and 4 above.

NOTE B

THE BOLSHEVIK DOCTRINE OF SELF-DETERMINATION

(a) *The Nineteenth-century Background*

THE French revolution abrogated the conception of the state as the personal domain of the monarch and substituted the conception of national or popular sovereignty. The idea of a proprietary right vested in the sovereign had been bound up with the feudal system of land tenure, and was incompatible with the new social and economic conditions created by the rise of industry and commerce and with the growth of a new non-feudal intelligentsia. The middle classes thus became the heirs of monarchy and the bearers of the new creed of nationalism.

> In aristocratic states [said Robespierre] the word *patrie* has no meaning except for patrician families who have seized the sovereignty. It is only under democracy that the state is truly the *patrie* of all the individuals composing it.[1]

The definition of the nation or the people as the repository of power, popularized and systematized by the French revolution, remained, however, purely bourgeois. Babeuf complained that the multitude " sees in society only an enemy and loses even the possibility of having a country ". Weitling connected the notion of country with the notion of property :

> He alone has a country who is a property owner or at any rate has the liberty and the means to become one. He who has not that, has no country.

The " nation " or " people " who constituted the state were the triumphant bourgeoisie. The workers had as little portion in it as in the days of the monarchy ; they still had, in a modern phrase, " no stake in the country ".

Such was the background of Marx's attitude to the national question and the ancestry of the aphorism in the *Communist Manifesto* that " the worker has no country ". This famous phrase was not, as is sometimes supposed, either a boast or a programme. It was a protest against the exclusion of the proletariat from the privilege of full membership of

[1] *Discours et Rapports de Robespierre*, ed. C. Vellay (1908), p. 328.

the nation. The first requisite laid down in the *Manifesto* was therefore that the proletariat of each country should " settle accounts with its own bourgeoisie ". Thus " though not in substance, yet in form, the struggle of the proletariat with the bourgeoisie is at first a national struggle ". And again :

> Since the proletariat must first of all acquire political supremacy, must rise to be the leading class of the nation, must constitute itself *the* nation, it is so far itself national, though not in the bourgeois sense of the word.

All this could take place within the framework of bourgeois democracy, the merit of which was to provide the proletariat with tools to undermine bourgeois supremacy.

But other and longer-term forces were at work. Marx did not, like Lassalle, stop short at national socialism. He had observed that the technical developments of production were profoundly affecting the nation-state, irrespective of whether bourgeoisie or proletariat was the dominant class.

> National differences and antagonisms between peoples are daily more and more vanishing, owing to the development of the bourgeoisie, to freedom of commerce, to the world market, to uniformity in the mode of production and in the conditions of life corresponding thereto.
>
> The supremacy of the proletariat will cause them to vanish still faster. United action of the leading civilized countries, at least, is one of the first conditions for the emancipation of the proletariat.
>
> In proportion as the exploitation of one individual by another is put an end to, the exploitation of one nation by another will also be put an end to. In proportion as the antagonism between classes within the nation vanishes, the hostility of one nation to another will come to an end.

The proletariat would hasten this process. It was the class in which, as Marx said in a rash early pronouncement, " nationality is already dead ", and which " represents the dissolution of classes and nationalities in contemporary society.[1] Clearly the process would be completed only after the overthrow of the bourgeoisie and the transition to socialism. There was, however, no inconsistency in exhorting the proletariat of each country to dispossess its own bourgeoisie and make itself the national class and in believing at the same time in the unity of workers in a classless and nationless society as the ultimate goal of the revolution. Most nineteenth-century thinkers, from Mazzini onwards, had treated nationalism not as the antithesis of internationalism but

[1] *Karl Marx-Friedrich Engels: Historisch-Kritische Gesamtausgabe*, 1ᵉʳ Teil, v, 50, 60.

as the natural stepping-stone to it.[1] In the same way it could be assumed that the nationalism of the bourgeois stage of the revolution would develop into the internationalism of the proletarian stage.

The doctrine of popular sovereignty carried with it by implication the doctrine of national self-determination, which seemed the logical and inescapable corollary of democracy. But the doctrine of self-determination as proclaimed by the French revolution implied primarily the right of peoples to constitute national states in defiance of the dynastic principle, and was a domestic as well as an international question. It certainly did not contemplate a wholesale process of secession and disintegration. In France the revolution had proved a uniting force, destroying the last traditional remnants of Breton, Norman and Provençal separatism. Elsewhere the nations in whose favour the principle was most often invoked in the next fifty years — the Poles, the Italians and the Germans — were dispersed peoples seeking reunion and reintegration with their brethren. Marx does not appear to have had any occasion to consider the question of national self-determination before 1848 ; but he would certainly have seen in it nothing to contradict the gradual process of unification, which was, in his view, dictated by modern conditions of production.

The year 1848 was a landmark in the issue of nationalism and national self-determination. The dynastic principle, destroyed in France in 1789, was shattered all over central Europe ; and, now that national sovereignty was being invoked everywhere as the basis of the state, new nations began to make their voice heard. Not only were the aspirations of the Germans, the Poles and the Italians for national unity stimulated, but the national claims of the Danes of Schleswig, of the numerous peoples of the Habsburg empire, and even of the Irish, began to be canvassed. These claims raised some altogether new problems. The claims of Germans, Poles, Italians (and, incidentally, Magyars) all threatened the integrity of the Habsburg empire. That empire, the backbone of the nefarious Holy Alliance, had been a target for all progressive thinkers since 1815 ; and the formation of German, Polish, Italian and Magyar national states could the more easily be represented as a progressive and constructive progress. But now German unity was also subject to challenge by Danes and Czechs, Polish unity by Ruthenians, Magyar unity by Slovaks and Croats, Italian unity by Slovenes, and British unity by the Irish. Nationalism

[1] By the beginning of the twentieth century this nineteenth-century assumption had been forgotten. Jaurès and Bernstein, correctly interpreting Marx's aphorism that " the worker has no country " as a complaint, claimed it as supporting national against international socialism ; Plekhanov (*Sochineniya*, xiii, 263-264) rejected the correct interpretation of Marx's phrase precisely because it seemed to lead to this obnoxious conclusion.

and national self-determination were being invoked for the first time as destructive, disintegrating and reactionary forces.[1] Marx and Engels did not attempt either at this or at any other time to formulate a complete theory of nationalism. When they were called on to express opinions on the events of 1848 their attitude to the national question was conditioned by the background of the bourgeois revolution, and did not differ sensibly from that of liberals and democrats generally. It was apparent to everyone that the line must be drawn somewhere. Claims to national independence could not be indefinitely multiplied. So far, all schools of thought were agreed. The interest lay in the criteria which were applied.

In the first place, Marx and Engels tended to accept claims which would lead to the building up of large and powerful units, and reject claims which would lead to the break up of large states in order to create small ones. This accorded with current liberal opinion [2] as well as with the view of the *Communist Manifesto* that the establishment of larger units was required by contemporary economic development.

---

[1] The year 1848 also saw the first shift from the conception of individual self-determination as a corollary of democracy (the proposition that " Ruritanians have a right to choose to what state they shall belong ") to the conception of nationality as an objective right of nations to independent statehood (the proposition that " the Ruritanian nation has a right to constitute itself an independent state "). The rights of man envisaged by the French revolution were transferred to nations. The Slav congress of June 1848 issued a manifesto " in the name of the liberty, equality and fraternity of European nations ". Rousseau's " general will " had come home to roost.

[2] Progressive nineteenth-century thinkers were as a rule unsympathetic for practical reasons to the claims of small nationalities. " Nobody can suppose ", wrote J. S. Mill in his *Considerations on Representative Government*, " that it is not more beneficial to a Breton, or a Basque of French Navarre, to be brought into the current of the ideas and feelings of a highly civilized and cultivated people — to be a member of the French nationality, admitted on equal terms to all the privileges of French citizenship, sharing the advantages of French protection and the dignity and prestige of French power — than to sulk on his own rocks, the half-savage relic of past times, revolving in his own little mental orbit, without participation or interest in the general movement of the world. The same remark applies to the Welshman or the Scottish Highlander as members of the British nation." A few pages later Mill expressed the hope that more enlightened administration of Ireland would soon make the Irish sensible " to the benefits which the less numerous and less wealthy people must necessarily derive from being fellow-citizens instead of foreigners to those who are not only their nearest neighbours, but the wealthiest, and one of the finest, as well as the most civilized and powerful, nations on earth ". Lenin took exactly the same view : " The nearer the democratic state comes to full freedom of secession, the rarer and weaker in practice will the strivings for secession be, since the advantages of great states are undoubted from the point of view of economic progress and from the point of view of the interest of the masses " (*Sochineniya*, xix, 39-40).

In an article of 1866 Engels drew a clear distinction between those
" large and well defined historical nations of Europe " (he specifically
named Italy, Poland, Germany and Hungary [1]) whose national aspirations were supported by all European democrats and those " numerous
small relics of peoples which, after having figured for a longer or shorter
period on the stage of history, were finally absorbed as integral portions
into one or other of those more powerful nations ". These minor
" nationalities " (" Serbians, Croats, Ruthenes, Slovaks, Czechs and
other remnants of bygone Slav peoples in Turkey, Hungary and Germany ") were inventions or instruments of Russian pan-Slavism,
and their claims deserved no manner of encouragement.[2] The later
liberal idealization of the small nation had not yet begun, and there
was no reason why Marx and Engels should be affected by this
sentiment.

Secondly, Marx and Engels tended to support claims whose realization might be supposed to further the scheme of world revolution set
forth in the *Communist Manifesto*, that is to say, the claims of countries
in which bourgeois development was well advanced and which might
thus provide a promising field for eventual proletarian activities. The
claims of Poland, the only country mentioned in the *Communist Manifesto* whose bourgeois revolution would have an agrarian rather than
an industrial character, were by exception admitted to this category,[3]
and were consistently supported in Marx's articles of 1848 on the
Frankfort Assembly. Other peasant nationalisms were treated as
naturally reactionary. It was in this spirit that Engels dismissed the
claim of the Danes to Schleswig on the ground that they were only
" a half-civilized nation " ; the German right to the duchies was the
" right of civilization against barbarism, of progress against stagnation ".[4] It is customary to attribute this judgment to Engels's German

[1] Engels here followed the commonly accepted list. The last belated echo
of the priority accorded by nineteenth-century liberal thought to the national
aspirations of these four peoples is to be found in Woodrow Wilson's Fourteen
Points. The Germans and Magyars were now enemies ; and the Italians and
Poles were the only peoples whose national claims were specifically recognized
in the Fourteen Points. Autonomy would suffice for the lesser nations, which
were not mentioned by name.

[2] Marx i Engels, *Sochineniya*, xiii, i, 154-157.

[3] The Cracow rising of 1846, which had been the prelude of the 1848
revolution, gave the Polish movement a " democratic " character on which Marx
constantly insisted at this period. Nevertheless, Marx and Engels were not
altogether happy about the place of Poland in the revolutionary scheme : their
not always consistent utterances on the subject are collected by Ryazanov in
Archiv für die Geschichte des Sozialismus und der Arbeiterbewegung (Leipzig), vi
(1916), 175-221.

[4] *Karl Marx-Friedrich Engels: Historisch-Kritische Gesamtausgabe*, 1ᵉʳ Teil,
vii, 353.

prejudice. But Marx, who can be acquitted of English prejudices, also failed at this time to support the claims of the Irish.[1] The claims of the Slav nations of the Habsburg empire, other than the Poles, were rejected with similar scorn in the two much-quoted articles against Bakunin written by Engels in 1849.[2] All these (except for the Czechs, whose revolutionary activities in 1848 were more than once praised by Marx and Engels [3]) were backward peasant nations. Their triumph would represent the subjugation " of the civilized west by the barbaric east, of the town by the country, of trade, manufacture and intelligence by the primitive agriculture of Slavonic serfs ".

Thirdly, it was the axiom of all progressive nineteenth-century thought that Russia was the most powerful champion of European reaction, and hostility to Russia was therefore a touchstone of revolutionary sincerity. It was primarily on this ground that Lenin explained the rejection by Marx and Engels of the claims of the small nationalities of the Habsburg monarchy :

> In 1848 there were historical and political grounds for distinguishing between " reactionary " and " revolutionary-democratic " nations. Marx was right to condemn the former and support the latter. The right of self-determination is one of the demands of democracy which must naturally be subordinated to the general interests of democracy. In 1848 and the following years these general interests consisted first and foremost in the struggle with Tsarism.[4]

By this token the claims of Poland, which could be pressed against Russia, were approved, and those of the lesser Slav peoples, which tended to lean for support on the Russian power, stood condemned.

Lastly, the attitude of Marx and Engels contained an element of sheer empiricism, and it would be foolish to attribute everything in it to a consistently considered theory. For example, the peasant Slavs of Austria for the most part regarded the Habsburgs as more remote, and therefore less obnoxious, masters than their Polish or Magyar landlords ; in 1848 they assisted the Habsburgs to resist those very

---

[1] In a manifesto of February 13, 1848, of which Marx was one of three signatories, satisfaction was expressed at the " close alliance between the Irish people and that of Great Britain " and at the chance to " break down that prejudice which prompted the Irish people to confound in one common hatred the oppressed classes of England with the oppressors of both countries " (*ibid.* vi, 652).

[2] Marx i Engels, *Sochineniya*, vii, 203-220.

[3] Notably in an article of June 18, 1848, where, however, it is added that German repression has driven the Czechs on to " the side of the Russians, the side of despotism against revolution " (*Karl Marx-Friedrich Engels : Historisch-Kritische Gesamtausgabe*, 1ᵉʳ Teil, vii, 68-70).

[4] Lenin, *Sochineniya*, xix, 43.

national claims which Marx and Engels, in common with most liberals, were concerned to maintain. It was this so-called " betrayal " of the national cause, quite as much as any theory about the reactionary character of peasant nations or about their supposed predilection for Russia, which prompted the denunciations of Engels. The attitude of Marx and Engels to Poland was also affected by the practical difficulties of reconciling German and Polish claims. Whether through national prejudice, or because Germany from the revolutionary standpoint seemed more advanced and therefore more deserving of support than Poland, Marx and Engels were constantly disposed to favour German territorial claims against Poland while ready to compensate Poland at the expense of Russia or of those small nationalities which inhabited the marches between Russia and Poland. It would be dangerous to draw theoretical conclusions from these empirical pronouncements.

Before 1850, therefore, Marx and Engels developed no distinctive theory of national self-determination, but were content either to follow broad democratic prescriptions or to take empirical decisions in particular cases. In his later life Marx was led to take some further interest in the national question by his direct contact with the workers' movement. The Polish insurrection of 1863 had been the occasion of the initial meeting between British and French workers from which the First International had sprung ; and sympathy for Poland was still lively in radical circles when the International was actually founded in the following year. Through these accidents national self-determination found its way into the programme of the International, which was adopted by the General Council on September 27, 1865, by a Polish side-door. " It is urgently necessary ", ran one of its articles, " to annihilate the growing influence of Russia in Europe by assuring to Poland the right of self-determination which belongs to every nation and by giving to this country once more a social and democratic foundation."

While, however, national self-determination had apparently been invoked only for the specific purpose of casting a stone at Russia, it was difficult to confine its application to Poland. Engels in due course was induced to revise his attitude towards the Danish claim to Schleswig ;[1] and Marx admitted a change of view about Ireland :

> Formerly I thought the separation of Ireland from England impossible. Now I think it inevitable, even if after separation it came to a federation.

He ultimately reached the conclusion that " *it is the direct absolute interest* of the English working class to get rid of their present connexion

---

[1] *Karl Marx-Friedrich Engels: Historisch-Kritische Gesamtausgabe,* III[ter] Teil, iii, 163.

with Ireland ",[1] and argued the case in the General Council of the International. The question of principle appears to have been raised only once. The French members of the International were Proudhonists almost to a man, and followed their master in rejecting the claims of nationalism. When the Prussian-Austrian war broke out in June 1866 the " Proudhonist clique ", as Marx reported to Engels, began to preach peace on the ground that " war was out of date and nationalities nonsense ".[2] When a few weeks later Lafargue, pursuing this line of thought, described nations in the General Council as " antiquated superstitions ", Marx launched a counter-attack by showing that Lafargue " by his denial of nationalities quite unconsciously understood their absorption in a model French nation ".[3] It was an argument which Lenin was one day to use against Austrian and Polish socialists and " Great Russian chauvinists ", who in denying the principle of national self-determination implicitly asserted their own national superiority.

The Second International from its foundation in 1889 down to 1914 was still less concerned than its predecessor with the doctrine of national self-determination. After 1870 interest in the question ebbed. No further troubles occurred in Poland or elsewhere to make it acute on the European continent ; and the voices of the oppressed peoples of other continents were only just beginning to be heard by the world at large. The fullest pronouncement on it was contained in a resolution of the London congress of the Second International in 1896 :

> The congress declares in favour of the full autonomy of all nationalities, and its sympathy with the workers of any country at present suffering under the yoke of military, national, or other despotisms ; and calls upon the workers in all such countries to fall into line, side by side with the class-conscious workers of the world, to organize for the overthrow of international capitalism and the establishment of international social-democracy.[4]

---

[1] *Ibid.* III[er] Teil, iii, 442 ; iv, 258. Lenin afterwards wrote that " the policy of Marx and Engels in the Irish question gave the first great pattern, which retains today its vast *practical* importance, of the attitude which the proletariat of oppressing countries ought to take to national movements " (*Sochineniya*, xvii, 464).

[2] *Karl Marx-Friedrich Engels: Historisch-Kritische Gesamtausgabe*, III[er] Teil, iii, 336.

[3] *Ibid.* III[er] Teil, iii, 341.

[4] *International Socialist Workers and Trade Union Congress, London, 1896* (n.d.), p. 31 ; the German version (*Verhandlungen und Beschlüsse des Internationalen Arbeiter- und Gewerkschafts-Kongresses zu London* (1897), p. 18) translates " autonomy " by *Selbstbestimmungsrecht* and is followed in the current Russian version (Lenin, *Sochineniya*, xvii, 455).

The first half of the resolution thus established the proletarian interest in the bourgeois doctrine of national autonomy or self-determination ; the second half recorded its faith in the ultimate international solidarity of the proletariat. But interest in it was perfunctory. No attempt was made to return to it at the subsequent congresses of the International before 1914.[1]

(b) Bolshevik Doctrine before 1917

The right of national self-determination had been proclaimed in the initial manifesto of the Russian Social-Democratic Workers' Party at its foundation congress in 1898. The party programme adopted at the second congress in 1903 recognized the " right of self-determination for all nations entering into the composition of the state ". The turn of phrase and the inclusion of this clause among others relating to Russian domestic policy showed that the reference was to the nationalities belonging to the Russian state.[2] The international implications of this simple formula were not raised either now or at any other time before 1914. But its party and its national implications were the subject of controversies throughout the period. These became more acute after the 1905 revolution ; and Lenin's own sense of the importance of the national question may well have been sharpened by his move into Austrian Poland in the summer of 1912. In the following year he noted that " the national question has at the present time emerged into a conspicuous position among questions of Russian social life ".[3] The major Bolshevik pronouncements on this question before the revolution belong to this period.

The first of the two main heresies which challenged party orthodoxy at this time was of Austrian origin. About the turn of the century, the leading Austrian Marxists, anxious to counteract the disruptive tendencies of a nationalism which threatened the ramshackle framework of the Dual Monarchy, propounded a project for replacing national self-determination, as a right recognized in social-democratic doctrine, by a non-territorial cultural autonomy, which could be enjoyed by national groups throughout the empire without destroying its political and

[1] It is noteworthy that the grievances of Finland against Russia, which acquired international notoriety after 1905, were discussed on a basis not of an abstract right of self-determination, but of constitutional law of the Russian Empire.

[2] Plekhanov, in his comments on Lenin's draft of this passage in the programme, proposed to substitute " empire " for " state ", in order to make the word applicable only to the Tsarist régime and to avoid committing a future bourgeois or socialist republic to a policy which might mean the dismemberment of Russia ; Lenin resisted this limitation (*Leninskii Sbornik*, ii (1924), 144).

[3] Lenin, *Sochineniya*, xvii, 133.

territorial integrity.[1] The first and most obvious corollary of this project was its application to the party itself. At its congress of 1897 the Austrian Social-Democratic Party decided to reorganize itself as a federation of six autonomous national parties — German, Czech, Polish, Ruthenian, Italian and Yugoslav. The next party congress, held at Brünn in 1899, passed a vaguely worded resolution in favour of the reorganization of Austria as a " federation of nationalities ". This was followed by a campaign, led by Karl Renner (writing under the pseudonym of Rudolf Springer) and Otto Bauer, in favour of an ingenious scheme of national cultural autonomy on a personal basis ; members of the different nationalities would be organized, irrespective of their place of residence, under national councils for the conduct of their educational and other cultural affairs, the political and economic unity of the monarchy and its administration remaining unaffected.

In Russia these ideas, in regard both to party organization and to the state, were eagerly taken up by the All-Jewish Workers' Union in Russia and Poland, commonly called the Bund. The Bund, the oldest social-democratic organization in Russia, had been admitted to the Russian Social-Democratic Party at its foundation congress in 1898 as " an autonomous organization independent only in questions especially affecting the Jewish proletariat ".[2] At the second congress in 1903, the delegates of the Bund fought to retain its prerogative as " sole representative of the Jewish proletariat in whatever part of Russia it lives and whatever language it speaks ".[3] Heavily defeated on the vote, they withdrew from the congress and from the party. They were re-admitted to it at the fourth congress in 1906 on an equivocal formula which settled nothing.[4] By this time the Lettish and Caucasian social-democratic parties were putting forward the same demands as the Bund. With the growing acuteness of the national issue in Russia, controversy within the party became constant and bitter, the policy of autonomy for national sections being opposed only by Lenin and the few Bolshevik stalwarts.

Throughout the controversy it seems to have been assumed on all sides that national autonomy within the party and cultural autonomy for nationalities within the state were principles that stood or fell

---

[1] Owing to the wide dispersal of Germans in Europe, German conceptions of nationality tended to have a personal rather than a territorial basis. The delegates to the Frankfort Assembly of 1848 represented not territories, but communities of Germans, some of them minorities in the territories inhabited by them ; the suggestion was even made, though not adopted, to admit delegates of the German community in Paris.

[2] *VKP(B) v Rezolyutsiyakh* (1941), i, 5.

[3] *Vtoroi S"ezd RSDRP* (1932), pp. 323-325 ; see p. 30 above.

[4] *VKP(B) v Rezolyutsiyakh* (1941), i, 81-82.

together.[1] Lenin, convinced that it would weaken the party to split it
on national lines, was equally convinced that the same was true of the
state ; and he fought the issue on state as well as on party lines. Early
in 1903, before the second congress, he had reproached an Armenian
social-democratic group with demanding a "*federal* republic" for
Russia as a whole and "autonomy of cultural life" for the Caucasian
nationalities. The proletariat, Lenin held, was not interested in
"national autonomy". It was interested only in two things : on the
one hand, in "political and civil liberty and complete equality of
rights", on the other, in "the right of self-determination for any
nationality" (meaning the right of secession).[2] Lenin thus quickly
came to occupy an uncompromising "all or nothing" position on the
issue of national self-determination, which was less paradoxical than it
appeared at first sight. The nation had a right to secede ; if it chose not
to exercise that right, then it had, as a nation, no other, though its
individual members naturally enjoyed a right to equality with other
citizens in matters of language, education and culture, such as they
enjoyed even in a bourgeois democracy like Switzerland.[3]

Lenin's attitude was therefore already defined at the beginning of
1903. It was ten years later, when the national question had become
acute, that he set Stalin, a young Georgian Bolshevik then visiting him
in Galicia, to demolish the Austrian thesis. Stalin's essay *The National
Question and Social-Democracy* was published in a party journal in the
spring of 1913.[4] External and internal evidence shows it to have been
written under Lenin's inspiration ; and it remained the standard work
in party literature on its subject.

[1] This point was afterwards argued at length by Stalin : "Type of organization . . . stamps an indelible impress on the whole mental life of the workers.
. . . When the workers are organized according to nationality they are isolated
within their national shells, fenced off from each other by organizational parti-
tions. The stress is laid not on what is *common* to the workers but on what
distinguishes them from each other. . . . National federation in organization
inculcates in the workers a spirit of national aloofness" (Stalin, *Sochineniya*,
ii, 365).

[2] Lenin, *Sochineniya*, v, 242-243. Stalin attacked the Armenian social-
democrats on the same ground (*Sochineniya*, i, 37).

[3] The principle enunciated by Lenin was adopted in the Versailles peace
settlement of 1919. National self-determination implied the right of a national
group to secede from an existing state and attach itself to another state or form
a state of its own. Where, however, for one reason or another, a national group
could not exercise the right of secession, it was entitled to no further recognition
as a group, though political and civil liberties and equality of rights were
guaranteed under the "minorities treaties" to its individual members.

[4] Stalin, *Sochineniya*, ii, 290-367, where it has the title *Marxism and the
National Question* ; English translation in J. Stalin, *Marxism and the National
and Colonial Question* (2nd ed. 1936), pp. 3-61.

The introduction to the essay deplored the growing " wave of nationalism ", and called on social-democrats to " protect the masses from the general ' epidemic ' . . . by bringing against nationalism the tried weapon of internationalism, the unity and indivisibility of the class struggle ". Stalin then proceeded to define the nation as " a historically evolved stable community of language, territory, economic life and psychological make-up manifested in a community of culture ". The Austrian definitions of a nation as " a cultural community no longer tied to the soil " (Springer) or " an aggregate of people bound into a community of character by a community of fate " (Bauer) were condemned as ignoring the objective quality of nationhood and the changing historical and economic conditions which produced it.   In fact " a nation is not merely a historical category, but a historical category belonging to a definite epoch, the epoch of rising capitalism "· The bourgeoisie " plays the leading rôle " in its creation ; and ·" the market is the first school in which the bourgeoisie learns its nationalism ".   Thus " the national struggle is a struggle of the bourgeois among themselves ". A national movement is " *in its essence* always a bourgeois struggle, one that is chiefly favourable to and suitable for the bourgeoisie ".[1]   The pattern varied between western and eastern Europe, where, thanks to the longer survival of feudal authority, multi-national rather than national states came into being.   But these broad generalizations about the rise of nations applied everywhere· The nation thus created must be considered as an objective and independent entity.   " Nations are sovereign and all nations are equal."

This view, which implied the right of nations to full self-determination and secession, assailed the Austrian thesis on two counts.   On the one hand, the Austrian thesis limited the rights of nations both by seeking to maintain the multi-national state in defiance of the right of self-determination and by endeavouring to substitute parity of cultural rights for sovereign political rights.   On the other hand, the Austrian thesis fostered nationalism not only by perpetuating national prejudices,[2] but by treating the nation as a fixed and permanent category, so that on this hypothesis even the future socialist order would " divide humanity into nationally delimited communities ".   It was in opposition to this dual heresy that Stalin propounded the dual view of the

[1] Lenin at the time fully endorsed this view : he found the " economic basis " of national movements in the fact that " for the complete victory of mercantile production it is indispensable for the bourgeoisie to conquer the domestic market ", and regarded the national state as " *typical* and normal for the capitalist period throughout the civilized world " (*Sochineniya*, xvii, 428).

[2] As an example of the reactionary implications of cultural autonomy Lenin observed that " in America in the southern, formerly slave-owning, states the children of negroes are to this day segregated into special schools, whereas in the north whites and negroes are educated together " (*ibid*. xvii, 93).

nation which took its place in the Bolshevik creed. On the one hand, the nation was the historically attested form of state organization in the period of the bourgeois revolution, and as such enjoyed an indefeasible right of self-determination in the form of secession from an existing multi-national state. On the other hand, the ultimate goal of socialism was the replacement of the division of the world into " nationally delimited communities " by the " principle of the international solidarity of the workers ". The distinction between the nationalism of the bourgeois revolution and the internationalism of the socialist revolution, here only faintly adumbrated, had important consequences which would become apparent later.

The second heresy against which Bolshevik doctrine reacted was mainly associated at this time with Polish social-democracy.[1] In the early 1890s a split occurred between two groups of Polish social-democrats on the national question. Out of one of these sprang the " patriotic " Polish Socialist Party of Pilsudski. The other, endorsing the ideas of Rosa Luxemburg, denounced " the demand for the restoration of the Polish state " as a " utopia ", and eventually became a section of the Russian party.[2] The controversy was reflected in a sharp article by Rosa Luxemburg in the social-democratic journal *Neue Zeit*,[3] which argued that national independence was a bourgeois concern and that the proletariat, being essentially international, had no interest in it. Rosa Luxemburg's argument was rebutted in later issues of the same journal by Kautsky, who in an article entitled " Finis Poloniae ? " sustained what afterwards became the Bolshevik position.[4] It is a curious symptom of the dependence on Russia felt in all sectors of the population of Russian Poland before 1914 that, while the landowning and merchant classes leaned on their Russian counterparts through fear of revolutionary stirrings in the Polish peasantry or the Polish proletariat, Polish revolutionaries equally scouted the idea of an independent Polish revolutionary party which would be too weak to make headway against a Polish ruling class. A long article of Rosa Luxemburg published in 1907–1908 in a Polish journal provided Lenin with the text for his most elaborate refutation of the Polish thesis.[5]

[1] It should be added that the same view was held by early Russian radicals and revolutionaries from Pestel to Chernyshevsky, nearly all of whom had been either hostile or indifferent to the claims of nationalism.

[2] The best account of this controversy from the Polish side, for those not having access to Polish documents, is an article in *Proletarskaya Revolyutsiya*, No. 2-3 (61-62), 1927, pp. 148-208.

[3] *Neue Zeit* (Vienna), xiv (1895–1896), ii, 176-181, 206-216.

[4] *Ibid.* xiv, ii, 484-491, 513-525.

[5] Lenin's article in reply to Rosa Luxemburg, *On the Right of Nations to Self-Determination* (*Sochineniya*, xvii, 427-474), was not published till the spring of 1914. Some of the arguments used in it appear in previous articles published

The Bolshevik reply to the Polish thesis turned on three main points. In the first place, " the formation of independent, national states is a tendency of all bourgeois-democratic revolutions ",[1] so that the recognition at this stage of the right of secession is a corollary of the doctrine of proletarian support for the bourgeois revolution. The proletariat could not at this stage reject or limit a right of self-determination accorded even in bourgeois principle and practice : the secession of Norway from Sweden in 1905 was constantly quoted by Lenin as a shining example of bourgeois self-determination.[2] Secondly, the denial by a ruling nation of the right of self-determination for other nations flouted the principle of equality among nations : the proletariat of a ruling nation could not properly be an accomplice in such a denial. Just as Marx had sought to goad the English workers into support of Irish independence and had denounced Lafargue's denial of nationality as a concealed way of asserting French national supremacy, so Lenin now argued that rejection of national self-determination by Russian social-democrats meant " subservience to the interests of the serf-owners and to the worst prejudices of the ruling nations ".[3] It was legitimate for a Polish democrat to reject the policy of secession for Poland, but this did not make it any less necessary for the party as a whole, and particularly for its Russian members, to proclaim the right of Poland to secede. This argument led up to the third point on which Lenin constantly insisted : the distinction between the right of national self-determination (including secession) and the decision to secede. To advocate the right of divorce did not, Lenin observed, mean to vote for divorce in a particular instance.[4] Those whose right to secede was recognized had still to make the decision whether secession was desirable or not. This distinction became highly important at a later stage.

The first full-dress party pronouncement on nationalism was contained in a resolution adopted at a meeting of the central committee at Poronin in Galicia, where Lenin was then living, in the autumn of

in the latter part of 1913 : *On the National Programme of the Russian Social-Democratic Workers' Party* (*ibid.* xvii, 116-121) and *Critical Notes on the National Question* (*ibid.* xvii, 133-159). Lenin was intensely preoccupied by the national question at this time.

[1] *Ibid.* xvii, 471.

[2] *Ibid.* xvii, 327, 441, 449-454.

[3] The identical phrase occurs twice in Lenin's articles of this period (*ibid.* xvii, 169, 446); the idea is repeated again and again. As Trotsky afterwards put it, " the desire of a ruling nation to maintain the *status quo* frequently dresses up as a superiority to ' nationalism ', just as the desire of a victorious nation to hang on to its booty easily takes the form of pacifism " (*Istoriya Russkoi Revolyutsii*, ii (Berlin, 1933), ii, 50).

[4] Lenin, *Sochineniya*, xvii, 119.

1913. The resolution fell into five sections, of which the three first were devoted to the Austrian and the two last to the Polish heresy. The following were the principal points :

(1) In capitalist conditions the main desiderata are equality of rights for all nations and languages, the absence of an obligatory state language, school instruction in the local language, and a wide measure of provincial autonomy and local self-government.

(2) The principle of cultural-national autonomy and of separate national school administrations within a given state is rejected as inimical to democracy in general and to the interests of the class struggle in particular.

(3) The interests of the working class demand the union of all workers of a given state in proletarian organizations not divided on national lines.

(4) The party supports " the right of the oppressed nations of the Tsarist monarchy to self-determination, i.e. to secession and the formation of an independent state."

(5) The desirability of the exercise of this right in any particular case will be judged by the party " from the point of view of the whole social development and of the interests of the class struggle of the proletariat for socialism ".[1]

The controversy was not ended by the resolution of 1913. Discussion about national self-determination was everywhere stimulated by the war, and not least in social-democratic circles. The manifesto issued by the Zimmerwald conference of anti-war parties in September 1915, which contained the usual recognition of " the right of nations to self-determination ", provoked an angry article in a Swiss journal by the Polish social-democrat Radek, who denounced as " illusory " the " struggle for a non-existent right of self-determination ".[2] In the following spring the controversy was carried into the columns of the *Vorbote*, the journal set up by the Zimmerwald Left, which in April 1916 carried two sets of theses for and against self-determination, the one by Lenin, the other by Radek. Radek argued that social democracy " can in no case come out for the setting up of new frontier posts in Europe or for the restoration of frontiers destroyed by imperialism " ; that to espouse national self-determination was a sure road to " social patriotism " ; and that the only acceptable slogan for social-democrats was " down with frontiers ".[3] A few weeks later, in another journal, Radek condemned the Dublin rising of Easter 1916 as a " putsch ".[4] Lenin summed up in another long article entitled *Results of the Discussion about Self-Determination*. Even Radek had declared against

[1] *VKP(B) v Rezolyutsiyakh* (1941), i, 210-211.
[2] Lenin, *Sochineniya*, xviii, 323.
[3] *Ibid.* xix, 37-48, 438-440.   [4] *Ibid.* xix, 268.

" annexations "; and to reject self-determination was to support annexation. If Germany annexed Belgium, would not Belgium be justified in reasserting her claim to independence in the name of self-determination? Was not the destruction of an independent Poland itself an " annexation "? To recognize the right of national self-determination was the only alternative to a condonation of national oppression.[1]

The resolution of 1913 had been specifically related to the " capitalist conditions " of the bourgeois period; and it was against this background that the whole controversy was conducted. For this reason little stress was laid on a point which was none the less indispensable for a clear understanding of Bolshevik doctrine. Lenin never departed from the Marxist conception of " national differences and antagonisms " as " vanishing ever more and more " before the approach of socialism. He therefore never allowed them any long-term or absolute validity. As early as 1903 he opposed the conditional recognition of national self-determination by social-democrats to its unconditional recognition by bourgeois democracy:

> The bourgeois democrat (and the contemporary socialist-opportunist who treads in his footsteps) imagines that democracy eliminates the class struggle and therefore presents all his political demands abstractly, " unconditionally ", from the point of view of the interests of the " whole people " or even from the point of view of an eternal moral absolute principle. The social democrat unsparingly unmasks this bourgeois illusion always and everywhere, whether it is expressed in abstract idealist philosophy or in the presentation of an unconditional demand for national independence.[2]

And ten years later, in the year of the Poronin resolution, he distinguished in the clearest terms the two stages in the Marxist attitude to the national question corresponding to the two stages of the revolution:

> Developing capitalism knows of two historical tendencies in the national question. The first is the awakening of national life and of national movements, the struggle against all national oppression, the creation of nation states. The second is the development and growing frequency of all sorts of relations between nations, the breaking down of national barriers, the creation of the international unity of capital, and of economic life in general, of politics, of science, and so forth.
> Both tendencies are the universal law of capitalism. The first predominates at the beginning of its development, the second characterizes mature capitalism as it approaches its transformation into a socialist society. The national programme of the Marxists takes account of both tendencies, defending in the first case the equal rights of nations and languages, the inadmissibility of any privileges

[1] *Ibid.* xix, 241-272.   [2] *Ibid.* v, 338-339.

of any kind in this respect and also the right of nations to self-determination, and, in the second case, the principle of internationalism.[1]

The distinction here drawn was between the period when the bourgeoisie was still struggling for its rights against the feudal order and the period after the bourgeois revolution had already been consummated. In the first period the national struggle was *par excellence* bourgeois and aimed at the creation of the nation-state. This did not mean that the workers were not interested in it and should not give it their support ; " limitation of freedom of movement, disfranchisement, suppression of language, restriction of schools and other forms of repression affect the workers no less, if not more, than the bourgeoisie ".[2] They would not, however, regard the demands of national self-determination as absolute. A claim to self-determination could never be set up against the claims of international socialism :

> The worker who places political unity with the bourgeois of " his own " nation higher than full unity with the proletarians of all nations acts against his own interest and against the interests of socialism and the interests of democracy.[3]

And again :

> Marxism is incompatible with nationalism, even the most " just ", " pure ", refined and civilized nationalism. Marxism puts forward in the place of any kind of nationalism an internationalism which is the fusion of all nations in a higher unity.[4]

The aim of socialist policy, Stalin had said in his famous essay, was to break down national barriers and to unite the peoples " in such a manner as to open the way for division of a different kind, division according to classes " ;[5] so long as the national issue stood in the way it diverted the attention of " the lower strata of the population " from the class struggle to questions momentarily " common " to them and to the bourgeoisie.[6] The principle of national self-determination must therefore always be accepted with full consciousness of its relative, conditional and temporary validity and with one eye firmly fixed on the ultimate international goal.

But while the doctrine of the two stages of the revolution had always been essential to the Bolshevik theory of self-determination, the national question had hitherto been treated for all practical purposes as a matter exclusively of the first or bourgeois stage, since the second stage still seemed to be in the remote future. The war of 1914 gradually brought Lenin to the view that the contradictions of the capitalist

---

[1] Lenin, *Sochineniya*, xvii, 139-140.   [2] Stalin, *Sochineniya*, ii, 308.
[3] Lenin, *Sochineniya*, xvi, 509.   [4] *Ibid.* xvii, 145.
[5] Stalin, *Sochineniya*, ii, 362.   [6] *Ibid.* ii, 309.

system had brought it near to breaking-point, and that the beginning of the second or socialist stage of the revolution was at hand ; and this called for a corresponding adjustment of the theory of self-determination. The study of world conditions under the impact of war introduced, however, a fresh complication. The stages of the revolution were successive in time. But, owing to the unequal development of capitalism, different stages might be reached in different parts of the world at the same time ; and these reacted on each other. Both these points were announced in Lenin's theses of April 1916 on *The Socialist Revolution and the Right of Nations to Self-Determination*.[1] The first of the theses boldly maintained that " all the objective prerequisites of the realization of socialism " had now been created ; and, since the first task of " victorious socialism " would be to bring democracy to its completion, it would have also to realize " the right of oppressed nations to self-determination, i.e. the right to free political secession ". But the most novel of the theses was the one which divided the world into " three chief types of countries ". The first comprised " the leading capitalist countries of western Europe and the United States " : here " bourgeois-progressive national movements are long ago finished ". The second group of countries covered eastern Europe " and especially Russia " : here " the 20th century has especially developed bourgeois-democratic national movements and sharpened the national struggle ". In the third category were " semi-colonial countries like China, Persia and Turkey and all colonies " : here " bourgeois democratic movements are either only just beginning or far from finished ".

Thus, at the moment when Lenin was groping his way towards the transition from the bourgeois to the socialist stage of the struggle for national self-determination, he also introduced a new refinement into the analysis of the bourgeois stage of the struggle. This was a direct corollary of the view propounded at this time in his famous pamphlet, *Imperialism as the Highest Stage of Capitalism*,[2] in which he traced the degeneration of competitive nineteenth-century bourgeois capitalism into exploiting twentieth-century bourgeois imperialism. The struggle for national liberation was essentially a bourgeois democratic struggle. In its characteristic nineteenth-century form it had been a struggle against the remnants of feudalism and autocracy ; and in this form it had not yet been completed in the countries of the second type, i.e. eastern Europe " and especially Russia ". In its characteristic twentieth-century form it was a struggle of the colonial and semi-colonial countries of the third type, no longer against feudalism and autocracy of the old kind, but against bourgeois imperialism. The foundation was thus laid for a working alliance between national move-

---

[1] Lenin, *Sochineniya*, xix, 37-48.   [2] *Ibid.* xix, 78-175.

ments of the second and third categories, between the victims of the
old nineteenth-century autocracy and the new twentieth-century
imperialism, between eastern Europe and Asia.

> To suppose [wrote Lenin later in 1916] that a social revolution is
> *thinkable* without a revolt of the small nationalities in the colonies
> and in Europe, without revolutionary outbreaks of the petty
> bourgeoisie with all their prejudices, without the movement of
> unconscious proletarian and semi-proletarian masses against the
> oppression of the nobility, the churches, monarchies and foreign
> nations — to suppose that is to *abjure the social revolution*.[1]

These refinements had, however, to be applied in the light of the
announcement also made by Lenin in the theses of April 1916 of the
impending advance from the bourgeois to the socialist application of
the principle of national self-determination.[2] Here, too, Russia occupied a central and a crucial position. In the transition period from the
bourgeois to the socialist revolution, the line between the bourgeois
and socialist stages of development in the national struggle had also
become blurred, with Russia, in particular, keeping a footing on both
sides of it. But Lenin was prepared with a working criterion for the
application of the bourgeois and socialist aspects respectively of the
doctrine of national self-determination.

> People who have not thought out the question find it " contra-
> dictory " that social-democrats of oppressing nations should insist
> on " freedom to *secede* " and social-democrats of oppressed nations
> on " freedom to *unite* ". But a little reflexion shows that there is
> not and cannot be any *other* road to internationalization and to the
> fusion of nations, any other road from *the present position* to that goal.[3]

On this somewhat nebulous foundation the October revolution was
left to build its theory and its practice in the burning issue of national
self-determination.

[1] Lenin, *Sochineniya*, xix, 269.

[2] Stalin wrote long afterwards that Lenin in the article of October 1916,
Results of the Discussion about Self-Determination (Lenin, *Sochineniya*, xix,
241-272), " declared that the essential point of the national question in general,
and of the right of self-determination in particular, was that they had ceased to
be parts of the democratic movement and had become vital constituents of the
proletarian movement, of the socialist revolution " (Stalin, *Voprosy Leninizma*,
9th ed. 1933, p. 183); Stalin's article in which this passage occurred originally
appeared in *Bol'shevik*, No. 11-12, June 30, 1925, but was dropped from later
editions of *Voprosy Leninizma* and from the collected works. The passage is not
a textual quotation. It fairly represents the implication of Lenin's article seen
in retrospect, but is more definite than anything Lenin actually said.

[3] Lenin, *Sochineniya*, xix, 262.

LIST OF ABBREVIATIONS

Cheka	=	Chrezvychainaya Komissiya (Extraordinary Commission).
Comintern	=	Kommunisticheskii Internatsional (Communist International).
GPU	=	Gosudarstvennoe Politicheskoe Upravlenie (State Political Administration).
IKKI	=	Ispolnitel'nyi Komitet Kommunisticheskogo Internatsionala (Executive Committee of the Communist International).
Narkomfin	=	Narodnyi Komissariat Finansov (People's Commissariat of Finance).
Narkomindel	=	Narodnyi Komissariat Inostrannykh Del (People's Commissariat of Foreign Affairs).
Narkomnats	=	Narodnyi Komissariat po Delam Natsional'nostei (People's Commissariat of Nationalities).
NEP	=	Novaya Ekonomicheskaya Politika (New Economic Policy).
OGPU	=	Ob"edinennoe Gosudarstvennoe Politicheskoe Upravlenie (Unified State Political Administration).
Rabkrin or RKI	=	Rabochaya i Krest'yanskaya Inspektsiya (Workers' and Peasants' Inspection).
RSFSR	=	Rossiiskaya Sotsialisticheskaya Federativnaya Sovetskaya Respublika (Russian Socialist Federal Soviet Republic).
Sovnarkhoz	=	Sovet Narodnogo Khozyaistva (Council of National Economy).
Sovnarkom	=	Sovet Narodnykh Komissarov (Council of People's Commissars).
SR	=	Sotsial-Revolyutsioner (Social-Revolutionary).
STO	=	Sovet Truda i Oborony (Council of Labour and Defence).
TsIK	=	Tsentral'nyi Ispolnitel'nyi Komitet (Central Executive Committee).
Uchraspred	=	Uchet i Raspredelenie (Account and Distribution Section).
Vesenkha	=	Vysshii Sovet Narodnogo Khozyaistva (Supreme Council of National Economy).

LIST OF ABBREVIATIONS

Vikzhel = Vserossiiskii Ispolnitel'nyi Komitet Sozyuza Zhelez-nodorozhnikov (All-Russian Executive Committee of Union of Railwaymen).

VKP(B) = Vsesoyuznaya Kommunisticheskaya Partiya (Bol'-shevikov (All-Union Communist Party (Bolsheviks)).

VTsIK = Vserossiiskii (Vsesoyuznyi) Tsentral'nyi Ispolnitel'nyi Komitet (All-Russian (All-Union) Central Executive Committee).

END OF VOL. I

Printed in the United States
79028LV00002B/45

9 780393 301953